EUI — Series A — 6

Teubner (Ed.), Juridification of Social Spheres

European University Institute
Institut Universitaire Européen
Europäisches Hochschulinstitut
Istituto Universitario Europeo

Series A

Law/Droit/Recht/Diritto

6

Badia Fiesolana — Firenze

Juridification of Social Spheres

A Comparative Analysis in the Areas of Labor, Corporate, Antitrust and Social Welfare Law

Edited by

Gunther Teubner

1987

Walter de Gruyter · Berlin · New York

Library of Congress Cataloging-in-Publication Data

Juridification of social spheres.
(Series A--Law ; 6)
Includes index.
1. Corporation law. 2. Labor laws and legislation. 3. Antitrust law. I. Teubner, Gunther. II. Series.
K1005.4.J87 1987 340'.2 87-8860
ISBN 0-89925-272-9 342

CIP-Kurztitelaufnahme der Deutschen Bibliothek

Juridification of social spheres : a comparative analysis in the areas of labor, corporate, antitrust, and social welfare law / ed. by Gunther Teubner. – Berlin ; New York : de Gruyter, 1987.
(European University Institute : Ser. A, Law ; 6)
ISBN 3-11-011137-3
NE: Teubner, Gunther [Hrsg.]; Istituto Universitario Europeo <Fiesole> : European University Institute / A

Dust Cover Design: Rudolf Hübler, Berlin. — Setting: Satz-Rechen-Zentrum, Berlin
Printing: K. Gerike, Berlin
Binding: Verlagsbuchbinderei Dieter Mikolai, Berlin.
Printed in Germany

Preface

The juridification of social spheres appears as a disquieting modern trend in several different national cultures. Although the large variety of national experiences with juridification cannot be summarized in a unifying formula, it is important to note that juridification is not to be understood primarily as a quantitative phenomenon of the growth of law and regulation. Rather, it has to be seen in its qualitative dimensions, that is, as the emergence of new structures of law to keep pace with the growth of the welfare state. To the degree that the law is used for the regulatory and compensatory purposes of the welfare state, extensive changes in the structure and function of law are involved. In addition, recent trends of crisis in regulatory law seem to be closely connected to the more general crisis of the welfare state. One fascinating aspect of the debate on the crisis of the welfare state and the law is the emergence not only of the concepts of delegalization and deregulation but also of alternatives to delegalization, that is, of forms of legal discourse which avoid certain fallacies of regulatory law without abandoning the idea of an active role of law in shaping social institutions.

The modern phenomenon of juridification was the central theme of a larger research project which Terence Daintith and I conducted at the European University Institute in Florence. The results of this project were presented in March 1985 at a conference on "Law and Economic Policy: Alternatives to De-Legalization". The contributions with an economic policy orientation are to be published separately in a volume on "Law as an Instrument of Economic Policy" edited by Terence Daintith; this volume instead concentrates on juridification in the fields of labor, industrial organization, antitrust and social security.

The book grew out of a close cooperation with the *Deutsche Gesellschaft für Rechtsvergleichung*. After a first workshop in Florence under the guidance of the European University Institute's President, Werner Maihofer, the Department of Fundamental Legal Research of the Comparative Law Association, directed by Friedrich Kübler, organized a session on juridification at its 1983 annual conference in Bonn. The results were published in a book by H. Zacher, S. Simitis, F. Kübler, K. Hopt and G. Teubner, *Verrechtlichung von Wirtschaft, Arbeit und sozialer Solidarität: Vergleichende Analysen*, Baden-Baden: Nomos, 1984. Subsequently the comparative and international aspects were systematically broadened with experts from several European countries and the United States being asked to compare their recent national experiences in juridification and to offer their theoretical interpretations. We have tried to provide a well-balanced selection of national approaches, but unfortunately, since the colleague invited from France had to cancel his participation at a late date,

French ideas on juridification will be expressed exclusively in more abstract terms in the general part of this book.

I would like to thank Eve Lerman, Constance Meldrum and Elizabeth Webb for their precise and thorough editorial assistance, and the Institute's Publications Officer, Brigitte Schwab, for her helpful activities in coordinating the publication.

January 1987 Gunther Teubner

Table of Contents

I

General Aspects

Juridification
Concepts, Aspects, Limits, Solutions

GUNTHER TEUBNER

Bremen, Firenze

Contents

1. Introduction

Juridification is an ugly word — as ugly as the reality which it describes. The old formula used to describe the excess of laws, *fiat justitia, pereat mundus,* at least had the heroic quality of a search for justice at all costs. Today we no longer fear that the proliferation of laws will bring about the end of the world but we do fear "legal pollution" (Ehrlich, 1976). The bureaucratic sound and aura of the word juridification indicate what kind of pollution is primarily meant: the bureaucratization of the world (Jacoby, 1969; Bosetzky, 1978: 52). To put it in the language of sociology: law, when used as a control medium of the welfare state, has at its disposal modes of functioning, criteria of rationality and forms of organization which are not appropriate to the "life-world" structures of the regulated social areas and which therefore either fail to achieve the desired results or do so at the cost of destroying these structures. The ambivalence of juridification, the ambivalence of a guarantee of freedom that is at the same time a deprivation of freedom, is made clear in the telling phrase "the colonialization of the life-world", which was coined by Habermas. Social modernization at the expense of subjection to the logic of the system and the destruction of intact social structures is the essence of this idea (Habermas, 1981: 522; 1985: 203).

Expressed in this extreme, dramatic form, juridification describes a reality which is not merely a problem of jurists, nor a national phenomenon. *Verrechtlichung* does not only spring from the well-known Teutonic tendency towards overregulation, so the discussion of the problem is not confined to German jurisprudence. Although national divergences exist (see Daintith 1987) the phenomenon is universal, and the debate international and interdisciplinary. In the United States in particular a lively debate is going on about the "legal explosion", the "regulatory crisis" and "delegalization" — a debate in which not only lawyers and jurists but sociologists and economists are particularly involved[1]. If one attempts — and this is the aim of this introductory essay — to bring together some of the different strands in this discussion, the results may be instructive for all who participate in the debate. National peculiarities will then be able to be seen in the light of their universal elements. Sociological generalizations can be corrected when viewed from within the laws if they are set against specific legal material. On the other hand a dynamization of the strictly juristic perspective could be hoped for if extralegal modes of interpretation are actually taken up and not simply dismissed. However, one must remain sceptical about the possibility that such learning processes will actually lead to perspectives for solutions. The problem of "juridification" is too abstractly formulated for this and as such is perhaps even insoluble. What *can* be achieved is tentative answers to three questions: How and to what extent is the expansion of law into the social environment contingent and reversible or necessary and irreversible, and how is it connected to wider societal developments? How and where are the limits of legal growth becoming apparent? And can guidelines for a kind of legal growth which is less damaging to the social environment be given? For each of these complexes of questions a proposition can be elaborated. The first complex concerns the *definition of the problem* of juridification. In the current debate, the term has come to designate so many diverse phenomena that it must be carefully delimited before any sensible pronouncements can be made about it at all. It is scarcely illuminating to subsume all tendencies towards

[1] For previous discussion of "creeping legalism", cf. Fuller, 1969: 3; Shuklar, 1964; Nonet, 1969; Friedman, 1975; Galanter, 1980: 11, 1981: 147; Abel, 1980: 27, 1982; Mitnick, 1980; Wilson, 1980; Breyer, 1982; Stewart, 1985. Cf. the results of a German/American conference on regulatory control, Trubek, 1984.

proliferation of law or all legal evolution under the heading "juridification". In such a case one would have to be content with a mere stock-taking of contradictory and heterogeneous developments under the relatively arbitrary heading "Developments in Law in the World of Industry, Work and Social Solidarity". The phenomenon of juridification becomes a subject which is analyzable, interpretable and strategically appropriate only when — and this is the first proposition — it is identified with the type of modern "***regulatory law***" in which law, in a peculiar fashion, seems to be both politicized and socialized. This type of law must then be related to Max Weber's concept of "***materialization of formal law***". This will provide an analytical framework in which both naive delegalization recommendations of the "alternatives to law" movement and politically motivated "de-regulation" strategies can be adequately and critically assessed. Here the changes which law itself, in its function, legitimacy and structure, has undergone in the process of juridification also become clear.

The second complex of questions relates to limits to the growth of regulatory law. Is it possible to discern fundamental limits of juridification in so far as certain juridification processes prove inadequate in the face of regulated social structures and/or constitute an excessive strain on the internal capacities of law? The argument I would like to propose here is that this is not merely a problem of the implementation of law, nor of the use of state power, nor merely of the efficiency of law in terms of the appropriateness of means to ends, but it is a problem of the "***structural coupling***" of law with politics on the one hand and with the regulated social fields on the other. Once the limits of this structural coupling have been overstepped, law is caught up in an inevitable situation which I propose to examine more closely under the heading "***regulatory trilemma***".

If, thus, the "regulatory crisis" is adequately interpreted, the third question that arises is how to assess the various proposed therapies and alternative strategies. Are there alternatives to juridification which at the same time do justice to the social guidance requirements of politics, the special properties of the respective social areas and the inner capacities of law? The proposition I would like to put forward here is that neither the various suggestions on improvements in the implementation of law nor the numerous recommendations on delegalization take adequate account of the problem of structural coupling. Intellectual attention and institutional energies should be concentrated on a series of conceptions which go beyond materialization and reformalization and amount to more abstract, more indirect control by law. What these conceptions have in common is that they look for models of "socialization of law". Among the relevant terms here are: "semi-autonomous social fields" (Moore, 1973: 719), "negotiated regulation" (Harter, 1982: 1), "officially sponsored indigenous law" (Galanter, 1980: 26), "proceduralisation of law" (Wiethölter, 1982a: 38, 1982b: 7; 1985), "ecological law" (Ladeur, 1984), "reflexive law" (Teubner, 1983: 239ff., 1985: 299ff., 1986b), and "relationing programmes" (Willke, 1983a: 62); in short: *legal control of self-regulation* (Teubner, 1983: 239ff.). This term refers to different legal programs which, sometimes more, sometimes less explicitly, define structural coupling as "legal self-restraint" and which, therefore, are appropriate as a means of reducing legal pollution.

2. Concepts

A precise use of terms and definitions is necessary, especially in the case of juridification, not just for the sake of terminological clarity but, as already indicated, to create a working framework in which to examine the complex phenomenon of juridification. Furthermore, when we are using a term as polemical as juridification it becomes clear that the term not only enables us to make definitions but also provides options. Options are empirical analyses of the historical situation on the basis of which evaluative assessments are made, strategies chosen and decisions taken (Luhmann, 1981: 118; Rottleuthner, 1985: 9ff.). Notions of juridification always contain a theory of the conditions in which it developed, an evaluation of its consequences and a strategy for dealing with it. A clarification of the term would therefore have to lay bare these three elements in the different ways in which the term is used. At the same time it would have to state the reasons why one of the options is finally chosen.

2.1 Legal Explosion

In legal discussion juridification is described primarily as a growth phenomenon[2]. Fear-laden terms such as "flood of norms" or "legal explosion" (Barton, 1975: 567) underline the disquieting effect which the rapid expansion of law has had on the legal profession and the general public alike. Especially in those areas of the law which cover the world of industry, labor and social solidarity — labor law, company law, antitrust law and social security law — the enormous quantitative growth of norms and standards is noted and criticized. From a certain threshold onwards, those involved are overtaxed. The enforcement of law is damaged, credibility suffers and a high level of dogmatic mastering of legal material becomes impossible (Heldrich, 1981: 814). In all four areas of law it can be observed from a comparative perspective that consistency control of norm and decision making material as well as the construction of conceptual structures — the two classical tasks of legal doctrine — is giving way to a new mode of thinking — "case-law-positivism" as Zoellner polemically terms it. This style of legal thinking is content to analyse developments in judicial decisions and to produce ad-hoc criticism of their "policies". As an observer from outside has noted: "The disastrous state of modern positive law lies in the incoherence of large numbers of norms which are produced procedurally in response to a particular situation and are

[2] Berner, 1978: 617; Boerlin *et al.*, 1978: 295; Hillermeier, 1978: 321; Weiss, 1978: 601; Vogel, 1979: 321; Starck, 1979: 209; Sendler, 1979, 227; Barton, 1975: 567.

then lumped together in disordered heaps. No adequate means of coping with this material intellectually has been developed" (Luhmann, 1972: 331; cf. also Hegenbarth, 1983: 67).

Of course with a term like juridification, if it is geared towards a crisis of growth, the therapy is implicitly contained in the term itself. Growth itself must be combatted. The prescription reads as follows: rationalize legislation, reduce the number of regulations, thin out the stock of laws — in short, simplify the law[3]. However, scepticism based on historical experience with such appeals is not unjustified, and perhaps makes one more receptive to the cynical proposal to try the exact opposite remedy: "growth-boosting hormone injections". The experiment has already been tried with weeds: acceleration of growth beyound an optimum level is a sure means of extermination (Luhmann, 1981: 73).

Yet it still seems too narrow an approach to concentrate on the expansion of legal material, on the extension and intensification of law. The current criticism of juridification processes under the general heading "flood of norms" scarcely seems an appropriate starting point because it limits the discussion in several respects. The term "flood of norms" merely stresses the quantitative aspect of the increase in legal material — a problem which could certainly be combatted by technical improvements in legislation. In fact, qualitative aspects are more important: what changes in the content of legal structures has the (alleged?) crisis of juridification brought about? The term "flood of norms" is also historically unspecific — throughout the centuries complaints have been made about the proliferation of laws and their intricacy (Nörr, 1974). Juridification processes should in fact be analysed in terms of the specific conditions of the modern social state, "the interventionist state". This at the same time excludes the law-centered and lawyer-centered perspective of the "flood of norms" school, which concentrates exclusively on the legal material as such. The problem to be addressed is broader in scope: the political and social appropriateness of juridification processes in various social areas (labor, market, company, and social security law). Finally, an attempt should be made to abstract from the national peculiarities of the flood of norms and, adopting a comparative perspective, to bring out the universal features of juridification processes and the problems which result from them.

2.2 Expropriation of Conflict

If one attempts to correct the myopia of the legal perspective by means of the optics of legal sociology juridification suddenly appears in a quite different light. The "politics of informal justice" in the U.S. and its European equivalent, "alternatives to law", come to the fore while problems of growth recede into the background (Abel, 1980: 27; Blankenburg *et al.*, 1980). Sociologists of law describe juridification as a process in which human conflicts are torn through formalization out of their living context and distorted by being subjected to

[3] Ehrlich, 1976: note 1. Cf. the references in note 2 supra.

legal processes. Juridification, as it were, is the expropriation of conflict. Christie (1976: 12) even uses the expression "conflict as property". This is certainly an extreme formulation, but it clearly indicates the direction of the analysis. Doubt is cast on whether law can fulfil what is generally regarded as its major function, the resolution of conflicts. Numerous socio-legal studies have pinpointed factors which constitute "obstacles to the adequate conflict resolution through law: barriers to access, fear of going to court, the length and cost of proceedings as well as processual inequality of chances of success" (Hegenbarth, 1980: 48). In this view juridification does not solve conflicts but alienates them. It mutilates the social conflict, reducing it to a legal case and thereby excludes the possibility of an adequate future oriented, socially rewarding resolution.

If conflicts are thus expropriated by juridification, the slogan of the delegalization movement is: expropriation of the expropriators[4]. As "alternatives to law", informal modes of dealing with conflicts are sought, modes which will take conflicts out of the hands of lawyers and give them back to the people. Certainly, the people will achieve a solution to the conflicts in the real social world, not only in the illusory world of legal concepts and procedures.

Institutional proposals and experiments (see Blankenburg, Gottwald, Strempel, 1982) range from reinforcement of the arbitration element in court proceedings[5] to the extension of out-of-court proceedings[6], to the establishment of "community courts" in big city neighbourhoods (Danzig, 1973: 1). Comparative legal and anthropological studies of Kbelle palavers in Africa, of arbitration phenomena in Japan and of social courts under real socialism are the inspiration behind these "alternatives to law".

These ideas of "communal law", as Galanter rightly terms it (Galanter, 1980), have been severely criticized in the socio-legal discussion. Abel provided the ideology-critical, Hegenbarth the conflict-theoretical and Luhmann the social-theoretical variants of this criticism (Abel, 1980, Hegenbarth, 1980; Luhmann, 1985). To put it briefly — a return to "informal justice" means, under today's conditions, surrendering conflict to the existing power constellations. Secondly, "alternatives to law" ignore crucial factors in dealing with conflict under modern conditions of role separation. Thirdly, they underestimate an indispensable function of law in functionally differentiated societies — which is to use the possibility of conflict in order to generalize congruent expectations throughout society. They may, of course, be able to formulate useful reform proposals which could certainly increase social potential for satisfactory conflict resolution, but they are scarcely appropriate as a general perspective for interpreting juridification and for

[4] A valuable analysis of the different directions in which the movements towards delegalisation is going is offered by Röhl, 1982: 15.

[5] E.g., active role of the judge, settlements, negotiations aimed at reaching an amicable agreement: see Giese, 1978: 117; Röhl, 1980: 279.

[6] E.g., arbitration courts, courts within companies and associations: see Bender, 1976: 193; Bierbrauer *et al.*, 1978: 141.

developing alternatives to dejuridification. This is ultimately because the current discussion in legal sociology has confined itself to the classical tasks of law (conflict regulation) and has only marginally concerned itself with the really explosive aspects of modern juridification (social regulation). Sociologists of law have concentrated their attacks on the unsatisfactory consequences for a continuation of harmonious social relations when human conflicts are delivered up to the court system. But how relevant is this criticism of the judicial system in face of the far more disquieting tendencies of a politically instrumentalized law, which threatens profoundly to change entire social spheres through its regulatory interventions. In comparison the legal-sociological formulation of the question seems somewhat harmless, and almost provincial.

2.3 Depoliticization

In view of these belittling definitions it is perhaps as well to look at the historical origins of the term. The word *Verrechtlichung* (juridification) was first employed as a polemic term in the debate on labor law in the Weimar Republic. Kirchheimer used it to criticize the legal formalization of labor relations, which neutralized genuine political class conflicts (Kirchheimer, 1933: 79). According to Fraenkel, juridification of labor relations means to "petrify" the political dynamics of the working class movement (Fraenkel, 1932: 255). Critical labor lawyers in West Germany have recently renewed this line of argument. The ambivalence of juridification — the guarantee and the simultaneous deprivation of freedom — is clearly worked out with examples from industrial relations law, codetermination, strikes and lockouts. On the one hand labor law protects and guarantees certain interests of employees and ensures that labor unions have scope for action. Yet on the other, the repressive character of juridification tends to depoliticize social conflicts by drastically limiting the labor unions' possibilities of militant action (Hoffmann, 1968: 92; Däubler, 1976: 29; von Beyme, 1977: 198; Erd, 1978; Voigt, 1980: 170). This kind of ambivalent juridification and its acceptance by labor unions is explained in terms of the interaction of the interests of specific trade union groups with state control interests: juridification reinforces "cooperative" trade union policies, just as it is reinforced by them. This interaction of course occurs at the expense of "conflictive" trade union policy (Erd, 1978: 19).

Here too, the counter-strategy is implied. Only when labor union policy changed to "conflictive" strategies and stressed autonomous representation of interests could juridification processes be reversed and labor conflicts repoliticized (Erd, 1978: 26, 251; Rosenbaum, 1982: 392). In fact this interpretation of the term has clear advantages over the lawyer-centred and judiciary-critical formulation of juridification. It takes account of the effects of the proliferation of laws on regulatory areas, stresses qualitative as well as quantitative aspects of change brought about by law, provides differentiated analyses of the ambivalence of the phenomenon and, with its concept of depoliticization, has certainly pinpointed one of the most important consequences of juridification processes.

Nonetheless, it is in several respects an over-simplification. Simitis has pointed out the, as it were, "voluntaristic" nature of this concept of juridification (Simitis, infra: 134 ff.). The key role of the "conflictive/cooperative" alternative implies that the dynamics of juridification are primarily a strategy problem of the labor unions: the concept is restricted to the politics of organised labor. Yet it is also necessary to point out a national limitation in this concept. Because tendencies of "cooperative" trade union policy are highly marked, especially in Germany, it is tempting to regard "juridification" as a "German speciality" (Unterseher, 1972: 190; v. Beyme, 1977: 198). This is a deficit in comparative legal terms, and it shows that the theoretical connection between "cooperative trade union policy" and juridification is far more relative than it appeared to be. The limitations of this perspective lead finally to a theoretical deficit. The attempt to explain juridification in terms of intra-union preconditions and the collusion between decision-making groups in trade unions with legislation and judiciary (Erd, 1978: 19; Moritz, 1980: 171) can perhaps be accepted as a particular explanation of interests and influences operating in this area, but cannot be regarded as a class theoretical analysis, let alone as a component in a social theory of juridification phenomena[7]. This concept of juridification hardly seems inappropriate, not so much because it is normatively limited to particular social interests but because it is limited to the labor union perspective and abstains from socio-structural explanations.

2.4 Materialization

We have examined and found wanting the juristic view of juridification as a "flood of norms", the concept of conflict expropriation propounded by sociologists of law and the political science perspective which sees juridification as restricting the room for manœuvre of social movements and interest groups. So to arrive at an adequate formulation of this problem we will have to go beyond those disciplines and draw on the great theories of legal evolution in the tradition of Marx, Maine, Durkheim and Max Weber, as continued by Parsons, Unger, Nonet and Selznick in the U.S. and by Habermas and Luhmann in Europe[8]. Of course we cannot even begin here to distangle the complexities of legal evolution. On the contrary, we will merely attempt to

7 This is not meant as an overall criticism of the very useful analyses of Erd. It simply seems noteworthy that Erd firstly makes a vehement criticism of the limited nature of rival explanations, and then for his part produces a very limited explanation. Interesting nuances of his explanation are found recently in Erd, 1984.

8 With respect of Parsons' theory of norms, which can only be reconstructed from scattered fragments, cf. Damm, 1976. For more recent theories of legal development in the U.S., see Unger, 1976; Nonet and Selznick, 1978; Habermas, 1976: 9, 1981: 322, 522, 1985: 203; Luhmann, 1972; 1981a. For a discussion of theories of evolution of law, see Rottleuthner, 1985.

take up a few strands from the tangle of theory and to combine them in such a way as to further our comprehension of juridification. And here the distinction introduced by Max Weber between "formal and material qualities of modern law" will play a crucial role (Weber, 1978: 644ff.).

Firstly, the wider historical context of juridification becomes clear, the context of the development of the modern welfare state. Habermas' analysis (1981: 522; 1985: 203) in particular shows how in the modern era law has responded to global social developments with various thrusts of juridification which in turn have influenced the developments to which they responded. Habermas distinguishes "in a rough fashion" between four epoch-making thrusts of juridification. The first thrust led to the bourgeois state, which in West Europe developed in the form of absolutism. Law reacted to the differentiation of the two great subsystems — economy and politics — and safeguarded their new autonomy in legal form. Here the modern formal system of civil law originated and formed the common starting point for the later differentiation between "materialized" areas of civil law such as labor law, antitrust law, company law and social security law. The classical system of civil law was "tailored to strategically acting legal persons who enter into contracts with one another ... This legal order bears the features of positivity, generality and formality, and is constructed on the basis of the modern concept of statutory law as well as the concept of the legal person, as one who can enter into contracts, acquire, dispose and bequeath property. The legal order has to guarantee the liberty and property of the private person, the certainty of the law (*Rechtssicherheit*) and the formal equality of all legal subjects before the law, and thereby the calculability of all legal-normed action" (Habermas, 1985: 205). The three thrusts of juridification which followed, of which the last is of particular interest for us, are described by Habermas as historical counter-movements to the differentiation of the economic and political system, more precisely as their legal, democratic and social constitutionalization. In Habermas's words this is to be understood as follows: "a life-world which was at first placed at the disposal of the market and absolutist rule little by little makes good its claims" (Habermas, 1985: 206). In the first thrust of legal constitutionalization the system of civil law was so coordinated with the exercise of power that the principle of the legality of administration could be interpreted in terms of the "rule of law". In a further thrust the democratization of the constitutionalized power of the state was introduced by law. Universal and equal franchise and freedom of organization for political associations and parties legalized the political process. The last thrust of juridification, that which occurred in the social state, is of crucial importance to our subject. There, the juridification of the modern world of industry and labor, the line of freedom-guaranteeing juridification was continued. Juridification in the social state means "constitutionalization" of the economic system. The social state controls the economic system in a similar fashion to that in which the two previous thrusts of juridification controlled the political system (Habermas, 1985: 208). The collective bargaining system, norms of employee protection, the complicated network of social security protection, the intensification of company constitutions as well as antitrust law interventions in the market are all part of this latest epoch-making thrust of juridification in which the intervening social state uses law as a means of control to constitutionalize the economy.

If this analysis is basically correct then two important conclusions may be drawn. First, our analysis of the problem of juridification should concentrate on the thrust of juridification in the social state[9]. Juridification cannot be usefully analysed as a universal historical phenomenon. Rather the task must be to analyse a specific form of juridification, which can only be understood in its proper historical context (see especially Clark and Wedderburn, infra). The most pressing problem at the moment is how to cope with the typical thrust of juridification which occurs in the welfare state, one in which law is used as a control medium for state intervention and compensation. The problem becomes one of the "legitimacy and desirability of state intervention" (Partington, infra). In this view, concepts of juridification discussed above appear either too abstract in their approach or as only partial aspects of a wider problem. The proliferation of law, for example, is not a phenomenon which can be analysed or even combatted as such but one which can only be understood in the context of social guidance in the social state. The "flood of norms" is not primarily a problem for law as such, but one for the interventionist state. Conflict expropriation by law does not come within the framework of analysis chosen here in so far as classical justice is concerned, but it becomes relevant again in so far as these are triggered by typical forms of welfare state intervention. Finally, the restriction of autonomous social groups is reduced to the status of one of several problems of juridification in the welfare state in which the ambivalence of the guarantee of freedom and the deprivation of freedom is expressed.

The second conclusion to be drawn is that — despite political formulae such as deregulation — delegalization cannot be seriously considered as a counter-strategy (Hopt, infra). If it is correct that juridification in the welfare state is part of an epoch-making thrust of development then it cannot be reversed by mere political decision, let alone by an isolated decision about more law or less law. The "flood of laws" cannot be stemmed by dykes and dams; at best it can be channelled. Nor can juridification processes in industrial relations be reversed, and certainly not by a shift of trade union policy from cooperative to conflictive strategies. And in the larger perspective of development any delegalization of conflicts is likely to be merely marginal. The already completed functional differentiation of societies with welfare state structures does not permit "alternatives to law"; at best it permits alternatives within law.

Radical demands for delegalization — which suggest that the juridification process as such could be reversed — are simply illusory. Indeed the juridification versus delegalization alternative should be abandoned completely and replaced by a formulation of the problem which recognizes

[9] Similar definitions are given in Voigt, 1984: 17; Dreier, 1980; 1983: 101; Ronge, 1984; Werle, 1982: 1; Simitis, infra: 113 f.

the juridification thrust within welfare states as a historical fact but also resolutely confronts its dysfunctional consequences. Certainly the problematic results of juridification in welfare states are far clearer to us today than they were when the process began. But this should not blind us to the freedom-guaranteeing function of juridification processes in the intervention state (Voigt, 1980: 15; Habermas, 1981: 530, 1985: 208; Heldrich, 1981: 824; Zacher, infra). Even from a normative perspective juridification in welfare states should be accepted as such and reforming attention should be directed to compensating for negative side-effects, although of course every compensation inevitably brings dysfunctional results in its train which in turn require correction, and so on and so on (Simitis, infra; Partington, infra).

3. Aspects

In order to examine more closely how law transforms itself in the thrust of juridification in welfare states, it is helpful to take up Max Weber's famous distinction (1978: 653ff.) between formal and material legal rationality. It makes clear what effects are produced when the rule-of-law orientation of classical law is overlaid by a welfare state orientation (1978: 868ff.).

More than half a century ago, Max Weber, whose main sociological interest was the tension between material and formal rationality in the most diverse areas of life, described modern European law, and to a lesser extent Anglo-American law, as formal-rational. The formalization of law is part of the great rationalization process of the modern era analysed by Weber, which developed parallel to the differentiation of economics, politics and science as spheres of action. The legal system is one of formal rationality to the extent that professionally trained lawyers orientate themselves by universal norms, or more concretely, to the extent that in legal procedures, "in both substantive and procedural matters, only unambiguous general characteristics of the facts of the case are taken into account" (Weber, 1978: 656). In modern legal formalism a conceptually "increasingly logical sublimation and deductive rigor of law" is paralleled by a procedural element, "an increasingly rational technique in procedure" (Weber, 1978: 882). Weber analyzed certain processes of legal development in which powerful social interests so influenced the law as to transform its orientation from the primarily material ethical, to the formal conceptually abstract and procedurally rationalized orientation.

Yet at the same time Max Weber also emphasised certain anti-formal elements in modern legal development. In the law of contract for example such rematerialization manifested itself in "an increasing particularization of law" and an increasing legislative and judicial control of the content of contracts. For Weber this meant a threat to formal rationality by norms of different quality: "the norms to which substantive rationality accords predominance include ethical imperatives, utilitarian and other expediential rules, and political maxims, all of which diverge from the formalism of the 'external characteristics' variety as well as from that which uses logical abstraction."

According to Weber, the inner quality of highly developed legal culture would be damaged; "the juristic precision of judicial opinions will be seriously impaired if sociological, economic, or ethical argument were to take the place of legal concepts" (1978: 894).

Weber traced this recent particularization of law to various causes. At force here were the "social demands of democracy" (1978: 886) for interventions of the welfare state. Material demands are made on law by interest groups, especially labor unions. Other interests in industry also bring about different materializations of formal law. And finally lawyers themselves bring about change "by new demands for a 'social law' to be based upon such emotionally colored ethical postulates as 'justice' or 'human dignity'" (Weber, 1978: 886).

However compared with the extremely powerful processes of the formal rationality of law, Max Weber regarded these material tendencies as all in all only marginal. In modern theories of development these tendencies are assessed very differently. "Materialization of formal law" today appears as the dominant development trend and evolutionary approaches are brought into play to explain it[10]. The trend towards juridification in welfare states, which expresses itself in the materialization of formal law characterizes large numbers of legal control interventions in areas classically regarded as self-regulating (Hart, 1983: 10) in the world of industry and labor. The main reasons for intervention — and this applies to labor law as well as to company, anti-trust and social security law — are the appearance of phenomena of economic power and/or a societal need for social protection. Juridification in welfare states can be further defined in terms of three processes of change with regard to formal law: change in the function of law, in its legitimation and in its norm structure[11].

3.1 Function

Compared with classical formal law, materialized law in the industrial world has taken on a new social function. It is no longer tailored only to the normative requirements of conflict resolution but to the political intervention requirements of the modern welfare state. It can be instrumentalized for the purposes of the political system which now takes on responsibility for social processes — and this means the definition of goals, the choice of normative means, the ordering of concrete behavioral programs and the implementation of norms. Instrumentalization is most evident in social security law, in the two dimensions for which Zacher (infra: 379 ff.) uses the terms externalization and internalization. Here the internalized changes, in which classical formal law is itself transformed for social purposes, are highly instructive. The same applies

[10] Eder, 1978: 247. For materialization trends in American law, cf. Unger, 1976: 192; Trubek, 1972: 11; Turkel, 1980-81: 41. For German analyses of processes of materialization, see Wieacker, 1967: 514; Wiethölter, 1982a, 1985; Assmann *et al.*, 1980.

[11] For these dimensions and their application to a third type of law i.e. reflexive law, cf. Teubner, 1983: 252, 1985: 305ff.

to individual and to collective labor law, both of which for reasons of social protection were brought into the sphere of political responsibililty (Simitis, infra: 121 ff.). Both company law and antitrust law must be seen in more relative terms. Cartel law of course, is also conceived as a state institution to ensure that genuine competition is maintained. The "visible hand" of the state intervenes in the operations of the market to break up existent market power, to limit market power and to exclude the abuse of market power. But its complete political instrumentalization beyond its function of guaranteeing competition is problematic and in any case controversial (Hopt, infra: 298 ff.). Interventionist instrumentalization seems not very clearly marked in the field of company law either; however, in certain areas such as the legal definition of corporate social responsibility, the norms on publicity and in particular the rules of codetermination and company constitution, the "activist state" intervenes massively in structures of company law (see Kübler, Buxbaum, Corsi infra). Perhaps the US-American development of corporation law following four stages of legal evolution — (1) facilitative rules; (2) fiduciary duties; (3) "soundness" rules; (4) "consumer protection" (see Clark, 1981 and Buxbaum infra) — provides the clearest example of the increasing role of massive public intervention in capitalist activities.

3.2 Legitimation

Materialized law at the same time derives a new inner legitimation from this new function. Whereas formal law clearly viewed itself to be confined to the delimitation of abstract spheres for private-autonomous action[12] material law legitimates itself by the social results it achieves by regulation. "La justice légaliste-libérale" is replaced by "la justice normative-technocratique" (Ost, 1984: 46). The legitimation shifts from autonomy to regulation. Even in the still more formally oriented areas of company and antitrust law, the rhetorics of direct regulation are breaking through. In company law an if anything obfuscating "ethicization" can be observed which basically amounts to regulations for the protection of shareholders and minorities (Wiedemann, 1980b: 147). The regulatory intention is far clearer in the case of regulations on codetermination on the supervisory boards (Kübler, infra). In antitrust law, legitimation is sought in the area of indirect rather than direct control of economic behavior. Yet here too regulations on market behavior and the abuse of market power are clearly phenomena of result oriented direct control (Hopt, infra: 298 ff.; Markovits, infra: 345 ff.).

3.3 Structure

This transformation of function and legitimation triggered by juridification processes in social states clearly also affects the norm structure and inner order of the law itself. The effects range from a weakening of the idea of generality to changes in methods of interpretation (see Wiethölter, 1985). In labor law,

[12] Kennedy, 1973: 351, 1976: 1685; Unger, 1976: 166; Heller, 1979.

the tendency towards particularization was observable at an early stage (Simitis, infra: 119 ff.). Classical formal law, in using the concept of the legal person, abstracted from socially relevant features and was therefore accused of covering up real power positions or indeed helping to force them through by this means. In contrast modern labor law deliberately extended the class of legally relevant features through its definitions of the employer and employee (Rottleuthner, 1985). Labor law thus made formal law material in the sense that it internalized features that were previously extralegal. This transposition of law from general norms to specific positional roles is probably one of the most significant changes in the course of modern juridification (Rehbinder, 1967: 197; Teubner, 1980: 50; Koendgen, 1981: 192). Here, too, labor and social security law are centrally affected, while the changes in company law and antitrust law are less striking. The counterpart to particularization in antitrust law is the process of gearing to specific market structures in which the same behavior may be judged differently depending on the market situation (Hopt, infra: 312 ff.). In company law too a growth in positionally specific thinking has been noted under the heading of "role and law" (Lutter, 1982: 565).

A further structural feature of juridification in social states is the unstoppable rise of "purpose in law". It is no accident that the teleological method was not included in Savigny's canon of methods: yet its domination over other methods is more or less generally recognized today[13]. Indeed the term "legal policies" goes even further and legitimates in Continental law too the policy thinking which is so popular in the U.S. (Steindorff, 1973: 217; 1979). Cartel law and company law may be considered two classical areas of the conflict between two modes of legal thinking. In both areas, policy oriented legal thinking is penetrating into areas of classical formal law and leading to difficult problems, such as the relation between codetermination law and traditional company law in Germany (Wiedemann, 1980a: 607; Kübler, 1981: 367) and the conflict between the civil law and the antitrust law concept of contract (Hopt, infra: 297 ff.).

As a general rule it can be said that the predominant rule orientation is being increasingly overlaid by an instrumental orientation. According to Selznick, "sovereignty of purpose" is the main feature of a responsive law which can only develop in the context of the social state (Nonet and Selznick, 1978: 78). Instead of strictly applying precisely defined legal norms (conditional programs), legal experts now tend to administer ill-defined standards and vague general clauses (purpose programs). This is causing a dramatic shift in the mode of legal thinking, a shift which can be adequately defined by the term 'result orientation'. However, the consequences of this shift for legal doctrine are far from being adequately worked out, let alone solved (Luhmann, 1974, 1987; Teubner, 1975: 179; Unger 1976: 193ff.; Rottleuthner, 1979: 97; Lübbe-Wolff, 1981).

[13] For a comparative law study of evolution of methods, cf. Fikentscher, 1975; Krawietz, 1978: 86. For the French situation, see Ewald, infra: 104 ff.

Result orientation leads us to a final consequence of juridification which has been noted with interest and disquiet in recent years. Social science thinking in the widest sense has been observed to exert increasing influence on the formation of legal concepts and on practical decision-making in the courts. This is especially true for antitrust law[14]. This applies not only to academic discussion but also deeply affects the decision-making practices of the regulatory agencies and the courts. Legal argumentation is heavily subsidized by the language of economics, whether the issue is the major ideological question of the function of competition (protection of freedom or economic results) (Reich, 1977: 29; Möschel, 1983: § 3), the issue of whether antitrust law can be instrumentalized for different economic ends, or the solution of technical problems relating to "as-if" competition in § 22 German Antitrust Statute (Klauss, 1975) and to the definition of market power. Indeed this could scarcely be otherwise, for how could antitrust law credibly demonstrate that it was seeking the maintenance or restoration of competition over and above the concrete case at hand if it disregarded available social science knowledge on the regulatory control of markets?

The situation is the same in the area of company law. In Germany, the great legal-political debates on corporate governance *(Unternehmensverfassung)* in the context of the larger political and economic constitution *(Wirtschaftsverfassung)* simply could not be conducted without the aid of social sciences. Whether explicit borrowings are made from organization theory as with terms such as "the company as organization"[15], whether efficiency prognoses are made disguised as constitutional law (Badura *et al.* 1977: 123; Kübler *et al.*, 1978: 145, 197), or whether company law, in apparently strict dogmatic style, is rethought in terms of basic concepts such as "organization" and "group" (Flume 1977: §§ 1, 4, 7) — theories of the interrelation between organization and market, politics and law, will always be needed. In the U.S., the influence of social science thinking, especially of economic analysis of law, can hardly be over-estimated (see Buxbaum 1984a, 1984b, 1986 for a critique). The everywhere evident opening of legal practice and doctrine to ideas from economics, sociology and political science cannot simply be dismissed as a passing fashion of the unruly sixties and seventies. Of course yesterday critical theory, system theory and "law and society" were the height of fashion, whereas today the trend is towards economic analysis of law, "property rights" and "public choice"[16]. Of course these are fashions, but the

[14] An example is provided by the discussion between Gotthold, 1981: 286 and Möschel, 1981a: 590; as an example in this volume see Markovits, infra: 345 ff.

[15] For the German discussion, see Raiser, 1969, 1980: 206. Even the critics cannot help basing themselves on extra-legal theories, cf. for example, Wiedemann, 1980a: 307. For the French discussion, see Farjat, 1986; for the American discussion, see Buxbaum, infra.

[16] As a more recent thorough survey , cf. the introductory essay by Walz, 1983: 1ff.; cf. as well, the various approaches of social science to legal analysis in Daintith and Teubner, 1986.

reasons for them lie deeper: the opening to the social sciences is closely connected with the phenomenon of juridification itself. For regulatory law regards itself as instrumental law, as a means of social guidance which aims to bring about certain social changes and therefore needs social knowledge.

In the self-image of classical formal law, on the other hand, particular effects were not regarded as significant. Classical formal law saw itself as having to provide only a formal framework within which social autonomy could develop, and no particular control effects were thereby intended. The tenacious survival of formal law can be explained in particular by the fact that it makes itself independent of particular effects on society and if it has any aim at all it is to bring about a state of universal freedom. The crisis of formal law cannot therefore be understood as a crisis of effect. In practice it has functioned splendidly according to its own conception of its identity. It is in terms of this internal model of formal law that Windscheid's confident dictum of the "lawyer as such" who is "not concerned with ethical, political or economic considerations" (Windscheid, 1904: 101) becomes plausible — a view that today appears arrogant or unwordly to us. As Max Weber showed, it was only by indirect means, through politics, which developed welfare state conceptions in response to the pressure of social problems and class movements, that formal law began to suffer from a crisis of identity. It was the conflict between political demands for compensation for the results of industrialization and the structures of classical formal law that triggered the crisis of formal law, to which law has responded with materialization tendencies. In contrast, materialized law as an instrument of political guidance regards itself as designed to produce social effects. If these effects are not achieved, this directly affects its legitimacy. Accordingly material law is forced to enlist the aid of implementation analyses. Social sciences therefore become directly relevant in that analyses of effects can shed light on the effectiveness of law. The extent of so-called sociologization of law cannot therefore be arbitrarily modified by lawyers according to intellectual fashion; on the contrary, it is connected with the transformations of law in the welfare state itself.

At this stage we may formulate a *first interim finding*: juridification does not merely mean proliferation of law; it signifies a process in which the interventionist social state produces a new type of law, regulatory law. Only when both elements — materialization *and* the intention of the social state — are taken together can we understand the precise nature of the contemporary phenomenon of juridification[17]. Regulatory law "coercively specifies conduct

[17] With some slight differences, this concept of regulatory control of the social state is at the basis of many of the contributions in these volumes. For example, Simitis, infra: 119, 121 ff. puts greater emphasis on the control of the social state, whether in the form of direct regulation or in other legal forms, while Kübler, infra: 219 ff., emphasizes rather the aspect of mandatory law with direct regulatory action. In my opinion, only the combination of both elements can make something of the difficult problem of regulatory control, i.e. if law is subjected to the combined requirements of political objectives and direct social regulation.

in order to achieve particular substantive ends" (Stewart, 1986). Regulatory law, which is characterized by material rationality as opposed to formal rationality, may be defined in terms of the following aspects. In its function it is geared to the guidance requirements of the social state, in its legitimation the social results of its controlling and compensating regulations are predominant. In its structure it tends to be particularistic, purpose oriented and dependent on assistance from the social sciences. As part of a greater historical process juridification cannot be reversed by political decision. The only approach worthy of serious discussion is that which seeks to mitigate dysfunctional problems resulting from juridification.

4. Limits

4.1 Regulatory Trilemma

What then are the dysfunctional problems resulting from juridification? With such an abstract formulation of the question we will have to concentrate on questions of principle — islands of safety where we can escape drowning in the flood of norms. Above, we have already discussed important problems resulting from juridification under headings such as proliferation of law, conflict expropriation and depoliticization — the list could be increased at will. In contrast to these partial aspects of the problem, the fundamental question is this: are there any signs that regulatory law has reached insurmountable limits of effectiveness? Has juridification today already reached its "limits of growth"?

In order to find our theoretical bearings, we will again draw on Max Weber's concepts of formal and material rationality of law, but this time we will examine them from a different angle. Weber (1978: 641ff.) described two conflicting developmental tendencies. On the one hand the legal system increases its "formal" specialization, professionalization and internal systematization; on the other hand it is exposed to increasing "material" demands from social interests, to the welfare-state demands of democracy etc. From the viewpoint of system theory this is to be reformulated as a conflict between the social *function* of law, namely to produce from conflicts social expectations in which it then specializes more and more, and the regulatory *performance* which the social environment demands from law[18].

This indicates that the materialization of formal law should be reinterpreted as a process in which two conflicting trends are intensified simultaneously. On the one hand the "formalization" of law is intensified in the sense that law partakes of the functional differentiation of society and develops its autonomy to a point which sociologists today refer to as autopoietic self-refer-

[18] For the distinction between function and performance in law, see Teubner, 1983: 272.

ence[19]. This concept cannot here be analysed in all its ramifications; a rough explanation will have to suffice. The official definition is: An autopoietic system of this kind in all its operations always refers to itself and produces its elements from the relations between its elements. In the field of law autopoietic self-reference means that its validity is based solely on legal normativity and that legal validity has definitively freed itself from all extralegal connections — politics, morality, science — as well as from justifications in terms of natural law. Law can therefore only reproduce itself intra-legally (Luhmann, 1985).

On the other hand, "materialization" of law increases with, and is indeed caused by, the increase in formalization. The more the legal system specializes in its function of creating expectations by conflict regulation, the more it develops and refines norms and procedures which can be used for future oriented behavior control. This can only be formulated in the following paradoxical terms: *law, by being posited as autonomous in its function — formality — becomes increasingly dependent on the demands for performance from its social* environment — materiality. And in today's conditions this means: autonomous, positive, highly formalized and professionalized law, when instrumentalized for purposes of political control, is exposed to specified demands of politics on the one hand and of regulated areas of life on the other.

This tension between increasing autonomy and increasing interdependence explains the necessity and the problem of modern juridification. The problem lies precisely in the "contradiction" between increasing autonomy and simultaneously increasing dependence. When certain sectors of society such as economy, politics, law, culture and science become so autonomous that they not only program themselves, but exclusively react to themselves, they are no longer directly accessible to one another. Within its own power cycle, politics produces binding decisions; law reproduces its normativity in the decision-rule cycle and the economy is, so to speak, short-circuited in the money cycle. Reciprocal influences do, of course, occur permanently but they do not operate according to a simple causal scheme. External demands are not directly translated into internal effects according to the stimulus-response scheme. They are filtered according to specific selection criteria into the respective system structures and adapted into the autonomous logic of the system. In terms of environmental influences on law, this means that even the most powerful social and political pressures are only perceived and processed in the legal system to the extent that they appear on the inner "screens" of legal reality constructions. Conversely, legal regulations are accepted by envi-

19 The terms self-reference/autopoiesis are used in biology as well as in the social sciences in order to identify a system which produces and reproduces the elements of which it is made. See in general, Maturana *et al.* 1980; Varela, 1979. For an application in the social sciences, cf. Hejl, 1982a, 1982b; Luhmann, 1984. For the legal system, see Luhmann, 1983; 1985; 1987; Teubner 1984, 1987.

ronmental systems only as external triggers for internal developments which are no longer controllable by law.

One is therefore forced to abandon ideas of effective outside regulation, the notion that law or politics could have a direct goal oriented controlling influence on sectors of society. The effect of regulatory law must be described in far more modest terms as the mere *triggering of self-regulatory processes*, the direction and effect of which can scarcely be predicted. Beer (1975) puts it well, saying that legal regulations do not change social institutions at all, they only offer a new challenge for their autopoietic adaptation. Cyberneticians use the term "black box" to describe this phenomenon (Glanville, 1979: 35). External influence on areas of social life is possible but — and this is crucial — only within the paths and the limits of the respective self-reproduction. These are described by the *regulatory trilemma: Every regulatory intervention which goes beyond these limits is either irrelevant or produces disintegrating effects on the social area of life or else disintegrating effects on regulatory law itself* (Teubner, 1985).

The matter is further complicated by the political instrumentalization of law. In the activist state legal regulation involves not only the legal system and the respective social area of life but invariably also the political system. However, the legal system and the political system in turn are autonomous self-referential social systems which cannot directly influence each other but can only reciprocally trigger self-regulating processes. This they can only do if they respect the limits of their respective self-regulation. If we adopt this perspective and regard juridification processes as complex relations between three self-regulating social systems, we begin to grasp why "regulatory failures" must in fact be the rule rather than the exception and that this is not merely a problem of human inadequacy or social power structures but above all one of inadequate *structural coupling of politics, law and the area of social life*[20].

The unlikely event of a successful structural coupling of political decision-making, legal norm-making and social guidance can only occur if relevance thresholds are successfully crossed and if the respective limits of self-reproduction are observed. If this structural coupling is not achieved, then law inevitably gets caught up in the regulatory trilemma mentioned above. We can now see more clearly that this trilemma of law applies both to the regulated area of life and to politics. For law must first pass through a complicated series of phases, beginning with the build-up of political power and the political guidance decision, moving on to legal norm-making and application and finally to the process of social implementation. First, the guidance decision is "legalized" in the political process, i.e., politics is translated into law. This first phase of juridification is itself problematic, for it must on the one hand satisfy the relevance criteria of law but on the other

[20] On the difficult concept of the structural coupling of autopoetic systems, see the introduction in Maturana, 1982: 20ff. See also Hejl, 1982: 63

must not interfere with the conditions of self-regulation either of law or of politics itself. In the second phase of "juridification" the social area of life is "legalized" by regulatory law. Here law must cross social relevance thresholds but must not cross the limits of its own self-regulation nor those of social self-regulation. In other words, the regulatory trilemma exists on both frontiers of the law, that which borders on politics and that which borders on the area of social life. The trilemma exists in three forms: first, as a problem of mutual indifference; second, as a problem of social disintegration through law; and third, as a problem of legal disintegration through society.

4.2 Mutual Indifference

Robert Fischer, president of the Cartel Senate of the Federal Supreme Court, has criticized the amendment practice of the German Antitrust Statute, arguing that the Law on Restraints of Competition is no longer a law but a novel, that paragraphs covering three pages are not litigable, that political compromises have left the application of law without bearings and that constant amendments have made doctrinal analyses of law obsolete (Fischer, 1978: 6). Fischer's criticisms are a drastic example of how politics can fail to achieve the relevance criteria of law. Hopt describes these normative guidelines of competition policy as one of the major reasons for the growth crisis in antitrust law (Hopt, infra: 315; for counter-arguments see Markovits, infra: 366). The reaction of law to this is an increasing indifference to political guidelines of this kind. The legislature is constantly producing amendments to indicate changes of direction. However, these signals no longer appear on the internal screen of the legal system; they vanish without trace. This indifference of law to politics is not confined to antitrust law. Precisely in the case of other laws designed to control the economy it has been noted that the inadequate litigability of modern legislative decisions on the micro and macro level make traditional legal control and regulation problematic (Brüggemeier, 1980: 80). This is an inevitable conflict in the structure of politics and law as systems with different self-reference. According to Luhmann "the political selection of legal decision-making premises by parliamentary legislatures is a permanent problem for legal systems" (Luhmann, 1981a: 45).

There are, however, two sides to this indifference. Not only must politics attune its decisions to legal relevance criteria; law too can and must change its relevance criteria with respect to politics. The increasing use of the method of "interest weighing" and the increasing policy orientation of legal decisions indicate such changes of direction in law itself. Accordingly, in some cases where politics seems to come up against legal indifference it has in fact merely reached relative limits of the coupling of politics and law. Law can change its concrete structures without affecting its self-reproductive organization (for this distinction in general see Maturana and Varela, 1980: 137 f.).

In the case of Germany, the conflicts between classical company law and the current laws on codetermination provide a good example of this situation (Wiedemann, 1980a: 607). In the literature it is said that company law has primacy over the codetermination law (Martens, 1976: 114). This would therefore be a case of such indifference of law to politically motivated change. The pioneering rulings on codetermination, particularly of the Federal Constitutional Court but to a lesser extent of the Federal Supreme Court as well (Bundesverfassungsgericht (BVerfGE) § 50: 290; Bundesgerichtshof Neue Juristische Wochenschrift (BGH NJW) , 1982: 525), show that relative limits as opposed to absolute limits of legal relevance are involved here. The codetermination law is a classical case of manifold political compromises which can however be productively legally processed — as the Federal Constitutional Court decisions demonstrate. Mutual indifference necessarily occurs only when the adjustment limits of law have actually been reached. In theory this point can be clearly defined: it is the point at which not mere structures but the self-reproductive organization itself is affected. Mutual indifference represents an important case of the application of the "symbolic use" of politics (Edelmann, 1964). In politics great reforms are introduced which never reach society because they disappear when they are translated into law.

Indifference may not occur until the second state of the juridification process in cases where policies have been translated into applicable law but legal norms then come up against an area of life whose structures simply prove resistant to legal change. It is the achievement of Philip Selznick to have pointed to the important connection between the "conceptual readiness" of the legal system and the "opportunity structure" of the social area (Selznick, 1968: 55ff). He illustrates this connection in the field of labor law and company constitution. In "Law, Society and Industrial Justice", (1969) Selznick demonstrates in detail that protection of basic rights and constitutional safeguards in the industrial sphere could only be successfully implemented because the internal bureaucratic decision-making structures of companies opened themselves, as it were, to external legal regulation (Ott, 1972: 372). In the special social area there must be what can be termed an order of relevance which is sufficiently receptive to legal signals. Law in turn must select control signals on a certain wave-length and these must be received and acted on in the area of regulation. Here, too, antitrust law provides examples of structurally related legal resistance. It is no coincidence that the Law on Restraints of Competition was once polemically described as a paper tiger (Wiethölter, 1968: 259), an image which underlines the merely symbolic use of law. Yet at the same time this image implies that only problems of power are concerned here. Of course problems of implementation arise from asymmetries of power, such as inadequate political and financial resources on the part of the Cartel Office or the equivalent regulatory agency when compared with the considerable power and financial resources of companies. Such asymmetries can only be tackled by reinforcing state control resources. Yet the obvious question of power should not blind us to the deeper structural problem, which is that areas of regulation react with indifference when regulatory law fails to achieve the relevance criteria of the social mechanism. If one reacts to this by increasing power resources, one can break the indifference but this does not necessarily lead to the desired structural coupling; indeed the result may be a partial disintegration of self-reproduction.

This much criticized effect of juridification will be examined later in greater detail. However, one misunderstanding must be cleared up first (Macaulay, 1983: 114; Reich, 1983). If the present article stresses self-reproduction and self-regulation of social spheres, to which regulatory legal interventions can only remain external, this should not be regarded as taking sides against political instrumentalization of antitrust law and in favor of a position such as that of Hayek, who views competition as a noncontrollable process of discovery which should on no account be interfered with by interventionist constructivism. On the contrary, the purpose is to underline the contradictory nature of juridification, (the fact that in many fields of politics juridification must cope with both the political instrumentalization of law and the resistence of self-regulating social systems at the same time); and to show that the essential task is to discover the limits of this improbable combination, with a view to defining the conditions of compatibility, of "structural coupling".

4.3 Social Disintegration through Law

"Colonialization of the life-world" — this was the dramatic heading under which Jürgen Habermas (1985: 203) analyzed the dilemma of juridification in welfare states. We have already looked at Habermas' analysis of juridification in social states — he sees it as the political-legal constitutionalization of the economic system. Regulatory law, by delimiting class conflicts and shaping the social state, has a freedom-guaranteeing character. Yet at the same time juridification reveals a dilemma. Tendencies to destroy life-world structures emanate from the very character of juridification itself in the welfare state and cannot be regarded only as undesirable side-effects of this process. Social security law itself is the most important instance of this dilemma. Modern social security certainly represents an improvement on traditional measures for care of the poor, yet bureaucratic procedures and the cash payment of legal entitlements have damaging effects on the social situation, on the self-image of those affected, and on their relations to their social environment. The alien "if.... then" structure of conditional law programs cannot react adequately, let alone preventively, to the causation of the facts requiring compensation. Legal subsumption and bureaucratic procedures subject the concrete life-problem to "violent abstraction" (Habermas, 1981a: 530-532; 1985: 209-210).

If one attempts to fit this example into our general framework, then the following limit of juridification becomes clear: law intervenes in self-regulating situations in a way which endangers the conditions of self-reproduction. Habermas views this as a general dilemma of juridification in the social state. In social law, family law and educational law it can be observed that juridification endangers the self-reproductive spheres of the life-world, i.e. the areas of socialization, social integration and cultural reproduction in their own conditions of self-reproduction (Tennstedt, 1976: 139; Pitschas,

1980: 50; Habermas, 1981: 540; 1985: 210). Even at the risk of falling short of Habermas' normative intention, we are obliged to pursue the abstraction even further. Dangers to self-organization and self-reproduction from regulatory interventions of law are not confined to the sphere of the "life-world". These disintegrating consequences of juridification are also observable in other self-regulating social areas which Habermas classifies as belonging to the "system". Fraenkel, for example, wrote that the price of juridification of labor relations would be a "petrification" of the political class conflict (Fraenkel, 1932). In fact, the above mentioned depoliticization argument leads to the limits of the juridification of politics. Of course, in the modern social state in particular political processes are legalized to a considerable extent, but in such a way that they make possible the build-up of power to produce binding decisions and are not replaced by legally-specific criteria of right and wrong. The same applies to the areas of labor and industry. Simitis has pointed to the dilemmatic structure of norms in juridification on health and safety at work: under the German Work Safety Law and under the American Occupational Safety and Health Act the worker gains increased protection of his health and safety, but he also has to accept the increasing revelation of his personal life area just as he is obliged to accept the consequences for his life style of measures introduced for his safety (Simitis, infra: 132). The same applies to the extension of constitutional safeguards in the field of labor. If in the case of dismissals, transfers and appointments employers are to be constitutionally bound to objective, verifiable criteria, this can lead to the creating of stereotypes which in turn force employees to conform (Simitis, infra: 133 f.).

4.4 Legal Disintegration through Society

A third limit of juridification is reached when regulatory law is itself exposed to the disintegrating demands of politics and society. This equally important phenomenon is often overlooked in the course of the debate on juridification, which has concentrated on the social effects of "creeping legalism". The juridification of society can have disastrous repercussions on law itself (Zacher, infra: 410 f.). Political and social demands for regulation push law to the limits of its effectiveness (Mitnick, 1983). This does not mean that the implementation of law is inadequate, quite the contrary. It is the successful attempts to increase the effectiveness of legal control that have repercussions on the internal structure of law, repercussions with which law may no longer be able to cope. Law is so to speak sandwiched — on one side by social state policy, which calls for legal enforcement and thus for the adjustment of law to the logic of political guidance and on the other by the regulated areas of social life, with their autonomous logic with which law must become involved if it is to be successfully implemented. These double demands on law can go so far as to endanger its own self-reproductive organization.

Niklas Luhmann (1985: 111) recently analyzed the paradoxical danger which juridification poses for law in its relation to the political system. He distinguishes between *normative* elements in law as representatives of the self-reference of law in which legal decisions are produced, and *cognitive* elements as representatives of the openness of law, in which law adapts to its environment. Both elements are necessary but they stand in precariously tense relation to one another. Now when law is enlisted for regulatory tasks in the social state, this precarious relation becomes so strained as to endanger the self-referential structure of law. In particular, Luhmann quotes two major instances of political overtaxing of law: the rapidity of change in political decisions on regulation, which do not allow case law and dogmatics sufficient time to develop independently, and the result orientation of political guidance, which burdens law with the problem of controlling its own results. Although one may disagree with Luhmann about whether these are absolute limits of strain or only relative limits — in which case law could adjust more, particularly with regard to result-orientation — one must in principle agree with his analysis. Even if law, by developing its own stop-rules of result control and by more abstract dogmatic concept formulation, can increase its adjustment and learning capacities — and there are signs that this is happening — it will at some stage come up against absolute limits at which normativity as such is in danger. Here too, a clear distinction must be made between structural changes within the framework of self-reproductive organization and changes in this organization itself, although this does not necessarily mean that the structural scope of self-reproductive organization can be defined in advance.

Yet this is only one side of the self-endangerment of law by juridification, that is, the enforced inclusion of political criteria in law. The normativity of law is equally strained by the inclusion of social criteria, by the enforced adjustment of law to the autonomous logic of the regulated social areas. Once more German antitrust law provides a good example. In his study of the control of abuses in § 22 of the Law on Restraints of Competition, Möschel has shown how the law on competition, for conceptual and practical reasons, has reached its limits (Möschel, 1981b: § 22,4). How is law to maintain its normativity and at the same time become involved in a structure of regulations whose elements are so interdependent that they become, as it were, "moving targets" when they are defined as aspects of the relevant market, of market power and of abuse, with the result that they completely defy any solid legal subsumption? (Möschel, 1974: 166, 171).

Of course to a certain extent economic analyses may be of assistance here. Cartel law, as already stated, provides a spectacular example of the inroads made by the social sciences into law (see Markovits infra). The phenomenon applies to a wide range of areas. "Norm area analyses", to use the term coined by Friedrich Mueller (1966: 168), are required in many areas in order to achieve the regulatory intention. But this "economization" and "sociologization" of law also has its limits (see Daintith and Teubner, 1986). In the case of economic analysis of law fears have been expressed that this "economization" of law could endanger its characteristic feature: its very normativity (Assmann, 1980b: 305). Yet precisely as a partisan of "sociological jurisprudence" one must examine closely such limits of law, in order to realistically estimate the opportunities and dangers of the opening of law towards the social sciences.

We can now formulate a ***second interim finding***: juridification raises many problems, such as inadequate effectiveness of regulation and unintended side-effects, whether in the regulation area or in other social sectors. But these are, so to speak, only the "everyday" problems of the phenomenon. To find out whether fundamental limits of effectiveness have been reached, one must concentrate on the problem of structural coupling of law with social state policies as well as with various social life areas. The deeper reason for this problem lies in the autonomy of social subsystems, which is so highly developed that as self-referential systems they cannot directly influence one another but can only affect self-regulatory processes that are uncontrollable from outside. The fundamental limits of structural coupling are reached either when relevance criteria are not met or when the conditions of self-reproductive organization are endangered. When juridification processes overstep the limits of structural coupling, law inevitably becomes caught up in a regulatory trilemma. This means: either law, politics and/or the social area of life will be mutually indifferent, or juridification will have disintegrating effects on politics and/or social sectors concerned, or, finally, law itself will be exposed to the disintegrating pressures to conform of politics and/or social sectors.

5. Solutions

There is no "solution" of the regulatory trilemma in sight. As already stated, the phenomenon of juridification as such is a partial aspect of societal evolution and cannot therefore be effectively reversed by delegalization strategies. The only approaches which can be taken seriously are those which seek to deal with the dysfunctional consequences resulting from juridification. The solutions proposed are very different, depending on whether juridification processes are regarded as positive or negative and on which problems are perceived as relevant. In the discussion which follows we will take as our criterion how far the various approaches seem capable of avoiding the regulatory trilemma by taking the problem of the structural coupling of law, politics and the area of regulation implicitly or explicitly into account.

5.1 Implementation

Partisans of comprehensive regulation through law will concentrate on the effectiveness of juridification. Their view of the problem has been most clearly formulated in a branch of socio-legal and political research known as "implementation" research (Mayntz, 1977: 51, 1980, 1983; Windhoff-Heritier, 1980, Sabatier and Mazmanian, 1980: 538). It takes as its starting point an "enforcement deficit" of regulatory law which is diagnosed again and again, in environmental, consumer protection, and other policy fields. Implementation research aims to pinpoint the causes of this enforcement deficit and to produce political recommendations on how to overcome them. The background theories here are frequently theories of political guidance of society, including guidance through law. The political system takes on overall responsibility for social processes and in particular is responsible for balancing out and compensating for false developments, particularly in economic life.

The problem of structural coupling is then reduced to a problem of technical effectiveness. If political regulation fails, then power resources and funds must be increased and the means of regulation refined to a point that will ensure the desired effects. In the U.S., this view is strongly supported by a new movement for "re-regulation" (Tolchin and Tolchin, 1983). According to this view, the crisis of regulatory law can only be overcome if the instrumental effectiveness of law is increased. Accordingly the task, then, is to reinforce cognitive, organizational and power resources so that law in fact will fulfil its regulatory functions. Thus legal dogmatics will have to shift even more from a primarily law-applying to a legal-political orientation, even in their conceptuality (Nonet and Selznick, 1978). Jurisprudence will definitively come to see itself as one of those social sciences which produce knowledge about social guidance (Ziegert, 1975). Law will then primarily be a matter of socio-technics (Podgorecki, 1974). In the attempt to achieve greater efficiency, economic and sociological analyses will have to be drawn on. This means in particular that law will have to take into consideration both its own implementation and its social consequences (Luhmann, 1974; Teubner, 1975: 179; Rottleuthner, 1979: 97; Lübbe-Wolff, 1981).

The boom in implementation research in recent years can be explained precisely in these terms: as the expression of an attempt to respond to the crisis of regulatory law by drawing increasingly on social science methods. Implementation research is based on a clearly instrumental notion of law which sees law as a means of social engineering designed to produce certain social changes. In political processes a goal is defined and translated into a legal program which in turn is meant to bring about changes in behavior among those whom it affects. Implementation research works with a relatively simple causal model: the goal determines the program; the program determines the behavior of the implementors and target groups; this in turn produces the required effect. Implementation research concentrates especially on the last links in this chain and attempts to find out why certain enforcement deficits occur, why certain programs do not result in the desired behavioral changes and the desired changes in the social situation. The major objective here is to increase the effectiveness of regulatory law by clarifying the causal connections in the implementation field, thus making them accessible to social engineering.

Renate Mayntz recently published a first appraisal of the achievements of implementation research in which she points out that the hopes pinned on it cannot be fulfilled and argues that corrections must be made in its basic approach (Mayntz, 1983: 7). These corrections point precisely in the direction of our notion of "structural coupling". This relates both to the theoretical and practical mastery of causal connections. Mayntz concludes that the scientific ideal of setting up testable causal hypotheses and developing an axiomatized theory can only be partially realized in implementation research. Instead one must be content with far more modest results: 1) conceptual identification of phenomena and the establishment of categories and typologies; 2) the use of the case-study method, which allows only very guarded generalizations; 3) the taking back of precise individual prognoses on the model of Hayek's pattern predictions, i.e., the mere prediction of general structural patterns. These deficiencies are all explained in terms of the great complexity implementation research faces.

This means quite simply that the most ambitious attempt so far to cope with the crisis of regulatory law by means of social science research on its effects will apparently fail because of the complexity of the subject which it is analyzing. Here again — this time on the basis of practical research experience — the limits of regulatory law become apparent. Social science is not yet capable, and is perhaps fundamentally incapable, of developing sufficiently complex models of reality to check and control in the necessary detail the probable effectiveness of regulatory law in the implementation field. From the standpoint of our approach, this is hardly surprizing. If it is correct that social regulation, because of the autonomy of social systems, can do nothing but trigger uncontrollable self-regulation processes, then simple causal models are inadequate as a means of analyzing and checking the results of legal regulations. In this case both the regulatory claim of law and the analytical claim of the social sciences must be restrained. But does restraint here also mean abandonment of the claim?

The various solutions which Mayntz herself proposes are interesting. Pattern predictions allow only prognoses of very general constellations. In the scientific study of implementation, causal models, it is argued, should be replaced by so-called congruence models. Public policy effectiveness would depend on a "congruent" relationship between structural properties ("the problem to be solved") on the one hand and contextual variables ("program characteristics") on the other. Regulatory law, in the narrower sense of direct regulation which is described as scarcely appropriate, ought to be replaced by incentive programs and persuasive strategies. Finally, hopes are pinned on the granting of calculated autonomy to implementors and target groups alike. She argues for a specific type of "procedural regulation" as an intraorganizational and interorganizational device.

5.2 Deregulation

Is deregulation then the solution? If an implementation expert such as Renate Mayntz, who is not in principle opposed to state intervention, is fascinated by Hayek's "pattern predictions", then we are not far from the normative consequence that juridification should be cut back to the classical framework for competition — a self-regulating process of discovery. However, careful distinctions are required if the "deregulation" movement's criticisms of juridification processes are to be adequately judged and institutional conclusions drawn from them (cf. Mitnick, 1980; Breyer, 1981). We must differentiate between at least three different strands of criticism: 1) cost-benefit analyses, (2) economic versions of "capture theories", and (3) political criticisms of "constructive interventionism".

In the U.S. in particular the regulatory agencies, such as the Securities Exchange Commission, which tackles problems of company law, the Federal Trade Commission which handles questions of antitrust law and the National Labor Relations Board, which deals with problems of labor law, have all been subjected to detailed cost-benefit analyses by economists (McCraw, 1975: 159). The verdicts on this kind of juridification are frank: "What the regulatory commissions are trying to do is difficult to discover; what effect these commissions have is, to a large extent, unknown; when it can be discovered, it is often absurd" (Coase, 1964: 194). Economic cost-benefit analyses have shown the costs of regulation in many cases to be horrendous: the estimated negative balance of the regulation of inshore water pollution in the U.S. from 1972 to 2000: 107 billion dollars; the regulation of transport goods: 4 to 8 billion dollars per annum; the regulation of medical drugs: 350 million dollars per annum (McCraw, 1975: 172; Feick, 1980: 51). Weidenbaum (1980) estimated that the annual costs of administering federal regulatory programs in the U.S. amounted to 6 billion dollars and the cost of compliance amounted to 120 billion dollars. These cost-benefit analyses are undoubtedly useful and their results should certainly be considered in the debate over the extent to which and the way in which regulatory juridification should take place. But of course economic cost-benefit analyses must be treated with caution and used only as one criterion among others. Economic burdens in the form of costs are relatively easy to measure, whereas the *social* benefits of regulation are often difficult, if not impossible, to quantify. One must be very wary of allowing economic criteria of efficiency to completely replace the legal or political weighing up of interests and values — a method which is usually more complex. Stewart (1986), for example, lists six principles which go beyond considerations of economic efficiency: (1) moral condemnation, (2) distributional equity, (3) noncommodity values, (4) assuming control over outcomes, (5) access to judicial remedies, (6) honoring expectations created by past regulation.

The second strand of arguments for deregulation is found in economic versions of the so-called "capture theories". Bernstein (1955), the best known representative of the political "capture theory", put forward the proposition that regulatory agencies are subject to a typical "life cycle". In the first stage of juridification, it is argued, they tackle their regulatory task with public support actively, if not aggressively; in the next phase, however, they degenerate into tired, inert organizations that can be easily captured by the economic interests they are regulating (hence the term "capture theories"). This thesis, which has been taken up and further developed by political-economic authors such as Kolko (1965), McConell (1966) and Lowi (1969), was surprizingly given further support by leading representatives of the Chicago School (Stigler, 1971: 3, 1972: 207, 1975). Stigler, for example, comes to the pointed conclusion that "regulation is acquired by the industry and is designed and operated primarily for its benefits" (Stigler, 1975: 114). Juridification is regarded as a resource supplied by politics and demanded by the regulated industry. In return for political support, industries interested in regulatory policies can receive the form of juridification which corresponds to their interests. Deregulation strategies based on such analyses do not appear at all unreasonable; they concentrate on dysfunctional consequences of juridification. However they hardly affect the fundamental limits of juridification with which we are concerned.

These limits are more likely to be touched on by a politically motivated deregulation strategy. Here, too, Chicago stands in the front line (e.g. Posner 1974; Stigler, 1976: 17; McCormick and Tollison, 1981). Regulatory state intervention is described as the "visible paw" of state economic policy, which prevents the invisible hand of market competition from developing its beneficial effects. The goal striven for here is a high degree of self-organization in society through markets. Milton Friedman says he would most like to see a "completely anarchic world" but he is content with "completely untrammelled capitalism" (Milton Friedman in *Der Spiegel*, No. 48, 1970: 153). Even clearly recognized deficiencies in the market are preferable to state intervention. The consequence of this philosophy is the demand for complete economic deregulation.

Von Hayek and his school propose a more sophisticated line of argument (v. Hayek, 1972, 1973-1979). Social state intervention through juridification is criticized as "interventionist constructivism". The criticism has been applied in particular to antitrust law but can also be generalized to cover every area of economic regulation (Hoppmann, 1972). This school holds that the connections which interventionists claim exist between market structures, market behavior and market results are based on inadequate theoretical premises and are not empirically testable. They work from the unrealistic assumption that complicated market processes can be depicted in simple models of causal relations between a few variables, one that is bound to lead to false economic policies. Hayek's school argues that the regulation of market results by interventions in market structures is fundamentally impossible and leads to arbitrary economic interventionism. Instead, the conception of "competition as a process of discovery" is advocated. Social structures and processes are interpreted as complex phenomena which cannot be reduced to simple so-called economic laws. The market is regarded as a complex, cybernetic system, the elements of which are individuals and companies, which interact spontaneously on the basis of general rules of behavior. The nature of the system is self-regulating, environmentally open and evolutionary.

This means that competition is a dynamic process which cannot be captured in static models. The data and information which go into this process cannot be grasped or pinpointed, so scientifically sound predictions can relate only to the emergence of a general structure but never to specific market results. This need not be a disadvantage, however, because the social institution of competition is consciously brought into play as a process of information, seeking and learning. Competition as a process of discovery is beyond the reach of any scientific method of discovery. It is therefore nonsensical to attempt to define the institutional preconditions of competition on the basis of its results, of the so-called economic competitive functions. The only sensible course is to introduce a system of general rules to guarantee the basic conditions of freedom of competition.

In my view this is a remarkable attempt to tackle the central problem of juridification, that of the structural coupling of juridification and the area of regulation — a remarkable attempt, but one which discredits itself in advance by its normative hypostatization. It is remarkable because it aims to define the absolute limits of effectiveness of juridification: interventionist interference in self-regulating systems cannot in principle be controlled from outside. At the same time an attempt is made to formulate the conditions of the structural coupling of law and competition in the concept of "pattern predictions" and of law as a system of general rules of the game. Thus, we have the possibility of acting in the political and legal spheres despite the limitations of human knowledge about complex self-regulatory processes. This is also the reason why the concept of pattern predictions is so attractive for implementation research, which has reached its cognitive and organizational limits. This concept of competition as a process of discovery could also be usefully applied to other self-regulating systems which are exposed to legal intervention (Gotthold, 1984b).

However, the manner in which this theory hypostatizes sectoral economic rationality is unacceptable. The absolute primacy of freedom of competition over other economic, social and political goals is normatively postulated. According to this view, the sole function of legal rules concerning the economy would be to safeguard freedom of competition. This is unacceptable to jurists on constitutional grounds alone. In terms of constitutional law it can be said that goal conflicts cannot be resolved by the absolute primacy of freedom of competition over other economic and social goals. On the contrary, the constitutional method normally used seems more practicable: the mediation of goals in terms of "practical concordance" — a method which allows greater legislative scope.

For social theory this position is again unacceptable because it hypostatizes the sectoral rationality of the economic system — market and competition — for the whole and refuses to see that it is precisely the task of juridification in welfare states to bring the rationality of other social subsystems into play against the economy (Habermas, 1981: 530; 1985: 209; Willke, 1983b). The function of law cannot be reduced to the mere preservation of self-regulating structures. On the contrary, the fact must be acknowledged that one important function of law is precisely to coordinate the sectoral rationalities of different self-regulating systems with one another (Teubner, 1983: 273). This function does not become redundant because self-regulatory systems defy direct control. It remains necessary — but is incomparably more difficult.

Our discussion has now reached a point at which the most interesting alternatives to juridification appear. Solutions to the problem of juridification are sought which assume *both the necessity of the socio-political instrumentalization of law and the necessity of structural coupling with self-regulating areas of life.* The problem can be formulated as follows: are there ways and means by which law can change from direct regulatory intervention to more indirect, more abstract forms of social regulation, i.e. to the politico-legal control of social self-regulation?

5.3 Control of Self-regulation

As alternative solutions going beyond the formalization and materialization of law, strategies are today being discussed which tend towards more abstract, indirect regulation by law. Law is relieved of its task of regulating social areas and is instead burdened with the control of self-regulating processes (Bohnert and Klitzsch, 1980: 200; Ronge, 1984).

The crisis of regulatory law is here diagnosed as a social immune reaction to legal interventions. The problems of juridification show that different social systems operate according to their own inner logic, which cannot easily be harmonized with the logic of other systems. Material legal programs have at their disposal modes of functioning, criteria of rationality and organizational patterns which are not necessarily adequate to the regulated areas. The background theories on which such ideas are based are frequently macro-theories of society and law, usually variants of system functionalism or critical theory or manifold attempts to combine the two (see Wiethölter, 1985; Buxbaum infra). Normatively, these approaches have highly different perspectives, from the emancipation of man to smoothly functioning system technology, depending on the theoretical context and normative preferences. Yet they all have one problem in common. Is normative integration still possible in a society characterised by inner contradictions, by distintegrating, indeed disruptive conflicts between the specific logic of highly specialized sub-systems? (Habermas, 1981: 334; Luhmann, 1975: 51). They all assume that neither the state nor law is capable of achieving this integration — as Durkheim perhaps envisaged in his notion of organic solidarity. However, politics and law have to bring about important structural preconditions for a new type of decentralized integration of society.

The proposed solution is to move to "constitutive strategies of law" (Stewart, 1986), i.e., to introduce structural legal frameworks for social self-regulation. The term "proceduralization", for instance, is used as an overall heading for this function of law, which is to encourage "social systems capable of learning" (Wiethölter, 1982a, 1982b, 1984, 1985). Essentially three matters are concerned here: 1) the safeguarding of social autonomy by an "external constitution" (Habermas, 1981: 544f.; 1985: 218f.), a legal guarantee for "semi-autonomous social fields" (Moore, 1973; Galanter, 1980; 1981); 2) structural frameworks for effective self-regulation, for instance along the lines of "external decentralization" of public tasks or in terms of internal reflexion of social effects (Lehner, 1979: 178; Teubner, 1983: 273; 1987; Hart, 1983; Gotthold, 1984a: 249; Buxbaum, infra); 3) the canalization of conflicts between systems by "relational programmes"

(Willke, 1983a: 62ff., 145) or neo-corporatist mediation mechanisms of "procedural regulation" (Mayntz, 1983; Streeck and Schmitter, 1985), by "negotiated regulations" (Harter, 1982; Reich, 1983), by semi-formal modes of procedure in the so-called "discovery process of practice" (Joerges, 1981: 111), or by legal coordination of different system rationalities (Scharpf, 1979; Assmann, 1980a: 324; 1980b; Ladeur, 1982a: 391; 1982b: 74; 1983: 102; 1984). In short: instead of directly regulating social behavior, law confines itself to the regulation of organization, procedures and the redistribution of competences.

What does this mean in concrete terms? "Negotiated regulation" is one heading under which such indirect regulations through law are discussed today (Harter, 1982; Reich, 1983). It includes "dependent bargaining" as well as "constitutive bargaining" (Stewart, 1986). Antitrust law, for example, contains a wealth of material to illustrate regulation through negotiation, in which solutions are reached through negotiation under the pressure of legal sanctions (Hopt, infra). The control of company mergers is an important example. Here, with the threat of a ban on the contemplated merger looming in the background, modifications of the merger proposals are worked out cooperatively.

"Bargaining in the shadow of law" describes a mechanism which has been demonstrated in many areas of law (Mnookin and Kornhauser, 1979: 950; Galanter, 1980). The mere existence of substantive law with its threat of sanctions creates negotiating positions for the parties — whether private individuals, organizations or state institutions — which ultimately affect the result of negotiations — an effect which would not have been achieved had the law not existed. The advantages here are clear to see: this method is more likely to lead to flexible, cooperative solutions geared to specific situations as opposed to rigid, approximative and authoritative solutions. The problem of structural coupling is tackled in such a way that the official function of law, which is to decree changes of behavior recedes into the background, whereas its latent function, which is to regulate systems of negotiation becomes crucial.

Numerous studies have analysed how widespread this phenomenon has become (e.g. Treiber, 1983). Events regularly take the following course. First, law is primarily used to bring about a certain kind of behavior by the threat of negative sanctions. However, enforcement deficits appear which oblige the parties concerned to transform the enforcement systems into negotiation systems. One can interpret this by arguing that in this case regulatory law is subject to a latent change of function. As direct regulation of human behavior it soon reaches its limits and is tacitly reinterpreted as a kind of procedural law. The threat potential of legal sanctions is not used. It is not so to say "liquidated", but in fact survives as a legally guaranteed power of negotiation within the self-regulating system of negotiation. Indeed there are even interpretations of regulatory law which warn against taking the implementation of law too seriously. "Strict enforcement by the book" often appears unreasonable and endangers the precarious regulation situation (Bardach and Kagan, 1982).

A critical point is reached when not only the parties concerned reinterpret regulatory law more or less openly and more or less legitimately as negotiation regulating law, but law itself abandons direct regulation to concentrate instead on structuring negotiation systems. Of course labor law provides the historical paradigm here (Simitis, infra; Wiethölter, 1985: 239; Mückenberger, 1980: 241). State legislation on safety at work and the mere regulation of free collective bargaining are, within certain limits, functional equivalents of the goals of employee protection. In many cases indirect regulation of the system of free collective bargaining has been preferred to substantive regulation because of the obvious advantages it brings. Without placing the emphasis on concrete substantive control state law here tends to regulate collective agreements only indirectly — by making legal recognition of negotiating parties dependent on certain structural conditions, by devising procedural norms for the system of negotiation and for disputes, and by extending or restricting the competences of the collective parties. In fact the attempt here is merely to control indirectly the quality of the negotiation results through a balancing of negotiating power. More important than rearrangements of social power by means of law are legal strategies designed to increase the "public responsibility" of parties involved in industrial disputes. Here I do not mean the rather naive attempts to impose public accountability on both sides of industry through a "public interest" clause. The development of reflection structures in the system of industrial conflicts, i.e. of structures in which the external social results are taken into account when action is being considered, is more likely to be achieved by institutional influencing of the size of organizations and their internal structures. Comparative empirical studies to a certain extent support the hypothesis that the overall social impact tends to be reflected more within the decision-making processes of the system of collective bargaining when collective labor law systematically favors a centralized "industrial trade union" as opposed to a decentralized system of shop stewards with professionally oriented trade unions (Streeck *et al.* 1978; Streeck 1979: 206, Groser, 1979: 258). Although here too one should be wary of generalizations, procedural law does show a certain superiority over material law (cf. Giugni, infra). As Simitis puts it: "Procedural rules are almost always symptomatic of a phase of juridification in which regulation by material rules is no longer sufficient, if only because of their fundamentally selective approach and their limited adaptability to changing social and economic conditions" (Simitis, 1984: 102).

Of course, the model of collective labor law cannot be universally applied throughout the world of industry and labor. Similar attempts in other areas to establish a system of negotiation based on countervailing power have proved only partially capable of development, especially in the field of consumer law (Hart and Joerges, 1980; Joerges, 1981: 52).

In the U.S. proposals for "negotiated regulation" have aroused considerable interest (Harter, 1982). As a means of preventing excessive "lawyering", which only intensifies conflicts, it is proposed that the groups concerned hold negotiations on regulation, to be presided over by a convenor who would mediate between the parties and be vested with certain legal powers. The intention here is clearly to draw on the experience gained in American labor law arbitration. Similar proposals have been made in France in connection with problems of rent and consumer law (Reich, 1983: 28). This generally amounts to the state-directed organization of a system of negotiation in which all the relevant interest groups participate. It is intended to lead to "accords negociés collectivement". The problematic of the parallel to collective labor law is evident: the organizational capacity of consumer associations are not even remotely comparable with those of trade unions.

Consumer law in particular, but other areas of contract law as well, show that "external decentralization" fails when social power and information asymmetries reduce legal control of self-regulating processes to a farce. The inevitable consequence is therefore specific legal reinforcement of negotiating power in order to counteract these asymmetries — but the likelihood of this achieving the desired effects must be regarded with scepticism. Functional equivalents, however, may be established if autonomous public institutions are "artificially" created with state aid — to provide consumer information or to organize effective representation of consumer interests (e.g. the creation of the "Stiftung Warentest", of consumer centres, state-funded representation of consumers) (Joerges, 1981: 133). Here, too, the role of state law would consist not of the material regulation of market processes but of procedural and organizational pre-structuring of "autonomous" social processes. Through the ordering of organizational norms, the law forces highly specialized, unilaterally oriented organizations to take the conflicting demands of their social environment into account when making decisions. (The consequence of this perspective in consumer law, which could overcome the weaknesses of direct legal interventionism is described by Joerges, 1983: 57, 65).

"Social contract" is the term used to define a trend in which the role of law is transformed from one of direct regulation of behavior to a more indirect regulation of procedures [21]. The social contract is merely a special case of the many "neocorporatist arrangements" which are attracting increasing interest internationally[22]. Unlike the pluralistic mediation of interests, in which social groups bring their interests to bear only in the forecourt of state power, the neocorporatist syndrome amounts to a form of voluntary cooperation between the state and social interests, and in particular to a decision-making symbiosis between the state, trade unions and industrial associations. The reasons for this development are essentially found in the increase of power and rationality of sectoral social systems, in the face of which classical legal forms of state regulation break down (Schmitter, 1977: 7; Winkler, 1976: 100). This "disenchantment of the state" (Willke, 1983a) leads to new forms

[21] For the emergence of different forms of "Social Contract" see Simitis, Giugni, Clark and Wedderburn, infra.

[22] See as an informative introduction, Alemann and Heinze, 1979; Alemann, 1981. For recent proposals in the U.S., see Industrial Policy Study Group, 1984.

of juridification, to "new legal forms of the intertwining of the state and the economy" (Gessner and Winter, 1982). According to Winter, the crucial feature here is the "avoidance of imperative intervention" through temporary cooperation in which the state gives up part of its domination and industry gives up part of its freedom. This takes the form of the permanent installation of state rationality in private organizations, of the repetition of social conflicts in the sectoral system itself and of the private "occupation" of state organizations. The concomitant loss of demarcation and generalization of the state apparatus can even lead to a form of intertwining in which the two parties are no longer distinguishable as organizations with structural and functional limits but which instead form a single identity (Winter, 1982: 28).

The term "relational program" has been introduced into the discussion to describe the new role of law in such neocorporatist arrangements (Willke, 1983a: 10; Teubner and Willke, 1984). It differs from the conditional program of classical formal law and the purpose program of social state regulatory law by being oriented towards organization and procedures for coordinating different rationalities of social sub-systems. It is no longer the classical forms of law — prohibitions and incentives — which predominate, but "procedural regulations" (Mayntz, 1983) in which the state involves social interests in procedures of program formulation, decision-making and implementation.

The juridification process is not stopped by such trends towards the reduction of direct state influence but merely steered into new channels. As Streeck and Schmitter (1985: 25f.) explain: "It is true that an associative social order implies a devolution of state functions to interest intermediaries. But this has to be accompanied by a simultaneous acquisition by the state of a capacity to design, monitor, and keep in check the new self-regulating systems" ("procedural corporatism"). There is another phenomenon worth noting here, as well, in connection with which Simitis (infra: 143) talks of a "second generation of employee protection rules" — but it is a phenomenon which is generalizable beyond this: the internal organizational consequences of neocorporatism. In the development of American labor law the duty to bargain has been supplemented by the duty of fair representation: the employer's duty to negotiate implies the duty of the trade unions to defend the interests of all their members. This was the starting point for a wave of juridification which affects the internal organization of trade unions and other organizations representing employees, which have hitherto been regarded as autonomous (see, e.g., Summers, 1977: 251). Even in Great Britain, Clark and Wedderburn (infra: 182) observe, in regard to the internal conduct of trade union affairs, "an unambiguous increase in state intervention in areas which were previously left to autonomous regulation". The phenomenon is generalizable from trade unions to all organized interests which are bound into neocorporatist negotiation systems. As a result of this binding a large number of social problems (the coordination of interests, the build-up of legitimation, the implementation of the policies worked out in negotiation) are shifted to the inside of the organization itself. This means a shift from "external" market coordination to "internal" political processes of organizations. The internal structure of the organization thus becomes the "Achilles' heel of corporatism"[23]. Thus the internal constitution of private organizations becomes a central regulatory problem of state law.

This leads directly to the last complex of problems: the role of law in relation to large private organizations. As Buxbaum, Kübler and Corsi (infra) have demonstrated, there is a tendency in company law towards a materialization of previously neutral formal law. However, state regulation and judicial control here seem to reach the limits of their control capacity, not only because of superficial changes in political trends but for structural reasons as well (Mayntz, 1979: 55). Our approach would not necessarily lead to a reinforcement of state power resources but rather to a shift towards more abstract guidance mechanisms: i.e., towards the design of legal norms which would systematically strengthen the development of "reflection structures" within the economic industry. "Company constitution" and "neocorporatist systems of negotiation" are the relevant terms here (see Hopt and Teubner, 1985). The question which remains unanswered is whether such control mechanisms can be directed in such a way that they will function effectively as a "corporate conscience", in other words, force the economic system or the company to "internalize" external social conflicts, and do so in such a way that internal decision-making processes also take into account non-economic interests of employees, consumers and the general public. Within the past decades, economic goal structures within companies have undergone considerable changes, from profit orientation to growth orientation. Is it completely inconceivable that they could change again so as to include problems of ecological balance in their set of goals? Does this have to be, as Christopher Stone (1975) puts it, the point "where the law ends"? Is it not rather precisely the point at which law receives its institutional opportunity: to bring about the "reflexive" control of economic behavior, which is capable of transforming external social "troubles" into internal organizational "issues" for the micro-policies of the company? Buxbaum (infra: 264 ff.) points out rightly that the success of such a legal strategy depends mainly on the "institutional setting" of adequate judicial and bureaucratic structures.

The main goal is not the reduction of power, nor an increase in individual participation in the emphatic sense of "participatory democracy" but the well-considered design of internal organizational structures which make the institutions concerned — companies, public associations, trade unions, mass media and educational institutions — sensitive to the social effects which their strategies for the maximization of their specific rationality trigger. The major function of such reflexive internal structures would be to replace interventionist state control by effective internal control. The creation of structural conditions for an "organizational conscience" which would reflect the balance between function and performance of the social system — this, in our definition, would be the integrative role of reflexive law.

[23] A discussion of the relationship of neo-corporatist structures and the internal structures of organization is found in Teubner, 1978b: 545, 1979: 487.

These various approaches and development trends appear at first sight to be extremely varied. What they have in common is that they tackle, though in very different ways, the problem of the structural coupling of law, politics and the regulated areas. "Structural coupling" is a term which could open up further perspectives for future theoretical and practical legal attempts to grasp the phenomenon of juridification. It seems essential for an adequate understanding of the relationship between law and society to draw conclusions from the social autonomy discussed above, or more precisely, from the autopoietic organization of social subsystems. Politico-legal intervention in complex self-reproducing systems would then have to abandon the model of hierarchic control relations and adapt itself to reticular interaction of communication systems with equal status. This refers legal intervention to the indirect method of "decentral context regulation" (Teubner and Willke, 1984: 4). This form of regulation is made necessary and possible by the high degree of autonomy of social subsystems: regulation impulses are only possible in the form of context conditions, which as observable differences constitute the information basis for the respective basal circularity.

And this means more than regulation in the classical liberal sense of residual context regulation which provides the social subsystems with the basic framework for their freedom of self-organization. What is required is an *internal legal modelling of the autopoietic organization of social subsystems*, with the goal of identifying strategic variables in order to change them and, by influencing them, to institutionalize environmentally appropriate reflection processes. The possibility that this would overtax the internal capabilities of law cannot be ruled out. However, theoretical considerations do not in principle invalidate this form of regulation; on the contrary they support it.

A second possibility of decentral context regulation consists of fully accepting the closure and intransparence of complex social systems as "black boxes" and concentrating legal regulation solely on the external relations, the interactive relations between the subsystems. The chances of legal effectiveness would then lie in the fact that law would not have to impose its mode of operation on other areas but could confine itself to the norming of the independent interaction systems. In this case no isomorphism of modes of operation would be required but only their "structural coupling". The necessary consequence of the social phenomenon of self-reference and self-reproduction is the adjustment of legal theory and legal practice to such concepts.

However, exaggerated hopes must be warned against[24]. It must be assumed that the move from direct legal control to indirect regulation of self-regulation would bring new, serious problems in its wake. "Inexactness" of legal regulation and increased coordination costs would almost inevitably be side-effects of a "proceduralization" of law (Kübler, infra: 134 ff.). Finally it

[24] Blankenburg, 1984, expends a great amount of energy in destroying illusions about "proceduralized" law, which in fact no one ever had in this form.

must be emphasized that the issue is not one of totally adjusting law to new forms of regulation. Just as classical formal law is not replaced, but at most overlaid, by materialization processes, here too it is only a matter of relative dominance. The most that can be expected is a shift of emphasis in legal regulation towards more flexible strategies. These strategies will not solve all the problems of juridification, nor will they reverse the process of juridification as such. On the contrary, the legal regulation of self-regulation can itself be seen as a continuation of the juridification trend, but — and this would be the crucial step forward — it would help steer the process into more socially compatible channels.

[Translated from the German by Paul Knight]

References

ABEL, Richard L. (1980) "Delegalization — A Critical Review of its Ideology, Manifestations, and Social Consequences," in E. Blankenburg, E. Klausa, H. Rottleuthner (eds.), *Alternative Rechtsformen und Alternativen zum Recht.* Opladen: Westdeutscher Verlag.

—(ed.) (1982) *The Politics of Informal Justice.* New York: American Press.

ALEMANN, Ulrich von (ed.) (1981) *Neokorporatismus.* Frankfurt: Campus.

ALEMANN, Ulrich von and Rolf G. HEINZE (1979) *Verbände und Staat.* Opladen: Westdeutscher Verlag.

ASSMANN, Heinz Dieter (1980a) *Wirtschaftsrecht in der Mixed Economy. Auf der Suche nach einem Sozialmodell für das Wirtschaftsrecht.* Königstein: Athenäum.

—(1980b) "Zur Steuerung gesellschaftlich-ökonomischer Entwicklung durch Recht", in H.-D. Assmann, G. Brüggemeier, D. Hart and C. Joerges, *Wirtschaftsrecht als Kritik des Privatrechts.* Königstein: Athenäum.

ASSMANN, Heinz-Dieter, Gerd BRÜGGEMEIER, Dieter HART and Christian JOERGES (1980) *Wirtschaftsrecht als Kritik des Privatrechts.* Königstein: Athenäum.

BADURA, Peter, Fritz RITTNER, and Bernd RUETHERS (1977) *Mitbestimmungsgesetz 1976 und Grundgesetz. Gemeinschaftsgutachten.* München: Beck.

BARDACH, Eugene and Robert A. KAGAN (1982) *Going by the Book — the Problem of Regulatory Unreasonableness.* Philadelphia: Temple University Press.

BARTON, John H. (1975) "Behind the Legal Explosion", 27 *Stanford Law Review* 567.

BEER, Stafford (1975) "Preface to 'Autopoiesis'", in: H. Maturana and F. Varela (1980) *Autopoiesis and Cognition.* London: Reidel.

BENDER, Rolf (1976) "Das staatliche Schiedsgericht — ein Ausweg aus der Krise des Zivilprozesses?", 54 *Deutsche Richterzeitung* 193.

BERNER, Georg (1978) "Inflation im Recht", 24 *Bayrisches Verwaltungsblatt* 617.

BERNSTEIN, Marver (1955) *Regulating Business by Independent Commissions.* Princeton: Princeton University Press.

BEYME, Klaus von (1977) *Gewerkschaften und Arbeitsbeziehungen in kapitalistischen Ländern.* München: Piper.

BIERBRAUER, Günter, Josef FALKE and Klaus Friedrich KOCH (1978) "Konflikt und Konfliktbeteiligung. Eine interdisziplinäre Studie über Rechtsgrundlage und Funktion der Schiedsmannsinstitution", in Bierbrauer *et al. Zugang zum Recht.* Bielefeld: Gieseking.

BLANKENBURG, Erhard (1984) "The Poverty of Evolutionism. A Critique of Teubner's Case for 'Reflexive Law'". 18 *Law and Society Review* 723.

BLANKENBURG, Erhard, Walter GOTTWALD and Dieter STREMPEL (eds.) (1982) *Alternativen in der Ziviljustiz.* Köln: Bundesanzeiger Verlag.

BLANKENBURG, Erhard, Ekkehard KLAUSA and Hubert ROTTLEUTHNER (eds.) (1980) *Alternative Rechtsformen und Alternativen zum Recht.* Opladen: Westdeutscher Vlg.

BOERLIN, Daniel, Gottlieb A. KELLER and Christoph ZUMSTEIN (1978) "Die Normenflut als Rechtsproblem", in K. Eichenberger, W. Buser, A. Metraux, P. Trappe (eds.), *Grundfragen der Rechtsetzung.* Basel.

BOHNERT, Werner and Wolfgang KITZSCH (1980) "Gesellschaftliche Selbstregulierung und staatliche Implementation politischer Programme" in R. Mayntz (ed.), *Implementation politischer Programme* I. Königstein: Athenäum.

BOSETZKY, Horst (1978) "Bürokratisierung in Wirtschaft und Unternehmung", in H. Geissler (ed.), *Verwaltete Bürger-Gesellschaft in Fesseln. Bürokratisierung und ihre Folgen für Staat, Wirtschaft und Gesellschaft.* Frankfurt a.M.: Ullstein.

BREYER, Stephen G. (1981) *Administrative Law and Regulatory Policy.* Boston: Little Brown.

—(1982) *Regulation and its Reform.* Cambridge: Harvard University Press.

BRÜGGEMEIER, Gerd (1980) "Probleme einer Theorie des Wirtschaftsrechts", in H.-D. Assmann, G. Brüggemeier, D. Hart, C. Joerges, *Wirtschaftsrecht als Kritik des Privatrechts.* Königstein: Athenäum.

BUXBAUM, Richard M. (1984a) "Corporate Legitimacy, Economic Theory, and Legal Doctrine", 45 *Ohio State Law Journal* 515.

— (1984b) "Federalism and Company Law", 82 *Michigan Law Review*

— (1986) "Federal Aspects of Corporate Law and Economic Theory", in T. C. Daintith and G. Teubner (eds.), *Contract and Organization.* Berlin: De Gruyter.

CHRISTIE, Nils (1976) "Konflikte als Eigentum", *Informationsbrief der Sektion Rechtssoziologie der deutschen Gesellschaft für Soziologie* 12.

CLARK, Robert (1981) "The Four Stages of Capitalism: Reflections on Investment Management Treaties", 94 *Harvard Law Review* 561.

COASE, Ronald H. (1964) "Comment", 14 *American Economic Review* 194.

DÄUBLER, Wolfgang (1976) *Das Arbeitsrecht* Bd. 1. Reinbek: Rowohlt.

DAINTITH, Terence C. (1987) "Law as Policy Instrument: A Comparative Perspective", in T. C. Daintith (ed.), *Law and Economic Policy: Comparative and Critical Approaches.* Berlin: De Gruyter.

DAINTITH, Terence C. and Gunther TEUBNER (eds.) (1986) *Contract and Organisation.* Berlin: De Gruyter.

DAMM, Reinhard (1976) *Systemtheorie und Recht. Zur Normentheorie Talcott Parsons'.* Berlin: Duncker und Humblot.

DANZIG, Richard (1973) "Toward the Creation of a Complementary Decentralized System of Criminal Justice", 26 *Stanford Law Review* 1.

DREIER, Horst (1983) "Rezension zu Voigt, Verrechtlichung", 4 *Zeitschrift für Rechtssoziologie* 101.

EDELMANN, Murray (1964) *The Symbolic Uses of Politics.* Urbana: University of Illinois Press.

EDER, Klaus (1978) "Zur Rationalisierungsproblematik des modernen Rechts", 29 *Soziale Welt* 247.

EHRLICH, Thomas (1976) "Legal Pollution", *New York Times Magazine* (February 8) 17.

ERD, Rainer (1978) *Verrechtlichung industrieller Konflikte. Normative Rahmenbedingungen des dualen Systems der Industrie.* Frankfurt a.M.: Campus.

—(1984) "Gesetzgebung oder Machtpoker? Das Beispiel der amerikanischen Gewerkschaften", in R. Voigt (ed.), *Abschied vom Recht?* Frankfurt: Suhrkamp.

FARJAT, Gerard (1986) "The Contribution of Economics to Legal Analysis: The Concept of the Firm" in G. Teubner and T. Daintith (eds.) *Contract and Organization.* Berlin: De Gruyter.

FEICK, Jürgen (1980) "Zur Kritik regulativer Politik in den Vereinigten Staaten", 21 *Politische Vierteljahresschrift* 43.

FIKENTSCHER, Wolfgang (1975) *Methoden des Rechts.* Tübingen: Mohr Siebeck.

FISCHER, Robert (1978) "Kurzinformation", 28 *Wirtschaft und Wettbewerb* 6.

FLUME, Werner (1977) *Allgemeiner Teil des Bürgerlichen Rechtes, Bd. I, Teil 1. Die Personengesellschaft.* Berlin: Springer.

FRAENKEL, Ernst (1932) "Die politische Bedeutung des Arbeitsrechts", in T. Ramm (ed.) (1966) *Arbeitsrecht und Politik.* Neuwied: Luchterhand.

FRIEDMAN Lawrence M. (1975) *The Legal System. A Social Science Perspective.* New York: Simon and Schuster.

FULLER, Lon L. (1969) "Two Principles of Human Association". 11 *Nomos* 3.

GALANTER, Marc (1980) "Legality and its Discontents: A Preliminary Assessment of Current Theories of Legalization and Delegalization", in E. Blankenburg, E. Klausa and H. Rottleuthner (eds.), *Alternative Rechtsformen und Alternativen zum Recht.* Opladen: Westdeutscher Verlag.

—(1981) "Justice in Many Rooms: Courts, Private Ordering and Indigenous Law", in M. Cappelletti (ed.), *Access to Justice and the Welfare State.* Alphen: Sijthoff.

GESSNER, Volker and Gerd WINTER (1982) *Rechtsformen der Verflechtung von Staat und Wirtschaft.* Opladen: Westdeutscher Verlag.

GIESE, Bernhard (1978) "Ansätze zur Tatsachenforschung und Rechtssoziologie des Prozessvergleichs", in G. Bierbrauer *et al. Zugang zum Recht.* Bielefeld: Gieseking.

GLANVILLE, Ranulph (1979) *The Form of Cybernetics: Whitening the Black Box.* Louisville, Kentucky.

GOTTHOLD, Jürgen (1981) "Neuere Entwicklung der Wettbewerbstheorie", 145 *Zeitschrift für das gesamte Handelsrecht und Wirtschaftsrecht* 286.

—(1984a) "Privatisierung oder Entbürokratisierung kommunaler Sozialpolitik zur Erfüllung von Aufgaben, die nicht durch Geld und Recht steuerbar sind", in R. Voigt (ed.), *Abschied vom Recht?* Frankfurt: Suhrkamp.

—(1984b) "Jenseits von Geld und Recht. Chancen und Grenzen kommunaler Sozialpolitik für soziale Brennpunkte", in Krüger and Pankoke (eds.), *Kommunale Sozialpolitik.* München: Beck.

GOTTWALD, Walter (1981) *Streitbeilegung ohne Urteil.* Tübingen: Mohr und Siebeck.

GROSER, Manfred (1979) "Stabilität und Wandel im System der Arbeitsbeziehungen", 20 *Politische Vierteljahresschrift* 258.

HABERMAS Jürgen (1976) *Zur Rekonstruktion des historischen Materialismus.* Frankfurt: Suhrkamp.

—(1981) *Theorie des kommunikativen Handelns* Vol. 1 and 2. Frankfurt: Suhrkamp.

—(1985) "Law as Medium and Law as Institution", in G. Teubner (ed.) *Dilemmas of Law in the Welfare State.* Berlin/New York: De Gruyter.

HART, Dieter (1983) "Contract and Consumer Protection: Organizing Countervailing Power — On the Development of Substantive and Reflexive Elements in Modern Contract Law", in D. Trubek (ed.), *Reflexive Law and the Regulatory Crisis,* Madison: University of Madison.

HART, Dieter, and Christian JOERGES (1980) "Verbraucherrecht und Marktökonomie", in H.-D. Assmann, G. Brüggemeier, D. Hart and C. Joerges, *Wirtschaftsrecht als Kritik des Privatrechts.* Königstein: Athenäum.

Harter, Philip J. (1982) "Negotiating Regulation: A Cure for Malaise", 71 *Georgetown Law Journal* 1.

Hayek, Friedrich A. von (1972) *Die Theorie komplexer Phänomene*. Tübingen: Mohr.

—(1973-79) *Law Legislation and Liberty*, vols. 1-3. London: Routledge & K. Paul.

Hegenbarth, Rainer (1980) "Sichtbegrenzungen, Forschungsdefizite und Zielkonflikte in der Diskussion über Alternativen zur Justiz", in E. Blankenburg, E. Klausa and H. Rottleuthner (eds.), *Alternative Rechtsformen und Alternative zum Recht*. Opladen: Westdeutscher Verlag.

—(1983) "Selbstauflösung des Rechtssystems", in R. Voigt (ed.), *Abschied vom Recht?* Frankfurt: Suhrkamp.

Hejl, Peter M. (1982a) *Sozialwissenschaft als Theorie selbstreferentieller Systeme*. Frankfurt: Campus.

— (1982b) "Die Theorie autopoietischer Systeme: Perspektiven für die soziologische Systemtheorie", 13 *Rechtstheorie* 45.

Heldrich, Andreas (1981) "Normüberflutung". *Festschrift für Zweigert*. Tübingen: Mohr und Siebeck.

Heller, Thomas C. (1979) "Is the Charitable Exemption from Property Taxation an Easy Case? General Concerns about Legal Economics and Jurisprudence", in D. Rubinfeld (ed.), *Essays on the Law and the Economics of Local Governments*. Washington D.C.: Urban Institute.

Hillermeier, Karl (1978) "Eindämmung der Gesetzesflut", 24 *Bayrisches Verwaltungsblatt* 321.

Hoffmann, Reinhard (1968) *Rechtsfortschritt durch gewerkschaftliche Gegenmacht*. Frankfurt a.M.: Europäische Verlagsanstalt.

Hoppmann, Erich (1972) *Fusionskontrolle*. Tübingen: Mohr Siebeck.

Hopt, Klaus and Gunther Teubner (eds.) (1985) *Corporate Governance and Directors' Liability*. Berlin: De Gruyter.

Industrial Policy Study Group (1984) *Promoting Economic Growth and Competitiveness*. London.

Jacoby, Henry (1969) *Die Bürokratisierung der Welt. Ein Beitrag zur Problemgeschichte*. Neuwied: Luchterhand.

Joerges, Christian (1981) *Verbraucherschutz als Rechtsproblem*. Heidelberg: Verlagsgesellschaft Recht und Wirtschaft.

—(1983) "Der Schutz des Verbrauchers und die Einheit des Zivilrechts", 28 *Aktiengesellschaft* 57.

Kennedy, Duncan (1973) "Legal Formality", 2 *The Journal of Legal Studies* 351.

—(1976) "Form and Substance in Private Law Adjudication", 89 *Harvard Law Review* 1685.

Kirchheimer, Otto (1933) Verfassungsreform und Sozialdemokratie (1972) in O. Kirchheimer (ed.), *Funktionen des Staates und der Verfassung*. Frankfurt: Suhrkamp.

Klauss, Gerd (1975) *Die Bestimmung von Marktmacht. Eine Untersuchung von Machtkriterien unter Berücksichtigung der Zusammenschlußkontrolle des "Gesetzes gegen Wettbewerbsbeschränkungen" in der Bundesrepublik Deutschland*. Berlin: Duncker und Humblot.

Köndgen, Johannes (1981) *Selbstbindung ohne Vertrag. Zur Haftung aus geschäftsbezogenem Handeln*. Tübingen: Mohr und Siebeck.

Kolko, Gabriel (1965) *Railroads and Regulation 1877-1916*. Princeton: Princeton U.P.

Krawietz, Werner (1978) *Juristische Entscheidung und wissenschaftliche Erkenntnis. Eine Untersuchung zum Verhältnis von dogmatischer Rechtswissenschaft und rechtswissenschaftlicher Grundlagenforschung*. Wien, New York: Springer.

KÜBLER, Friedrich (1981) *Gesellschaftsrecht.* Heidelberg: C.F. Müller.

KÜBLER, Friedrich, Walter SCHMIDT and Spiros SIMITIS (1978) *Mitbestimmung als gesetzgebungspolitische Aufgabe. Zur Verfassungsmäßigkeit des Mitbestimmungsgesetzes.* Baden-Baden: Nomos.

LADEUR, Karl-Heinz (1982a) "Konsensstrategien statt Verfassungsinterpretation?", 29 *Der Staat* 391.

—(1982b) "Verrechtlichung der Ökonomie — Ökonomisierung des Rechts?" in V. Gessner, G. Winter (eds.), *Rechtsformen der Verflechtung von Staat und Wirtschaft.* Opladen: Westdeutscher Verlag.

—(1983) "Politische Ökonomie verwaltungsgerichtlicher Planungskontrolle", in R. Voigt (ed.), *Gegentendenzen zur Verrechtlichung.* Opladen: Westdeutscher Verlag.

—(1984) *Abwägung — Ein neues Paradigma des Verwaltungsrechts.* Frankfurt: Campus.

LEHNER, Franz (1979) *Grenzen des Regierens.* Königstein: Athenäum.

LITAN, Robert E. and William D. NORDHAUS(1983) *Reforming Federal Regulation.* Yale: Yale University Press.

LOWI, Theodore (1969) *The End of Liberalism.* New York: Norton.

LÜBBE-WOLFF Gertrude (1981) *Rechtsfolgen und Realfolgen.* Freiburg: Alber.

LUHMANN, Niklas (1972) *Rechtssoziologie.* Reinbek: Rowohlt.

—(1974) *Rechtssystem und Rechtsdogmatik.* Stuttgart: Kohlhammer.

—(1975) "Die Weltgesellschaft", in *Soziologische Aufklärung.* Opladen: Westdeutscher Verlag.

—(1977) *Funktion der Religion.* Frankfurt a.M.: Suhrkamp.

—(1981a) *Ausdifferenzierung des Rechts.* Frankfurt a.M.: Suhrkamp.

—(1981b) "Selbstreferenz und Teleologie in gesellschaftstheoretischer Perspektive", in N. Luhmann *Gesellschaftsstruktur und Semantik 2.* Frankfurt: Suhrkamp.

—(1981c) *Politische Theorie im Wohlfahrtsstaat.* München: Olzog.

—(1984) *Soziale Systeme. Grundriß einer allgemeinen Theorie.* Frankfurt: Suhrkamp.

—(1985) "The Self-Reproduction of the Law and its Limits" in G. Teubner (ed.) *Dilemmas of Law in the Welfare State.* Berlin: De Gruyter.

—(1987) "The Unity of the Legal System" in G. Teubner (ed.), *Autopoiesis in Law and Society.* Berlin: De Gruyter.

LUTTER, Marcus (1982) "Rolle und Recht", in *Festschrift für Helmut Coing.* München: Beck.

MACAULY, Stewart (1983) "Private Government", in D. Trubek (ed.), *Reflexive Law and the Regulatory Crisis.* Madison: University of Madison-Wisconsin.

MARTENS, Klaus Peter (1976) "Allgemeine Grundsätze zur Anwendbarkeit des Mitbestimmungsgesetzes", 21 *Aktiengesellschaft* 113.

MATURANA, Humberto R., Francisco E. VARELA and R. URIBE (1980) *Autopoiesis and Cognition.* Boston: Reidel.

MAYNTZ, Renate (1977) "Die Implementation politischer Programme: Theoretische Überlegungen zu einem neuen Forschungsgebiet", 10 *Die Verwaltung* 51.

—(1979) "Regulative Politik in der Krise?", in J. Matthes (ed.), *Sozialer Wandel in Westeuropa.* Frankfurt: Campus.

—(1980) "Die Implementation politischer Programme", in R. Mayntz (ed.), *Implementation politischer Programme I.* Königstein: Athenäum.

—(1983) "Zur Einleitung: Probleme der Theoriebildung", in R. Mayntz (ed.), *Implementation politischer Programme II. Ansätze zur Theoriebildung.* Opladen: Westdeutscher Verlag.

MCCONNELL, Grant (1966) *Private Power and American Democracy.* New York: Vintage Books.

McCormick, Robert E. and Robert D. Tollison (1981) *Politicians, Legislation and the Economy.* Boston: Nijhoff.
McCraw, Thomas K. (1975) "Regulation in America, A Review Article", 49 *Business History Review* 159.
Mitnick, Barry (1980) *The Political Economy of Regulation. Creating, Designing and Removing Regulatory Forms.* New York: Columbia University Press.
Mitnick, S. Shep (1983) *Regulation and the Courts. The Case of the Clean Air Act.* New York: Brookings.
Mnookin, Robert H. and Lewis Kornhauser (1979) "Bargaining in the Shadow of the Law. The Case of Divorce", 88 *Yale Law Journal* 950.
Möschel, Wernhard (1974) *Der Oligopolmißbrauch im Recht der Wettbewerbsbeschränkungen.* Tübingen: Mohr und Siebeck.
—(1981a) "Neuere Entwicklungen der Wettbewerbstheorie", 145 *Zeitschrift für das gesamte Handelsrecht und Wirtschaftsrecht* 590.
—(1981b) "Zu § 22 IV", in U. Immenga and E.J. Mestmächer: *Kommentar zum Gesetz gegen Wettbewerbsbeschränkungen.* München: Beck.
—(1983) *Recht der Wettbewerbsbeschränkungen.* Köln: Heymann.
Moore, Sally F. (1973) "Law and Social Change: The Semi-Autonomous Social Field as an Appropriate Object of Study", 7 *Law & Society Review* 719.
Moritz, Klaus (1980) "Begrenzung gewerkschaftlicher Politik durch Arbeitsrecht", in R. Voigt (ed.), *Verrechtlichung.* Königstein: Athenäum.
Mückenberger, Ulrich (1980) "Der Arbeitskampf als staatlich inszeniertes Ritual" *Blätter für Steuerrecht, Sozialversicherung und Arbeitsrecht* 241.
Mueller, Friedrich (1966) *Normstruktur und Normativität. Zum Verhältnis von Recht und Wirklichkeit in der juristischen Hermeneutik, entwickelt an Fragen der Verfassungsinterpretation.* Berlin: Duncker und Humblot.
Nonet, Philippe (1969) *Administrative Justice.* New York: Russel Sage Foundation.
Nonet, Philippe and Philip Selznick (1978) *Law and Society in Transition.* New York: Harper.
Nörr, Dieter (1974) *Rechtskritik in der römischen Antike.* München: Beck.
Ost, François (1984) "Entre jeu et providence: le juge des relations économiques", in A. Jaquemin and B. Remiche (eds.), *Les magistratures économiques et la Crise.* Brussels: CRISP.
Ott, Claus (1972) "Die soziale Effektivität des Rechts bei der sozialen Kontrolle der Wirtschaft", 3 *Jahrbuch für Rechtssoziologie und Rechtstheorie* 345.
Pitschas, Rainer (1980) "Soziale Sicherung durch fortschreitende Verrechtlichung? — Staatliche Sozialpolitik im Dilemma von aktiver Sozialgestaltung und normativer Selbstbeschränkung", in R. Voigt (ed.), *Verrechtlichung.* Königstein: Athenäum.
Podgorecki, Adam (1974) *Law and Society.* London: Routledge and Kegan.
Posner, Richard (1974) "Theories of Economic Regulation" 5 *Bell Journal of Economic and Management Science* 335.
Raiser, Thomas (1969) *Das Unternehmen als Organisation: Kritik und Erneuerung der juristischen Unternehmenslehre.* Berlin: De Gruyter.
—(1980) "Unternehmensziele und Unternehmensbegriffe", 144 *Zeitschrift für das gesamte Handelsrecht und Wirtschaftsrecht* 260.
Rehbinder, Manfred (1967) "Wandlungen der Rechtsstrukturen im Sozialstaat", in E.E. Hirsch and M. Rehbinder (eds.), *Studien und Materialien zur Rechtssoziologie.* Opladen: Westdeutscher Verlag.
Reich, Norbert (1977) *Markt und Recht.* Neuwied: Luchterhand.
—(1983) "The Regulatory Crisis: Ideology or Reality?", in D. Trubek (ed.), *Reflexive Law and the Regulatory Crisis.* Madison: University of Wisconsin.

Röhl, Klaus F.(1980) "Der Vergleich — eine Alternative zum Recht?" in E. Blankenburg, E. Klausa and H. Rottleuthner (eds.), *Alternative Rechtsformen und Alternative zum Recht.* Opladen: Westdeutscher Verlag.

—(1982) "Rechtspolitische und ideologische Hintergründe der Diskussion über Alternativen zur Justiz", in E. Blankenburg, W. Gottwald, D. Stempel (eds.), *Alternativen in der Ziviljustiz.* Opladen: Westdeutscher Verlag.

Ronge, Volker (1984) "Entrechtlichung oder äquifunktionale 'Alternativen zum Recht'"?, in R. Voigt (ed.), *Abschied vom Recht?* Frankfurt: Suhrkamp.

Rosenbaum, Wolf (1982) "Die Wirkungen des Arbeitsrechts auf die Beziehungen zwischen Arbeitnehmern und Arbeitgebern im Betrieb", 10 *Leviathan* 392.

Rottleuthner, Hubert (1979) "Zur Methode einer folgenorientierten Rechtsanwendung", *Archiv für Rechts- und Sozialphilosophie, Beiheft 13.*

—(1985) "Theories of Legal Evolution: Between Empiricism and Philosophy of History", *Rechtstheorie Supplement* 9.

Sabatier, Paul and Daniel Mazmanian (1980) "The Implementation of Public Policy: A Framework of Analysis", 8 *Policy Studies Journal* 538.

Scharpf, Fritz (1979) "Die Rolle des Staates im westdeutschen Wirtschaftssystem: Zwischen Krise und Neuorientierung", in v. Weizsäcker (ed.) *Staat und Wirtschaft.* Berlin: Duncker und Humblot.

Schmitter, Philippe C. (1977) "Modes of Interest Intermediation and Models of Societal Change in Western Europe", 10 *Comparative Political Studies* 7.

Selznick, Philip (1968) "Law. The Sociology of Law", 9 *International Encyclopedia of the Social Sciences* 50.

—(1969) *Law, Society and Industrial Justice.* New York: Russell Sage.

Sendler, Horst (1979) "Normenflut und Richter", 12 *Zeitschrift für Rechtspolitik* 227.

Shklar, Judith N. (1964) *Legalism.* Cambridge: Harvard University Press.

Simitis, Spiros (1984) "Zur Verrechtlichung der Arbeitsbeziehungen", in H.F. Zacher, S. Simitis, F. Kübler, K. Hopt and G. Teubner, *Verrechtlichung von Wirtschaft, Arbeit und sozialer Solidarität.* Frankfurt: Suhrkamp.

Starck, Christian (1979) "Übermaß und Rechtsstaat?" 12 *Zeitschrift für Rechtspolitik* 209.

Steindorff, Ernst (1973) "Politik des Gesetzes als Auslegungsmaßstab im Wirtschaftsrecht", in: *Festschrift für Karl Larenz.* München: Beck.

—(1979) "Legal Consequences of State Regulation", 17 *International Encyclopedia of Comparative Law,* Ch. 11. Tübingen: Mohr und Siebeck.

Stewart, Richard (1981) "Regulation, Innovation and Administrative Law. A Conceptual Framework", 69 *California Law Review* 1263.

—(1986) "Regulation and the Crisis of Legalization in the United States", in T. Daintith (ed.), *Law as an Instrument of Economic Policy: Comparative and Critical Approaches.* Berlin: De Gruyter.

Stigler, George Joseph (1971) "The Theory of Economic Regulation", 2 *Bell Journal of Economics and Management Science* 3.

—(1972) "The Process of Economic Regulation", 17 *Anti-Trust Bulletin* 207.

—(1975) *The Citizen and the State: Essays on Regulation.* Chicago: University of Chicago Press.

—(1976) "The Sizes of Legislation", 5 *Journal of Legal Studies* 17.

Stone, Christopher D. (1975) *Where the Law Ends? The Social Control of Coporate Behaviour.* New York: Harper & Row.

Streeck, Wolfgang (1979) "Gewerkschaftsorganisation und industrielle Beziehungen", in J. Matthes (ed.), *Sozialer Wandel in Westeuropa.* Frankfurt: Campus.

STREECK, Wolfgang and Philippe C. SCHMITTER (1985) "Community, Market, State — and Associations?" in W. Streeck and P.C. Schmitter (eds.), *Private Interest Government: Beyond Market and State.* Beverly Hills/London: Sage.

STREECK, Wolfgang, Peter SEGLOW and Pat WALLACE (1978) *Railway Unions in Britain and West Germany. Structural Sources of Crossnational Differences and Similarities.* Frankfurt: Campus.

SUMMERS, Clyde W. (1977) "The Individual Employee's Rights under the Collective Agreement: What Constitutes Fair Representation?" 126 *University of Pennsylvania Law Review* 251.

TENNSTEDT, Florian (1976) "Zur Ökonomisierung und Verrechtlichung in der Sozialpolitik", in A. Murswieck (ed.), *Staatliche Politik im Sozialsektor.* München: Piper.

TEUBNER, Gunther (1975) "Folgenkontrolle und responsive Dogmatik", 6 *Rechtstheorie* 179.

—(1978a) *Organisationsdemokratie und Verbandsverfassung. Rechtsmodelle für politisch relevante Verbände.* Tübingen: Mohr und Siebeck.

—(1978b) "Zu den Regelungsproblemen der Verbände. Neo-Korporatismus und innerverbandliche Opposition", *Juristenzeitung* 545.

—(1979) "Neo-korporatistische Strategien rechtlicher Organisationssteuerung", 10 *Zeitschrift für Parlamentsfragen* 487.

—(1980) "Kommentierung des § 242", in *Alternativkommentar zum Bürgerlichen Gesetzbuch.* Neuwied: Luchterhand.

—(1983) "Substantive and Reflexive Elements in Modern Law", 17 *Law and Society Review* 239.

—(1984) "Autopoiesis in Law and Society: A Rejoinder to Blankenburg" 18 *Law and Society Review* 281.

—(1985) "After Legal Instrumentalism? Strategic Models of Post-regulatory Law" in G. Teubner (ed.) *Dilemmas of Law in the Welfare State.* Berlin/New York: De Gruyter.

—(1987) Autopoietic Law, in G. Teubner (ed.) *Autopoiesis in Law and Society.* Berlin: De Gruyter.

TEUBNER, Gunther and Helmut WILLKE (1984) "Kontext und Autonomie: Gesellschaftliche Selbststeuerung durch reflexives Recht", 5 *Zeitschrift für Rechtssoziologie* 4.

TOLCHIN, Susan J. and Martin TOLCHIN (1983) *Dismantling America: The Rush to De-regulate.* Boston: Houghton Mifflin.

TREIBER, Hubert (1983) "Regulative Politik in der Krise", in D. Trubek (ed.), *Reflexive Law and the Regulatory Crisis.* Madison: University Wisconsin-Madison.

TRUBEK, David (1972) "Toward a Social Theory of Law: An Essay on the Study of Law and Development", 82 *Yale Law Journal* 11.

—(1983) (ed.) *Reflexive Law and the Regulatory Crisis.* Madison: University of Madison Press.

TURKEL, Gerald (1980-81) "Rational Law and Boundary Maintenance", 15 *Law & Society Review* 41.

UNGER, Roberto Mangabeira (1976) *Law in Modern Society.* New York: Free Press.

UNTERSEHER, Lutz (1972) "Arbeitsrecht — Eine deutsche Spezialität", in O. Jacobi *et al.* (eds.), *Klassenkampf. Kritisches Jahrbuch.* Frankfurt: Fischer.

VARELA, Francesco J. (1979) *Principles of Biological Autonomy.* New York: Elsevier.

VOGEL, Hans-Jochen (1979) "Zur Diskussion um die Normenflut", *Juristenzeitung* 321.

VOIGT, Rüdiger (1980) "Verrechtlichung in Staat und Gesellschaft", in R. Voigt (ed.), *Verrechtlichung.* Königstein: Athenäum.

—(1983) "Gegentendenzen zur Verrechtlichung. Verrechtlichung und Entrechtlichung

im Kontext der Diskussion um den Wohlfahrtsstaat", in R. Voigt (ed.) *Gegentendenzen zur Verrechtlichung*. Opladen: Westdeutscher Verlag.
—(1984) *Abschied vom Recht?* Frankfurt a.M.: Suhrkamp.
WALZ, Rainer (1983) "Sozialwissenschaften im Zivilrecht", in R. Walz (ed.), *Sozialwissenschaften im Zivilrecht*. Neuwied: Luchterhand.
WEBER, Max (1978) *Economy and Society*. Berkeley: University of California Press.
WEIDENBAUM, Murray (1980) *Cost of Regulation and Benefits of Reform*.
WEISS, Hans-Dietrich (1978) "Verrechtlichung als Selbstgefährdung des Rechts", 31 *Die öffentliche Verwaltung* 601.
WERLE, Raymond (1982) "Aspekte der Verrechtlichung", 3 *Zeitschrift für Rechtssoziologie* 2.
WIEACKER, Franz (1967) *Privatrechtsgeschichte der Neuzeit*, (2nd ed.). Göttingen: Vandenboeck und Ruprecht.
WIEDEMANN, Herbert (1980a) *Gesellschaftsrecht*. München: Beck.
—(1980b) "Rechtsethische Maßstäbe im Unternehmensrecht", 2 *Zeitschrift für Unternehmensrecht und Gesellschaft* 147.
WIETHÖLTER, Rudolf (1968) *Rechtswissenschaft*. Frankfurt, Hamburg: Fischer.
—(1982a) "Entwicklung des Rechtsbegriffs", in V. Gessner and R. Geinter (ed.), *Rechtsformen der Verflechtung von Staat und Wirtschaft*. Opladen: Westdeutscher Verlag.
—(1982b) "Wissenschaftskritische Ausbildungsreform — Anspruch und Wirklichkeit", in R. Francke, D. Hart, R. Lautman and P. Thoss (eds.), *Einstufige Juristenausbildung in Bremen. Zehn Jahre Bremen Modell*. Neuwied: Luchterhand.
—(1985) "Materialization and Proceduralization", in G. Teubner (ed.), *Dilemmas of Law in the Welfare State*. Berlin: De Gruyter.
WILLKE, Helmut (1983a) *Die Entzauberung des Staates. Überlegungen zu einer sozietalen Steuerungstheorie*. Königstein: Athenäum.
—(1983b) "Gesellschaftliche Kritierien ökonomischer Rationalität". Bielefeld: Manuscript.
WILSON, James (1980) *The Politics of Regulation*. New York: Basic Books.
WINDHOFF-HERITIER, Adrienne (1980) *Politikimplementation. Ziel und Wirklichkeit politischer Entscheidungen*. Königstein: Athenäum.
WINDSCHEID, Bernhard (1904) "Die Aufgaben der Rechtswissenschaft", in B. Windscheid, *Gesammelte Reden und Abhandlungen*. Leipzig: Duncker.
WINKLER. John T. (1976) "Corporatism", 17 *European Journal of Sociology* 100.
WINTER, Gerd (1982) "Literaturbericht zum Thema", in V. Gessner and G. Winter (eds.), *Rechtsformen der Verflechtung von Staat und Wirtschaft*. Opladen: Westdeutscher Verlag.
ZIEGERT, (1975) *Zur Effektivität der Rechtssoziologie. Die Rekonstruktion der Gesellschaft durch Recht*. Stuttgart: Enke.

Juridification and Disorder

BRIAN BERCUSSON
London, Firenze

Contents

1. Introduction

The problems of juridification, which are the subject of the papers in the volume, are, it will be argued here, a reflection of the disorders which threaten legally supported society. Moreover, disorder in society is reflected not only in the functioning of law in different spheres, but also in the realm of legal theory.

The first part of the paper, concerning the relation between problems of juridification and social disorder, analyses Teubner's concept of "dejuridification", and his proposed solution, in the light of a study which utilised the framework developed by Daintith (1987) to analyse state implementation of economic policy through law. That study argued that there were striking parallels between *state* instruments and measures, and the processes and outcomes reflected in the activity of major *private* actors pursuing their economic objectives (Bercusson, 1987). This line of argument allows for insights into the areas of law discussed in this volume. For example, the search for private functional equivalents of state regulation reveals that the concepts of competition law make the "regulation of competition" almost a contradiction in terms. State regulatory law notions of "competition" are invoked to suppress the private regulatory workings of the economy — to implement the abstract concept of the market. One (regulatory competition law) does not mirror the other (the privately regulated economy) — they both are to reflect an abstract conception.

The area of social law similarly seeks, in Zacher's words, the "correct" juridification level of social law (Zacher, infra: 409). Rather than posing an abstract ideal (as competition law does the "market"), this view accepts the real workings of social life and points to the tide of positive law which threatens to engulf it and change its quality (metamorphosis). The solution is not, however, the re-assertion or re-establishment of an ideal of social life, because there is no such ideal. The historical evolution of, for example, the family, notions of health, education, work and social security precludes such a fixing of an ideal to which law should strive[1]. Rather, law and society are perceived as each possessing qualities which can threaten each other. Too much law threatens the social life form, but also threatens the coherence and values of legal ordering (Zacher, infra 411). In Part 2 of this paper I examine the problems of juridification and disorder, and the proposed solution to them.

Part 3 of the paper, concerning the relation between disorders in society and confusion in the realm of legal theory, begins with a summary of the place of legal theory in the education and practice of lawyers in the U.K. and the uncertainty as to the very concept of legal theory which is manifest in legal textbooks on jurisprudence. The specific connection between social disorder and legal theory will be developed through analysis of a central element in the leading text on legal theory currently used in the teaching of the subject in British law schools: H.L.A. Hart's *The Concept of Law.* This element, Hart's notion of the "internal aspect" of rules, will be argued to be highly dependent on a notion of "order", and correspondingly unable to cope with disorder. An attempt is then made to understand the confusion in British legal theory by looking to T.S. Kuhn's theory of scientific development (Kuhn, 1970). Using Kuhn's theory, R. Cotterrell has sought to develop a link between confusion in legal theory and social and political conflict — i.e. disorder (Cotterrell, 1986). The paper concludes with some reflections on the "ideological" nature of legal theory.

2. Juridification and disorder: state and private ordering

2.1 Problems of disorder

Whether private orderings of social life share certain qualities with state orderings of social life was one object of my study "Economic Policy: State and Private Ordering". To the extent that they share certain qualities (state

[1] It is as if social lawyers were trained in the Annales School whereas competition lawyers were trained in Chicago. Cf. F. Ewald's comments (Ewald, 1985) on the ever-changing content of "droit social", in contrast with the fixed quality of a "Code civil": by comparison, social law is "un droit obsolescent". "La juridiction de droit social".

and private actors, state instruments and measures and private processes and outcomes), the notion of mutual threat seems contradictory — unless the law and/or society, state and/or private ordering threatens itself.

The notion of law and/or society threatening points to a common element of both state and private legal orderings — that they are both *orderings*. Implicit in them is the notion of order, rule, standard, consistency, patterns and so on of behavior, and yet within that concept lies its own contradiction — disorder. For order is incomprehensible without disorder. In the same sense, law is incomprehensible without illegality — breakdowns in legal order. The concern that is expressed over juridification or the "regulatory crisis" is a response to the disorder which is threatening the legal ordering of collectives of capital (companies), social security, labor and competitive economies. Lawyers have taken too literally the slogan "the medium (law) is the message". The message is not that law is breaking down. It is that the legally supported order is breaking down. It is breaking down as competition is strangled by private economic regulation; as social security is threatened by attacks on the welfare state; as companies are racked by economic recession; and as labor is undergoing the agonies of unemployment.

These illustrations should make it clear that the present problems of disorder will not necessarily lead to anarchy. The "problem" of juridification raises the fundamental issue of what constitutes a problem. A problem is not a scientific artefact; it is a sociological construct. It is a perception by a group of a state of affairs that is threatening that group's interests. Whether a state of affairs (juridification) constitutes a problem depends on the group selected and on the definition of its interests. The "regulatory crisis" as a problem poses the question whether those who privately regulate, and those who are to be deregulated are in fact the same people[2]. Thus Sir Geoffrey Howe, now a senior Conservative Party Minister in the U.K. government, argued in 1977 against "legislative pollution" counterposing "law makers" and "wealth creators" (Jordan, 1984: 126). Defining the problem becomes difficult when the wealth creators *are* the law makers.

2.2 Problems of juridification

To what extent can these discontents be attributed to juridification? Teubner's "regulatory trilemma" is premised on the argument that the three sub-systems of politics, law and social life are autonomous, that they are self-referential and so cannot directly influence each other, except within limits described as triggering off self-regulation by the autonomous system, and that when these limits are exceeded by the legal system, the crisis of juridification occurs (Teubner, supra: 19 ff.). As I see it, this crisis takes three forms, each affecting

[2] To adapt Coldthorpe's famous comment on Flanders' proposal that management regain control from shop stewards by sharing it: "the question which must arise is that of whether those with whom control is to be shared and those over whom control is to be reimposed are in fact the same people" (1974: 440).

one of the three sub-systems (Teubner, supra: 22). First, indifference, in that politics "disintegrates" in the sense that the implementation of policy through law has no impact. Policy is ignored by both the law and the social life form which the political system intends to affect: each is indifferent to policy. Secondly, social forms "disintegrate" under the impact of the legal implementation of policy. Thirdly, the law disintegrates. Scrutiny of these consequences throws light on Teubner's critique and his solution.

What Teubner characterises as the "indifference" of both law and social forms to policy projected from the political system could be perceived quite differently as a form of *resistance* to policy[3]. Teubner conscientiously denies any intention to take sides against purposive law, but merely seeks to discover its limits. The solution is not to increase the pressures of policies on law (for example, by exchanging lawyers for laymen, or courts for tribunals) or on social forms (by increasing resources of policing, administration and control). As Teubner says: "one can break the indifference but this does not necessarily lead to the desired structural coupling; indeed the result may be a partial disintegration of self-reproduction" (supra: 23 f.).

It may be, however, that at a high level of abstraction and generality, one would *desire* the disintegration (partial or otherwise) of a particular self-reproducing society. And in the context of a specific and concrete social form (for example, a company failing to contribute towards the national insurance system protecting its employees, to take an illustration from both company and social law), one might well *wish* the policy to achieve not simply a "desired structural coupling", but a disintegration of the social form of any law (court interpretation) which avoided it. The notion of there being limits to the achievement of the policy, the limits being "conditions of compatibility, of 'structural coupling'", (Teubner, supra: 24) is bound to be perceived as, intentionally or otherwise, a *policy restriction* (albeit cast in terms of means, not ends).

The parameters of this restriction need, therefore, to be very delicately drawn, as their political implications are apparent. For example, it could be argued (as has been recently in the U.K.) that imposing personal liability on a director of an insolvent company which did not pay its employees' national insurance contributions is "incompatible" with (a) the law of separate corporate existence and (b) the social form which is that of a complex institution where the director cannot control everything. Or, to take another example from the manpower area, that the requirement that companies contribute an amount levied by a tripartite Industrial Training Board in the U.K. towards training in their industry is "incompatible" with (a) the law which opposes this form of "private taxation" and (b) social forms where employers are unwilling to be subject to the decisions of trade union and inde-

[3] Indifference is not the only, and not the most extreme form of resistance. Cf. resistance by social forms to policy which leads to disintegration of law, or resistance by lawyers and courts to policy (by narrow interpretation, constitutional blocking, or qualification by other "public policy", and so on).

pendent representatives fixing the levy. On the other hand, however, it could be argued that the policy of directors' liability in the case of national insurance contributions is "compatible" in that (a) the legal rights of employees should not be deflected by the legal device of incorporation and (b) directors formally, and some in practice do, control the company. Or that the policy with respect to the training levy is "compatible" with (a) the law allowing administrative delegation of revenue raising for specific purposes, and (b) the social fact that employers alone will not fix an adequate levy because their short-term interest works against high expenditure on long-term training[4].

The question is whether the explanation of the success or failure of specific and concrete policy choices in terms of "structural coupling" or "compatibility" is useful. Or whether this explanation itself obscures the political forces which, it is submitted, really determine the success or failure of the policy. And it is difficult to shift the terrain upwards to the general and abstract. For while the threat to, for example, competition policy as a whole of legal and social indifference may be real, it becomes very difficult to specifically and concretely pinpoint *parts* of competition policy which can be identified as the sources of "incompatibility" *which could not be interchanged* with other parts, similarly "incompatible". The individual compatible parts become part of an incompatible whole. Disaggregation will not be on the basis of sorting the incompatible from the compatible. It will be done on political grounds. And, perhaps, once some parts have been demolished, then the rest, *mirabile dictu*, will be seen as "compatible".

Similar arguments could be developed as to the other two parts of the "regulatory trilemma": that *disintegration of the social form* under the impact of law is not failure, but political and legal success. The social form's resistance to the policy has successfully been broken down using the law[5]. As to *disintegration of law*, the negative connotations may not be borne out, for the loss of legal control does not necessarily mean anarchy. The political implications are apparent from the following comment: "What is described ... as a loss of integration could from another perspective be analysed in terms of encroaching control — a response to inequalities no longer regarded and accepted as legitimate" (Eldridge, 1973: 165). The values implicit in the quotation can be reversed if one drops the "in" from "inequalities".

The issues could be otherwise formulated as follows: what *is* the social life form, for example, in the case of industrial training? In the U.K., prior to "legislation" by the Industrial Training Act 1964, the system of industrial

[4] In the event, it has now been proposed in the U.K. that the liability of company directors for national insurance contributions will not be enforced; and as of 1981, the training levy can be imposed only by a majority vote of the employers in the tripartite Industrial Training Board.

[5] This assumes disintegration occurs by virtue of non-compliance. If it occurs through compliance, either this is the object of the law (success again), or the non-intended result of the law — in which case the social form would be driven to non-compliance.

training took a variety of forms. First, employers would unilaterally organise training schemes within their establishments, though there was wide variation between industries and among different employers within industries. Secondly, there were joint trade union and employers' association training agreements, dealing usually with apprenticeships. Thirdly, there were some government centres for re-training adult workers displaced from contracting industries, established under the Employment and Training Act 1948. Finally, in addition to these formal mechanisms, there was the informal training described in colloquial language as learning by "sitting next to Nellie". Use of trainees in industries dominated by craft unions was often regulated by "dilution" agreements. The inadequacies of this system were reflected in shortages of skilled labor and wide variations in quality and standards of training (Lindley, 1983; Donovan Report, 1968).

The problem, according to Teubner, is to discover the requisite "structural coupling" of this social form with the law and politics sub-systems. But to define the social form of industrial training, prior to juridification, one usually has to resort to legal or normative language. The relations among employers, their associations, their employees and trade unions are governed by rules concerned with "poaching" trained workers, seniority, bonus and merit systems for trained personnel, apprenticeship schemes organised by unions and employers, demarcation agreements and so on.

This system was "self-regulating" for many years. Unfortunately, it had certain consequences which were undesirable in the view of many politicians in the early 1960s. The law which resulted was not an imposition of juridification on a normless, non-legal social form. It was a *change in the legal/normative structure of an existing social form involving a higher degree of state rather than private control.* The "structural coupling" is not, therefore, between social and legal forms, but between one legal form (privately dominated) and another (in the event, a tripartite structure was imposed by the 1964 Act). The "coupling" is between "state law" and "private law", not between legal and social forms.

As to the success of the "structural coupling", whether the social form which remains continues to be self-reproducing in a different legal form is a separate question from that of whether the old social form continues. It may be that the social form remains unaltered — it continues self-reproduction. This is the "indifference" scenario. It may be that the old form disintegrates and is replaced by a new self-reproducing form — the "social form disintegration" scenario — but this is the desired outcome of the policy. The possibility that the old form disintegrates and that the new form does not continue is another result of the "social form disintegration" scenario — but is not the politically desired outcome. It is, perhaps, the third scenario — the disintegration of law — but only in the sense that failure of this kind might throw the law into disrepute.

This is not to deny the fact, which is at the heart of Teubner's thesis, that the implementation of policy through law requires the most delicate appreciation of the internal orderings (actors, processes and outcomes) of social life forms, and the greatest sophistication in choosing from old and developing new legal orderings (instruments and measures). The whole of this research project on legal implementation of economic policy is concerned with these problems. But the matching of social life forms and legal orderings, while a task of sublime importance for lawyers, is not, in my view, at the heart of the discontents which go under the title of "juridification".

My argument is that private ordering (social life forms) and state ordering (law) have in common certain qualities (instruments = processes; measures = outcomes). Their nature and relation as systems, as orderings, is fundamentally threatened not by incompatibility *between* them, but by incompatibilities, disorders, *within* them.

2.3 Solutions to juridification

In my view, therefore, the problem identified in Teubner's analysis (supra) must affect the solution he appears to support: "The proposed solution is to introduce structural legal frameworks for social self-regulation... instead of directly norming social behaviour, law confines itself to the regulation of organisation, procedures and the redistribution of regulation rights". Applied in the field of manpower policy, it might read something like this: "One can think of legislation in principle which determines analytically only the managing organs of employment, the scope of their competence, the incentive and disincentive inducements they can use to affect the behaviour of subjects in the labour market, and which determines instead a few fundamental things... leaving all further specifications to be made to the organs given subordinate normative powers, such as regional authorities, and to commissions in which are represented the interests in the field" (Garofolo, 1982: 32-33).

But even the most delicate and sophisticated "structural coupling" of law with the social system is constrained by political conflicts within the social system being regulated. Structural coupling either reflects these strains (the current balance of power) or it does not. In either event, problems will arise as the balance of power changes, or as powerful actors resist the structural coupling, by indifference or mutual disintegration: "In theories of advanced capitalism, the antagonism between private decisions and social effects is not considered a primary cause of crisis in the system. Instead, interest is centred on an analysis of mechanisms, such as collective bargaining, which help to balance the antagonism" (Offe, 1972). "The limited effectiveness of these mechanisms, however, leads to increasing discrepancies between social problems and the ability to deal with them" (Hartman and Conrad, 1981: 220). Rather than elaborate the point in theory, I will briefly illustrate it by reference to what Teubner called "the historical paradigm here" — collective labor law (supra: 35).

As Teubner puts it: "state law here tends to regulate collective agreements only indirectly — by making legal recognition of negotiating parties dependent on certain structural conditions, by devising procedural norms for the system of negotiation and for disputes, and by extending or restricting the competences of the collective parties. In fact the attempt here is merely to control indirectly the quality of the negotiation results through a balance of its negotiating power" (supra: 35). It is precisely this "structural coupling" of law with the labor relations system which has come under ideological attack in recent years. The conventional form of "structural coupling" in this area has been described as characteristic of "the pluralistic society with the least possible statutory regulation of employment relations. Through the mechanisms of freedom of contract, freedom of association, an unrestricted traffic in ideas and ideologies, combined with a strong preference for voluntary action, there develops a wide variety of relatively autonomous but interacting norm-creating groups and agencies. The result is a multiplicity of separate normative systems..."[6]. The ideological critique of "pluralism in industrial relations" has focussed on precisely that quality of "structural coupling" which Teubner emphasised in the title of a recent article: the contrast between "substantive and reflexive elements in modern law" (Teubner, 1983). The criticism is of "the tendency to evaluate procedural rights far above substantive interests" (Hyman, 1978: 32 note 18). It was brought out in a recent American critique of the "industrial pluralist view of the National Labor Relations Act":

"The fact of negotiations alone, however, does not ensure that one party has not dictated terms to the other. Labor and management have different powers at the bargaining table, powers partially determined by the law itself... In addition, the agenda of the negotiations — that is, what issues are put up for discussion — is constrained by practical and legal barriers... In order to retain the protection of the law, the union must surrender many of its economic weapons... The law restricts the sphere of joint sovereignty by limiting the scope of the duty to bargain" (Van Wezel Stone, 1981: 1544-47).

Alan Fox (1974) put it more sharply: "In the field of work... pressures develop from below for some voice in these decisions. But the essential protections for wealth, privilege and power are still largely accepted by those mounting these pressures. Their aspirations are for marginal improvements in their lot, not for eliminating private property, hierarchy, extreme division of

6 Fox and Flanders (1969: 158). This is posed as one extreme, the opposite of which is that: "The tasks of norm creation and enforcement are wholly centralized, thus preventing a free market in ideas and values and precluding the existence of autonomous groups at liberty to challenge the ruling norms. In industrial relations this would imply one universal system that attempts fully to regulate employment relations on a unified and consistent basis, within work establishments, between establishments in the same industry, and between all industries and occupations. Such a comprehensive order could only be imposed by dint of *force majeure*, that is, by the coercive powers of the state. Tensions and instability might develop within the system when subject groups rebel or seek some measure of autonomy, but even the mildest forms of disorder become a threat to the state and must be suppressed".

labor, and the principles and conventions which support great inequalities of wealth, income and opportunities for personal fulfillment"[7].

Teubner argues that reflexive law does not seek to determine substantive results. It is acknowledged that leaving matters to autonomous independent action of individuals or groups does often dictate certain results[8]. Is it not the case that the adoption of particular structures of coupling will also dictate certain results, by shaping the procedural and structural parameters of lawful action? Hence, even if not intended to shape substantive results (and in many cases this is intended), reflexive law does shape substantive outcomes — albeit not as explicitly as substantive law.

Clegg's defence of pluralism was simply to assert that "it is not easy to see how (the law) could equalise power..." (Clegg, 1975: 315). Teubner too recognises the limits of law to correct social and power inequalities (supra: 36). However, the solution is not to put forward proposals based on "structural coupling" which understate the significance of the power balances between the different actors in the arena (and indeed the definition of the arena itself is critical). As Richard Hyman said, presciently, in 1978: "Economic crisis and recession are in no way an opportune context for the peaceful and orderly accommodation of opposing interests: social and economic antagonisms are necessarily sharpened, the process of give and take becomes a more manifestly zero (or even negative) sum" (Hymann, 1978: 35 note 26). The crisis of juridification is attributable primarily to these sharpened antagonisms, and solu-

[7] Fox (1969: 278). He continues: "This is partly because they have been sufficiently socialized by power-holders to continue legitimising this basic framework; partly because they see the power arrayed against them as so overwhelming as to make that basic framework appear inevitable, or challengeable only at disproportionate cost to themselves and things they value. These perceptions and acceptances make it possible for power-holders to concede subordinate groups or representatives a voice in certain limited kinds of decision-making, since they can be confident that their more fundamental prerogatives will not be attacked. If this expectation were not fulfilled they would seek to withdraw the concession, at whatever cost in social conflict".

[8] Teubner, (supra: 36): the powerful individuals win, as cited in Abel. Thus Teubner talks of the "limits of the arena", structured by reflexive laws, and speaks of "political responsibility" and "desired degree of social accountability", while insisting that certain outcomes are not specified. What is the difference between the "boundaries of acceptability" and "specified outcomes"? Is it sufficiently great to distinguish reflexive law from substantive law? Teubner insists there are major differences. But what are they? Labor law is a particularly unfortunate illustration as the assertion as to "balance" is precisely at the heart of the critique. As Hyman puts it: "The mere participation in job regulation may of course be wholly compatible with the stagnation or deterioration of material conditions". Or by way of a concrete example, where a multi-national proposed to close a plant: "There is little evidence that (Massey-Fergusson's) conformity to most of the formal requirements of consultation and negotiation and disclosure offered any major advantage to the workers at Kilmarnock". Henderson *et al.* (1984).

tions to the crisis must reflect these and consciously weigh them in considering the role of law in society and the disorders which threaten it.

2.4 Solutions to disorder

My paper on "Economic Policy: State and Private Ordering" did not propose solutions. It sought rather to highlight the parellel orders of private actors, processes and outcomes and the state, its instruments and measures. Here, I venture the conclusion that the problem is not that of juridification or dejuridification. It is that of the present order — or another[9].

My argument is that the social life form which is said to be juridified by state intervention is only comprehensible in terms of a set of private rules. State intervention does not, therefore, juridify; it simply changes the set of private rules by introducing, perhaps, new actors, processes and outcomes. Cries of "disorder" are only polemical devices hurled by those who benefitted from each of the two orders against each other.

One major, and perhaps the central, difference lies in that state ordering is based primarily on force, whereas most private ordering is based primarily on wealth. Each order also depends, to a much lesser extent, on respect. If this distinction among resources used to maintain order is warranted, then the choice between state order using force and its corollary, fear, on the one hand, and private order, dictated by the wealth of major private actors and the need of the rest, on the other, is a matter of preference. A choice between submission to force or to wealth is not, however, inevitable. There is the possibility of using respect as a resource to maintain order — and actors who rely on this resource are perhaps more worthy than others. But the powers of wealth and force are still dominant. Until we can eliminate need, or until we can mobilise respect, we may have to live with force.

3. Juridification and disorder: society and legal theory

The problems of juridification are not specific to any one field of law. As the papers in this volume indicate, the issue is a live one in social security, labor, competition and company law. The general papers in this volume are an attempt to address the issue on a theoretical level, and the first part of this paper was written as a response to that of Teubner. In this part of the paper, I discuss the difficulties British lawyers in particular have in coming to grips with the problems of juridification at the level of theory.

3.1 Legal theory and lawyers in Britain

Why is it that jurisprudence is taught only as a minor element in courses of legal education? Why is it considered that the theory of law merits only one

9 "Disorder", again, need not mean chaos or anarchy. It can mean a different order (of social security, competition, company or labour law) which will in turn face its challenge of "disorder".

quarter of one year's courses in a three or four year program for training and educating lawyers?[10] And this in an academic institution. Those lawyers who did not go through university would not even obtain that proportion of formal intellectual preparation in the subject. Is this an accurate reflection of the status of legal theory? Of its considered role and utility in the work of lawyers, judges and the law. Do other disciplines, if that is what law is, spend similarly little time on the theoretical underpinnings of their subject? Do others spend so much time on the particular, on methodology and problem solving techniques, with little or no attention paid to general principles?[11].

But it is not only in legal education that legal theory takes such a backward place. In the work and practice of lawyers and others concerned with law, it seems that general theoretical questions do not suggest themselves overmuch[12]. As Dicey put it succinctly: "Jurisprudence is a word which stinks in the nostrils of the practising barrister". The jurisprudence texts are fond of citing cases where judges have addressed themselves to large questions of theory. But these are rare indeed. The attitudes of the proud Philistines of the 19th century bar prevail. The emphasis is on the requirements of legal practice and training in the techniques required of the practicioner.

The traditional dichotomy in legal education circles — whether one wants to train lawyers or provide a broad education — was the background to the work of the Ormrod Committee (1971). Ormrod accepted that legal education was split into academic and professional compartments. In its conclusion, the Committee were keen that the academic side of this process should mix in nicely with the professional to produce full fledged lawyers:

> (1) For the purpose of training for the legal profession, academic and vocational legal education should as far as possible be integrated into a coherent whole.
>
> (2) The scheme of legal education should reflect the *profession's* continuing need to recruit men and women of widely differing character, temperament and attainments.
>
> (3) Legal education should not attempt to equip the lawyer at qualification with a comprehensive knowledge of every subject he may encounter in practice; instead, it should concentrate on providing him with the best

[10] This is the case in law faculties of England and Wales; there is greater attention paid to jurisprudence in Scottish universities.

[11] Cf. the statement by J.W. Harris (1980: 4), that "I have expressed the controversial opinion that general jurisprudence is not a necessary part of the training of a lawyer *qua* lawyer". Harris' book, according to the survey of the teaching of jurisprudence in 1984 (Barnett and Yach, 1985) was the most frequently recommended text after Hart's *The Concept of Law*.

[12] The connection between "altruism and economism" — the market situation in the legal profession and in academic jobs — in legal practice and curriculum reform is critically analysed in Bankowski and Mungham, (1976). For an argument that nineteenth century legal theory had a similar inspiration, see Sugarman, (1986: 28ff.).

possible general introduction so as to enable him, with the help of experience and continuing education after qualification, to become a fully equipped *member of the profession.* (Para. 185).

Despite the genuflection towards integration of academic legal education with the vocational, Ormrod's customer orientation towards professional training is apparent. It even comes out in its description of the "objective of the academic stage" of legal education. Students are to be provided with:

(i) a basic knowledge of the law, which involves covering certain 'core' subjects, and acquiring a sound grasp of legal principles and the ability to discover for himself the law on any subject which he is likely to be called upon to deal with in his early years of practice.

(ii) an understanding of the relationship of law to the social and economic environment in which it operates. (Para. 185).

The attempts to provide for the academic component of legal education have gone in various directions. For example, one relates to methods of instruction and learning — clinical legal education as practised at, e.g. the University of Kent. Or the sandwich course providing for work stages at Brunel University. Again, there has been an expansion in the subjects taught as well as variations within the content of traditional courses. Sometimes this is simply a shift of emphasis — administrative law tends to concentrate more on race, civil disobedience and industrial relations than it did some ten years ago. Property rights may now include rights to welfare benefits. However, one must be cautious in estimating how fundamental a shift in understanding is conveyed by a replacement of entails with the provisions of social security benefit. There are, of course, critiques of how much such shifts and changes reflect attempts at analysis and understanding of the theoretical foundations of law — and how much is simply acceptance of the old traditions with an added dose of liberal amelioration: black letter law topped with social reform [13].

This has led to some pressure on teachers of jurisprudence to provide the challenge to unstated ideology which seems to pervade legal education. The subject by its very nature seems to question the underlying base of law systems and legal rules. This is not to say that jurisprudence has achieved or even sought a critical stance toward ideology in law. The recent surveys on the teaching of jurisprudence indicate that many courses are only slowly emerging from a "legal thought from Plato to Dworkin" model. Some, of course, do not see it as their purpose, in what they consider to be a branch of philosophy, to pay heed to questions of ideology. These are the concerns of sociologists

[13] Two leading texts will be used to illustrate this argument below: *Introduction to Jurisprudence*, 1979, by Lord Lloyd of Hampstead, and *Jurisprudence*, 1976, by R.W.M. Dias. A survey (Cotterell and Woodliffe, 1974) of basic textbooks used in British law school courses on jurisprudence and legal theory in 1973 found that the most widely read books were Dias and Lloyd, as well as Hart's *The Concept of Law*. By 1984, another survey (Barnett and Yach, 1985) showed that Hart remained in first place, but now followed by Harris's *Legal Philosophies*, 1980, and Lloyd's *Introduction to Jurisprudence.*

and political scientists, not lawyers. Lawyers can get very excited about particular laws, but not about theory. They will defend to the death the right to physical integrity and security — and imprison thieves and hang murderers. They will condemn fraud, but condone speculation; insist on the protection of property, and the right to destroy property; on the freedom of contract, and the legal relationship of master and servant. There may be only limited opportunities available within particular areas of law study for a total analysis of the nature and function of law in society. Hence jurisprudence courses are currently seen as the place where this critical evaluation of the ideology of the law can take place. To some extent, this is facilitated by the extreme lack of definition of the subject matter of jurisprudence in British law schools. It is quite startling that a subject should be as indefinite as many of the leading textbooks in use in jurisprudence courses describe it[14]. One would have thought that so ancient a discipline might have achieved some degree of clarity as regards its subject matter. But Lloyd begins his *Introduction to Jurisprudence* by answering the question: "What is Jurisprudence?" as follows:

"To ask this question is to be reminded of the old adage, *quot homines, tot sententiae.* For not only does every jurist have his own notion of the subject-matter and proper limits of jurisprudence, but his approach is governed by his allegiances, or those of his society, by, what is commonly referred to nowadays as, his 'ideology'" (Lloyd, 1979:1).

Dias begins his book on *Jurisprudence* by adverting that "Jurisprudence was the first of the social sciences to be born", adding, "Its province has been determined and re-determined because the nature of the subject is such that no delineation of its scope can be regarded as final" (Dias, 1976:1). He concedes that the standard textbooks on the subject do not give much definition to the subject, and explains:

"Books called 'jurisprudence' vary widely in subject-matter and treatment. The reason is that these writings concern thought *about* law on the broadest possible basis, rather than expositions of law itself. thus, jurisprudence deals with the structure, uses and functioning of law and legal concepts... Thought about law is also a story of movements in outlook and ever-changing ideas, and developments are taking place in contemporary physical, moral and other social sciences, which make it difficult to decide once and for all in what way, if at all, jurisprudence should take account of them. So the answer to the question, What is 'jurisprudence'?, is that it means pretty much whatever anyone wants it to mean — a depressing start indeed" (Dias, 1976:1).

[14] Austin (1954). Austin's work was derived from Jeremy Bentham's writings, which only surfaced after World War Two. As Lloyd comments: "there is little of Austin...which is not foreseen in Bentham...No doubt lawyers will still read Austin as the fount of nineteenth century positivism... But there is no doubt who is the master, who the student". (1979: 173).

3.2 Law and disorder: Hart's concept of law

Despite the prevailing uncertainty as to the scope and definition of legal theory in British law schools, surveys of the teaching of jurisprudence confirm that "Professor Hart's *Concept of Law* remains a central focus in jurisprudence teaching in the U.K. In 1973, 26 out of 28 law schools dealt with this book 'fairly fully'; similarly in 1984, the corresponding figure being 50 out of 57" (Barnet and Yach, 1985: 158).

Hart's concept of law is built upon a critique of the theory expounded by John Austin (1954): this critique occupies three chapters in *The Concept of Law*[15]. The Austinian school has been the dominant one in English jurisprudence since the end of the last century. This is evidenced by the space afforded to Austin in the conventional textbooks. Lloyd devotes considerable space to a criticism of Austin's theories, and Dias distinguishes the approach taken by Austin (and earlier Bentham) by the title "British" theories (Lloyd, 1979: Ch 4; Dias, 1976: Ch 15) But while others have, often successfully, shown up the fundamental flaws of Austinian theory, few have done so as effectively as Hart. He demonstrates not only the flaws, but also points up the aspects which have led to the strength of the theory, what it is about Austin's view which gave it the dominant position it held. He then goes on to present his own concept on the ruins of Austin's definition of law, which may be summarised as including the following elements: law is characterised by a habit of obedience to the commands of a superior having the power to threaten and inflict sanctions. According to Hart, Austin's definition is inadequate because it does not include the "idea of a rule" a standard which functions as a "reason or justification" for doing or not doing certain things. The *legal* ("normative") structure of society is said to be distinguished by a "critical reflective attitude" — this is the famous "internal aspect" of rules. Such an attitude presupposes the existence of rules; and these rules are used as standards for the evaluation and justification of social conduct. The idea of a *rule* is required to explain any legal structure of authority and obligation. The meaning of either of these terms entails that those participating in such a structure (of authority or obligation) not only do certain things, but seek to justify what they do as well. And because both authority and obligation are features of every legal system, without the idea of a rule, "we cannot hope to elucidate even the most elementary forms of law"[16].

It is not my intention here to describe either Austin's theory or Hart's critique. Rather, I want to analyse a central aspect of Hart's concept of law, so dominant in British legal theory, which provides an analogy with the critique of the debate over juridification which I presented in Part 2 of this paper. This aspect of Hart's theory is highlighted in an essay by P.M.S. Hacker which

[15] Hart, 1961: 78.

[16] Hacker (1977: 1). The paragraphs which follow are derived from Hacker's exposition at pp. 8-18.

examined the context in which Hart's ideas emerged [17]. In contrast to classical positivism, Hacker shows how Hart differed from the prevailing "methodological monism" — that human and social phenomena could be explained and described, so far as their logical structure was concerned, by following the patterns in the physical sciences. The converse doctrine was that human and social phenomena are essentially intentional and teleological: what is termed hermeneutics. Hence Hart would declare in the Preface to the *Concept of Law*:

"one of the central themes of the book is that neither law nor any other form of social structure can be understood without an appreciation of certain crucial distinctions between two different kinds of statement, which I have called 'internal' and 'external' and which can both be made whenever social rules are observed" (Hart, 1961).

One of the salient themes of hermeneutics is that description of distinctively human phenomena must involve understanding the situation described as it is apprehended by the agent whose behavior is to be explained and understood. So it must make reference to the conceptual framework of the agent. A central feature of Hart's analysis is that legal phenomena can only be understood if reference is made to the attitudes of human beings towards their behavior. So if social behavior is to be characterised as "legal", then it must be grasped as being seen by at least some of its participants as conforming to, or deviating from, general standards of conduct. The "internal point of view" — which must characterise legal phenomena — is manifested in specific ways — in demands for conformity, criticism of deviation, acceptance of the legitimacy of criticism, and distinctive kinds of justification of action expressed in "ought" language. Hart's focussing on this "internal" aspect, on the marking of *legal* phenomena by such a sign, has to be seen as a decisive deviation from classical positivism, which attempted to explain legal relations between individuals largely in terms of certain probabilities, patterns and predictions of behavior. At most they would countenance some psychological (but not an "ought") connection (e.g. obedience under threats).

Hart's deviation is not complete: like the classical approach, Hart looks to specific, albeit complex, social facts — critical attitudes and dispositions as manifested in patterns of behavior and response. But he totally rejects the imperatival analysis of law. Laws are rules, not imperatives; not expressions of will backed by threats. Hart focusses on trying to describe what it is for a rule to exist. His analysis of social facts has this end in mind. This constitutes a major advance, in Hacker's view, over his predecessors. Hacker explains that rules, according to Hart, have an "internal aspect", which habits do not. Rules, with their internal aspect, allow for two distinct points of view with respect to them: an external and an internal point of view. Corresponding to the different points of view, different types of statement can be made. These

[17] Dare one say there are echoes here of the debate between the adherents of "instrumental" and "reflexive" law. See Teubner (supra: 27 ff.).

different types will be made depending on whether the speaker has one or the other pont of view. So these types of statement are distinguished by the terms "internal" or "external" statement; or "statement made from the internal (external) point of view."

Hacker points out that Hart is concerned with the description of social behavior that is rule governed (whether the behavior conforms to the rules or not). One can distinguish different kinds of descriptions of such behavior along a spectrum of increasing complexity. Thus, at one extreme, one can describe such an action simply in terms of physical behavior in a given circumstance — and give a similar description of the actions which commonly accompany its non-performance in the circumstances. Now such descriptions do not involve any elements of intention or purpose on the part of the actors: "ought" statements are not part of the description. Hacker observes that such descriptions would, in most cases of distinctively human action, display complete lack of understanding of the action.

Hacker elaborates that further along the spectrum of possible descriptions of such behavior lie increasingly complex descriptions of intention or purpose of the actors — these describe the action as intentional in various ways; they may specify the intention with which the action was done, give the actor's reason for doing it, and specify the social context of the action. For an example of a minimal level of intentionalistic description, Hacker posits an anthropologist encountering an alien society. Viewed "externally", the social behavior exhibited there would seem obviously purposeful (teleological) — but as yet unintelligible. If more complex intentionalistic descriptions were used, a large number of factors relating to the actor's conception of his action and goals might be posited. If one went to a complex level indeed — and that is the level of interest for the purposes of Hart's analysis of law — the description would display an understanding of the action by referring to such features as the agent's beliefs, values and desires with respect to the social institutions which involve him. As an illustration, Hacker takes the case of a person who can be described as making scratches on paper, at one simplistic level, or as making a will on another level. Again, behavior could be described as emitting sounds, or as pronouncing a judicial verdict. In sum, Hacker states, the normative (legal) descriptions are the ones of a person who understands the significance of what he describes. Such understanding, from an "internal point of view", is a prerequisite to explaining the agent's behavior (in motivational terms). The complex descriptions will use many normative words. These characterise the social practices which the agent himself understands as the social context of his actions.

Having identified that there may be at least two attitudes towards social phenomena, one can then try to elaborate them with regard to the concept of rules. With regard to rules, a person may have a range of views — not just a single "internal" point of view. Two in particular concern Hart. He distinguishes two attitudes towards rules: acceptance and rejection. The circumstances which justify asserting that an agent accepts a rule divide into two main types: instances in which the rule applies to the agent (actor) on a particular occasion; and instances where the rule does not apply to the agent on a given occasion. One can examine each of these two situations. Where it is not the actor's behavior which is to be measured against the rule; i.e. where his own rule-conformity or violation is not in view — he may nonetheless manifest his acceptance of it by his attitude towards the actual or possible behavior of others. He must, if the rule is accepted, criticise the behavior by reason of it. His rationale for so doing must manifest respect for the rule — be it moral, social or legal.

Where the agent's own behavior is in view, his acceptance of the rule is to be seen from the additional reasons which, together with the operative facts, constitute his complete reason for conformity. Again, the key is in the respect manifested for the rule. Acceptance of a rule does not require complete conformity — but non-conformity must be accompanied by certain types of excuse and justification. The actor must make such gestures — or at least feel guilt, shame and remorse as the natural consequence. Moreover, where criticism is directed at him for his rule-violation, he must view it as legitimate.

These are all features of the circumstance where the actor's behavior is characterised by an internal attitude of acceptance of the rule. Rejection would entail the opposite. In addition, his attitude is characterised by the consideration by him of "external" reasons for conforming to the rule. Conformity is determined by reference to incentives or disincentives (e.g. approval of others, or sanctions). Either may follow compliance or non-compliance respectively. But these are the reasons which enter into his attitude towards the rule: mainly the wisdom, advisability or otherwise of incurring the disadvantages of non-conformity. Again, rejection of a rule by no means requires uniform violation of it.

The above account of what Hart argues it means for a rule to exist is an essential part of his refutation of the classical Austinian theory. There are some related elements — the idea that critical response must occur has some analogies with the idea that sanctions must apply. But there is a fundamental difference in Hart's focus on the internal point of view, and its appreciation of normative "ought" language. The ordinary use and understanding of normative language — duties, rights, oughts and must nots — these are much more congruent with Hart's concept of a rule than with the Austinian approach through commands and habits[18].

It is at this point that I believe a major *caveat* must be made to Hart's theory, which links it to the debate concerning juridification and disorder. Lawyers and academics teaching law are all very familiar with the concept of a rule, and

[18] For a similar distinction between these two notions, see F. Ewald, (1985) who also reflects the concern expressed here about the acceptance (the internal attitude) of those subject to law: "la loi en vient à perdre, ce qui avait pu... sembler être une de ses charactéristiques essentielles: l'obligation. Les lois obligent, sans doute, mais de manière en quelque sorte facultative, sous la condition suspensive de l'accord de ceux à qui elle s'adresse".

share understanding of the responses it evokes. These responses might be qualified by the adjectives "critical and reflective". What I think must be questioned is the attitudes of those who are familiar with Hart's theory, and lawyers and academics generally; whether their acknowledgement of Hart's description of what it means for a rule to exist — a description based on critical reflective attitudes — is a description adequate to describe what ordinary people understand by rules, and particularly, legal rules?

I think this problem comes out well in Hart's discussion of a certain type of rules — those concerning the conferral of authority to legislate, which arose in his analysis of Austin's concept of the sovereign who commands. It is, as Hart concedes, "one of the strong points of Austin's theory". The discussion relates to this specific rule about legislative authority, but its implications go further. Hart says:

"we spoke as if most ordinary people not only obeyed the law but understood and accepted the rule qualifying a succession of lawgivers to legislate. In a simple society this might be the case; but in a modern state it would be absurd to think of the mass of the population, however law abiding, as having any clear realization of the rules specifying the qualification of a continually changing body of persons entitled to legislate. To speak of the populace 'accepting' these rules... would involve putting into the heads of ordinary citizens an understanding of constitutional matters which they might not have. We would only require such an understanding of the officials or experts in the system; the courts, which are charged with the responsibility of determining what the law is, and the lawyers whom the ordinary citizen consults when he wants to know what it is" (Hart, 1961: 59-60).

What we have here, it seems to me, is rather a giant step backward from Hart's original assertion that the existence of rules posits a critical reflective attitude. It is this attitude on the part of people which is said to distinguish the existence of rules — and Austin's command theory is criticised for its failure to account for this. Yet here Hart goes on to say about this mental attitude of people to rules that problems arise when people are ignorant of the rules. And more: what is meant when we say that people *accept* rules? Hart says:

"Plainly, general acceptance is here a complex phenomenon, in a sense divided between official and ordinary citizens, who contribute to it and so to the *existence* of a legal system in different ways. The officials of the system may be said to acknowledge explicitly such fundamental rules conferring legislative authority: the legislators do this when they make laws in accordance with the rules which empower them to do so: the courts when they identify, as laws to be applied by them, the laws made by those thus qualified, and the experts when they guide the ordinary citizens by reference to the laws so made. *The ordinary citizen manifests his acceptance largely by acquiescence in the results of these official operations.* He keeps the law which is made and identified in this way, and also makes claims and exercises powers conferred by it. But he may know little of its origin of its makers: some may know nothing more about the laws than that they are 'the law'. It forbids things ordinary citizens want to do, and they know that they may be arrested by a policeman and sentenced to prison by a judge if they disobey. ***It is the strength of the doctrine which insists that habitual obedience to orders backed by threats is the foundation of a legal system that it forces us to think in realistic terms of this relative passive aspect*** of the complex phenomenon which we call the existence of a legal system. The weakness of the doctrine is that it obscures or distorts the other relatively active aspect, which is seen primarily, though not exclusively, in the law-making, law-identifying, and law-applying operations of the officials or experts of the system". (Hart, 1961: 59) (My emphasis.)

What has become of the acclaimed "internal aspect"? It seems that as regards some rules, at least, some watering down is in order. It is difficult to have a critical reflective attitude about something you are ignorant of or scarcely understand. How many "rules" of law — what parts of the legal system — are susceptible to such a critical reflective attitude by ordinary people? It seems we must distinguish between ordinary people and "officials" — legislators, judges and lawyers. These latter have the proper attitude — the others have no attitude at all — they acquiesce in the application of rules by the officials. This acquiescence is rather more akin to Austin's habit of obedience than Hart would perhaps care to admit. I makes his theory of what law is more of a theory with only certain individuals (officials) in mind. They can appreciate it while the ordinary mass cannot. It might be said here that we have something along the lines of an "ideology" — a theory of law produced for the gratification of certain segments of society, the old command theory no longer proving satisfactory. Ordinary people don't have to understand law; they cannot be expected to criticise it in any informed manner. They have to accept it by acquiescence. If this is true of the mass of the people, which is the more accurate description of rule-governed behavior: Hart's or Austin's?

A similar aspect (also "ideological") arises from Hart's (1961: 78-88) analysis of the idea of obligation. Hart begins by reiterating the fact that even Austin's coercive theory was correct in its appreciating that where there is law, there human conduct is made in some sense non-optional or obligatory. Hart is concerned to examine precisely what is meant when we say that conduct is obligatory. He uses his "gunman situation": A orders B to hand over his money and threatens to shoot him if he does not comply. According to the theory of coercive orders, this situation illustrates the notion of obligation or duty in general. And *legal* obligation, looking to Austin's theory, would be this situation generalized to all society — the gunman situation writ large it is sometimes said. Only A is the sovereign habitually obeyed, and the orders must be general, prescribing courses of conduct, not single actions.

Hart says the plausibility of the claim that the gunman situation displays the meaning of "obligation" lies in the fact that it is certainly one in which we would say that B, if he obeyed, was "obliged" to hand over his money. But, Hart points out, we would be mis-describing the situation if we said, on these facts, that B "had an obligation" or a "duty" to hand over the money. So it seems we need something else for an understanding of the idea of obligation. There is a difference between the assertion that someone *was obliged* to do something (bear in mind the Austinian model of coercive orders), and the assertion that he *had an obligation* to do it[19].

The statement that B *was obliged* is often a statement about the beliefs and motives with which an action is done: B was *obliged* to hand over his money — means that he believed some harm or other unpleasant consequences would befall him if he did not, and he handed it over to avoid those consequences (though if the threatened harm was trivial, or unlikely to happen, we might not say that B was *obliged*).

Whatever the problems about the facts leading to B's belief that he was obliged — Hart makes clear that the statement that someone "had an obligation" to do something is of a very different type. So, e.g., no matter what the facts are in the gunman situation, no matter what B's beliefs or motives were — they are *not sufficient* to warrant the statement that B had an obligation to hand over the money. Moreover, it is clear that facts about beliefs or motives are *not necessary* in order to say that a person has an obligation to do something. That a person *has an obligation* e.g. to tell the truth or report for military service is true regardless of whether he believed he could get away without doing it. He has an obligation even though he may not be obliged in the circumstances, or at least felt he is not obliged.

Hart points out that Austin, and others, did *not* regard *obligation* in terms of the *subjective* motivation of people. Rather it was defined in terms of the *chance* or *likelihood* of punishment in the event of disobedience. A person has an obligation, regardless of his feelings, if he will suffer at the hands of another for disobeying the order. Now Hart concedes that it is true, in a normal legal system, where sanctions are exacted for a high proportion of offences that an offender usually runs the risk of punishment. So usually, he admits, the statement that a person has an obligation, and the statement that he is likely to suffer for disobedience will both be true together. Indeed, he goes on to say that connexion between these two statements is even stronger: it may well be true that in a legal system, *unless in general* sanctions were likely to be exacted from offenders, there would be little point in making statements about peoples' *obligations.*

Nonetheless, Hart objects to this view of obligation. He does not go so far as to say it is wrong, but he says that it ignores the central element of *rules* — which is, of course his own key to the science of jurisprudence. He says that to understand the idea of "obligation", one has to involve the concept of rules. Rules must be the background for the statement that a person has an obligation. Moreover, the *function* of the statement that a person has an obligation is *that a rule applies to him.*

Hart then goes into a detailed discussion of how not *all* rules imply obligations (e.g. rules of etiquette or correct speech). Only when there is a "general demand for conformity" which is insistent and "the social pressure brought to

[19] For criticism of Hart's concept of the "internal aspect" of rules from a sociological standpoint, see Cotterrell: (1983, 695-696) especially footnotes 70-75.

bear upon those who deviate or threaten to deviate is great". He goes on to distinguish moral rules (pressure through feelings of shame, remorse and guilt) and legal rules (physical sanction). But the key to whether rules give rise to obligations is the *seriousness* of the social pressure behind them. Then they are though of as giving rise to obligations.

So far I think the two concepts of obligation put forward by Austin and Hart differ principally in that in Austin's case, breach of the *order* is likely to lead to sanctions; while with Hart, the *rule* is accompanied by social pressure of a serious kind. But the key difference lies, as it did in the previous discussion, between the concept of a *rule* on the one hand, as distinguished from an order or command on the other. But Hart does not underestimate the difference:

"The difference may seem slight between the analysis of a statement of obligation as a prediction, or assessment of the chances, of hostile reaction to deviation, and our own contention that though this statement presupposes a background in which deviations from rules are generally met by ***hostile reactions***, yet ***its characteristic use*** is ***not*** to predict this ***but to say that a person's case falls under such a rule.*** In fact, however, this difference is not a slight one. Indeed, until its importance is grasped, we cannot properly understand the whole distinctive style in human thought, speech, and action which is involved in the existence of rules and which constitutes the normative (legal) structure of society" (Hart, 1961: 86).

What Hart is saying is that when a person makes the statement that B has an obligation — he usually, characteristically ***means*** to say something about a ***rule*** — ***not*** about the consequences of the action — of a deviation, for example. Here once again we come to that aspect of rules which was marked out as having certain ideological connotations — the internal aspect. The ideological aspect comes out in the rather misleading way Hart describes the ***external*** point of view: as that of an "observer", who does not himself accept the rules. The "observer" is one who is "content merely to record the regularities of observable behaviour", to assess the chances of a deviation meeting with punishment (1961: 87). These strange beings, possessed of the external view only, cannot conceive of, because they have no need of, concepts of obligation. Hart is, however, prepared to admit:

"The external point of view may very nearly reproduce the way in which the rules function in the lives of certain members of the group (***quaerel*** society), namely those who reject its rules and are only concerned with them when and because they judge that unpleasant consequences are likely to follow violation" (Hart, 1961:88).

Fortunately, Hart reassures us that these outsiders, these outlaws, are indeed mistaken as to the way which "obligation" is normally perceived (by decent men and women):

"What the external point of view, which limits itself to the observable regularities of behavior, cannot reproduce is the way in which the rules function as rules in the lives of those who are normally the ***majority*** of society. These are the officials, lawyers, or private persons who use them, in one situation after another, as guides to the conduct of social life... For them the violation of a rule is not merely a basis for the prediction that a hostile reaction will follow but a reason for hostility" (Hart, 1961: 88).

Once again one is struck by the way Hart looks to officials and lawyers as the archetypal possessors of the internal point of view. Those who truly understand what *law* is, what *rules* mean. To make up his majority, of course, he must not reduce himself to these minority groups — so he includes private persons. A wide category indeed — though presumably, it will include some, many, indeed perhaps a majority of those who do not know what the rules are. Though, apparently they are sufficiently conscious of them to guide their behavior not by fear of the consequences, but solely because the rule indicates what their obligation is. I have no doubt that Oxford and other places are peopled by such law-abiding individuals. What I wonder is whether such persons are quite as common as Hart thinks. Whether *rules* comprise such an important element in the lives of most people, or whether fear of the consequences, hostility, social pressure, or sanctions under any other name are the reason for many people's behavior. Much depends on how you regard society, I suppose. It may be an extension of a tea or sherry party, with the rules observed by pleasant people, educated in the niceties of rule-observance, whose encounter with deviance, with sanctions, with police, is rare. In such society, people follow the rules because they are rules. Life in such society consists of encounters with others who are similarly civilized. Clearly, all of these are possessed of the internal point of view. What one wonders is whether Hart's view of society, of law, is applicable outside such small circles. Perhaps even Hart doubts. For he goes on to say:

"At any given moment the life of any society which lives by rules, legal or not, is likely to consist in a tension between those who, on the one hand, accept and voluntarily co-operate in maintaining the rules, and those who, on the other hand, reject the rules and attend to them only from the external point of view as a sign of possible punishment. One of the difficulties facing any legal theory anxious to do justice to the complexity of the facts is to remember the presence of both these points of view and not to define one of them out of existence. Perhaps all our criticisms of the predictive theory of obligation may be best summarised as the accusation that this is what it does to the internal aspect of obligatory rules" (Hart, 1961: 88).

So here is the revenge of the civilized man. A theory which purports to define his observance of law in jungle terms — that he only behaves as he does for fear of the consequences imposed by some commander — is unacceptable. It fails to allow for the finer feelings, the internal aspect. The *fact* that people, *civilised* people, do things out of *noblesse oblige*, their voluntary acceptance of the rules of the game, of society. No coercion is needed, no need for threats or force. Law is the internalised acceptance of rules by civilised people. Of course, there will always be the *minority* of others, those who do not possess this internal point of view. Outsiders. Society is torn by the tension between the two. But, Hart explains, one need not fear:

"Though such a society may exhibit the tension, already described, between those who accept the rules and those who reject the rules except where fear of social pressure induces them to conform, it is plain that the latter cannot be more than a minority, if so loosely organised a society of persons, approximately equal in physical strength, is to endure: for otherwise those who reject the rules would have too little social pressure to fear (especially lawyers and officials) — or, as Austin would have it — obedience through threats, enforced by the sovereign. Or, as other would have it, through a minority class enforcing their will on the majority"[20].

3.3 Rules, juridification and legitimacy

In the tension which Hart posits "between those who, on the one hand, accept and voluntarily co-operate in maintaining the rules, and those who, on the other hand, reject the rules and attend to them only from the external point of view as a sign of possible punishment" (1961:88), there are echoes of two themes which appeared in Part 2 of this paper. First, that tension parallels the argument there that: "The concern that is expressed over juridification or the 'regulatory crisis' is a response to the disorder that is threatening the legal ordering of collectives of capital (companies), social security, labor and competitive economies"[21]. Is this disorder attributable to the increasing number of those involved in these fields who adopt the "external" rather than the "internal" point of view about the rules which regulate their activities? Is the acceptance shading off into acquiescence, or even into rejection? If so, the social ordering of rules of law would be threatened with disorder. The problems of juridification would be due to the changing attitudes to rules, not to the proliferation of rules. (Cf. Teubner's trilemma, including the "indifference" and the "disintegration" (rejection) scenarios supra: 19 ff.). The issue becomes one of *legitimacy* of the rules; disorder follows their illegitimacy.

A second theme echoed in the section on Hart's concept of law is found in the critique of industrial relations pluralism described in Part 2 of this paper. This critique characterises the general condition of the area of job/employment/work/labor relations as one of inequality in authoritarian hierarchies (Hyman and Brough, 1975: 157 ff.). The question is why it is that those employed in uncongenial circumstances, in conditions of subordination, do not revolt. One approach is that there are social processes which shape the prevailing beliefs and values of workers in a manner favorable to social stability and the interests of those in positions of power and privilege. The radical critique posits the study of industrial relations as in large measure the study of those institutions and processes which contribute to this accommodation. Industrial relations pluralists recognise conflicts of interests between different groups in industrial relations, but assume that none possesses a *disproportionate* concentration of power. Their theory is predicated on the assumption of an underlying balance of power and interests. The order that

[20] Supra.

[21] Further parallels may be sought in my paper on "Economic policy: State and private ordering".

results is deemed to be a compromise freely conceded by the parties negotiating it as the best result in the circumstances where none can get all it wants. Of course, if one removed that presumption of balance of power — what is conceived of as negotiated order might be seen to rest in actuality on coercion or manipulation (Hyman and Brough, 1975: 164; note 26).

The parallel between the acquiescence, on the one hand, of the subordinated worker and of the accommodated trade union before the power of the employers and management respectively, and, on the other, that of the "minority" with the external point of view in Hart's society, is an obvious one. The assumptions of Hart as to equality, and that of the industrial relations pluralists as to balance, are both questionable. The challenge to Hart and the industrial relations pluralists is from those who question the legitimacy of the rules which govern society and industrial relations.

To give a practical demonstration of the process of juridification, and its connection with concepts of "rules" and legitimacy, I propose to examine a phenomenon of British industrial relations which has caused great difficulty to those concerned with theorising about industrial relations and labor law: "custom and practice".

The determination of terms and conditions of employment in British industry is largely a function of collective bargaining between representatives of the workers and those of employers. A variety of actors appears on each side. Collective bargaining structures are to be found on many levels (national, industry-wide, regional, craft-wide, enterprise, workplace) and with many kinds of personnel (management, employers' associations, full-time and lay officials of trade unions). These actors engage in processes of collective negotiation — some of which are formally regulated by legal rules requiring, e.g. consultation and disclosure of information or time off for union officials to carry out various industrial relations duties (Employment Protection Act (1975) Sects. 17 ff. and 99 ff.; Employment Protection (Consolidation) Act (1978) Sects. 27 ff.). The outcomes of the processes engaged in by these actors are collective agreements of greater or less formality, with a variety of legal effects, which set out the terms and conditions of employment of individual workers and the rules governing the relations between the collective parties.

The phenomenon of custom and practice is of great significance to workers, but is neither captured within the structure of collective bargaining, nor adheres to the formal process of collective negotiation, nor is to be found embodied in the collective agreements which are the outcome. The difficulty of precisely defining what custom and practice is may be seen from the following attempt:

"...custom and practice rules (are) those transactional rules of job regulation which arise, not from any explicit and formal negotiation, but from a process whereby managerial error or omission establishes a practice that workers see as legitimate to defend. Besides being a type of job regulation rule, custom and practice is used as a claim and an excuse in circumstances where powerful work-forces interact with un-coordinated managements.

The importance of custom and practice should be emphasized. Whatever it is called, the phenomenon is evident in most of industry. In some industries it provides the basis and origin of rules of job regulation. It does not just augment formally negotiated rules; it supplants them. Even many ostensibly solid formal agreements are not more than the temporary recording of the current state of custom and practice rules. Once signed, these agreements may become battered by managerial deviation and worker pressure and finally dissolve into the broad flux of custom and practice.

If, in much of industry, custom and practice is king, its reign is curiously blind. Its rules do not emerge from any of the conscious bargaining processes with which industrial relations theories concerned themselves. They do not arise from intention, deliberation or conspiracy. They are the product of management error and worker power" (Brown, 1972).

A practical illustration may clarify the workings of custom and practice in industrial relations, H.A. Clegg posits the case of a small plant with only one union lay representative (shop steward) for all the workers (Clegg, 1972: 248-50). The relationship between the steward and management is informal: each sees the other when they want to. It may be that on one occasion the union representative persuades the manager that one group of workers should be paid an extra $1 per day, and this may be implemented by a verbal instruction to the wages clerk — without more. Or in connection with the allocation of overtime, the manager may ask the union representative to keep a rota of workers willing to do it — and the representative may take on the task and thereafter organise the distribution of overtime. Moreover, this might arise from the union representative's initiative without management consciously deciding anything, but acquiescing in the representative's decision to organise the allocation of overtime among the workers he represents. These understandings and arrangements are commonly called custom and practice. As Clegg states:

"There is no clear line between bargaining of this kind and consultation. The decision is an agreement if the manager accepts that he cannot change it without the consent of the steward. The manager may be forced to do so if he finds that the men are prepared to strike or if the steward appeals to his full-time officer and through him to the industry's disputes procedure. But in any particular instance in which it has not been put to the test there may be doubt as to whether a particular managerial decision is an agreement or merely an exercise of managerial prerogatives after consultation with the steward" (Clegg, 1972: 249).

The essence of custom and practice appears to be that some degree of rule-governed behavior is acknowledged to exist (restraints on management; concessions by workers). The development of custom and practice appears as a process of juridification of industrial relations — the development of rules or norms governing the behavior of the actors involved. But the stability of the order thus established is unclear, as is its legitimacy in the eyes of the participants in the order.

The difficulty of theories of industrial relations and of labor law in coming to terms with custom and practice is analysed by S. Hill (1974; 1981: Ch. 7) in a way which contributes to an understanding of our concern with juridification and Teubner's analysis of it. Hill asserts that the problem lies with the traditional perspective of academic commentators who located rule-making at the level of formal institutions outside the workplace — and relegated the workplace itself to secondary importance, despite the fact of its increasingly dynamic role in the generation of rules. The need is to develop concepts which explain the creation and maintenance of rules at the workplace. It is worth quoting Hill's proposals at length for they link up the themes of juridification, rules and legitimacy:

"(one explanation of rules and normative regulation) presupposes an analysis of actual behaviour in specific situations, focussing attention on the relationships of workers with management and with each other. This is an interactionist perspective which lays emphasis on the nature of social relations within a social system. In this case, norms are treated as the expressions of regularities arising out of interactive behaviour rather than imposing regularity on this...

Norms serve primarily to codify and formalize these interactions. There is no reason why such norms should necessarily become more than mere statements about the regularity of behaviour, because the internalization of norms as morally binding or desirable is not the necessary consequence of such interaction. Interaction can and does become habitual and can be stable over time without either party attaching moral value to it or treating it as legitimate in terms of social values. The regularity of interaction and the growth of norms can be matters of indifference to either party, or they can be regarded as illegitimate by one side which does not, however, have the resources to change the situation. Situations where management feels itself dominated by the labour force, or vice versa... are characterised by regularity of interactions and the existence of norms or rules but not by sentiments of legitimacy.

On the other hand, it is possible that interaction may develop into something which is normatively internalised... the regularities can become invested with legitimacy and develop a morally binding force if continued over time. In some instances, it is possible to talk of a moral obligation to follow the rules which derives from their regular, or customary, nature...

The moral force which some rules accumulate over time can make them to some extent independent of interaction, however, so that the rules themselves can be appealed to if behaviour deviates from, say, customary practices. But changes in interaction ultimately change the rules: for example, if a work group consistently breaks a rule and has the power to prevent management enforcing this, then the new action becomes the norm and the old rule ceases to operate as a standard for behaviour. The dialectical nature of this process indicates that some rules become as it were detached from interaction and exert an independent force of their own which partially constrains future actions, but that changes in the interactive base ultimately modify the norms to accord with the new reality. The structure of the workplace social system is neither inherently stable nor static, since it represents the regularities of past interactions which are modified by new ones: it is a continually evolving, adaptive process. Norms have force to the extent that they embody these previous regularities: they are taken into account, but do not necessarily determine behaviour in relationships.

Such an emphasis does not necessarily imply disorder, though the scheme can of course explain this should it occur. The difference between this perspective and those of systems theorists or value and normative integrationists is that stability and integration are not made part of the taken-for-granted background assumptions of the scheme. However, it may often be the case that 'orderly', static and stable, industrial relations result from interaction, both because the bases of interaction remain stable over time and so ensure regularity of behaviour and because norms generated in interaction can exercise some independent effect of their own on social relationships" (Hill, 1974: 230-32).

Hence, the development of custom and practice is a process of juridification, but the "rules" developed are not characterised by the actors' having a stable "internal" or "external" point of view, as Hart posits. Rather, not only does the "tension" *between* different groups' attitudes to the rules exist (and power relations are very important in determining which attitude, and whose, prevails over the other), but, more importantly, the attitudes of the actors themselves are neither stable nor entirely coherent or clear. Their attitudes may be confused and change, depending on such factors as the balance of power and the duration of the custom and practice. The nature of juridification is thus contingent, not permanent. Custom and practice can develop rule-governed orderings — but can also break them down into disorder.

Hill's analysis of custom and practice as contributing to both order and disorder throws light on the relationship between juridification and the stability of social forms. The issue of stability is linked closely with that of legitimacy: order or disorder is a function of the legitimacy attached to the rules by those governed by them. In this connection, custom and practice in industrial relations can again throw light on processes of juridification. The legitimacy of rules in industrial relations is traditionally ascribed to managerial prerogative. As Brown puts it:

"The nature of managerial prerogative is complex. Fox's discussion of the matter traces its power basis to the control of resources and its authority to 'a measure of normative agreement which, to the extent that it prevails, enables subordinates to legitimize management's superordinate role and the use of sanctions'. Flanders emphasizes that management is a decision-making body first and foremost and that workers can never expect to be anything more than an 'official opposition' to management's 'Government'. This is not to deny that managerial prerogatives can in fact be eroded almost out of sight. The key point is that there is a prevailing assumption that any particular matter concerned with the conduct of work will be regulated by management unless management has specifically handed over to workers powers of joint or unilateral regulation. Managerial prerogative means that management has the legitimate right to determine rules of job regulation unilaterally, whether or not it has the power" (Brown, 1972: 48)[22].

However, Brown goes on to note that "There is another source of legitimacy present in the industrial context, one that is very different from the managerial type. This is based on custom... and long-practice" (1972: 49). The question of "under what circumstances (custom and practice) becomes important and over-rides managerial legitimacy" was set aside by Brown in his paper, but was addressed by M. Terry in the following passage:

"Rules which differ in form, content, and authorship often apply in the same area of job control. The potential conflict thus implied is only brought to the surface when each side invokes the rule to which it adheres in a dispute situation. In these situations it then becomes possible to see that these different rules may carry different degrees of support and allegiance with the different groups involved. Consider the common case of a dispute situation in which management base their case on a formal rule, and the shop floor base theirs on a custom and practice understanding" (Terry, 1977: 78).

Terry illustrated the position by a conflict over the transfer of a worker — attempted by management invoking prerogative, but resisted by workers invoking custom and practice — and resolved by conceding the workers' claim (custom and practice), while emphasising that it was a "special case" and not a diminution of management's general prerogative. As Terry summarises:

"The cumulative effect of such decisions tends to be to reinforce the legitimacy of the formal provision in the minds of management and to confirm the usefulness of the custom in the minds of the stewards and the shop floor. Such situations can, and do, lead to a situation typical of many workplaces, namely that the legitimacy and authority of rules purporting to regulate the work situation are not constant across those to whom they apply and by whom they are applied. Different groups attach different importance to different rules.

To put the same point more systematically, *the hypothesis can be advanced that a rule will carry the greatest authority with the group or individual who fought for, negotiated, or guarded, that rule. This implies that groups or individuals further away from the authorship or care of such rules will be more prepared than the authors or guardians to challenge such rules.* Thus in the workplace custom and practice should carry greater authority for the shop floor workers than any other group, and for these workers, such rules may well carry greater authority than any other rule or set of rules, with another source or author. Further, the strength of shop-floor allegiance to custom and practice suggests that, from the shop-floor perspective, it is irrelevant whether or not the authors of such rules have any written dispensation, either from management or the union outside, to negotiate or enforce such rules" (Terry, 1977: 78) (My emphasis).

[22] For another example of legal abdication confirming and legitimizing management control, see the Employment Protection (Consolidation) Act 1978, section 62, and Bercusson (1979).

This analysis of industrial relations custom and practice may be of value to the debate over juridification by illustrating the case of the development of rules in one context. The features highlighted include the unstable nature of social orders where power conflicts lead to the rules emanating from different power sources, with consequently differing degrees of legitimacy — and hence varying points of view (external and internal as Hart would have it) towards the rules.

Even more tentatively, if one was to draw an analogy between management prerogative and state power, and work-group power and lower level social forms — the example of industrial relations custom and practice has implications for the solution propounded by Teubner to the problems of juridification structural coupling between social life forms and state ordering (or control of self-regulation) (See Teubner, supra: 33ff.; Habermas, 1985: 203). On the one hand, the devolution of power to those involved in the day-to-day working of the social life form (lower management and workers and their representatives at the workplace) gives a major role to custom and practice, and if these rules command a larger claim to legitimacy from the actors (who thereby manifest Hart's internal attitude, as required for rules to govern behavior successfully) — the achievement of social order is promoted. On the other hand, the problem remains of the maintenance of control (state or management), in circumstances where power conflicts are endemic. Ewald provides a good illustration when he discussed the judicial control of management prerogative to discipline or dismiss workers (Ewald, 1985). Either this results in the judges undertaking a task for which they are not, as lawyers and not industrial relations experts, equipped. Or they opt for a strategy of self-restraint: they use their power to control management very sparingly. This, it is important to note, is *more* than just an abdication of power to management which *appears* to be subject to the control of judicially enforced legal standards. By refusing to intervene when complaints are made concerning the exercise of management prerogative, the judges are *legitimising* that power — and thus reinforcing it as a source of rules against other sources (e.g. custom and practice) [23].

Unsuccessful attempts at "structural coupling" are likely to result in an unstable and constantly shifting balance between the imposition of control and the demand for self-regulation. Indeed, the conditions within which self-regulation takes place may simply replicate these problems at a lower level, insofar as Teubner's and Habermas's proposed solutions are based on a view of "undistorted or unconstrained discourse" among the participants. As described by H. Rottleuthner, such discourse is marked by three features: "there is no compulsion other than the compulsion of argumentation; no form

[23] I do not pretend that this is the sole meaning or use of the term "ideology", nor does it do justice to the richness and scope of the concept. See Lichtheim, (1967: 46), who would characterise the definition adopted here as "the ideology concept of contemporary positivism. Its limited practical relevance ought not to veil its incompatibility with the intellectual tradition (ultimately rooted in classical thought) that is intended when one speaks of the philosophy of history". See also Plamenatz (1970).

of domination exists; every participant has an equal opportunity to choose and perform the possible speech acts; and every participant can freely change the linguistic levels (putting forward propositions, norm formulations, intentional/self-representative expressions, and so on)".

One must recognise the practical difficulties in adjusting the development of workplace custom and practice to this ideal. It is no less an ideal, however, than that of Hart's society peopled with civilized bearers of the "internal attitude", or my own advocacy of the need to mobilise respect as a resource (rather than force or wealth) to maintain social order (supra).

3.4 Disorder, ideology and legal theory

There have been a number of references to the "ideological" nature of legal theory in preceding sections, and I want here to clarify what is meant by "ideology", and how the use of this term affects my argument. I intend to use the term "ideology" to mean a secular and political creed, in particular, one carrying the implication that the truth of what is said is *relatively* unimportant, compared with its effects on those who hear and believe it, and compared with the social origins of the creed[24]. This last element further implies that a social class or group will select the evidence for or slant language about the creed so as to protect their own interests or performances — hence the connection between ideology and value considerations. So when it is said that legal theory is ideological, what is claimed is that the theories put forward by lawyers or legal theorists are proferred in order to defend the interests or values of some group or other, and, moreover, that their effectiveness in doing so accounts both for their production and their reception[25].

It was Marx who put forward the most famous and influential account of the nature and effects of ideology — an account which still stirs fears among social scientists. His attack on religion, moral beliefs, political science and economic theory all had the common feature that, as ideologies, they served to hide the *truth* of exploitation and misery from the working class. This was done by painting a picture of the world in which the existing incumbents of powerful positions were doing the best job they could, and were only taking their due reward for so doing.

[24] This is not to confuse theory and method, nor to denigrate the role of theory — rather to criticise the ideological character of much legal theory. As Cotterrell (1983: 686) says of the confusion of legal analysis with legal theory, the former "makes no reference to any specific explanatory aims of theory". He later adds: "The conditions of modern legal practice suggest that conceptual rationalisation is properly seen as the lawyer's necessary attempt to maintain the stability of legal doctrine in conditions of continual legislative change dictated by complex political, economic and social conditions. Lawyers' pragmatic doctrinal rationalisations, in contemporary conditions, need, and can receive, little technical aid from general theory.

[25] The relevance of this comparison of natural and social sciences is highlighted by the resort of legal theorists to models of the natural sciences for inspiration: Habermas to Piaget and Kohlberg; Teubner to Maturana; not to mention the less reputable antecedents of Herbert Spencer's "Social Darwinism". See Blankenburg, (1984) a critique of Teubner's case for "reflexive law"; and Teubner's reply (1984).

Ideology in the sense above is defined could be instrumental in what Marx terms "false consciousness". By false consciousness, Marx appears to have meant a set of mistaken beliefs about matters important to them shared by a whole group of persons or even a whole community. False consciousness is pervasive and has extensive social consequences. It consists of a number of closely related illusions common to all or nearly all persons whose situations or roles in society are the same. Bourgeois ideas — to take an example from the field of jurisprudence — about the state are, so Marx believed, an example of false consciousness. For example, the beliefs about the essential functions of the state were illusory. Marx considered that these false beliefs were necessary to enable the state to carry out its real functions. If the state is to be what it really is, if it is to favor the interests which in fact it does favor, there must be false beliefs more or less widely accepted about what it is, about the interests it favors. For example, it must be widely held that it favors interests common to all who are subject to its authority — whereas in fact, according to Marx, it favors the interests of one class to the detriment of others.

By formulating his concept of ideology, Marx created some terrible problems for social theory. In particular, the problem of how to distinguish between ideology and truth about social life, Marx himself plainly never doubted that there was a clear distinction to be drawn. Thus, he did not use the word ideology to refer to his own theory — even though it was a theory in line with the class interests of the proletariat, and therefore a theory which the proletariat would gradually come to accept as it learned to recognise its class interests. Marx and Engels did not call their theory an ideology presumably because they did not think of it as a form of false consciousness. The proletariat, according to them, is in one respect a uniquely privileged class: the beliefs about society and the course of social change that favor its interests are true beliefs. It is their destiny to be the only class that understand the course of social change and rises above false consciousness.

Though Marx and Engels may have risen above doubt, later social theorists have become entangled in some very awkward questions about the relativity of social truth and the apparent subjectivity of all social theory and observation (including, of course, legal theory). Many contemporary social and political scientists tend towards the view advanced by Karl Popper in resolving this problem. Briefly, on the face of it, the claim that a doctrine is ideological and not scientific ought to be susceptible of a simple enough test — at any rate in principle. This test would take the following form. Where we are offered an explanation, we cast it into the form of a hypothesis. We then try to derive from its assumptions testable predictions about social life. When we have done this, we can perform the appropriate tests and see whether the generalisations on which the explanation was based can stand up to the evidence. If a proposition has *no* testable consequences, then it is not a scientific proposition at all. The Popperian view states that it will then very likely turn out to be a moral demand which we may either accept or reject. Or it may be a metaphysical proposition which can be turned into the kind of methodological claim which can be indirectly tested by way of the fruitfulness of its recommendations — or which can be rejected as meaningless.

When one confronts the Popperian view, as outlined above, however, certain doubts creep in as to whether indeed the tests which it posits can be applied as simply as the theory imagines. One wonders whether as a matter of fact social scientists can live up to the demands of the Popperian view of objectivity. A common starting point shared by many sociologists today is the observation that a person's social position determines to a large extent what kinds of moral and political creeds he espouses, what kinds of beliefs he will hold about the way in which society ought to be organised. This is not simply an allegation of bias, for it goes much deeper. It is not simply that the social position of a writer or a scientist will prejudice him in favor of some beliefs against others. It is also the assertion that a person's whole way of life is bound up with the way he thinks, in such a way that thought and action together form an integral whole.

To take an example, I have sought to analyse the legal perspective on labor law generally, and picketing in particular, from this viewpoint (Bercusson, 1977). Legal commentators rarely affirm the perspective they adopt in their writings. It is an unfortunate consequence that they thereby appear to give their analysis an objective character. Frequently, however, and almost invariably in modern times, their analysis, description and criticism of labor law are predicated on an acceptance of the conventional wisdom. This presumes the inherent desirability, justice and continuity of a system of industrial relations based on collective bargaining. This implies the corollaries of management rights, union responsibilities and individual workers' freedoms. The preliminary acceptance and often conscious welcoming of a continuing division of industrial society into capital and labor contradicts the purportedly objective character of their discussion. It colors not only the substance of their analysis and the nature of the arguments brought to bear, but even the language in which they are expressed and the strength of their criticisms. The perspective adopted is one of constantly seeking to balance the opposing forces of capital and labor in a particular state of equilibrium. The state of equilibrium idealised by the legal perspective has traditionally been characterised by two fundamental concepts: the master-servant relationship of employment, and the ownership and control of the means of production by the employer. The idealisation of this state of equilibrium is bound to influence the analysis of strikes and picketing, which of their nature threaten to disturb the equilibrium. In my article, I sought to indicate how the legal perspective reveals its bias in the law of picketing.

Marx's account of the inter-relationship of economic circumstances and how they determine the intellectual and moral superstructure have become part of what is known as the "sociology of knowledge". It is an account of how as a matter of fact the social, economic and eventually political circumstances in which we live make it harder or easier for us to discover the truth about social life. Because in any understanding of the world we have to select some aspects and ignore others we are necessarily vulnerable to the *pre-selection* of significant detail which the *existing* social organisation of our society involves. It is thus the case both that the social world will be organised according to some particular brand of principles — and that we will be predisposed to see some principles embodied in it, to the neglect of other principles, which are perhaps even more significantly at work.

Marx thought that sociological knowledge was especially vulnerable to this kind of blinkering. Indeed, he goes rather further than this. He went on to argue that the dominant social class will hire intellectuals, artists, priests and philosophers to put about its social view as *the* social view; its account of the truth as *the* truth. It is for this reason that Marx often refers to ideology as false consciousness. For when the non-dominant class sees its own situation in the terms which the dominant class has imposed on it, then it *mis*perceives its situation, and cannot be aware of the truth about its condition.

Now Marx himself was well aware of his own position as a bourgeois critic of the bourgeois order — and how this might seem paradoxical and inexplicable — but only on a rigid account of ideological influences in social theory. His argument was only meant to hold for the most part and in the majority of cases. It was not only meant to imply a kind of bourgeois original sin whereby any member of the bourgeoisie would be inexorably tainted and quite unable to tell the truth about social life. Rather Marx meant that since the truth meant unmasking the exploitation and wholesale cheating practised by the bourgeoisie, it would be irrational to suppose that large numbers of bourgeois would commit large quantities of the resources of the bourgeoisie to such a task. Social science was always in danger of being corrupted. Marx did, as mentioned above, suppose that the proletariat would see its social world more clearly than their oppressors — an assertion that rarely fails to kindle outrage among them.

In preceding sections of this paper I have sought to examine the state of British legal theory which is revealed from the examples of the textbooks of Lloyd and Dias to be in a condition of confusion. Theories abound, and their relation to each other is difficult to establish, since they often fail to agree that their subject matter, let alone the approach to it, has anything in common. Certainly none of them qualifies as objective scientific truth in the Popperian sense — neither Dias nor Lloyd awards this accolade. I have also, using the concept of ideology, attempted to analyse the idea of objective truth in social theory. I want to try to link these two strands together by contrasting two views of the process of change in scientific theory — drawn from the natural sciences but with equal relevance in the social sciences [26].

[26] Kuhn, 1970: 82-83. The similarity between this process and a crisis of the English common law in the last century was remarked upon by A.W.B. Simpson, who described the latter crisis as follows: "When, however, cohesion has begun to break down, and a failure to achieve consensus becomes a commoner phenomenon, interest will begin to develop in the formulation of tests as to how the correctness of legal propositions can be demonstrated, and in the formulation of rules as to the use of authorities — that is to say warrants or proofs that this or that is the law". See Twining (1986: 23).

The Popperian view rests on the fundamental assumption that the business of science, social and natural science alike, is the confrontation of hypothesis with fact. And the less obstacle there is to this confrontation, the greater the chance of establishing the truth and thus distinguishing science from mere ideology. This whole presumption is called into question by the account of science presented by T.S. Kuhn (1970). He begins by criticising the image of science now possessed by most people:

"That image has previously been drawn, even by scientists themselves, mainly from the study of finished scientific achievements as these are recorded in the classics and, more recently, in the textbooks from which each new scientific generation learns to practice its trade. Inevitably, however, the aim of such books is persuasive and pedagogic; a concept of science drawn from them is no more likely to fit the enterprise that produced them than an image of a national culture drawn from a tourist brochure or a language text... we have been misled by them in fundamental ways" (Kuhn, 1970: 1).

Kuhn points out how historians of science have been challenging the orthodox view that science develops by the accumulation of individual discoveries and inventions. They are finding it difficult to distinguish the "scientific" component of past theories from what is labelled by contemporary science as "error" and "superstition". Their conclusion is that "those once current views of nature were, as a whole, neither less scientific nor more the product of human idiosyncrasy than those current today" (1970:2). Kuhn describes the consequences of the approach of historians of science to their subject: "Rather than seeking the permanent contributions of an older science to our present vantage, they attempt to display the historical integrity of that science in its own time". (1970: 3)

This view of the nature of scientific development has implications for the perception of contemporary science. As Kuhn states:

"Normal science, the activity in which most scientists inevitably spend almost all their time, is predicated on the assumption that the scientific community knows what the world is like. Much of the success of the enterprise derives from the community's willingness to defend that assumption, if necessary at considerable cost. Periodically, there are problems which resist solution, or anomalies are produced by equipment and experiment which cannot be aligned with professional expectation. These are often initially suppressed and ignored, until they cannot any longer be evaded". Then, says Kuhn "when, that is, the profession can no longer evade anomalies that subvert the existing tradition of scientific practice — then begin the extraordinary investigations that lead the profession at last to a new set of commitments, a new basis for the practice of science" (1970: 5). These extraordinary episodes are what he calls scientific revolutions. "They are the tradition-shattering complements to the tradition-bound activity of normal science" (1970: 6). The absorption and working out of this revolution takes a long time and involves many people — which feed the tendency to regard such changes as imputable to a single event. The implications of these revolutions in science are quite staggering. For "normal science" defines not only what entities the universe does contain, but also what it does not — by implication. The conceptions are altered by unexpected discoveries.

Kuhn's conclusions are relevant to perceptions about states of knowledge about law, legal theory, or as Dias would have it, "thought about law". He rejects the confirmation or falsification procedures made familiar by our usual image of science. He states categorically that "no process yet disclosed by the historical study of scientific development at all resembles the methodological stereotype of falsification by direct comparison with nature" (1970: 77). His view is rather that our image of science is better obtained through a theory of scientific enquiry. As he states:

"Competition between segments of the scientific community is the only historical process that ever actually results in the rejection of one previously accepted theory or in the adoption of another... 'Normal science' means research firmly based upon one or more past scientific achievements, achievements that some particular scientific community acknowledges for a time as supplying the foundation for its further practice...

Their achievement was sufficiently unprecedented to attract an enduring group of adherents away from competing modes of scientific activity. Simultaneously, it was sufficiently open-ended to leave all sorts of problems for the redefined group of practicioners to resolve.

...the act of judgment that leads scientists to reject a previously accepted theory is always based upon *more* than a comparison of that theory with the world. The decision to reject one paradigm is always simultaneously the decision to accept another, and the judgment leading to that decision involves the comparison of both paradigms with nature *and* with each other" (Kuhn, 1970: 8, 10, 77).

The present confusion over the scope of jurisprudence, and the proliferation of "paradigms" — legal theories, is symptomatic of a state which Kuhn describes in relation to scientific theory as a "crisis". This crisis stage occurs when the existing paradigm produces an anomaly, which must be of a substantial, or even fundamental kind. As Kuhn says:

"The scientist who pauses to examine every anomaly he notes will seldom get significant work done. We therefore have to ask what it is that makes the anomaly seem worth concerted scrutiny, and to that question there is probably no fully general answer" (Kuhn, 1970: 82). But once the anomaly has come to command sufficient attention, as Kuhn states: "the transition to crisis and to extraordinary science has begun". It is worth quoting Kuhn's description at length:

"When, for these reasons or others like them, an anomaly comes to seem more than just another puzzle of normal science, the transition to crisis and to extraordinary science has begun. The anomaly itself now comes to be more generally recognised as such by the profession. More and more attention is devoted to it by more and more of the field's most eminent men. If it still continues to resist, as it usually does not, many of them may come to view its resolution as *the* subject matter of their discipline. For them the field will no longer look quite the same as it had earlier. Part of its different appearance results simply from the new fixation point of scientific scrutiny. An even more important source of change is the divergent nature of the numerous partial solutions that concerted attention to the problem has made available. The early attacks upon the resistant problem will have followed the paradigm rules quite closely. But with continuing resistance, more and more of the attacks upon it will have involved some minor or not so minor articulation of the paradigm, no two of them quite alike, each partially successful, but none sufficiently so to be accepted as paradigm by the group. Through this proliferation of divergent articulations (more and more frequently they will come to the described as *ad hoc* adjustments), the rules of normal science become increasingly blurred. Though there is still a paradigm, few practicioners prove to be entirely agreed about what it is. Even formerly standard solutions of solved problems are called in question"[27].

The legal profession, both its academic and practising branches, does not compare, of course, with the scientific profession in the concern it expresses for legal theory in Britain. Few men, even the most eminent, are devoting much attention to the chaotic state of jurisprudence. Most are not concerned overmuch what the state of the science is.

The solutions to scientific crisis are classified by Kuhn as three:
"Sometimes normal science ultimately proves able to handle the crisis-provoking problem despite the despair of those who have seen it as the end of an existing paradigm. On other occasions the problem resists even apparently radical new approaches. The scientists may conclude that no solution will be forthcoming in the present state of their field. The problem is labelled and set aside for a future generation with more developed tolls. Or, finally... a crisis may end with the emergence of a new candidate for paradigm and with the ensuing battle over its acceptance" (Kuhn, 1970: 84).

Neither the first nor the third of these solutions has been forthcoming in legal theory. No existing paradigm has evoked acceptance. Nor have previous paradigms proved adequate in the eyes of those of the profession who are bothered to concern themselves with the state of the art. On the other hand, the problem has certainly not been labelled and put aside. Those who are concerned continue to fret. Any proposed new approach, however radical, should therefore be seen in the light of an attempt to resolve the anomalies and problems of legal theory. The rough and ready state of such attempts should be appreciated — paradigms are not created overnight or by a single person.

Above all, Kuhn's prescriptions as regards scientific theory should be borne in mind: "if any and every failure to fit were ground for theory rejection, all theories ought to be rejected at all times. On the other hand, if only severe failure to fit justifies theory rejection, then the Popperians will require some

[27] Hart stated in the Preface to *The Concept of Law* that "Notwithstanding its concern with analysis the book may also be regarded as an essay in descriptive sociology". Cf. Twining's comment: "To the more sociologically minded the least convincing of Hart's claims was the statement that *The Concept of Law* was an essay in descriptive sociology"; in W. Twining (1983: 3).

criterion of 'improbability' or of 'degree of falsification'..." (1970: 146-47). In considering the theories of law one must remember, as Kuhn states:

"To the historian, at least, it makes little sense to suggest that verification is establishing the agreement of fact with theory. All historically significant theories have agreed with the facts, but only more or less. There is no more precise answer to the question whether or how well an individual theory fits the facts. But questions much like that can be asked when theories are taken collectively or even in pairs. It makes a great deal of sense to ask which of two actual and competing theories fits the facts *better*..." (Kuhn, 1970: 147).

Of course, there remains the problem of which *facts* fall within the territory of jurisprudence. As Dias says: "A lawyer will find a definition valuable if its logical implications correspond with the actual ways in which judges and lawyers think and act in deciding disputes". He quotes Holmes as saying: "The first call of a theory of law is that it should fit the facts". Dias regrets that: "Not all the implications of a definition of 'law' have ever corresponded with the actual language and behavior of lawyers"... "which is unfortunate since efforts should be made towards bridging the gulf that regrettably exists between jurisprudents and practicioners" (Dias, 1976: 11). The problem of expanding the area of *facts* beyond the limited world of lawyers and judges to achieve a theory of law can easily be appreciated. It is one particular contribution of the sociology of law to have greatly expanded the area of facts relevant to legal theory[28].

The confusion in legal theory, as an illustration of Kuhn's theory of the development of (social) science, has parallels with the view of law as an ideology in the sense ascribed above. The notion of an "ideology" has been linked closely with the interests of groups or classes — as having, therefore, clear political implications. The political implications of Kuhn's theory are developed in part of a paper by R. Cotterrell (1986) which suggests that, with respect to Kuhn's theory:

"...for knowledge-fields such as law and sociology there is only what we might call a 'discipline-effect' — a mirage of disciplinary integrity — not the actual conditions of practice for an integrated intellectual discipline... Thus critical writing in jurisprudence importing perspectives from philosophy or various social sciences has, despite some extremely cogent demonstrations of the inadequacies of prevailing modes of legal thought, often failed to achieve any lasting reorientation of legal thinking... The possibility of intellectual advance in this context probably has to be viewed much more modestly. It may mean (putting the matter in Kuhnian terms) a reduction in the range of

[28] Cotterell (1986: 8-9). Cotterrell also draws on the analysis of Michel Foucault who "is explicit in his writings that the character of the social sciences and of law as a knowledge-field is shaped by the intricate relationship between knowledge and power; that these knowledge-fields are structured by their direct relevance to particular configurations of power in society" (1986: 4). Cotterrell acknowledges other views of the peculiar resistance of legal theory: Luhmann's description of the legal system as a "normatively closed system" (1986: 8).

seriously competing exemplars (paradigms), or clarification of their appropriateness, power or scope" (Cotterell, 1986).

The political implications of Kuhn's theory for legal theory lies in his view that "normal science" is the preserve of the "old guard" of the scientific community, and "scientific revolutions" occur when this old guard cannot resist the new theory. As Cotterell (1986: 4) puts it: "The actual decision to reject the established order of a discipline — the occurrence of what Kuhn terms a scientific revolution — seems to be very much a matter of personalities, power and environment". The peculiar resistance of the "old guard" of legal theory, in particular its resistence to the contributions of other disciplines, may, Cotterell suggests, be due to the fact "that the relationship of legal knowledge with configurations of power in society is so firm, direct and fundamental that the power-knowledge interpenetration provides an exceptionally strong demand for and guarantee of the maintenance of the autonomy of the legal field and its discipline-effect"[29].

The "opening of an intellectual space", to use Cotterell's phrase, or, as he puts it:

"... the only way in which knowledge in the human sciences generally (including the study of law) can escape being limited by the particular configurations of power in the human activities which make possible each of these specific disciplines is by confrontation ***between*** disciplines, or — to put it another way — the effective challenging of the mechanisms sustaining the discipline-effect of these fields ... It should also follow, if disciplines are understood as social constructs in the ways outlined above, that a confrontation of disciplines will never be a confrontation of 'pure' knowledges or methodologies with its outcome determined by intellectual criteria (methodological rigour, sophistication of theoretical analysis, depth of empirical reference, etc.). Such a confrontation will always ultimately be a *social* conflict (in certain aspects, a political conflict in the sense of a competition for power or an attempt to exercise power). It is thus not possible to bring about any such confrontation merely by intellectual argument, unless the social conditions for such a confrontation arise" (Cotterell, 1986: 5).

In other words, there is a link between "disorder" and developments in legal theory. This argument is illustrated by the link which I attempted to demonstrate between the theory of juridification and disorder (or changing order) in the first part of this paper. To play on one of my own conclusions: "Cries of juridification are only polemical devices hurled by those who stand to lose or benefit by changes in the existing order (or disorder)" (cf. supra: 58).

In a book in which he discusses the role of ideology, M. Shaw observes how the increasing complexity of modern society — its bureaucratisation in particular — affects the activity of the production of theory and knowledge (Shaw, 1975: 6-7, 13). This is the case first of all with knowledge of the

[29] For an argument that legal theory in England, as formulated by Bentham to be inherently a matter of political debate, was gradually squeezed out to "appear apolitical", see Cotterell, 1986: 686-687.

natural sciences, but also with regard to social scientific knowledge. The production of such knowledge is no longer a general attribute of the ordinary social activity of ordinary people and groups — albeit largely undeveloped. Nor has it become a secondary function of intellectual groups outside ordinary productive activity. Instead, it becomes *both*; first, a distant function *within all* other branches of production, *and* secondly, and increasingly, a branch of production in its own right. It becomes not only a specific and acknowledged attribute of all productive workers, but also the sole activity of specialised groups of productive worker. Hence the general concern with legal theory, the increasing concern among the legal profession and the growing specialisation amongst academics.

The development of legal theory — its production — is a consequence of the problematic nature of the social goals of the organisation of production — and society generally. The proliferation of legal theory is a consequence of needs at various levels. First, for some consciousness of law and order at the basic level of ordinary productive activity. Secondly, for layers of administrators and educators trained in the legal ideology to mould the work force outside production. Finally, for a more sophisticated justification of the existing social order. Shaw argues that modern capitalism, in all its complexity, creates an unprecedented requirement for special means whereby the ruling class maintains its "hegemony" — i.e. its non-coercive control, over the subject population. Social science generally, and legal theory in particular, contributes to this set of mechanisms. All the more so as the mechanisms of coercion become concentrated in the hands of the state. Legal theory can be an instrument of justification and legitimation — a means of expanding both the efficacy of state coercion and the hegemony of the ruling class.

The concept of ideology can be used to explain the multiplicity of different — and indeed conflicting — theories of law and legal systems. The key to the inadequacies of legal theory — the current paradigms in the terminology of Kuhn — is the failure to account for, explain or reflect reality. In Kuhn's words, there is an increasing number of anomalies or problems which resist solution. Shaw quotes Lukacs who emphasised the effects of this kind of increasingly strained rationalisation on the possibilities of knowledge. Speaking of modern science, and by analogy with legal "science", Lukacs said:

"The more highly developed (it) becomes and the more scientific, the more it will become a formally closed system of partial laws. It will then find that the world lying beyond its confines, and in particular the material base which is its task to understand, its own concrete underlying reality lies, methodologically and in principle, beyond its grasp" (Shaw, 1975: 68).

Legal thought which seeks to understand the reality of law and legal systems abandons this task in favor of the goals of systematic, formal knowledge. Legal theory comes to offer formal rational and abstract conceptual systems — but these are only subjectively founded. The most they can achieve is "to set up a formal typology of the manifestations of history and society using historical facts as illustrations. This means that only a chance connection links the theoretical system to the objective historical reality that the theory is intended to comprehend" (Shaw, 1975:73).

An even more dangerous consequence is that the content of social reality which neglects to conform to the formal theory must increasingly appear as irrational. It is possible and necessary, for both scientific and polemical purposes, to extricate partial knowledge, information and ideas — even from legal theories committed to the existing social and intellectual framework. But the limitations implicit in that commitment should always be borne in mind.

References

AUSTIN, John (1954) *The Province of Jurisprudence Determined.* London: Weidenfeld and Nicholson.

BANKOWSKI, Zenon and Geoff MUNGHAM (1976) *Images of Law.* London: Routledge and Kegan Paul.

BARNETT, Hilaire and Diana YACH (1985) "The Teaching of Jurisprudence and Legal Theory in British Universities and Polytechnics", 5 *Legal Studies* 151.

BERCUSSON, Brian (1977) "One hundred years of conspiracy and protection of property: time for a change" 40 *Modern Law Review* 268.

—(1978) "Commentary on Employment Protection Consolidation Act 1978" in B.A. Hepple and P. O'Higgins (eds.) *Encyclopedia of Labour Relations Law* (loose-leaf). London: Sweet and Maxwell.

—(1987) "Economic Policy: State and Private Ordering", in T.C. Daintith (ed.), *Law as an Instrument of Economic Policy: Comparative and Critical Approaches.* Berlin: de Gruyter (forthcoming).

BLANKENBURG, Erhard (1984) "The Poverty of Evolutionism. A Critique of Teubner's Case for 'Reflexive Law'", in D. Trubek (ed.) *Reflexive Law and the Regulatory Crisis.* Madison: University of Wisconsin-Madison, Law School.

BROWN, William (1972) "A Consideration of Custom and Practice", 10 *British Journal of Industrial Relations* 42.

CLEGG, Hugh A. (1972) *The System of Industrial Relations in Great Britain* (2nd Ed.). Oxford: Blackwell.

—(1975) "Pluralism in Industrial Relations", 13 *British Journal of Industrial Relations* 309.

COTTERRELL, R.B.M. (1983) "English Conceptions of the Role of Theory in Legal Analysis", 46 *Modern Law Review* 681.

—(1986) "Law and Sociology: Notes on the Constitution and Confrontations of Disciplines", 13 *Journal of Law and Society* 1.

COTTERRELL, R.B.M. and John C. WOODLIFFE (1974) "The Teaching of Jurisprudence in British Universities" 73 *Journal of the Society of Public Teachers of Law* 87.

DAINTITH , Terence C. (1987) "Law as Policy Instrument: A Comparative Perspective", in T.C. Daintith (ed.), *Law as an Instrument of Economic Policy: Comparative and Critical Approaches.* Berlin: de Gruyter (forthcoming).

DIAS, R.W.M. (1976) *Jurisprudence* (4th Ed.). London: Butterworth.

ELDRIDGE, John E.T. (1978) "Pluralism, Procedural Consensus and Collective Bargaining", 16 *British Journal of Industrial Relations* 34.

EMPLOYMENT PROTECTION ACT (1975) ss. 17ff and 99ff.

EMPLOYMENT PROTECTION [CONSOLIDATION] ACT (1978) ss. 27ff.

Ewald, François (1985) "La Juridication de Droit Social", Presented at the Conference on *Law and Economic Policy — Alternatives to Delegalisation*, European University Institute, Florence (March 26).
Fox, Allan (1974) *Beyond Contract: Trust, Power and Work Relations*. London: Faber.
Fox, Alan and Alan Flanders (1979) "The Reform of Collective Bargaining: From Donovan to Dürkheim", 7 *British Journal of Industrial Relations* 151.
Garofolo, Mario G. (1982) "Collocamento, integrazioni guadagni, mobilità: un profilo storico", in M. G. Garofolo and C. Legala (eds.) *Collocamento e Mercato del Lavoro*. De Donato: Bari.
Goldthorpe, John H. (1974) "Industrial Relations in Great Britain: A Critique of Reformism", *Politics and Society* 419.
Habermas, Jürgen (1985) "Law as Medium and Law as Institution", in G. Teubner (ed.) *Dilemmas of Law in the Welfare State*. Berlin: de Gruyter.
Hacker, Peter M.S. (1977) "Hart's Philosophy of Law", in P.M.S. Hacker and J. Raz (eds.), *Law, Morality and Society*. Oxford: Clarendon Press.
Harris, James W. (1980) *Legal Philosophies*. London: Butterworth.
Hart, H.L.A. (1961) *The Concept of Law*. New York/London: Oxford University Press.
Hartman, Heinz and Wolfgang Conrad (1981) "Industrial Relations in West Germany", in P.B. Doeringer (ed.) *Industrial Relations in International Perspective*. London: Macmillan.
Henderson, Stewart, Christopher Baldry, Nick Haworth and Harvie Ramsay (1984) "Multinational Closure and the Case of Massey-Ferguson, Kilmarnock", 15 *Industrial Relations Journal* 17.
Hill, Stephen (1974) "Norms, Groups and Power: The Sociology of Workplace Industrial Realtions", 12 *British Journal of Industrial Relations* 213.
—(1981) *Competition and Control at Work*. London: Heineman Educational.
Hyman, Richard and Ian Brough (1975) *Social Values and Industrial Relations*. Oxford: Blackwell.
Jordan, Grant "Enterprise Zones in the UK and USA: Ideologically Acceptable Job Creation?" in J. Richardson and R. Henning (eds.), *Unemployment: Policy Responses of Western Democracies*, Vol. 8. London: Sage Modern Politics Series.
Kuhn, Thomas S. (1970) *The Structure of Scientific Revolutions* (2nd Ed.). Chicago: University of Chicago Press.
Lichtheim, George (1967) *The Concept of Ideology*. New York: Random House.
Lindley, Robert M. (1983) "Active Manpower Policy", in G. Bain (ed.), *Industrial Relations in Britain*. Oxford: Blackwell.
Lloyd, Dennis (1979) *Introduction to Jurisprudence* (4th Ed.) London: Stevens.
Luckacs Georg (1971) "Reification and the Consciousness of the Proletariat", in *History and Class Consciousness*. London.
MacCormick, Neil and William Twining (1986) "Theory in the Law Curriculum", in W. Twining (ed.), *Legal Theory and Common Law*. Oxford: Blackwell.
Offe, Claus (1972) *Strukturprobleme. Der kapitalistische Staat*. Frankfurt: Suhrkamp.
Ormrod Committee On Legal Education. (1971) Report. London: HMSO.
Plamenatz, John (1970) *Ideology*. London: Macmillan.
Royal Commission on Trade Unions And Employers' Associations 1965-1968 (1968) Donovan Report. London: HMSO.
Rottleuthner, Hubert (1981) "The Contribution of the Critical Theory of the Frankfurt School to the Sociology of Law", in A. Podgorecki and C.J. Whelan (eds.), *Sociological Approaches to Law*. London: Croom Helm.
Shaw, Martin (1975) *Marxism and Social Science: The Roots of Social Knowledge*. London: Pluto Press.

Simpson, A. W. Brian (1986) "The Common Law and Legal Theory", in W. Twining (ed.), *Theory in the Law Curriculum.* Oxford: Blackwell.

Stone, Katherine Van Wezel (1981) "The Post-war Paradigm in American Labor Law", 90 Yale Law Journal 1509.

Sugarman, David (1986) "Legal Theory, the Common Law Mind and the Making of the Textbook Tradition", in W. Twining (ed.), *Theory in the Law Curriculum.* Oxford: Blackwell.

Terry, Michael (1977) "The Inevitable Growth of Informality", 15 *British Journal of Industrial Relations* 78.

Teubner, Gunther (1983) "Substantive and Reflexive Elements in Modern Law", 7 *Law and Society Review* 239.

—(1984) "Autopoiesis in Law and Society: A Rejoinder to Blankenburg", in 18 *Law and Society Review* 274.

Twining, William (1986) *Theory in the Law Curriculum.*Oxford: Blackwell.

Justice, Equality, Judgement: On "Social Justice"

François Ewald
Paris

Contents

1. Introduction

The articulation I wish to propose between these three terms — *justice, equality, judgement* — has not only a theoretical interest, that of restoring the original sense of the word "justice" in the occidental tradition. It has a more practical aim connected with the understanding of the notion of "social justice".

That the notion of justice must go in parallel with that of equality goes without saying. It is less obvious that it has to do with the issue of judgement, of just judgement, i.e. legal judgement. This in fact amounts to opposing a whole tradition that has conceived of justice as a moral or political value.

Attaining an understanding of the necessary articulation between *justice, equality and judgement* should allow us to go beyond the positions of F. Hayek on the notion of "social justice" (an object of political philosophy), and also those of Kelsenian positivism (object of legal philosophy). More concretely, raising the question of justice as having to do with the issue of judgement may allow appropriate conceiving of the relationships between law and history, of historicity of one of the essential dimensions of law, which is indubitably one of the major tasks facing a philosophy of law today.

Let us recall Hayek's and Kelsen's positions. Hayek concludes, most rigorously, from his philosophical construction of liberalism, that the "notion of social justice", an essentially critical and polemical concept, cannot have any positive definition that is not totalitarian. The determination of a "value for society" that it presupposes could in fact emerge only from the constructivist ideology that brings with it the demise of the open society. For Hayek, belief in a value for society, in the existence of a common social measure, is a dangerous imposture (Hayek, 1980:75).

Hayek's position is very confining, since it makes justice into an epistemological problem. On his ground, the ground of a theory of justice, his position is very hard to get round. But this is not the way the problem of justice has been raised in the Western tradition. If Aristotle, who gave the word the meaning it is still given today, is to be believed, justice is characterized by the fact that when there is no possible theoretical solution (the just not being definable *a priori*), there is always a practical solution. As long as there is society, community, there is a common measure. Aristotle gives the example of money: while there is no one to set the value of values, while it even seems impossible for anyone ever to set it, goods are exchanged according to a common measure, namely money. The problem of justice is not in the theoretical definition of what is just, but in the curious relationship between theory and practice that it displays. Justice designates a practice of assessment; as such, it can only be peculiar to a polity at a particular moment of its existence. And the theory of justice can be nothing but a way of reflecting its practice, which no doubt in turn has its effect on it. The articulation I wish to propose between *justice, equality and judgement* aims at restoring this peculiar relationship between theory and practice in the question of justice; it should allow an understanding of how the practices of justice may be diverse, without thereby being destroyed; how they do not have to be bound to any one particular theoretical form.

The way Kelsen posed the question of the relationships between law and justice (or more exactly, the non-relationship between law and justice) is no longer tenable (Kelsen, 1962). We feel the need for a limitation of law, for a distinction between law and legality, for a superiority of right over law, in a word the need to allow justice again to play a part in positive law. This tendency has to do not only with a vague ideological movement external to the law, since it is inspired by positive legal practices, as is shown by the success of the category of general principles of law. Legal practice today engenders, as it were by itself, the instruments for its own critique; the term, clearly, being understood in the Kantian rather than the sociological sense.

For a long time the question of justice was put in terms of natural law. The epistemological complex born with the 20th century has made this approach impossible. It was Kelsen's merit to note this, while committing the error of interpreting the constraints of a particular situation as an expression of an essential divorce. That the question of justice can no longer be posed in terms of a universal morality does not imply that the idea of thinking about relationships between law and justice should be definitively abandoned. Specifically, Kelsen did not see that natural law's being formulated as morality did not come from an evil wish to have law dominated by morality, but from the epistemological conditions in which, at a certain point in time, the question of law was posed. The problem of justice is not a moral problem, but a problem falling within the issues of legal judgement itself. It is not a content coming in from the outside to constrain it, but rather its very form. I wish to bring this out by considering the relationships between justice and judgement.

That is my program: an ambitious one. Too ambitious, no doubt. But the game is worth the candle, since what lies behind this question of justice and judgement is the question of the meaning to be given to the expression of social law: *Can there be a legal positivity that would be specific to social law?*

2. What is to be Understood by Justice?

The term justice designates three different things: 1) a *virtue*: the quality of a man that causes him to be called just. "All classical definitions show that justice was conceived of as resident in, or which ought to be resident in, souls," explains B. de Jouvenel, who clarifies: "Thus, the institutes of Justinian say 'justice is a firm, perpetual will to accord to each his right', so that justice appears as a mode of being of the will; St. Thomas goes further: "justice is a habit which maintains within us a firm and perpetual will to accord to each his right". He thus goes along with Aristotle, for whom "Justice is the moral condition of the just man, which renders him able to choose with justice as regards attributions between himself and another or between two others" (Jouvenel, 1955: 184). But as the same author rightly notes, "The justice spoken about today is no longer that virtue of the soul; it is a state of things. The word no longer brings to mind a way of being of men, but a certain configuration of society; it is no longer applied to personal attitudes, but aimed at collective arrangements".

In fact, use of the term justice to describe a certain type of social arrangement is itself very old. It is in this sense that Plato uses it in the *Republic*, in accordance, it would seem, with a long tradition: justice qualifies, firstly, a type of State or political system where "each individual need exercise only one employment in society; the one for which nature has given him most aptitude.... Justice consists in occupying oneself with one's own affairs without occupying oneself with those of others" (Republic, Bk. IV, 433a). This proposition is commented on by Karl Popper in these terms: "For us, justice presupposes a certain equality in the treatment of *individuals*, whereas Plato does not regard it as applying to relations between individuals, but as a property of the *State as a whole*, having its foundation in a relationship between classes" (Popper, 1979: 83). In this sense "justice" describes a political and social order, an ideal, perfect order, the good order which, for this reason, must remain invariable. In practice, whatever be the foundation that one gives to this just order — nature or convention — what is just will be defined by the law of the polity. Justice will be legal; to be just, for the individual, will amount to behaving in all circumstances in accordance with what the good order of the polity requires. This conception of justice as designating the principle of order in society leads to confusing morals, law and politics. If it is not necessarily totalitarian, it does fundamentally carry that risk.

Finally, in a third sense, justice designates no longer an order, a construction or a political regime, but simultaneously a certain type of "distribution of honors, of money or of anything that can be distributed among the men in the political community" and "order in relationships among individuals" (Nicomachean Ethics, Bk. V, 11296). This is the justice that Aristotle calls "particular": it corresponds to the various modalities of the relationship of individuals among themselves in the polity. By contrast with the foregoing, it aims less at respect for *legality* than *equality*. It is this that corresponds to the definition we are familiar with of law and justice: *suum cuique tribuere*, "to attribute to each his own". It seems that the paternity of this distinction between legal or total justice and particular justice is to be attributed to Aristotle; it is essential, since it amounts to conferring upon the legal order an autonomy by comparison with the order of power and its imperatives. This distinction between the relationship of law and legality indicates, then, nothing less than the birth of law in the Western sense of the term (Villey, 1978: 58).

Aristotle defined "particular justice" in Book V of the *Nicomachean Ethics*. From that famous text, what has above all been retained is Aristotle's distinction between distributive justice and corrective and/or commutative justice. The essential, perhaps, lies elsewhere: in the statement of what one might call the three archeological components of the concept of justice.

The first has to do with the notion of equality: justice lies essentially in a relationship of equality; it is "a principle of action according to which the beings in a single essential category must be treated in the same way" (Perelman, 1972: 26). But Aristotle goes on to clarify, and this is the important point, that this equality may take different forms: equality corresponding to a geometrical proportion, a way of establishing a relationship of equality between unequal things; equality obeying the rule of arithmetical proportion, when the justice of an exchange among equivalents is to be assured. In other words, the relationship of equality is posited by Aristotle as an abstract form, capable of being institutionalized in manifold concrete configurations. Justice is not bound up with one particular type of equality. This means that a relationship of justice is not a way of imposing equality (of right) where reality is made up of inequalities, but that it is never anything but a way of articulating equality *and* inequalities without one having to be sacrificed to the other. The legal idea of equality, which allows law to be conceived of as something distinct from mere respect for legality, thus does not exclude consideration of differences. Quite the contrary; justice designates an always specific way of establishing a relationship of equivalence between necessarily unequal, distinct and different things; and therefore of combining equality and inequalities. The demand for social justice enjoys no privilege here. Ancient law had its way of compromising between equality and inequalities; the law of 1789 proposed another; in the name of social justice, yet another is being proposed. So much is this true that Aristotle's text constitutes, well *ante litteram*, a refutation of the critique, which some people have regarded as pertinent, made by Marx of the law: that it is incapable of satisfying justice because it is incapable of respecting the fact of inequalities.

The second notion bound up with that of equality is that of *common measure* (Nicomachean Ethics, Bk. V, 1133a). The idea of justice (and of law) presupposes the solution of the apparently insoluble problem of the comparison of the most dissimilar things. There can be no justice without a measure, a rule that makes them comparable and allows equality between them to be conceived of. This is the problem of determining a *general equivalent* that allows one to conceive the respective value of things and people, at least in the context of the polity, or again the problem of defining a principle that would allow *the value of all values* to be assessed. This decisive and mysterious problem cannot find its solution in things, but only in the reason; it is always solved practically. The greatest minds have always struggled with it, and the more so the more reforming or revolutionary will they had. Moralists posited it in the form of the Highest Good, some seeing in utility the determining principle of values, others seeing it in pleasure, virtue or happiness. The notion of sovereignty was, in politics, a way of, if not solving it, at least naming it. And it is well known that there is a discipline particularly called upon to give an account of the solutions that practice "naturally" gives it and to correct what appears in it as unjust: political economy. Determining what should be the general equivalent constitutes a considerable endeavor, since it would give the possibility (if it existed) of scientifically defining, under the guarantee of the nature of things, the true hierarchy of values, and thus of generating right (the obligations and rules of exchange) from the mere consideration of facts. As we know, this was Marx's ambition in writing *Capital*: to determine the principle of the value of values (identified by him with labor power), which would allow, from the mere description of the objective function of the economy, the production of a text that could at the same time specify good and evil, the just and the unjust.

Aristotle gives a third description of the concept of justice: "It is no less true," he says, that in "the associations of trade, which maintain the community, it is this type of justice, the reciprocal one, which is understood, certainly, in terms of proportion and not on the basis of strict equality. For what makes a polity survive is that each renders the equivalent of what he has received. Has someone done us wrong? One seeks to repay, and if one cannot, one feels oneself in the position of a slave. And good? If one does not repay it, there is no longer exchange, and yet it is exchange that binds us indissolubly one to another" (Nicomachean Ethics, Bk. V, 1132b). At a first approach, one finds it hard to see what this notion of *reciprocity* adds to the two previous definitions of the concept of justice. It localizes it in the polity. The choice of (and respect for) a common measure is "what makes the polity survive". The rule of justice is, in fact, what makes possible the exchange of things (and hence the mutual satisfaction of needs) and what allows men to find their mutual *identity*: the rule of justice that designates their place in the order, *ipso facto* conferring on them their identity. If the rule of justice is not at the foundation of the political association (which Aristotle, like Plato, locates in the division of labor), it is what makes these necessary relationships, instead of being only successions of conflicts, able to take on the form of a mutually desirable association: no longer merely undergone, like a fatality of nature, but desired; that the *de facto* solidarity that links men to each other becomes transformed into a community of law. It is this transformation of solidarity that Aristotle calls reciprocity. One might equally well speak of passage from a state of war or opposition to a state of peace or harmony. It is why Aristotle says that justice "maintains" the community (and not that it founds it) or even that it allows "the exchange which indissolubly links us one to another". It is in fact the identity of the common evaluation of the value of things that allows the rule of justice which makes exchange possible. "Justice is, then, *the rule of rules* of a society; it is what comes to give a moral value to respect for regulations of all kinds, even when these are not, in themselves, specifically moral rules. It is therefore *par excellence* the moral rule that guarantees the very existence of the social group, since it is what brings moral blame on the culprit of any breach of the rules of the group, of whatever nature these rules may be" (Dupréel, 1967: 486).

In his *Politics* Aristotle states that the rule of justice (in the specific case, the rule of distributive justice), on which one must agree in order for the polity to live as a harmonious whole, is also the most problematic thing there is. The definition of the criterion of equality — and therefore of the measure — is in fact much more the object of conflict than of agreement. This has to do with the nature of "political judgement": "one believes that justice is equality, and it is so in fact, not for all, but only for the equals; inequality then seems to be just, and is in fact so, not for all, but only for the unequal individuals. But if one omits this 'for whom?' one judges badly. The reason is that here one is judging one's own case; but the majority of men are in general bad judges of their own affairs".

"In consequence, since justice is relative to persons and a distribution must be made, keeping the same proportion concerning things and persons, as was already said in the *Ethics*, there is ready agreement on the equality of things, but difference on that of persons in a case, precisely for the reason just given, namely that one is a bad judge about oneself and also because, in speaking only of what is just up to a certain point, both the ones and the others believe they are speaking about absolute justice. The ones, in fact, if they are unequal on a specific point, for instance wealth, believe themselves unequal in everything; the others, if they are equal on a specific point, for instance liberty, believe themselves equal in everything" (Politics, Bk. III, 1280a). There is, then, a two-fold reason why the rule of justice is more a ground for dispute than for agreement: everyone is a bad judge of himself; everyone tends to assert what distinguishes him from others — a specific difference that never relates to more than *one* criterion — as a superiority in everything.

"Everyone is a bad judge of himself". It is, basically, on a consideration of the same type that the theoreticians of modern natural law were to build the contractual doctrine. This brings us back to a situation before political society. The problem is that of intersubjectivity: in the judgement which men naturally bring to bear on themselves, there is a principle of conflict and of dispersion; it seems that there is a fundamental solipsism preventing them from being able to agree to a common measure — the rule of justice — which would at once make possible life in common, exchange and communication. The institution of the rule of justice, and hence of the *polis*, is, in an expression of Aristotle's, marked by a "circle": it supposes that men managed in a certain sense to emerge from themselves, to agree on a *common rule of judgement* that would allow their judgement about themselves, by gaining a certain objectivity, to become reciprocable; though the judgement that one naturally brings to bear on oneself seems always to have to reject this agreement. In other words, the agreement on the rule of justice that allows an end to be put to the conflict of inequalities is what this conflict renders most unlikely. It presupposes in fact that each should recognize his just identity, which is not in itself possible unless each judges himself in terms of the rules. For the agreement to be reached, each would have to bring to bear on himself the point of view of the whole or of the common good; but this is precisely what the agreement is about.

The rule of justice, which is the object of the "social contract", by allowing a relationship of equality to be conceived of, makes possible a just distribution of duties and burdens, is firstly what permits communication, the having of a common language. It is also what, as a rule of judgement, articulates the individual and the collective, morals and politics. It is thanks to this that the judgement which you make of yourself, far from separating you from the others, brings them closer to you; that whereby the animal that cannot attain his own good without others, namely man, can in fact attain it.

The problem of justice, then, is not in the determination of a good, but in the gaining of that *objectivity* of judgement about oneself (and about others) which is the true political good. Justice thus has to do with an issue of judgement. Objectivity is the condition of the justice of the judgement, of the existence of a just judgement, and therefore of a *right*, of a practice of judgement whose constraint will not be merely undergone, but demanded, as making peaceful collective life possible.

Justice has more to do with a science of being than of duty. The search for it has not in the first instance to do with the faculty of desiring, but with the faculty of knowing. The realm of justice is at bottom subordinate to the possibility of a true knowledge of men and of things. Laying down the law is always dependent on a type of telling the truth. The problem of justice comes down to an *epistemology*. So much so that one may make the assumption that there were historically as many ways of conceiving the problem of justice as there were different espistemological configurations. And *ipso facto* that there could be no new way of conceiving of justice except in correlation with the emergence of a new configuration of knowledge. Thus, the problem we set ouselves concerning "social justice" would come down to determining what might be the epistemological configuration behind it.

3. Three Images of Justice

Equality, common measure, convention: these, then, are the three essential components of the concept of justice. Each of its historical realizations will offer a particular combination of them, bound up with particular historical circumstances.

3.1 Classic Natural Law

An initial articulation of these three elements is supplied by the construction of *classical natural law*, a term that may serve to designate the philosophy of law developed by Aristotle and St. Thomas, to which the practice of Roman law would have corresponded (Villey, 1979: 123).

The essential point of this conception lies in the notion of *nature* that appears in the expression *natural law*. The "nature" appearing here has nothing to do with the mechanistic conception of nature familiar to us today. Nature has to be understood in the sense of Aristotle's *Physics*. A being is not in nature; it has (is) a nature that is the principle of its own development, that makes it be what it is, makes it, in the contemporary vocabulary, "realize itself", "actualize its potentialities". The idea of nature is fundamentally bound up with that of *finality*: "Nature acts towards an end, and that end is nature itself" (Mansion, 1945: 251). If not hindered, a natural being will tend to accomplish its nature: it will attain the end, and therefore perfection, that is in it. This means at the same time that each being has a destination appropriate to it, which defines for it its own good, and that nature also exists as a finalized *totality* of natural beings. The finality embodied in nature is at the same time a principle of totalization for nature, i.e. a principle of order, harmony and regularity. "The world, for the Aristotelian ... is a 'world', a *nature* or a hierarchicalized and well-ordered set of *natures*, a very stable, very firm whole that has a being of its own; that even has it in its *own* right" (Koyre, 1966a: 28).

In the context of this *episteme*, that which underlies justice and defines the commensurable and the value of values has to do with a physics, in the sense of an ontology or even of a theology. On the one hand, the idea of cosmic order implies "belief in the existence of principles of order in virtue of which the whole set of real beings forms a whole (naturally) well ordered" (Koyre, 1966b: 18). There are beings of different nature; the difference of nature underlies the hierarchy of beings. The inequality, which is natural, is not merely difference, but a hierarchy of values. The idea of a natural order is not expressed, as for us, in the fact that all things obey fixed, immutable laws, but more in the constitution of a world ordered towards an end — God, its prime mover or its perfection. On the other hand, this type of thought excludes the possibility of evaluating the respective value of things and people according to a yardstick external to them. Nature is made up of *qualities*. There is a value of things that is in them, and is therefore objective and does not depend on the judgement that evaluates them, but on the contrary has to be sought in that judgement: "*Bonum est in re.* The good or the beautiful are qualities inherent in the real itself. Their existence does not depend on our evaluation" (Villey, 1979: 139).

The same is true of people: they are not all the same; they do not all have the same qualities nor the same dispositions. Though they belong to the same type, they do not all realize its perfection to the same degree: "the one," says Aristotle in the *Politics*, "who thanks to his intelligence is capable of foreseeing, is leader by nature, master by nature; the one who, thanks to his physical strength, is capable of working, is subordinate, is slave by nature (Politics, Bk.

I, 1252a). The identification of men as belonging to the same species — and therefore equal from that point of view — does not exclude their being assessed according to their specific natural difference.

In this epistemological framework, the question of justice, i.e. of the determination of this principle of commensurability, the basis of political association that allows the equality of things and the identity of people to be conceived, passes first of all via the determination of this *nature* to which the rule of justice may be appropriate. The latter, and this is an essential difference from the future doctrines of the social contract, is not the individual but the community, the political collectivity. "It is clear", writes Aristotle, "that the *polis* is a natural reality and that man is by nature a being intended to live in a *polis* (*political animal*)" (Politics, Bk. I, 1252b). Just as "the whole is necessarily antecedent to the part", it is clear that the *polis* is antecedent to each individual. There is an ontological privilege of the whole over its parts. Man is a naturally incomplete being, able to reach his own good, to fully realize himself, only by belonging to a community, which in itself constitutes a natural being oriented to a good of its own: the *common good.*

The common good is precisely, in the context of this epistemology, the category in which the common measure is reflected, the principle of evaluation to which the citizens have to agree and which confers on them their identity. There is a sort of even-handed relationship between common good and the rule of justice: it is on the basis of the common good that the rule of justice has to be laid down, and the common good is nothing other than an agreement as to the rule of justice: "that which is 'just' must be understood as 'in conformity with equality' and that which is just 'in conformity with equality' must aim at the general interest of the whole of the *polis* and the common good of the citizens" (Politics, Bk. III, 1283b). The rule of justice that governs the distribution of power, honor or wealth must itself be in conformity with the nature of the *polis* where it is to be applied. For the definition of justice and of the common good given *in abstracto*: it depends on the particular nature of each *polis,* on its history, its geography, the number of its population, the peculiar qualities of the citizens making it up. The epistemological model of classical natural law is not of the mathematical type: the natural law does not, as for us, designate a universal law able to remain identical to itself whatever be the situation; it is instead a law whose nature implies that it be adapted to each situation. For Aristotle it is the nature of natural law to be of variable content.

The consequence is that to the extent that it is defined as a way of treating equal things equally, justice in the *polis* must first of all be expressed in the form of a relationship of equality corresponding to a geometrical proportion, an equality of relationships that will allow unequal things and individuals to be treated equally: the justice that St. Thomas was to call "distributive", which concerns "distributions of honor, money or whatever can be distributed among the members of the political community" (Nicomachean Ethics, Bk. V, 1130b). This rule of proportional equality must, for its own conservation, be paralleled by a rule of arithmetical equality that governs exchanges, ensuring that trade among men does not upset the hierarchies established among them.

From this definition of justice, finally, there can be deduced a special type of *juris-diction*, a specific way of laying down the law. The law designates what is justly to go to each in the divisions and distributions. It is not a capacity, but a certain relationship founded in the nature of things. The law is not a power, the quality of a will. It is a "thing". Moreover, it is not determinable *a priori*, once and for all. It cannot be expressed in the form of universal propositions. Nature, in fact, in the sense of classical natural law, and in particular the nature under discussion here, that of the political community, is mobile, changeable, unstable and indeterminate: what it is appropriate to do for the common good must always be specified in situations and events that are always particular. The art of the legislator cannot therefore be that of the geometer. It calls for other qualities than those needed by science: the political virtue that Aristotle calls "prudence", which reappears in the expression "juris-prudence".

Thus, classical natural law offers a first definition of justice characterized by the series: *ontology, physics* and *theology* (as type of knowledge or locus of truth), *common good* (as *common measure*), *geometrical proportion* (as type of equality), *prudential law* (as type of jurisdiction).

3.2 Modern Natural Law

A second conception of justice can be deduced from the construction of modern natural law, the formation of which is associated with such great names as Grotius, Hobbes or Locke, to name but a few. The epistemological conjuncture supporting this new conception of natural law is well known. It was the one that saw the birth of modern science. Here is how A. Koyre describes the changes brought about by the revolution of the 17th century: "These can, it seems to me, be reduced to two chief factors, closely linked with each other, namely the destruction of the cosmos and the geometrization of space, i.e. (a) the destruction of the world conceived of as a finished, well-ordered whole, in which the spatial structure incarnated a hierarchy of value and perfection, a world in which, 'above' the heavy, opaque earth rose the celestial spheres of the imponderable heavenly bodies, incorruptible and luminous, and its replacement by an indefinite, indeed, infinite universe, no longer with any natural hierarchy, united only by the identity of the laws governing it in all its parts, and by that of its ultimate components, all located on the same ontological level; and (b) the replacement of the Aristotelian conception of space as a differentiated set of intramundane places by that of the space of Euclidean geometry — a homegeneous and necessary infinite extension — now regarded as identical, in structure, with the real space of the universe. This in turn implied the rejection by scientific thought of all considerations based on notions of value, perfection, harmony, meaning or purpose, and finally the complete devaluation of being, the total divorce between the world of values and the world of facts" (Koyre, 1962: 2).

The essential point here is that the nature objectivized by modern physics is no longer the one bequeathed by antiquity to the Middle Ages. "The great book of nature is written in the language of mathematics", wrote Galileo, going beyond the prohibition imposed by Aristotle. The search for *causes* is abandoned in favor of that for *laws.* And the law itself no longer designates a principle of development internal to a being: it is, to use Montesquieu's words, "a necessary relationship deriving from the nature of things". The law comes to be a description of the function of a mechanism: "The whole of nature is a machine, as the machine is nature" (Jacob, 1970: 42). The law is no longer a teleological principle. The principle of inertia replaces the ancient finalities. Nature has no meaning: "thenceforth people would no longer believe in explaining a thing by saying 'what it is for'; its existence and its mechanism have their laws independently of man" (Lenoble, 1969: 316). Nature and the phenomena in nature obey an order, the expression of the regularity of its laws. No doubt it had God as a creator. But God's will itself is bound by the laws it imposed at creation: He cannot deny himself, make two plus two not equal to four, or make nature obey other laws than its own. This secularization of science and nature is reflected in the famous formula of Grotius: "Everything we have just said would in some way happen even if one were to agree, which cannot be without horrible crime, that there is no God, or that if there is one, he is without interest in human affairs" (Grotius, 1724: 13).

Finally, though man does have a body, which like any other, obeys the laws of nature, his true nature, thought, opposes him to a nature of which he now sees himself "master and possessor", and the penetration of whose secrets he may imagine is no longer more than a question of time and the good administration of science. "By a logical development of the consequences of mechanism, nature, as material substance, no longer has anything to teach man about the destiny of his soul: he and it are no longer on the same plane at all" (Lenoble, 1969: 324). Nature is no longer a guide for man; the idea of living in accordance with nature no longer has meaning. "Never, perhaps, in history have man and nature been so radically separated in their destinies" (Lenoble, 1969: 332). And Descartes was to imagine the new situation of man and nature as like that of a traveller lost in a forest, who can hope for salvation only from his firmness of will. The same epistemological movement that made possible the scientific knowledge of nature makes it useless to man for the conduct of his life. "The eternal silence of these infinite spaces terrifies me", as Pascal said.

A new world, then, a new *episteme*, a new way of thinking, came along, within which the question of law and of justice, of values and their comparability, was to be posed on completely renewed bases. With the disappearance of the cosmos, in fact, the principle of totalization that constituted the idea of a finalized natural order finished. The old way of conceiving of the relationship between the whole and its parts was overturned: it was no longer possible to start from the idea of the whole of nature and deduce an adequate knowledge of the destination of its parts. The new method forbade thinking about the question of values and of justice on the basis of the hypothesis, till then decisive, of a common good.

There was a two-fold consequence for law and politics: the existence of a rule of justice, of a common measure unifying the *polis*, could no longer be a datum of nature. What the classics conceived of as natural, the *polis*, became for the moderns a problem to be explained, a riddle to be solved; a state of nature must have preceded the existence of civil societies, and it had to be demonstrated what the idea of the state of nature makes most unlikely — the birth of civil society, the institution of a common rule of justice — had been able to take place.

Human life could in fact no longer be conceived of, in its origins, except in terms of a scattering of individuals. It made little difference whether men in the state of nature were imagined as living in bands or isolated; those were merely different ways of representing a fundamental dispersion, the correlate of a single methodological schema. Since nature did not contain any principle of totalization in itself, only the individual, the discrete element that analysis finally comes up against, could have a real existence. This methodological individualism can be found both in the rules of the Cartesian method of compounding simple ideas and in the juridical individualism typical of the conception of modern natural law.

No possible viewpoint of society on itself exists; there can only be individual, localized, situated and therefore limited viewpoints on the whole. Each is linked with the group only in terms of an interest, a passion or a need which can never be other than personal to him. Society is never anything but a mediation between an individual need and its satisfaction. There is no good other than that proper to each. And this good is both the cause and the goal of political association. The wish to make society's goal some common good would never be anything but a way of ensuring the domination of one particular interest over all others.

The characteristics of this epistemological scheme can be expressed in terms of the problem of judgement as formulated by Aristotle. Aristotle had said: "One is a bad judge of oneself", and explained that the rule of justice was what conferred objectivity on the judgement of oneself by oneself. What now had to be said was: "one is necessarily the sole judge of oneself". Irremediably. This in no way implied that individuals were bound to such a rigorous solipsist position that they could not enter into relationship with their fellows. On the contrary, man in a state of nature is, at least potentially, a social being; he recognises others as other selves; he has an awareness of belonging to the same species; he does not cease comparing himself to them, and therefore judging himself in his relationship to others and judging the others on a basis of the awareness he has of himself. But he does so with a judgement that cannot find reference in any natural objectivity, that can have no other measure than himself, i.e. that seems to rule out any common measure for the multiplicity of judgements that each makes of himself and others (cf. in particular, Smith, 1960; Locke, 1977: 146).

No one can accept being subject to the judgement of another. Seeking to generalize the judgement that each makes of himself and others, under the pretext that what is true for one must be for the other, can only provoke defiance and conflict. Each is his own law unto himself, without there being able to be a law of these laws; each is a unique principle of valuation, without any principle being imaginable that would set the value of values; each, naturally the sole judge of his right, cannot but reject a common judge that could be nothing but one particular judge. How, in these conditions, can an end be put to the infinite rivalry of egoisms? How can dispersed humanity be transformed into a political unity, their "aggregation into an association"? In a word, how and where can a *common rule of judgement* be found that would allow the peaceful articulation of individual identity and social identity? Everything in the way that one now objectivizes the nature of man seems to imply that he can never emerge from a state of war, which is as natural as it is irremediable. A natural impasse, a *lusus naturae*: the solution will come from it, but will be arrived at against it. In order for man to find peace, nature will have to break with itself, to set up a sort of counter-power: political power, sovereign power, aimed at containing it, bridling it, subjecting it to its *law*.

Barred from the viewpoint of the search for a content, of the definition of a particular order, the solution had to be found in a consideration of the very fact of the interdependence of men; in the notion of social relationship as pure relationship. Can the very concept of "society" not be deduced from a certain number of purely formal rules that would allow the co-existence of freedoms to be organized without imposing any particular direction on them? One, at least, has the requisite rational obviousness: *do not do to others what you do not want done to you* (Hobbes, 1971, sees this as "the rule that constitutes, for the laws of nature, a criterion easy of application").

It was asked how the individualism of judgement could ever allow the existence of a common judgement. How could the multiplicity of individuals unite around a principle that did not at the same time imply totalization? How could a common judgement be possible that was domination of some particular judgement? The proposition: "*do not do unto others...*", which has immediately the legal form of a commandment, testifies to this possibility and indicates its form and style: there, one has a rule whose characteristic is to be able to be imposed on all without imposing anything in particular on anyone. What is it, then, that gives it this power? The fact that it has no other content than to state a form: *reciprocity*. It imposes no act on anyone; it merely indicates to each that, whatever he may wish, he must do it while in some sense putting himself in the position of every other. It does not oblige me to come out of myself; it makes the other into another of myself. It does not alienate my will into that of another; it merely obliges me to regard myself as another for the other. It does not hierarchicalize; on the contrary, it supposes that each is equal to the other.

If the requirement of reciprocity is the sole content of a law of the type: "*do not do unto others...*", its principle, as we have seen, lies in a certain idea of *equality*. It objectivizes each as being the equal of every other; and it cannot be formulated except in a judgement regulated by the principle of equality. This new idea of equality is based on a two-fold argument. The first is of a factual nature: the inequalities that naturally exist among men are never very significant. Hobbes states that they are never big enough to prevent each having the power to kill every other (Hobbes, 1981: 82). The second is more legal. It amounts to saying more or less that *men must judge themselves as equal* — not so much because they are so in fact but *because none would accept being unequal to the others.* "Supposing", writes Hobbes in his *Elements of Natural and Political Law,* "there be so great a difference of nature that it is not the consent of men but inherent power that would make one be master and the other servant, there is a question on which these men will never agree: who has the superiority of power over the others, and who is so stupid that he cannot rule himself? In fact, everyone naturally considers that he is at least as capable of ruling another as the other is of ruling him" (Hobbes, 1981: 219). This argument is more or less reciprocal to the foregoing one: supposing even that in fact men are unequal, they would have to be considered as equal, because there is no common measure that would allow these differences to be evaluated and hierarchicalized. The type of thought at work here is radically different from Aristotle's: he started from the fact of inequality and drew consequences for the law; nature played the role of reference. Now, on the contrary, it is more the absence of any reference that reigns. Because of this absence, an equality (in law) must be accepted; moreover, it is known that it is wellnigh compatible with the facts. Hence the formula that keeps coming up, that men must "*regard themselves as being* (*and not are*) naturally equal to each other". The objectivity thus conquered derives less from a finding of what is than from a pure decision: one will act *as if.* Equality is thus very exactly posited as a *rule of judgement.* What characterizes it is the reintroduction into legal and political judgement of the objectivity that the consideration of nature is no longer capable of supplying. In this rule of equality we have the rule of justice that was to be the one of modern natural law: a common measure that would allow comparison of each with every other without anyone having to pronounce upon the value of any.

It is characteristic of this conception of justice that it confuses itself with the existence of a legal order. Law is no longer deduced from a knowledge of the common good; the common good, the possibility of a common measure, is in the existence of a law, itself posited as a rational order resolutely separated from the factual one. This fundamental split between *fact* and *law* characterizes jurisdiction in the sense of modern natural law. The law is ordered by reason, since it is reason alone that can supply the legal judgement with its objectivity. The legal order is to be of the hypothetical, deductive type. Whatever be the objects to which it is applied or the solutions adopted, the legal rules must respect the fundamental principle of equality. Hence the characteristics of law bound up with this type of jurisdiction: universality and invariability.

3.3 Social Justice

To be sure, this consideration of the two images of justice bound up with the two, classical and modern, conceptions of natural law should be gone into in more detail. However, it is adequate for illustrating the thesis that the question of justice has to do with an issue of judgement, and that in consequence it is not bound up with the affirmation of a certain type of values. What remains to be dealt with is the last element of the program set out, concerning the notion of *social justice*. Does this have no other meaning than to be the critique of the position of modern natural law, or does it correspond to a positive, and therefore alternative, idea of justice?

The notion of social justice is contemporary with the transformation in *episteme* that gave birth to the human sciences (Foucault, 1966: 229ff.). The first characteristic of this *episteme* is that the knowledge that it establishes is not referred to any *nature*, not even to a human nature, but to history. Everything fluctuates in an irreducible historicity: the life of men, the forms of sociability, the most elementary rules of law, the apparently most indestructible values. Nothing can resist: everything is condemned, perpetually, to change. This change may be conceived of as progress or as pure, structural transformation; it matters little. The essential point is that the life of men is deprived of any reference that might be external to its empirical forms. Everything is now referred to "society", a reference that has no other reference than itself, which is also subject to change. "Society" is both the foundation and the structure: indissolubly the principle of identification and the principle of destabilization, of dissolution, of the same identities whose establishment it permits.

The second characteristic of this *episteme* is what Foucault calls "the analytics of finitude". Man discovers himself as a finite, limited, situated being, whose being must constantly be relocated in the particular positivity that has given him birth and is regarded as explaining him. "The experience that takes shape at the beginning of the 19th century locates the discovery of finitude no longer within the thought of the infinite, but at the core of those contents which are, by a finite knowledge, given as the concrete forms of finite existence. Thence comes the unending action of doubled reference" (Foucault, 1966). And this generalized dance cannot be escaped from by the knowledge that perceives it. It must always know itself to be caught up in what it states. That is its truth. It is the era of "isms": sociologism, psychologism, historicism, in brief, generalized *relativism*. Knowledge is caught up in this game of indefinite regress between its statements and their formulation that is displayed in the "I am lying" paradox. "Since the human being has become historical through and through, none of the contents analysed by the human sciences can remain stable in itself, nor escape the movement of the Historian" (Foucault, 1966). Telling truth implies a sort of perpetual twisting of every statement back on to itself. A statement cannot in fact be true as such but only to the extent to which it admits its own conditions of enunciation. This exhausting acrobatics is the price that now has to be paid to gain access to truth. Thus, we see the human sciences perpetually engaged in founding themselves upon endless quarrels of method. Or, on the contrary, as attached to recalling that they do not say what they say, that their statements are valid only under such and such conditions. One may no doubt see these practices as concern for scrupulous honesty; one may also discern in them the impotence of a knowledge never capable of asserting anything. The age of guilty knowledge; the age when truth itself brings guilt. A dramatic age where truth telling, powerless to affirm anything that is not cancelled out in its own enunciation, seeks its positivity in *denunciation*: the desperate struggle to reduce every statement to the finitude of its enunciation.

This game cannot be escaped from by what was the foundation of the possibility of the rule of justice in the framework of natural law: the reason, the transcendental subject itself. Nothing of the subject can hope to escape from the forms of finitude and of "back reference". The form of the universal is denounced in the conditions of its possibility: it can never do anything but betray a wish for particular domination. No doubt there exist values, good and evil, just and unjust, but it would be a deceit for them to assert themselves as valid forever and everywhere; for them to claim to escape from their historical and geographical conditions of birth, from the finitude of the interest that supports them.

The new *episteme*, to the extent that it reduces the transcendental to the empirical, seems to make dispersion and conflict somehow insuperable: it is impossible to see how the assertion of particularities as irreducible can allow the establishment of a rule of justice which must by definition be common to them. Does one not at bottom have to, as it were, fall back on a state of war similar to what the theoreticians of the social contract described as having preceded the institution of civil society? One would be back in a situation that would not be the absence of law, but what those authors described as that of law in the state of nature: disputed, precarious, a ground for infinite litigation. And no solution could be foreseeable.

The model deserves to be tried out. But that should not lead to forgetting that the actors of social law are no longer those of natural law: individuals, isolated in their individuality, have been succeeded by groups, collectivities, which each have their own interest, but are constituted by the relations of interdependence that link them together. If, then, there is a sort of state of war among these groups, it is of a special type: here the dispersion is nothing but the other side of a relationship of mutual dependence. Conflict and solidarity are like heads and tails. War is no longer opposed to peace. We are in an order of infinite pacification, where peace is no longer separate from war, where war is within peace.

In other words, in the context of the new *episteme*, the problem of the conditions for the possibility of a common rule of justice, the contractualists' problem, no longer arises. The principle of agreement is practically given, and only its content is to be negotiated. The problem is shifted from the *principle* of the agreement — sociologically always given — to its *terms*. The rule of social justice does not have the task of giving cohesion to civil society; it must allow each to assess whether the relative place he occupies in the interplay of social solidarities is just or not. The relationship between rule of justice and political association is the inverse of the foregoing image: the rule of justice is not what has first to be determined in order for association to be possible; instead, it is that in terms of which each, from his own viewpoint, has to draw up the cost-benefit analysis of his belonging to the association. The novelty is not in the problem of balance, which was already constitutive of the social contract, but in its practice: in the case of the social contract, balance took the form of a wager on the future that committed you once and for all; now, the balance has continually to be drawn and redrawn. It is no longer at the origin of the constitution of civil society, but of its continuing reform. The problem of social justice is to know whether there can be a role on which there can be agreement, allowing each to compare himself with others and measure the price of solidarity. This is with a view not to final consent, but to perpetual claiming.

This rule does exist: it is the *norm.* Social justice is a justice of the norm. In societies based on solidarity in the framework of the welfare state, the norm plays the role of common measure that might previously have been played by the notion of the common good on the one hand, and of the principle of equality on the other. Being just today is no longer attributing to each his own in terms of a hierarchy grounded in nature, nor is it asserting one's right while equally respecting that of others; it is — and let us accept that it is less glorious — keeping to the norm. (On the notion of *norm* in the sense we mean here cf. Canguilhem, 1966 and Foucault, 1975).

a) The norm designates, firstly, a specific way of conceiving the issue of *equality,* and of bringing relationships of equality and inequalities to terms: not under a proportional rule or a principle of formal equality, but in relation to ideas of *mean* and of *equilibrium,* that is, without reference to a fixed, transcendent measure, but through a regular statement of society's relationship with itself.

The rule of justice of modern natural law articulated equality and inequalities round the opposition between fact and law. There was reciprocity between law and equality: what made equality conceivable made law possible and, conversely, the law was merely the pronouncement of equality. The norm has a very different epistemological structure: it is supposed to be experimental; it keeps to the facts whose differences, divergencies and hierarchies it privileges. It multiplies inequalities and brings them out wherever it takes hold: inequalities in face of death, in face of sickness and knowledge etc. It does so not so much because the norm reveals a particularly inegalitarian society, but because it "unequalizes", because it is set up on the basis of its capacity to locate the most minimal disparities. Correlatively, the equality to which the norm refers back does not correspond to anything in reality: an average man exists no more than does a normal man. The norm is a pure instrument of comparison, a yardstick that society equips itself with in order to follow its own transformations, and that transforms itself, and this is the point, along with the transformations that it describes.

If the norm, like the principle of equality in modern natural law, is a fiction, it is so in quite a different sense. The principle of equality found its condition of possibility in the *a priori* structure of the subject. It was a category of reason, which rendered legal experience possible. The principle of equality had, then, like reason itself, to be universal and immutable. The norm refers back to a very different experience of the subject: it has no subject; it is a rule without subject. In it, the subject is at the same time constituted as object of perpetual observation, object of examination, and subjected to a permanent labor of individualization. Correlatively, the norm offers the differentiated subject a way of asserting his relationship with others in the form of an insatiable demand for equality.

Aristotle, who regarded inequalities as natural, sought for a rule that would respect them. The norm follows a more complex object: it locates the inequalities, but with the idea that they are not natural, that they are never given, but always acquired, in some way or other the effect of previous normative processes. The norm does not aim to fix them in the form of a right; instead, it tends to bring about their destabilization, their denaturalization. The point is to mobilize the inequalities in order to combat them. Is this with a view to setting up equality? No, if what is understood by equality is *de facto* equality, a contradictory concept in a normative order which in principle unequalizes; yes, if the point is to reduce inequalities regarded as "abnormal", that is, as going beyond certain limits or thresholds, which are themselves variable.

b) The norm is the *common measure* whereby, in societies based on solidarity, each can assess his value, his identity and his respective place in society. In a quasi-experimental manner, the norm solves the problem of judgement of oneself by oneself raised by Aristotle: it confers on it the objectivity of the statistical procedures that allow its definition. The norm socializes judgement and identities. It makes the judgement that one makes of oneself and that which "society" makes about one come together. It reduces the "for oneself" to the "for others"; it makes each into a being for the other.

The norm is the imaginary point where what lives dispersed in society can see itself as one: the mirror of solidarities. It is a principle of totalization no longer of the type either of the general interest or of the common good. It does not have the form of an end: there is no meaning in "wishing the norm"; nor does it designate anything that might be common to the members of society. It is the locus where "society", in practice divided into simultaneously antagonistic and solidary elements, can represent the fact of solidarity to itself. It is thus the spriritual counterpart of the solidarities: the indicator of their state and the instrument of their operation.

c) Finally, the norm is the modern form of the social bond. The societies of solidarity have their coherence assured by economic and sociological positivities. They are not founded on a contract like the "social contract"; this could never enter in except in second place, as a way of administering already given solidarities. The norm defines the conditions of what takes the place of the social contract in the solidarity societies: *consensus*. It is both the reference and the object of consensus. It indicates the price to be paid for the advantages of solidarity; it allows the cost-benefit balance sheet of belonging to society to be drawn up. The norm serves as a reference for a negotiation which it makes permanent. It is also the thing the negotiation has to correct.

In solidarity societies, the norm performs the *three* traditional functions of the rule of justice. The norm is the rule of judgement that allows objectivity of judgement of oneself by oneself — a specifically social objectivity. The norm is the form that the rule of justice takes on in the age of social law, when justice becomes social justice.

The norm is a rule of judgement of a new type. Its epistemology rejects the opposition between fact and law which was so decisive in the construction of modern natural law. The norm is an endeavour to reconcile fact and law. The articulation of law around the norm is to allow a juridification of the fact: to assert the fact, in particular the fact of inequalities, in law. The norm raises the problem of a legal rationality whose categories are no longer definable *a priori*, but only *a posteriori*. This is an impossibility from the viewpoint of the epistemology of modern natural law. While statutes in that legal construction were in principle formal, the norm is always substantive. And we know that it is a characteristic of social law to seek to reverse legal reasoning: to think about a situation no longer in terms of the abstract legal categories of civil law, but in terms of its concrete characteristics. This is, in a sense, the extraction of law from the fact. The legal subject gives way to the wage earner, the consumer, the professional; the notion of contract breaks down into a multiplicity of types of contract, each capable, like the labor contract, of being governed by a special regulation.

Just as the common good or the principle of reciprocity was linked with a certain type of jurisdiction, the norm presides over its own one: ***the jurisdiction of social law***. Its characteristics, peculiar in relation to civil law jurisdiction, are well known: loss of the privileged nature of statute as a source of law; the inflation and obscelescent nature of regulations, the sociologization of judgement. They only testify to the new relationship between fact and law implied by the epistemology underlying the norm.

The chief characteristics of the three images of justice considered may be summarized in the following table:

	Classical Natural Law	Modern Natural Law	Social Law
Epistemology	Ontology	Physics	Sociology
Common Measure	Common Good	The Law as Form of Reciprocity	Norm
Equality	Geometrical Proportion combined with Arithmetical Proportion	Equality of Rights	Mixture of Geometrical and Arithmetical Equality
Jurisdiction	Prudential Law	Separation of Fact and Law	Reconciliation of Fact and Law in a Jurisdiction of Sociological Type

This table illustrates the thesis maintained, namely 1) that justice is not bound up with any particular way of conceiving of equality; 2) that, being bound up with issues of the objectivity of judgement, its conceptions vary along with whatever, in different epistemological circumstances, makes such objectivity possible; and 3) that the notion of social justice does refer back to a positive rule, to which there corresponds what does have to be recognized as a type of jurisdiction alternative to the civil law: *social law.*

[Translated from the French by Iain Fraser]

References

All cites are to the French translations of works as given in this section.

ARISTOTLE, *Politique.*

—*Ethique à Nicomaque.*

CANGUILHEM, Georges (1966) *Le Normal et le Pathologique.* Paris: Presses Universitaires de France.

DUPRÉEL, Eugène (1967) *Traité de morale.* Bruxelles: Presses Universitaires de Bruxelles.

FOUCAULT, Michel (1966) *Les mots et les choses.* Paris: Gallimard

—(1975) *Surveiller et Punir.* Paris: Gallimard.

GROTIUS, Hugo (1724) *Le droit de la guerre et de la paix.* Translation by Jean Barbeyrac. Amsterdam.

HAYEK, Friedrich A. (1980) *Droit, Législation et Liberté.* Translation by Raoul Audouin. Paris: Presses Universitaires de France.

HOBBES, Thomas (1971) *Léviathan.* French edition: François Tricaud. Paris: Sirey.

—(1977) *Les Eléments du droit naturel et politique.* Louis Leroux, Lyon edition: Editions L'Hermès.

—(1981) *Decive.* Translation by Samuel Sorbière. Paris: Sirey.

JACOB, François (1970) *La logique du vivant.* Paris: Gallimard.

JOUVENEL, Bertrand de (1955) *De la Souveraineté.* Paris: Editions Génin.

KELSEN, Hans (1962) *Théorie pure du Droit.* Translation by Charles Eisenmann. Paris: Dalloz.

KOYRE, Alexandre (1962) *Du monde clos à l'univers infini.* Paris: Presses Universitaires de France.

—(1966a) *Etudes d'histoire de la pensée scientifique.* Paris: Presses Universitaires de France.

—(1966b) *Etudes galiléennes.* Paris: Hermann.

LENOBLE, Robert (1969) *Histoire de l'idée de nature.* Paris: Albin-Michel.

LOCKE, John (1977) *Deuxième traité du gouvernment civil.* Berhard Gilson edition. Paris: Jean Vrin.

MANSION, Augustin (1945) *Introduction à la Physique aristoltélicienne,* 2nd Ed. Louvain and Paris: Editions de l'institut supérieur de philosophie — Jean Vrin.

PERELMAN, Chaim (1972) *Justice et raison.* Bruxelles: Editions de l'Université de Bruxelles.

PLATO, *République.*

POPPER, Karl R. (1979) *La société ouverte et ses ennemis.* Translation by Jacqueline Bernard et Philippe Monod. Paris: Editions du Seuil.

SMITH, Adam (1960) *Théorie des sentiments moraux.* Translation by Ms. S. de Grouchy. Paris: Guillaumin et Cie.

VILLEY, Michel (1978) *Philosophie du droit* Vol. I. 2nd Ed. Paris: Dalloz.

—(1979) *Philosophie du droit* Vol. II. Paris: Dalloz.

II

Labor

Juridification of Labor Relations*

Spiros Simitis
Frankfurt

Contents

1. Premises

1.1. Background

"Juridification" is a term that occurs increasingly, in the widest range of contexts (for a comprehensive discussion of various uses (see Voigt, 1980: 19). Its use, however, is probably nowhere more justified than where the structure and objectives of labor regulation are being discussed. Labor law constitutes the classic paradigm for juridification. Both the background and evolution of the juridification process can therefore best be understood by looking at the origin and development of labor law.

The term, which admittedly seems vague at first to some, and to others absolutely nebulous, reflects a changing concept of state functions. It

* The following paper is an abridged version of "Zur Verrechtlichung der Arbeitsbeziehungen", a study first published in Zacher, Hans F., Spiros Simitis, Friedrich Kübler, Klaus Hopt and Gunther Teubner (1984), Verrechtlichung von Wirtschaft, Arbeit und sozialer Solidarität: Vergleichende Analysen, Baden-Baden: Nomos.

expresses the displacement of the "contemplative" by the "activist" state[1] and thus marks the path from the undisputed priority of contractual agreements to a "law-driven" society (see also Ackerman, 1984; Damaska, 1984.). More precisely: under the impact of industrialization the legal framework of economic and social processes is, as labor law reflects, reformulated. Labor is no longer just one of many marketable and marketed goods. The labor market is increasingly distinguished from the market generally, and subjected to specific rules. These, rather than simply aiming at the protection of individual contracts, lay down binding requirements carefully adapted to the particular characteristics of labor relations, to which all agreements concerning the supply of labor must conform. The more the juridification of labor relations is accentuated, the more labor law assumes its own distinct form. Each of its provisions deliberately interferes with the conditions of work, thus restructuring the scope of both employers' and employees' activities.

The steering function may not be discernible at the start. However, the control intention determines the very first steps of juridification, the so-called "workers' protection" laws. Irrespective of whether they restrict child labor, limit hours of work, introduce minimum wages or regulate payment methods, they establish barriers against the consequences of industrialization. Their obvious purpose is to make corrections and to prevent future problems. Through each of these statutes the law redefines the division of competences for dealing with economic and social problems. Once the "worker question" is seen as a *question sociale* the binding distinction between intentionally minimized state functions and a virtually unlimited area reserved to the individual falls away. The *question sociale* leads to a state policy aimed at long-term social changes regarded as the only means, in the end, of reducing or eliminating sources of conflict. The "juridification" of labor relations is one of the most important elements of such a policy. No wonder, then, that the various "workers' protection" laws have been repeatedly justified by pointing at the necessity of "social pacification" [2]. Legislators are, as the continuously increasing interference with labor relations illustrates, no longer prepared to simply accept or sanction economic and social developments. They see intensified intervention as their primary task, in order to adapt these developments to their political and social objectives.

1.2. Universality

"Juridification" is still usually described as a national peculiarity[3]. To some it reflects a typical German legalism, (Unterseher, 1972: 190 ff.; 1970: 140 ff.)

[1] On the "activist" state, see the contributions to the symposium organized by the *Yale Law Journal*, 92 (1983) 1083-1620.

[2] See for instance the critical analysis of the parliamentary debates in Germany by Benöhr (1977: 212), or by François (1977: 53 ff.) for Belgium.

[3] For a good example of the tendency to "nationalize" the juridification process see von Beyme (1977: 198).

to others a no less characteristic French *juridicisme* (Adam and Reynaud, 1970). But, even where its characterization is not so precise, juridification is frequently seen as the main feature distinguishing the Continental European from the British regulation of industrial relations[4]. Great Britain is in fact considered as more or less the only country which is largely immune from juridification. None of these assumptions corresponds, however, to the history of labor relations. Industrialization may have followed very different paths, nevertheless, it was and is not a specifically national phenomenon. Where, therefore, the industrialization process begins there is no alternative to juridification. Hence, labor relations have developed in Great Britain, as well as in any other country, under the constant impact of "the one indubitably fundamental and irreversible trend ... the ever-increasing extent of the legal regulation"[5]. The long road from the Factory Act of 1833 to the Employment Act of 1982 is a single confirmation of progressive juridification.

However, though the starting point, industrialization, and its consequences coincide, the juridification process by no means follows the same path everywhere[6]. Restrictions on child labor, the prohibition of the truck system, attempts to avoid health risks through elementary safety precautions and the limitation of working hours, are nearly always the first signs of a steering interference within labor relations. The regulations, vary neverthless substantially. The United States, France, Italy and Germany, for example, in contrast to Great Britain, tend to rely on comprehensive regulations affecting all employees. Where the British legislature, as in the case of the Coal Mines Act of 1908 or the Trade Boards Act of 1909, addresses the particular problems of a specific workers' group, most of the other laws opt for generally applicable protective provisions. Thus, the French legislature never hesitated to treat minimum wages as a requirement completely independent of a particular type of work or the characteristics of a particular group of employees (Code du travail Art. L. 141 ff.; Javillier, 1981: 388). The same applies to German rules on working hours. Their primary aim is to fix a binding maximum in the interest of all employees (Arbeitszeitordnung Sections 1, 3).

Many differences which were originally sharp disappear, however, in the course of the juridification process, as in the case of protections against dismissal. Continental European laws took up the problems created by the dissolution of employment relationships at a rather early stage. The freedom

4 Particularly Kahn-Freund's discussion of the development of labor law points in this direction, see for instance (1979: 29 ff.; 1954: 42 ff.; 66 ff.).

5 Lewis (1976: 15; 1979: 202; 1983a: 372), see also Wedderburn (1971: 13 ff.; 160 ff.; 1983: 53 ff.; 1984: 19), Hasselbach *et al.* (1982: 38 ff.); Davies and Freedland (1979: 3 ff.); Dunlop and Yalenson (1978: 83).

6 Hence, only as long as the different ways are carefully considered the obviously ever-present temptation to develop abstract schemes and thus to transform all attempts of a comparative analysis into a mere legitimacy instrument for the export or the import of certain rules can be successfully restricted, see also Wedderburn (1984: 16), Kahn-Freund (1974: 186 ff.).

to end contracts, an otherwise essential element of all individual agreements, was long ago replaced by mechanisms that determine both the grounds and procedures of dismissal. Though most of thee provisions have been thoroughly and repeatedly revised, none of the modifications has ever challenged the original intent, which was to introduce a mandatory alternative to the employers' free decision. But the rules included both in the first German and Swiss attempts to restrict dismissals in case of illness (see Hug, 1927: Vol. 2, 109 ff.; Jedzig, 1984: 3 ff., 25 ff.), as well as in the later far more extensive regulations, clearly demonstrate the wish to offer employees a minimum of protection against uncontrolled loss of their jobs.

Dismissal by now is also a leading topic of British labor law, the legislature has, however, chosen a distinctly different approach. The accent was originally placed on some of the most obvious cases of job loss, close-downs and rationalization (Redundancy Payments Act 1965). The immediate object, therefore, was not so much prevention or even substantial delay of termination, but financial compensation in a few situations with particularly far reaching consequences. Only a long-term labor market policy providing job security, however, can in the end really restrict redundancy. Thus where at first just the individual fate of what can, admittedly, be a substantial number of employees seems to be at stake, it soon becomes apparent that both the structure and the development of the labor market are deeply affected. The redundancy cases underline best the potentially destabilizing effect of dismissals. Due to the considerable increase in unemployment, the political implications of lack of job security can hardly be overlooked.

Compensation payments as guaranteed by the Redundancy Payments Act 1965 are, in fact, a deliberate attempt to control and reduce these implications. But even if redundancy payments alleviate unemployment to a certain extent, they never protect against loss of jobs. Any state policy conscious of unemployment effects will therefore sooner or later consider measures modifying the procedures governing dissolution of the employment relationship. Redundancy rules are, in other words, at best an intermediary regulation. The stricter the requirements for a dissolution are and the more complicated the procedure, the greater the discouragement of the employer and the better the chances of the employee to keep his job. This is exactly why the German legislature, in the course of the juridification process, assigned a key role to a dissolution scheme. By creating a series of carefully planned obstacles to dismissal plans the legislature, in its own words, has protected the *status quo* and at the same time unburdened the labor market[7]. Dismissal provisions have, accordingly, a highly directive function. They are instruments of a state-guided market policy well aware of the social risks of unemployment and of the need to limit the decision-making power of employers.

[7] See Regierungsentwurf zum Kündigungsschutzgesetz, Recht der Arbeit 1951, p. 61, 64, but also Bundesarbeitsgericht (BAG). Arbeitsgerichtliche Praxis sec. 620 BGB, Befristeter Arbeitsvertrag No. 16, sec. 7 Kündigungsschutzgesetz No. 20, Wolf (1981: 311), Reuter (1982: 165 ff.).

Against this background the attempts of the British legislature to complete the redundancy provisions with an elaborate employment protection law appear perfectly logical. The result is, however, once more a striking concordance. By acknowledging, for instance, the employee's right "not to be unfairly dismissed"(Employment Protection (Consolidation) Act 1978, Sec. 57) British law proceeds in the same way as the French labor code, where a *cause réelle et sérieuse* is asked for (Code du Travail Art. L. 122-14-2), and in the direction of the German statute as well, which explicitly rejects all "socially unjustified" dismissals (Kündigungsschutzgesetz Sec. 1). In each of these cases the employer is expected to adapt his personnel policy to criteria basically hostile to the dissolution of the employment relationship. For example, as long as the employee, despite reduced ability to work can be given another job, there is no *cause réelle et sérieuse* (see Javillier, 1981: 315 ff., 343 ff.). In addition, dismissals resulting from the introduction of new production methods or changing market structures remain clearly "unfair" and "socially unjustified" if they are not preceded by a choice based on the personal implications for each employee concerned (Employment Protection (Consolidation) Act 1978, Sec. 59; Kündigungsschutzgesetz Sec. 1, Par. 3). In short, the law replaces unilateral decisions by the employer with an increasingly objectivized decision-making process. Whatever the employer's motives may be, they are only taken into consideration on condition that they conform to mandatory criteria set down by the law and confirmed through judicial examination.

It can certainly not be seriously contested that dismissal laws are far from having achieved their aims. Reinstatement is still absolutely exceptional (see for West Germany, Falke *et al.*, 1981: 149, 774 ff.; for Great Britain, Dickens *et al.*, 1981:160 ff.). Compensation, at best, not job security, is what dismissal regulations have succeeded in providing (see also Coen, 1979: 21 ff.; Ellermann-Witt *et al.*, 1983: 2295 ff.; Becker, 1984: 842). It would nevertheless be mistaken to conclude, based on this inefficiency (see for example Erd, 1982a: 367 ff.), that the juridification process is irrelevant. Each step in the process signals, first and foremost, a change in attitude leading to increased regulation of labor relations in order to fulfill the purposes of an interventionist policy. The activist state establishes a detailed legal regime regarding these relations in order to ensure their adjustment to a series of specific economic and social goals. But the choice of a particular regulation at not point entails its effectiveness, either in the context of a decidedly interventionist or clearly abstentionist policy. Consequently, effectiveness considerations have always been understood as challenging the means, not the aims, of an interventionist policy. They reflect the search for better means of implementation, and thus implicitly accept the motives and purposes of intervention. Whether therefore, the various dismissal statutes have really led to structural change is a secondary question. In any case, even purely in terms of "effectiveness" the juridification process by no means has proved to be a failure. Reinstatements may indeed rarely occur, but the provisions on dismissal have nevertheless substantially changed the conditions of termination especially as shown by the demand for "deregulation" (see Reuter, 1979: 405 ff.; 1982: 165;

Schwerdtner, 1977: 76 ff.). The employer, though perhaps only because of the procedures foreseen by different laws, must overcome a series of obstacles that at least greatly delay a binding decision. In West Germany, for instance, up to four years may elapse before the final judgment of a court definitively severs an employment relationship. Personnel planning, therefore, can not simply ignore existing regulations, but must instead develop strategies of compromise (see also Russig, 1983: 288). Their result may be far from the original intention of the law, they nevertheless reflect the impact of these regulations on employer attitudes.

The convergence of the regulatory instruments and thus of the juridification process is, however, not always easy to discern. Though "juridification" everywhere reflects the shift to increasingly outspoken interventionism, the circumstances under which the interference is exercised are often very different. Thus, industrialization leads not only to a series of new provisions specifically adapted to the employment relationship, it also activates mechanisms developed in the preindustrial period in order to alleviate social distress. The law of the poor accordingly remains perfectly relevant wherever industrialization results in pauperization of the workers (see Hutchins and Harrison, 1926: 1ff.; François, 1974: 20 ff.). But at the same time, as traditional mechanisms undergo functional change, they provide the elements for the juridification process. The *question sociale* generates a *droit social*, which on the one hand projects the law of the poor into labor relations, and on the other produces an increasing number of additional regulations directly related to particular workplace problems (see also François, 1974: n. 26; Javillier, 1981: 15ff).

Belgium is probably the best example of juridification through a *droit social* that continuously combines the opportunities offered by the preindustrial approach with regulations developed in view of the changing structure of work and the particular implications of industrialization (for a detailed discussion see François, 1974: 129ff). The opposite is true of Germany. The history of German labor law is marked by its increasing independence from social legislation. While labor law has developed into a system of rules solely dedicated to labor relations and therefore only understandable in relation to specific labor conflicts, social legislation has evolved into much broader regulation with widely differing objectives[8]. Social security, however important it may be for employees, is by no means related only to their position or to their problems. It can only succeed in dealing with the risks typical of an industrialized society if the *question sociale* is clearly separated from the "workers' question", in order to include, through its own genuine mechanisms, all those who remain outside the boundaries of labor law (see also Zacher, 1976: 7 ff.; 1977, 29ff; Müller-Volbehr, 1978: 254). Irrespective of what is at stake — the welfare of the elderly, better educational chances for young people, or the needs of the disabled — social legislation reformulates

[8] The various stages of social legislation are described and analyzed by Zacher (1974a: 19 ff.; 1976: 18 ff.), see also Stolleis (1976: 18 ff.)

throughout the conditions as well as the scope of state intervention and at the same time demonstrates its emancipation from labor law.

The changes in perception regarding the tasks of social legislation do not, however, affect the juridification process. Whether attention is focused on genuine labor law instruments (like the rules on dismissal) or regulations located in the grey area between labor and social legislation (maternity protection or social security, for example) is unimportant. The label may change but the result is the same: substantial elements of labor relations are subjected to conditions included in a scheme imposed by the state, thereby deliberately interfering with individual relationships and replacing personal agreements with mandatory rules of behavior. Whenever, therefore, both the development and the implications of juridification are described, specific labor law provisions are only part of the picture. Labor law must in fact be seen within the frame of a *droit social* covering the whole labor relationship. Only then does the universal character of juridication, as well as its true extent, become visible and capable of being correctly appreciated (see also Javillier, 1981: 16 ff.; Dunlop and Galenson, 1978: 72 ff.).

1.3. Development

The juridification process begins with a clearly reactive phase. State interventions during this period are punctual responses to a few peculiar consequences of industrialization. Labor relations are still regarded as a perfectly individual affair and decisions are left to the parties involved. Criticisms followed by interventions are directed throughout against a restricted series of "abuses". The interference of the state aims at eliminating and preventing the effects of clearly identifiable "excesses" of contractual regulation. The list of statutes may be long, from the prohibition of the truck system, to the child labor laws and the regulation of working hours. Each of its items is, nevertheless, no more than a carefully limited reaction presented and defended as a regrettable but unavoidable and by all means exceptional restriction of the otherwise untouched individual decision-making power.

The various interventions, however, are increasingly integrated into an overall policy concept aimed at a long-term regulation of economic and social development (a point stressed also by Ghera, 1982: 607 ff.). Consequently, interest shifts more and more to the potential causes of conflict and thus from reaction to prevention. The protection from dismissal, for instance, is gradually supplemented with provisions to promote employment and therefore openly qualified as part of an "active labor market policy"[9]. State controlled, institutionalized employment agencies, the carefully built-up promotion of occupational training, as well as detailed measures for the preservation of already existing jobs and the creation of new ones (see, for instance, Arbeitsförderungsgesetz Sects. 4 ff., 33 ff. 63 ff.) are essential elements of a strategy pursuing greater flexibility of the labor market and

[9] In the case of the West German Arbeitsförderungsgesetz, see Gagel and Jülicher (1979: sec. 1 note 1 ff.).

better adaptation to changes due either to structural modifications or general economic conditions.

But even where the link between the juridification of labor relations and long-term labor market policy is relatively obvious, the result is not necessarily a comprehensive regulation including all or even most aspects of the employment relationship. On the contrary, the regulatory intention is, as the example of the British Employment Protection Consolidation Act of 1978 shows, usually expressed in particularly sensitive fields by amplifying the objectives of the various laws. Employment protection amounts, in fact, to decidedly more than a set of rules exclusively dealing with the grounds and details of dismissal. Hence, the legislature combines dissolution provisions with measures countering unemployment due to rationalization or maternity. It thus attempts not only to secure stability of employment for a particular group of employees, but to compensate for changing production methods as well. It is therefore not surprising that all similar regulations have been described as an obvious expression of a *politique économique de l'emploi*, the main objective of which is to restructure the labor market (see Javillier (1981: 143 ff.).

Significantly, the National Labor Relations Act in the U.S. completes the acceptance process of collective bargaining by setting up a National Labor Relations Board[10]. Labor relations thus may depend on decisions taken in the course of negotiations between employers and employees, but they always evolve within a labor market characterized by the presence and intervention of a government agency. As in the case of the West German rules on the promotion of employment, the legislature does not regard the labor market as being in a fixed state. On the contrary, it seeks to establish binding normative and administrative data in order to guarantee as "conflict-free" an evolution as possible. The structure and rights of agencies like the National Labor Relations Board, the Agence Nationale pour l'Emploi, and the Bundesanstalt für Arbeit may thus differ, but they all illustrate a state policy that considers the economic and social order to be a controllable process and accordingly uses the juridification of labor relations as a means to enforce a series of policy objectives[11].

Directive interference aimed at the macrostructure of the labor market maximizes the complexity of its regulation but at the same time reduces the lifetime of the various rules and increases the pressure for legitimation of the interventionist measures. Thus, provisions linking dismissals to mandatory periods of notice, which at first seemed perfectly sufficient, are supplemented by a whole series of rules obliging employers to carefully compare and

[10] National Labour Relations Act of 1935 sec. 20 ff., Labour Management Relations Act of 1947 sec. 3 and 10. For a discussion of the history and the importance of the Board see Getman and Blackburn (1983: 28 ff., 47 ff.), Murphy (1968: 113 ff.).

[11] For a discussion of the various tasks of an "agenzia del lavoro" see also Ghera (1982: 630 ff.).

evaluate employees' work conditions as well as by detailed administrative measures against an overburdening of the market through an excess of lay-offs. Another equally instructive example is safety provisions. The original rudimentary rules have been gradually replaced by a long list of mandatory standards and control mechanisms that guarantee both the transparency and permanent monitoring of employers' activities.

However, the more marked the tendencies to influence the structure and the development of labor relations are, the more the legislature is forced to continuously control and revise its own decisions. In Great Britain, for example, the dissolution problems were dealt with in a period of seven years by three consecutive laws (Employment Protection Act 1975; Employment Protection (Consolidation) Act 1978; Employment Act 1982). Their enactment not only reflects policy changes, but also the attempt to profit from experiences gained in the intervening period, in order to refine regulatory tools and increase the effectiveness of control mechanisms (see Mellish and Collis-Squires, 1976: 164 ff.; Clark and Wedderburn, 1983: 187 ff.; Hepple, 1983: 408 ff.). Because the various instruments are designed for regulatory purposes, the credibility of state policy depends largely on their ability to fulfill particular policy aims. Irrespective of whether the compensation rules of the 1982 British Employment Act, the employment promotion measures of the 1969 West German Act, or the control mechanisms of the American Occupational Safety and Health Act are considered, all can be justified only so long as they really reduce the risks they are supposed to cope with. Hence, never before has the use of legal instruments for economic and political purposes been so outspoken, and the expectation as to what they could accomplish so high (see also Wiethölter, 1982a: 53 ff.; Assmann, 1980a: 220 ff.; 1980b: 268 ff.).

1.4. Methods

Laws are, understandably, the normal vehicle of juridification, at least as long as the initial situation is considered. The prohibition of child labor, the reduction of work hours, and the first steps towards improved work place safety did not occur within a legal vacuum. In each case the hitherto undisputed and explicitly guaranteed regulation prerogatives of the contracting parties were questioned. By interfering with the economic and social process the state displaced contractual commitments, restricted the decision-making power of the parties and thus changed the level of regulation. Governments increasingly claim exclusive competence in an area for which the individuals originally assumed sole responsibility. Binding conditions of work, the basic requirement for effective correction of the labor market, however, demand a uniform model. Statutory regulation guarantees the necessary uniformity. Hence, specific legal provisions appear to be the most appropriate regulatory instrument. Even where, as the example of auxiliary regulations shows (for a discussion of this type of legislation see Kahn-Freund, 1983: 60 ff.), the legislature is willing to accept the parties' decisions, they must be taken against a background clearly defined by the standards set by law.

Juridification, nevertheless, does not only consist of a substantial increase in legislation. Administrative measures also play an important role, in connection with safety standards or the promotion of employment, for example. In fact, they make up the core of regulatory efforts. A third, no less relevant factor is the influence of the courts. Their contribution is visible even when they act within the traditional framework of the interpretation of exisiting laws. Thus, the decisions of the West German Federal Labor Court on employee liability demonstrate how original contractual rules were gradually modified in order to diminish, if not eliminate, employee responsibility for damages typical for a particular job (see Bundesarbeitsgericht (BAG), Arbeitsgerichtliche Praxis Sec. 282 No. 6; Sec. 611 BGB No. 37; Gamillscheg and Hanau, 1974). But the real tests for the courts' participation in the juridification process are the cases in which the judiciary has openly substituted for the legislature. Collective labor law, in particular, is a main area of court-determined juridification of labor relations. The less the political authorities are prepared to deal with social conflicts, the more the tendency towards legislative escapism prevails. Judicial activism in this situation replaces legislative inactivity. The advantage, for both government and parliament, is rather obvious. They can successfully avoid involvement in ongoing conflicts and assume a spectator's role while the juridification process continues (see also Hart and Joerges, 1980: 186ff.; Kissel, 1982: 1779). Criticisms, as sharp as they may be, will be directed only at the courts. Finally, as a result of the at least formal separation of the courts and the government, chances of legitimation are better than if state agencies directly interfere. Consequently, the attention paid to the individual case and its peculiarities lessens, the language of the judicial decisions becomes increasingly abstract and the courts start to openly treat the principles they formulate in exactly the same way as statutory rules.

Direct intervention by legislation, administrative measures and judicial decisions are supplemented by indirect steering based on carefully delegated decision-making power. The traditional protective provisions, in other words, are but one aspect of the juridification process. The other, no less relevant, is the acknowledgment of autonomous regulatory mechanisms, collective agreements being the most significant example. It cannot be contested that collective bargaining is by no means a regulatory instrument developed and put at the disposal of the parties by law. Illegality, on the contrary, was the decisive initial characteristic of bargaining. It grew out of the workers' deliberate opposition to a legal system that regarded the individual contract as the only conceivable or admissible means of regulating labor relations. The open rejection of the traditional mechanism was, for the workers, a substantial condition for an approach permitting real consideration and respect of their interests. Hence, collective bargaining not only changes the structure of negotiations, but more importantly, displaces traditional legal rules and by that prevents the intervention of a judiciary prepared to fit labor relations into the contractual scheme (see also Sinzheimer, 1976: Vol. 1, 150ff.; Kahn-Freund, 1943: 143; 1954: 42 ff.; Wedderburn, 1971: 160 ff.).

Legalization of collective bargaining, however, shifts the accent. Collective agreements are from then on integrated into a regulatory system governed by state intervention. Thus, the "convention collective" becomes a complementary instrument. The change is probably nowhere better expressed than in the Norris-La Guardia and National Labor Relations Acts. Both laws aim to restore and ensure the effectiveness of the labor market by guaranteeing and institutionalizing "collective laissez-faire" [12]. This is, at first, a perfectly logical continuation of the ruling market principle, but with a slight difference. Whereas elsewhere the individual aspect predominates, the labor market is governed by a collective approach. The legislature, however, does not simply acknowledge the importance of "collective laissez-faire". The National Labor Relations Act at the same time foresees a duty to bargain (National Labour Relations Act Sec. 8(a) 5). The employer hence has no choice. Once the unionized employers opt for collective bargaining, the employer cannot, even if he so wishes, withdraw to the level of individual negotiations. The demand for a collective agreement is privileged by law and enforced by sanction mechanisms provided and controlled by the state. Consequently, the law tries to free negotiations from potential obstacles by enumerating, for instance, the subjects of bargaining[13]. The legislature thus establishes a regulation model based on active participation of the parties within precisely defined fields. Collective bargaining, in other words, is instrumentalized. Employer and employees exercise an authority expressly given to them and relieve the legislature of the necessity for direct intervention. The collective agreement is no longer the *ordo ordinans*, but merely an *ordo ordinatus*. To the extent to which there is no need for immediate interference by the state, employers and employees have the right but also the duty to determine the modalities of employment in a collective agreement. Each of these agreements results, therefore, from a carefully calculated autonomy.

The same tendency can be observed in a less traditional field of collective bargaining: agreements between employers and works councils, as foreseen by the West German Works Constitution Law (Betriebsverfassungsgesetz). Section 87 in particular prescribes that all decisions in the cases listed must be taken in common by the employer and the council. The employer is thus deprived of strictly unilateral decision-making power and is subjected to a duty to bargain. Whatever his motives may be for shortening work hours, for example, they are irrelevant as long as they have not been discussed with the

[12] See sec. 1 of the National Labour Relations Act, but also Justice Frankfurter in NLRB v. Insurance Agents Int'l Union, 361 U.S. 477, 506 (1960), Wellington (1968: 38 ff.), Cox (1958: 1408 ff.), Bernstein (1950: 100), Taylor (1948: 5).

[13] National Labour Relations Act sec. 8 (d), see also Wooster Division of Borg-Warner v. NLRB, 356 U.S. 488 (1958), Fibreboard Paper Products Corp. v. NLRB, 379 U.S. 488 (1979), Wellington (1968: 50 ff.), Feller (1973: 663 ff.), Getman and Pogrebin (1984: 90 ff.)

workers' representatives and acknowledged in a regulation formulated and agreed upon by both parties. In addition, the initiative for particular regulations is no longer reserved to the employers. The works councils are equally entitled to raise the question of overtime or of additional safety measures. Thus the employer is again confronted with a requirement of negotiation. In two essential respects, however, the Works Constitution Act differs from regulations like the National Labor Relations Act or the Swedish Codetermination Act (1976). The mere existence of a works council restricts the decision-making power of the employer. Hence, anytime five or more persons are employed and a works council has been elected, the employer operates under fundamentally changed conditions. As soon as his policies touch upon the areas mentioned by the law, all further steps depend on the results of negotiations with the works council. The price, however, for the unequivocal acknowledgment of a codetermination right is the equally unmistakable loss of the right to strike with respect to all matters assigned to the works council (Betriebsverfassungsgesetz Sec. 74).

Codetermination rights, as granted by West German law in particular, are thus no less significant for the increasing juridification of labor relations than the general provisions on collective bargaining. In both cases the impression is given that decision-making power is left to the parties directly concerned. In reality, their activity triggers mechanisms established by the legislature under its view of long-term regulation of the labor market. Instead of simply prescribing the content of certain conditions of work, the legislature compels the employer to accept a procedure permitting the employees to insert their experiences and expectations into a regulation directing all further steps of the employer. Both the introduction of particular representation forms for the employees, like the works councils, and the calculated reduction of employers' powers are part of a concept viewing structural change of the enterprise as an instrument at least as important for effective treatment of labor conflicts as the statutory provisions on collective bargaining or direct legislative regulation of employment conditions.

1.5. Contents

A directive regulation of the individual activity presupposes substantive provisions. An interventionist policy therefore entails increasingly dense materialization of the law[14]. While the law's content was originally confined to a few provisions guaranteeing the individual's right to establish contractual relationships according to criteria selected and approved by the parties, the later stages of legal regulation are characterized by a constantly growing number of detailed standards of conduct. The legislature determines tolerance limits for wages and for hours of work, defines the composition of the work force in specific industries, and enumerates safety requirements. Thus, for instance, all the *Code Civil*, had to offer regarding employment relations, were two hardly

[14] For a discussion of the materialization problems, see Hart and Joerges (1980: 187 ff.), Assmann (1980: 251 ff.), Wiethölter (1982a: 39 ff.), Teubner (1983: 250 ff.).

noticeable, extremely abstract provisions (Code Civil Art. 1779, 1780; for a discussion see Tissier, 1904: Vol. 1. 85 ff.). The *Code du Travail* replaced these with a comprehensive regulatory system including a long list of protective measures, rules securing and promoting employment and institutionalized control of work conditions. The *citoyen* is displaced by the *employeur* and the *travailleur.* It is their particular position and comportment not the role indifferent citizen that interests the legislature. Social conflicts are no longer hidden behind purely formal regulation, but are openly addressed through clearly substantive provisions. The juridification of labor relations to that extent amounts to structural change in the law.

The substantive rules, however, at an early stage are supplemented by procedural measures, as the legalization of collective bargaining shows[15]. The state establishes carefully delimited areas of jurisdiction, enforces bargaining procedures, rearranges organizational structures and thus operates on a level distinct from the actual conditions of work. The aim, nevertheless, is once more to conform the labor market to specific state policies. The longer the time span between the first consequences of industrialization and state intervention, the more procedural measures dominate. Substantive rules mitigate acute conflicts and therefore favor the development of social and economic conditions under which purely procedural regulation can fully expand. The employees' bargaining positions change drastically once they are able to act against a background of legally guaranteed minimum standards of work. In addition, the growing complexity of social and economic development renders the legitimation of detailed substantial provisions increasingly difficult. By delegating decision-making to the parties directly concerned, the legislature can successfully avoid most complications[16]. There are, however, no general rules for the relationship between substantive and procedural regulation mechanisms. Weights are primarily distributed according to historical, political and legal factors determining the evolution as well as the structure of the specific law.

Where, as in the United States for example, constitutional law confines the Federal Government's margin of intervention to a narrow field, procedural mechanisms, are by far the better, if not the only means of interference[17].

[15] For the tasks and scope of procedural mechanisms, see Wiethölter (1982a: 42; 1982b: 8 ff.), Teubner (1983: 254 ff.), Voigt (1983: 24 ff.).

[16] See also Scharpf (1978: 16). Procedural mechanisms are insofar prototypical for a soft law. Their introduction marks the beginning of a reductionism reaching its peak once the ambivalences and deficits of state interventionism cannot any more be repressed.

[17] On the importance of the Commerce Clause for the development of labour law in the U.S., see Hammer v. Dagenhart, 247 U.S. 251 (1918), Schecter Poultry Corp. v. U.S., 295 U.S. 495 (1935), NLRB v. Jones and Laughlin Steel Corp., 301 U.S. 1 (1937), but also the far more general remarks of Kitch (1981: 14 ff.). The particular historical and constitutional conditions and not a "tradition of social darwinism" have therefore, contrary to the assumption of Reuter (1983: 586), determined the structure of the regulation of industrial relations in the U.S.

Thus, the duty to bargain to a large extent compensates for the Federal authorities' lack of power to enforce uniform substantive rules. Procedural measures are to this extent the reverse side of nonexistent or scarcely existent materialization (see Wiethölter, 1982a: 45 ff.). The strength and the structure of trade unions are no less relevant. As long as the membership is relatively unimportant, substantive rules, in the end, are the only effective means of regulation. The low degree of organization restricts the effects of collective agreements to a few groups of employers[18]. The smaller the groups, however, the less suitable the agreements for a labor market policy which, in order to be successful, must take into account the position of the entire labor force. Finally, the political representation of employees plays a decisive role (see in particular Kahn-Freund, 1983: 51 ff.). It can, as the German example shows, facilitate the acceptance of substantive rules, and reinforce their weight, and as the Swedish experience illustrates, promote procedural mechanisms.

2. Criticism

2.1. Starting points

The juridification of labor relations has been frequently and thoroughly criticized. In fact, the whole juridification discussion began as a sharp criticism of a process considered undesirable and dangerous (see Kirchheimer, 1928: 593 ff.; but also Neumann, 1967: 254 ff.). However, as in the case of analysis of the process itself, the arguments can only be correctly appreciated against the background of an increasingly interventionist policy. All criticisms of juridification in reality reflect a critical evaluation of state interventionism. The discussion is, nonetheless, frequently conducted in a technocratic way. Slogans like "overproduction of law", "flood of norms" or "legislative perfectionism" (see for example Bühler, 1959:297 ff.; Mayer-Maly, 1969) are as characteristic of this approach as the demand for strictly "consequence-oriented" application of legal norms (see Mayntz, 1979: 55 ff.; 1980; 1983; Wälde, 1979). After deploring the apparently endless increase in regulation as well as the inefficiency of the law, all attention is focused on ways and means of rationalizing law production and thus improving its effectiveness. However instructive some of these reflections may be, they concern purely secondary phenomena. The "flood of norms" cannot be reduced to a solely technical problem. Both the quantitative increase and growing complexity are inevitable side effects of an interventionist policy marked by the structural problems and specific conflicts of a highly industrialized, technical society (on this point, see Kübler, 1969: 647; Simitis, 1970: 33 ff.; Voigt, 1980: 16 ff.; 1983: 18 ff.). Any modification of the juridification process presupposes, under these circumstances, a change in perception of the conditions of economic and social development. Whatever criticism or

[18] A good example are the debates on the necessity of a statute for the protection against unjust dismissal in the U.S., see Summers (1976: 480 ff., 519 ff.).

demand is advanced, therefore, can only be discussed in the context of a reappreciation of activist state policy. The aims pursued may nevertheless be very different, or even diametrically opposed to one another.

2.2. Deregulation

Juridification is viewed in a particularly critical light by those who favor reprivatization of the labor market (see for instance Benoit, 1978: 65 ff., 268 ff; Stoffaes, 1979: 22 ff; Kronberger Kreis, 1983: 10 ff.; Epstein, 1983: 1357). "Deregulation" is seen as the only means of restoring the effectiveness of a market systematically destroyed by interventions that deliberately ignore the working principles of market mechanisms. Labor relations should therefore be subject to the very same rules that govern all other private agreements. In other words, they should be directed by the expectations of the parties, not by standards of conduct decreed by the state. Consequently, regulations like the provisions on the protection against dismissal are among the most frequently quoted examples for a policy fundamentally opposed to market principles and thus incompatible with the priority of solutions found and agreed to by the parties (see Stoffaes, 1979: 22; Kronberger Kreis, 1983: 12 ff.).

None of these arguments, however, was put forward as long as an economy marked by what many assumed would be everlasting prosperity concealed the implications of juridification for the employer's scope of activity. Where the employer has to deal with a constant shortage of labor, he is primarily interested in incentives that discourage employees from changing jobs, not in the implications of a mandatory protection against dismissal. Not the stimulation but the prevention of mobility is, therefore, the employer's main concern (for a comprehensive discussion, see Dorndorf, 1979: 175 ff.). Hence, particular rewards, like long-service bonuses, were supplemented by a legal framework more or less openly based on the idea of "job-ownership" (see Meyers, 1964: 12 ff.; Turner *et al.*, 1967: 337 ff.; Wedderburn, 1971: 137 ff.; Hepple 1983: 408 ff.). The employee's legally guaranteed claim to a specific job, for many the counterpart of the employer's right to be protected against all interferences with his on-going business (see for instance, Herschel, 1960: 121; 1977: 31 ff.; but also Reuter, 1982: 167 ff.), appears to be the next step in a path already marked out by the traditional rules on dismissal. But expectations change with the first signs of a crisis. The reduction of labor costs, either through new production methods, as in the printing industry, or by closing down more and more plants, as in the textile and shipping industries, is seen by employers as an essential condition for adjustment to a changing market structure. All attempts to reduce the number of personnel collide, however, with dismissal rules. They at the least prevent immediate reaction and delay entrepreneurial adaptation efforts. Hence, provisions which for a long time were considered a necessary correction of employer decision-making power are increasingly disqualified as utterly uneconomic impositions that prevent employers from pursuing economically reasonable policies (see in particular, Reuter, 1983: 575 ff.; 1982: 180 ff.; but also Mestmaecker, 1978: 702 ff.; Russig, 1983: 284 ff.).

In short, just as "job-ownership" was put forward and defended in a period of full employment and economic prosperity, the controversy over the necessity and limits of dismissal regulation reflects a recessive economy. However, in contrast with the initial stages of protective legislation, the criticisms are formulated against the background of an elaborate system of unemployment benefits. Job loss, therefore, is no longer a purely individual risk, but one which is at least temporarily socialized (this is openly admitted by Reuter, 1982: 181). Thus, deregulation may relieve the employer of a series of obligations, but only at the expense of the state, the intervention of which is harshly criticized.

Every step limiting the protection against dismissal nevertheless diminishes the influence of the state on labor relations and reinforces the decision-making power of the employer. Binding substantive rules are replaced with regulations relying once more upon the contractual agreement between an employer and the individual employee. Deregulation thus reformalizes the employment relationship (for a discussion of reformalization tendencies see Teubner, 1983: 254 ff.; supra: 29 ff.).

However, contrary to all appearances, the "activist" state is by no means dismissed. Reformalization does not indicate a return to the preinterventionist period. The intention is rather to correct the consequences of what is regarded as a false policy framework and to establish an economic order altering the role of the state but not denying its responsibility for both social and economic development (see Kronberger Kreis, 1983: 5 ff.; Reuter, 1983: 578 ff.; 1982: 185 ff.). Far from simply rejecting all interference, the state is assigned the task of setting the elementary conditions for a functioning market. Thus, instead of viewing the market as a more or less natural event, the market is seen as a goal to be achieved through adequate competition oriented mechanisms, safeguarded and supervised by the state. Hence, what is sought is a policy that insists on the rentability of enterprises, connects wage costs to profits, and maximizes the mobility of employees (see Kronberger Kreis, 1983:13).

Consequent deregulation, however, in view of these aims, can not stop at substantive rules, but must equally include procedural mechanisms, which are the second, no less important, set of juridification instruments. Hence, collective bargaining has been sharply criticized, in particular the attempts to establish a duty to bargain, as well as the provisions institutionalizing representation of employees within the enterprise (see Epstein, 1983: 1364 ff.; Kronberger Kreis, 1983: 11 ff.; Woll, 1983). Interference of the state it is said, has, despite the usual assertions, not led to negotiations truly taking into account the parties' positions, but in fact has prevented them from reaching solutions corresponding to their interests. Even if statutes like the Norris-La Guardia or Wagner Acts carefully avoid regulating the content of collective agreements, the state undermines the bargaining positions by defining the negotiations as a means to secure "acceptable terms and conditions of employment" (Norris-La Guardia Act Sec. 2; see also Cox, 1960: 8; Wellington, 1968: 38 ff.) for the employers (Epstein, 1983: 1370 ff.). Both capital and labor should instead be treated as individual goods, granting a right to negotiate free of all state interferences. Hence, the state's primary and decisive obligation consists of strict observance of an absolutely neutral position, irrespective of whether employers' expectations or employees' demands are at stake (Epstein, 1983: 1371 ff.).

Consequently, employers and employees should, as far as their negotiations are concerned, first and foremost be entitled to choose the method which they believe conforms to their interests. The employer thus must have the right to insist on individual bargaining and to refuse to conclude an agreement as long as the employees insist on being represented by a union. For the same reason, the employer should be free to support all organizations which in his view are prepared to take his interests and expectations into account, thus more willing to reach compromises on the basis of his expectations (Epstein, 1983: 1391). Instead, the legislature has not only opted for compulsory bargaining, but has established a monopoly in bargaining for organizations structured by law in a way deliberately excluding all employer influence. The price, according to critics, is an extremely complicated, highly bureaucratic regulation maximizing bargaining and agreement costs that is simply unacceptable. Only a return to normal contractual procedures could, therefore, restore the market mechanisms and at the same time radically reduce costs (see Epstein, 1983: 1394 ff.; but also Posner, 1977: 65 ff.; Kronberger Kreis, 1983: 11 ff.).

The deregulation demand clearly challenges nearly all the principles governing labor law. The uncompromising attitude is, however, easy to explain. It arises out of the basic assumption that parties meeting in the labor market, as in any other market, are perfectly rational individuals well aware of how to profit from their resources (see in particular Epstein, 1983: 1358 ff.). The legislature's task under these circumstances can only be to remove all obstacles to a rational process of decision-making. Hence, procedural rules, like provisions on collective bargaining, appear to be counterproductive and to that extent an inadmissible attempt to displace legitimate individual decisions by imposing expectations on the parties which ignore their interests.

Both the elaborate criticisms and detailed demands contrast, however, with complete disregard of the social and political background of state interference. Though, for instance, the costs of mandatory regulation of labor relations are extensively discussed, the specific conditions that lead to command-and-control intervention are not even hinted at. No wonder of course, since the very premise of the demand for deregulation blocks off any recourse to the history of labor law. Whoever departs from the assumption that the individual is perfectly free to decide whether to become an employer or an employee (Epstein, 1983: 1366), can see neither the sense of, nor use for, references to the history of employment. Once contractual agreements are presumed to be to the advantage of the parties concerned, because they necessarily initiate and effectuate changes in the positions of the parties (Epstein, 1983: 130, 1383), reflections on earlier periods of labor law appear to be as irrelevant as remarks on inequalities in bargaining strength. Hence, it would be completely mistaken to insist on the social and economic situation of the parties as a relevant criterion for the regulation of employment. The law, on the contrary, must limit itself to securing undisturbed use of mutual resources in precisely the way indicated by the contracting parties.

References to the history of labor relations are indeed far less persuasive than they used to be. The once hardly disputed link between the development of labor law and the economic and social predominance of the employer has lost much of its plausibility. In fact, the rediscovery of freedom of contract is closely connected with often emphatically expressed doubts about the employee's "need of protection", especially in view of evident changes in income, the dense social security network and the ever present, sometimes even constitutionally guaranteed trade union activity (see for instance Ruethers, 1973: 1649 ff.; Zoellner, 1976: 221 ff.; Reuter, 1979: 413 ff.; 1983: 598 ff.). The more the necessity of protection is contested, the more the existence of particular regulations becomes questionable. The reflections on a new "social model" for labor law reintegrating its provisions into the traditional civil law framework (for a comprehensive discussion, see Westermann, 1978: 158 ff.; Lieb, 1978: 196 ff.; but also Assmann, 1980a: 34 ff.) are no less typical for the changing approach than the so-called "neo-civilistic" tendencies (see in particular Couturier, 1975: 151 ff.). In both cases labor law is emancipated from its history and increasingly regarded as one of many examples of "occupational" regulation, requiring a series of particular rules but nevertheless belonging to the law of contracts (see Reuter, 1979: 413 ff.; 577 ff.). The once dominant *question sociale* is obviously no longer the incentive for regulatory intervention, but only the label for a long over period in the history of labor relations.

Both precise deregulation demands and more general criticisms of the juridification process, irrespective of whether the arguments and expectations are shared, are unmistakable signs of the legitimation crisis of labor law. As long as it was possible to grasp the connection between regulatory instruments and acute social problems, intervention could easily be justified. Mandatory reduction of work hours, protection against dismissals, and institutionalization of collective bargaining, all derive their legitimacy from visible individual consequences of the employment relationship and equally discernable implications of the economic and social dependence of employees. Certainly, long and heated controversies preceded each of these regulations (for a detailed analysis see Benoehr, 1977: 187 ff.; 1981: 95 ff.; François, 1974: 29 ff.). But as sharp as these may have been, they clearly illustrate the close relationship between all regulatory interferences and a socially as well as economically critical situation, from the aftermath of industrialization (as in the case of the first factory laws) to the effects of the first world war (as in the case of many of the provisions on dismissal), and to the economic crisis of the late twenties and early thirties (as with the New Deal labor legislation). Under the influence of increasing juridification leading to guaranteed minimum protection standards and secured collective representation of employees, the connection, however, fades away. Hence, the reference to social and economic handicaps loses its legitimizing effect and becomes a ritualized formula accompanying most general reflections on the structure and necessity of labor law. But the reference does not reappear in a substantiated form when the details of the various regulatory mechanisms are discussed.

The lack of precise legitimation is particularly detrimental where regulatory instruments developed in order to reduce dependency are blamed for worsening the position of employees by sabotaging all attempts for a better defence and enforcement of their individual interests (see Reuter, 1983: 345 ff.; 1979: 1 ff.; 1982: 180 ff.; Schwerdtner, 1977: 47 ff.; Benoit, 1978: 268 ff.). It is indeed difficult, if not impossible, to overlook the dialectics of protection. Provisions restricting dismissal, for instance, make it harder to terminate employment relationships, but at the same time they substantially reduce the employment chances of all those who still have no job (see also Reuter, 1979: 410; 1982; 180 ff.; Stoffaes, 1979: 22 ff.; Simitis, 1978: 14 ff.). In fact, the more sophisticated the regulation is, the better it protects "job-owners" at the expense of the unemployed. Terms like "lay-off" clearly illustrate the ambivalence (see in particular Summers, 1976: 481 ff.; Youngdahl, 1975: 297 ff.). Dissolution is seen as a temporary interruption of the employment relationship, distinct priorities being thus fixed, as seniority clauses in the U.S. and selection criteria under both West German and French law demonstrate[19]. Where the dismissal is seen and treated as a lay-off, the labor force is split into privileged and neglected parts. The legitimacy of a regulation depends increasingly on its ability to correct the implications of improved job security and thus avoid transforming the initial conflict between employer and employees into a dispute between different groups of employees.

In addition, all further development of labor law intensifies its concentrative effect. As experience with most regulatory mechanisms shows, only big firms can, in the end, fulfill their requirements. The long and complicated road from the first protective measures for women and children to the detailed provisions of the Occupational and Safety Act in the U.S. or the West-German Arbeitssicherheitsgesetz, and the institutionalized activity of the Comités d'hygiène et de sécurité marks the gradual transition to a regulation assuming a minimum business size, even if this is not explicitly admitted by the legislature. The costs of interventionism can only be met within the organizational framework of large-scale enterprises. Their financial and organizational means enable them to adjust the conditions of work to the demands of the various regulatory mechanisms, but also to counteract their implications with strategies aimed at long-term structural changes, both in the production and service sector[20]. In

[19] Significantly enough, Wiedemann (1979: 659) speaks of "values" clearly established by the provisions on protection against dismissal, justifying all attempts to foresee job guarantees in favour of the already employed workers and thus to disregard openly all outsiders.

[20] Big firms have consequently adapted their personnel policy to the statutes on the protection against dismissal quicker and easier than most of the small enterprises, see Verhandlungen des 52. Deutschen Juristentages, Wiesbaden (1978, Sitzungsbericht M 138 ff., 183 ff.).

brief, the main purpose of intervention (to reduce conflicts by increasing mandatory protection) favors the elimination of smaller firms and accentuates concentration tendencies (see also Kronberger Kreis, 1983: 25; Jeammaud, 1980: 217 ff.; Reuter, 1983: 581; Russig, 1983: 288). Hence, the same mechanisms meant to alleviate the consequences of dependency, create the conditions for a market structure that aggravates the employee's position.

The legitimacy of labor law rules is thus again questioned. However, as long as the degree of juridification remains low, the dilemma is scarcely noticed. The costs of intervention must, in other words, assume a proportion which is usually attained as soon as the regulatory mechanisms imply long-term organizational changes. It is not surprising that the ambivalence of labor law became particularly evident in the course of the deregulation debate. The quest for a radical revision of existing legal structures is expressed against the background of an already highly juridified labor market and in view of the potential overall economic implications of well-developed regulatory intervention. But once the dilemma has been clearly outlined, further reflections on labor law cannot avoid asking how the intended protection can be reconciled with preferential treatment of a part of the labor force and the tendency towards concentration, irrespective of whether the premises and consequences of the deregulation demand are accepted or not.

2.3. Colonialization

"Colonialization" describes an entirely different but no less critical assessment of the juridification process (Habermas, 1981: Vol. 2, 520; 1985: 208). The ever increasing number of substantive rules, and the various agencies set up to control labor relations have established patterns of life to which individual employees must adapt in order to share the protection offered by regulatory mechanisms. Each step towards more perfected and detailed regulations amounts to an interference with the employee's life world and colonizes his behavior by forcing it into a prefixed scheme that excludes alternatives. Mechanisms which were meant to ensure the employee's self-determination, develop the pathological side effect of bureaucratizing the employee's life and jeopardizing the very freedom the mechanisms are supposed to guarantee (see Habermas, 1981: Vol. 2, 530 ff.; 1985: 208 ff.).

The implications of the constantly growing information pressure on employees are a good example of colonialization tendencies. The more sophisticated the protective system, the wider the range of information requirements concerning the employee's personal situation (for a detailed discussion see Simitis, 1980: 7 ff.). Statutes like the Occupational Safety and Health Act and the Arbeitssicherheitsgesetz deliberately aim at extensive collection and retrieval of individual health data. This data constitutes, on the one hand, an important element of the information permitting identification and prevention of certain occupational risks. To that extent, the employees' duty of disclosure appears to be a necessary prerequisite of a no less indispensable protective measure (see for instance *United States* v. *Westinghouse Electric*

Corp., 638 F. 2d 570 (1980) (3rd Circuit); but also Simitis, 1983: 257 ff.). On the other hand, this same data is part of a continuous information process that culminates in a series of abstract standards for determining both the conditions of access to various jobs and entitlement to legally guaranteed protection. The employee, therefore, has no choice. The opportunity to work, as well as compensation for employment risks, depend on his readiness to conform with the expectations resulting from an increasingly dense safety network.

The same tendency can be observed wherever the law intervenes in order to force employers to solve personnel problems as objectively as possible. Irrespective of whether dismissals, transfers or even engagements are concerned, the legislature attempts, either through mandatory criteria or by establishing a duty to bargain, to increase transparency and ensure the controllability of the employer decision-making process. But the quest for objectivity presupposes depersonalized standards[21]. Where, for instance, as in connection with redundancies, age or strain may play an important role under the old system, the first and foremost task is to define, in a generalized, abstract way, both the precise meaning of each of these criteria and the particular situations in which decisions can or must be based on them. Any definition, however, reflects the stereotypes that govern the attitudes of the legislature, courts, and bargaining parties and transforms them into orientation points that deeply influence the employee's perception of his personal situation. The juridification process thus once again confronts the employee with standardized patterns of behavior, reshaping his lifeworld in accordance with the peculiar characteristics of these patterns and initiating increasingly internalized adaptation.

The pressure for conformity becomes even more noticeable when state agencies directly interfere in order to reduce labor market risks. Most laws, for instance, foresee unemployment benefits but reject any payment obligation so long as, under West German law for example, an opportunity for "reasonable" occupation exists (Arbeitsfoerderungsgesetz Sec. 103), or, as the Federal Unemployment Tax Act puts it, "suitable work" can be found and there is no ***motif legitime*** for a refusal (Code du Travail Art. L. 351-4). The remarkable similarity of all these provisions reflects a noteworthy concordance of expectations. The unemployment benefit presupposes the readiness of the individual to revise his personal pattern of life in order to conform to a series of preset, strictly standardized criteria.

Colonialization thus appears to be the unavoidable consequence of a juridification process resulting in progressive occupation of the individual's lifeworld. But however critical the reactions are, they neither lead to the quest for a more technocratic reappraisal of state intervention nor serve as an argument

[21] West German labour courts have, therefore, especially in the case of redundancies, tried to complete the legislative criteria for dismissal by elaborate, strictly formalized schemes of evaluation. See, for a detailed discussion, Bundesarbeitsgericht, Betriebs-Berater 1983: 1665, Becker (1984: 593 ff.).

for a deliberate return to the supremacy of individual bargaining strategies. The reverse side of the colonialization reproach is in fact the question how, despite the necessity of regulatory intervention, the original aim of ensuring the individual employee's freedom of action can be pursued, either with the help of substantive rules or through the establishment of procedural mechanisms. Hence, the real alternative to "colonialization" is a gradual "reindividualization" of the employment relationship. Only to the extent to which the individual employee is offered the chance of self-determination and given the power to govern his lifeworld, can the expectations legitimizing state intervention from the employee's standpoint be fulfilled. "Colonialization" therefore marks the dilemma of all juridification efforts: because of the close interconnection between the guarantee and the withdrawal of freedom, the juridification process must be stopped and redesigned whenever protective mechanisms threaten to turn into a machinery of patronage[22]. Protection must be constantly measured against its foremost task: to establish and secure the individual employee's competence for decision.

2.4. Devolution

Juridification, finally, has often been criticized as a deliberate use of legal instruments for lasting domestication of the unions. The legislature and above all the courts, over the years, have systematically limited trade union activities and steered the unions into a binding legal framework, securing continuous control over them, as well as their adaptation to the government's economic policy (see in particular Erd, 1978: 1 ff., 118 ff., 238 ff.; 1982b: 13 ff.; 1983: 197 ff.; Daeubler, 1980: 49 ff.; 1981: 80 ff.; Rosenbaum, 1982: 392 ff.). Though, for instance, unions are officially acknowledged as the sole representatives of employees, West German law has not hesitated to expand the power of the works councils and thus establish a competing system of representation. Besides, even if collective bargaining is still guaranteed as the primary means of regulating the conditions of work, the courts have time and again limited the number of conflicts which can be settled by collective agreement, usually by restricting the legality of strikes. Labor disputes are indeed seen as the most significant example of regulatory intervention. The illegalization of wild-cat strikes, the insistence on specific procedures for beginning a strike, and the increasingly reluctant acceptance of solidarity actions, as well as the confinement of such actions are considered cornerstones of an intentional, long-term policy juridifying the employee's activities by establishing clear limitations in labor disputes.

However important these examples may be, both the extent and the implications of the juridification process can only be understood, according to critics, when viewed in the context of a distinctly "cooperative" union policy (see

[22] Instead, therefore, of accelerating the juridification process, law must primarily be used to correct a dysfunctional development, see Wiethölter (1982b: 10 (18)), Habermas (1981: Vol. 2, 547).

Bergmann *et al.*, 1975: 143 ff.; Jacobi, 1982: 101 ff.). "Conflict based" strategies, which under the influence of a prosperous economy pushed employers to make a series of concessions were gradually abandoned. In their place, a continuous process of negotiations together with a substantial number of statutory regulations was adopted as the only promising way to balance the interests of capital and labor.

Behind these considerations there is a strong feeling of disappointment in an economic and social policy which, in the late 60s and early 70s aroused high expectations with its ambitious reform programs but never really assessed the methods, costs, or risks of implementation (see also Zacher, 1977: (note 1) 67 ff.; Voigt, 1983: 24 ff.). The harsh, often polemic criticisms are the counterpart of excessive promises. As the failure of state policies became more evident the quest for an alternative policy basis grew. The "legitimacy crisis" of the state entails the entitlement, if not the duty, of nongovernmental institutions to take up and bring to an end the process of social reform. Thus, it is not surprising that all hopes concentrate on the unions. Their activity is seen as the main chance for a new and better start. Consequently, regulatory interventions by the state are perceived as memories of a disenchanting past, and radical dejuridification appears as the true sign of a promising future (see for instance Luhmann, 1981: 94 ff.; Voigt, 1983: 36 ff.)

It is precisely this background that prevents a correct analysis of the juridification process. By concentrating all attention on the unions, collective labor law is overestimated and individual labor law decidedly underestimated. As important as the role of the unions may be, they never and nowhere had an exclusive regulatory competence. On the contrary, labor law began with legislative measures, and still is largely shaped by statutory provisions. With each mandatory rule the legislature modifies the range of collective bargaining as well. As long as the constant interplay between substantive statutory rules and procedural mechanisms is not taken into account, neither the conditions of work nor the scope of collective activity can be correctly appreciated. Even if the legislature contents itself with auxiliary regulation, standards that prejudice all future union policies are set (see infra Sec. 1.4). Hence, wherever the regulation of labor relations is more or less exclusively identified with union activities, history as well as social reality are repressed.

It can, therefore, hardly be contended that both the intensity and the details of the juridification process depend on the unions. Their legalization is inevitably linked to the integration of their activities into an interventionist policy that relies on substantive rules and procedural mechanisms. Once the necessity of collective representation is acknowledged and guaranteed, the activity of the unions is deliberately disciplined. The very act of acknowledgement constitutes the basis for constant monitoring and continuous interference[23]. Irrespective of whether the "golden formula" of the British Trade Disputes Act of 1906 (for a comprehensive discussion see

[23] The guarantee is, in other words, functionalized and the unions thus "incorporated", see Preuss (1979: 97 ff.), Erd (1982b: 18), von Beyme (1977: 198 ff.).

Kahn-Freund, 1983: 291 ff.; Wedderburn, 1971: 316 ff.; 1983: 37 ff.; Lewis, 1983b: 362 ff.), the extensive regulation of union organization in the National Labor Relations Act (see in particular Getman and Blackburn, 1983: 55 ff.; Getman and Pogrebin, 1984: 26 ff.), the precise definition of collective representation in the *Statuto dei diritti dei lavoratori* (see the detailed analysis of Giugni, 1979: 32 ff., 59 ff.), or the "social mightiness" required by the German Federal Labor Court[24] is examined the result is the same. The law does not indiscriminately sanction all collective activities, but only those of organizations whose structures and policies fit into the scheme determined by the legislature and the courts. There are certainly considerable differences between purely "negative statutory protection", as foreseen by the "immunities" of the Trade Disputes Act of 1906 (see Wedderburn, 1983: 37; 1984: 12), and openly "positive protection", as guaranteed by the detailed provisions of the Greek Trade Union Law (Law No. 1264 of June 30, 1982; see in particular Karakatsanis, 1982: 97 ff.) as well as the criteria contained in decisions of the West German Federal Constitutional Court (see for instance Entscheidungen des BVerfG Vol. 2, 107; Vol 18, 28; Vol. 50, 368). But even a regulation like the Trade Disputes Act of 1906, which intentionally limits itself to excluding compensation claims in labor disputes, integrates both the freedom to combined and collective bargaining into a system established and secured by the law and thus juridifies labor relations.

Employees' representatives therefore everywhere face the same dilemma: the very rules that permit them to codetermine the employee relationship and that grant their agreements a maximum of effectiveness force them to conform to a system of organization and negotiation laid down by the legislature and the courts. However, the dilemma does not only illustrate the ambivalence of all union activity, it also shows how illusory is the assumption that unions are perfectly free to reverse the juridification process (see also Streeck, 1981: 354 ff.; Kittner and Breinlinger, 1981: 56 ff.).

Such assertions are, nevertheless, neither fortuitous nor surprising. They have, on the contrary, a long tradition, that begins with Otto von Gierke's (1985: Vol. 1 Secs. 58-78; 1902) and Hugo Sinzheimer's (1907: Vol. 1, 61 ff.; 1916: 181 ff.; 1927: 79 ff.; see also Kahn-Freund, 1976: 7 ff.) concept of corporate autonomy and continues with Otto Kahn-Freund's impressive pleading for "collective laissez-faire" (1943; 1954: 43 ff.; 1959: 224 ff.; but also Wedderburn, 1983: 40 ff.; Lewis, 1983a: 613 ff., 202 ff., 366 ff.) — a demand which also played an important role in the course of New Deal legislation[25]. Both the terminology and reasoning are a striking reminder of early discussions on freedom of contract. Just as individual autonomy was

[24] BAG, Arbeitsgerichtliche Praxis Sec. 2 Tarifvertragsgesetz No. 26, Sec. 97 Arbeitsgerichtsgesetz No. 2; see also Duetz (1976: 65 ff.).

[25] Conseil d'Etat, Droit Social (1973: 514), see also Lyon-Caen (1973: 89 ff.), Javillier (1980: 510). A similar idea is expressed by the assumption of the existence of a particular "Arbeitsverfassung" (employment-constitution), see Scholz (1979: 514 ff.), Ramm (1977: 1 ff.; 1978: 361 ff.).

presented and defended as a "natural right" existing independently of all state action, corporate autonomy and "collective laissez-faire" are described as principles inherent in the structure of society and therefore clearly separated from state activity. With "collective laissez-faire" a new "natural right" typical of industrialized society was established.

Consequently, the principle enunciated with respect to freedom of property and contract is literally repeated in the case of collective autonomy: "what the State has not given, the State cannot take away" (Kahn-Freund, 1959: 244). The purpose in both cases is identical: to defend and uphold a fiction aimed at the priority and exclusivity of a specific regulation of individual relations in general and labor relations in particular. Collective autonomy is, in other words, an instrument with whose help the claim of unions to act for employees and represent their interests is defended against traditional contractual rules and all attempts of the state to discipline unions.

In brief, the unions exercise their functions within a regulatory system that combines guarantees of activity with control measures intended to secure the adjustment of the labor market to general economic and social policy. The employers' representatives operate under the constraint of a specific *ordre public économique et social*[26] and are thus expected to respect the "public interest" by pursuing "socially responsible collective bargaining" (see OECD, 1975; Cooper, 1982: 72). Hence, readiness to acknowledge the primary competence of the unions for the regulation of labor relations and thus to limit intervention to the establishment of a procedural mechanism essentially depends on the degree of concordance between the objectives of bargaining and the leading principles of state economic policy. As long as employers and employees contribute through their agreements to the implementation of these principles, their regulatory competence remains unquestioned. Where however bargaining proves to be the source of widening discrepancy, "public interests" are increasingly invoked (see for instance Reuter, 1983: 578 ff.; 1982: 194 ff.; Scholz, 1979: 513 ff.). They are the means by which the state gradually revokes bargaining competence and replaces it with direct interference.

"Public interests", *Gemeinwohl*, and *ordre public économique et social*, to repeat some of the most common terms, are instruments of adaptation as well as scales of reference for measuring the intensity of intervention. The more extensive their use, the sharper the restriction of union activity. Thus British courts set aside all doubts as to whether injunctions are really compatible with the very structure of labor disputes by pointing at "public interests"[27]. At the same time, the courts outlined increasingly detailed regulations, imposing on the unions rules that progressively limited their decision-making power and forced them to adapt their activity to expectations motivated and dictated by

[26] See NWL Ltd. v. Woods (1979) I.C.R. 867, Duport Steels Ltd. v. Sirs (1980) I.C.R. 161, Clark and Wedderburn (1983: 136 ff.), Lewis (1983: 386 ff.).

[27] All three are in fact typical examples of a regulatory model intentionally aiming at a "tripartism", see Cooper (1982: 13 ff.), but see also Schmidt (1977a: 77 ff.).

considerations openly reflecting general economic and social policy. Another, no less significant example, are the Italian provisions on the reduction of costs resulting from the employment relationship (Decreto-legge numero (d.l.n) 12/1977; see also Giugni, 1982: 395). The legislature carefully avoided interfering directly with wage agreements. All regulation efforts concentrate instead on accessory costs. Though, for instance, the law foresees compensation for dismissals, it at the same time excludes all negotiations on the compensation sum by fixing a mandatory amount. In addition, the law attempts to increase the flexibility of personnel policy in economically critical situations (D.l. n. 80/1978 Art. 1; n. 795/1978 Art. 4-bis; see also Giugni, 1982: 396). Again, dismissals are linked to clearly regulated compensation. Unions and employers can nevertheless bargain, but only to reduce the amount foreseen by the law in view of the enterprise's particular difficulties. Collective bargaining thus remains an essential instrument for the regulation of labor relations. However, because of the "public interest" in enforcing an economic policy that favors a gradual reduction of employment costs and accelerates the modernization process of industry, bargaining is surrounded by mandatory rules steering employers' and unions' decisions in a direction determined by state economic policy, thus intentionally instrumentalizing their agreements.

It is therefore hardly surprising that even explicity constitutional guarantees of the freedom to collectively negotiate work conditions, like Art. 9 para. 3 of the West German Constitution or Art. 39 of the Italian Constitution, have never prevented controversies over the scope of collective bargaining. They underline the dilemma well illustrated by repeated statements of the West German Federal Constitutional Court that the Constitution, though it certainly does not prohibit statutory regulation of labor relations, definitely excludes all interferences with the "core" of collective bargaining (see Entscheidungen des Bundesverfassungsgerichts (BverfG) Vol. 19, 321; Vol. 28, 304; Vol. 38, 393; Vol. 50, 368; Vol. 57, 245). An exact description of the "core" has, however, neither been given, nor can it be provided. In reality, the Court has done no more than indicate that the limits of state intervention cannot be determined in an abstract way but only from case to case, ultimately by the Court itself. One conclusion can be drawn: constitutional provisions, like the guarantees foreseen by both the West German and Italian constitutions, establish a clear priority (see also Giugni, 1979: 43 ff.; Runggaldier, 1983: 86 ff.; Simitis, 1978: 20 ff.). Regulation is first and foremost a task entrusted to unions and employers, to be fulfilled through collective bargaining. Hence, solely state intervention and not the regulative competence of parties to a collective agreement must be justified. The more this priority is reversed, the clearer the authoritarian features of the economic and social policy. Thus the distribution of competences between the state and collective bargaining parties, far from simply concerning organizational questions, affects the very structure of society. At the same time it demonstrates the fragility of a democratic system and illustrates just how fluid the boundaries between a democratic and an authoritarian welfare state are.

The quest for regulatory models that reinforce the position of the unions, under these circumstances, is at least understandable. The "Social Contract" between the Labour Party and the Trade Union Congress is by now probably the classic example of such a model (for a comprehensive discussion see in particular Clark *et al.*, 1980: 20 ff., 62 ff.; Clark and Wedderburn, 1983: 184 ff.). ff.). Similar tendencies can be found in the agreement signed in Rome on January 22, 1983 by the government, trade unions and employers association (the tendencies preceding it are analyzed by Treu, 1983: 184 ff.), as well as in the establishment of institutions like the Labor Foundation and the Social and Economic Council in the Netherlands (see Social-Economische Raad, 1976; Pels, 1966; Windmuller, 1969: 436 ff.; Cooper, 1982: 24 ff.), or the National Labor Council in Belgium (see Blanpain, 1982: 34 ff.; Kommission der europäischen Gemeinschaften, 1982: 76 ff.). There are, however, certainly important differences. For instance, the range of participants, when compared to the "Social Contract" is obviously wider[28]. Besides, while in both the Netherlands and Belgium a long-term institutional approach has been taken, the Italian and British attempts were far more informal and intended to cope with a series of particular conflicts. But despite these differences the purpose is everywhere the same. The terms used in connection with the activity of the Belgian National Labor Council, the development of an efficient "social programming", have the same purpose as those used by the Trade Unions Congress, namely, a "coherent economic and social strategy ... designed both to overcome the nation's grave economic problems, and to provide the basis for cooperation between the Trade Unions and the Government" (Trade Union Congress Report, 1974: 284; see also Joint Statement, 1979). The unions are thus involved as early as possible in a centralized decision-making process with direct or indirect participation of the government[29] in order to ensure, particularly through a series of trade-offs (see also Peper, 1979: 139; Cooper, 1982: 13), the effectiveness of an economic policy aimed at monetary stability, increased productivity and the highest possible level of employment.

Each of these models suggests the existence of an alternative to the juridification of labor relations. Consequently, the very first words of the Trade Union and Labour Relations Act 1974, "The Industrial Relations Act 1971 is hereby repealed", which openly reject attempts to establish a mandatory legal regime for union activities were considered as probably the most important achievement of the "Social Contract" (see in particular Wedderburn, 1983: 54 ff.; but also Kahn-Freund, 1975: 186 ff.). The repeated efforts to dissociate the various attempts of a "concertation" of government, unions and employers, from the traditional legal forms of cooperation, and to underline their "ex-

[28] The interference thus indeed assumes the form of a "persuasive dirigisme", see von Beyme (1977: 252; 1979: 235 ff.).

[29] The West German Federal Government explicitly described its draft for a statute on "premature retirement", in view of the intended reduction of unemployment, as an offer for a "labor pact", Bundesrat-Drucksache 552/83.

tra-legal" character (see for instance Giugni, 1982: 373; Treu, 1983: 84) are no less significant. However, in none of these cases was the juridification process weakened or even stopped. On the contrary, juridification climaxed under the "Social Contract" (see Clark and Wedderburn, 1983: 185 ff.; Wedderburn, 1978: 435; Lewis, 1976: 1 ff.; 1983a: 373 ff.). If measured against its own objective of removing industrial relations from state control, the Social Contract was a failure. Juridification has not decreased, but significantly increased. The list of new regulations is impressive. From dismissal to maternity and health protection, as well as to specific discrimination cases, an increasingly detailed legal scheme for labor relations was designed. It cannot be disputed that at least two statutes enacted in 1974, the Health and Safety at Work Act and the Arbitration and Conciliation Service Act, provide conflict solving mechanisms based on participation of the unions (on this point see Clark and Wedderburn, 1983: 186 ff.). But precisely these mechanisms demonstrate the change. The legislature, far from abstaining from any interference, fits labor relations into a framework that intentionally incorporates the unions. Their activity is just as much a part of the system of labor relations defined and established by law as any other mandatory rule of the statutes concerned.

The increase in regulation is the price for cooperation. For both the unions and the government, statutes not only offer the advantage of solving a series of conflicts, but also demonstrate the efficiency of cooperation and therefore stabilize it by improving its chances of legitimation. But again, even if union participation changes the objectives and content of juridification it does not alter its implications. On the contrary, unions are even more intensively integrated into a regulatory system that adjusts the conditions of work to the expectations of the general economic policy. Consequently, the really dominant feature of all "concerted actions" (for a discussion of the West German experience see von Beyme, 1977: 352 ff.; 1979: 236 ff.; Schlecht, 1968; Hoppmann, 1971; Streeck, 1979: 206 ff.; Jacobi, 1982: 117 ff.) and "labor pacts"[30] as well as of the various attempts to institutionalize cooperation with the help of an "economic and social council" (for a description see Cooper, 1982: 16 ff.; von Beyme, 1977: 302 ff.), is the unmistakable "corporatist" tendency involved (see also Middlemas, 1979: 19 ff.; Crouch, 1979: 186 ff.; White, 1982: 149 ff.; Cooper, 1982: 68 ff.; but also Lewis, 1983b: 117 ff.). The implications are once more best illustrated by the "Social Contract". Government and trade unions were, in the end, the only decisive factors of the political decision-making process. Their negotiations determined the main policy objectives and thus the framework of state activity. The consensus with the unions was, accordingly, both the basis and the limit of all governmental action.

Social as well as political expectations, under these circumstances, will only

[30] This is illustrated by both the Trade Union Congress (TUC) reports (1974: 284 ff.; 1975: 460 ff.) and the Labour Party Manifesto (1974: 12) see also Cooper (1982: 42 ff.).

be seriously considered if the unions and the ruling political forces are prepared to take them into account [31]. Agreements like the "Social Contract" therefore filter the political reflections and steer the course of all further discussion (see also Treu, 1983: 84; Himmelmann, 1983: 71). Both parliamentary proceedings and collective bargaining are thus reduced to a mere ratification of the aims and rules defined by the "pact" (social conflicts are insofar indeed "depoliticized", see Offe, 1979: 72 ff.). Furthermore, a decision-making process increasingly confined to negotiations between government and the unions, tends to become more and more arcane. The really relevant opinions are almost exclusively formed in the course of discussions within the bodies constituted by the cooperating parties with a view to establishing and ensuring their consensus. At the same time weight is shifted within the unions. The leadership, because of the overall social and economic importance of the negotiations, claims the right to make unilateral decisions, thus progressively depriving union members of their influence and pushing them further and further to the periphery of the organization (on this point see in particular Streeck, 1979: 207 ff.; Scharpf, 1978: 20 ff.; Cooper, 1982: 70 ff.). Both the "Social Contract" and the other various forms of "labor pacts" therefore favor strictly hierarchic organization structures and, consequently, further professionalization of leadership[32].

However, both the increased hierarchy as well as the diminishing influence of membership are by no means restricted to the cases where the state seeks to ensure support of the unions for a specific economic and social policy through direct agreements or with the help of particular institutionalized procedures. These follow, in fact, from the guarantee of the unions' right to represent employees and negotiate on their behalf. The clearer the bargaining monopoly, the more the position of union leadership is reinforced. Once the union is, by law, the only body entitled to conclude collective agreements, it can also claim exclusive competence to define the employees' interests. The claim may not be obvious as long as bargaining is decentralized, but it hardly can be overlooked as soon as national or even regional agreements predominate (see also Scharpf, 1978: 20 ff.; Streeck, 1979: 208 ff.; Cooper, 63 ff.). Where, as in the case of the Belgian National Labor Council, for example, negotiations are deliberately situated at the highest possible organizational level, there is in the end no way to express the employees' expectations other than through the demands of national leadership. Each of the provisions establishing the bargaining monopoly of the unions may thus at first be seen as a necessary consequence of regulation of labor relations based on the autonomy of unions and their competence to develop and enforce

31 Significantly enough, unions are confronted in the context of such agreements with the expectation "'to educate' their members to the current economic realities", Cooper (1982: 63 ff.).

32 See for instance Steel v. Louisville and Nashville R.R., 323 U.S. 192 (1944), Humphrey v. Moore, 375 U.S. 335 (1964), Vaca v. Sipes, 386 U.S. 1717 (1967); Hines v. Anchor Motor Freight, 424 U,S. 1717 (1976).

conditions of work corresponding to the employees' interests. But they also underline the ambivalence of all tendencies aimed at maximizing autonomy: while the employees' opportunities to influence their work conditions increase, and the degree of direct, if not indirect, state intervention diminishes, the trend to an organizational structure that alienates members from their leadership while expanding their power at the expense of true representation is accentuated (see also Cooper, 1982: 42; Teubner, 1979: 487 ff.).

The bargaining monopoly is therefore completed by rules aimed at "fair representation". Significantly, as the example of the National Labor Relations Act shows, none of the traditional regulations went that far. For the legislature it was indeed perfectly sufficient to combine the unions' right of representation with the employers' duty to negotiate. The Supreme Court and the National Labor Relations Board, however, asked for more[33]. They expect negotiations to reflect the interests of all members. The "duty of fair representation" thus limits bargaining power by intentionally excluding discrimination[34]. Members are given the right to interfere with bargaining policy and to ensure that their particular situation is taken into account. Hence, the union may still have exclusive bargaining competence, but both the negotiation and enforcement of the agreement must be based on careful appreciation of the problems faced by the membership as a whole.

The duty of fair representation shows only too clearly that the juridification process does not simply end once the devolution of the power to regulate labor relations is guaranteed. Readiness to respect the autonomy of the unions merely changes the direction of this process. Intervention concentrates increasingly on a correct representation of the employee's interests (see also Kahn-Freund, 1979: 1 ff.; von Beyme, 1977: 107 ff.). Irrespective of whether priority is given to the rights of individual employees or to the mandatory establishment of mechanisms ensuring the participation of members in the decision-making process[35], the apparently autonomous organization is, with respect to its internal structure, progressively subjected to legally binding rules.

The more, therefore, the autonomy of the unions is stressed, the clearer the

33 See Local 12, United Rubber Workers v. National Labor Relations Board (NLRB), 368 F.2d 12 (1966) (5th Cir.), cert. denied, 389 U.S. 837 (1967), United Packinghouse Workers Int'l Union v. NLRB, 416 F. 2d 1126 (District of Columbia Circuit), cert. denied, 396 U.S. 903 (1969); but also Summers (1977: 251 ff.); Getman and Pogrebin (1984: 136 ff.).

34 For a discussion of the experiences with collective bargaining, see for instance Heinze *et al.* (1981a: 19 ff.).

35 The West German works councils, for example, did not hesitate to consider the fact that both spouses had a job as a perfectly valid criterion for establishing a top priority in view of dismissals due to the deteriorating market conditions (sec. 1 par. 2 Kündigungsschutzgesetz), but restricted its application to women, see Landesarbeitsgericht Hamm, Beschlußsache (Bsa) 1327/83. for the experience with seniority-clauses, see Russig (1982: 260 ff.), Cooper and Solo (1969: 1598 ff.), Poplin (1975: 194 ff.).

quest for a second generation of employee protection rules. Their target is not the employer but the employee representatives. The aim, however, in both cases, is to guarantee the employee a minimum of rights, regardless of whether his interests have to be defended against the employer or secured in the course of negotiations conducted by his own representatives. Traditional employee protection rules mark the beginning of the juridification process, whereas rules like the duty of fair representation are symptomatic of a period in which the regulation of labor relations is largely determined by the bargaining policies of already established employee organizations.

3. Outlook

3.1. Recomposition of the labor force

Juridification is as a rule considered to be a process having long passed its peak. The motives no less than the structure and the possible fields of regulatory interferences seem to have been sufficiently clarified in the course of the long and complicated history of state interventionism. The more interferences are projected into the past, however, the less the implications of a changing labor market can be correctly assessed. The consequences of the increasingly modified position of women and older employees illustrate the difficulties.

Protective regulations for both groups are classic examples of the juridification of labor relations (for a detailed description see for instance François, 1977: 70 ff.). They were and are seen as necessary reactions to risks specific to the employment of women and older employees. Each of these regulations, however, reflects a particular view of the two groups as well. Despite all contrary assertions they are not considered "normal" employees. In fact, their presence on the labor market is linked either to a "sexual" or "age" reservation setting clear employment priorities. They marginalize women and older employees and bar access to the market whenever jobs become scarce (see for instance Bundesanstalt für Arbeit, 1978: 221, 227; Lehr, 1984: 284 ff.; Offe and Hinrichs, 1977: 3 ff.; Pohl, 1976: 9 ff.). Thus, full employment is the only situation in which their presence is unconditionally tolerated or desired. Discriminatory treatment is usually justified by pointing at "natural" alternatives: housework for women, or retirement for older employees. Hence, employment is seen as a deviation from the "proper" life model. In short, the employment chances of both groupst when compared to all other employees, are burdened with an additional risk which is rationalized through the presumed availability of alternative life patterns.

A labor market structure based on the "double" role of women and older employees, however, is scarcely compatible with any law clearly rejecting discrimination. The conflict, as experience shows, can be repressed for an often substantial period of time. In the case of women, for instance, it remained largely unnoticed as long as all efforts concentrated on the elimination of the many other forms of legal discrimination, from the denial of voting rights to monocratic, patriarchal family structures. With each step towards equality, the criticisms of labor market practices inevitably grew. Where obstacles to active participation in the political decision-making process are removed, barriers to the various professions cleared away, educational opportunities ameliorated, and family relations freed from "natural" male domination, the woman's "double role" can no longer be easily invoked. Higher qualifications, increased professional experiences, and political activity also strengthen resistance to discrimination in the labor market.

However, despite growing consciousness of the necessity to revise employment conditions, the traditional conflict solving mechanisms failed. In fact, the codetermination right granted to the works-councils (Betriebsverfassungsgesetz Sec. 95) did not prompt them to improve women's employment opportunities and the duty to bargain failed to bring about a policy excluding discrimination [36].

On the contrary, personnel decisions ignoring existing discrimination or even creating greater discrimination were repeatedly sanctioned in the course of collective bargaining. The very same attitudes and prejudices that for a long time determined legislative policy today dominate collective agreements, having transformed them into instruments stabilizing and perpetuating discriminatory treatment. Dismissal procedures as well as seniority clauses that intentionally disregard the interests of both women and older employees are among the most common examples [37]. The justifications given, of course, avoid all references to factors which might arouse the suspicion of discrimination. Consequently, the need to balance the interests of all employees or the exceedingly difficult position of those with particularly heavy family duties are emphatically stressed. Strangely enough, however, both the "overall interest" of the employees and various "social" reasons nearly always lead to the dismissal of women or older employees.

The intervention of the legislature thus appears to be the only way to restrict discrimination. Hence, a series of statutes beginning with the 1964 Civil Rights Act in the U.S. not only expressly prohibits discriminatory practices in employment, but also foresees particular administration efforts meant to ensure equal opportunities (for a comprehensive discussion see for instance Hohmann-Dennhardt, 1982: 25 ff., 53 ff., 71 ff.; Seeland, 1982: 298 ff.; Mockenhaupt, 1984: 34 ff.). The legislature refuses to confine its interference to a comprehensive list of possible violations. Nor does it find it sufficient to establish standards of conduct positively implementing equal treatment, like equal pay for equal work, or job advertisements that avoid all discriminatory wording [38]. It regards the antidiscrimination policy as a long term task which

[36] For a comprehensive discussion, see for instance, Hohmann-Dennhardt (1982: 25 ff.; 53 ff.; 71 ff.), Seeland (1982: 298 ff.), Mockenhaupt (1984: 35 ff.).

[37] See for instance, the directive of the European Communities of February 9 1976, (76/207) and the decision of the European Communities Court of April 10 1984, Neue Juristische Wochenschrift (1984: 2021).

[38] For a critical appreciation, see for instance Koral (1979/80: 473 ff.), Bryner (1982: 411 ff.); Hohmann-Dennhardt (1982: 53 ff.), Mockenhaupt (1984: 45 ff.).

can only be successfully completed by continuously influencing employers through the activity of special agencies. It is their function to adopt the statutes to everyday experiences and to transform them into demands directly affecting personnel policy (for a critical appreciation see for instance Koral, 1979/80: 473 ff.; Bryner, 1982: 411 ff.; Hohmann-Dennhardt, 1982: 53 ff.; Mockenhaupt, 1984: 208 ff.). Therefore, instead of simply reprimanding employers for adverse practices, the regulatory intervention deliberately aims at an organizational structure that both corrects and prevents discrimination[39].

The need for regulatory measures may be less evident in the case of older employees. However, in a society where life expectancy increases and the number of older persons constantly grows it becomes increasingly difficult to present retirement as a true alternative to employment (see Kendig, 1978: 10 ff.; Shuck, 1979: 27 ff.; Steffen and Niestrath, 1977: 93 ff.; Lehr, 1984: 313 ff.). The traditional, and for many still perfectly normal practice of marginalization, can not conceal the knowledge that the aging process depends to a great extent on the opportunity to work (see in particular Wolfgang, 1978; Lehr, 1984: 240 ff., 313 ff.). As important as the function of retirement may have been within a developing industrial system, it must be judged differently when the changing health and employment picture excludes uncritical application of traditional "disablement" standards (see also Lehr, 1984: 240 ff.; Steffen and Niestrath, 1977: 98). Besides, even if employment is linked to continuous strain, retirement does not necessarily result in improved living conditions. On the contrary, experience shows that no matter what the type of work, termination of employment has considerable emotional and physical implications. No society, and no law pretending to condemn discriminatory practices, therefore, can continue treating older employees as a disposable segment of the labor force. Social degradation and mental alienation can only be avoided as long as equal employment opportunities are secured. In order to achieve a policy anticipating conflicts which destabilize social and economic development, it is essential to interfere in the employment relationship and thereby modify the conditions of employment.

Despite the differences between regulations aimed at eliminating discriminatory practices against women and older employees, both systems illustrate (for an appreciation see in particular Erickson, 1979: 591; Bryner, 1982: 411 ff.; Mockenhaupt, 1984: 40 ff.) that juridification is entering a new stage. The goals pursued by the legislature do not fit easily into the traditional scheme of interventionist policy. Besides, the legislature's intervention reflects the inability of the existing procedural mechanisms, and particularly of collective bargaining, to correct practices deeply rooted in a series of social

[39] It is therefore not surprising that the "affirmative action" proved to be the main regulatory instrument. For a discussion see Smith-Abrams (1981: 33), Milkovich (1981: 42 ff.), Seeland (1982: 298 ff.), Thomas (1983: 208 ff.).

prejudices and well established attitudes. The interference of the legislature is therefore mainly a sign of qualitative change within the juridification process.

3.2. High-risk technologies

Regardless of whether early protective provisions, the guarantee of collective bargaining, or the various regulatory measures of the labor market are considered, juridification throughout its development has been marked by the effort to solve conflicts typical for employees. The social and political implications of the employee's position trigger state intervention and determine both its structure and evolution. But, what up to now was thought to be perfectly obvious, appears to be increasingly questionable, as the example of the nuclear and chemical industries shows.

In each case, the use of new substances and energy sources has maximized the risks for society in general. The need for measures to restrict the dangers, therefore, is scarcely contested. However, all attempts to reduce, for instance, effects on the environment, inevitably result in steps directly affecting production. This is the obvious source of the dangers and hence the natural object of all policies intending to control and diminish risks. But once the production process becomes the target of regulatory intervention, the conditions of work are implicated no less than any other production factor. Irrespective of whether the machinery, the substances used, the waste products, or the tasks of the individual employee are concerned, tolerance limits are increasingly dictated by environmental risks. Thus where dangers emerge, employment is determined more and more by regulatory interferences based on the requirements of risk-free production.

The consequences are particularly evident in the nuclear industry (for a detailed description see Simitis and Rydzy, 1984; Lewis, 1978). Detailed mandatory procedures govern the selection of employees and ensure permanent monitoring. Understandably enough, special attention is paid to skill. Sophisticated regulations carefully relate expectations to the various positions and provide for constant improvement as well as continuous supervision. "Reliability", however, is not judged on the basis of skill and physical ability alone. Equal importance is attached to emotional factors (see Fechner, 1978: 74 ff.; 1980: 249 ff.; Simitis and Rydzy, 1984: 28 ff.). Both the capacity to react adequately in critical situations and to deal with conflicts within and without the enterprise must be tested. Finally, the political and social activities of the employees are meticulously examined (for a description of the various procedures and their implications see Simitis and Rydzy, 1984: 30 ff.).

The regulations also interfere with the organization of the enterprise (see Simitis and Rydzy, 1984: 32 ff.). The various tasks of the employees must be determined exactly and included in a plan submitted to a particular government agency. Besides, the employer must comply with a series of demands concerning, for instance, structuring of the workplace, the number of persons to be employed in different sectors, the conditions of access to different parts of the enterprise, and its partition into zones according to the intensity of risk.

Each of these regulations penetrates a domain otherwise reserved to collective bargaining. Regardless of whether the employer negotiates with the unions or the works council, the agreement is supposed to precisely determine those conditions of work which constitute the subject of the numerous statutes and administrative guidelines concerning the nuclear and, to a lesser extent, the chemical industry (see Simitis and Rydzy, 1984: 41 ff.). To what extent for instance, employees can be tested and monitored, and under what circumstances the employer is entitled to enforce an organization plan with far reaching consequences for work conditions depends, outside these industries, largely on consent between the employer and the employees' representatives (see for example, Betriebsverfassungsgesetz Secs. 87 par. 1, 94 par. 2, 95). Hence, in the case of high-risk technologies the state obviously disregards the existing regulatory principles and deliberately imposes on employers and employees a mandatory scheme of behavior that excludes negotiations and thus all chances of influencing work conditions. These schemes are a part of regulations provided, or at least approved, by the state on the basis of an appraisal of the technology risks and not in view of the employee's position. Consequently, as revealed by the various reliability tests, the political screening and exhaustive controls, the employee is subjected to procedures that restrict his freedom of action and interfere with his personal life to an extent unknown or even inadmissible in other branches of industry.

The dangers accompanying the use of high-risk technologies can certainly not be disputed. It nevertheless seems difficult, at least at first, to reconcile the far reaching intervention of the state with its repeatedly acknowledged readiness to guarantee the priority of regulations negotiated between the employers and employee representatives. Collective agreements owe their legitimacy not only to the fact that they contain rules initiated and consented to by the parties, but also to the conviction that both the procedure and its result correspond best to the general interests of society. It is for precisely this reason that collective bargaining, in the case of industries using high-risk technologies, appears to be a no less appropriate means of regulation than in any other sector (see for instance Heinze *et al.*, 1981b: 345 ff.; but also Teske, 1983: 192 ff.).

A functioning bargaining process presupposes, however, the existence of parties able and determined to defend their particular interests[40]. Hence, the collective agreement can only fulfill its task as long as the parties are aware of their special situation and regard the agreement as a means to solve

[40] "It must be realized that collective bargaining, under a system where the Government does not attempt to control the results of negotiations cannot be equated with an academic collective search for the truth — or even with what might be thought to be the ideal of one. The parties — even granting the modification as that may come from a realization of economic interdependence — still proceed from contrary and to an extent antagonistic viewpoints and concepts of self-interest", NLRB v. Insurance Agents Int'l Union, 361 U.S. 477, 488 (1960); see also Streeck (1981: 359 ff.); Simitis (1978: 22 ff.).

problems arising out of this situation. Consequently, unions must introduce into the bargaining process the experiences and expectations of the employees concerned. As their representatives, the unions must first and foremost adopt policies based on the day to day involvement of employees in the work environment and aimed at corrections and changes necessary from their standpoint (see also Ulman, 1955; Atherton, 1973; Flanagan, 1983: 230 ff.). Unions must of course develop, in the interest of the employees, long-term strategies that anticipate possible changes of the enterprise structure as well as of the economy in general. But even if all such strategies restrict the impact of the employees' immediate expectations regarding the bargaining process, their hopes and wishes must remain the ultimate incentive for and legitimation criterion of, the unions' policies.

Quite understandably, therefore, unions and works councils focused their attention on the implications of the various regulations related to the use of high-risk technologies for the employees concerned (see in particular Teske, 1983: 193 ff.). Reliability tests and constant control were seen as unacceptable monitoring of the employees. The reaction to demands for higher qualifications was equally unequivocal. These were rejected as an inadmissible restriction of the employee's opportunity for advancement. Each of these criticisms obviously collides with employment criteria derived from the need to prevent high-technology risks. Collective bargaining may, therefore, still be in the interests of the employee, but it can not claim to ensure regulation protecting society from the dangers of the production process (for a discussion of this conflict see also Schmidt, 1977b: 243 ff.; Kahn-Freund, 1979: 63 ff.; and the critical remarks of Wedderburn, 1984: 7 ff.). As long as both unions and works councils act as genuine employee representatives they cannot be forced into a role which, in the end, entrusts them with an appreciation for the implications of high-risk technologies for society's future and thus confines the reactions to the negotiations between the unions or works councils and the employers. Neither internal trade union debates nor collective bargaining can substitute for public discussion and, in particular, the parliamentary decision-making process. They do not offer, therefore, an alternative to political action based on parliamentary decision and exercised through the interference of government. Any other interpretation amounts to a falsification of the union's function as well as of the peculiar tasks of collective agreements (see also Streeck, 1981: 362). They both have their own priorities marked by the specific interests of the parties concerned and consequently can not provide adequate solutions where, as in the case of high-risk technologies, adequate rules can only be found at some cost to the parties directly involved.

Hence, the premises of the juridification of labor relations change once more. To the extent to which clearly risk oriented regulation is aimed at, the employees' position ceases to be the decisive intervention factor and the employment relationship is subject to a mandatory regime intentionally excluding both the employers and employees from decisions on employment conditions. The legislature, however, limits itself to a few provisions establishing the framework for continuous admininstrative interference. It is precisely this expansion of purely adminstrative regulations that indicates, more than anything else, the intensity of the juridification process. As long as the employees' behavior constitutes a risk factor, there is virtually no aspect of the employment relationship that can escape mandatory adminstrative rules. Both the conditions and the extent of the juridification process are thus deeply modified. Where intervention is motivated by threats of physical harm to society rather than by social and political implications of the employee's position, the adminstration of employment becomes a part of public administration.

3.3. Relocation of work

The changing aspects of the juridification process are illustrated, finally, by the already discernible trend of job relocation. With the transition to new information and communcations techniques the traditional integration of employees into a technical as well as organizational unit reflecting the specific objectives of each enterprise becomes, especially in the services sector, increasingly unnecessary[41]. Teletext equipment enables the employee to perform his tasks without having to leave his home. When technical requirements, both inside and outside the enterprise, are fulfilled, telework constitutes, at least for the employer, an attractive alternative to usual work conditions. Expenses for buildings, workplace equipment as well as a large part of incidental labor costs can be substantially reduced. Besides, the entrepreneur for the first time has the chance to exhaust all the opportunities offered by the labor market. He is, for instance, no longer confined to a particular region, and can organize work far better than before in a way largely eliminating disturbances related to employee absence or sudden increases in demand.

However, enterprises are, despite these rather obvious advantages, still sceptical or even openly disinterested, for very good reasons. Whether a relocation of work is really worthwhile depends to a large extent on communication costs (see also Huws, 1984: 14). Telework, in order to be seriously considered, must be less expensive than traditional workplace methods. The technical infrastructure, therefore, is of primary importance. The denser the cable network and the cheaper its use, the better the chances that telework will be utilized (see also Braun, 1981).

In addition, because of early experiences the importance of telework is often underestimated. Relocation was originally confined to relatively simple, routine office work. But in the meantime, particularly in the case of insurance companies, telework has been successfully extended to far more complicated services as well as to managerial tasks (see Braun, 1981: 570 ff.; Olsen, 1982; Huws, 1984: 16 ff.; Shirley, 1979). The potential impact of telework can

[41] For a description and a first discussion, see the Braun Report submitted in 1981 to the French Premier (Droit Social (1981: 205 ff.); also Olson (1981; 1982); European Foundation (1984); Grewlich (1983: 20 ff.); Huws (1984: 14 ff.).

therefore only be correctly estimated, if the relation between the services sector and the total number of employees is considered. Statistics, at least in the case of highly industrialized countries, are absolutely clear. The services sector is not only constantly growing, it already covers the majority of employees[42]. Hence, techniques aimed at relocation challenge the conditions of work of by far the largest group of employees (see also Huws, 1984: 16 ff.).

Telework is, finally, of considerable interest to certain employees who up to now have faced great difficulties in finding and keeping a job. Significantly, women, the disabled, and inhabitants of remote regions are particularly prepared to support activities favoring relocation. Consequently, the British Equal Opportunities Commission, in the course of its consideration of policies counteracting discrimination, has given special attention to telework (see Huws, 1984: 15 ff.). The more each of these employee groups comes to understand the importance of telework, the greater the political pressure for relocation will be.

Hence, for more than one reason, the unity of home and workplace emerges as probably the most striking feature of the future development of labor. Industrial society thus returns, at precisely the moment when it has reached its technological peak, to its long forgotten earliest phases. Video and personal computers stand where the loom and the sewing machine used to be placed. Whereas industrial production methods forced employees to move from their homes to the factory, the new communcation and information techniques drive them back.

It is certainly too early to describe the exact consequences. A few tendencies are nevertheless already discernible. Relocation, for instance, affects methods of payment. With the change to telework the employee is no longer bound to specific times. He can determine his working hours according to his own expectations and commitments. Under these circumstances the employer's attention is focused wholly on the result of the employee's work. Consequently, payment by piece appears, at least in the large majority of cases, to be the only adequate method of remuneration. An important aspect of employment is thus subjected to practices which in the course of long and complicated bargaining processes had been gradually overcome.

Relocation also intensifies control of the employee. The same technical means that render the employee more independent with respect to organization of his work, record all his moves and thus permit the employer to retrace at any moment all the employee's activities. The employer, therefore, not only has better control, but is also provided with information enabling him to continuously adjust his demands and hence force the employee to adapt himself to the employer's expectations more than ever before.

Finally, as the experience in the U.S. has shown (see Huws, 1984: 15), relocation incites employers to transform their employees into small entrepre-

[42] According to the 1982 Statistical yearbook for the Federal Republic of Germany, International Part: 647 ff., more than 60% of the employees in Canada, Sweden and the U.S. work in the services sector.

neurs. Anyone interested in telework must first acquire the necessary equipment and accept contractual conditions typical for the suppliers of goods and services.

The closer telework is looked at, the clearer it becomes that teleworkers do not fit into traditional labor concepts. None of its mechanisms, in fact, can be separated from the conditions of work characteristic of industrial production. It is industrialization that led to the gradual development of specific rules for the employment relationship and it is industrial production that moulded the provisions governing this relationship. The long list of mandatory safety measures, for instance, is only understandable against the background of the risks generated by factory work. It is equally obvious that both the development and structure of collective activity are clearly linked to the particular experiences accompanying industrial production. Whenever, therefore, as in the case of telework, integration into a collective workplace is reversed and work is shifted back to the employee's home, labor law is deprived of its basis.

Home work, it is true, has never been ignored[43]. In fact, there is virtually no law that does not include at least a few provisions dealing with the specific problems of home workers. All these rules, however, either concern genuine preindustrial relics or a few peculiar types of work — in short — purely exceptional situations (see also Drygala, 1978). Telework, on the contrary, despite its actual singularity, signals the transition to a new normality. Employment structures, in the end, are modified as radically as they were by industrialization. Provisions designed in an entirely different context and for different purposes are therefore inapplicable.

But as necessary as new regulations adjusted to the particularities of telework may appear to be, the difficulties should not be underestimated. The question is not content, as the requirements can be rather easily described. The real obstacle is their monitoring. However convincing the demands, regulations are of little use as long as their fulfillment cannot be reliably checked. Traditional mechanisms are unable to guarantee satisfactory control as the case of the unions already shows. Because of the lack in job concentration and because of extremely restricted communication, the readiness for collective activity as well as its effectiveness are substantially reduced. In fact, unions risk, as experience with existing forms of home work illustrates, being transformed into pure bureaucratic agencies [44]. In addition, the complexity of state control mechanisms, as demonstrated by both the establishment of special records and the elaborate inspection system (see for example Heimarbeits-

[43] For examples of the actual forms of homework and a detailed discussion see for example, Schwägerl (1982); Cragg and Dawson (1981); Hakim and Dennis (1982).

[44] The West German Heimarbeitsgesetz, for example, foresees (Sec. 17) a particular form of written agreement between the unions and the employers in order to cope with the homeworkers. Similarly the Code du Travail (Art. L. 721-19) grants the unions a right to sue employer and attempts thus to guarantee at least a control. See also Wlotzke (1974: 2254).

gesetz Secs. 5-9), is multiplied. But even if such regulations function in the few exceptional home work cases, neither the records, nor the number of inspectors and their rights can be extended at will without modifying the political structures of society.

However, as considerable as the difficulties may be, they do not affect the juridification process. They only underline the need to develop new approaches adapted to the changing structures of work. All three examples — recomposition of the labor force, the implications of high-risk technologies, and the relocation of work — confirm, therefore, that far from being completed, juridification is, regardless of all contrary assertions, still an on-going process.

References

ACKERMAN, Bruce A. (1983) "Law in an Activist State", 92 *Yale Law Journal* 1083.

ADAM, Gérard and Jean Daniel REYNAUD (1978) *Conflits du travail et changement social.* Paris: Presses Universitaires de France.

ASSMANN, Heinz Dieter (1980a) "Wirtschaftsrecht in der Mixed-Economy. Auf der Suche nach einem Sozialmodell für das Wirtschaftsrecht", in H.D. Assmann, G. Brüggemeier, D. Hart and Chr. Joerges, *Wirtschaftsrecht als Kritik des Privatrechts.* Königstein: Athenäum.

— (1980b) "Zur Steuerung gesellschaftlich-ökonomischer Entwicklung durch Recht", in H.D. Assmann, G. Brüggemeier, D. Hart and Chr. Joerges, *Wirtschaftsrecht als Kritik des Privatrechts.* Königstein: Athenäum.

ATHERTON, Wallace (1973) *Theory of Union Bargaining Goals.* Princeton: Princeton University Press.

BECKER, Friedrich (1984) "Commentaries to § 1, 9-12", in F. Becker, G. Etzel, H.W. Friedrich, K. Grüninger, W. Hillebrecht, F. Rost, H. Weigand, M. Wolf and I. Wolff, *Gemeinschaftskommentar zum Kündigungsschutzgesetz und sonstigen kündigungsschutzrechtlichen Vorschriften,* 2nd Ed. Neuwied, Darmstadt: Luchterhand.

BENÖHR, Hans-Peter (1977) "Wirtschaftsliberalismus und Gesetzgebung am Ende des 19. Jahrhunderts," 8 *Zeitschrift für Arbeitsrecht* 187.

— (1981) "Soziale Frage, Sozialversicherung und Socialdemokratische Reichstagsfraktion (1881-1889)", 98 *Zeitschrift der Savigny-Stiftung für Rechtsgeschichte. Germanistische Abteilung* 95.

BENOIT, Francis-Paul (1978) *La démocratie libérale.* Paris: Presses Universitaires de France.

BERGMANN, Joachim, Otto JACOBI and Walter MÜLLER-JENTSCH (1975) *Gewerkschaften in der Bundesrepublik.* Frankfurt, Köln: Europäische Verlagsanstalt.

BERNSTEIN, Irving (1950) *The New Deal Collective Bargaining Policy.* Berkeley: University of California Press.

BEYME, Klaus von (1977) *Gewerkschaften und Arbeitsbeziehungen in kapitalistischen Ländern.* München, Zürich: R. Piper & Co.

— (1979) "Der Neo-Korporatismus und die Politik des begrenzten Pluralismus in der Bundesrepublik", in J. Habermas (ed.), *Stichworte zur "Geistigen Situation der Zeit". 1: Nation und Republik.* Frankfurt: Suhrkamp.

BLANPAIN, Roger (1982) "Belgium," in *International Encyclopaedia for Labour Law and Industrial Relations.* Ell-Suppl. 29. Deventer: Kluwer.

Braun, Gérard (1981) "Le télétravail," in 7 *Droit Social* 569.
Bryner, Gary (1982) "Congress, Courts and Agencies: Equal Employment and the Limits of Policy Implementation," 96 *Political Science Quarterly* 411.
Bühler, Ottmar (1959) "Grundsätzliches zum Thema der 'Gesetzesinflation' und der 'aufgeblähten Verwaltung'," 14 *Juristenzeitung* 297.
Bundesanstalt für Arbeit (1978) *Überlegungen II zu einer vorausschauenden Arbeitsmarktpolitik*. Nürnberg: Bundesanstalt für Arbeit.
Clark, Jon, Heinz Hartmann, Christoph Lau and David Winchester (1980) *Trade Unions, National Politics and Economic Management: A Comparative Study of the TUC and the DGB*. London: Anglo-German Foundation.
Clark, Jon and Kenneth William Wedderburn (1983) "Modern Labour Law: Problems, Functions, and Policies," in K.W. Wedderburn, R, Lewis and J, Clark (eds.), *Labour Law and Industrial Relations: Building on Kahn-Freund*. Oxford: Clarendon Press.
Coen, Martin (1979) *Das Recht auf Arbeit und der Bestandsschutz des gekündigten Arbeitsverhältnisses*. Köln: Bund.
Commission of the European Communities (1982) *Report on Social Developments* Luxembourg: Office for Official Publications of the European Communities.
Cooper, George and Richard B. Solol (1969) "Seniority and Testing under Fair Employment Laws: a General Approach to Objective Criteria of Hiring and Promotion," 82 *Harvard Law Review* 1958.
Cooper, Martha R. (1982) *The Search for Consensus. The Role of Institutional Dialogue Between Government, Labour and Employers. The Experience of Five Countries*. Paris: OECD.
Couturier, G. (1975) "Les techniques civilistes et le droit du travail. Chronique d'humeur à partir de quelques idées reçues," *Dalloz* 1975 Chronique 151.
Cox, Archibald (1960) *Law and the National Labor Policy*. Los Angeles: University of California, Institute of Industrial Relations.
Cragg, A. and Dawson T. (1981) *Qualitative Research among Homeworkers*. London: Department of Employment, Research Paper No. 21.
Crouch, Colin (1979) *The Politics of Industrial Relations*. London: Fontana.
Damaska, Mirjan (1983) "Activism in perspective," 92 *Yale Law Journal* 1189.
Dübler, Wolfgang (1980) "Arbeitsbeziehungen und Recht in der Bundesrepublik — Eine Skizze," in *In Memoriam Sir Otto Kahn-Freund*. München: C.H. Beck.
Davies, Paul and Mark Freedland (1979) *Labour Law: Text and Materials*. London: Weidenfeld & Nicolson.
Dickens, Linda, Moira Hart, Michael Jones and Brian Weekes (1981) "Re-employment of Unfairly Dismissed Workers. The Lost Remedy," 3 *Industrial Relations Journal* 160.
Dorndorf, Eberhard (1979) *Freie Arbeitsplatzwahl und Recht am Arbeitsergebnis*. Baden-Baden: Nomos.
Drygala, Renate (1978) "Die soziale und rechtliche Situation der Heimarbeiter in der Bundesrepublik Deutschland," 33 *Blätter für Steuerrecht, Sozialversicherung und Arbeitsrecht* 356.
Dütz, Wilhelm (1976) "Soziale Mächtigkeit als Voraussetzung eines einheitlichen Koalitionsbegriffs?," 24 *Arbeit und Recht* 65.
Dunlop, John T. and Walter Galenson (eds.) (1978) *Labor in the Twentieth Century*. New York, San Francisco, London: Academic Press.
Ellermann-Witt, Rolf, Hubert Rottleuthner and Harald Russig (1983) (eds.) *Kündigungspraxis, Kündigungsschutz und Probleme der Arbeitsgerichtsbarkeit. Beiträge zur Regelung und Praxis in der Bundesrepublik Deutschland, in Grossbritannien und den USA*. Opladen: Westdeutscher Verlag.

Epstein, Richard A. (1983) "A Common Law for Labor Relations: A Critique of the New Deal Labor Legislation," 92 *Yale Law Journal* 1357.

Erd, Rainer (1978) *Verrechtlichung industrieller Konflikte. Normative Rahmenbedingungen des dualen Systems der Interessenvertretung.* Frankfurt, New York: Campus.

— (1982a) "Kündigungsschutz und Wirtschaftskrise," 15 *Kritische Justiz* 367.

— (1982b) "Die Modernisierung des Arbeitsrechts im korporatistischen Verbund," in U. Billerbeck, R. Erd, G. Jacobi and E. Schudlich (eds.), *Korporatismus und gewerkschaftliche Interessenvertretung.* Frankfurt, New York: Campus.

— (1983) "Gesetzgebung oder Machtpoker? Das Beispiel der amerikanischen Gewerkschaften," in R. Voigt (ed.), *Abschied vom Recht.* Frankfurt: Suhrkamp.

Erickson, Nancy S. (1979) "Equality between the Sexes in the 1980's," 28 *Cleveland State Law Review* 591.

European Foundation for the Improvement of Living and Working Conditions (1984) *Telework: Impact on Living and Working Conditions.* Dublin: Loughlinston House.

Falke, Josef, Armin Höland, Barbara Rhode and Gabriele Zimmermann (1981) *Kündigungspraxis und Kündigungsschutz in der Bundesrepublik Deutschland.* Bonn: Bundesminister für Arbeit und Sozialordnung.

Fechner, J.B. (1978) "Eignungsuntersuchungen für Schichtpersonal in Kernkraftwerken," *Atomwirtschaft* 74.

— (1980) "Schutzbarriere Mensch im Kernkraftwerk: Anforderungen aus der Sicht des Bundesministers des Inneren," *Atomwirtschaft* 299.

Feller, David E. (1973) "A General Theory of the Collective Bargaining Agreement," 61 *California Law Review* 663.

Flanagan, Robert J. (1983) "Workplace, Public Goods and Union Organizations," 22 *Industrial Relations* 224.

François, Lucien (1974) *Introduction au droit social.* Liège: Faculté de Droit.

Frankfurter Institut für Wirtschaftspolitische Forschung (F.I.W.F.) (eds.) (1984) *Mehr Mut zum Markt.* Bad Homburg: F.I.W.F.

Gagel, Alexander and Friedrich Jülicher (1979) *Arbeitsförderungsgesetz.* München: C.H. Beck.

Galenson, Walter and Robert S. Smith (1978) "The United States", in J.T. Dunlop and W. Galenson (eds.), *Labour in the Twentieth Century.* London, New York: Academic Press.

Gamillscheg, Franz and Peter Hanau (1974) *Die Haftung des Arbeitnehmers,* 2nd Ed. Karlsruhe: Verlag für Versicherungswirtschaft.

Getman, Julius G. and John D. Blackburn (1983) *Labor Relations,* 2nd Ed. Mineola, New York: The Foundation Press.

Getman, Julius G. and Pogrebin (1984) *Understanding Labor Law.* Manuscript.

Ghera, Edoardo (1982) "Mercato del lavoro: Prospettive di riforma," IV *Giornale di diritto del lavoro e di Relazioni Industriali* 607.

Gierke, Otto von (1895) *Handbuch des deutschen Privatrechts.* Vol. 1. München, Leipzig: Duncker & Humblot.

— (1902) *Das Wesen der menschlichen Verbände.* Berlin: Gustav Schade (Otto Francke).

Giugni, Gino (1979) *Diritto sindacale.* Bari: Cacucci.

— (1982) "Il diritto del lavoro negli anni '80," 4 *Giornale di Diritto del Lavoro e di Relazioni Industriali* 373.

Grewlich, Klaus W. (1984) "Introduction and Synthesis of Conference Results," in K.W. Grewlich and F. H. Pedersen (eds.), *Power and Participation in an Information Society.* Luxembourg: Commission of the European Communities.

Habermas, Jürgen (1981) *Theorie des kommunikativen Handelns.* Frankfurt: Suhrkamp.

— (1985) "Law as Medium and Law as Institution," in G. Teubner (ed.), *Dilemmas of Law in the Welfare State.* Berlin: de Gruyter.

HAKIM, C. and R. DENNIS (1982) *Homeworking in Wages Council Industries.* London: Department of Employment, Research Paper No. 37.

HART, Dieter and Christian JOERGES (1980) "Verbraucherrecht und Marktökonomik: Eine Kritik ordnungstheoretischer Eingrenzung der Verbraucherpolitik," in H.D. Assmann, G. Brüggemeier, D. Hart and Chr. Joerges, *Wirtschaftsrecht als Kritik des Privatrechts.* Königstein: Athenäum.

HASSELBALCH, Ole, Alan C. NEAL and Anders VICTORIN (1982) *A Perspective on Labour Law.* Stockholm, London, New York: Almquist & Wiksell, Sweet & Maxwell, Transnational Publishers.

HEINZE Rolf G., Karl HINRICHS, Claus OFFE and Thomas OLK (1981a) "Einheitsprobleme der Einheitsgewerkschaft. Überlegungen zum Zusammenhang von Arbeitsmarktmacht und organisationspolitischen Vertretungschancen verschiedener Kategorien von Arbeitnehmern," 32 *Soziale Welt* 19.

— (1981b) "Interessendifferenzierung und Gewerkschaftseinheit. Bruchlinien innerhalb der Arbeiterklasse als Herausforderung für gewerkschaftliche Politik," *Gewerkschaftliche Monatshefte* 336.

HEPPLE, Bob (1983) "Individual Labour Law," in G. Bain (ed.), *Industrial Relations in Britain.* Oxford: Blackwell.

HERSCHEL, Wilhelm (1960) "Die Betriebszugehörigkeit als geschütztes Rechtsgut," 13 *Recht der Arbeit* 121.

— (1977) "'Recht auf Arbeit' und Kündigungsschutz," 32 *Betriebsberater* 708.

HIMMELMANN, Gerhard (1983) "Öffentliche Bindung durch neokorporatistische Verhandlungssysteme?" in *Öffentliche Bindung von Unternehmen. Beiträge zur Regulierungsdebatte.* Baden-Baden: Nomos.

HOHMANN-DENNHARDT, Christine (1982) *Ungleichheit und Gleichberechtigung.* Heidelberg: C.F. Müller.

HOPPMANN, Erich (ed.), (1971) *Konzertierte Aktion. Kritische Beiträge zu einem Experiment.* Frankfurt: Athenäum.

HUG, Walther (1927) *Das Kündigungsrecht,* Vol. 2. Aarau: Sauerländer.

HUTCHINS, B. Leigh and Amy HARRISON (1926) *A History of Factory Legislation,* 3rd Ed. London: P.S. King & Son.

HUWS, Ursula (1984) "New technology homeworkers," *Employment Gazette* 13.

JACOBI, Otto (1982) "Industrielle Beziehungen und Korporatismus in der Bundesrepublik Deutschland," in U. Billerbeck, R. Erd, O. Jacobi and E. Schudlich (eds.), *Korporatismus und gewerkschaftliche Interessenvertretung.* Frankfurt, New York: Campus.

JAVILLIER, Jean-Claude (1980) "Dits et non dits sur le droit de travail," in *In Memoriam Sir Otto Kahn-Freund.* München: C.H. Beck.

— (1981) *Droit du travail,* 2nd Ed. Paris: Librairie Générale de Droit et de Jurisprudence.

JEAMMAUD, A. (1980) "Les fonctions du droit du travail," in F. Collin, R. Dhoquois, P.H. Goutierre, A. Jeammaud, G. Lyon-Caen and A. Foudil (eds.), *Le Droit capitaliste du travail.* Grenoble: Presses Universitaires.

JEDZIG, Joachim (1984) *Der Bestandsschutz des Arbeitsverhältnisses im Krankheitsfall.* Heidelberg: R. v. Decker's Verlag, G. Schenck.

KAHN-FREUND, Otto (1943) "Collective Agreements under War Legislation," 6 *Modern Law Review* 112.

— (1954) "Legal Framework," in A. Flanders and H.A. Clegg (eds.), *The System of Industrial Relations in Great Britain.* Oxford: Blackwell.

— (1959) "Labour Law," in M. Ginsberg (ed.), *Law and Opinion in England in the 20th century.* London: Stevens.
— (1968) *"Labour Law": Old Traditions and New Developments.* Toronto: Clark, Irwin.
— (1975) "The Industrial Relations Act 1971 — Some Retrospective Reflections," 4 *Industrial Law Journal* 186.
— (1976) "Hugo Sinzheimer (1875-1914)," in *Hugo Sinzheimer, Arbeitsrecht und Rechtssoziologie. Gesammelte Aufsätze und Reden,* Vol. 1. Frankfurt, Köln: Europäische Verlagsanstalt.
— (1979) *Labour Relations. Heritage and Adjustment.* Oxford: Oxford University Press.
— (1983) *Labour and the law,* 3rd Ed. P. Davies and M. Freedland (eds.), London: Stevens & Sons.
KARAKATSANIS, Alexandros (1982) "Skepsis ja to sistima ton sillogikon simvaseon ergasias me aformi kai to n. 1264/1982," 1 *Dikaio kai politiki* 97.
KENDIG, William L. (1978) *Age Discrimination in Employment.* New York: AMACOM.
KIRCHHEIMER, Otto (1928) "Zur Staatslehre des Sozialismus und Bolschewismus," 17 *Zeitschrift für Politik* 593.
KISSEL, Otto-Rudolf (1982) "Grenzen der rechtsprechenden Gewalt," 35 *Neue Juristische Wochenschrift* 1777.
KITCH, Edmund W. (1981), "Regulation and the American Common Market," in A. Tarlock (ed.), *Regulation, Federalism and Interstate Commerce.* Cambridge, Mass.: Oelschlaeger.
KITTNER, Michael and Axel BREINLINGER (1981) "Gewerkschaften und Recht," 2 *Zeitschrift für Rechtssoziologie* 53.
KORAL, Alan M. (1979/80) "Practical Application of the Uniform Guidelines: What to do 'Till the Agency Comes'," 5 *Employee Relations Law Journal* 473.
KRONBERGER KREIS (1983) Mehr Mut zum Markt. Frankfurter Institut für wirtschaftspolitische Forschung. Schriftenreihe vol. 1. Bad Homburg: Frankfurter Institut für wirtschaftspolitische Forschung.
KÜBLER, Friedrich (1969) "Kodifikation und Demokratie," 24 *Juristenzeitung* 645.
LEHR, Ursula (1984) *Psychologie des Alterns.* Heidelberg: Quelle & Meyer.
LEWIS, Roy (1976) "The Historical Development of Labour Law," 14 *British Journal of Industrial Relations* 1.
— (1978) "Nuclear Power and Employment Rights," 7 *Industrial Law Journal* 1.
— (1979a) "Collective Agreements: The Kahn-Freund Legacy," 42 *Modern Law Review* 613.
— (1979b) "Kahn-Freund and Labour Law: An Outline Critique," 8 *Industrial Law Journal* 202.
— (1983a) "Collective Labour Law," in G. Bain (ed.), *Industrial Relations in Britain.* Oxford: Blackwell.
— (1983b) "Method and Ideology in the Labour Law Writings of Otto Kahn-Freund," in K.W. Wedderburn, R. Lewis and J. Clark (eds.), *Labour Law and Industrial Relations: Building on Kahn-Freund.* Oxford: Clarendon Press.
LIEB, Manfred (1978) "Sonderprivatrecht für Ungleichgewichtslagen? Überlegungen zum Anwendungsbereich der sogenannten Inhaltskontrolle privatrechtlicher Verträge," 178 *Archiv für die civilistische Praxis* 196.
LUHMANN, Niklas (1981) *Politische Theorie im Wohlfahrtsstaat.* München, Wien: Olzog.
LYON-CAEN, Gérard (1973) "Négociation collective et législation d'ordre public," *Droit Social* 89.
MAYER-MALY, Theo (1969) *Rechtskenntnis und Geseztesflut,* München: Pustet.
MAYNTZ, Renate (1979) "Regulative Politik in der Krise?" in J. Matthes (ed.), *Sozialer Wandel in Westeuropa.* Frankfurt: Campus.

— (1980) "Die Implementation politischer Programme," in R. Mayntz (ed.), *Implementation politischer Programme.* Königstein: Athenäum.
— (1983) (ed.), *Implementation politischer Programme,* Vol. II. Opladen: Westdeutscher Verlag.
MELLISH, M. and N. COLLIS-SQUIRES (1976) "Legal and Social Norms in Discipline and Dismissal," 5 *Industrial Law Journal* 164.
MESTMÄCKER, Ernst-Joachim (1978) *Recht und ökonomisches Gesetz.* Baden-Baden: Nomos.
MEYERS, Frederick (1964) *Ownership of jobs: A Comparative Study.* Los Angeles: University of California, Institute of Industrial Relations.
MIDDLEMAS, Keith (1979) *The Politics in an Industrial Society.* London: André Deutsch.
MILKOVICH, George T. (1981) "The Male-Female Pay Gap: Need for Reevaluation," 104 *Monthly Labor Review,* 42.
MOCKENHAUPT, Ines-Maria (1984) "Gleicher Lohn für 'gleiche' Arbeit oder für 'vergleichbare' Arbeit," 15 *Zeitschrift Arbeitsrecht* 31.
MÜLLER-VOLBEHR, Jörg (1978) "Der Begriff des Sozialrechts im Wandel," 33 *Juristenzeitung* 249.
MURPHY, William P. (1968) "The National Labor Relations Board — An Appraisal," *Labor Law Developments* 113.
NEUMANN, Franz (1967) *Demokratischer und autoritärer Staat.* Frankfurt, Wien: Europäische Verlagsanstalt, Europa Verlag.
ORGANISATION FOR ECONOMIC CO-OPERATION AND DEVELOPMENT (OECD) (1975) *Socially responsible wage policies and inflation.* Paris: OECD.
OFFE, Claus (1979) "Die Institutionalisierung des Verbandseinflusses. Eine ordnungspolitische Zwickmühle," in U. von Alemann and R.G. Heinze (eds.), *Verbände und Staat. Vom Pluralismus zum Korporatismus.* Opladen: Westdeutscher Verlag.
OFFE, Claus and Karl HINRICHS (1977) "Sozialökonomie des Arbeitsmarktes und die Lage 'benachteiligter' Gruppen von Arbeitnehmern," in C. Offe (ed.), *Opfer des Arbeitsmarktes.* Neuwied, Darmstadt: Luchterhand.
OLSON, Margaret H. (1961) *New Information Technology and Organisational Culture.* New York: New York University, Center for Research on Information Systems.
— (1982) *Remote Office Work.* New York: New York, Center for Research on Information Systems.
PELS, P.S. (1966) "La coopération des organisations centrales d'employeurs et de travailleurs et la planification aux Pays-Bas," 94 *Revue Internationale du Travail* 313.
PEPER, Bram (1979) "Trade-offs and politicisation," in *Collective bargaining and government policies.* Paris: OECD.
POHL, Hans Joachim (1976) *Ältere Arbeitnehmer. Ursachen und Folgen der beruflichen Abwertung.* Frankfurt, New York: Campus.
POPLIN, Caroline (1975) "Fair Employment in a Depressed Economy: The Layoff Problem," 23 *University of California Law Review* 177.
POSNER, Richard A. (1977) *Economic Analysis of Law,* 2nd Ed. Boston, Toronto: Little, Brown and Company.
PREUSS, Ulrich K. (1979) *Die Internalisierung des Subjekts.* Frankfurt: Suhrkamp.
RAMM, Thilo (1977) "Die Arbeitsverfassung der Bundesrepublik Deutschland," 32 *Juristenzeitung* 1.
— (1978) "Probleme der Arbeitsverfassung," *Zeitschrift für Arbeitsrecht* 361.
REUTER, Dieter (1979) "Grundlagen des Kündigungsschutzes — Bestandsaufnahme und Kritik," in *25 Jahre Bundesarbeitsgericht.* München: C.H. Beck.
— (1982) "Reichweite und Grenzen der Legitimität des Bestandsschutzes von Arbeitsverhältnissen," 33 *Ordo* 165.

— (1983) "Gibt es eine arbeitsrechtliche Methode?" in *Festschrift M.L. Hilger und H. Stumpf*. München: C.H. Beck.

ROSENBAUM, Wolf (1982) "Die Wirkungen des Arbeitsrechts auf die Beziehungen zwischen Arbeitnehmern und Arbeitgebern im Betrieb," 10 *Leviathan* 392.

RÖTHERS, Bernd (1973) "Arbeitgeber und Gewerkschaften — Gleichgewicht oder Dominanz," 26 *Der Betrieb* 1649.

RUNGGALDIER, Ulrich (1983) *Kollektivvertragliche Mitbestimmung bei Arbeitsorganisation und Rationalisierung*. Frankfurt: Metzner.

RUSSIG, Harald (1982) "Sozialversicherungs- und arbeitsrechtliche Rahmenbedingungen für die Ausgliederung älterer und/oder leistungsgeminderter Arbeitnehmer aus dem Betrieb," in K. Dohse, U. Jürgens and H. Russig (eds) *Ältere Arbeitnehmer zwischen Unternehmensinteresse und Sozialpolitik*. Frankfurt, New York: Campus.

— (1983) "Anmerkungen zum Verhältnis von Kündigungsschutzdiskussion, betrieblicher Beschäftigungspolitik und arbeitsmarkttheoretischen Kontroversen," in R. Ellermann-Witt, H. Rottleuthner and H. Russig (eds.), *Kündigungspraxis, Kündigungsschutz und Probleme der Arbeitsgerichtsbarkeit*. Opladen: Westdeutscher Verlag.

SCHARPF, Fritz W. (1978) *Autonome Gewerkschaften und staatliche Wirtschaftspolitik: Probleme einer Verbändegesetzgebung*. Frankfurt: Otto Brenner Stiftung.

SCHLECHT, Otto (1968) *Konzertierte Aktion als Instrument der Wirtschaftspolitik*. Tübingen: J.C.B. Mohr (Paul Siebeck).

SCHMIDT, Folke (1977a) *Law and Industrial Relations in Sweden*. Stockholm: Almquist & Wiksell.

— (1977b) "From Socialism to Labourism," *Scandinavian Studies in Law* 243.

SCHOLZ, Rupert (1979) "Bundesarbeitsgericht und Arbeitsverfassung," in *25 Jahre Bundesarbeitsgericht*. München: C.H. Beck.

SCHUCK, Peter (1979) "The Graying of Civil Rights Law: The Age Discrimination Act of 1975," 89 *Yale Law Journal* 27.

SCHWÄGERL, Adolf (1982) "Beschäftigungssituation," 10 *Bundesarbeitsblatt* 19.

SCHWERDTNER, Peter (1977) "Die Garantie des Rechts auf Arbeit — Ein Weg zur Knechtschaft?" 8 *Zeitschrift für Arbeitsrecht* 47.

SEELAND, Rolf (1982) "Das Gleichberechtigungssystem in den USA und in den Mitgliedsstaaten der EG unter besonderer Berücksichtigung des Verhältnisses von Männern und Frauen im Arbeitsleben," 81 *Zeitschrift für vergleichende Rechtswissenschaft* 286.

SHIRLEY, S. (1979) "The remote control of projects". Presented at the Euro-IFIP Conference of the International Federation of Information Processors.

SIMITIS, Spiros (1970) *Informationskrise des Rechts und Datenverarbeitung*. Karlsruhe: C.F. Müller.

— (1978) "Sind im Interesse einer gerechteren Verteilung der Arbeitsplätze Begründung und Beendigung der Arbeitsverhältnisse neu zu regeln?" in *Verhandlungsberichte des 52. Deutschen Juristentages*, Wiesbaden 1978, Sitzungsbericht M. München: Beck.

— (1980) *Schutz von Arbeitnehmerdaten. Regelungsdefizite — Lösungsvorschläge*. Bonn: Bundesminister für Arbeit und Sozialordnung.

— (1983) "Zur Informationspflicht des Arbeitgebers. Einige rechtsvergleichende Bemerkungen zum Verhältnis von Arbeitgeber und Arbeitnehmervertretung," in *Ius inter nationes. Festschrift Stefan Riesenfeld*. Heidelberg, Karlsruhe: C.F. Müller.

SIMITIS, Spiros and Wilhelm RYGSZY (1984) *Von der Mitbestimmung zur staatlichen Administration: Arbeitsbedingungen bei riskanten Technologien*. Baden-Baden: Nomos.

SINZHEIMER, Hugo (1907) *Der korporative Arbeitsnormenvertrag*, Vol. 1. Leipzig: Duncker & Humblot.

— (1916) *Ein Arbeitstarifgesetz*. München, Leipzig: Duncker & Humblot.

— (1927) *Grundzüge des Arbeitsrechts*, 2nd ed. Jena: Gustav Fischer.
— (1976) "Der Tarifgedanke in Deutschland (1915)," in H. Sinzheimer, *Arbeitsrecht und Rechtssoziologie. Gesammelte Aufsätze und Reden*, Vol. 1. Frankfurt, Köln: Europäische Verlagsanstalt.
SOCIAL-ECONOMISCHE RAAD (1976) *Industrial Organisation under Public Law in the Netherlands.*
STEFFEN, Margaret and Friedrich-Hermann NIESTRATH (1977) "Die Ausgliederung älterer Arbeitnehmer aus dem Arbeitsmarkt — Individuelles Versagen oder gesellschaftliche Notwendigkeit?" in C. Offe (ed.), *Opfer des Arbeitsmarktes.* Neuwied, Darmstadt: Luchterhand.
STOFFAES, Christian (1979) "Le libéralisme jusqu'où?" 28 *Revue de l'entreprise et Revue de la formation permanente* 22.
STOLLEIS, Michael (1976) *Quellen zur Geschichte des Sozialrechts.* Göttingen: Musterschmidt.
STREECK, Wolfgang (1979) "Gewerkschaftsorganisation und industrielle Beziehungen," in J. Matthes (ed.), *Sozialer Wandel in Westeuropa.* Frankfurt: Campus.
— (1981) "Einheitsorganisation und Interessendifferenzierung — Anmerkungen zum Begriff der Vereinheitlichung," *Gewerkschaftliche Monatshefte* 354.
SUMMERS, Clyde W. (1976) "Individual protection against unjust dismissal: Time for a statute," 62 *Virginia Law Review* 480.
— (1977) "The Individual Employee's Rights under the Collective Agreement: What constitutes Fair Representation?", 126 *University of Pennsylvania Law Review* 251.
TAYLOR, George W. (1948) *Government Regulation of Industrial Relations.* New York: Prentice-Hall.
TESKE, Guido (1983) "Arbeitnehmer zweiter Klasse? Fachtagung der Betriebsräte in Kernenergieunternehmen," 29 *Die Mitbestimmung* 192.
TEUBNER, Gunther (1978) *Organisationsdemokratie und Verbandsverfassung.* Tübingen: J.C.B. Mohr (Paul Siebeck).
— (1979) "Neo-korporatistische Strategien rechtlicher Organisationssteuerung. Staatliche Strukturvorgaben für die gesellschaftliche Verarbeitung politischer Konflikte," 10 *Zeitschrift für Parlamentsfragen* 487.
— (1980) "Ordnungspolitische Optionen im Recht privater Organisationen," in W. Dettling (ed.), *Die Zähmung des Leviathan.* Baden-Baden: Nomos.
— (1983) "Substantive and Reflexive Elements in Modern Law" 17 *Law and Society Review* 239.
TEUBNER, Gunther and Helmut WILLKE (1980) "Dezentrale Kontextsteuerung im Recht intermediärer Verbände," in R. Voigt (ed.), *Verrechtlichung.* Königstein: Athenäum.
THOMAS, Clarence (1983) "Current Litigation. Trends and Goals at the EEOC," 34 *Labor Law Journal* 208.
TISSIER, A. (1904) *Le code civil et les classes ouvrières*, Vol. 1. Paris: Rousseau.
TRADES UNION CONGRESS (1974) *Annual Report.* London: Trades Union Congress.
— (1975) *Annual Report.* London: Trades Union Congress.
TRADES UNION CONGRESS AND THE GOVERNMENT (1979) *The Economy, the Government, and Trade Unions Responsibilities.* Joint Statement.
TREU, Tiziano (1979) "Comment on Peper's paper," in *Collective Bargaining and Government Policies.* Paris: OECD.
— (1983) "L'intervento del sindacato nella politica economica", 5 *Giornale di diritto del Lavoro e di Relazioni Industriali* 67.
TURNER, H.A., Grafield CLACK and Geoffrey ROBERTS (1967) *Labour relations in the Motor Industry: A Study of Industrial Unrest and an International Comparison.* London: Allen & Unwin.

Ulman, Lloyd (1955) *The Rise of the National Trade Union*. Cambridge, Mass.: Harvard University Press.
Untersehér, Lutz (1970) "Funktionen des gewerkschaftlichen Legalismus," 3 *Kritische Justiz* 141.
— (1972) "Arbeitsrecht — eine deutsche Spezialität," in O. Jacobi, W. Müller-Jentsch and E. Schmidt (eds.), *Gewerkschaften und Klassenkampf*. Kritisches Jahrbuch 1972. Frankfurt: S. Fischer.
Voigt, Rüdiger (1980) "Verrechtlichung in Staat und Gesellschaft," in R. Voigt (ed.), *Verrechtlichung*. Königstein: Athenäum.
— (1983) "Regulatives Recht im Wohlfahrtsstaat," in R. Voigt (ed.), *Abschied vom Recht*. Frankfurt: Suhrkamp.
Wälde, Thomas (1979) *Juristische Folgenorientierung*. Königstein: Athenäum.
Wedderburn, Kenneth William (1971) *The Worker and the Law*. 2nd ed. Harmondsworth: Penguin.
— (1978) "The New Structure of Labour Law in Britain," 13 *Israel Law Review* 435.
— (1983) "Otto Kahn-Freund and British Labour Law," in K.W. Wedderburn, R. Lewis and J. Clark (eds.), *Labour Law and Industrial Relations: Building on Kahn-Freund*. Oxford: Clarendon Press.
— (1984) "Current Directions in Labour Law," 1 *Arbetsrättliga uppsatser* 7.
Wellington, Harry H. (1968) *Labor and the legal process*. New Haven, London: Yale University Press.
Westermann, Harm Peter (1978) "Sonderprivatrechtliche Sozialmodelle und das allgemeine Privatrecht," 178 *Archiv für die civilistische Praxis* 150.
White, Richard (1982) "Community and Organisation," in K.W. Wedderburn and W.T. Murphy (eds.), *Labour Law and the Community. Perspectives for the 1980's*. London: University of London, Institute of Advanced Legal Studies.
Wiedemann, Herbert (1979) "Leistungsprinzip und Tarifvertragsrecht," in *25 Jahre Bundesarbeitsgericht*. München: C.H. Beck.
Wiethölter, Rudolf (1982a) "Entwicklung des Rechtsbegriffs," in V. Gessner and G. Winter (eds.), *Rechtsformen der Verflechtung von Staat und Wirtschaft*. Opladen: Westdeutscher Verlag.
— (1982b) *Materialisierungen und Prozeduralisierungen von Recht*. European University Institute. Florence, December 1982.
— (1985) "Materialization and Proceduralization in Modern Law," in G. Teubner (ed.), *Dilemmas of Law in the Welfare State*. Berlin: de Gruyter.
Windmuller, John P. (1969) *Labor relations in the Netherlands*. Ithaca: Cornell University Press.
Wlotzke, Otfried (1974) "Neuerungen im gesetzlichen Arbeitsrecht", 27 *Der Betrieb* 2254.
Wolf, Manfred (1984) "Allgemeine Grundsätze des Kündigungsrechts und des Kündigungsschutzrechts," in F. Becker, G. Etzel, H.W. Friedrich, K. Gröninger, W. Hillebrecht, F. Rost, H. Weigand, M. Wolf and I. Wolff, *Gemeinschaftskommentar zum Kündigungsschutzgesetz und sonstigen kündigungsschutzrechtlichen Vorschriften*, 2nd ed. Neuwied, Darmstadt: Luchterhand.
Wolfgang, Marvin E. (ed.) (1978) "Planning for the Elderly," 193 *The Annals of the American Academy of Political and Social Science* 1.
Woll, Arthur (1983) *Das Ende der Stabilitätspolitik*. Tübingen: J.C.B. Mohr (Paul Siebeck).
Youngdahl, James E. (1975) "How can Seniority, Antidiscrimination and Affirmative Action be reconciled in a Layoff Economy: The Union Viewpoint," 28 *New York University Conference on Labor* 297.

ZACHER, Hans F. (1974) *Materialien zum Sozialgesetzbuch. Die Entwürfe der Bundesregierung und die Verhandlungen des Bundestages mit einer Einführung*. Percha: R.S. Schulz.
— (1976) "Grundfragen theoretischer und praktischer sozialrechtlicher Arbeit," 4 *Vierteljahresschrift für Sozialrecht* 1.
— (1977) "Vorfragen zu den Methoden der Sozialrechtsvergleichung," in H.F. Zacher (ed.), *Methodische Probleme des Sozialrechtsvergleichs*. Berlin: Duncker & Humblot.
ZÖLLNER, Wolfgang (1976) "Privatautonomie und Arbeitsverhältnis," 176 *Archiv für die civilistische Praxis* 221.

Juridification — a Universal Trend? The British Experience in Labor Law

Jon Clark and Lord Wedderburn
Southampton LSE, London

Contents

1. Introduction: The 'Universality' Thesis and the Case of Britain

Juridification is not a term which readily comes to mind when one thinks of British industrial relations or of the literature upon them. As Spiros Simitis has stated that "juridification is frequently seen as the main feature distinguishing the Continental European from the British regulation of industrial relations[4]. Great Britain is in fact considered as more or less the only country which is largely immune from juridification" (Simitis, supra 115)[1]. The system of industrial relations in Britain, above all during its so-called 'golden age' (1906 to 1963, or, more broadly, 1871 to 1971), is generally viewed as one where voluntary procedural regulation and collective autonomy predominated over state regulation (see Kahn-Freund, 1959). In historical terms, collective autonomy was to a large extent the product of struggle by the (predominantly industrial) labor movement. In sociological terms, the rules governing employment were determined by the social and economic power of employers (capital), modified by the collective social power of trade unions (organized labor) and by voluntary collective bargaining.

In contrast to most other democratic societies, the basic cornerstones of British industrial relations were not established as positive legal or constitutional *rights*, but as negative *immunities* or *freedoms* from legal restraints and liabilities (freedom to organize, to bargain, and to strike). In addition, 'regulatory legislation' was confined traditionally to areas not thought to be readily susceptible to collective bargaining, e.g. health and safety, or where collective bargaining was weak, e.g. minimum wage legislation (see Kahn-Freund, 1977: 24f.; Wedderburn, 1971: 314, 326f.; Wedderburn, 1983: 37). 'Auxiliary legislation' promoting collective bargaining and employee representation at the workplace was also relatively underdeveloped (see Kahn-Freund, 1977: 45-7). All these factors seemed only to reinforce the view that Britain was a deviant case as far as juridification was concerned.

Simitis does not share this view. In his paper he argues that British industrial relations in the 1980s are no longer 'immune' from juridification, if they ever were. Industrialization excludes alternatives he insists, (Simitis, supra: 115), and the process of juridification of industrial relations is a universal tendency in all democratic industrial societies. "Hence, labor relations have developed in Great Britain as well as in any other country, under the constant impact of 'the one undubitably fundamental and irreversible trend is the ever-increasing extent of the legal regulation of ... industrial relations'[2]. The long road from the Factory Act of 1833 to the Employment Act of 1982 is a single confirmation of progressive juridification". (Simitis, supra 115).

In this paper it will be argued that the volatile and uneven development of British labor law and industrial relations does not in fact represent a "single confirmation of progressive juridification". Instead, the development of juridification, even since the late 1960s, will be shown to be much more contradictory, complex and open than suggested, and to have been at times a reversible process. Before attempting this, however, it is necessary to clarify what is meant by the term juridification, and to outline a detailed strategy for applying it to industrial relations and labor law in both a national and comparative framework. It is hoped that the development of such a general framework will make a contribution to comparative analysis as well as provide the basis for an empirical study of the juridification of industrial relations in one country.

[1] At certain points, reference will be made to the more extended German version of this paper, which will be cited as Simitis (1984). For a critical discussion of the German version, see Clark (1985a).

[2] This is a quotation by Simitis from Lewis (1976: 15). For a different view, see Clark and Wedderburn (1983: esp. 184-91); also Kahn-Freund (1977: 46 n. 55).

2. Juridification: Definitions, Conditions, Effects

2.1 Definitions

Juridification can be defined as a process (or processes) by which the state intervenes in areas of social life (industrial relations, education, family, social welfare, commerce) in ways which limit the autonomy of individuals or groups to determine their own affairs. In the most general terms, it is about the relation between state and society, and the balance between their relative influence on the way human beings conduct their lives. All juridification involves state intervention, but not all state intervention necessarily involves juridification. It is thus possible to envisage state intervention which decreases the influence of the state and increases the autonomy of particular individuals and groups. It will be argued below that this is exactly what happened in 1974 in Britain in the field of collective bargaining and trade union activity, with the repeal of the 1971 Industrial Relations Act and the passing of the Trade Union and Labour Relations Act.

This distinction between the concepts of juridification and state intervention will be crucial to the analysis of British industrial relations and labor law to be carried out below. However, this general definition of juridification requires further elaboration before it can be applied empirically. A useful starting point in this respect is Voigt's assertion, quoted approvingly by Simitis, that juridification is concerned with the "conditions for, and limits of, the effectiveness of the law as a steering mechanism" (Voigt, 1983: 20). In the next section we shall outline some of the most important *conditions* which influence the process and extent of juridification of industrial relations in Britain, and this will be followed by an examination of some of the problems involved in evaluating its *effects*.

2.2 Conditions

In a comparative discussion of what he called "the borderline between legislation and collective bargaining" (Kahn-Freund, 1977: 38f.), Otto Kahn-Freund suggested five main factors which might explain the particular location of this "borderline" in different countries. Slightly adapted and extended, these factors provide a conceptual focus for investigating the conditions for the development of the process of juridification of industrial relations:

— industrialization (pace and volume)
— political and economic history (national and international)
— constitutional system (relation of labor law to basic constitutional or statutory rights, and to other areas of 'social law')
— trade unions (history and political allegiance)
— collective bargaining (structure and scope)

This is not the place to apply these factors in detail, but such a 'checklist' does enable us to pinpoint the main choices open to us in analyzing the conditions for the development of juridification.

In Simitis' paper, industrialization is quite clearly the most important, indeed the overriding, factor in explaining the 'universal' trend toward juridification. While he admits that juridification may take different forms and proceed irregularly and at different paces, his fundamental argument is that these differences become less significant as industrialization progresses. His programmatic statement "Industrialization excludes alternatives" (Simitis, supra 115) seems to suggest that the primary condition which determines the extent and process of juridification is the advance of industrialization.

In contrast, those (like Kahn-Freund) who have argued that the main difference between industrial relations in Britain and in continental Europe is the relative lack of juridification in Britain, have tended to attach equal if not greater weight to the other factors. These include the fact that in Britain the industrial revolution preceded the extension of the franchise to the working class, and that the trade unions were founded and legally recognized long before they developed any significant degree of political organization and representation (see Kahn-Freund, 1977: 39f.; Wedderburn, 1980: 65, 66-75; also Fox, 1985: 161-4, 433-5). Even the great quantitative increase in British labor legislation since 1963 is explained by Kahn-Freund as much in terms of political and social developments in Britain as by economic changes and advancing industrialization.

These matters, particularly developments in British labor law since 1963, will be examined in more detail below. What is important here is to outline a conceptual focus for analysis, to establish the multiplicity of causal factors which might shape the process and extent of juridification, and to note that Simitis has suggested that one of the factors, industrialization, provides the key to explaining what he believes to be a universal trend toward juridification.

2.3 Effects

Juridification cannot simply be measured by pointing out the quantitative increase in legal regulation ('more law') or the fact that the law has become increasingly complex ('more complex law'). An adequate assessment of the extent of juridification also requires some qualitative judgment as to the *effects* of the law (on this point see also Simitis, supra 119 ff.). The strategy being advanced in this paper for examining this question involves distinguishing between the effects of legal regulation at various levels and in different areas of industrial relations, and examining these separately. The overall nature and extent of juridification can then be assessed by weighing up the relative importance of these different levels and areas for the conduct of industrial relations as a whole.

There are at least three levels at which the effects of legal regulation on industrial relations might be examined: the level of public policy, the 'symbolic' level, and the level of day-to-day industrial relations. The term 'public policy' covers such widely differing areas as government policy and legislation, the judiciary, the policy of political parties and pressure groups, the debate in the mass media, and 'public opinion'. The question to be addressed here is to what extent policy and practice regarding industrial relations in these areas has been 'juridified'. In the 'golden age' when collective labor relations developed with immunity from common law regulation in Britain (1906 to the 1960s), there was widespread, if never complete, acceptance at the level of public policy that the law, and particularly the courts (see Wedderburn, 1980; also Clark and Wedderburn, 1983: 166-73), should play only a secondary role in industrial relations[3]. Whilst for much of its existence "the traditional framework of British labor law really rested upon a middle-class acquiescence in the current balance of industrial power" (Wedderburn, 1972: 270, 275), it was only towards the end of this period that any political party or pressure group in Britain advocated major changes in the largely non-interventionist framework of industrial relations[4].

From the end of the 1950s, there were growing signs that public policy might be changing, but the first major break to result in legislation came in 1971 with the explicit commitment of the newly elected Conservative government that the law was to be the 'main instrument' in a fundamental reform of industrial relations (for further details see Clark and Wedderburn, 1983: 127f.). This was a clear example of the juridification of public policy toward industrial relations in Britain, but it should be stressed that, in itself, this says little or nothing about the effects of Conservative party policy and legislation on the day-to-day conduct of industrial relations at the occupational level. In fact there is strong evidence that the effects of the legislation at this level were extremely limited (see Weekes *et al.*, 1975; Thomson and Engleman, 1975).

Before we go on to discuss the question of the effects of legal regulation at this level, we should perhaps mention the effects of state intervention at the ideological or 'symbolic' level, since this provides a bridge between public policy and the day-to-day conduct of industrial relations. A good example of the effect of the law at this level relates to developments in Britain since 1979 (see on this Clark, 1985; Wedderburn, 1985). In the months preceding the general election of 1979, certain forms of trade union activity in Britain (picketing, 'secondary action', the closed shop, and 'political' strikes) were heavily criticized by the Conservative party, and became central issues in the election campaign which led to the defeat of the Labour government in May 1979. In other words, labor legislation was part of a 'populist' strategy which identified trade unions as one of the primary causes of Britain's industrial

[3] The exceptions to this rule were during the two World Wars, and between 1927 and 1946 in respect of the rights of civil servants to organize and strike.

[4] The first major post-war proposals of this kind were in *A Giant's Strength*, a document produced by the Inns of Court Conservative and Unionist Society in 1958. After the General Strike of 1926, the Conservative Party Prime Minister Stanley Baldwin had rejected employers' calls for overall regulation of the unions. See on this point Fox (1985): "The most significant aspect of the episode (the 1926 strike) was the way it revealed the continued predominance on both sides of those forces and traditions that were anxious to contain, rather than bid up, class conflict" (p. 334).

weakness, and which built on undoubted widespread public opposition to certain contemporary examples of trade union action. In these circumstances the government needed to be seen to enact legislation limiting the freedom to picket, even if in practice the effect of the new legal regulations proved to be by no means as strong as expected or intended.

This wider ideological importance of trade union legislation is well captured in the following passage taken from an empirical study of the effects of the picketing sections of the 1980 Employment Act: "Few of the managers we spoke to expected the law would have any direct effect... Nevertheless, it was essentially a popular piece of legislation, and to the extent that it met a felt need it had already worked at one level ... we noted a psychological gratification on the part of the managers that at last a government was 'on their side'. It was, many said, an encouragement to take control of the reins more vigorously. In a small way it was a reinforcement of the managers' 'right to manage'" (Kahn *et al.*, 1983: 193)[5]. As the authors of this study went on to argue, this type of psychological or symbolic effect of labor legislation is extremely difficult to measure. However, it does clearly constitute 'juridification' of industrial relations, which is related to but somehow distinct from the other levels.

The third, and probably the most crucial, level at which the effects of legal regulation need to be assessed is that of the day-to-day conduct of industrial relations by employers, employees and their representatives. In sociological terms, the question being addressed here is how far the social behavior and values of the actors in industrial relations are shaped by legal norms, and whether it is possible to discern a secular trend toward the juridification of the rules and processes governing the employment relationship. These issues will be discussed in detail in the third section of this paper.

This leads us directly to the question of the effects of the law on *different areas of industrial relations*, such as collective bargaining, health and safety, dismissal and trade union organization. This issue will also be discussed in the third section of the paper. At this stage, it is important to note the need for a separate analysis of different areas of industrial relations and the different legal forms, substantive provisions, and remedies which apply to them. The remedies are perhaps particularly important, since they frequently determine the concrete effect which the law is likely to have. Simitis, for example, suggests four main forms or methods of juridification: statutory regulation, administrative regulation, judicial decision, and 'indirect steering' (Simitis, supra 121 ff.). He also distinguishes between collective and individual labor law, between substantive and procedural regulation, and between different sanctions and remedies. We shall argue below that the different legal forms, substantive provisions, and remedies applying to different areas of industrial relations are highly relevant to any evaluation of the process and extent of

5 This book provides extensive evidence of the difference between the law as stated and the law as perceived by workers, unions and employers.

juridification, as is the relative importance of different areas for the system of industrial relations as a whole.

This last point deserves special emphasis. It will be argued below that the area of state intervention in collective bargaining is so fundamental to the system of industrial relations in democratic industrial societies, or at any rate in Britain, that it should be a more weighty indicator of the trend toward juridification than, say, the effects of legal intervention on unfair dismissal. An overall qualitative assessment of the extent of the juridification of industrial relations requires not only a separate analysis of different levels and areas of state intervention, but an evaluation of the relative importance of these different levels and areas for each industrial relations system as a whole. One small section of one Act of Parliament may be qualitatively more important than hundreds of pages of regulations.

3. British Industrial Relations and Labor Law: Contradictory Trends

In this section of the paper, a number of issues will be discussed which have a direct bearing on the question of the juridification of industrial relations in Britain. Where possible an attempt will be made to examine particular questions in the context of more general problems of juridification.

3.1 The State and Autonomy: the Legalization of Trade Unions and Collective Bargaining

In a crucial section of his paper, Spiros Simitis discusses the juridification of industrial relations via what he calls the 'indirect steering' of industrial relations by the state (see Simitis, supra 122). By this he means the recognition and guaranteeing by the state of 'autonomous' or social methods of regulation, of which the most important example is the collective agreement. Simitis argues that collective bargaining in most industrialized countries was initially developed outside the legal system. In fact in most cases it was initially illegal. When it was 'legalized', however, Simitis suggests that the relationship between the state and collective bargaining was fundamentally changed. In essence he asserts that the legalization of collective bargaining integrates the collective agreement into a wider system of rules determined by state intervention.

He cites as a classic expression of this process of juridification the National Labor Relations Act (1935) in the U.S., which sees institutionalized collective bargaining as a guarantee of the effective functioning of the labor market. In addition, the Act imposes on the employer a duty to bargain if this is demanded by organized labor, and lays down the issues about which bargaining must take place in such circumstances.

For Simitis (supra 123) this is an example of the state 'instrumentalizing' collective bargaining by employers and trade unions and using it as a means to its own end. In legalizing bargaining the state delegates to employers and employees the right and obligation to determine working conditions by collective agreement. Simitis calls this a policy of 'calculated autonomy' (Simitis, supra 123), in which the state affirms self-determination and self-regulation on the one hand, and on the other ties it into the system of rules governing the labor market which it (the state) has determined.

Simitis recognizes that this process of indirect steering takes different forms in different countries such as Sweden, the U.S. and West Germany, and stresses in particular the importance of this form of juridification for West German industrial relations. However, despite recognizing differences between different countries, Simitis implies that the policy of 'calculated autonomy' is common to all industrialized countries and is an important example of juridification.

How far does this analysis apply to Britain? The first approach to this question is at the level of historical and legal analysis. Historically, of course, there is no legally or constitutionally guaranteed right to organize, to bargain, or to strike in Britain, nor does the state place a duty to bargain on the employer or define the issues about which bargaining must take place. The legal framework of collective bargaining and trade union activity in Britain was established between 1871 and 1906 in the form of a series of immunities from certain criminal and civil liabilities and from common law doctrines such as 'restraint of trade' and 'inducing breach of contract'[6]. In this respect the form and substance of legal provisions serve to underline the relation between the state and autonomy in the development of this crucial area of industrial relations. The legalization of collective bargaining and trade unions in Britain was not so much 'granted' or 'guaranteed' by the state, as conceded under pressure from various social and political forces, particularly the trade unions themselves. To this extent, the state could be said to have ratified a kind of 'historical compromise'.

This process can now be seen as part of a seamless web of British (especially English) social history in the nineteenth century. When "working people" felt that they had "erected their unions by themselves" (Phelps Brown, 1983: 47) they were appealing both to the historical fact of struggle and to the social myth of 'freedom' strongly entrenched in the *laissez faire* legends of their society. The 'organic relationship' between law and collective bargaining fashioned in this British formative period reflected, in particular, the nature of its labor movement, surely always a critical factor, at least in Western Europe (see Wedderburn, 1980: 65, 69-79). The addition of the 'new' unionism to the 'old' in the 1880s and 1890s made Britain's unionism unique, not least because on the continent trade unionism developed simultaneously with the mass political labor movement and its parties (see Hobsbawm, 1984: 152-3).

6 See on this point Wedderburn (1983): "Statutes of 1875 and 1906 decreed ... that ... liabilities based upon combination, economic pressure, and consequent interference with contracts shall not apply to acts done 'in contemplation or furtherance of a trade dispute', the golden formula of British Labour law" (p. 38).

The compromise was all part of a process of 'mutual accomodation', in which "the failure of certain patterns of political thought and vocabulary to take root in British industrial and political relations" derived less from "intellectual *naïveté* or an inability to grasp complex foreign ideas", than from "the fact that they have not had functional usefulness for its practitioners" (Fox, 1985: 164 and *passim*)[7]. After all, at the very moment when the non-interventionist system was to be confirmed by the Trade Disputes Act of 1906, there were influential voices which advocated the importation of the most legally regulated systems then known in industrialized countries, those of New Zealand and Australia[8]. In fact, it was exactly in this period (1890-1906), during which industrial relations in Australia leapt from crude, often violent, adversarial 'voluntarism' straight to a highly legalistic system of obligatory conciliation and arbitration[9], that Britain contemporaneously jettisoned compulsory arbitration in favor of a 'voluntary' role for the Board of Trade[10].

Indeed, the Australian perspective is helpful in more general terms. Because trade unions there were seen "as being part of a set of systems of compulsory arbitration", they also came to be "seen as existing primarily to serve public purposes" with only a "quasi-autonomy" in relation to the state (see Rawson, 1982: 2-3). That was not the case with British unions, nor it seems with other European unions. In fact, the specific historical-legal analysis of British labor law raises a more fundamental question about the legal recognition of collective bargaining and trade union activity in countries apart from Britain. Is there any logical or historical reason why the legal or constitutional *recognition* of these activities should necessarily imply that the freedom to bargain and join a trade union has somehow been *granted* by the state? To adopt this view would be to suggest that collective bargaining and trade unions in advanced industrial societies always receive their legitimacy ultimately from the state, and not primarily from the individuals, groups, and social classes who participate in them.

7 Fox (1985: 164 and *Passim*). Others speak of these developments as "the politics of class collaboration, inaugurated by franchise reform and favourable labour legislation". Gore (1982: 50).

8 For example, Webb (1906: 18). There was by then a long history of proposals for compulsory, or semi-compulsory, arbitration in industrial disputes: see Amulree (1929). However, the tide had turned in favor of essentially 'voluntary' methods after the ineffective Councils of Conciliation Act 1867 (Lord St. Leonard's Act).

9 Once again, a critical factor was the "distinctive political development of the Australian labour movement". Turner (1979: 16-17) and Creighton, Ford and Mitchell (1983: 5-9).

10 With reference to the passing of the Conciliation and Arbitration Act of 1896, Phelps Brown writes: "So it was decided that British industrial relations were to consist of voluntary negotiations between employers and employees". Phelps Brown (1959: 187). See too Wedderburn and Davies (1969).

3.2 The Juridification of Collective Bargaining (1971-79)? : "The Most Interventionist Intervention is Non-intervention" (Talleyrand)

A comparison between two recent short periods in the development of British industrial relations illustrates most clearly the need for a number of the conceptual distinctions outlined in the second part of this paper. The contrast between the period of the Industrial Relations Act (from 1971 to 1974) and the 'Social Contract' labor legislation shows in particular the crucial importance of distinguishing between state intervention and juridification, between juridification at different levels (public policy, ideology, day-to-day industrial relations) and in different areas (collective bargaining, trade union organization, employment protection, such as protection from unfair dismissal), and between different legal forms, substantive provisions and remedies. Many of these issues will be taken up in the next section of this paper, which examines different dimensions of juridification in a wider historical perspective. In this section we shall concentrate on collective bargaining, an area which we have suggested above is central to any assessment of the juridification of industrial relations systems as a whole.

We have already noted that the Conservative government which was elected to office in 1970 immediately announced its intention of radically changing the entire system of British industrial relations, with the law as the 'main instrument' of reform. The provisions of the Industrial Relations Act (1971) have been analyzed in detail elsewhere, and need not be summarized here (see Clark and Wedderburn, 1983: 131-5, 199-201; Simpson and Wood, 1973; Weekes *et al.*, 1975; Thomson and Engleman, 1975). In the field of collective bargaining law, the Act represented a "radical break with the tradition of free voluntary collective bargaining" (Kahn-Freund, 1972: 123), and a break with the public policy tradition of support for voluntary collective negotiation in the public and private sectors which went back to the beginning of the century and had been given all party support in the Whitley Committee Reports (1917-19)[11]. Under the 1971 Act the collective agreement, previously binding in honor only, was presumed to be a legally enforceable contract, unless the parties expressly agreed that it was not intended to be so. The Act also introduced into British industrial relations a range of statutorily defined "unfair industrial practices", and employers were "in effect invited to use the law as a tactic in industrial disputes with the object of securing restraining orders and financial compensation" (Clark and Wedderburn, 1983: 133-4) in actions before a newly established National Industrial Relations Court. Legal remedies open to the Court included not only injunctions and damages, but the imposition (on application from the government) of 'national emergency' cooling-off procedures and strike ballots, supplemented by the application of

[11] Cf. Wedderburn (1971): "The original Whitley Committee of 1916 inaugurated a new era of voluntary joint negotiation, in both the civil service and industry. Seventy-three Joint Industrial Councils were set up between 1918 and 1921" (p. 102).

quasi-criminal sanctions for contempt of court in cases where individuals or organizations refused to obey the Court's orders.

In the area of collective bargaining, then, this legislation marked a major qualitative increase in the juridification of industrial relations *at the level of public policy*, as represented by Conservative party policy and positive (statute) law. With one or two exceptions, however, the effect of the legislation on day-to-day industrial relations was small. As Kahn-Freund wrote, "the provisions of the 1971 Act on the legal enforcement of collective agreements as contracts were a complete failure. They were resisted by the unions and not supported by management. They had no effect on the improvement of labour relations at all" (Kahn-Freund, 1977: 131). In this particular case, it was not industrialization which was the main factor shaping the process and extent of juridification of industrial relations at a concrete level, but trade union action bolstered by employer acquiescence in, and even positive support for, the traditional system of voluntary collective bargaining. As a result, the 1971 Law as it applied to collective agreements became discredited. It should perhaps also be stressed at this point that attempts between 1972 and 1974 to control autonomous wage bargaining by an 'incomes policy' directly established by legislation failed, as under the Labour government between 1966 and 1969, to take over the voluntarist structures of British labor law[12].

To summarize the argument so far, state intervention in collective bargaining in Britain was greatly intensified during the period of the 1970-74 Conservative government. This led to a significant increase in the extent of juridification of collective bargaining at the level of public policy, but there was no significant increase in the juridification of collective bargaining at the level of day-to-day industrial relations.

One of the first acts of the Labour Party after its return to government in March 1974 was to 'intervene' to restore the traditional non-interventionist framework of voluntary collective bargaining which had governed most of British industrial relations since 1906 and before. In many ways, this involved bringing public policy back into line with the reality of day-to-day industrial relations. The state intervened to recognize or sanction a 'non-juridified'

[12] It is in fact true that all British governments from 1948 to 1979 pursued fiscal and social policies that can be thought of as within the *genus* of Keynesian 'incomes policy', and it has been suggested recently that more attention should be paid to the effect of those central governmental concerns upon labor law. See Davies and Freedland (1983: 3-10). Whilst incomes policy had its effect upon 'public policy', however, the remarkable fact emerges that incomes policy never took over the 'voluntarist' structures of British labor law, even in those periods (1966-69, 1972-74) when wages were controlled by norms directly established under legislation. Indeed, the 'auxiliary legislation' found in these structures was used to render areas of bargaining immune to incomes policy norms. See Wedderburn (1984: 74-78). Despite the anxiety, even obsession, with inflation in these decades, incomes policy law could not swallow up labor law. In 1979, of course, both traditional labor law policy and interventionist incomes policy were (ostensibly) disavowed by government.

system of negotiating, concluding and enforcing collective agreements (on the Social Contract legislation in general, see Clark and Wedderburn, 1983: 184-98).

In two ways, therefore, the 1974 legislation (Trade Union and Labour Relations Act) on collective agreements represented a 'de-juridification' of industrial relations compared with the 1971 Act. First, at the level of public policy, it represented a clear rejection of the juridified framework of collective bargaining advanced by the Conservative government of 1970-74 and enshrined in statute law. Second, it restored one of the central aspects of industrial relations systems (collective agreements) to voluntary social regulation. When this is taken together with other provisions in the 1974-76 legislation which restored, and even strengthened, trade union freedoms in areas such as the closed shop and the scope of lawful strike action, there appears to be powerful evidence in support of the view that the Social Contract labor legislation reaffirmed the non-interventionist voluntary framework of the industrial relations system as a whole.

This view is in some contrast to that of Spiros Simitis, who states: "If measured against its own objective of removing industrial relations from state control, the Social Contract was a failure. Juridification has not decreased, but significantly increased" (Simitis, supra 140). There appear to be three possible reasons for this difference in interpretation, two of which relate directly to the evaluation of the Social Contract against its own objectives[13].

First, there is a tendency, particularly in the German version of the paper (see Simitis, 1984: 135ff.), to apply the term juridification in the case of the Social Contract to any intervention of the state which involves some kind of legal regulation of industrial relations, however 'non-interventionist' this might be. In an important section of the German paper, Simitis argues that, even where the task of the 1974 legislation was to "reverse the process of juridification" enshrined in the 1971 Act (i.e. in the areas of collective bargaining and trade union law), it nevertheless led "in reality" to the establishment of a legally regulated system of industrial relations in Britain which was "just as guaranteed" (Simitis, 1984: 138) by the state as in 1971. Here the terms 'state intervention' and 'juridification' appear to be used synonymously.

The second main reason that Simitis advances to support his view that there was an increase in juridification under the Social Contract relates to the whole range of other areas of industrial relations which became regulated by law in the 1974-78 period. While it is undoubtedly true that the legislation of 1974-78 initiated a great increase in statute law in a number of areas, it cannot necessarily be concluded that these new statutory provisions 'juridified' British industrial relations in an unambiguous fashion. In fact, although it is sometimes suggested that there has been a major increase in the legal regulation of

13 The third, and important, reason relates to the 'corporatist' tendencies within the Social Contract, its 'intensification' of the division between union leaders and members, and the increasing tendency of the state to intervene in the internal affairs of trade unions to protect individual union members from abuse by their leaders.

British industrial relations since the mid-1960s, the period from 1942 to 1962 also shows a significant, if not quite so great, increase in the number of labor law statutes (see Appendix for list of statutes). As before, the argument being advanced in this paper is that it is the type of law and its effect at various levels that matters.

Nevertheless, both in its own terms and in its impact on collective industrial relations, Simitis hypothesizes that the Social Contract legislation in areas such as unfair dismissal, maternity, health and safety, discrimination, and conciliation and arbitration, was all part of a clear trend toward the juridification of British industrial relations (Simitis, 1984: 138). This hypothesis will now be examined by looking at some of these areas in more detail.

3.3. Dimensions of Juridification: History, Form, Substance and Remedy

(1) Unfair Dismissal and the System of Industrial Tribunals

The history of industrial tribunals and unfair dismissal legislation in Britain seems to confirm the thesis of a growing trend toward the juridification of industrial relations. Until 1964 there were no separate labor courts or industrial tribunals in Britain, but by the mid-1980s such institutions were receiving around 30,000 complaints a year about disputes on "a wide range of statutory rights mainly across the spectrum of individual employment protection law" (Clark and Wedderburn, 1983: 176), including redundancy, unfair dismissal, itemized pay statements, guarantee payments, employer's action short of dismissal, rights to time off, maternity rights, sex and race discrimination, equal pay, health and safety notices, safety representatives' rights, questions relating to occupational pension schemes, and (after 1980) exclusion or expulsion from trade unions. Most of these rights were first granted under the Social Contract legislation[14], although rights on unfair dismissal, which normally account for around 80% of complaints received, were first introduced in the Industrial Relations Act of 1971[15].

This significant extension of employment protection rights represented clearly a qualitative increase in the juridification of industrial relations at the level of public policy (see on this, and more generally, Dickens *et al.*, 1985: 252-55). But to assert that this also entailed a qualitative increase in juridification of industrial relations more generally, it would be necessary to demonstrate two further things. First, that behavior, attitudes and outcomes in cases affected by these new rights were now likely to be determined more by reference to the law than by traditional 'voluntary' methods, such as collective

[14] For a more detailed examination of the development of the industrial tribunal system in Great Britain, see Clark and Wedderburn (1983: 173-84).

[15] In fact, the vast majority of trade union members of industrial tribunals boycotted them between 1971 and 1974 as an expression of their hostility to the Industrial Relations Act (1971), so that only after the repeal of the Act in 1974 did the new provisions on unfair dismissal lead to a large number of cases in the tribunals.

action, disciplinary and grievance procedures (on the significance of formal disciplinary and dismissal procedures, see Daniel and Millward, 1983: 159-76), custom and practice, or the social power of the employer vis-à-vis the employee. Second, that the areas affected by these new rights were of great relative importance in the industrial relations system, and that therefore the juridification of these areas would contribute significantly to the juridification of the system as a whole. These questions will be discussed in relation to the area of unfair dismissal, which, as we have already noted, accounts for the vast majority of all references to the industrial tribunals.

The right of individual employees to appeal to an industrial tribunal against unfair dismissal by the employer has been enacted in the form of a statutory protection. Analytically, therefore, it is a form of 'regulatory legislation' (Kahn-Freund, 1977: 24f.), through which the state has intervened formally to regulate an area of industrial relations which was previously determined almost exclusively by autonomous regulation. But can we conclude from this that the behavior of employers in practice is now 'regulated' by these new statutory norms, that employers conform in their behavior to the legal norms established by the state? The answer to this question would appear to depend, at least to some extent, on the force of the legal remedy, on the effectiveness of the legal sanction in practice.

The most powerful remedy which can be imposed on the employer in cases of unfair dismissal is the reinstatement of the dismissed employee. This involves a return to the *status quo ante*, which clearly represents a significant reduction in the autonomous social power of the employer to dismiss the individual employee. In practice, however, reinstatement is a remedy in Britain in only around three per cent of cases where the tribunal finds that the employee has been unfairly dismissed (see Dickens *et al.*, 1985; also Williams, 1983)[16]. In the overwhelming majority of such cases, in fact, the remedy of the tribunal is a requirement that the employer pay monetary compensation to the employee. The median award in 1984 was around 1300 pounds sterling, around one-fifth of present average annual earnings in Britain. This can hardly be regarded as a powerful remedy likely to modify substantially the behavior of employers or to protect significantly the individual employee.

The British experience remains that the 'non-legal' grievance procedure dependent upon the 'non-legal' collective agreement can provide the remedy of reinstatement for dismissal, but much less easily compensation, while the 'legal' procedures through 'judicial' tribunals can provide compensation, but only rarely reinstatement to the job. That contrast remains valid even in regard to complaints of unfair dismissal settled in the 'conciliation' procedures of the tribunals[17]. In short, unfair dismissal appears to be an area where

[16] For further discussion of this issue, see Dickens *et al.*, (1981); also Williams (1983). Williams writes: "Perhaps the most disappointing feature of the whole jurisdiction has been its signal failure to promote real job security" (p. 163).

[17] In 1983, out of 10,051 such settlements by conciliation, only 301 included re-employment of the workers. See Department of Employment Gazette (November, 1984: 490).

the introduction of legal regulation does not necessarily lead to a qualitative increase in juridification even if recently there has been a growing formalization of dismissal procedures (see Daniel and Millward, 1983: 163f.) Put positively, the form, substantive provisions and remedy of legal regulations are important factors shaping the outcome of the process of juridification.

It should perhaps be noted that the above assessment has not taken into account the extent to which the legal norms on unfair dismissal act as a reference point in the behavior and thinking of managers, employees and trade unions. It could be argued, for example, that the recent growth in the number of 'non-legal' dismissal procedures in British industrial relations is mainly a response by worried personnel managers to the new legislation in an attempt to conform to the procedures now required in law if a dismissal is to be deemed fair. In addition, we have not discussed whether the very existence of legal norms and procedures may have contributed, in the words of a recent study, "to a greater acceptance on the part of trade unions of legal regulation in areas where it was resisted previously and of judicial institutions" (Dickens *et al.*, 1985: 253). Overall, though, evidence seems to suggest that, although there has been "some shift from settlement of problems in negotiating procedure to settlement via judicial process" (Wedderburn, 1978: 435), the shift has not led to a qualitative increase in juridification, nor to the replacement of autonomous by legal regulation as the main factor determining behavior, attitudes and outcomes in cases of unfair dismissal and in other areas of individual employment protection.

What is the relative importance of the entire range of employment protection legislation for industrial relations as a whole? So far in Britain, employment protection legislation has "attempted, to a great extent successfully, to draw a line between 'individual' and 'collective' labour law for the tribunals, even if the boundary is somewhat uncertain at times" (Clark and Wedderburn, 1983: 178). For example, tribunals have traditionally been precluded from determining collective issues such as the reasonableness or merits of a strike (which might have led to a dismissal)[18]. Some 'hybrid' rights, it is true, such as the rights of 'individual' trade unionists to time off for 'collective' industrial relations and trade union duties, have important implications at

[18] Thus, so long as the employer does not discriminate amongst them or victimize only some of them, his dismissal of *all* the workers who are on strike at one establishment cannot be challenged as an 'unfair dismissal' before an industrial tribunal. The tribunal has no 'jurisdiction' to hear such a case on the complaint of a dismissed striker. This policy has, however, been departed from by the 1980s legislation, under which a non-unionist dismissed by an employer after industrial pressure by a union can 'join' the union as a defendant in the tribunal, which must then decide what proportion of the compensation it is 'reasonable' to award against the union having regard to the threat of industrial action. Cf. Clark and Wedderburn (1983): "When it intervenes in a case of unfair dismissal of a non-unionist to make the union (by reason of its industrial 'pressure') pay a 'just' share of the compensation awarded, the law crosses a legal and ideological Rubicon" (p. 207).

the collective level. In addition, certain provisions in recent Conservative government legislation allow employees for the first time to sue the trade union for its part in an unfair dismissal and for 'unreasonably' excluding individuals from union membership (see Clark and Wedderburn, 1983: 199f.).

At the level of public policy these developments represent a significant incursion of the law into specific areas of industrial relations. What effect they will have on the day-to-day conduct of industrial relations remains to be seen.

In summary, it is indeed true that recent developments in employment protection legislation have been one of the factors promoting more formality in certain industrial relations procedures, e.g. grievance procedures about discipline and dismissal, and more specialization in management (Brown, W., 1981, chs. 3 and 4; Daniel and Millward, 1983: 296f.). Nevertheless, reliance on 'custom and practice' and the rejection of the distinction between 'conflicts of interests' and 'conflicts of rights'[19] appear to have survived (see Clark and Wedderburn, 1983: 188f.; Dickens *et al.*, 1985), particularly where strong trade union organization in the workplace is maintained (on this point, see Batstone, 1984). However paradoxical it may seem, individual employment protection legislation in Britain has been framed largely with a view to protecting the primacy of voluntary collective bargaining. There is as yet no evidence that it has significantly undermined the primacy of the voluntary system.

(2) Health and Safety Legislation

Another paradox of labor law in Britain, and perhaps in other countries too, is that parallel to the development of autonomous collective bargaining as the main method of regulating basic terms and conditions of employment, the area of health and safety at work was increasingly subjected to legal regulation. By 1974 in Britain, when previous legislation was consolidated and re-fashioned in the Health and Safety at Work Act, there were many volumes of regulations covering most areas of industry.

To what extent did the legislation of 1974 represent an intensification of a trend towards the juridification of this area of industrial relations?

Clearly, by broadening the coverage of regulations to include another eight million employees, the Act extended the juridification of health and safety at work, at least at the level of public policy. The state's main enforcement agency, the Factory Inspectorate, was also given new powers, for example to issue 'improvement notices' and 'prohibition notices', although the relatively small number of inspectors suggests that their ability to enforce the new regulations will certainly be less than comprehensive. However, the main innovations in labor law and industrial relations brought about by the Act lay in its promotion of tripartite and bipartite regulation and enforcement. First, the Act was an enabling Act, in which the legislature provided a general structure, while leaving the elaboration of detailed regulations to a new tripartite

[19] A distinction which, as Allan Flanders pointed out, "is fundamental in European labour law". Flanders (1965: 28).

agency. Second, this agency, the Health and Safety Commission, was governed by an Executive composed of an equal number of employer and trade union representatives and a third group of 'independents', and was charged by Parliament with overseeing policy developments in the area of health and safety at work. Third, employers were obliged by law under the Act to consult with safety representatives and safety committees composed of trade unionists.

These innovations raise a number of important questions for our evaluation of the process and extent of juridification. First, the provisions on health and safety representatives and committees are analytically not an example of 'regulatory' legislation, but of 'auxiliary' legislation (on the distinction between these two terms see Kahn-Freund, 1977: 24f., 48). In other words, although such legislation has traditionally been regarded as 'regulating' in intention and in effect, this aspect of the 1974 Act was another example of the state intervening to support and promote autonomous regulation. Second, the establishment of a tripartite administrative agency is but one example of an institutional feature of industrial relations, namely tripartism, which cuts across the conceptually neat divide between state and society, between legal and autonomous regulation. The implications of tripartism for the process and extent of juridification is an issue which needs further exploration. One field in which it can be directly explored is the area of conciliation and arbitration.

(3) Conciliation and Arbitration

The Advisory, Conciliation and Arbitration Service (ACAS) was established under the Employment Protection Act of 1975. The statute stated expressly that it was not "subject to directions of any kind from any Minister", and was charged with the "general duty of promoting the improvement of industrial relations, and in particular of encouraging the extension of collective bargaining and the development and, where necessary, the reform of collective bargaining machinery" (EPA, section 1). As Kahn-Freund pointed out, its social 'autonomy' was not simply a matter of law, but enshrined in its constitution. This followed the "traditional pattern of British self-governing institutions in the field of labor relations" (Kahn-Freund, 1977: 79), with a self-governing tripartite Council composed of employer and trade union representatives, and independents. In this respect it represented to some extent a break with previous forms of conciliation and arbitration in Britain, which until then had been located in the Ministry of Labour and its successor, the Department of Employment.

The system of conciliation and arbitration administered by ACAS is now exclusively 'voluntary', requiring the consent of both parties to any dispute. Interestingly, under the Social Contract legislation, ACAS was given exceptional powers to oblige the employer to recognize and bargain with a trade union. However, even in this case, the remedy stopped short of direct legal sanctions, and the relevant provisions proved largely ineffective in practice. On behalf of the ACAS Council, the ACAS Chairman effectively invited the

Conservative government in 1979 to repeal this particular statutory provision, which it did in 1980. As has been suggested elsewhere, it turned out to be astonishing but true that "even this small degree of intervention" was "too strong a burden for the traditionally 'voluntary' system of collective labour law to bear" (Wedderburn, 1978: 456; see also Wedderburn, 1983: 54-55).

To what extent, then, can the establishment of ACAS[20] under the Social Contract labor legislation be interpreted as part of a trend towards the juridification of industrial relations? The answer, in short, is that it was not, either at the level of public policy or at the level of day-to-day industrial relations. ACAS is an independent tripartite agency, a self-governing institution with no compulsory powers, charged with improving industrial relations, particularly by encouraging the extension of collective bargaining. On the one issue where it was given compulsory powers, albeit without a strong legal remedy, it proved ineffective. Here again, the state intervened to promote autonomous regulation. ACAS thus embodies a continuation of the traditional resistance to the juridification of conciliation and arbitration in British industrial relations going back to the 1890s.

3.4 British Labor Law in the 1980s: Contradictory Trends

Developments in labor law and industrial relations in Britain since the return of a Conservative government in 1979 provide conflicting and contradictory evidence about the process and extent of juridification. Most of these developments have been examined in detail elsewhere (see Clark and Wedderburn, 1983: 136-44, 162-65, 198-210; Wedderburn, 1985; Hepple, 1983; Lewis, 1983), so in this section we shall concentrate on trying to assess their relevance for the 'juridification' debate.

At the general level of program and ideology, Conservative government policy towards industrial relations since 1979 has had the express aim of reducing the power and protections ('immunities') of the trade unions and restoring the primacy of the market in regulating the employment relationship. However, the way it has gone about implementing this policy, i.e. the legal forms, substantive provisions and remedies, in different areas is crucial to any assessment of its implications for juridification. Our discussion will focus on these issues in five separate but related areas: state support for collective bargaining (auxiliary legislation); direct statutory intervention in the employment relationship (regulatory legislation); individual employment protection; the internal conduct of trade union affairs; and the legality of trade union action (particularly the freedom to strike).

The reduction of state support for collective bargaining has been a hallmark of Conservative government labor law policy since 1979. Already in 1979, one of the statutory periods within which employers must consult with trade unions over redundancy was reduced (in the so-called 'July Orders') and in

20 A more comprehensive analysis would include a similar discussion of other tripartite agencies such as the Manpower Services Commission, the Health and Safety Commission, Equal Opportunities Commission, and so on.

the 1980 Employment Act the two most important procedures promoting collective bargaining in the 1975 Employment Protection Act were repealed. We have already noted that the 'recognition' procedure in the 1975 Act was not widely used, so its repeal was of greater symbolic than practical importance. Schedule 11 of the same act had contained unilateral arbitration provisions enabling a union to compel an employer to observe minimum collectively bargained conditions of employment. However, even though research has suggested that some groups of low paid workers were assisted by such arbitration, the government argued that Schedule 11 represented a restraint on the operation of the market mechanism and that it should therefore be repealed. A Minister declared in 1980: "We want to get back to the voluntary system and we think that Schedule 11 is standing in the way there" (Gowrie, 1980). In this case the government spokesman was invoking the language of 'non-intervention' to justify the dismantling of statutory protections and a return to market principles.

Against this background it was hardly surprising when the government announced that it was to rescind the Fair Wages Resolution from September 1983, even though this involved denouncing ILO Convention 94 of 1949 which requires fair wages clauses in public contracts and "which was passed largely on the precedent of British practice since 1891" (Wedderburn, 1985)[21]. On top of this, the government has diluted significantly a number of EEC directives and proposals (e.g. concerning workers' rights on the transfer of undertakings and concerning disclosure of information to employees in large undertakings, especially multinational companies) to the point where, in effect, employers are relieved of important legal responsibilities to consult (let alone negotiate with or protect) their employees in the face of changes in the market (see Clark and Wedderburn, 1983: 209f.). In the area of auxiliary legislation, therefore, there is a clear tendency since 1979 towards the de-juridification of industrial relations, and the promotion of the market rather than collective bargaining in the regulation of the employment relationship.

[21] The Fair Wages clause set minimum conditions and also provided for the freedom to join trade unions. A measure of the changing climate of industrial relations can be gauged by recalling the atmosphere in which the Fair Wages Resolution was initially enacted. Kahn-Freund wrote in 1959: "This Resolution had been drafted by a Committee on which the British Employers' Confederation, the Trades Union Congress and the Government were represented, and they passed the draft unanimously. When the Resolution was debated in the Commons, not a single voice was raised against the Resolution in general or against this freedom of association clause in particular" (pp. 230-31). Kahn-Freund went on: "The unanimity with which the House accepted the principle that respect for the workers' freedom of association should be a condition for the privilege of obtaining government contracts, together with the lack of pressure for the implementing of the ILO Convention, shows the change in the climate of opinion since Dicey's day" (p. 231). Something similar could be said about the change in the climate of opinion from 1946 to 1985!

As for statutory intervention in the employment relationship via 'regulatory' legislation, a similar tendency is in evidence. All statutory protection for individual workers under the Truck Acts is now to be repealed. The government has also announced its intention to reduce the power of, and in some cases abolish, the wage councils by 1985-6, thus removing the statutory guarantee of a minimum wage for specified groups of workers in industries with low pay and low levels of trade union organization. Here again, the government is intervening to reduce statutory intervention in particular aspects of the employment relationship.

In the areas of individual employment protection, a similar trend can be detected, particularly as regards unfair dismissal. By the 'July Orders' of 1979, workers were excluded from their rights to compensation for unfair dismissal until they had one year of continuous service rather than 26 weeks, and under the 1980 Employment Act, the conditions under which employees in small firms and on fixed-term contracts could claim unfair dismissal were made more rigorous. At the same time the amounts of compensation were reduced. Overall, maternity rights for women employees were also reduced in the 1980 Act, although in one area (time-off for antenatal care) their rights were increased. The one area where there has been a clear and unambiguous extension of individual employment protection since 1979 has been in relation to the rights of non-unionists in respect of unfair dismissal. The promotion of non-unionism has been one of the cornerstones of the 'new' labor law (see Clark and Wedderburn, 1983: 141-43, 181, 207-09; Wedderburn, 1985).

To summarize the analysis so far: in the areas discussed above, the state has intervened since 1979 to reduce statutory support for collective bargaining and to reduce statutory protection for individual employees, with the exception of non-unionists, whose rights have been increased. In general, the policy in these areas has been one of "deregulation" or "reprivatization of the labor market", to use the terms of Spiros Simitis (Simitis, supra 127 ff.). These are examples of state intervention to reduce legal intervention in industrial relations, to promote the social power of the employer and the economic 'laws of the market' as determinants of the employment relationship.

When we turn to the question of the internal conduct of trade union affairs, however, there is an unambiguous increase in state intervention in areas previously left to autonomous regulation. For example, section 3 of the 1982 Employment Act, which came into force in November 1984, requires regular ballots of all employees on 'union membership agreements' (closed shops or compulsory union membership) and overwhelming support in their favor if lawful dismissal of a non-unionist is to be permitted. This is a classic example of what Spiros Simitis has called the increased "legal scrutiny" of the internal affairs of trade unions in situations where they have exclusive bargaining rights, albeit in these cases guaranteed not by the state, but by autonomous regulation via collective agreement (see Simitis, supra 142 ff.; Clark and Wedderburn, 1983: 137f., 178, 199f.).

However, the Trade Union Act (1984) goes much further in terms of statutory intervention in internal union affairs. This is particularly the case with Part I of the Act, which establishes in great detail the way in which trade unions must carry out internal elections of their executive committees. In Part III unions are also required to hold successful ballots at regular intervals if they are to operate lawful 'political funds', which are the most important source of finance for the British Labour Party and which allow unions to carry out political campaigns and activities in support of their members' occupational interests. In this area, the 1984 Act makes the terms of legality of a political fund tighter, although of course the whole question of the political activity of trade unions has been subject to legal regulation since the *Osborne* judgment of 1910 and the 1913 legislation which responded to it (see *Amalgamated Society of Railway Servants* v. *Osborne* [1910] A.C. 87 H.L.; Trade Union Act (1913); see also Clark and Wedderburn, 1983: 210-11; Wedderburn, 1985). It is too early as yet to assess the practical effects of this intervention, but at the level of public policy and positive law, and to different degrees in different areas of internal union activity, a tendency towards juridification can be detected.

The 1984 Act also establishes in great detail the procedures trade unions must adopt in the calling and ending of strikes if they are to continue to enjoy some degree of immunity from the common law and its associated liabilities. This takes us directly to the question of recent developments in trade union immunities and the freedom to strike. The objective behind government intervention in this area since 1979 is undisputed: to reduce the power of the trade unions in the labor market. The way it has done this, however, is quite distinct from the 1971 Industrial Relations Act, and has important implications for our assessment of juridification. The 1971 Act established the right of government to intervene directly in certain industrial disputes, introduced a whole new range of 'unfair industrial practices', and set up a new court, the National Industrial Relations Court, to enforce the new requirements. Since 1979, in contrast, the government has enacted a series of measures which have the same aim as in 1971, to restrict the scope of trade union action, but it has used a very different legal method of achieving its aim, that of "manipulating 'non-interventionist' institutions" (Clark and Wedderburn, 1983: 213).

Probably the clearest example of this is the narrowing of the definition of 'trade dispute', so that a number of types of industrial action which were previously lawful no longer enjoy immunity from legal liability. Under the 1982 Employment Act, for example, the concept of trade dispute is restricted to disputes 'wholly or mainly' related to industrial matters (previously only *a* connection was necessary); and disputes between workers and workers, and disputes not strictly between an employer and his own employees, are excluded. Under the 1982 legislation, too, trade union funds are now, for the first time since 1906, no longer protected from civil law claims for damages in the ordinary courts (see Clark and Wedderburn, 1983: 198f.).

The new legislation also removes protection in trade disputes from those organizing 'secondary' action, i.e. any industrial action by workers whose 'employer' is not party to the dispute[22], and from picketing, however peaceful, other than at the worker's place of work. It also renders illegal all industrial action which induces an employer to induce others (e.g. his sub-contractors) to consult or negotiate with trade unions. "One thread runs through these legal developments: The collective strength of workers is to be limited by the boundaries of the employment unit" (Wedderburn, 1985).

The legal form chosen by the government to achieve its objectives is, as we have noted, to reduce the traditional statutory protections of the trade unions, the 'immunities'. As a result, it has reintroduced, as it were by default, common law doctrines and principles into the regulation of the employment relationship. The common law, of course, assumes the 'equality' of the parties to the employment contract, and thus acknowledges openly the subordination of the employee to the employer. The significance of this trend towards the reintroduction of common law doctrines and principles into industrial relations will be examined further below.

When we turn to the practical 'effects' of the new labor law on day-to-day industrial relations a complex picture emerges. This picture can be pieced together by examining a number of examples.

The new legal provisions on picketing in the 1980 Employment Act appear to have had only a marginal effect on the conduct of disputes in their first years of operation. According to a detailed study carried out between 1980 and 1982: "Of all the disputes we have followed, the law has been used in ... a miniscule proportion of cases. Its infringement, on the other hand, has been a very common occurrence indeed" (Kahn *et al.*, 1983: 196). Probably the most tangible 'effect' of the new provisions on employee behavior and thinking during this period was the recommendation, not in the statute, but in the accompanying Code of Practice, of a maximum of six pickets. According to the authors of the study, this was "the aspect of the new law most frequently in the minds of the workers" (Kahn *et al.*, 1983: 193). Thus, the major effect of the picketing legislation was, as we have suggested above (section 2.3), to be found at the symbolic or ideological level, at any rate until February 1985. Then, however, the High Court granted injunctions against the mineworkers' union specifically restricting peaceful picketing to a number "not exceeding six" at each relevant pit (*Thomas* v. *National Union of Mineworkers (South Wales Area)*, [1985] 2 W.L.R. 1081). At this advanced stage in the dispute, the union decided to obey the injunction, thus marking an important step in the development of the practical effects of the picketing legislation.

When we look at the practical effect of the provisions on 'secondary action' in the 1980 Employment Act and on the narrowing of the trade dispute immunities in the 1982 Act, a similarly complex and changing picture emerges. On the one hand, there are a number of well documented cases[23],

[22] This includes any company in a group which is separate from the subsidiary company employing its workers in dispute.

[23] E.g. Mercury Communications Ltd. v. Scott-Garner [1983] 3 W.L.R. 914 (C.A.); Messenger Newspaper Group Ltd. v. N.G.A. [1984] I.R.L.R. 397; see on these cases Wedderburn (1985) and Clark (1985).

where trade unions have ended industrial action as a result of injunctions taken out against them and under threat of sequestration of their assets for contempt of court. On the other hand, there are a number of other cases where injunctions have been ignored and not enforced by the employer (see Younson, 1984). In March 1984, for example, the employer in the nationalized mining industry, the National Coal Board (NCB), applied in court for an injunction against the Yorkshire Area of the miners' union (NUM) on the grounds of unlawful 'secondary picketing'. The injunction was granted, but it was ignored by the union. The NCB then started an action for contempt against the union, which could have led to large fines and even the imprisonment of union leaders. However, the contempt action was not activated because the NCB believed that such an action would promote unity among its employees and within the union, and inflame the dispute rather than resolve it. In this case, the law was not shown to be ineffective as much as counter-productive from the point of view of the employer in the wider context of industrial relations as a whole.

Yet another example from the miners' dispute shows a different effect of the new legislation. In this case, road hauliers, whose lorries carrying coal were affected by peaceful pickets at coal mines other than those at which the picketing miners worked, pursued the union in the High Court after an injunction prohibiting the picketing was disobeyed. The court fined the union; and when the fine was unpaid, the court, on the application of the companies, ordered the sequestration of the union's entire assets (*Read (Transport) Ltd.* v. *National Union of Mineworkers (South Wales Area)* [1985] I.R.L.R. 67).

The prolonged mineworkers' strike also gave rise to litigation launched by dissident members of the union. In one line of cases, members who complained of picketing which harrassed them on their way to work were granted injunctions on the ground that the union was liable in 'tort' for the pickets (*Thomas* v. *National Union of Mineworkers (South Wales Area)*, [1985] 2 W.L.R. 1081). In other cases, members argued that the strike was in breach of the area union's own rules and were granted injunctions to prevent this breach of contract (*Taylor and Foulston* v. *National Union of Mineworkers (Yorkshire Area)* [1984] I.R.L.R. 445; *Taylor* v. *National Union of Mineworkers (Derbyshire Area)* [1984] I.R.L.R. 440). In one case, the court ordered the entire assets of the National Union of Mineworkers to be taken over by a receiver to prevent any further breach of 'trust' It has not gone unnoticed that the terms of some of the injunctions sought, for example in the *National Union of Mineworkers (South Wales Area)* cases in 1985, were precisely the same terms as in the injunctions granted to the NCB in March 1984.

Two other examples of the use of the law to influence the conduct of the miners' dispute ought to be mentioned here before we attempt to draw some tentative conclusions about recent developments. First, there has been an extensive use of criminal law in the dispute, with some 8,000 prosecutions for offences ranging from 'obstruction' and 'breach of the peace' to 'intimidation' and 'unlawful assembly', the creation of a national police reporting center to co-ordinate police activities during the dispute, the imposition of standard bail conditions, delayed trials, police road blocks preventing miners from leaving their own area of England to give support to fellow workers elsewhere, and so on. Second, aspects of social security law have been changed which have put pressure on striking miners and their families. For example, procedures for strikers to reclaim taxes have been made more difficult, and the Department of Health and Social Security now deducts 16 pounds sterling from the social security benefit of the families of strikers whether or not the union concerned pays any strike pay (the National Union of Mineworkers does not).

How can we summarize recent developments in labor law, and their implications for the juridification of industrial relations? In the period 1979 to 1983 there appears to have been a reticence on behalf of 'primary' employers to take legal action against their own employees and unions (see Kahn *et al.*, 1983: 193f.; Younson, 1984). Unlike during the period of the Industrial Relations Act (1971-74), however, there has not been a uniform reluctance of employers, even large employers, to sue (see Evans, 1983). Indeed, there have been a number of legal actions of great significance for industries such as shipping and printing (e.g. *Dimbleby & Sons* v. *N.U.J.* [1984] 1 W.L.R. 427 (H.L.); *Merkur Island Shipping Corporation* v. *Laughton* [1983] 2 A.C. 570 (H.L.); *Shipping Company Uniform Inc.* v. *I.T.W.F.* [1985] I.R.L.R. 71; *Messenger Newspapers Group* v. *N.G.A.* [1984] I.R.L.R. 397). Perhaps one of the most crucial developments has been the escalating use of the legal procedure known as the 'interlocutory injunction'. In interlocutory procedures cases are normally brought at short notice, evidence is submitted all on affidavit and is not subject to legal cross-examination, and the plaintiff simply needs to prove that there is a "serious question to be tried" for the judge to award an interim injunction against the union. As we have argued elsewhere, "this 'discretionary' remedy is in theory an 'interim' measure maintaining the status quo until trial. But an employer or other plaintiff ... has rarely wanted to pursue any remedy other than this order to stop the union from continuing with its industrial action" (Clark and Wedderburn, 1983: 136)[24].

Once again, the legal forms and the legal remedy are important factors in assessing the process and extent of juridification. Public policy in labor law, at least since 1906, has traditionally shielded trade unions from restrictive judicial doctrines. By reducing the trade union 'immunities', the new labor law allows the courts to impose the doctrines of the common law, well known for their ignorance of collective realities of day-to-day industrial relations and generally hostile to the legality of trade unions. We suggested in 1983: "Restriction of trade unions' industrial rights by way of reducing the immunities inevitably invites the 'labor injunction' to flood back into industrial relations at the choice of employers and other plaintiffs in whose favor the judges will

[24] There has recently been a significant number of injunctions in other sectors apart from shipping and printing, including road transport, teaching and the car industry (Austin Rover), but most of these cases are not fully 'reported' by reason of the procedures.

normally dispense their discretion" (Clark and Wedderburn, 1983: 137). Since that time, there has been a growing use of the labor injunction, in breach of contract actions (such as the civil miners' cases) as well as in 'tort' cases arising from the reduction in trade dispute immunities.

4. Conclusion

British labor law in the 1980s presents a complex picture with a number of contradictory trends (for a more detailed elaboration, see Wedderburn, 1985). There has been a clear weakening of individual employment protection. There has also been statutory encouragement of non-unionism. Many traditional 'props' to collective bargaining have been abolished. There has been an increase in legal intervention in internal union affairs, but a dismantling of many statutory protections for trade union action and the reimposition of common law civil liabilities. At the same time, two of the central features of the 'non-interventionist' voluntary system of British industrial relations have not been subject to legal restrictions, namely the collective agreement which is not legally enforceable as a contract, and the voluntary system of trade union representation at the workplace based on shop stewards.

So far we have not discussed what might be called the 'threat effect' of recent legislation, the extent to which workers and unions have been deterred from taking some form of action which they knew to be unlawful. This 'effect' of legislation is extremely difficult to measure, but it does raise probably the most complex question surrounding the issue of juridification, namely how far law can be isolated in terms of cause and effect, and how far other factors, such as unemployment, wider government policy, international and national market forces, may be regarded as equal, or more important factors shaping employer, employee and trade union behavior in industrial relations. To attempt an answer to this question would take us beyond the confines of this paper. What is clear, though, is that there is no clear trend towards the juridification of industrial relations in Britain, but rather a number of contradictory and parallel developments. The juridification of industrial relations is therefore not an irreversible trend, but an open process.

APPENDIX

Labor law statutes in Britain: A comparison between two recent periods

1942–62

1942 Restoration of Pre-War Trade Practices Act

1944 Disabled Persons (Employment) Act

1945 Wages Councils Act
Law Reform (Contributory Negligence) Act

1946 Trade Disputes and Trade Unions Act
Dock Workers (Regulation of Employment) Act

1948 Agricultural Wages Act

1950 Shops Act
Arbitration Act
Restoration of Pre-War Trade Practices Act

1954 Mines and Quarries Act
Baking Industry (Hours of Work) Act

1956 Agriculture (Safety, Health and Welfare) Act
Police, Fire, Probation Officers Remuneration Act

1957 Nurses Act

1959 Terms and Conditions of Employment Act
Wages Councils Act
Fire Services Act
Factories Act (consolidated 1961)

1960 Payment of Wages Act
Local Employment Act

1961 Factories Act

1963–83

1963 Contracts of Employment Act
Offices, Shops and Railway Premises Act

1964 Industrial Training Act
Trade Unions (Amalgamations) Act
Emergency Powers Act

1965 Trade Disputes Act
Redundancy Payments Act
Remuneration of Teachers Act
Race Relations Act

1966 Prices and Incomes Act

1967 Prices and Incomes Act

1968 Prices and Incomes Act

1969 Employers' Liability Compulsory Insurance Act
Employers' Liability Defective Equipment Act

1970 Merchant Shipping Act
Equal Pay Act

1971 Industrial Relations Act
Attachment of Earnings Act

1972 Contracts of Employment Act
Local Employment Act
Employment Medical Advisory Service Act
Counter-Inflation (Temporary Provisions) Act

1973 Counter-Inflation Act
Employment Agencies Act
Employment and Training Act

1974 Health and Safety at Work Act
Mechant Shipping Act
Trade Union and Labour Relations Act

1975 Sex Discrimination Act
Employment Protection Act

1976 Trade Union and Labour Relations (Amendment) Act
Race Relations Act
Dock Work Regulation Act

1977 Job Release Act

1978 Employment Subsidies Act
Employment Protection (Consolidation) Act
Shipbuilding Redundancy Payments Act

1979 Wages Councils Act

1980 Employment Act

1981 Redundancy Fund Act
Employment and Training Act

1982 Industrial Training Act
Employment Act

References

AMULREE, LORD (1929) *Industrial Arbitration in Great Britain.* Oxford: Oxford University Press.

BATSTONE, Eric (1984) *Working Order, Workplace Accomodation and Conflict Since the 1960s.* Oxford: Blackwell.

BROWN, William (1981) *The Changing Contours of British Industrial Relations.* Oxford: Basil Blackwell.

CLARK, Jon (1985) "Die Gewerkschaftsgesetzgebung 1979 bis 1984 und ihre Folgen für die Politik der Gewerkschaften", in O. Jacobi and H. Kastendiek (eds.), *Staat und industrielle Beziehungen in Grossbritannien.* Frankfurt a.M.: Campus.

—(1985a) "The Juridification of Industrial Relations: A Review Article", 14 *Industrial Law Journal* 69 June 1985.

CLARK, Jon and Kenneth William WEDDERBURN (1983) "Modern Labour Law: Problems, Functions and Policies," in Kenneth William Wedderburn, Roy Lewis and Jon Clark (eds.), *Labour Law and Industrial Relations: Building on Kahn-Freund.* Oxford: Clarendon Press.

CREIGHTON, W. Breen, William FORD and Richard MITCHELL (1983) *Labour Law, Materials and Commentary.* Sydney: Law Book Company.

DANIEL, William and Neil MILLWARD (1983) *Workplace Industrial Relations in Britain.* London: Heinemann Educational.

DAVIES, Paul Lyndon and Mark FREEDLAND (1983) "Editors' Introduction", in P.L. Davies and M. Freedland (eds.) *Kahn-Freund's Labour and the Law* (3rd ed.). London: Stevens.

DICKENS, Linda, Moira HART, Michael JONES and Brian WEEKES (1981) "Re-employment of Unfairly Dismissed Workers: 'The Lost Remedy'", 10 *Industrial Law Journal* 160.

—(1985) *Dismissed: A Study of Unfair Dismissal and the Industrial Tribunal System.* Oxford: Blackwell.

EVANS, Stephen (1983) "The Labour Injunction Revisited", 12 *Industrial Law Journal* 129.

FLANDERS, Allan David (1965) *Industrial Relations: What is Wrong with the System ? An Essay on its Theory and Future.* London: Faber.

FOX, Alan (1985) *History and Heritage: Social Origins of the British Industrial Relations System.* London: Allan and Unwin.

GORE, Van (1982) in C.J. Wrigley (ed.), *A History of British Industrial Relations 1875-1914.* London: Harvester.

GOWRIE, Earl of (1980) in *Parliamentary Debates* (House of Lords), 20 May 1980, column 902.

HEPPLE, Bob (1983) "Individual Labour Law", in G.S. Bain (ed.), *Industrial Relations in Britain.* Oxford: Blackwell.

HOBSBAUM, Eric J. (1984) *Worlds of Labour.* London: Weidenfeld and Nicolson.

KAHN, Peggy, NORMAN Lewis, ROLAND Livock and Paul WILES (1983) *Picketing — Industrial Disputes, Tactics and the Law.* London: Routledge and Kegan Paul.

KAHN-FREUND, Otto (1959) "Labour Law", in M. Ginsberg (ed.), *Law and Opinion in England in the 20th Century.* London: Stevens.

—(1972) *Labour and the Law* (1st ed.). London: Stevens.

—(1977) *Labour and the Law* (2nd ed.). London: Stevens.

LEWIS, Roy (1976) "The Historical Development of Labour Law," 14 *British Journal of Industrial Relations* 1.

—(1983) "Collective Labour Law", in G.S. Bain (ed.), *Industrial Relations in Britain.* Oxford: Blackwell.

Phelps Brown, Ernest Henry (1959) *The Growth of British Industrial Relations; A Study from the Standpoint of 1906-14.* London: Macmillan; New York: St. Martin's Press.

—(1983) *The Origins of Trade Union Power.* Oxford: Clarendon Press.

Rawson, Donald W. (982) "British and Australian Labour Law: The Background to 1982 Bills", *Industrial Relations Papers.* Australian National University.

Simitis, Spiros (1984) "Zur Verrechtlichung der Arbeitsbeziehungen," in H. Zacher, S. Simitis, F. Kübler, K. Hopt and G. Teubner (eds.), *Verrechtlichung von Wirtschaft, Arbeit und Sozialer Solidarität — Vergleichende Analysen.* Baden-Baden: Nomos.

Simpson, Robert Cecil and John Crossley Wood (1973) *Industrial Relations and the 1971 Act.* London: Pitman.

Thomson, Andrew William John and S. R. Engleman (1975) *The Industrial Relations Act: Review and Analysis.* London: Martin Robertson.

Turner, Ian (1979) *Industrial Labour and Politics: the Dynamics of the Labour Movement in Eastern Australia 1900-1921.* Sydney: Hale and Iremonger.

Voigt, Rüdiger (1983) "Gegentendenzen zur Verrechtlichung", 9 *Jahrbuch für Rechtssoziologie und Rechtstheorie* 20.

Webb, Sidney (1906) "Memorandum", in *Report of the Royal Commission on Trade Disputes and Trade Combinations.* London.

Wedderburn, Kenneth William (1971) *The Worker and the Law* (2nd ed.). London: Penguin. New edition forthcoming 1986.

—(1972) "Labour Law and Industrial Relations in Britain", 10 *British Journal of Industrial Relations* 270.

—(1978) "The New Structure of Labour Law in Britain", 13 *Israel Law Review* 435.

—(1980) "Industrial Relations and the Courts", 9 *Industrial Law Journal* 65.

—(1983) "Otto Kahn-Freund and British Labour Law", in K.W. Wedderburn, R. Lewis and J. Clark (eds.), *Labour Law and Industrial Relations: Building on Kahn-Freund.* Oxford: Clarendon Press.

—(1984) "Labour Law Now — A Hold and a Nudge," 13 *Industrial Law Journal* 73.

—(1985) "The New Policies in Industrial Relations Law," in P. Fosh and C. Littler (eds.), *Industrial Relations and the Law in the 1980's.* Farnborough: Gower.

Wedderburn, Kenneth William and Paul Lyndon Davies (1969) *Employment Grievances and Disputes Procedures in Britain.* Berkeley: University of California Press.

Weekes, Brian, Michael Mellish, Linda Dickens, and John Lloyd (1975) *Industrial Relations and the Limits of the Law: the Industrial Effects of the Industrial Relations Act, 1971.* Oxford: Blackwell.

Williams, Kevin (1983) "Unfair Dismissal: Myths and Statistics", 12 *Industrial Law Journal* 157.

Younson, Fraser (1984) "Who's been using the law in industrial disputes?" *Personnel Management,* June 1984.

Juridification: Labor Relations in Italy

GINO GIUGNI
Roma

Contents

1. The Fiction of Contractual Regulation

Analytical research on the high degree of juridification in the area of industrial and labor relations ought first to determine the causes of this phenomenon. The alternative to legal rules is the absence of rules. In the legal ideology of the industrial revolution, the absence of legal rules was linked with reliance on the market as a means of regulating the work relationship and achieving an optimum allocation of resources. But even in this case it is not correct to speak of an absence of rules. A free market presupposes the existence of freedom of contract, enforceable through the courts. This is the legal foundation of capitalism (Commons, 1924). However, the contract is subject to judicial control only as regards the procedures of its formation, i.e., the free expression of the will of the parties. The content is unassailable: *Qui dit contractuel dit juste.*

Customary rules and contractual practices constitute an alternative to legal rules and the market. These played an important role in preindustrial labor relationships, but were generally destroyed in the new industrial structure. They remained important in highly skilled labor, where trade practices were transferred from the craft workshop to the capitalist factory. Indeed, they were often consolidated through the craft unions. They retained considerable importance in the labor markets of Anglo-Saxon countries, as well as imperial Germany and Habsburg Austria. However, they found it hard to resist the impact of the Taylorist Revolution, though they did last longer in the U.S., and especially in Britain, than in other countries. In Italy, craft practices have been much less important, due to the lateness of industrial development and the formation of the working class (Giugni, 1961).

In the context of free labor markets, however, the contractual relationship is almost devoid of significance for workers. Although, in theory, enforceable rights may derive from it, access to the courts is, in fact, impossible. For this reason, the employment relationship, before the birth of modern "social legislation" is best described as *de facto*. It is of little importance whether it can be fitted into the *locatio operarum*. The capacity of this relationship to act as an effective source of subjective rights is in fact entirely theoretical.

In this phase, accordingly, one may say that the degree of juridification reached is zero.

2. The Birth of Labor Law

As is well known, the *Sozialfrage* rendered debatable the theory of equilibrium on the labor market, at least as regards its capacity to bring about an optimum allocation of resources. It became clear that contractual regulation as described above, or better, the fiction of contractual regulation, was not enough. Instead, a process of juridification began along two lines: (a) the effective enforceability of workers' rights, achieved mainly through the setting up of special tribunals (in Italy, the Probiviri, in 1893) and (b) the laying down of prohibitions and obligatory terms in the employment relationship. This was the most important innovation. It put at issue the general principles of civil law regarding contracts, and gave birth to a special branch of law, namely labor law. Thus a crisis was opened in the traditional civil law system.

At this stage, a reduction in the contractual freedom of the individual began. Alongside the norms of law, collective bargaining clauses appeared with increasing frequency. These enjoyed a rich development in Italy between the beginning of the century and the start of Fascism (Barbadoro, 1973; Degli Innocenti, 1984; Antonioli and Bezza, 1974). Some legal writers went so far as to throw doubt on the very existence of a contract of employment. In Italy, however, a powerful influence was exerted by Barassi (1915-17). A conservative civil lawyer, Barassi was the first to penetrate the unknown jungle of employment relationships, thereby making a decisive contribution to a legal construction that kept the employment relation within the area of contract and of contractual freedom. It was likewise Barassi who had the merit (or fault) of opposing a law on employment contracts, a fact which considerably slowed the process of juridification of the relationships concerned. A law on employment relations was finally promulgated in 1919, but was limited to white collar workers, who had hitherto functioned mainly under customary rules. Uniform legal rules for blue collar workers remained absent until the 1942 Civil Code was adopted.

3. The Corporatist System under Fascism

The seizure of power by the Fascists between 1922 and 1943 and the accompanying construction of the totalitarian state gave impetus to juridification in the area of industrial relations. This became almost total, but only in a seemingly indirect manner, since next to the many social protection laws, the most important normative role was assumed by collective contracts concluded by unions organized by the corporate state and controlled by the government (Jocteau, 1979-80). These could not be departed from and were effective *erga omnes.* Thus in reality they were instruments of normative centralization within the state, where they performed a function entirely similar to that of law or, as some have maintained, of administrative orders, but in any case, of state norms. The result was the extension of state law norms as an instrument for regulating labor relations. Moreover, one year before the fall of the regime, the new Civil Code introduced uniform regulation of employment, although many references to collective contracts were made. These regulations are still in force and consists of some 40 articles, plus numerous later amendments.

This large-scale juridification, however, did not consist solely of an increase in statutory or quasi-statutory norms; it was accompanied by a development of the legal doctrine in both a legalistic and formalistic sense. In the universities, labor law was called corporative law, and was devoted to a description of the social institutions of the regime. Finally, the special jurisdiction of the Probiviri was eliminated, and the judicial function in work matters was entrusted to a special section of the ordinary magistracy which contributed towards emphasizing and generalizing the legal approach to the handling of industrial relations.

4. The Post-Corporatist Period

The end of Fascism began a new cycle which will be briefly considered here in historical sequence, and afterwards analyzed as a "model" in force, with projections and proposals regarding future developments.

The fall of the Fascist regime had as an immediate consequence the delegalization of collective labor relations. In fact, even in 1944, before the end of the war, a decision was taken to dissolve the labor unions and employers' associations which had been set up in accordance with the corporative regime. As for the collective, so-called corporative contracts, which performed the quasi-legislative function described above, once the entities empowered to conclude them had been abolished they ought to have expired on their various expiry dates. Instead, they were prolonged *sine die*, a situation which in theory may still exist today in some branches of industry. (In 1959, a law attributed statutory effectiveness to almost all of the collective agreements concluded from 1944 until then, thereby bringing about the abrogation of the majority of the so-called corporative contracts). An outstanding example is the contract of the metalworking and engineering industry, which dates back more than 40 years and is still at least formally in force. The obsolescence of the corporative contract resulted from two factors. The first was inflation, which deprived the wage scales of any practical effect. The second was the immediate spread of so-called "common law", or more simply "post-corporative collective agreements", which almost always resulted in better conditions for workers and therefore, through a consistent approach by the courts, prevailed as a derogation from the corporative contracts.

All this will appear clearer after a brief description of the legal conditions of the unions after the Fascist regime. When the corporate system was abolished the free trade unions had already been re-established in the part of Italy under Allied government. These immediately began to conclude agreements, generally with emergency content. These unions were recognized as having the same nature as those existing before Fascism, that is of unrecognized or *de facto* associations, and as such were lacking legal personality. Without specific norms, the situation could not have been different. In turn, the collective agreements concluded by them were treated as common contracts of civil law, with an effectiveness limited to the contracting parties and their members.

5. The 1948 Constitution

The situation regarding the unions and collective agreements has continued until the present, although various alterations have been made. A peculiar system of relations has resulted in which the legal factor, or better, the statutory factor, has played a secondary role. The condition of hyper-juridification characteristic of the Fascist system was overturned by the sudden *deregulation* of industrial relations in Italy in 1944 and 1945 which still exists today.

The same condition of near absence of law was characteristic of industrial action at least up until the 1948 Constitution. The latter, while it failed in its attempt to construct a new legal system for unions and collective agreements, introduced a decisive innovation with the explicit recognition of the right to strike (Art. 40) and the entrusting of the task of determining implementing rules to the ordinary laws. However, since such ordinary laws were not thereafter issued (with a few, sectorial exceptions, Decreto del Presidente della Repubblica No. 185/1964; Law No. 242/1980 on nuclear plants), here too there was a vacuum of norms, which was filled by court decisions. The juridification which took place, therefore, was a weak one (Carinci, *et al.*, 1983).

As regards unions and collective agreements, the Constitution (Art. 39) had instead sketched out a very precise model: the unions and employers' associations would become incorporated bodies and, more importantly, have the right to conclude collective contracts with quasi-legislative effect. Given the trade union pluralism on the workers' side, the Constitution provided for the formation of unitary, proportional representation.

The model never came into force for a number of reasons, both political and practical. Some years later, accusations were even made that the object had been to reintroduce a corporative scheme (Mancini, 1963). Parliament recently began discussions on a proposal for radical amendment aimed at adapting the Constitution to the *de facto* system which has been developing through self-regulation during these decades. (Commissione parlamentare, 1985).

6. Slow Juridification of Collective Labor Law

The juridified *stratum* of industrial relations is, then, very limited. The union is an unrecognized association, not subject to special obligations. The courts have rarely been called on to intervene in cases of internal union conflict and the existing precedents in terms of breaches of statutes, etc. are so few that there can be no notion of a consistent trend. Indeed, there is a doctrine that argues in favor of union immunity from judicial intervention in internal union conflicts (Carabelli, 1984). On responsibility towards third parties there are no doubts, but here there have not yet been any *causes célèbres.*

Juridification of some relevance, however, was brought about in 1970 through legislation supporting union activities (Law No. 300/1970 on Workers' Statute). This concerns certain recognized rights, (particularly for the most representative confederations) such as the right to call meetings on company premises and to paid leave for union activities. The recognition of union rights has given rise to many legal cases, notably because the 1970 law introduced an injunction procedure giving the union itself the right to act directly before the courts (Art. 28). The juridification originating in the Workers' Statute and in the special procedure it introduced has been intensive, but not extensive, in the sense that it has mainly concerned the area of relationships connected with rights or privileges granted by the law itself to labor unions in regard to activities.

The legal condition of the collective contract has likewise been regulated by civil law, according to which a contract can bind only the participating parties. Therefore, a union or employers' association acting as agent for its members, can bind only the latter. Moreover, on the basis of principles of civil law, collective contracts, in the past, could not prevent the conclusion of different agreements between individual employers and individual workers. This lacuna was, however, immediately filled by the courts which affirmed that collective contracts could not be departed from, and that any derogations were void and would be replaced by the corresponding clauses of the collective agreement itself.

The problem was also partly resolved through interventions by Parliament, and particularly, through a creative interpretation of the law in force. In 1959, as already mentioned, a law laid down procedures for converting existing contracts into legal norms. Those concluded subsequently were to contain only those clauses more favorable to the workers than the ones previously in force. The difficulty of comparison created the basis for intense legal dispute, especially regarding non-economic clauses in the contracts. But a more general and permanent form of indirect lawmaking took place through the courts. In the first place, they found that if an employer declares his intention to apply a collective contract to his employees, that declaration will become binding. Still more important is the principle of treating the constant application of the collective contract as conduct which would allow intention to be presumed. Secondly, and more conspicuously, the wage clauses of the collective contracts were construed as expressions of the principle of the right to fair wages, established in general terms by the Constitution (Art. 36), which, given its source, is of general efficacy. This has extended the effects of the contracts well beyond the sphere assigned by the Civil Code.

Towards the end of the 1970s and later, many laws were brought into the hitherto almost virgin territory of bargaining, especially in the form of specific constraints imposed in connection with incomes policy objectives. In most cases, however, these restrictions were agreed upon by workers' confederations and the law served to give general effect to these agreements. The most notorious case, politically speaking, came in 1984, when Parliament slowed down the contractual machinery for cost of living adjustments without a full consent on the unions' side. The meaning of this new trend, particularly in connection with the practice of social consultation or of neo-corporatist agreements, will be treated in more detail in Section 15.

7. De-facto Self-Regulation in Collective Labor Law

The most important characteristic of the rules in force, however, lies outside the legal area. Instead of being viewed as a deregulated system, Italian industrial relations should be seen as a rather rare example of a self-regulated system. The instruments of this self-regulation are: clauses in collective agreements, contractual practices, and the by-laws and decisions of organizations. Legal doctrine has contributed to the identification of this legal framework by setting up the theory of "ordinamento intersindacale" (Giugni, 1960; Vardaro, 1984) — a systematic ordering of the set of rules governing the industrial relations.

Contractual rules chiefly concern relationships between levels of bargaining, i.e. the links between interbranch agreements and those within each branch of industry, and the links between the latter and the company or plant agreements. In the 1960s the system was co-ordinated by norms of competence expressly contained in the contracts at various levels, with "references" from one to another. In the subsequent decade growing union militancy led to a refusal to lay down norms of competence and self-restraint. Today these have reappeared, specifically in the important general agreement between government, unions and employers' associations of January 22, 1983 (Diritto del Lavoro. Italy, 1985). It includes, for instance, a clause banning wage bargaining at the plant level for 18 months, and one laying down the principle that any issue negotiated at one level cannot be renegotiated at another.

The unwritten norms of conduct are subject to varying degrees of recognition, and hence of effectiveness, with the result that they are more unstable. On the other hand, while those indicated earlier are at least theoretically enforceable in the courts, though this may be rare in practice, these unwritten rules instead have only social effectiveness. An example of this hs the norm of industrial peace for the duration of a contract, which after a brief period of formalization in the 1960s was no longer written into contracts nor regarded as an implied term. It was nevertheless fairly consistently observed, and indeed recognized as a "political commitment" (Federazione Lavoratori Metalmeccanici, 1973). Most important of all, however, is the practice of representative self-legitimation, whereby bargaining,with only a few exceptions, takes place with the three big union confederations (CGIL, CISL and UIL) though there is no legal norm on the recognition of the bargaining agent.

Finally, industrial conflict (Aaron and Wedderburn, 1972), dealt with by law only in terms of principle, through constitutional recognition of the right to strike, has in the public utilities area given rise to full scale codes of fair practice. The most developed code has been operating since 1984 in public and private transport, and consists of an agreement between the Minister of Transport and the Transport Unions belonging to the most representative confederations (ILO, 1985). The limit to this "self-regulation" lies in the fact that the code is not binding on workers not members of these unions. However, since strikes in "essential" public utilities, according to the Constitutional Court, are subject to implicit norms of *bona fide* conduct, it is likely that in any civil or penal action, the force of the self-discipline clauses will be recognized as an exemplification of the "implicit" restrictions on the right to strike in public utilities.

8. Legislative and Judicial Interventions in Individual Labor Law

The situation regarding individual employment relationships is very different. In this connection there has been growing juridification, which has increasingly restricted individual autonomy and hence the regulatory function of the market. The Fascist corporate system, as has been seen, gave strong stimulus to the extension of norms, but mainly through the "statutorized" collective agreements. After this system was replaced the role of legal norms as such increased; however, this took place to a limited extent through parliamentary intervention, and to a much greater extent following an increase in the number of cases before the courts.

Parliamentary intervention, at least during the first 20 years, was confined to "anti-fraud" laws, which combatted abuses by employers in specific cases such as fixed period contracts or contracting out, or dismissals of women after marriage. A greater impact resulted from judge-made law. The rise in the number of cases resulted from the fact that, though a formalized system of legal aid did not exist, the unions provided workers with defending lawyers, who were usually paid only if the court found in the employee's favor. Since collective contracts were less effective than corporative contracts during the Fascist period, there was a "squeezing" of statutory norms in order to extract the greatest possible benefit from them for the workers, through interpretations or interpretative manipulations. In addition to results that increased protection for workers, there were also negative effects, much criticized today, such as the creation of conflicts between statutory law and the more elastic norms of the new collective contracts, which were considered a rank below statutory law itself. This produced a consolidation of legal principles capable of considerable expansion by the courts, outside all controls of the Parliament or collective bargaining. The most noted example was the formation of a unified, "omni-comprehensive" concept of pay, which, starting with an *a priori* definition of the latter, applied it to different structures (various allowances, overtime, Christmas bonuses, etc.) that had been introduced with reference to more restricted bases (for instance, the basic hourly rate alone).

9. The Impact of the "Workers' Statute"

A real expansion in the legal regulation of new and significant areas took place with the Workers' Statute (Law No. 300/1970). This was preceded by the 1966 law on individual dismissals (Law No. 604/1966), which gave legal definition to the motives for dismissal and brought them under the control of judges, thereby moving away from the civil law principle of the irrelevance of motives. The Workers' Statute in turn, apart from the norms supporting union activities already mentioned, marked a step forward in the expansion of legal protection into the new areas of workers' "freedom and dignity" (an expression used in Art. 41 of the Constitution). Specifically, this involved norms for the protection of privacy, against discrimination, on due process in disciplinary proceedings, and against excessive controls (use of private police, closed circuit TV, continuous recording of work performance, body searches, etc.).

Even the broad interpretation by the courts, particularly the judges of first instance (the "pretori"), many of whom were openly inspired by pro-labor ideologies, gave further stimulus to juridification (Treu, 1975; 1984). In some cases, such as work accidents, penal sanctions were applied, which meant an increase in penal juridification.

10. New Developments in Labor Law

In this paper, labor law in Italy has been characterized as being at a fairly low level of juridification in terms of collective relationships, and a very high level in regard to individual ones. A parallel picture can be presented, taking account of the currently prevailing trends and dominant philosophies. The main approach under discussion today centers on flexibilization and the revision of guaranteeism (Giugni, 1982), and, in a rather inexact manner as we shall see below, that of deregulation. This approach is generally accepted in principle, being regarded as the only one capable of adapting the system to the processes of technological change while dealing with the extremely serious problem of unemployment. In any case, the philosophy of flexibilization should not be confused with that of neo-liberalism, which has no great following in Italy at the present time, in any of its varieties. Only a limited number of business people openly propose a return to the market, with a drastic reduction in legal protection and in collective bargaining itself (Federmeccanica, 1985).

In terms of flexibilization, some thresholds have already been crossed, as in the agreement between the social partners and the government signed in January 1983 (Diritto del Lavoro). Apart from wage, tax and other provisions, this agreement laid down conditions for intervention to render the legal norms more elastic by: cutting back on the obligation to take workers onto state labor exchange lists, allowing broader recourse to fixed-term contracts; partially devolving norm-making authority on hiring to tripartite regional commissions; recognizing part-time employment; establishing of a new work-training contract; and reducing the percentage of physically handicapped people that firms have the obligation to hire.

The main area of intervention in the direction of flexibilization was, then, in hiring practices and in defining various types of employment relationships.

11. Flexibilization

As has been stated, the problem has not, at least for the moment, been raised in the context of neo-liberal philosophy, but rather as a tentative response to trends in development of the market and in industrial relations that have been going on for some time. Examples of these include:

a) segmentation of the labor market, due to the formation over a period of at least 15 years, of a very broad "submerged economy", giving employment, on uncertain estimates, to between 2 and 4 million workers. These workers are of different types; for example: moonlighters (Istituto di Sociologia, 1979), laid-off workers (with "Cassa integrazione" indemnification), highly skilled independent workers, home workers, (usually female), students etc. This sector is completely deregulated in the sense that neither protective laws nor collective agreements apply within it. Beside the "submerged", deregulated market, there is a broad semi-guaranteed sector, of regular firms immune from various legal restrictions because of size (with varying thresholds, from 5 employees for the restrictions on hiring to 15 or 35 for those on dismissals, etc.). Juridification of employment relationships is, then, unequally distributed.

b) a more recent change in the expectations of workers on the labor market, who are no longer exclusively oriented, as was the case until a few years ago, towards stable, full-time jobs. Particularly among young people, an important socio-cultural shift is going on (Accornero, 1980), which is expanding the labor supply for short-term contracts, part-time jobs, self-employment and co-operative work. On the demand side, there is a response to this increased supply, which is certainly more suited to the present drastic phase of technological change. Of course, it is not easy to distinguish between cases where a stable job is no longer desired and those which are necessary adjustments to job scarcity. However, in the area that interests us, there is broad consensus on the advisability of adapting the legal framework to the present structure of labor demand and supply. The issue of telework is still premature: home work is mainly of traditional type, though considerable developments can be expected in the not too distant future.

c) changes in employee skills and a parallel socio-cultural shift towards higher valuation of individual contractual freedom in determining the terms of employment. This phenomenon of course concerns the highest skills, and is caused by the need to regain differentials evened out by the unions' egalitarian policies and by inflation. The deeper component, however, is the socio-cultural aspect mentioned above, common also to other countries.

d) a fairly widespread awareness of the need to lighten the normative overloading that is one of the symptoms of the crisis of the welfare state. This attitude draws justification from the finding that some normative instruments have proved unable to govern labor relationships. As will be seen, this is true especially in regard to the legal restrictions on the hiring of workers and on the choice of type of employment relationship. The spread of the submerged economy has constituted the most dangerous challenge to the system of guarantees consolidated, in particular, in the Workers' Statute.

e) the development of a neo-corporatist model of industrial relations (Regini, 1984; Rusconi, 1984; Giugni, 1985). This has taken place unevenly, but for the area that concerns us has resulted in indirect participation by the social partners in legislative policy, and hence a blurring of the dividing lines between law and collective agreements. This has not promoted a true process of state withdrawal from intervention, but has outlined new self-regulatory areas. Moreover, it has limited devolution to judges (Treu, 1984).

12. Deregulation

The lines of development in legal policy can be characterized, from the viewpoint adopted here, as moving in three directions: deregulation, reregulation (or reformalization), and devolution of the sources of norms. The first two trends mainly affect individual relationships, while the third, in terms of our subject-matter affects the relationships between law and collective bargaining or similar forms of participation by the social partners in the normative process. Full-scale deregulation, meant to restore the market equilibrium has no scientific foundation. Its use would be the realization of an ideological program inspired by an orthodox conception of the market, which would only produce distorting effects since it does not correspond to the reality of the labor market. Genuine deregulation is conceivable only in limited cases, where a norm has proven ineffective, or where the problem it was meant to resolve has disappeared.

For this reason, deregulation in this context should not be understood as an abolition of norms and a return to the individual contract (see Section 1), but as a flexibilization of the normative process outside it. However, the statement that a deregulation therefore reformalizes the employment relationship (Simitis supra) requires correction, since the abolition of "external" rules for the latter may instead increase the space for the exercise of the employer's unilateral prerogatives.

It is however evident that any reformalization or devolution shifts the object of the norm and thus may result in partial deregulation in certain situations. Accordingly, the boundaries between the three trends indicated are not clear-cut.

A case of authentic deregulation is emerging in relation to the severe (but almost solely theoretical) restrictions imposed by the laws on hiring, which, with a few exceptions for highly skilled jobs, are supposed to be enforced by government offices on the basis of priority lists laid down by them. In reality, this system has almost never operated "at full steam", that is, in accordance with the legislature's intention. Evasions, avoidance, and in more recent years, exceptions laid down by the law itself, have almost completely demolished the enforcement machinery. Adaptation of the law to the *de facto* situation is now prevented only by differences between unions and employers regarding the new set-up to be enforced and particularly by the administrative bureaucracy, which is interested in retaining its own control positions (Ichino, 1984).

An example of reregulation aimed at flexibility would instead be the legislation on working hours, going back to 1923 (Law No. 692) and that on holidays, which is fairly old as well (Law No. 370/1934). While in bargaining there is a marked trend towards annual or flexible hours and flexitime, the legal restrictions appear to be an obstacle to normative modernization. Since the problem, however, is not to change the amount of time worked but rather its distribution; the usual regulatory scheme, based on the classical relationship between rule of conduct, finding of breach, and punishment, is lacking appropriate mechanisms for adjustment and ought to be replaced by a new normative technique.

A third case deserves attention. According to an opinion widespread in business circles (Federmeccanica, 1985), the most serious reason for rigidity or "hyper-guaranteeism" is related to dismissals. In plants with more than 15 worker the consequence of individual dismissals with no justified motive is reinstatement of the worker. The impact of this rule depends largely on the speed of court decision-making. This factor has been emphasized by a Court of Cassation ruling that requires continued compliance with a first instance decision to reinstate an employee until final appeal to the Court of Cassation has been made, even if the verdict is overturned by the Appeal Court. This process can take several years. In case of collective dismissals for economic reasons, however, the sole restrictions consist of procedures for consultation with the unions as provided for by collective agreements: Italy has, indeed, been condemned by the European Court of Justice for being below the guaranteed standards laid down by the EEC directive (Directive 75/129 on collective redundancies). The inelasticity of company staffing is caused, therefore, more by union resistance than by legal norms or contractual clauses.

In conclusion, it seems realistic to characterize the case of dismissals as part of the trend towards corrective reregulation rather than deregulation.

13. Reregulation

The problem of reregulation is largely a political one, since every proposal aimed at changing the institutions of the labor market and of industrial relations is undoubtedly politically inspired. For some issues, however, the autogenous pressure of the normative system should not be underestimated. It expresses demands for rationalization, which can be classified in three categories:

a) a demand for correction directed at improving the performance of the norm. The example of dismissals mentioned earlier is in fact ambivalent — the demand for liberalization is the expression of the political pressure from business, while that for rationalization corresponds to requirements of internal functionality within the existing system of guarantees;

b) a need for harmonization of the labor laws in Italy, which have been adopted over a period of 60 years under three different political regimes;

c) a gap between norms and technological progress which has raised problems difficult to solve even by evolutionary interpretation of the existing norms.

Among the problems under c), two examples deserve mention: first, the division of workers into categories (blue collar, white collar, and management) increasingly hard to distinguish, especially following the formation of intermediate bodies, and second, the growing potential for interference with workers' privacy, through the use of computers and by stiffening systems of control. In connection with this, the Workers' Statute in 1970 placed restrictions on the use of closed circuit television to monitor workers, a move which for Italy was almost akin to science fiction. Fifteen years later, the courts are facing the problems that have arisen from supervision through the recording of data concerning the work itself and are seeking to adapt the norm of the Statute to this new case, with controversial results. After fifteen years, the Statute is already old.

14. Devolution

In connection with reregulation, however, not only does the problem of changing norms arise, but also that of changing the process of making norms, which is of greater relevance here.

The basic assumption is as follows: labor law consists mainly of norms regulating behavior, binding on both individuals and collective entities.

Moreover, the norms are almost always applied directly. Only occasionally do they refer to administrative regulations as, for example, in the case of exceptions to minimum hours of work standards or, more broadly, in the area of plant safety (Cassese, 1984).

Rarely in a system based on the separation of powers is reference made to adaptation by judges. However case law has played an important role in this area precisely because certain norms are outdated, and as a result of organic defects in the legislative system mentioned earlier. Among other things, it has extended the effectiveness of contractual wage tariffs, as mentioned in Section 6.

It has been noted that the case law in the area of wages seems inspired, as during the Weimar period (Clark *et al.*, 1983), by visions of *Sozialmitleid.* In a noticeable change, however, groups of young magistrates began in the 1970s, to broaden union powers through the use of evolutionary interpretation, thus entering the area of collective relations and of the rules governing them. This trend has continued, though sporadically.

Notwithstanding its breadth, devolution to the judiciary has always been considered pathological, anomalous or temporary. The laws make very cautious use of the same "general clauses" which in other systems have, instead, constituted the foundation of government by the judiciary.

Wider use of devolution techniques, however, is now increasingly proposed as a way of achieving increased flexibility while avoiding so-called "wild" deregulation. Possible methods include:

a) the devolution of powers to depart from law through administrative acts. This was recently relied on to authorize departures from the ban on fixed-period contracts (Law No. 876/1977). Under some recent rules, the administrative organ (work inspector) is obliged to consult the most representative unions or ask their agreement before making such departures (Law No. 36/1979).

This mechanism has both advantages and drawbacks: the latter relate to the notorious slowness of the Italian bureaucracy (for example, administrative regulations provided for by law are issued only after long delays) and to the fear of responsibility that makes Italian administrators postpone decisions or refer them to a higher level which is in turn unable to cope with the resulting overload.

b) devolution to regional legislation. This is already in force for some matters like professional training (Law No. 845/1978). Other matters however do not fall within the constitutional power of the regions. Only the "special statute" regions have broader powers, especially labor market legislation, which is in fact handled locally in Sicily and Trentino-Alto Adige. A widening of the regions' powers could be achieved through delegation by national legislation, but is improbable in the area under discussion. In some regions, however, administrative organization work has been intense and innovative. For example, information centers on job supply and demand have been created, etc.

c) devolution to collective bargaining, which may be direct or indirect. The Workers' Statute, inspired by the philosophy of union support legislation, had the indirect aim of stimulating plant bargaining, through the plant units of the most representative unions. Here the law aimed at generating structural preconditions which would make the process of bargaining more effective. In this direction, it secured highly satisfactory results. The achievements result from the following causal chain: strengthening of the union in the enterprise (through recognition of union rights, cf. Section 6) — an increase in bargaining power — the extension of plant or company bargaining, even of the informal variety.

Direct devolution to collective bargaining may be of two types. The first is the complementary remittal, in use since the period of the corporate state. Its effectiveness is limited by the fact that the range of binding observance of collective contracts is much narrower than that of law, though this limit is less important than it might seem on the basis of formal normative data (see Section 6). Among the most prominent cases, one can mention Art. 35 of the Workers' Statute, which provides that the application of the law itself in the area of sea and air navigation shall be remitted to collective agreements.

The other type of devolution, with more complex aspects, is that of derogations from the law. The principle is that if a matter is regulated by law, collective contract clauses must fail in favor of legal norms, unless they contain conditions more favorable to the workers than those norms. The technique of derogation, in the opposite direction as well, has been defined as semi-imperative (Kahn-Freund, 1958), and has been increasingly applied even if only in circumscribed areas. An important example is Law No. 903/1977 on sex discrimination under which the collective contract may be used to lift the ban on assigning women to night shifts.

d) devolution to bipartite or tripartite commissions (a variant of remittal to bargaining). These commissions, which perform administrative tasks, are numerous. In some cases they are given real regulatory powers. Here too it may be appropriate to distinguish between complementary remittal and derogative remittal. Important examples of both types are found in Law No. 140/1981, which introduced an experimental employment system giving broad regulatory powers to regional employment commissions in those Southern regions hit by the 1980 earthquake (Campania and Basilicata), even in derogation from national legislation.

15. Neo-Corporatist Proceduralism

In Italy in recent years, as in other European countries, concertation practices among government, labour and employers' associations have arisen. These practices, which have been described as neo-corporatist, have created an equilibrium between state intervention and self-regulated systems which is a very different result from that of the systems of "conflictual pluralism" (or collective *laissez-faire* (Kahn-Freund, 1959; Lewis, 1983). In the latter, the law lays down ground rules substituting collective *laissez-faire* for individual *laissez-faire*, in the law of the market (Section 1). However, it maintains neutrality between the parties, especially in mediatory interventions, even if the government itself is not always neutral, as has been the case in Italy since 1969. In contrast, in the areas of neo-corporatist models, law and contract are overlapping. This creates a need for new, stricter ground rules, especially regarding (a) legitimation of contracting parties (b) effectiveness of agreements and (c) the management of conflicts (Duran, 1983). The self-regulatory mechanisms that dominated for more than 30 years were proving inadequate for this purpose.

The confusion resulting from the overlap between law and contract mentioned above has occurred in various areas. Above all, new legal rules have come into existence which are contractually binding even against contractual provisions more favorable to the workers. (e.g. Law No. 91/1977, Law No. 297/1982, both on severance payments). In 1984, the government intervened directly in wage developments by placing a temporary ceiling on indexing. These interventions have almost always taken place with the consent of the most representative unions. Only in 1984 was there serious conflict between the government and a part of the trade union movement. This strengthening of the law, which goes in an opposite direction to the one of devolution previously described, however, has been compensated for by a more frequent use of remittal of the law to bargaining, as described in section 14.

In the opposite direction, there has been a broad extension of "bargained" law, not unknown previously, but of limited use over time or for matters of importance. All of the restrictive interventions mentioned above were negotiated, either formally or informally.

The 1983 tripartite agreement (Section 7) bound the government to bring before Parliament bills concerning employment relations, as well as income tax, social security, family allowances, national health service and utility tariffs. The following year's agreement extended the earlier one's scope to legislation on crisis areas and to various measures meant to promote employment. Of course, this practice has raised problems in relations with Parliament which has sometimes delayed, or rejected or amended the government's commitments. A recent ruling of the Constitutional Court has stated that these "neo-corporative" agreements are not covered by the constitutional guarantee of trade union freedom (Art. 39), which has been held to protect freedom of negotiation as well. According to the Constitutional Court such agreements fall within the public sphere since the government is party to them (Corte Costituzionale, 1985). This latter statement, however, raised widespread criticism among legal writers.

The need for new rules of the game has not yet given rise to significant innovations, but the need for these is very much felt. Above all, there is the problem of the effectiveness of plant agreements on redundancies, which regulate the quantity, procedure and timing of lay-offs and dismissals. Moreover, though no true "concessionary bargaining" to cut wages have been achieved, the so-called "solidarity contracts" aimed at reducing wages in order to cut working hours and absorb redundancies are being used more widely. An *ad hoc* legal framework has even been introduced for these (Law No. 863/1984).

The lack of sure rules is felt particularly in regard to the representativeness of the unions and their power to conclude agreements that deal with redundancies. Many agreements in this area have been assailed in the courts by workers or groups of workers who have suffered under them, for instance, by being included on lay-off lists, and many rulings have declared the agreements themselves invalid. A recent bill has proposed a ratification procedure according to which agreements must be accepted by the workers in a bargaining unit before they will be recognized as binding. (Giugni *et al.*, 1985).

In conflict management too, neo-corporative or social concertation, as already mentioned, has introduced some rationalizing norms regarding the links between different levels of bargaining such as tripartite, national and plant agreements. Obviously this also implies a consistent rationalization of conflict behavior. In a recent agreement regarding the large state holding company, IRI (Institute for Industrial Recovery), signed in December 1984, cooling off and conciliation procedures were finally introduced. Mention should also be made of the consolidation of self-regulation in public transport (section 7) though this is a parallel development not part of the policy of social concertation.

The trend is still, however, to intervene in order to support rather than to replace (Streeck and Schmitter, 1984). That is, the law ought to state the conditions for the introduction of adequate procedures, but not impose compulsory models of conduct that look like an effort by the state to colonize the area of autonomy. More generally, a trend can be discerned in doctrine right now (Liso, 1981), and to some extent in case law as well, to give workers protection against employers' decisions through binding procedures rather than by enforcing subjective rights against the employers. This is a further direction of growth of the procedural method (Mayntz, 1983), or reflexive law, which fits in with the more general revision of basic ground rules concerning both collective and individual relationships. The objective is in both cases is to promote self-regulation instead of a substantive or regulatory law (Teubner, 1983). In the past the latter, by dictating direct norms of conduct, have severely restricted the self-regulatory capacity of individuals and, though to a lesser extent in Italy, of social groups themselves.

[Translated from the Italian by Iain Fraser]

References

Aaron, Benjamin and Kenneth William Wedderburn, (eds.) (1972) *Industrial Conflict. A Comparative Legal Survey.* London: Longman.

Accornero, Aris (1980) *Il lavoro come ideologia.* Bologna: Il Mulino.

Antonioli, Maurizio and Bruno Bezza (1974) *La Fiom dalle origini al fascismo.* Bari: De Donato.

BARASSI, Ludovico (1915-17) *Il contratto di lavoro.* Milano: SEL.
BARBADORO, Isidoro (1973) *Storia del sindacalismo italiano*; Vol. I and II. Firenze: La Nuova Italia.
CARABELLI, Umberto (1984) *Libertà e immunità del sindacato.* Napoli: Jovene.
CARINCI, Franco, Paolo TOSI and Tiziano TREU (1983) *Diritto del Lavoro,* Vol. I "Il diritto sindacale". Torino:UTET.
CLARK, Jon (1983) "Towards a Sociology of Labour Law: An Analysis of the German Writings of O. Kahn-Freund", in: K.W. Wedderburn, R. Lewis, and J. Clark (eds.) *Labour Law and Industrial Relations: Building on Kahn-Freund.* Oxford: Clarendon Press.
CAMERA DEI DEPUTATI — SENATO DELLA REPUBBLICA (1985) *Relazione della Commissione parlamentare per le riforme istituzionali.*
COMMONS, John (1924) *Legal Foundations of Capitalism.* New York: Macmillan.
DEGLI INNOCEENTI, Maurizio (1984) *Geografia e istituzioni del socialismo italiano.* Napoli: Guida.
DURAN LOPEZ, Federico, (1983) "Dalla democrazia industriale all'economia concertata", 59 *Mondoperaio*
FEDERAZIONE LAVORATORI METALMECCANICI (FLM) (1973). *Report of Executive Committee* April 10, reported in *Annuario Sindacale.* Milano: Franco Angeli.
FEDERMECCANICA (National Federation of Mechanical Industry) V National Conference "The Labour Issue". Florence March 22-23, 1985. Introduction: *Relazione Industriale* 83.
GIUGNI, Gino (1960) *Introduzione allo studio dell'autonomia collettiva.* Milano: Giuffrè.
— (1961) "Il progresso technologico e la contrattazione collettiva dei rapporti di lavoro", Centro di Prevenzione e Difesa Sociale (1961) *Lavoratori e sindacati di fronte alle trasformazioni del processo produttivo.* Milano: Feltrinelli.
— (1982) "Il diritto del lavoro negli anni '80", 15 *Giornale di diritto del lavoro e di relazioni industriali* 373.
— (1985) "Concertazione sociale e sistema politica in Italia", 25 *Giornale di diritto del lavoro e di relazioni industriali* 1.
GIUGNI, Gino *et al.* (1985a).
GUIDI, Eugenio *et al.* (1974) *Annuario sindacale.* Milano: F. Angeli Editore.
ICHINO, Pietro, (1984) "Politiche del lavoro e strategie di deregulation" *Rivista italiana di diritto del lavoro* 590.
ILO (1985) "In Focus: Italy", in *Social and Labour Bulletin* 4.
ISTITUTO DI SOCIOLOGIA (ed.) (1979) *Lavorare due volte* Torino: Università di Torino press.
JOCTEAU, Giancarlo, (1979-1980) "La contrattazione collettiva. Aspetti legislativi e istituzionali 1926-1934" Annali Feltrinelli *La classe operaia durante il fascismo,* XX. Milano: Feltrinelli.
KAHN-FREUND, Otto (1958) "Rapports collectifs du travail. Rapport général", *Actes du II Congrès international de droit social,* I, Bruxelles.
— (1959) "Labour Law", in M. Ginsberg (ed.) *Law and Opinion in England in the Twentieth Century.* Berkeley: University of California Press.
LEWIS, Roy (1983) "Method and Ideology in the Writing of Otto Kahn-Freund", in: K.W. Wedderburn, R. Lewis, J. Clark (eds.) *Labour Law and Industrial Relations: Building on Kahn-Freund.* Oxford: Clarendon Press.
LISO, Francesco (1981) "Modifiche dell'organizzazione e contratto di lavoro", 12 *Giornale di diritto del lavoro e di relazioni industriali* 359.
MANCINI, Federico (1963) "Libertà sindacale e contratto collettivo erga omnes" *Rivista trimestrale di diritto e procedura civile* 570.

MAYNTZ, Renate (1983) "The Conditions of Effective Public Policy: A New Challenge for Policy Analysis", 11 *Policy and Politics* 123.
REGINI, Marino (1984) *I tentativi italiani di patto sociale a cavallo degli anni '80.* Bologna: Il Mulino.
CASSESE, Sabino (Chairman) (1984) Report of the Commission on *delegificazione* appointed by President of the Council, March 1984.
RUSCONI, Gian Enrico (1984) *Scambio minaccia decisione. Elementi di sociologia politica.* Bologna: Il Mulino.
STREECK, Wolfgang and Philippe S. SCHMITTER, (1984) *Community, Market, State and Associations.* Firenze: European University Institute Working Paper No. 94.
TEUBNER, Gunther (1983) "Substantive and Reflexive Elements in Modern Law", 17 *Law and Society Review* 239.
TREU, Tiziano (1975) *L'uso politico dello statuto dei lavoratori.* Bologna: Il Mulino.
— (1984) "Una ricerca empirica sullo statuto dei lavoratori negli anni '80", 23 *Giornale di diritto del lavoro e di relazioni industriali* 497.
VARDARO Gaetano (1984) *Contrattazione collettiva e sistema giuridico.* Napoli: Jovene.

III

Corporations

Juridification of Corporate Structures*

Friedrich Kübler
Frankfurt

Contents

* This study is indebted in numerous ways to the exchange of information and ideas with colleagues and friends of the International Faculty for Corporate and Capital Market Law. Special thanks are owed to Dean Robert H. Mundheim and his research assistant, Stephen W. Smith of the University of Pennsylvania, to Professor Barthelemy Mercadal, Paris, and to Professor Misao Tatsuta, Kyoto.

The attempt to cover, in a brief comparative law study, the quantitative and above all qualitative changes in company law which are hinted at by the term "juridification", is paradoxical in the sense that the phenomenon of expansion and differentiation is made the object of systematic abbreviation and reduction. The need to simplify extremely complex fact situations has been taken into account in two ways. First, the following discussion concentrates almost exclusively on the law of the United States and the Federal Republic of Germany; other legal systems are mentioned only occasionally. Second, the presentation does not follow the traditional pattern. Instead it is ordered according to an outline of problems which was presented to the members of the working group by the project coordinator. Finally, it should be noted that the present text is half the length of the German original, and has not been abbreviated as a whole, but shortened by omitting or simply referring to entire sections.

1. Trends in Growth: Juridification as Quantitative Increase in Law

In the most important nonsocialist industrial states, the continuous expansion of company law is frequently discussed and often criticized. Empirical observations can be made based on the rising tide of law gazettes, reports, and journals, as well as other commentaries, text books and publications seemingly unaffected by the recession in the publishing industry. Quantifying information, however, is scarce and of questionable value. (Data available for France indicate that during the period from 1907 to 1970 some 2,600 judgements were made in commercial company cases. It seems more useful to measure the expansion of law by its increasing regulatory functions. Models of classical company law can be taken as a starting point (infra, 1.1). Only in terms of historical comparison can the internal (infra, 1.2) and external (infra, 1.3) increase in functions be reasonable assessed.

1.1 The Area of Conrol Under Classical Company Law

Classical company law is organizational law. It controls the legal relationships of associates in a business in relation to one another as well as to the entity itself, which is also based on company law. These structures create the legal status and duties of shareholder representatives (directors, or *Aufsichtsräte*), and of appointed managers (officers, or *Vorstände*). Shareholders can be simple investors, i.e., stockholders or limited partners, but in some cases may also be owners managing their own businesses. Company law is concerned, however, not only with the internal structure of organizations, but also with their relationships with the outside world, through provisions that regulate business transactions and above all protect creditors.

(1) U.S. Law

Company law in the U.S has traditionally been state law (Conard, 1976: 3; infra, 1.3 (2) and 3.1 (1)). This is true of the law governing both partnerships and corporations. The importance of partnership is slight in comparison with Germany so this form will not be discussed further here. (Most of the states have adopted the Uniform Partnership Act of the National Conference of Commissioners of Uniform State Law. Jennings and Buxbaum, 1979: 2). Classical corporation law is set out in individual state business corporation codes (the most important of these codes are listed in Conard, 1976: XXXVV), which are based on a control model which can be summarized as follows (Eisenberg, 1976: 1): shareholders have the authority to decide on "major corporate actions", i.e., on "fundamental" or "extraordinary changes", and they may elect "directors" whom they may not instruct and who may be dismissed only on serious grounds. These "directors" form the board which formulates "business policy", delegates management duties to the officers as its agents, and supervises these officers in their functions. There are two subcategories within this model (Eisenberg, 1976: 316. For a substantially more detailed differentiation see Conrad, 1976: 52):

(a) The "closely-held" or "close" corporation has relatively few shareholders. These control the business, either together or by majority. The most important regulatory problem is the protection of the minority from fundamental decisions made by the majority.

(b) The "publicly held" or "public" corporation's shares are widely distributed and in most cases are the object of stock exchange or over-the-counter trading. The company is not controlled by the shareholders but by a board, or more precisely, a group of directors who simultaneously act as the main executive officers of the corporation[1]. The most important regulatorly problem is the

[1] The composition of the board is described in detail and extensively illustrated by Herman (1981: 30). The difference in comparison with German law, which is not so much fundamental as related to technical problems of organization lies in the fact that the management and regulatory functions are not allocated to separate institutions. Cf. Vagts (1966/67: 23 and 52); Großfeld and Ebke (1977: 57 and 94).

protection of shareholders and, in the case of publicly traded stock, the protection of investors (infra, 3.3 (2)) from corrupt practices and/or incompetent management.

(2) German Law

The classical concept of German company law is formally based on the idea of codification. The traditional forms of partnerships (*offene Handelsgesellschaft (offG) and Kommanditgesellschaft (KG)*) and stock corporations (*Aktiengesellschaft (AG)*) were both offered by the Commercial Code as models of organizations which to a large extent could be modified by and substituted for one another. The structure of codification was shaken first by the introduction of the GmbH (*Gesellschaft mit beschränkter Haftung*), a form of private limited company under German law very similar to the close corporation, and later again by reform of the stock corporation law during the 1930's. The expansion of corporation law could be achieved only by means of special legislation. In contrast to the situation in the United States, the legal form of the partnership as well as mixed forms of partnership and corporation (*GmbH & Co. KG*) have remained significant even for medium-sized and larger firms (Kübler, 1981: 41). The link between legal form and actual fact has become increasingly loose and even the public company may now occur in the form of a partnership (Wiedemann, 1980a: 114 and 121).

1.2 Increasing Differentiation Within the Classical Control Area

The following discussion will center on how company law has changed its traditional focus. The analysis is restricted to the corporation, and to the finer points of corporate accountability and creditor protection.

(1) Corporate Accountability

The term "corporate accountability" here refers to the problem of making the management of a corporation effectively conform to the wishes and requirements of the shareholders. The problem appears most acutely in the phenomenon first described by Berle and Means as the "split between ownership and control" in the case of the typical public corporation (Berle/Means, 1937). The observation that the growing dispersion of shares makes it easier for managements to escape control by shareholders has been confirmed for Germany (Mestmäcker, 1958: 78,91; Wiethölter, 1961: 270). In both Germany and the U.S. this finding has been associated with wide-ranging expectations of a fundamental change in the socio-economic system[2]. This so far has not occured. (On this point detailed and, even for the German situation, plausible explanations appear in Herman, 1981: 85). Legislative policies aimed at elimination of the split between ownership and control through the

2 As to the expectation of Marx, Schumpeter and Renner, that managers will function "objectively as the grave-diggers of the capitalist system", cf. Pross (1965: 29). In the U.S., Burnham (1941) forecast far reaching changes in the orientation of company objectivities.

institutionalization of "shareholder democracy", are regarded with increasing scepticism (Cf. Eisenberg, 1976: 19 and Wiedemann, 1980a: 352, both with further references. On the current reform discussion in the U.S. see Manning, 1980: 9,2). This can be easily supported by the fact that the cost involved for a small shareholder in effectively exercising powers of control and participation is not matched by an even approximately equivalent chance of return. The transaction costs incurred, however, are not invariable. They can be influenced by modifying institutional framework conditions, which is the aim of several policies:

(a) Their bases are the powers of the general meeting as separated from the powers of management, (board, or *Aufsichtsrat* and *Vorstand*)[3]. Both legal systems start from the principle that ordinary business transactions are the responsibility of management, while all fundamental changes come within the power of the general assembly (Eisenberg, 1976: 85; Kübler, 1981: 193). This delimitation, though clear at first glance, has proved increasingly difficult in the context of business practices determined by new methods of financing, grouping, and take over bids. Allocation of authority may depend on the purpose of a contemplated action. Thus board decisions may exceed the board's proper authority if they are aimed at modifying existing opportunities for control or at maintaining these against changes that would otherwise occur, e.g., control by foreign capital[4]. On the other hand, the formal nature of a measure is no longer solely determinant of its legal qualification; increasing importance is being attached to its economic impact (see *Aiple* v. *Twin City Barge & Towing Co.*, 274 Minnesota Reports (Minn.) 38, 143 North Western Reporter (N.W.) Second Series (2d) 374 (1966) and the *Tiefseehafen* decision of the Federal (Supreme) Court in 1982 Entscheidungen des Bundesgerichtshofs für Zivilsachen (BGHZ) 83: 122).

(b) When a general meeting is required to make a decision, the large public company is confronted with the technical problem of a voting procedure in which hundreds of thousands and sometimes millions of shareholders may be taking part. This has been solved in the U.S., as in Germany, by allowing for proxy votes (Großfeld/Ebke, 1977: 95). The proxy voting right is exercised in Germany by the major banks and in the U.S. by management, though this is not mandatory. There is a risk of conflicts of interest in both practices. In order to reduce this risk the authority of the proxy is restricted in that he must fully inform the person he represents and seek binding instructions[5]. In the

[3] The possibility of changing this distribution of powers is most clearly demonstrated by the proposals to take away the voting rights of shareholders in general. For the U.S., cf. Manning (1958); for Germany, cf. Roth (1972: 225).

[4] Cf. the cases discussed in Eisenberg (1976: 91). In German law a different view still appears in Bundesgerichtshof Entscheidungen in Zivilsachen (BGHZ) 33, 175, 186, though some regard the ruling as erroneous. See Mestmäcker (1958: 139); Wiethölter (1961: 122); Lutter (1971: § 186 Rn. 50).

[5] In Germany this rule is based on secs. 128 and 135 Aktiengesetz (AktG) and in the U.S. on the proxy rules of the Securities Exchange Commission (SEC). For a more detailed discussion see *infra* 1.3 (2).

U.S. there is furthermore a concern to prevent the proxy machinary, financed by corporate funds, from being used by management for its own purposes instead of for the benefit of the stockholders (see Eisenberg, 1976: 97, for a detailed discussion). In Germany the "Gessler" Commission investigated the phenomenon of power concentration in big banks, in part from the perspective of proxy voting rights, and recommended "appropriate improvements of current regulation". A minority of the Commission pleaded furthermore, for "fundamental reforms" (Bericht der Studienkommission, 1979: 384).

(c) The wide dispersion of stock ownership is associated with the further difficulty that shareholders are no longer in a positon to monitor management acting on their behalf. For this purpose, German company law has for a long time required the setting up of supervisory boards (*Aufsichtsrat*), to which it has given additional functions under the codetermination laws. In the U.S. the board of directors was originally responsible for policy decisions, but this function has been increasingly transferred to the chief executives, and thus the former have come to assume the supervision ("selecting, monitoring, and removing") of the latter as their main task (Eisenberg, 1976: 139 ff., particularly: 170; Leech/Mundheim, 1976: 3). This distribution of authority has proved questionable in both legal orders. For public companies, in fact, it is management, which should be subject to control, that decides on who is to be appointed director or member of the supervisory board (Mestäcker, 1958: 78; Wiethölter, 1961: 270; Kübler, 1981: 173; Eisenberg, 1976: 170; Herman, 1981: 17 ff. particularly: 52) The considerable increase in the number of outside directors in the U.S. has changed the situation little.[6] Comparable difficulties arise from the fact that the monitoring entities generally do not have their own substructure and therefore are dependent on information supplied by management. This has become a legal problem provoking lively discussion far beyond the law of accounting (Eisenberg, 1976: 188; Lutter, 1978; Mertens, 1980: 67).

(d) The by now almost traditional difficuties involved in ensuring effective control of management through organizational provisions constitute a plausible explanation for the increasing importance of civil liability. The fact that it has played no role in Germany for a long time is due not only to the small number of true public companies, but also to relatively unfavorable procedural conditions. Apart from the risk of costs there is, above all, the fact that individual shareholders lack the right of action. It seems to be all the more

[6] For figures concerning this increase cf. Herman (1981: 39). It obviously results from several circumstances: pressures from the SEC, see Leech and Mundheim (1976: 5), and for a critical view, Karmel (1982: 160), and from the stock exchanges. Thus the New York Stock Exchange requires, for the listing of a corporation, "an Audit Committee comprised solely of directors independent from management", Herman (1981: 38) "For the most part, however, outside directors do not have substantial power in the corporation ... A friendly, helpful but definitely unthreatening, and perhaps really compliant and passive, board may be the norm," (1981: 37).

noteworthy that the civil responsibility of *Aufsichtsrat* and *Vorstand* has recently, with increasing frequency, been the object of cases decided by the Federal (Supreme) Court (see e.g. Bundesgerichtshof (BGH) Neue Juristische Wochenschrift (NJW) 1980, 1628 "Schaffgotsch" and BGH 79, 38 "Poullain"). In the U.S. the derivative suit gives every stockholder the opportunity to involve the management in litigation, and the case material, abundant by now, has for a long time been the most important basis for determining managements' and directors' duties of care and of loyalty (Wiethölter, 1961: 200; Großfeld, 1968; Conard, 1976: 380; Jennings/Buxbaum 1979: 168).

(2) Creditor Protection

The extraordinary growth in the number of corporations is based to a considerable extent on the possibility of limiting liability, and thus risk, to the invested capital. For creditors this entails the risk that losses of the company will be passed on to them. Therefore the institution of "stated capital" and the regulations intended to guarantee its contribution and maintenance have become part of classical corporate law. In both American and German law the extent to which such provisions must be constantly supplemented and extended by the courts is striking. In Germany this tendency is illustrated, above all, by a line of important decisions dealing with shareholders' loans to corporations[7]. The attempt made in the most recent amendment of the GmbH statute, to transform rules evolved by the courts into legal provisions (sections 32a nd 32b Gesetz betreffend die Gesellschaften mit beschränkter Haftung (GmbHG)) can obviously not be understood as a definitive solution due to the fact that the provisions do not fully comply with pre-existing rules of case law (See Hueck, 1983: 345 and Farrenkopf/Cahn, 1983). Thus it must be assumed that judicial evolution will not be held back by this legislation (Cf. the most recent judgements BGHZ 81, 252, 311 and 365; 90, 370 and 381). However, the question as to whether creditors in other cases of undercapitalization can also hold shareholders responsible has so far not been clarified[8]. In this respect case law in the U.S. has gone a step further (Clark, 1977; Jennings/Buxbaum, 1979: 976, and Schanze, 1975: 96), generally on the basis of the doctrines of "alter ego" and "disregard of corporate entity".[9] Shareholders' loans are treated as being contributions to capital, which in the case

[7] BGHZ 31, 258, 272; 67, 171, 174ff; 69, 274, 281; 75, 334, 337; 76, 326, 329; 81, 252, 255 and 311, 317ff; 90, 370, 375 and 381, 385.

[8] In the negative the strongly criticized decision of (the VIII. instead of the II. Civil Senate of the BGH competent for company law) BGHZ 68, 312; opposite in many cases the lower courts (e.g. Oberlandesgericht (OLG) Hamburg Betriebsberater (BB) 1973, 1231 and OLG Karlsruhe Wertpapier-Mitteilungen (WM) 1978, 692) and at least in result also BGHZ 54, 222; cf. Wiedemann (1980a: 224 and 570).

[9] These formulas correspond to the "*Durchgriffs*"-*Konzept*. Their "main function, ... lies... in the increase in the creditor protection which is only inadequately established in the individual state corporation laws". Rehbinder (1969: 127).

of bankruptcy must serve to meet the claims of actual creditors (See *In re Mader's Store for Men, Inc.*, 77 Wisconsin Reports (Wis.) 2d 578, 254, N.W. 2d 171 (1977); *Tanzi* v. *Fiberglass Swimming Pools, Inc.*, 414 Atlantic Reporter (A.) 2d 484 (1980)). Furthermore "inadequate capitalization" in a number of situations may lead to a finding of unlimited liability on the part of controlling shareholders [10].

(3) Corporate Organization and Juridification

From this brief survey the conclusion can be drawn that management by nonshareholders and limited liability, as structural principles of corporate law, inevitably generate problems relating to the protection of shareholders from management incompetence and/or disloyalty, and to the protection of creditors from the misuse of the corporate form by shareholders. Present legislative provisions, which constitute the response to a history of previous abuses are offen inadequate. At least under current framework conditions, the regulatory objectives of shareholder and creditor protection, both of which are essential for the corporation as an institution, can obviously not be achieved by a definitive list of narrowly and clearly stated rules. These can only be attained through general clause ("catchall") provisions which will permit flexible responses to constantly changing situations and thus allow for progressive differentiation of relevant rules. What would seem to be less clear are the conditions causing this type of juridification. It may arise out of the complexity of corporate organizational structures imbedded in a market controlled environment.

1.3 Development of New Areas of Law and Their Overlapping

The above discussion was concerned with trends in the growth of company law in relation to its traditional regulatory problems. This could be called the "internal" expansion of the relevant law. We shall now consider some aspects of the ways in which corporate law has gone beyond these classical limits with juridification becoming practically "external" to the areas of classical corporation law. The following phenomena should be noted:

(1) Intercompany Law

Instead of the simple corporation, organizational structures which are interlocked in increasingly complicated ways have appeared. These are designated as *Konzerne* in German law and as "megasubsidiaries" (among other terms) in the U.S. (Eisenberg, 1976: 277; for actual development: 217). In both

[10] For example Minton v. Cavaney, 56 California Reporter (Cal.) 2d. 576, 364, Pacific Reporter (P.) 2nd 473 (1961): "The equitable owners of a corporation ... are personally liable ... when they provide inadequate capitalization and actively participate in the conduct of corporate affairs". Cf. also De Witt Truck Brokers, Inc. v. W. Ray Flemming Fruit Co., 540 Federal Reporter (F.) 2d 681 (4th Circuit (Cir.) 1976) and in re *Mobile Steel Co.*, 563 F. 2d 692 (5th Cir. 1977).

countries these generate a great number of problems concerning the protection of investors, minorities, and creditors, which are taken into account in different ways.

(2) Securities Regulation and Capital Market Law
The system of controls termed "securities regulation", which is interwoven in many ways with company law, has envolved into an extensive area of law since its beginnings during the New Deal. It no longer exclusively serves the regulatory objective of investor protection (cf. infra 2.1. (2)), and for some time has generated a demand for deregulation (cf. infra, 3.1 (4)). The development of a corresponding German "capital market law" is still in the initial stages.

(3) Accounting Law
Accounting law, in the course of its development, has also assumed new functions relating to the protection of creditors, shareholders, the capital market, and the general public. This is another aspect of juridification of company structures.

(4) Tax Law
Tax law is increasingly proving to be a factor which determines not only the practice but the structure of corporate law (Walz, 1980: 234 ff., 253 ff.).

(5) Codetermination
Finally, with respect to certain European countries, we must take codetermination (the statutory requirement that employees be represented on company boards which are subject to company law) into account (Wiedemann, 1980a: 598). Here again we find a continuing process of growth which would appear to be of particular interest because of its qualitative aspects, i.e., its contribution to the progress of mandatory law.

2. Materialization: the Gradual Process of Mandatory Law

Based on Max Weber's distinction between the "formal" and the "material" rationality of law (Weber, 1967, in particular § 4 and 8), one can explain the law's modern development as a process of materialization: a movement from 19th century formal law subject to an abstract ethos of freedom, to a new law, inspired by the idea of the welfare state (Wieacker, 1953: 18; 1967: 539; Assmann, 1980b: 239 and 251; Wiethölter, 1982: 38; Teubner, 1983: 239-40). In analyzing company law it is advisable to define precisely two aspects of this method of explanation. Materialization means that the rule of law is designed to achieve specific economic results and/or social conditions. Thus its validity is removed from the influence of those directly concerned: the law becomes mandatory. At the same time, the purposes of materialization are so complex that a sweeping reference to the welfare state would appear to be of limited use. This is particularly true when the progress of mandatory law can be explained by the need for regulation inherent in economic development.

2.1 Replacement of Optional by Mandatory Law: the Problem of Transaction Costs

(1) Evolution from Optional to Mandatory Company Law

The general evolution of company law can be summarized by saying that classical company law is fundamentally optional, while the provisions which result from the processes of expansion of law described in section 1 are fundamentally mandatory. This change is traditionally explained in terms of needs for protection:

(a) Those doing business with a company must be able to rely on the extent of authority of any agents authorized to represent the company[11].

(b) Creditors need assurance that working capital will be maintained.

(c) Small shareholders in public corporations need to be protected by rules of mandatory law, although in close corporations optional rules are sufficient[12].

(d) Potential investors need assurances that relevent information is disclosed as well as accurate. Thus, securities regulation is basically mandatory[13].

(e) The same logic applies to employee protection requirements and the mandatory character of codetermination law.

(2) Transaction Costs and Allocative Efficiency

The above listed specific protection requirements indicate that there are different interests both within and relating to individual companies. This does not, however, explain the purpose of or the necessity for mandatory rules. It would be erroneous to regard optional law as simply an early form or transitory phenomenon of a predetermined evolution since it can be explained according to its own terms of rationality. It resulted from negotiation of concrete organization rules in the market place; in other words: in the classical liberal concept of company law, it is up to the (potential) entrepreneurs, the employees, and the financiers (in the role of both investor-shareholder and creditor) to agree on the legal form for the reciprocal relationships according to their respective needs. Optional corporation law supplies them with proven models and also saves them the trouble of providing for all eventualities by contract. To the extent that the market machanism functions,

[11] German law for a long time has known provisions governing all commercial companies. In the U.S. the abolition of the *ultra vires* doctrine, which links the power of representation to company objectives took considerably more time; cf. Jennings and Buxbaum (1979: 116 and 132).

[12] For German law this is provided by sec. 23 V AktG; for American law, cf. Eisenberg 1976: 316.

[13] Regarding the current discussion in the U.S. as to the need for or obsolescence of mandatory disclosure rules, see *infra* 3.1.(4).

mandatory law is not essential, and therefore its appearance requires an explanation. Several can be offered:

(a) One theory which has been proposed refers to "standards of legal ethics" ("rechtsethische Maßstäbe") "correcting the freedom of action of individuals for the sake of prevalent values" (Wiedemann, 1980b: 147 and 149). Protection of minorities and prospectus liability are given as examples[14]. No explanation, however, is given for the foundation of these standards nor their ranking[15], so no further discussion appears to be necessary.

(b) Mandatory law is often explained in terms of the social and political need to protect the individual (see Weitnauer, 1975) and is frequently based on the "social state" clause of the German Constitution. In some fact situations this explanation appears to be plausible, as in the case of tort creditors of companies whose interests, unlike those of (loan-) contract creditors, are not taken into account when organization and capital structures are worked out by agreement. This example shows that we are dealing with issues of distributive justice. The problem lies in how far one should generalize this protection of the individual. The desired protection benefits a variety of entities like banks and suppliers which are, in fact, in a position to look after themselves. It thus is questionable whether the public should be burdened with the costs of mandatory regulation.

(c) Commentators increasingly view mandatory law as a protective instrument not only for the individual but for functions and institutions as well (Raiser, 1963: 145; Steindorff, 1974: 521; Großfeld, 1968: 193; 1977: 78; Hopt, 1975: 51). Under this theory, provisions which protect creditors also provide the essential guarantee of the credit-worthiness of a corporation. Protection of shareholders and investors has the additional aim of creating and maintaining the trust necessary for thrift and capital investments. This concept has the advantage that it goes beyond contractual reciprocity and looks towards the functional efficiency not only of institutions, e.g., stock corporations, but of credit and capital markets as well. It remains vague, however, insofar as it fails to explain under what conditions confidence in the integrity and functionality of market controlled institutions must be ensured by the intervention of mandatory law.

(d) This gap is being increasingly filled by a series of recent and closely related theorems of microeconomics. These center on the concept of "transaction costs"[16]. The "theory of the firm", established by Coase, explains the origin

[14] Wiedemann, (1980b: 155ff. and 158).

[15] This may, above all, be due to the fact that it is not a question of establishing material criteria for decisions, but the complete denial of the view "that only a marxist economic system can develop moral force", Wiedemann (1980a: 176). For a critical view of this position see also Buxbaum (1983): "Wiedemann likes the adjective '*rechtsethisch*' ... I do not know what it means, but I like most of the proposed rules...".

[16] A basic discussion can be found in Coase (1953: 146, and particularly 164); cf. also Demsetz (1975: 23); Wegehenkel (1980: especially 20); as to private law implications see Assmann *et al.*, (1978: 21) and Kübler (1984).

of the company as a reaction to increasing costs of negotiating contracts. If the number of reciprocal exchange relationships required for the establishment of a business exceeds a certain level, it is cheaper to replace the exchange of individual goods and services with a coordinated system of long-term loan and partnership contracts. Through these, capital and labor factors are integrated in the enterprise organization (Coase, 1937: 386; also Kirchner, 1983: 137, and Schanze, 1983: 161). But the long-term commitment of capital, in the form of debt or equity, increases the risk to creditors and investors. Thus they try to improve their position by agreeing on appropriate protective measures. This results in further transaction costs, i.e., those involved in collecting information about a planned project and its promoters, and negotiating respective conditions. If a company wishes to obtain a large loan or equity capital from many depositors it will endeavor to reduce costs by standardizing conditions, i.e., by offering uniform capital preservation terms to all potential creditiors, uniform rights of information, control, participation and minority protection to all potential shareholders. Thus, both groups will find themselves faced with the further difficulty of complicated differences in the details of legal conditions when making decisions as to which rival offer to accept. The granting of credit extension would have to be made dependent on accounting requirements, and the purchase of shares on the scope of information and voting rights under company articles. This means that even the cost in terms of time and money (for professional advice, etc.) necessary for the evaluation of these variable framework conditions would prevent many economically desirable transactions and projects, or burden them with the risk of avoidable misallocations[17]. Therefore, there are several reasons for assuming that mandatory law may promote the development of private autonomy. In routine transactions it removes the burden of cumbersome negotiations, of complex assessments of contractual fairness, and — in the case of unequal power distribution — costly self-organization of weaker parties (Olson, 1973).

(3) Limits of Economic Explanation of Juridification

The observation that mandatory corporation law in many respects aims at improving allocative efficiency by reducing transaction costs is frequently underestimated in relation to juridification of enterprises. The restriction of private decision making through mandatory rules is determined neither by theoretically unexplained maxims of "legal ethics" nor by arbitrary majority decisions motivated by redistributive justice. Rather, it is based on testable rules of economic rationality. Mandatory law is used in order to simplify

[17] For a more detailed discussion see Brinkmann and Kübler (1981: 681); cf. also Dahlmann (1979: 141, 161). The issue is also discussed by Kirchner (1982: 154-55) who regards the advance of mandatory law as an historical experience of "reforms under the aspect of repairs particularly in company law" and who raises the "question as to the economic sense of the overall result achieved", without going into the aspect of transaction costs.

complex fact constellations and thus structure alternatives for economically rational decision-making. This conclusion at the same time illustrates the determinant evolutionary forces: the process of "juridification", manifest in the progress of mandatory law and interpreted by a broad body of opinion as being a product of political efforts directed against private autonomy and the free market system (Mertens, 1982: 29), is in fact completely determined by the inherent dynamic of economic development. When market contracts (upon which the existence of the individual as well as the community is based) become increasingly numerous and complicated, the need to stabilize necessary framework conditions by eliminating uncertainty grows. According to all available evidence, progress in economic development leads to an increased number, and differentiation, of contractual relationships and at the same time to their partial transformation into organizational structures (Eschenburg, 1978: 10, and Wegehenkel, 1980: 18), the economic rationality of which in turn is based increasingly on legally guaranteed reliability. This observation, which is fundamental to an understanding of modern legal development, can only be broadly outlined here. It requires modification in two ways:

(a) The statement that mandatory company law is often aimed at reducing transaction costs must not be understood to mean that it is necessarily successful in this. The cost-saving may be more than counterbalanced by misallocations or resulting administrative costs. Clear conclusions are hardly possible in this respect: "...the question of whether a given law is worth the costs (in terms of better resource allocation) is rarely susceptible to empirical proof. This does not mean, of course, that the best we can do is to adopt a *laissez faire* policy and let the market do the best it can. It is precisely the province of good government to make guesses as to what laws are likely to be worth their costs" (Calabresi, 1975: 204, 206). Current research is mainly concerned with regulations which also aim at other objectives[18]. Therefore one must at least ask whether the comparative observation of parallel rules of law in different legal systems cannot be evaluated as an indicator of objective needs. In the U.S. prospectus liability has been introduced by legislation, whereas in Germany the judiciary has filled the legislative gap[19]. The functional equivalence of these regulations, produced in such different ways, appears to justify the (refutable) assumption of their social usefulness.

(b) Finally, it must be remembered that mandatory company law may additionally, or exclusively, have more than purely allocative objectives. From the viewpoint of juridification, the above mentioned areas of securities regulation and codetermination are particularly interesting. They offer examples of policies designed for the achievement of several regulatory purposes. (This aspect is explained under D. III in the (original) German version of this paper).

[18] In the U.S. the primary question is the extent to which the mandatory disclosure required by the SEC improves allocative efficiency. The focal point of the German discussion is the evaluation of the cost and benefits of participation.

[19] For a detailed comparative law account see Assmann (1984).

2.2 Problems of Enforcement

Whenever mandatory law is introduced because economically rational contractual rules would cause excessive transaction costs for the parties concerned, and the public as a whole, the question arises as to the real efficiency of these regulations. Private law in general relies on the person benefiting from its rules to ensure its implementation. In the context of highly differentiated exchange and organizational relationships, this expectation is implausible. This is illustrated by the example of shareholder and investor protection. For the buyer and owner of just a few shares, it is generally not worthwhile to bring an action in the courts against clearly provable violations of prospectus requirements or profit calculation rules. The cost, in terms of time, stress, risk and expenditure bears no rational relationship to the benefit that can be expected from even the most favorable outcome. As a result, we can observe the genesis and growth of additional regulations which are specifically intended to permit the effective implementation of mandatory law.

(1) Facilitating the Bringing of Actions

These may be aimed directly at removing the economic barriers which stand in the way of bringing claims before the courts. German company law simply relies on the power of the court to reduce the cost of litigation (§ 247 II Aktiengesetz (AKtG). American law goes considerably further, in that "class action" and "derivative" suits allow for individual enforcement of collective interests. These options, combined with costs rules favoring private suits, have considerably stimulated "shareholder litigation" as an institutionalized element in the revitalization of company law (Conard, 1976:379, in particular 394; Homburger, 1975: 9, 69 and 78; Großfeld/Ebke, 1977: 97)

(2) Auditing and Disclosure of Balance Sheets

It is primarily where information processes are to be institutionalized that the sanctioning potential of private law damage remedies has been overlaid with more complex enforcement mechanisms. In German law, accounting, auditing, and the publication of balance sheets provide examples of this process. In the U.S. these three areas are closely connected to securities regulation. The Securities Exchange Commission (SEC) has at its disposal a considerable arsenal of formal sanctions and informal means of action (Karmel, 1982: 318). These are primarily concerned with issuing corporations and financial institutions subject to SEC supervision under the securities laws, such as stock exchanges [20], brokers, investment advisers and investment trusts.

[20] The National Association of Securities Dealers (NASD) is similarly affected. NASD is a professional organization of securities dealers and brokers trading on the over-the-counter-market. It is endowed with powers of self-regulation but comes under the general supervision of the SEC.

(3) Disciplining of Lawyers

It is particularly interesting that the SEC does not restrict its activities to the administrative supervision of corporations and institutions controlling transactions on the capital market. The Commission has extended its functions to cover independent advisers of issuing public corporations. The legal basis for this is provided by rule 2(e), introduced by the SEC itself, which allows for the exclusion of all persons who lack the necessary qualifications or integrity, or who have deliberately violated federal securities laws, from their professional activities, either temporarily or permanently. This rule was originally intended to provide authority to act against systematic obstruction ("contempt"), and as an instrument for disciplining unreliable auditors (Karmel, 1982: 175). In the early 70's the SEC extended its sanction to lawyers practising before that agency who failed to notify the commission in good time of irregularities known to them in the prospectuses and balance sheets submitted by their clients. Considering the high level of specialization of such lawyers, this is equivalent to disbarment[21]. One of the federal courts of appeal has confirmed this much criticized practice in an *obiter dictum* (*Touche Ross & Co.* v. *SEC*, 609 Federal Reporter (F.) 2d 570 2d Cir, 1979). This has strengthened the potential enforcement of securities regulation, above all in cases in which those obliged to disclose are financially at the end of their tether and therefore no longer fear the sanctions of the SEC. What has been questioned is the equating of lawyers, who are above all responsible for representing the interests of their clients, with certified public accountants, who in the final analysis are responsible to the public. This interpretation may infringe on the constitutional guarantee which protects lawyers from state prosecution implicit in the "due process" clause (Karmel, 1982: 179). It is also feared that the serious threat of sanctions against lawyers, who are generally averse to risk, may have a negative influence on the inclination of their clients to invest[22]. This means that the increase in efficiency will be paid for not only through higher social costs, but allocative losses as well[23].

[21] SEC v. National Student Marketing Corp. 457 Illinois Supplement (I. Supp.) 682 (D.D.C. 1978); *Keating, Meuthing and Klekamp, Securities Exchange Act Release Number (Sec. Exch. Act Release No.) 15922 (1979); in re Carter and Johnson*, Sec. Exch. Act Release No. 17597 (1981).

[22] Karmel (1982: 183): "Successful imposition of the new professional obligations will make lawyers even more conservative in their advice to corporate clients, and have a detrimental effect on the exercise of business judgement by corporation".

[23] German law does not go this far. It is true that auditors and lawyers under BGHZ 77, 172, 176 ff. are in principle subject to prospectus liability on the basis of *ulpa in contrahendo*. This, however, is based on their "creating a particular — and additional — basis for trust because of the evident participation in the drawing up of the prospectus" (p. 176).

2.3 Summary: Causes and Limits of Materialization

The conclusion to be drawn from this somewhat provisional and fragmentary analysis, is that the materialization of company law in the sense of its increasing transition towards mandatory law, is based to a considerable extent on structural changes in the economic system. The increasing density of the network of economic relationships requires a reduction in the costs of individual transactions. This is not least achieved through mandatory law by establishing a growing number of framework conditions for the organizational structures to be agreed on. Particular rules can in many cases be understood as measures inspired by distributive and welfare policies for the protection of "small" creditors, investors, or consumers. From an objective point of view, however, we are faced with a trend towards the improvement of allocative efficiency through the reduction of transaction costs, in order to increase the efficiency and stability of the free market system. It seems that at present the final limits to this development cannot be seen, although factors can be discerned which are slowing the process. For example, the implementation of mandatory law is subject to additional mechanisms of enforcement which for their part contribute to the cost burden. Theoretically a state of equilibrium is conceivable in which no further mandatory law would arise because the expected benefit (reduction in transaction costs) would cease to cover the necessary expenses (increase in transaction costs). Presumably this standstill will only be reached if the system of economic relationships itself stops changing significantly. Such a stage of consolidation and stagnation of economic development is so far not evident.

3. Proceduralization: The Vertical Differentiation of Regulatory Powers

The still vague term "proceduralization" (Teubner, 1983: 254; Wiethölter, 1982: 42) refers primarily to functional changes in the law: desired purposes are supposed to be achieved not through the direct imposition of legal sanctions, but indirectly, through the institutionalization of procedures. This, however, implies change in the structure of law as well. Procedures are based on allocations of power and their institutionalization therefore results in increasing vertical differentiation between levels of regulation and areas of control. For company law, as "private" organization law, this seems to be a promising perspective; even if the phenomena of proceduralization are in many ways heterogeneous.

3.1 Differentiation of Levels as Juridification of Law-Making

Classical company law was based on statute. It is understood to be the expression of the sovereign regulatory will of the legislative bodies. New sources of company law have emerged which will be discussed below under the headings of "federalization", "constitutionalization", "judicial regulation" and "bureaucratic regulation". This implies at least two aspects of juridification. First, regulatory powers must be attributed, which in the constitutional state is only possible by means of law. Second, the substance of legal rules must be coordinated, even if no direct (hierarchical) powers of correction exist. The result is legal ties in which formal elements are combined with substantive ones[24].

(1) Federal Integration

"Federalization" refers to the process of ending territorially determined differences in traditional company law by implementing common regulations. The most important example of this is provided by the federal security laws and their accompanying regulations in the U.S. These were introduced in an effort to overcome an economic crisis (Securities regulation is an important element of the "New Deal". Cf., Karmel, 1982: 38), and were supplemented by efforts to introduce federal corporate law to deal with inconsistencies inherent in the *status quo* (Fleischer, 1964/65: 1146, 1172). Further functions have been added over time: For example, the prevention of "sensitive payments" and "foreign corrupt practices". (Cf., Karmel, 1982: 147 ff.; Branch and Rubright, 1982: 1447). A process which is comparable in many ways has been taking place within the European Community. Directives drawn up by the commission and adopted by the Council of Ministers give rise to a rules structure which overrides the laws of the member states and for which the term "European Company Law" is coming into use. (For survey and data see Wiedemann, 1980a: 48). The main object of common rules is economic integration, i.e., the promotion of international economic transactions through harmonization of the framework condition to which these transactions are subject. In both the U.S. and the E.C. uniform regulations of a central authority are superimposed, though with greatly varying intensity, on a multiplicity of local company laws.

(2) Constitutional Governance

"Constitutionalization" is taken here to mean that company law legislation is subjected, in substance, to the text of a given constitution. It is related to "federal integration" because the distribution of legislative powers in federal states and confederations requires a basic arrangement, but can at the same time mean that the structural elements of company law are fixed by substantial constitutional guarantees. An illuminating example is provided by the "codetermination" decision of the German Federal Constitutional Court (Bundesverfassungsgericht). The court found it permissible to cut shareholders' powers, which are protected by the guarantee of private property, because the

[24] More precisely, the binding effect arises out of the formal authority of the "source of law" and at the same time out of the persuasive authority of the respective regulatory program.

statutory institutionalization of codetermination is aimed at the promotion of the common interest[25], and because the legislature has made sure that this objective can be achieved: "It must have exhausted the sources of information available to it in order to be able to assess as reliably as possible the foreseeable effects of its laws and to avoid a violation of the Constitution. It is thus rather a question of procedural requirements. If these are satisfied, they fulfil ... the requirement that their content be acceptable..." (Bundesverfassungsgericht-Entscheidungen (BVerfGE), 50: 334). Wiethölter has pointed out this approach implies proceduralization. The court "gives the politically legitimate legislature the freedom to impose new rules provided it bases its law-making on *all* previous experience and available opinions *convincingly*... It must of course correct its statutes if the reality should prove to be different from what was expected" (Wiethölter, 1982: 47; emphasis in original).

(3) Juridical Regulation

"Juridical regulation" refers not so much to the increase in the number of judicially settled disputes (Conard, 1976: 408), as to the increasing importance of judicial rule-making in company law[26]. This role of the judiciary was not foreseen in the classical concepts of company law. It has developed in the U.S. since the turn of the century (Conard, 1976: 380) and in Germany, above all, over the last three decades[27]. Its relationship to parliamentary legislation can no longer be described as merely filling in gaps or adapting to changing circumstances. Certainly, the application of legislatively determined norms to new fact situations plays a particularly important role. Examples of this can be found in U.S. law governing intercorporate relationships (cf. supra, 1.2 (1)), and in the "Vorgesellschaft" under German law (Kübler, 1981: 309 with references and more recently BGHZ 80: 129 and 182). In addition there are cases in which high court decisions introduce new "policies" into the legal system,

[25] Bundesverfassungsgericht-Entscheidungen (BVerfGE) 50, 290, 351. Cf. also BVerfGE 14, 263, 282 ("Feldmühle": "The legislator might also consider it desirable, on important grounds of general welfare, to place less emphasis on protection of the property of the minority shareholders than on the common interest in free development of business initiatives within the corporation". Similar tendencies of structural development are evident in the American discussion in relation to whether and to what extent corporations have the basic right to freedom of expression (vis-a-vis legislative restrictions). Cf. First National Bank of Boston v. Bellotti, 435 I.S. 765 (1978) and Brudney (1981).

[26] It is "juridification in the form of acts of jurisprudence" and signifies "the increasing displacement of political decisions and initiatives towards the judiciary", Voigt (1980: 15 and 21).

[27] This has given rise to a lively discussion in recent literature. Cf. Stimpel (1969: 15); Fischer (1971); Schulte (1969: 95, 1974: 525); Westermann (1975: 376, 407); Wiedemann (1980a: 43).

for example, in the area of liability for insider trading under American law,[28] and in Germany in cases restricting the validity of indemnity clauses (Kübler, 1981: 90 with references). Court decisions function increasingly as forerunners of legislation, which is content to convert court-made standards into statutory provisions. (As to the example of transforming share-holder loans into equity by the GmbH-amendments cf. supra 1.2 (2). Sometimes the courts intervene as well when legislative initiatives have failed. (For example, the German decisions relating to prospectus liability, which have taken the place of rules which did not get through law making processes; cf. Assmann, 1985). In these cases it is increasingly likely, however, that judicial activism will become an excuse for legislative inactivity. The great number of available examples reinforce the impression of a growing discrepancy between the objective social need for more legal rules, and the capacity of legislative processes to produce them. The similar picture drawn from major countries by findings of comparative law studies is not the least of the indications that the judiciary is being forced by the evolving interdependence of economic differentiation, social needs, and legal and political institutionalization, to act as a rule-making body.

(4) Bureaucratic regulation

"Bureaucratic regulation", is taken here to mean the generation of regulations relevant to company law by administrative bodies. The textbook example, which has been copied many times (primarily by Japan, France and Belgium,), is the regulatory power of the SEC (Karmel, 1982: 38). Its functioning can be abstractly described as follows: "purpose programs" which are formulated vaguely, on a long-term basis, by the legislature are from time to time converted by the regulatory agency into "conditional programs" which provide precise practical instructions (cf. in general, Voigt, 1980: 19) using the terminology introduced by Luhmann (1969: particularly 130). Administrative rule-making thus meets two needs which the legislative process is increasingly unable to fulfil. It can go into great detail, and at the same time adapt rapidly to changing circumstances and requirements (cf. Scharpf, 1970: 62). Necessary integration into the structure of the legal and political system, however, does not take place only via the normative framework provided by securities laws. Important guidance impulses are also transmitted via personnel and budget decisions (Scharpf, 1970: 62). At the same time, however, the SEC is an independent agency. It functions as an expert body which is continuously collecting information and experience concerning the area of control for which it is responsible, and converting

28 The leading case is SEC v. Texas Gulf Sulphur Co., 401 F. 2d 833 (2nd Civ. 1968), cert. denied, 394 United States Reports (U.S.) 976 (1969). For more recent developments cf. Chiarella v. U.S., 445 U.S. 222 (1980). The draft of a Federal Securities Code of the American Law Institute (ALI) provides for codification of the rule; see Hawes *et al.* (1982: 353).

these into new regulations or into modifications of already existing ones. In the simplified terminology of the analytical model introduced above (cf. supra, 2), the SEC can be said to react in a flexible and pragmatic way to new transaction cost problems as they arise. In the ideal case the advantages of market rationality are thus combined with those of bureaucratic rationality (in the sense of Max Weber's *Rechtssoziologie* (1967, 2nd. ed., sec. 6)). It is true that American literature does not give the impression that the status quo corresponds, even approximately, to such an ideal. Criticism of the expansive practice of the SEC and the demand for "deregulation" form the focal point of discussions on the juridification of corporate law and securities regulation. (Cf. apart from Karmel and Kripke, 1979; the contributions of Schotland *et al.*, 1979; Benston, 1980: 37; Fiflis, 1980: 70). Several observations can be made:

(a) The term "deregulation" has more than one meaning (Schotland, *et al.*, 1979: 115), and complaints about the Commission's activity appear to be, in some ways, diffuse. Widely differeing aspects of the Commission's practice are presented as particularly problematic and in need of change[29]. This dispersion relates to the question, which will not be discussed here, of the extent to which securities regulation is aimed at achieving something other than purely economic control objectives.

(b) The limitation of the American juridification discussion to deregulation of the securities market gives support to the idea that the institutionalization of "bureacratic" law-making can be considered ambivalent. In so far as the competent authority is equipped with adequate resources it constitutes a factor of additional regulation. But the task of making decisions which are rational and, as far as possible, empirically justified, stimulates reflection and discussion about the limits of useful regulation. At the same time the process of administrative rule-making, in contrast to judicial rule-making, remains politically controllable. The correction of "overregulation" can be achieved

[29] As a rough simplification: Kripke (1979), taking an extreme position, denies the value of mandatory disclosure in general, arguing that market forces would ensure adequate publicity (177) and that it cannot be assumed that the activity of the SEC improves allocative efficiency (134). For a critical view of this thesis see Sommer (1980: 119-22) within the context of a panel-discussion on "The SEC and Corporate Disclosure" Benston (1980: 49ff.) argues on the basis of a cost-benefit analysis and concludes, "that the costs to society of government-required disclosure exceed the benefits that may be derived therefrom" (67). For a critical view see Fiflis (1980: 87ff). In Schotland *et al.* (1979), some individual facets of the activity of the SEC are studied, the value of securities regulation in general being confirmed by most of the contributors. The book by Roberta Karmel (1982) (a summary of her practical experiences as an SEC commissioner) complains above all that the SEC does not concentrate on its task within the context of economic policy of improving capital build-up of companies but pursues different aims (in particular: 101 ff., 139 ff., 187 ff.). For a more detailed account see also *infra* M.3 (2) and (4).

above all through personnel decisions[30] and by cutting budgets, thus often avoiding the extremely complicated process of achieving the same effect by legislative change. This again illustrates the high degree of flexibility characterizing regulation by administrative agency.

(c) For an understanding of the deregulation discussion in the U.S., reference must also be made to the basic distinction between "old regulation" (OR) and "new regulation" (NR) (Herman, 1981: 172). OR relates to natural monopolies and in each case to a specific branch of commerce. (Typical examples are the Interstate Commerce Commission (ICC) and the Federal Communications Commission (FCC); re its efficiency see Hoffmann-Riem, (1981: particularly 177)). It generally has effects which restrict competition, and is therefore severely criticised by economists[31]. Over a period of time the purpose of regulation tends to be identified with the interests of the sector under control [32], to which it frequently owes not only its origin but its political survival. NR, which is often referred to as social regulation, typically arises as a reaction to economic or social abuses and results in a general limitation of business opportunities. (Typical examples are — apart from the SEC — the Environmental Protection Agency (EPA), the Occupational Safety and Health Agency (OSHA) and also the Federal Trade Commission (FTC, re see Reich (Zentrum für Europäische Rechtspolitik (ZERP)), Discussion Paper 2/82)). Most economists are in favor of it [33], and most of those affected disapprove[34]. The SEC, whose expert competence is generally acknowledged even

[30] The five Commissioners are appointed by the President for five years in each case and their appointment requires the approval of the Senate, see Karmel (1982: 46). In fact the term of office is in many cases considerably shorter (cf. the survey by Karmel (1982: 343).

[31] Herman (1981: 175) "...the really large social costs of business regulation are attributable to the OR... where cartel regulation has resulted in inflated prices and substantial resource misallocation. In these cases, private costs are not offset by any significant public benefits — the only beneficiaries are the private firms that are regulated and protected by the government-sponsored cartel".

[32] This identification is based not least on a personal intertwinement between "regulatory agency" and "regulated industry", called the "revolving door": the Commissioners (and in many cases also the staff) come from the companies subject to their regulation and go back to the companies after their term of office is over; re Federal Communications Commission (FCC) cf. also Noll *et al.* (1973: 123).

[33] Herman (1981) "The NR, as the OR, involves direct regulatory costs ..., but these are offset by potentially large public benefits, so that at worst the social deficit would be small and the potential for large positive net results under efficient management seems clear".

[34] Herman (1981: 175) "The fact that 'regulation' has become an acknowledged massive and threatening evil only with the rise of NR. and that the NR — not the really costly OR — is the subject of so much of the animus and criticism, tells us a great deal about the preferences and power of the business community".

by its critics (cf. Kripke, 1979: 126 and Karmel, 1982: 16, 47, 73, and 296), must be considered as forming part of NR[35].

3.2 The Instrumentalization of Areas of Autonomy

In the classical model of company law, the law defines the area left to private autonomy. Within this sphere of action legal subjects are free to pursue the aims which they have set themselves by all legally acceptable means. Vertical differentiation between different regulatory powers, however, is not limited to the state bodies discussed in Section 3.1. It has increasingly entered the area of private autonomy: thus private regulation is being transformed into an instrument of public policy.

(1) Regulation by Self-Regulation

A particularly important area of application of this strategy is designated in the U.S. as "regulation by self-regulation". The stock exchanges present a significant example. They were created as institutions under private law and only much later were integrated into emerging systems of administrative supervision. At the same time the original freedom to establish and organize such institutions was transformed into a derived power. In Germany there is a right to self-government subject to the constraints of stock market law, which is granted within the framework of a public institution and no longer based upon freedom of action under private law (see the thorough discussion in Schwark (1976, Einleitung, Rundnummer (Rn.) 28-33 in particular 29). In the U.S., section 19 of the Securities Exchange Act of 1934 determines the relationship between the SEC and the stock exchanges in a comparable way. The result is termed "self-regulation". Self-regulation supplements the powers of regulation and action at the disposal of the SEC (Karmel, 1982: 112). The instrumental nature of this institutional arrangement is made clear not least by subsequent amendments. In 1938 the Malony Act created a similar self-governing body, the National Association of Securities Dealers (NASD), for the over-the-counter market outside the stock exchange. In 1975 the SEC's powers of control over the stock exchanges were greatly increased, "largely because Congress believed that continued operation of the New York Stock Exchange as a private club was not in the public interest" (Karmel, 1982: 133). In a similar way accounting is also controlled by the SEC via self-regulation: the American Institute of Certified Public Accountants (AICPA) supervises and disciplines auditors and the Fair Accounting Standard Board (FASB) formulates rules governing balance sheets which

[35] The SEC has been successful in eliminating elements descending from OR its sphere. The most important example relates to the fees for stock exchange transactions: the system of commission rates set by the stock exchanges was abolished in 1975 by common action of Congress and the SEC, since when the level of commission rates has been left to the market (cf. Karmel 1982: 118).

approximately correspond to the German "good book-keeping principles" (Grundsätze ordnungsmäßiger Buchführung)[36]. Self-regulation is understood as a means of unburdening and replacing regulation (Karmel, 1982: 112). According to the available evidence, however, it is not to be expected that "regulation by self-regulation" will make any considerable contribution to the slowing down of juridification in company law.

(2) Control Mechanisms Set Up by Agreement

Self-regulation, however, should not necessarily be conceived as a functional element of administrative regulation. It can also be designed as a private institution outside and independent of all mechanisms of government supervision. By far the most important example is presented by the City Code on Take-Overs and Mergers in force in Great Britain since 1968, which supplements the Department of Trade Regulations with 14 general principles and 39 rules. The City Panel was formed to enforce the Code, and was integrated in 1978 into the newly established Council for the Securities Industry — a "voluntary, and extra-statutory, "watchdog" organization to supervise all forms of financial dealing by City institutions" (Gower *et al.*, 1979: 55 (the citation) and 694). A German parallel is provided by insider trading rules drawn up by national business federations and the association of stock exchanges, conformity to which is ensured by the watchdog commissions set up inside individual stock exchanges[37]. These regulatory mechanisms have the common feature of being valid only by force of private consent or subjection. The resulting lack of legally enforceable sanctions is generally criticized. (Gower *et al.*, 1979: 55; Schwark, 1976: 498). The private law form, however, must not be allowed to obscure the public policy features upon which both texts are based: The objective was and is not only to prevent abuses, but above all to anticipate legislative measures and thereby make them superfluous[38]. This aspect is made clear by the functional equivalents in other legal systems: prohibition of insider trading operates in Germany by agreement, in Great Britain and France by formal penal law (Hawes *et al.*, (1982: 338) (re the British Companies Act) and 341 (re French Law No. 70-1208 of 23 Dec. 1970)), and in the U.S., as mentioned above, by law and judicial decisions

[36] Kripke (1979: 149) and Karmel (1982: 325). Kripke, who in general argues in favour of deregulation, complains here that the SEC has abandoned the responsibility for determining accounting standards by the delegation of self-regulatory powers.

[37] These are — together with the dealer and adviser rules and the procedures for the examining commissions — printed in annex II of Schwark (1976: 481) and also commented on briefly.

[38] For insider trading rules, this is confirmed by the way they originated: the association agreement was due to a recommendation from the stock exchange commission set up by the federal government, Schwark (1976: 494), Hopt (1982: 171, 173).

which are based on a rule adopted by the SEC (cf., supra, 3.1). It is also evident that such voluntary regulations may be capable of relieving the otherwise overburdened enforcement mechanisms of government policy. Even if the question of their efficiency cannot be answered definitively at this time, one can assume that in the future voluntary regulations will play a considerable role.

(3) Codetermination as Legal Use of Private Autonomous Initiatives

A very different form of the legal utilization of possibilities of independent private initiative can be found in employee participation in company management. Its introduction is an act of redistribution of regulatory powers under company law aimed at legal and political objectives which lie, for the most part, outside the objectives of company law rules (cf. BVerfGE 50. 290: 350).

3.3 The Institutionalization of Legal Change

(1) Benefits of Proceduralization

The typical function of rules of law determines their time dimension. Classical formal law is intended to be of long-term validity, because, for example, highly abstract rules serve as a permanent, stable and thus calculable, framework for market operations. "Materialized" law is designed for concrete regulatory purposes which change with economic and social developments. The growing number of market relationships and the consequent increase in density of organizational structures generate additional transaction costs and externalities which can no longer be contained and reduced by the market alone, but increasingly call for mandatory rules. Proceduralization of law as a vertical differentiation of control levels can be explained as a structural consequence of this functional transformation, that is to say, as a reaction to the growing need for adaptability.

(a) There is first of all the question of relieving the mechanisms of legislation which are institutionalized by constitutional law and thereby bound to be a complicated and slow procedure with an output capacity that cannot be greatly expanded and a mode of operation which is directly determined by political priorities (cf. supra 1.1). Judicial and bureaucratic regulation, and the systematic institutionalization of self-governing bodies, shift the creation of necessary or desirable legal rules to a level below the legislative process, where such regulation can be achieved rapidly and at reduced cost. At the same time, the settlement of conflicts and the elaboration of rules designed for that purpose, are brought into direct contact with areas of life to be regulated, and are thus opened up to the influence and cooperation of experts and of the parties concerned. (To this extent we can speak of phenomena of "reflexive law"; cf. Teubner, 1983: 254-55 and 270-73 in particular). The court, competent because of its expertise, or the highly specialized administrative body, comes to a policy decision only after a thorough discussion of possible consequences with representatives of the interests concerned. (As to the possibilities and limits of the judicial taking into account of consequences cf. the different views of Luhmann (1974); Sambuc (1977); Wälde (1979)). In the case of "self-regulation" those directly concerned at the same time represent the expert knowledge required. At this point, however, the risk of conflicts of loyalty and interest must be taken into account. The possibility that the desirable solution, which would most likely benefit all, will be sacrificed to the particular interests of those directly involved illustrates the necessity for control and correction by a superior body.

(b) This indicates that the function of proceduralization (i.e., the vertical differentiation of stratified levels of regulation and control) is not simply to increase the adaptability of company law. The contingency implied by modern law (cf. Luhmann, 1972: 31, 207, 251), the emergence of a flexible normative structure, confronts the risk of arbitrary and/or disparate and poorly functioning rules. For this reason, there is a need not only to facilitate legal change, but to stabilize the framework conditions of the economy. This can be brought about with the influence of a constitution that subjects changes in the law to minimum requirements of a rational establishment of facts and forecasting of consequence (cf., supra, 3.1 (2)). Comparable results can be achieved through a federal system that endeavors to facilitate and promote the integration of large economic territories with the harmonization of particularly important bodies of regulation (cf. supra, 3.1 (1)).

(2) Costs of Proceduralization

A price must be paid for proceduralization even where it succeeds in guaranteeing the rational adjustment of law with simultaneous stability of the overall structure. Institutionalization of legal change confronts those who are its subjects with considerable risks which they must meet by paying for information about imminent changes[39] and for protection against unexpected new rules. Even more important are the effects on the legal system. Proceduralization creates the need to adjust the sectoral changes which take place on individual levels of regulation to one another and to harmonize them over the longer term. For this purpose, overall planning of legal policy is required, which is generally entrusted to independent experts. The visible expression of this development is the growing number of commissions set up to investigate complex relationships between rules[40]. No less significant would appear to be

[39] These increased needs for information correspond to new forms of communication, in particular the growing number of conferences and similar discussion events, at which the participants involved in the process of law making signal the orientation and impulse for imminent legal changes.

[40] Some German examples are: die Börsensachverständigenkommission, see Schwark (1979: 236), die Sachverständigenkommission zur Auswertung der bisherigen Erfahrungen bei der Mitbestimmung (Mitbestimmungskommission, Schlußbericht: Mitbestimmung im Unternehmen, Bundestagsdrucksache VI 334); die Unternehmensrechtskommission (cf. Bundesministerium der Justiz (ed.) Bericht über die Verhandlungen der Unternehmensrechtskommission (1980)). For the U.S., see in particular SEC, Report of Special Study of Securities Markets, House of Representatives Document No. 95, Pf. 1, 88th Congress (1968); Disclosure Policy Study of the SEC (Wheat-Report, 1969); Report of the Adivsory Committee on Corporate Disclosure to the SEC, Comm. Privat 95-29, 95th Congress 1st Session (1977).

the efforts of the American Law Institute (ALI), a private institution founded and run by the American Bar Association in cooperation with judges and legal experts (description and explanation in Zweigert/Kötz (1971: 306). In 1980 it bought out the comprehensive draft with commentary of a "Federal Securities Code", which integrates the substance of the securities laws, the rules developed by the courts, and the most important rules of the SEC, in a systematically organized body of regulation. Even if Congress, as the competent legislative body, cannot be expected to adopt and enact this code, the achievement of the ALI should have considerable influence on future practice in the establishment of rules by legislatures, courts and adinistrative agencies. In 1982 the ALI submitted to its members and the public the preliminary draft of restatement of substantive company law as well. This is not a draft ready for decision, but a summary of the substance of state corporation law combined with recommendations for the harmonization and further evolution of the relevant rules.

(3) The Shrinking Contrast Between Government Regulation and Private Regulation

Finally, proceduralization lessens the contrast between government regulation and regulation by private agreement. This can be confirmed by numerous observations. For example, one can note the displacement of optional law by stereotyped patterns of articles of incorporation and by-laws (see in general, Assmann (1980a: 217); re: specific company law aspects, Kübler (1981: 269), by self-regulation (cf., supra, 3.2 (1)), and finally by legal, judicial and voluntary regulation (cf. supra, 3.1 (3)), regarding prospectus liability and 3.2 (2), regarding insider trading). This finding supports the conclusion that the increase, intensification, and differentiation of company law corresponds to a considerable degree to objective needs which arise, above all, out of continuing development of the economic system. To this extent, flat demands for a "limitation" of juridification, or for "deregulation" appear to offer few prospects of success. Their implementation would probably achieve nothing but the shift of regulatory problems from one level of regulation to another. Such an approach risks the pushing aside of a question which will be increasingly important in the future: on which of the available levels can desirable rules be made most effectively and beneficially, i.e., be attained and enforced at the lowest cost?

[Translated from the German by John Hearsum]

References

Advisory Committee on Corporate Disclosures to the SEC *Report*, Comm. Privat 95-29, 95th Cong. 1st Sess. (1977).

American Law Institute (1980) *Federal Securities Code*, 2 Vols.

— (1982) *Principles of Corporate Governance and Structure: Restatement and Recommendations*, Tentative Draft No. 1.

ASSMANN, Heinz-Dieter (1980a) *Wirtschaftsrecht in der Mixed Economy.* Königstein: Athenäum.

— (1980b) "Zur Steuerung gesellschaftlich-ökonomischer Entwicklung durch Recht", in D.H. Assmann, G. Brüggemeier, D. Hart and C. Joerges (eds.), *Wirtschaftsrecht als Kritik des Privatrechts.* Königstein: Athenäum.

— (1985) *Prospekthaftung.* Köln: Carl Heymanns.

ASSMANN, Hans-Dieter, Christian KIRCHNER and Erich SCHANZE (eds.) (1978) *Ökonomische Analyse des Rechts.* Kronberg: Athenäum.

BENSTON, George J. (1980) "The Costs and Benefits of Government-Required Disclosure: SEC and FTC Requirements", in D. A. De Mott (ed.), *Corporations at the Crossroads: Governance and Reform.* New York: McGraw-Hill.

BERLE, Adolph and Gardian MEANS (1937) *The Modern Corporation and Private Property.* New York: Macmillan.

BRANCH, George S. and James A. RUBRIGHT (1982) "Integrity of Management. Disclosure Under the Federal Securities Laws", 37 *The Business Lawyer* 1447.

BRINKMANN, Tomas and Friedrich KÜBLER (1981) "Ökonomische Analyse von Unternehmensrecht", 137 *Zeitschrift für die gesamte Staatswissenschaft* 681.

BRUNDNEY, Victor (1981) "Business Corporations and Stockholders' Rights Under the First Amendment", 91 *Yale Law Journal* 235.

BUNDESMINISTERIUM DER JUSTIZ (ed.) (1980) Erfahrungen bei der Mitbestimmung (Mitbestimmungskommission, Schlußbericht: Mitbestimmung in Unternehmen, *Bundestags-Drucksache VI* 334) und die Unternehmensrechtskommission, Bericht über die Verhandlungen der Unternehmensrechtskommission.

BUXBAUM, Richard (1972) *Die private Klage als Methode zur Durchsetzung wirtschaftspolitischer Rechtsnormen.* Karlsruhe: C.F. Müller.

BURNHAM, James (1941) *Managerial Revolution.* New York: John Day.

CALABRESI, Guido (1975) "Transaction Costs, Resource-Allocation and Liability Rules — A Comment", in H. Manne (ed.), *The Economics of Legal Relationships.* St. Paul: West Pub. Co.

CLARK, Robert (1977) "The Duties of the Corporate Debtor to Its Creditors", 90 *Harvard Law Review* 505.

COASE, Ronald H. (1953) "The Nature of the Firm", 4 *Economica* n.s. 386.

CONARD, Alfred F. (1976) *Corporations in Perspective.* Mineola: Foundation Press.

DAHLMANN, Roger Clayton (1979) "The Problem of Externality", 22 *Journal of Law and Economics* 141.

DEMSETZ, Harold (1975) "Toward a Theory of Property Rights", in H. Manne (ed.), *The Economics of Legal Relationships.* St. Paul: West Publishing Co.

EISENBERG, Melvin Aaron (1976) *The Structure of the Corporation, a Legal Analysis.* Boston: Little Brown.

ESCHENBERG, Rolf (1978) "Mikroökonomische Aspekte von Property Rights", in K. E. Schenk (ed.), *Ökonomische Verfügungsrechte und Allokationsmechanismen im Wirtschaftssystem.* Berlin: Duncker und Humblot.

FARRENKOPF, Stefan and Andreas CAHN (1983) "Die Rechtsprechung des BGH zu den sogenannten kapitalersetzenden Gesellschaftsdarlehen bei der GmbH" 1983, *Die Aktiengesellschaft* 151.

FIFLIS, Ted J. (1980) *Economic Analysis as one Phase of Utilitarianism.*

FISCHER, Robert (1971) *Die Weiterbildung des Rechts durch die Rechtsprechung.* Karlsruhe: C.F. Müller.

FLEISCHER, Arthur (1964/65) "'Federal Corporation Law': An Assessment", 78 *Harvard Law Review* 1146.

GOWER, L. B. C., A. J. EASSON, K. W. WEDDERBURN (1979) *Gower's Principles of Modern Company Law*, 4th Ed. London: Stevens & Co.
GROSSFELD, Bernhard (1968) *Aktiengesellschaft, Unternehmenskonzentration und Kleinaktionär.* Tübingen: Mohr.
— (1977) *Zivilrecht als Gestaltungsaufgabe.* Heidelberg, Karlsruhe: Müller.
GROSSFELD, Bernhard and Werner EBKE (1977) "Probleme der Unternehmensverfassung", in: *Die Aktiengesellschaft* 94.
HAWES, Douglas, Peter LEE and Marie-Claude ROBERT (1982) "Insider Trading Law Developments: An International Analysis", 14 *Law and Policy in International Business* 353.
HERMAN, Edward S. (1981) *Corporate Control, Corporate Power.* Cambridge, New York: Cambridge University Press.
HOFFMANN-RIEM, Wolfgang (1981) *Kommerzielles Fernsehen.* Baden-Baden: Nomos.
HOMBURGER, Adolf (1975) "Private Suits in the Public Interest in the USA", in H. Homburger and L.H. Kötz (eds.), *Klagen Privater im öffentlichen Interesse.* Frankfurt a.M.: Metzner.
HOPT, Klaus J. (1975) *Der Kapitalanlegerschutz im Recht der Banken.* München: Beck.
— (1982) "Deutsche Landesreferate zum Privat- und Handelsrecht", XI *Internationaler Kongress für Rechtsvergleichung in Caracas* 171.
HUECK, Götz (1983) *Gesellschaftsrecht*, 18th Ed. München: Beck.
JENNINGS, Richard W. and Richard M. BUXBAUM (1979) *Corporations, Cases and Materials*, 5th Ed. St. Paul: West Publshing Company.
KARMEL, Roberta S. (1982) *Regulation by Prosecution, The Securities and Exchange Commission vs. Corporate America.* New York: Simon and Schuster.
KIRCHNER, Christian (1982) "Interkulturelle Rechtsvergleichung und Ökonomische Analyse". Frankfurt a.M.: Manuscript.
— (1983) "Analyse des Unternehmensrechts: Ein Forschungsansatz", in E. Boettcher (ed.), *Neue Politische Ökonomie als Analyse von Institution.* Tübingen: Mohr and Siebeck.
KRIPKE, Homer (1979) *The SEC and Corporate Disculsure: Regulation in Search of a Purpose.* New York: Law Business Inc.
KÜBLER, Friedrich (1981) *Gesellschaftsrecht, Die privatrechtlichen Ordungsstrukturen und Regelungsprobleme von Verbänden und Unternehmen.* Karlsruhe: Müller.
— (1984) "Was leistet die Konzeption der 'Property Rights' für aktuelle rechtspolitische Probleme?" 140 *Schriften des Vereins für Sozialpolitik* 105.
LEECH, Noyes and Robert H. MUNDHEIM (1976) *The Outside Director of the Public Corporation.* Philadelphia: Center for Study of Financial Institutions.
LIVINGSTON, J. A. (1958) *The American Stockholder.* Philadelphia: Lippincott.
LUHMANN, Niklas (1969) *Legitimation durch Verfahren.* Darmstadt: Luchterhand.
— (1972) *Rechtssoziologie.* Reinbek: Rowohlt.
— (1974) *Rechtssystem und Rechtsdogmatik.* Stuttgart, Berlin: Kohlkammer.
LUTTER, Marcus (1971) in *Kölner Kommentar zum Aktiengesetz.* Köln: Heymann.
— (1978) *Information und Vertraulichkeit im Aufsichtsrat.* Köln, Berlin: Heymann.
MANNE, Henry (1975) *The Economics of Legal Relationships.* St. Paul: West Publishing Company.
MANNING, Bayless, (1958) "Book Review: Livingston, 'The American Stockholder'", 67 *Yale Law Journal* 1477.
— (1980) "Thinking Straight about Corporate Law Reform", in D.A. De Mott (ed.), *Corporations at the Crossroads: Governance and Reform.* New York: McGraw-Hill.
MERTENS, Hans-Joachim (1980) "Berichtspflicht des Vorstands gegenüber dem Aufsichtsrat", *Die Aktiengesellschaft* 67.

— (1982) "Leges praeter legem", *Die Aktiengesellschaft* 29.
MESTMÄCKER, Ernst-Joachim (1958) *Verwaltung, Konzerngewalt und Recht der Aktionäre.* Karlsruhe: Müller.
DE MOTT Deborah A. (ed.) (1980) *Corporations at the Crossroads: Governance and Reform.* New York: McGraw-Hill.
NOLL, Roger G., Merton J. PECK and John J. MCGOWAN (1973) *Economic Aspects of Television Regulation.* Washington: Brookings Institution.
OLSON, Mancur (1973) *The Logic of Collective Action.* New York: Schocken Books.
PEHLE, Rudolf and Walter STIMPEL (1969) *Richterliche Rechtsfortbildung unter besonderer Berücksichtigung des gewerblichen Rechtsschutzes und des Personengesellschaftsrechts.* Karlsruhe: Müller.
PROSS, Helge (1965) *Manager und Aktionäre in Deutschland.* Frankfurt a.M.: Europäische Verlagsanstalt.
RAISER, Ludwig (1963) "Rechtsschutz und Institutionenschutz im Privatrecht", *Summum ius — summa in iuria* 145. Tübingen: Mohr und Siebeck.
REHBINDER, Eckard (1969) *Konzernaußenrecht und allgemeines Privatrecht.* Bad Homburg: Gehlen.
REICH, Norbert (1982) *Marktversagen und Politikversagen.* Bremen: Zentrum für Europäische Rechtspolitik
ROTH, Günther H. (1972) *Das Treuhandmodell des Investmentrechts.* Frankfurt a.M.: Athenäum.
SAMBUC, Thomas (1977) *Folgenerwägungen im Richterrecht.* Berlin: Duncker und Humblot.
SCHANZE, Erich (1975) *Einmanngesellschaft und Durchgriffshaftung.* Frankfurt a.M.: Metzner.
— (1983) "Theorie des Unternehmens und ökonomische Analyse des Rechts", in E. Boettcher (ed.), *Neue politische Ökonomie als Analyse von Institutionen.* Tübingen: Mohr.
SCHARPF, Fritz W. (1970) *Die sozialen Kosten des Rechtsstaates.* Tübingen: Mohr.
SCHOTLAND, Roy, Simon LORNE, Morris MENDELSON, Lee A. PICKARD, Michael KEENAN, Edward J. O'BRIEN, Lawrence G. GOLDBERG and Lawrence J. WHITE (1979) *The Deregulation of the Banking and Securities Industries.*
SCHULTE, Hans (1969) "Zur Methode revisionsrichterlicher Rechtsprechung auf dem Gebiete des Gesellschaftsrechts", in *Festschrift Otto Kunze.* Berlin: Duncker und Humblot.
— (1974) "Zu den Gesichtspunkten des BGH bei der Fortbildung des Gesellschaftsrechts", in *Festschrift Harry Westermann 525.* Karlsruhe: C. F. Müller.
SCHWARK, Eberhard (1976) *Kommentar zum Börsengesetz.* München: Beck.
— (1979) *Anlegerschutz durch Wirtschaftsrecht.* München: Beck.
SOMMER, A. A. (1980) "The SEC and Corporate Disclosure", 36 *The Business Lawyer* 119.
STEINDORFF, Ernst (1974) "Wirtschaftsordnung und -steuerung durch Privatrecht", in *Festschrift Ludwig Raiser* 521. Tübingen: Mohr.
STIMPEL, Walter (1969) *Richterliche Rechtsfortbildung unter besonderer Berücksichtigung des Personengesellschaftsrechts.* Karlsruhe: C.F. Müller.
STUDIENKOMMISSION "GRUNDSATZFRAGEN DER KREDITWIRTSCHAFT" (1979) Bericht.
TEUBNER, Gunther (1983) "Substantive and Reflexive Elements in Modern Law", 17 *Law and Society Review* 239.
VAGTS, Detlev (1966/67) "Reforming the 'Modern Corporation', Perspectives from the German", 80 *Harvard Law Review* 23.
VOIGT, Rüdiger (ed.) (1980) *Verrechtlichung.* Königstein: Athenäum.

WÄLDE, Thomas (1979) *Juristische Folgenorientierung*. Königstein: Athenäum.

WALZ, Rainer W. (1983) *Steuergerechtigkeit und Rechtsanwendung*. Heidelberg: R. v. Decker.

WEGEHENKEL, Lothar (1980) *Coase-Theoren und Marktsystem*. Tübingen: Mohr.

WEITNAUER, Hermann (1975) *Der Schutz des Schwächeren im Zivilrecht*. Karlsruhe: Müller.

WESTERMANN, Harry (1975) "Kautelarjurisprudenz, Rechtsprechung und Gesetzgebung im Spannungsfeld zwischen Gesellschafts- und Wirtschaftsrecht", 175 *Archiv für Presserecht* 376.

WIEACKER, Franz (1953) *Das Sozialmodell der klassischen Privatrechtsgesetzbücher und die Entwicklung der modernen Gesellschaft*. Karlsruhe: Müller.

— (1967) *Privatrechtsgeschichte der Neuzeit*, 2nd Ed. Göttingen: Vandenhoeck und Ruprecht.

WIEDEMANN, Herbert (1980a) *Gesellschaftsrecht, Ein Lehrbuch des Unternehmens- und Verbandsrechts*, Vol. I. München: Beck.

— (1980b) "Rechtsethische Maßstäbe im Unternehmensrecht", *Zeitschrift für Unternehmens- und Gesellschaftsrecht* 147.

WIETHÖLTER, Rudolf (1982) "Entwicklung des Rechtsbegriffs", in V. Gessner and G. Winter (eds.), *Rechtsform der Verflechtung von Staat und Wirtschaft* 38. Opladen: Westdeutscher Verlag.

ZWEIGERT, Konrad and Hein KÖTZ (1971) *Einführung in die Rechtsvergleichung*. Tübingen: Mohr.

Juridification and Legitimation Problems in American Enterprise Law

RICHARD M. BUXBAUM
Berkeley, California

Contents

1. Introduction

The juridification theme of this volume is designed to test certain social and systems theories associated with the work of Habermas and Luhmann respectively, theories which are pitched at various but fairly high levels of abstraction. Empirical inquiry on the basis of hypotheses found in this theoretical literature requires substantial preliminary problem definition, much of it also speculative in its formulation of intermediate hypotheses[1]. The present set of papers, while already benefiting from several prior studies (Kübler *et al.*,

[1] This brief textual statement about the legitimacy and role of empirical inquiry in the development of general social theories obviously does not begin to do justice to the problem of validation, let alone to the issue whether validation is a critical touchstone of this form and level of theory. The problems here hinted at are highlighted, for the subject under discussion, by the following authors, to whom reference can be made for more detailed (and conflicting) argumentation: Habermas (1981: 523; 1985: 203); Schmid (1982: 171ff); and Teubner (1985a: 376 f.).

1984), is necessarily also still involved in this intermediate task — evaluating the explanatory power of certain primary hypotheses in a variety of substantive legal areas.

The major social-theoretical elements most often used as touchstones for the discussion of legal issues are the "legitimation crisis" and "colonialization of life spheres" concepts, as these have been explored and defined by Habermas (1975; 1979; 1981; 1985), and the "differentiation" and "self-reproduction" phenomena of social subsystems developed from a more system-theoretic perspective by Luhmann (1982; 1985). To honor the assignment of considering their utility in comprehending the evolution of particular legal fields requires, at the outset, not only careful definition of the specific subject matter, but also equally careful statements, or at least assumptions, about the specific subject's historical evolution. The present paper is on "enterprise law", which I define rather narrowly, however, to include not all of the relations gathered under its original German rubric, *Unternehmensrecht*, but primarily the relationship of private household savers with non-governmental firms which use those savings to produce goods and services. This definition has an advantage beyond that of narrowness. It offers both a better historical view and a better-controlled "subsystem" view of enterprise activity than does a definition including employee-employer, customer-supplier and even producer-environment relationships. Yet, as will be seen below, it does not in the end ignore the problems these wider definitions seek to address (Buxbaum, 1984a).

The examination of the juridification and legitimation-crisis phenomena[2] in the field of company/enterprise law will focus on two themes of this group of social theories: the "colonialization of life spheres" concept and the system-theoretic argument (especially as developed by Teubner) that some of the excesses of juridification can be curbed without falling into the trap of socially dubious deregulation, by means of reflexive-law concepts and mechanisms that internalize socially desirable goals within the decision-making processes of social organizations (Teubner, 1983; supra: 33 ff. Teubner and Willke, 1984).

The "colonialization" theme is of particular interest to this field of enterprise law because a major, indeed animating aspect of that theme is best developed within the context of the "legitimation crisis" postulated by Habermas, a concept that in turn is directly related to the relationship of the private enterprise system with the state. While these "colonialization" and "legitimation crisis" hypotheses are well-known and hardly need my exegesis (McCarthy, 1978; Thompson and Held, 1982), a brief review of how I understand them nevertheless is appropriate as an introduction to the following discussion of enterprise law. The passively democratic social welfare state has

[2] For a fascinating internalization of these critical insights, legitimating the colonialization hypothesis by defining the "conflicted" state as "constructivist" and its new law — and lawyers — as "Constructive", (sic), see Ackerman (1984). Compare, from the perspective of Critical Legal Theory adherents, Frug (1984a) and, especially on the Ackerman theses, Frug (1984).

to pick up the task of redistribution of use-values that the private sector enterprise system cannot solve and to some degree creates (Habermas, 1975). Both the handling of the state's relationship with the private capitalist system and the handling of its relationship with the population generate systemic complexity, "system" being shorthand for the arrangements required by the extreme functional and role differentiations found in a society marked by the division (and "alienation") of labor and by the accumulation of capital. This system's complexity leads to the imposition of formal, law-suffused rules and imperatives upon a life world of earlier-developed, more personal relationships which maintained themselves by communicatively structured, "symbolic" manifestations of social integration. This is the phenomenon of the shift from the "mediatization of the life world" to the "colonialization of the life world", and an important medium of this process is *Verrechtlichung* — juridification (Habermas, 1981: II, 522ff; 1985: 203ff). Juridification comprises both the expansion of formal rules into communicatively structured, symbolically visible situations previously ruled informally, and the intensification of formal rules to bear ever more specifically on specific social situations [3].

Habermas seems to have two specific types of juridification phenomena in mind, at least in his work on the legitimation crisis in capitalism. The first is what I would call rules of eligibility, which determine participation in the social welfare net or in the redistributive process, and which at their pathological extreme reduce the freedom of action of those who are to be assured the material conditions needed to permit them to enjoy freedom of action. The second is what I would call rules of control, which check the unwanted emanations of the private enterprise system, and which at their pathological extreme are exemplified by the vision of the bureaucratic *Doppelgänger* who dogs every footstep of the shirt-sleeve entrepreneur and smothers the allocative efficiency, wealth-creating function on which the society and even the state rely (Habermas, 1975: 45ff, 61ff).

My view as to the applicability of the "colonialization-legitimation crisis" hypotheses to enterprise law is affected by two particularities of the enterprise system of economic activity that distinguish it from other social structures, including even other structures of economic activity. Enterprise activity, as defined below, is not a primordial form of social activity; it was not colonialized by some modern version of its own earlier prototype. By the same token — and in any event since by definition law is not a self-starting social organization — its legal framework is not one imposed by modern forces on an earlier legal framework. The social activity and its embedding law grew up

[3] On the legitimacy of combining these (juridification and legitimation) issues, see McCarthy (1984: xxxiv). Wiethölter (1985b: 131f) identifies Otto Kirchheimer as the source of the *Verrechtlichung* label. Habermas (1981: 182) himself explains the borrowing of Husserl's *Lebenswelt* (phenomenological) concept; the importance of this connection is stressed by Jay (1984: 32f). Finally, one should not overlook the alternative development of mediatatizion associated with Polanyi (see Gretschmann, 1981: 121).

together, and are natural albeit contingent forms of the historical period characterized by division of labor and accumulation of capital. Furthermore, alone among social subsystems, even other economic ones, the enterprise form of economic activity serves the modern mechanisms of societal reproduction without ambivalence (but cf. Deutsch, 1983). The family, to pick a contrasting system, is not "intended" to serve that reproductive function but is driven by exigent forces — colonialized — to do so. For a different reason, the same is even true of social forms that in other respects are modern creatures of the industrial age, like the union (Winter, 1963; compare Feller, 1973 with Klare, 1982). "Intended" by the mechanisms of modern liberal capitalism to redistribute wealth by reallocating certain balances of power, it nevertheless is forced into at least partial accommodation with or even cooptation by its protagonist. That is not the case with the enterprise or with the enterprise system of economic activity. These are not forced to adapt to the modern societal reproductive process which is marked by differentiation of labor and accumulation of capital — they are the embodiment of that process and of that differentiation and accumulation. As a result, as I hope to demonstrate in this paper, the relationship of the enterprise system and of enterprise law to the state's legitimation problems is unique.

Habermas, of course, distinguishes between the roles of law as a "medium" of intrusive steering of life spheres and as an ideal (an "institution") which helps maintain that world against the colonialization process engendered by the modern state and economy systems (Habermas, 1981: II, 536; 1985: 212). This distinction, however, persuasive or not as it may be in that context, is not applied by him to the question of the legal governance (or facilitation) of the subsystems of the economy, in particular of the private enterprise structure. Yet the tensions inherent in this ambivalent nature of law have their mirror image there: the intrusion of symbolic life world values, via law, on the systems. In the argument that follows, I hope at least to identify some possible consequences of this reverse ambivalence, in part because that focus may help to clarify whether the basic distinction between "law as medium" and "law as institution" is useful.

The second particularity of the enterprise subsystem bears on the reflexive-law hypotheses derived by Teubner (supra: 33 ff.) from Luhmann's as well as Habermas' discussion of the increasing autonomy of and methods of interaction among social subsystems. The organizational forms embodying enterprise activity are well-suited to assimilate reflexive, self-learning and self-steering processes because their internal hierarchical structures in any event rely heavily on the kind of indirect governance associated with reflexive law concepts. In historical reality, however, these forms happen to be structured to wrestle the external environment into exactly the socially dubious trap of deregulation which the reflexive law proponents claim or hope to avoid. This dilemma is due in part to the societal acceptance and legitimation of the "blind" drive of enterprise towards profit maximization. Paradoxically, however, it is also due to the power consciously held and consciously used in the real here and now specific large, wealthy and powerful enterprises.

Both particularities of the enterprise subsystem of economic activity will be developed in further detail below. First, however, some sense of geographic, historical and economic context is needed to set the stage for a more detailed argument.

2. The Historically Specific Enterprise Context: Background and Assumptions

It is obviously difficult to generalize about a subject as protean as enterprise activity, let alone about its evolution. At the least it is necessary to limit the following sketch, which is also intended to serve as the sketch of assumptions on which to base the later discussion of current law, to the situation in the U.S. leaving for later, and to others, the question of its general validity. The chronological if not historical setting can be organized in several ways. I find the following conceptual scheme by Clark (1981: 562ff) so fruitful for present purposes that I take the liberty of quoting it at some length:

The history of capitalist enterprise in the United States over the last two hundred years can be meaningfully organized into four distinct stages ... (E)ach stage is characterized by a distinctive set of problems to which the legal system has tried to respond by employing regulatory strategies appropriate for that stage ...

The four stages are like generations. They overlap with one another — indeed, none are dead, and all may continue indefinitely — but each in turn has had its own time of rapid growth ... The first stage is the age of the entrepreneur, the fabled promoter-investor-manager who launched large-scale business organizations in corporate form for the first time in history ... The objective correlate of this activity was the rise of the corporation as a form of business organization. Its legal correlates were the increased enactment of general incorporation statutes and "enabling" laws.

The second stage, which reached adulthood in the first few decades of the twentieth century, is the age of the professional business manager. He appeared when the entrepreneurial function was split into ownership and control ... The characteristic institution of the age was the modern publicly held corporation. The second stage required the legal system to develop stable relationships between professional managers and public investors, ostensibly aimed at keeping the former accountable to the latter, but also placing full control of business decisions in the managers' hands. A major legal correlate was the enactment of the federal securities laws during the Depression ...

The third stage of capitalism ... is the age of the portfolio manager, and its characteristic institution is the institutional investor or financial intermediary. As the second stage split entrepreneurship into ownership and control, and professionalized the latter, so the third stage split ownership into capital supplying and investment, and professionalized the investment function ...

The increasing separation of the decision about how to invest from the decision to supply capital for investment is one of the most striking institutional developments in our century ...

One fumbles for an apt label (for the fourth stage), but perhaps it could be called the age of the savings planner. Just as the third stage split the capital ownership function into the decision to supply capital funds and active investment management, and professionalized the latter, so the fourth stage seems intent upon splitting capital supplying into the possession of beneficial claims and the decision to save and professionalizing the savings-decision function. Today, decisions about whether and how much to save are increasingly being made by group representatives on behalf of a large number of group members, rather than by each individual whose present consumption is being deferred in favor of future consumption ... Today, the decision to save is only indirectly controlled by many of the workers who are to benefit from these plans (which can no longer accurately be described as 'fringe' benefits), just as the decision to invest in particular financial claims is only rarely controlled by public suppliers of capital to financial intermediaries...

(E)ach shift from one stage to the next is marked by two features: increased division of labor, and increased participation in the fruits of capitalist enterprise ... Each later stage splits off and professionalizes a certain analytically distinct aspect of the capital-mobilizing process, and creates a set of institutional arrangements that make it practical for a significantly greater portion of the population to share in capital income. If by 'capitalists' we mean only those who have a direct or indirect claim on capital income, then ... (s)tage four capitalists include all participants and beneficiaries in employee benefit plans. They now constitute a significant portion of the population and their investment claims are substantial.

But this sharing, or potential[24] sharing, of the benefits of capitalist enterprise has been accompanied by an ever greater concentration of important discretionary powers in the hands of professional managers and group representatives. Increased sharing in benefits and decreased sharing in power: one wonders whether any of the early commentators on capitalist enterprise, from Adam Smith to Karl Marx, correctly anticipated that this would be the evolutionary pattern of the capitalist system.

[24] It is not clear that the growth of stage three and stage four institutions has significantly altered the overall distribution of wealth or income in American society ... Obviously, many other trends and forces are relevant to the distribution of wealth.

Clark ascribes this evolution to two causes, which in fact might well be seen as one larger notion. First, the increasing division of functions, not to mention the increasing concentration of managerial power, has occurred and persists because it is efficient (Clark, 1981: 568). This may not have been a sufficient condition — the developments also may have been achievable only because of the concurrent, general increase in wealth over two centuries, which has permitted a larger degree of surplus savings formation and thus of participation in capital-derived income — but it is a necessary condition. Secondly, he ascribes this evolution to the conscious, "intentionalistic" choice of forms, and of facilitative legal rules for those forms, that is the result of "the cumulative decisions of rationally self-interested capitalists." (Clark, 1981: 569).

Clark remains instructive as we begin to move from the historically oriented description of the enterprise phenomenon (or at least of that aspect interesting in the present context) to the role of legal rules. It is already clear from the foregoing that the legal strategy — if the accumulation of rules in the 19th century deserves that conscious characterization — has moved away from limiting the power of corporate entities per se (e.g., ultra vires rules) or from providing Marquis of Queensbury rules for the battles between entrepreneurs.

It has even moved away from the early 20th century "strategy" of providing fiduciary rules for the newly-empowered professional agents of now publicly-held corporations, while simultaneously providing transparency (through federal securities regulation) to the second-stage capital raising process. Today, for the third stage, as Clark (1981: 571) says, our "basic regulatory approach ... can be summed up in the concept of soundness. By a variety of methods, public suppliers of capital are insulated from the consequences of financial failure of intermediaries."

Most interesting is his perception that for the fourth stage it is necessary to move "beyond power limits and fair play, beyond disclosure and fiduciary duties, and beyond soundness regulation, to what might be called consumer protection" (Clark, 1981: 571). That, for reasons elaborated in the following part, seems to me indeed to be a clear mandate derived from the current realities of surplus formation. It stems from the fact that an ever larger proportion of the decisions to save, let alone the decisions to invest those savings, is being made on an involuntary or at least on a collective basis. Third-stage soundness regulation, now even more important because of this involuntary or collective process, is not enough. It needs to be and is being supplemented by fourth-stage supervision of the substantive fairness of the terms of the savings and investment decisions imposed upon — made for — the individual, involuntary capital supplier.

This four-stage history clearly is specific to the American experience. It reflects the generation of surplus in a young state, large in space and small in population, favored in natural resources and climate but needing foreign capital. (Jenks, 1927) It reveals a young state, moreover, whose administrative structures could barely stand up against social structures that reflected a select, energetic, self-seeking population (a democratic brotherhood of self-seeking adventurers, Tocqueville called it in one of his few ungenerous moments, (Tocqueville, 1945: I, 297)). Its infrastructure, still publicly or at least communally owned in the earliest decades of the 19th century, expanded during the important mid-century years only after being recast in private ownership form (indeed the transportation infrastructure was the prototypical example of private enterprise during this important formative period after 1850). Its financial sector, also, not only was essentially in private hands but was and remains enormously decentralized, an aggregate of thousands of individual units. The concept of a national bank did not survive the Jacksonian Era, and even today the Federal Reserve Board is only a pale shadow of a modern central bank (Hammond, 1957; Sharp, 1970). Even its industrial sector, while not so nationally specific, was at least as diversified and decentralized as the nation's size and regional differences would suggest.

These are some of the nationally specific characteristics that we would expect to see reflected in nationally specific federal and state legal regimes in the general field of enterprise law. But there are also some characteristics of the American enterprise scene which are shared with its Western European counterparts. Perhaps in time these will turn out to be the more important characteristics, and they should suggest some commonalities among those regions' legal regimes (Buxbaum, 1984a). The economies are not organized along socialist lines, and thus the state sectors do not directly generate wealth or surplus. Important private sectors have come within the private control of ever larger firms. At the least, therefore, these sectors and firms have become subject to the attempts of states to impose missions, constraints and even operational methods upon them. Often seen in antitrust terms, this development rather is a result of the fact that important social welfare obligations, increasingly understood by society as being legitimate, have become substantially externalized (or internalized — take your choice) onto these private firms. That type of neo-syndicalist (rather than corporatist) pressure is accompanied, however, by the mutual and public acknowledgement of the legitimacy of the functions of the private enterprise sector by both parties to this relationship (Chirelstein, 1974; Buxbaum, 1984a).

As a result of these country-specific and economic organization-specific attributes, market-driven legal regulation always has been and to this day remains both a material and an ideological necessity. "So viel Markt wie möglich, so viel Staat wie nötig" is a slogan invented by a public official[4], but it could hardly have been improved on by private sector apologists. The logic of our historical situation and our economic philosophy has generated an inherent and persisting paradox as the underlying principle of enterprise law: No matter how regulatory the legal rules serving the passive investor (let alone the involuntary saver-investor) may be, they also need to be, and need to appear to be, facilitative of privately organized, profit-maximizing enterprise activity (Buxbaum, 1972: 27ff). The apologetics may be more or less sophisticated — from Chicago School economics to "what is good for GM is good for the US" — but even the most detailed and investor-protective regulation always has had to proclaim its congruence with the ability of the enterprise to function effectively in its profit-maximizing capacity.

3. Argument

3.1 The Framework

Enterprise law is concerned with enterprise activity, or at least with certain aspects of it. I suggest that the "colonialization of life spheres" argument does not apply to the life sphere of enterprise activity in the way it applies to, say, the family or to any other social sphere that predates the historical period from which "colonialization" springs. The "enterprise" itself is a form of social organization presupposing and only made possible by the division of labor and the accumulation of capital; i.e., by the modern era as such. It is a child of modern life, not an earlier-born adult adapted by the exigencies of a changed external environment to function differently. An enterprise has no more innate relation to pre-capitalistic owner-operator households

[4] On information and belief, a remark attributed to Finance Minister Schiller of the Federal Republic of Germany.

occasionally producing goods or services for occasional exchange than a collection of guest workers living in an auto assembly plant dormitory has to a family. It is the family living in a suburban apartment which indeed may have been "colonialized" by the same phenomena that produced the enterprise, and have adapted its form and functions to that exchange-driven life which the enterprise exemplifies. The enterprise, however, is the product of, not an adaptation to, that new life. This difference in characterization, I believe and hope to demonstrate, should provide a better perspective on the juridification phenomenon in the sphere of enterprise law than is provided by an undifferentiated "colonialization" characterization.

Furthermore, actual enterprise law of the first and second stages in a sense does not regulate relations between human beings, or even relations between human beings and organizations. Of course individual human beings may be investors, but the individual's surplus savings, invested either in a large enterprise or in a mutual fund, typically are only a small element of that person's personality, psyche or life. The worker investing eight hours a day for decades has a deeper relationship with the employer than the investor occasionally investing disposable income representing a small fraction of total income. And the occasional wealthy investor can diversify the investment portfolio and distribute risks, an option not available to the worker. In short, on a scale of loss of a finger nail, a finger, an arm or a life, the investor-enterprise relationship may go so high as the second level, the worker-enterprise relationship to the highest. It is in this perhaps exaggerated sense that I emphasize the impersonal aspect of enterprise law as against, say, labor law or consumer protection law. Another way to put the point is to characterize the investor-shareholder, in that capacity, as "only" an instrumental actor, limited, by the dedication of these savings, to profit maximization, in the same legal sense that the enterprise created through these pooled savings is characterized as a "merely" instrumental actor and legal subject (von Gierke, as cited in Wiethölter, 1961: 136f; Dan-Cohen, 1985: 23). Stage Two enterprise law provides the framework for a capital market, and the market in turn protects investors; the ostensibly more personal legal rules, in all their detail, are only ancillary to that function.

Of course this characterization is valid more for large enterprises than small ones, and I admit at the outset that shareholder-manager relationships among the latter, and their governing law, well might partake of the intensity (and when appropriate, of the protective attributes) of labor law or consumer protection law. But since the major concerns animating both the juridification and legitimation discussions as they bear on enterprise law arise from passive investment in large enterprises, it is legitimate to leave the close or owner-operated enterprise and its legal regime out of the following discussion.

It is also true — and this is a more significant qualification — that the fourth stage postulated by Clark may require re-evaluation of this "cool" perception of enterprise law. The internalisation/imposition of the costs of funding pension payments onto the wage-earning process and thus onto the employee may move that component of the overall enterprise law regime up on the intensity scale of the involvement of the person in the investment-enterprise relationship. That process, therefore, for the first time potentially invests the regime of enterprise law with some of the characteristics of consumer or worker protection. At the same time, however, this is the relationship in Clark's differentiated-structure scheme farthest removed, and most easily separated, from the overall structure of enterprise law created by the overlapping succession of the three prior stages. It bears more on the generation of savings than on their investment; therefore, although it is at least of quantitative significance to the investment process and thus to the enterprise law regime, it has no direct place in that regime. While this stage assuredly will call for "substantive" protection, in Clark's terms, it nevertheless need not and perhaps will not intrude directly upon the "facilitative", the "fiduciary/transparent" and the "intermediary insulation/soundness" rule patterns respectively characterizing the enterprise law of the first three stages. Below I discuss how it may intrude on the overall legitimation function of enterprise law regimes; here I only argue that it will do so vaguely and indirectly.

3.2 The Relation of Enterprise Structure to Enterprise Law in the Context of the Relation of Enterprise Law to System Legitimation

The modern forms of economic activity required the functional attributes of continuity of entity life, transferability of ownership interests, centralization of management and — later — limitation of shareholder liability. (Blackstone, 1765: I, 475) These, in turn, required facilitative legal regimes beyond those made available by pre-existing concepts of "contract" and "trust". (Maitland, 1911) Merchants and middle classes admittedly participated in voluntary passive stock investment even two hundred years ago, but it was not until there occurred, in the middle of the 19th century, the technological and organizational revolutions described by Chandler in The Visible Hand (1977) that large-scale passive savings were needed by and flowed to these firms. Thus, it was not until then that legal rules speaking to the rights of shareholders and to the responsibilities of managers began to appear. Even then, these rules originally and understandably bore more on the role of the promoter and on original capitalization and investment questions (i.e., on promoters' fraud and ultra vires) than they did on operational questions.

(1) The first period of facilitative legislation has its tentative origins in a New York statute of 1811 and a firmer base in the better-known but still inadequate Connecticut statute of 1837 [5]. Its first modern incarnation, however, is a New Jersey statute of 1875, which offered a simplified enabling act that attracted New York capital; this was followed by the notorious 1889/1892 recodification engineered by Dill, counsel to the Standard Oil Trust, and originally intended to supply a holding-company exception to the looming

[5] The following review is based on Chapter II of R. Buxbaum and K. J. Hopt (forthcoming).

Sherman Act prohibition of cartelization in trust form. Its proponents were interested mainly in rules to ease the formation and capital augmentation of companies; facilitation of managerial discretion and majoritarian shareholder decision still lay in the future. Rather, the New Jersey statute gained its temporary domination because of its usefulness in the creation of the promoter-driven horizontal integration of the 'Nineties, and of the (especially public utility) enterprise pyramids of the "Roaring 'Twenties."

A temporary moratorium on New Jersey's legislative pandering, imposed during Governor Woodrow Wilson's gubernatorial tenure between 1906 and 1914, led to the entrance of rivals, of whom Delaware, a competitor since 1899, had by 1932 become the dominant player. For a while a somewhat more paternalistic though still flexible enabling law regime remained in contention in the form of the first generation Model Business Corporation Law of the American Bar Association, enacted in more or less faithful detail by roughly half the states. But with its total about-face in the revision of 1950, with New York's revision of 1961, and above all with the Delaware revision of 1967, the typical American state corporation code, while not a single uniform pattern in all details, had become a total facilitative structure roughly by mid-century. What impulses the Crash of 1929 and the Great Depression of the 1930s generated were almost totally caught up and absorbed by the more explicitly regulatory regimes adopted by the federal Congress.

(2) That federal regime, one of the two hallmarks of Clark's second stage of American capitalism, has been lucidly summarized by Kübler as part of his earlier study and needs no elaboration here (Kübler, supra***). This set of laws and regulations discloses one feature, however, that strongly confirms the suggested ambivalence of any norm purporting to regulate enterprise behavior in the name of enterprise efficiency: its underlying principle of regulation by mandating disclosure, rather than by mandating behavior. (Loss, 1983: 154ff; but see Kripke, 1979). As has often been noted, the philosophy of the 1933 and 1934 statutes is that everything is permitted provided only that it is disclosed. Obviously no self-respecting administrative organization is going to accept such a limitation at face value, and if the SEC is anything it is a self-respecting agency. Thus a good deal of low-level substantive behavior control has been insinuated into the machinery, the two most noteworthy examples of which under the two respective statutes being the creative use of the discretionary acceleration power to make registration statements effective under the first (Jennings and Marsh, 1982: 182) and the only partially successful insistence on certain shareholder voting and director nomination processes under the second (Jennings and Buxbaum, 1979: 294ff). But it is revealing that these efforts and others like them typically have been clandestine and their legal justification typically has been defensive. Even under the most enforcement-minded Supreme Court regime they have been halting, and tentative; and they have been substantially disabled with the Burger Court's bland decision in *Santa Fe Industries*, 430 U.S. 46 (1977), to pull back the analogous extension of the Rule 10b-5 private remedy from its application to overreaching managerial behavior, and to limit its application to fraudulent behavior.

The state law half of this "Stage Two" set of enterprise laws was until recently common law in form and state level in origin — the fiduciary duties of care and loyalty. In oversimplified form, and in retrospect, one can characterize this state common law regime as providing the minimal behavorial constraints on managerial and controlling-shareholder actions needed to supplement the mandated transparency of decision-making which the federal regime imposed not only on the capital formation but also on much of the operational process.

These fiduciary rules, however, being based on historically specific notions of typical behavior, were bound to change as the structural conditions of industrial organization underlying that behavior changed. Increasing size of individual enterprise, increasing complexity of internal structure, increasing professionalization and thus opaqueness of management, and increasing independence of enterprise from public capital markets and their discipline (as tax-supported reinvestment of profits substituted for externally supplied funds) — all these had their influence on corporate agents' behavior and on judicial responses to that behavior. The self-dealing transaction of a board member with "his" corporation once was a random (though hardly an isolated) event, and when uncovered could be treated "with rough hands." (Lattin, 1971) The open and recurring transactions of a partly-owned, vertically if partially integrated subsidiary with its controlling parent were bound to win acceptance and to change the rules applicable to them simply because of their open and recurrent — eventually their typical — nature (Ballantine, 1946: 171; Jennings and Buxbaum, 1979: 466ff) The bank president failing to notice his subordinates' embezzlements could be seen as personally falling below a community standard of personalized care and attention to duty. The chief executive officer sitting at the top of a deep and wide pyramidal enterprise hierarchy, let alone his only occasionally convened, absentee board of directors, can no more be held responsible for wrongful behavior several steps down the scale than is the case in analogous political sectors (*Graham* v. *Allis-Chalmers Mfg.* Co., 41 Del. Ch. 78, 188 A.2d 125 (Sup.1963)).

In time this erosion of judicial scrutiny went so far as to embolden the state bar committees which typically draft state legislation to subsume the remnants of the fiduciary duty rules within the statutory regimes, and thereby quite consciously if paradoxically to convert them from constraints into elements of facilitative enabling structures (Eisenberg, 1974). The statutory treatment of conflict-of-interests transactions, whatever the motivation of their originators in the California of 1931, (Ballantine, 1931: 475f) today are and are openly acknowledged to be "curative" statutes (Jennings and Buxbaum, 1979: 457f). And the decision of the Model Act drafters finally to codify the quintessentially common law duty of care was taken not in order to generate a rule of scrutiny, but to provide a set of "safe harbor" provisions of operational specificity, adherence to which promised to move the transaction within the deferential and facilitative *non liquet* known as the business judgment rule. (Jennings and Buxbaum, 1979: 174ff, 190ff).

This simplified history at least suggests the accuracy of the differentiation aspect of Clark's evolutionary sketch (1981: 570): "The second stage required the legal system to develop stable relationships between professional managers and public investors, ostensibly aimed at keeping the former accountable to the latter, but also placing full control of business decisions in the managers' hands."

(3) The preceding characterization of the federal and state law regimes discloses an unsurprising divergence between them when viewed, now, from the perspective of system legitimation and its problems. In Clark's frame of reference the state law provides initially robust, later increasingly feeble control of managerial decision making; still the emphasis remains on the issue of supervision of management control. Shifting emphasis to the difference between the state and the federal legal regimes, however, points up an interesting and significant fact. The burden of legitimating the enterprise system has come to fall upon the federal regime, which for almost half a century managed to maintain and even to increase its hold on at least the investment-related if not the operational activities of enterprise. The operational functions of enterprise, which, as already noted, were only partially controllable by the federal disclosure system, have displayed a tendency to disengage themselves from legal control and to establish themselves as autonomous, almost literally lawless spheres of activity. The capitalization-related functions, by contrast, remain not only under the telescope of the SEC and the magnifying glass of the private plaintiffs' bar, but under manifold and exquisitely detailed affirmative duties of reporting, accounting and explaining — to agency and to investors (see, critically thereto, Kripke, 1979). With the fiduciary-rule constraints fading as the principal legal reflection of society's involvement with the (relatively) internal aspects of enterprise activity, the transparency-rule constraints have become ever more prominent in the role of expressing social concern with the corporation; and, in the paradoxical sense of successfully allaying that concern, in the role of providing social legitimation of the enterprise. The enterprise subsystem, however, is more than a capital market phenomenon; it impacts upon more, and more important, environments and subsystems. Because it is so explicitly focused on the limited segment of investment and investor relationship, the "extra" legitimation function now imposed on the federal legal regime, by default of state law, is an overload, one that cannot be carried by a legal system standing, as it were, on one leg (Buxbaum, J., 1981: 50).

In one sense this is not too critical, a conclusion that can be demonstrated if we now revert to the explicitly narrow definition of enterprise law offered at the beginning of this paper. The American legal response to enterprise activity, as compared with at least the German version of the European response, always has been sharply divided between the private law control of owner-manager (or principal-agent) relationships and the public law control of the external effects of the enterprise on its environment. This, of course, has its specific historical as well as general legal-cultural grounds. Already in 1890, the heyday of unfettered capitalism, the Sherman Act marked the debut of public law concern with the industrial organization element of enterprise activity — almost the exact point in time at which the facilitative enabling-law regime of modern corporation statutes arrived. And the employee-employer relationship, was brought under federal collective bargaining regimes (the quintessential paradigm of external public law constraint) during the Depression of the early 1930s, exactly at the time that the disclosure-and-transparency provisions of the federal securities regulation regimes also came into the picture. It is, I believe, hard to overestimate the importance of these major laws as mechanisms to insulate corporation law in the strict sense from the pressure to internalize public concern about enterprise behavior. Even concern about enterprise relations with those groups enjoying a specifically close and enduring relation with the enterprise, and often in need of legal help to obtain adequate bargaining leverage with corporate management — labor, suppliers, customers — basically has not penetrated the American versions of corporation law.

If I read European developments correctly, the dubious but persistent characterization of labor law as the private law of employer-employee contract relationships indirectly and paradoxically may have helped keep corporation law imbued with social values; i.e., with public law elements. It apparently has been easier to internalize worker-owner or worker-manager relations as part of corporation law just because these, as well as owner-manager relationships, traditionally have been doctrinally categorized as private, contract law. In addition, a specific German institutional focus — "das Unternehmen an sich" — whose spotty history needs no review here, of course also plays a role. In its presently dominant version (i.e., from Rathenau (1918) through Netter (1932) to Wiethölter (1961: 38ff) and perhaps Raiser (1969)), it may have provided a doctrinally acceptable impetus to the infusion of social issues other than those of the owner-management genre into the pigeonhole of corporation law, creating this "enterprise-law variant."

That twin cultural and doctrinal particularity is missing from the American scene. There the old, persistent separation of public concerns and private concerns has permitted the American version of corporation law, lacking an "enterprise-law variant", to flourish to this day[6]. (The only significant amelioration, that which is inherent in the continuing vitality of the common law adjudication process, is separately treated below; in any event, it has little bearing on this question of the subject matter scope of corporation law.) That separation of public and private concerns in turn becomes a significant consideration for the legitimation as well as for the juridification discussions. It has an obvious bearing on the problematical legitimation of deregulation; or, more precisely, on the efficiency-based argument that market constraints better serve all relevant interests than do legal constraints.

In the U. S. this latter argument, rampant today, should have an easier time of it than in Europe, for (among other, probably more important reasons) the

6 An interesting explanation based on the personification of the corporation in anthropomorphic terms is offered by Arnold (1937: 188f).

historical reason that American corporation law always has been understood as limited and "private" in the above sense. If at least Stage One and, as I have here suggested, even Stage Two corporate law regimes have had the benefit of this long-standing culturally embedded excuse not to carry their share of the larger legal system's burden of legitimation of enterprise activity (and of the latter's impact on distributive and redistributive functions), then the "legitimation crisis" postulated by Habermas would to that extent be more successfully — more "diffusively" — absorbed or rendered less critical by the American version of current corporation law than by, say, the German enterprise version. The burden at least would be shifted away from corporation law, including, n.b., from the first generation of securities regulation. It would shift substantially to the hydra-headed monster of public law. There it would be diffused in turn among the large number of separate statutes spawned by the New Deal and the New Frontier, statutes whose variously good and bad records of implementation could absorb ten times the amount of public interest and energies presently devoted to them. With this jungle of public laws demanding attention, the only slightly rank garden of corporation law can be left more or less safely to languish in obscurity.

Of course this is an overstated distinction, and of course the European scene is not so divergent from the American as the sketch suggests — if only because a fair number of comparable public law statutes can be found there, too. Nor is the cause of such divergence as does exist attributable solely or even primarily to these differences in the doctrinal evolution of corporation law. (Assmann, 1980: 253f). Nonetheless, an important conclusion as to the viability of state-economy system separation, and thus of state-economy system legitimation, lurks in even a weak form of the stated argument. If the American private law of corporations has been only partially responsible for the successful separation of enterprise activity from the larger socio-political system and its legal reflection (Stone, 1985: 123), that success carries within it some implications for the future. In particular, there are implications for the expectable persistence of some current tendencies, briefly reviewed next, and for the expectable forms which the legal regime reflecting Clark's Stage Three and particularly Stage Four may come to take along with the expectable legitimation role that regime may come to play.

(4) During the past decade the counter-revolution wrought in economic law by the Burger Court has found a major impetus in, and provided a major impetus to, this classic separation between the private, facilitative sphere of corporation law and the public, regulative sphere of enterprise law. Using, of all things, the Stage Two federal regulatory regime as its justification, the court has begun to insist on efficiency criteria as the constitutional touchstone with which to test member state substantive regulation of enterprise activity, under both supremacy and commerce clause principles. It has done this while not hesitating at the same time to narrow earlier, more generous interpretations of these same federal statutes, within their own field of application. Thus, in *Edgar* v. *MITE Corporation,* 457 U.S. 624 (1982), the court invalidated state regulations requiring prior approval of mergers involving

local corporations, on the argument that such legislation violated the commerce clause though no federal statute under the commerce clause had purported to regulate these transactions on an exclusive basis. It found a violation in the state's temporary ban of the share exchange between the bidding corporation and the tendering shareholders of the target corporation, because by such a ban the "reallocation of economic resources to their highest-valued use, a process which can impose efficiency and competition, is hindered."

And in *Southland Stores, Inc.* v. *Keating*, 104 S. Ct. 852 (1984), the Court invalidated a state statute prohibiting arbitration of disputes arising out of franchise investments, on the ground that the Federal Arbitration Act pre-empts anti-arbitration rules of this sort under the supremacy clause of the Constitution. Some of the justices may have joined in the opinion for institutional reasons, such as overload of the judiciary; their prior opinions in economic law matters were not averse to substantive regulation, even regulation based on distributive rather than allocational considerations. Others, however, apparently found this "free market" result (for given the realities of the arbitration process, such it is) congruent with their overall philosophy that the "micro-economic morality in which value is perceived as strictly individual, private and subjective" (Michelman, 1979: 139; see also 1978a, 1978b) should at least inform if not govern even constitutional interpretation.

If these two examples are accepted as indicating the American legal system's present response to legitimation problems in the twilight of Stage Two, they suggest two in themselves contradictory developments as our objective organization of households and firms moves towards Stage Four. First, to the degree that this legal ambiance is not in fact dysfunctional, but congruent with the economic structures and processes it purports to govern, these developments suggest that a legitimation crisis is not yet perceivable on the American scene. Why this should be so is beyond my competence and my subject. The buffer of a racially specific surplus labor population, the temporary relative increase in income associated with the massive entry of women from two-spouse households into the workforce, the geographically vast American labor and firm market that decentralizes and diffuses opportunities and breakdowns, the culturally related mobility of surplus labor, the culturally related personal and organizational habits and temperaments of a people still relatively (though diminishingly) different from those of other societies: All are candidates for at least partial explanation, as are objectively given factors of natural resources and even climate (Buxbaum, 1984a: 1166f). In any event, whatever the explanation, one could fairly argue that both in reality and in perception the systemic separation of the state and the economy persists in the U. S. to a degree not found in Europe. And it persists, one would have to say, in the teeth of actual state involvement in the economic sphere that by no means is less than that found in Western Europe (Buxbaum, 1971).

The second, quite different conclusion pertains to the possible crumbling of this resilient and productive illusion as the American version of capitalism enters Stage Four. (I relegate to separate treatment my view that in its operative detail and in its effects on these legitimation issues Stage Three can be treated as a variant of Stage Two — at least, that its legal reflection is a variant of the federal regime of securities regulation developed at Stage Two). That transition needs somewhat more detailed description and evaluation.

(5) This development is recent enough, and Clark's review thereof sketchy enough, to justify more discursive treatment of these Stage Four phenomena at this point. Two strands need to be followed, though it is their combined effect that then needs to be evaluated: the strand relating to employees, and the strand relating to firms.

Social security was not introduced in the U. S. until the New Deal, when the four elements comprising the system were introduced: the Old Age and Survivor's Insurance Trust Fund, the Disability Insurance Trust Fund, the Hospital Insurance Trust Fund, and (later) the Supplementary Medical Insurance Trust Fund. Beginning in the 1950s, privately funded retirement plans (as well as privately funded medical insurance plans) began to appear, both at the executive and, more significantly, at the wage-earner level (the latter typically introduced through the collective bargaining process), (Kolodrubetz, 1971). While the sense of crisis which now suffuses the entire state social security regime is of more recent origin (and began with medical, not retirement issues), the federal government early encouraged the growth of these private schemes, in the main through fiscal incentives. The plans were of two types: "pattern plans", negotiated by the major unions with industry-wide adoption, provided flat dollar benefits (though increasing with length of service); and "conventional plans", at first found in the higher employee echelons, provided income-related benefits. It is significant from the standpoint of social attitudes, discussed below, that the latter type of plan has come to predominate at all employment levels and that employer contribution of premium payments predominates over employee contribution.

Already by 1970 government and public were aware of the significance of this phenomenon. By then there existed about 200,000 separate plans, covering 30 million private sector employees, over 45% of all private sector employees (and a substantial though lesser proportion of state and local government employees also had won such supplemental pension coverage). Concomitantly, a substantial percentage of newly retired workers — over 25% of the private sector group — had begun to receive at least some compensation from these private plans by then (ibid.).

A decade later the phenomenon was in full flower. Today well over 80% of all private sector employees are covered, as is a significant proportion of public sector employees, by the more than half million existing plans. Almost 40% of all newly retired employees, and over 50% of the private sector ones, are receiving private pension payments in addition to their social security pensions. (Maxfield and Reno, 1985). In addition, 70% of all private sector employment retirement plans now are income-based rather than flat rate (Maxfield, 1982; Beller, 1983).

It is the destination of these insurance funds, as investments, that brings the foregoing factual discussion to our point of departure. Before the advent of this phenomenon, retirement, unemployment and medical coverage was funded by direct taxation of employer and employee, and by the statutorily mandated investment of these funds in the same governmental fisc, now in its capacity as borrower. It was the justified fear of the eventual insolvency of this system of investment in unproductive resources, particularly as the population stabilized and aged, demographically speaking, that sparked the conscious move to privatization of this major social welfare obligation, and not only among the (decreasingly) unionized segment of the population. "Integrated retirement plans" — private pension plans integrated, in their packaging of actual retirement benefits, with the governmental social security pension system — are the modern form. (U.S. Dept. of Labor, 1984: 42-56) It is because of their "interim" investment modalities that they are relevant to the discussion of the legitimation question to which the preceding review of earlier stages of enterprise activity and enterprise law was devoted.

These private pension plans can meet their payment obligations only through the income augmentation of the basic premium funds that is generated by their tax-driven investment in the capital markets. (Wharton School, 1980: 2f, 15ff). Already by the early 1980s these private, state and local government pension plans owned almost 20% of all publicly traded equity securities and were acquiring 50% of all newly issued equity securities. (New York Stock Exchange, 1983). Projections provided by the Department of Labor, based upon financial reports filed by these plans, suggest that by the year 2000 these plans will own roughly 50% of all outstanding equity shares. I agree with Clark that the well-known slogan, "pension plan socialism", coined by Drucker (1976), is not accurate; as Conard has pointed out (1984: 1487), federal law inhibits investment of single-firm funds in the employing firm's shares, and rules of prudence governing the administrators of all funds further dictate investment diversification and introduce a mild bias in favor of investment in the larger and more widely-held firms. Furthermore, the larger firms' direct pension funds typically are manager (firm)-run, not jointly let alone union-managed. Nevertheless, as to the large public sector funds and the only slightly smaller union-managed ones, new institutionally owned and institutionally managed holdings are a fact of life with implications for the owner-enterprise relationship.

The consequences of this major change in the form in which private savings are invested in firms are obviously significant to the management of those large enterprises. Management faces totally new issues of strategy and relation with such new investors, and particularly with the specific institutional forms of intermediaries who nominally own, or who on behalf of those nominal intermediate owners or of their ultimate beneficiaries manage, those massive investments, and with the specific instruments of control those investments unavoidably carry with them (Buxbaum, 1984a). Some knowledgeable observers suggest that institutional investors are passive investors, even though for many major corporations institutional investment — a broader concept than pension-plan investors — may be reaching 50% of the ownership of their equity securities (Lowenstein, 1983: 296ff). More recently, a distinction between their passivity as to operational issues and their increasing activism in the important but special area of managerial defensive manœuvres against takeover bids, manœuvers that directly and seriously threaten the investment value of large bloc holdings, has been noted[7]. These issues have spun a web of concerns together involving the increasingly critical relationship of enterprise management, and indeed of enterprise performance, with these new forms of enterprise ownership.

That increasingly critical relationship is a problem only on the system side of Habermas' life-world system division. The "disturbed" actor is the manager of private enterprise. The "disturbing" force or element is the newly structured and newly powerful intermediary-owner of private enterprise. The role or absence of legal rules as a medium for restabilization, however, is not directly connected to the use of the legal system as legitimating communicator between the subsystem "private economy" (and its power-medium "money") and the life world. While Habermas differentiates between law as an institution and law as a medium in so far as its differential influence on the life world is concerned, he provides no similar differentiation as to its influence on the two major systems, state and economy. His major interest is in law, as a derivative medium carrying the messages of those systems' primary media, power and money, in more palatable form to the life world addressees. In this scheme there is little room for considering law as an intrasystemic medium, though of course law is a significant if derivative steering mechanism for the state's primary medium of power even vis-à-vis the economy.

If, however, we follow Wiethölter's criticism of the law-as-medium/law-as-institution distinction beyond his charge that it is too vague and blurred to be useful, and in particular if we follow his assertion that law inherently demonstrates "institutional" characteristics associated with concepts like proportionality and equality, a different picture of law as an intrasystemic, system-internal medium may emerge (Wiethölter, 1985a; 1985b). For one thing, a "reverse-juridification" influence, transmitting life world symbolic concepts into the two systems, may be at work. This not only may temper excessively instrumental intrasystemic rulemaking, in order to protect the life world from its spillover effects, but it may even be immediately influential in tempering the relation — and perception — of the system actors' with — of — each other. Obviously this is no more than a fragmentary speculation, but I believe that both the juridification concept and our general sense of the legitimation issue might be enriched by more work in this direction. The future utility of the reflexive law concept, in particular, may be enhanced if this

[7] I base this on numerous journalistic reports of the reactions of institutional investors to anti-takeover tactics of incumbent management. The much-discussed action of California State Treasurer Unruh, on behalf of state employee pension funds, in organizing a national activist Council of Institutional Shareholders, is reviewed in Egelko (1984).

dimension of law as a two-directional (or autonomous — *eigenwillig*) steering mechanism is further explored; I attempt some suggestions in that regard below, in the discussion of the judicial role in reflexive law.

The central location of the legitimation problem, however, is on the other side of the coin.

(6) So long as the decision to save was a voluntary one, and so long as the investment of voluntary savings could voluntarily be through personal or collective intermediation, the fact that rational risk distribution (portfolio) considerations led many savers to delegate specific investment decisions to pool managers, for collective intermediation, still could be accommodated within the neutral, "microeconomic" frame of reference characteristic of Stage Two let alone of Stage One. Once, and to the degree, that even the decision to save is collectivized, however, all bets are off. The foregoing suggestions concerning the neutrality and sanctity of the enterprise sphere, in its operational as well as in its capital-formation aspects, now will be open to question. Contractarian apologetics cannot stretch to accommodate the need to enter the workforce. The argument that the laborer freely enters the marketplace to bargain for his hire did not survive the 1930's and stands no chance of being revived today.

Clark suggests that "soundness" regulation and consumer protection now will have to enter corporation law. When the worker is required to become a capital supplier, and to live in substantial part off his passive income, the state will not be able to avoid the descent into the marketplace. This prediction can be formulated in Habermas' terms as a legitimation question. A crisis of legitimation may come about, but not because the state has had to take over the balance wheel functions of the ideal super-capitalist among the contending rivals structured as private firms. Rather, it will come about because the particular firms themselves are the willing or unwilling subjects of the state's decision — and it is a decision — to authorize the appropriation of labor for the purpose of direct capital formation (in part, ironically, through the process of collective bargaining).

It is not self-evident, however, that this shift in the way in which social security benefits are funded and channelled is inherently more erosive of the symbolic legitimation of the private enterprise subsystem than is that which existed before or might realistically exist today in place of what we have. Neither the objective reality of social security claims satisfaction nor the perception of the relation of their satisfaction to the functions of state and enterprise systems is directly put in question by the organization of Stage Four capitalism. Especially the latter problems, those of perception, can give rise to quite conflicting speculations (Lesnoy and Leimer, 1985: 27). For example, the actual and incontrovertible relation of the maintenance of social security to the performance of the enterprise system nevertheless is not a close one. It is, on the contrary, uncoupled by the separation of the shareholder's claim to market value and income stream from the beneficiary's claim to a stable and predictable retirement income. In time failure in the first sphere will be felt in the second, but a wide range of good or less good performance in the first can be absorbed, because of this uncoupling, by the second (Edwards, 1979: Ch. 11). By contrast, direct ownership of income-producing claims on enterprise, by retirees, would subject them to constant uncertainty and the enterprise as well as the state system to considerable legitimation stress. In short, this and perhaps other specifics of the Stage Four phenomena may turn out to be no more than examples of that "segmentation of the labor market and fragmentation of consciousness" which Habermas and Held see as ways by which a legitimation crisis can, at times and for a time, be deferred (Held, 1982: 190ff; Habermas,1982: 281).

Whether and how these new forms of capital organization will generate new problems of enterprise governance, and new threats of that ever-impending legitimation crisis, is not answered merely by identifying these new phenomena. At the least, however, they are congruent with Habermas' prediction that both an increasing need for juridification of the life world and a concomitant erosion of the illusions of inevitability of contingent system-forms, may be empirically demonstrable.

With that admittedly provisional and incomplete inquiry into the relevance of Habermas' colonialization and legitimation arguments to enterprise law, it is now appropriate to turn to the second particularity of the private enterprise system of economic activity — its mission and structure. This focus may help identify whether and how enterprise mission and structure may bear on the possibility that reflexive law concepts could ameliorate potential excesses of juridification and crises of legitimation.

4. The Capacity of the Enterprise to Operate Under Reflexive Law Modalities

4.1 Reflexive Law and the Mission and Structure of the Enterprise System

Reflexive law steers with a light hand, rules its subjects indirectly. Stripped of value connotations and viewed simply as a general concept of systems or organizational theory, it is little more than an institutionally specific recharacterization of the concept of the legitimacy of the state as a necessary condition of the authority — and thus of the survival, and thus of the very definition — of the state. Seen in the evolutionary but not yet value-specific terms of ever-increasing functional differentiation of subsystems, reflexive law is both a reflection of and a reaction to the social complexity of modern life (Luhmann, 1982; Murphy, 1984).

It is only when a value orientation is added to the concept that its relation to the foregoing discussion becomes apparent. Viewed from that orientation, reflexive law, in Teubner's formulation, could be seen as an institutional counterpoint to Habermas' theory of communicative ethics, as a framework for the practical discourse of social actors under the best conditions of unconstrained and undistorted intersubjectivity that can be attained in a real, highly "systematized" world (Habermas, 1981; 1985). Teubner merges systems-theoretic arguments, concerning the danger of subsystems' self-perpetuation and the need for inter-(sub)system interaction, with a still vague concept of a system-generated, ethically animated "strategic model" of law that can "produce normative criteria for a conscious self-transformation of the law", in a way that suggests, at least to me, a possible variant on the mentioned theory of communicative ethics (Teubner, 1985a). It is beyond my competence to evaluate this larger merged concept in general, (especially its debatable roots in cybernetics and biology; cf. Teubner, 1985a: 377f) but some speculations on the suitability of Teubner's more explicit reflexive law concept either to explain or to prescribe developments in corporation (or enterprise) law are in order. This is especially valid since Teubner's own first effort to operationalize the reflexive law concept in the above-described sense lies in the field of enterprise law (Teubner, 1983; 1985c; supra: 38).

In an appealing but in the end problematical sense the corporation is an ideal social phenomenon through which to speculate on the operational (steering) modalities of the concept of reflexive law, as well as on its "external functions" in Teubner's terms, (Teubner, 1983: 255) though I do not indulge in the latter exercise here. Any person or group may act on the basis of internalized norms derived from the larger society's preferred values, or at least from the society's sense of the values it wishes that social actor to internalize and base its actions on — i.e., anyone may be a good citizen. The corporation, however, can only function as a "good citizen" in a way that differs from that of other actors, because of the particular modes of action generated by its internal hierarchy of decision-making (Stone, 1975: 122ff). "It" is a good citizen only in consequence of a complex aggregation of individual decisions,only some of which are even known to, let alone controlled by, let alone made by its collective owners or its Board of Directors or even its Chief Executive Officer (Kagan and Scholz, 1980; Coffee, 1977: 1129). "Reflexive" behavior, therefore, occurs in two dimensions, and thus reflexive law, as applied to the corporate phenomenon, entails the application of two somewhat different steering or legitimating concepts.

Indeed, one needs to take this dual function of reflexive law in the corporate context further. "It" — the corporation —strictly speaking makes no choices or decisions, since in Blackstone's (and perhaps Habermas') terms it "has no soul." (Blackstone, 1765: 477 (quoting Coke)). Its choices are those made by human beings along various ascending stages of the corporate hierarchy. Yet in an important, socially legitimate, sense none of these persons is a free moral agent, or, put in a less extreme way, a person free to disregard the consensual constraints established by the raison d'etre of the corporation; i.e., by its economic instrumental function of profit maximization. An individual is free to listen to societal suggestions of how to exercise dominion over personally owned property. The corporate agent for the owners (shareholders) is not. The discretion inherent in representative decision-making provides some room for that kind of morally responsive action on a derivative basis (Stone, 1985) but agent discretion that transcends this instrumental limitation would be doubly illegitimate: unacceptable in principle[8] and uncontrollable in practice (Eisenberg, 1985). Not even the shareholder is free to transcend this limit, assuming the capability to do so based on substantial stock ownership. The co-ownership of the corporation constrains each owner's freedom of action through the limiting condition of profit maximization, the common ground for the co-owners' joint investment, as surely as that condition constrains their common agent,the manager.

As a result, reflexive law instruments face two significant though not necessarily disabling obstacles to their successful insinuation into corporate decision-making structures. The first is the well-known problem addressed by bureaucratic or organizational theory; namely, how to shape the myriad decisions of many, hierarchically arranged actors holding complex personal as well as organizational values into the desired whole (see especially Kraakman, 1984). The second is how to do this when that aggregate of decisions, even taken as a coherent whole, is designed and expected to be taken in large part on the basis of conflicting social values — the social value of efficiency achieved by the enterprise drive towards profit maximization, and the social value(s), let us call them distributive values, which are typically though not necessarily jeopardized by the enterprise system's very success in achieving the first value of efficiency (Buxbaum, 1984a: 518f; Kraakman, 1984).

When applied to the enterprise form of economic activity, reflexive law instruments thus are both inherently compromised by their ambivalence, and susceptible of sabotage by the complexity of the structure they are required to steer. It may of course be argued, as Teubner has argued, that this ambivalence and this complex object-structure are the grounds for the failure of direct social intervention via public law, and the reasons for the move towards indirect intervention via reflexive law in the first place (Teubner, 1983: 268). That again, however, treats as one what in fact are two separate problems faced by law as it faces complex social organizations, and some separation of Teubner's argument is necessary[9].

The first ground for the failure of traditional public law, it is said, lies in the burden the plethora of such rules and regulations imposes on the enterprise, to the detriment of its accepted mission of efficiency. That is very much an empirical question, which has not yet been broken down into specific problems capable of being empirically addressed, let alone answered. A first sub-issue that needs attention in this debate is the differential impact of this much-disparaged albatross of legal rules on enterprises of different size and power. The large, or at least the large and market-powerful, enterprise simply

[8] This is particularly true of any suggestion that social goals are feasible for the oligopolistic corporation operating in an imperfect market environment, which seems to be Teubner's justification (1985: 161). Nor can — should — one hide behind the argument that use of a long-range profit maximization melts the problem away.

[9] From somewhat different perspectives, cf. also Blankenburg (1984) and Galanter (1980).

adds whatever capacity is needed to meet these obligations and more or less transfers the costs thereof to its prices and thus to the consumer society. The small, or at least the small and relatively powerless, enterprise cannot follow the same path and thus is disadvantaged in the maintenance of its market position vis-à-vis its more powerful rivals. Even this question requires a major functional separation of legal rules bearing on capital formation and maintenance from rules bearing on operations, especially since the very forms and channels of capital formation and maintenance may differ for the large (public) and small (private) corporation.

The second issue, however, is one of action and reaction. There is an implicit if not explicit assertion, within Teubner's larger argument, that direct confrontation between societal values, as reflected in "external" and directly impinging public law, on the one hand, and the enterprise decision-making system on the other, does not work. Apparently, for this is not entirely clear, it does not work in part because it causes dysfunctional reaction and overreaction from within the enterprise, and in part because in their substantive content these outside norms cannot be sophisticated or informed enough about the actual operation of the enterprise system to be effective in holding the system to a socially acceptable type of decision-making.

The first objection — confrontation is counterproductive — implies a disturbing concession: that the enterprise system is too powerful in present-day reality to be managed except through guile. Matthew's injunction to be "subtle as the serpent, harmless as the dove" may have been appropriate advice to the Apostles embarking on their proselytizing mission in a hostile environment, but it seems misapplied to societal efforts to create an appropriate regulatory structure for enterprise activity. The second objection, that society, by its laws, is not wise enough to tell the enterprise system how to act, is irrelevant to the direct-reflexive law distinction. If lack of substantive knowledge or sophistication is responsible for failure of direct legal regulation, the same deficiency may cause even more abject failure in the case of indirect, reflexive regulation; at least, there is no *a priori*, logical way to dismiss this possibility. What indirect governance saves through jettisoning the need for knowledgeable detail may be lost through the enterprise actors' ability to drive significant specific decisions through the interstices of open-ended reflexive steering guidelines[10]. Again, this is an issue for empirical study, though one with long time frame requirements and considerable difficulties of problem formulation. Stone's proposals (1975: 236ff) and Teubner's enquiry into corporate social responsibility (1985c; cf. also Teubner, 1985b, on codetermination) are examples both of this kind of work and of its complexity.

4.2 Reflexive Law in its Institutional Setting

Reflexive law no more than pre-reflexive law exists in a vacuum. It exists within pre-existing legal-institutional structures that carry out law-making

[10] For persuasive analogues from the field of administrative law, see Breyer (1979). For a Marxist characterization of this tension, see Hever (1985).

and law-applying functions. It may find that older structures, shaped by and adequate to carry earlier versions of law (both pre-modern, "mediatizing" law and early modern, Weberian purposive-instrumental law), are inadequate and dysfunctional from its perspective (cf. Nonet and Selznick, 1978). Teubner suggests that reflexive law most likely will use and further develop certain quite specific structures or institutions of law, structures and institutions so far brought together under the abstract concept of "proceduralization" (Teubner, 1985a; supra: 33 ff.).

"Proceduralization" is advanced in part as an inevitable development, once juridification — the symptom of the degeneration of Weberian "material (purposive) law" into system-supporting, merely "consequentialist" law — renders the previous stage of legal control of enterprise systems dysfunctional. It is also advanced as a desirable development in its own right, i.e., even in system-rational terms. The thorough and critical evaluation of the concept by Kübler, (supra) who has studied its manifestations in the field of corporation law, permits us to move directly to consideration of its positive value as a prime instance or at least as a prime institutional embodiment of the kind of reflexive law envisaged by Teubner.

The principal manifestations of proceduralization[11] turn out to revolve around a specific and limited range of institutions. Putting aside federalization and constitutionalization, which are double-edged swords as much capable of introducing reductionist forms of deregulation as they are of facilitating sophisticated, indirect governance, Kübler identifies proceduralization with its institutional embodiment in courts (judicialization) and administrative agencies (bureaucratization). I should like to hypothesize that the latter — in the American context specifically the SEC and its rules — are the harbingers of rule-oriented process requirements, whereas courts reflect fact- or result-oriented process requirements; and I believe that the availability of both institutions is a necessary condition for the realization of the socially beneficial promises of reflexive law. This hypothesis, however, is based, again, on the American legal-cultural scene; whether it is accurate in the European setting is very much open to argument (compare Bydlinski, 1982).

Bureaucratization describes a situation in which there exists a closer, more flexible (reality-reactive) and more sophisticated relationship between the law-maker and the social object than is the case for the traditional (legislative) law-maker and the social object of those laws. This closer relationship permits the use of indirect steering mechanisms or processes that cannot be effectuated in the traditional setting. A major example is the much-remarked case of the imposition of independent audit committees and nominating committees by SEC regulation as a substitute for substantive regulation of the decisions of boards of directors (Jennings and Buxbaum, 1979: 186ff). A second, equally important and closely related example is the semi-coerced involvement of legal

[11] To the "...izations" subsumed in the formal concept of proceduralization, and to the latter's own "content" from the functional perspective, see, critically, Wiethölter (1982).

and accounting professionals in the supervision of directorial (and lower-ranking) decision-making, and the imposition of direct sanctions for breakdowns in this supervisory relationship not on the enterprise but on these professionals. Debated as they were, and perhaps no longer fully operative in the present climate of substantive deregulation, these are subtle processes, fraught with risks as well as with rewards. They could only be instituted, I would argue, at the bureaucratic level and they can only be maintained and monitored at that level. Legislatively ordained, and maintained without agency intermediation, they would have been (even) less subtle and more useless than they have been in fact. That, I would argue, is demonstrated by the legislative enactments, at the state law level, of procedural "curative" mechanisms which today control the duties of care and of loyalty in an excessively open-ended way (Jennings and Buxbaum, 1979: 457f).

Judicialization, too, can generate process-oriented rules; indeed, a substantial portion of the Delaware jurisprudence is of that sort: "guest voting" by the majority of the disinterested shareholders on structural transactions like mergers, simulated arms'-length bargaining between representatives of the outside shareholders and the dominant corporate parent on the terms of similar mergers, etc. (see particularly *Weinberger* v. *UOP*, Inc., 457 A.2d 70 (Del. 1983); Yale Note, 1984). The inherent function of courts, however, at least in the common law system, is to rule on events. While nominally, in a non-common law setting, they are to rule on events by applying the event-typicizing rules produced by legislatures and called "laws", the reality is more complex than that. A legislature or even an administrative agency that rules too concretely on facts is not *systemgerecht* and at least in major parts of the corporate law field courts are driven by the justice of the concrete event to engage the governing statutory law and even the administrative regulation in a constant reciprocal-influence wrestling match. This is substantive, "material" law, but at a specific institutional level — the court as mediatizing instance, as both inventor and user of reflexive law.

4.3 The Courts as the Mediatizing Institution of Reflexive Law

The exigent demands of societal reproduction in a world of extreme system-differentiation, a world marked by division and alienation of labor and accumulation of capital, can only be mediatized to the life world, in Habermas' terms of reference, by social institutional channels hospitable to the necessary conditions of a communicative ethic. By suggesting that in some legal cultures courts are either inherently structured or at least adaptable to this function, I suggest a specific connection between the theory of communicative action and the concept of reflexive law.

In a complex and functionally differentiated social world, the unconstrained discourse of the communicative ethic is more likely itself to be embedded within functionally specific institutional mechanisms than to be an open-air process carried on between random individuals. The most likely cause of any given dispute itself, after all, at least in most enterprise law settings, is going to be one of the subsystem-specific relationships between the disputants.

Courts function in two stages, and the second stage of all judicial processes is that of coercion, of assuming the mantle of the state in imposing the judicial decision. But the first stage of the process, as Shapiro recently has demonstrated for a wide variety of cultures, (Shapiro, 1981) provides the setting for the carrying on of rational, uncoerced discourse between free parties in order to legitimate the necessary later imposition of the will of one of them, to a greater or lesser degree, on the other.

If law inherently contains life-world supporting institutional characteristics, as Wiethölter's comments on Habermas' "institution" concept suggest, (Wiethölter, 1985a; cf. also same, 1985b) then courts may inherently be the specific institution that realizes this institutional function of law (cf. Cappelletti, 1984). It should therefore be no surprise that the function of courts recently has become most problematical for students of adjudication in the arena of intrasystemic litigation. Dan-Cohen's development of a regulatory, forward-looking model of adjudication as against an adjudicatory, backward-looking model, for example, (Dan-Cohen, 1985) is based exactly on the difference between organizational and personal litigation and bears witness to the difficulty of realizing Habermas' "institutional" role of law in the setting of intrasystemic conflict. That very problem, however, should be a signal that at least in life-world system (litigated) conflicts, and, I suspect, in many intrasystemic conflicts, conflicts which by definition are unresolved at the legislative or administrative levels and therefore are carried to the courts for resolution, it is, to use Habermas' terms law-as-institution and not law-as-medium that is looked to for legitimate dispute resolution (cf. Fuller, 1978; Eisenberg, 1978). The actors, even the system actors, have become reflective actors as a result of the dispute. Reflection on the dispute before a disinterested forum not inevitably but more often than not leads to the rhetorical use of those immanent features Wiethölter adumbrates as the inherent attributes of law-as-institution. This is not inconsistent with the simultaneous rhetorical use of those instrumental, purposive arguments that are features of law-as-medium, but it does suggest an inherent ambivalence of legal concepts once they are at issue before courts.

At best this is an ambivalent notion, as Tocqueville's prediction that in the U.S. all political processes become judicialized suggests (Tocqueville, 1945: 280). And Shapiro's study of courts vividly illuminates this ambivalent, at worst hypocritical, role of courts — free discourse as a genuine prerequisite to the search for consensus on facts and values, but also as a symbolic prerequisite to the legitimation of a coerced result. (Shapiro, 1981: 25f) In some sense, however, this strikes me as not more than an institutional reflection of the perennial object-consciousness dilemma, whose perennial cry for resolution engages us all.

If reflexive law not only is indirect in its steering function but redundant, and not excessively concrete in its substantive detail, a judicial system hospitable to those imperatives (liberal, e.g., as to standing rules and implied remedies) (Buxbaum, 1972) may be the best warrant for the success of reflexive law.This is admittedly an ideal formulation. It is very much derived from the American apotheosis of court-law as the secular version of those European universals of religion and civic bureaucracy which are the necessary legitimating requirements of statehood (cf. Kelly, 1972: 7). It is also in some jeopardy even in the U. S., as courts concerned about the legitimacy of private litigants who challenge enterprise managers are tempted to succumb to a raison d'entreprise deference that in any event finds powerful support in some of the economic-analysis-of-law literature (Buxbaum, 1984a: 537ff).

In the long run, however, this kind of judiciary may turn out to be a necessary condition for the successful functioning of at least the enterprise law component of a legal system that supports rather than erodes the legitimacy of the state in the eyes of its citizens. The use of independent courts in the implementation of the process of reflection suggested semantically by the concept of reflexive law may be at least a necessary condition for the social goal of attaining those improved levels of social discourse that underlie the theory of communicative action.

References

ACKERMAN, Bruce (1984) *Reconstructing American Law.* Cambridge, Massachussetts: Harvard University Press.

ARNOLD, Thurman W. (1937) *The Folklore of Capitalism.* New Haven: Yale University Press.

ASSMANN, Heinz-Dieter, Gert BRUGGEMEIER, Dieter HART and Christian JOERGES (1980) *Wirtschaftsrecht als Kritik des Privatrechts.* Königstein: Athenäum.

BALLANTINE, Henry (1931) "Questions of Policy in Drafting a Modern Corporation Law", 19 *California Law Review* 465.

— (1946) *On Corporations.* Chicago: Callaghan and Company.

BELLER, Daniel (1983) *Estimates of Participants and Financial Characteristics of Private Pension Plans.* Washington, D.C.: U.S. Department of Labor.

BLACKSTONE, Sir William (1765) *Commentaries on the Laws of England,* Vol. I. Oxford: Clarendon Press.

BLANKENBURG, Erhard (1984) "The Poverty of Evolutionism: A 30 Critique of Teubner's Case for 'Reflexive Law'", 18 *Law & Society Review* 273.

BREYER, Steven (1979) "Analyzing Regulatory Failure: Mismatches, Less Restrictive Alternatives, and Reform", 92 *Harvard Law Review* 549.

BUXBAUM, James (1981) *The Corporate Politeia — A Conceptual Approach to Business, Government, and Society.* Washington: University Press of America.

BUXBAUM, Richard M. (1971) "Economic Law in the United States of America", in G. Rinck (ed.), *Begriff und Prinzipien des Wirtschaftsrechts.* Frankfurt: Metzner.

— (1972) *Die private Klage als Mittel zur Durchsetzung wirtschaftspolitischer Rechtsnormen.* Karlsruhe: C. F. Müller Verlag.

— (1984a) "Corporate Legitimacy, Economic Theory, and Legal Doctrine", 45 *Ohio State Law Journal* 515.

— (1984b) "Federalism and Company Law", 82 Michigan Law Review.

BUXBAUM, Richard and Klaus J. HOPT (forthcoming) *Legal Harmonization and the Business Enterprise: Corporate Law and Capital Market Harmonization Policy in Europe and the U.S.A.*. Berlin/New York: de Gruyter.

Bydlinski, Fritz (1982) *Juristische Methodenlehre und Rechtsbegriff.* Vienna: Springer Verlag.

Cappelletti, Mauro (1984) *Guidici Legislatori?* Milan: Giuffrè.

Chandler, Alfred D. Jr., (1977) *The Visible Hand.* Cambridge, Massachusetts: Belknap Press.

Chirelstein, Marvin A. (1974) "Corporate Law Reform", in J. W. McKie (ed.), *Social Responsibility and the Business Predicament.* Washington: Brookings Institution.

Clark, Robert (1981) "The Four Stages of Capitalism: Reflections on Investment Management Treatises", 94 *Harvard Law Review* 561.

Coffee, John C., Jr. (1977) "Beyond the Shut-Eyed Sentry: Toward a Theoretical View of Corporate Misconduct and an Effective Remedy", 63 *Virginia Law Review* 1099.

Conard, Alfred (1984) "The Supervision of Corporate Management: A Comparison of Developments in European Community and United States Law", 82 *Michigan Law Review* 1459.

Dan-Cohen, Meir (1985) "Bureaucratic Organizations and the Theory of Adjudication", 85 *Columbia Law Review* 1.

Deutsch, Jan G.(1983) "Corporate Law as the Ideology of Capitalism", 93 *Yale Law Journal* 395.

Drucker, Peter (1976) *The Unseen Revolution: How Pension Plan Socialism Came to America.* New York: Harper & Row.

Edwards, Richard (1979) *Contested Terrain.* New York: Basic Books.

Egelko, Robert (1984) "California's Takeover Climate", *California Lawyer* 59.

Eisenberg, Melvin (1974) "The Model Business Corporation Act and the Model Business Corporation Act Annotated", 29 *Business Lawyer* 1407.

— (1978) "Participation, Responsiveness and the Consultative Process: An Essay for Lon Fuller", 92 *Harvard Law Review* 410.

— (1985) "Corporate Legitimacy, Conduct, and Governance — Two Models of the Corporation", 17 *Creighton Law Review* 1.

Feller, David (1973) "A General Theory of the Collective Bargaining Agreement", 61 *California Law Review* 663.

Frug, Gerald E. (1984a) "The Ideology of Bureaucracy in American Law", 97 *Harvard Law Review* 1276.

— (1984b) "The Language of Power" (Book Review), 84 *Columbia Law Review* 1881.

Fuller, Lon L. (1978) "The Forms and Limits of Adjudication", 92 *Harvard Law Review* 353.

Galanter, Marc (1980) "Legality and Its Discontents: A Preliminary Assessment of Current Theories of Legalization and Delegalization", in E. Blankenburg, E. Klausa and H. Rottleuthner (eds.), *Alternative Rechtsformen und Alternativen im Recht.* Opladen: Westdeutscher Verlag.

Gretschmann, Klaus (1981) *Steuerungsprobleme der Staatswirtschaft.* Berlin: Duncker & Humblot.

Habermas, Jürgen (1975) *Legitimation Crisis* (translation: Thomas McCarthy). Boston: Beacon Press.

— (1979) *Communication and the Evolution of Society* (translation: Thomas McCarthy). Boston: Beacon Press.

— (1981) *Theorie des kommunikativen Handelns.* 2 vols. Frankfurt: Suhrkamp.

— (1982) "A Reply to My Critics" in J. Thompson and D. Held (eds.), *Habermas Critical Debates.* London: Macmillan (1982).

— (1984) *The Theory of Communicative Action: Vol. 1. Reason and the Rationalization of Society* (translation: Thomas McCarthy). Boston: Beacon Press

— (1985) "Law as Medium and Law as Institution" in G. Teubner (ed.) *Dilemmas of Law in the Welfare State.* Berlin: Walter de Gruyter.

HAMMOND, Bray (1957) *Banks and Politics in America: From the Revolution to the Civil War.* Princeton: Princeton University Press.

HELD, David (1982) "Crisis Tendencies, Legitimation and the State", in: J. Thompson and D. Held (eds.) *Habermas Critical Debates.* London: Macmillan.

HEUER, Uwe-Jens (1985) (Book Review of Wirtschaftsrecht als Kritik des Privatrechts), 71 *Archiv für Rechts- und Sozialphilosophie* 274.

JAY, Martin (1984) *Adorno.* Cambridge: Harvard University Press.

JENKS LELAND H. (1927) *The Migration of British Capital to 1875.* New York: Alfred Knopf.

JENNINGS, Richard and Richard M. BUXBAUM (1979) *Corporations — Cases and Materials* (5th ed.). St. Paul: West Publishing Company.

JENNINGS, Richard and Harold MARSH, Jr., (1982) *Securities Regulation: Cases and Materials* (5th ed.). Mineola: Foundation Press.

KAGAN, Robert and John SCHOLZ (1980) "The 'Criminology of the Corporation' and Regulatory Enforcement Strategies", in E. Blankenburg and K. Lenk (eds.), *Organisation und Recht.* Opladen: Westdeutscher Verlag.

KELLY, G.A. (1972) "Hegel's America", 2 *Philosophy and Public Affairs* 3.

KLARE, Karl E. (1982) "The Public/Private Distinction in Labor Law", 130 *University of Pennsylvania Law Review* 1358.

KOLODRUBETZ, Walter (1971) "Trends in Employee-Benefit Plans in the Sixties", 34 *Social Security Bulletin* 21.

KRAAKMAN, Reinier (1984) "Corporate Liability Strategies and the Costs of Legal Controls", 93 *Yale Law Journal* 857.

KRIPKE, Homer (1979) *The SEC and Corporate Disclosure: Regulation in Search of a Purpose.* New York: Law and Business.

LATTIN, Norman (1971) *Corporations* (2d ed.) Mineola: The Foundation Press.

LESNOY, Selig and D. LEIMER (1985) "Social Security and Private Saving: Theory and Historical Evidence", *Social Security Bulletin* 14.

Loss, Louis (1983) *Fundamentals of Securities Regulation.* Boston: Little, Brown.

LÖWENSTEIN, Lewis (1983) "Pruning Deadwood in Hostile Takeovers: A Proposal for Legislation", 83 *Columbia Law Review* 249.

LUHMANN, Niklas (1982) *The Differentiation of Society.* New York: Columbia University Press.

— (1985) "The Self-Reproduction of Law and Its Limits", in G. Teubner (ed.), *Dilemmas of Law in the Welfare State.* Berlin: Walter de Gruyter.

MAITLAND, Frederick W. (1911) "Trust and Corporation", in H. A. L. Fisher (ed.), *The Collected Papers of Frederick William Maitland.* Cambridge: Cambridge University Press.

MAXFIELD, Linda Drazga (1983) "The 1982 New Beneficiary Survey: An Introduction", 46 *Social Security Bulletin* 3.

MAXFIELD, Linda Drazga and Virginia RENO (1985) "Distribution of Income Sources of Recent Retirees: Findings from the New Beneficiary Survey", 48 *Social Security Bulletin* 7.

MCCARTHY, Thomas (1978) *The Critical Theory of Jürgen Habermas.* Cambridge, Massachusetts: MIT Press.

— (1984) "Translator's Introduction", in Jürgen Habermas: *The Theory of Communicative Action,* Vol. 1, *Reason and the Rationalization of Society.* Boston: Beacon Press.

MICHELMAN, Frank I. (1978a) "Norms and Normativity in the Economic Theory of Law", 62 *Minnesota Law Review* 1015.
— (1978b) "Political Markets and Community Self-Determination: Competing Judicial Models of Local Government Legitimacy", 53 *Indiana Law Journal* 145.
— (1979) "Microeconomic Appraisal of Constitutional Law: A Methodological Preface", in D. Rubin-Feld (ed.), *Essays on the Law and Economics of Local Governments.* Washington: Urban Institute.
MURPHY, W.T. (1984) "Modern Times: Niklas Luhmann on Law, Politics and Social Theory", 47 *Modern Law Review* 603.
MYERS, Robert (1983) "Financial Status of the Social Security Program", 46 *Social Security Bulletin* 3.
NETTER, Oskar (1932) "Zur aktienrechtliche Theorie des Unternehmens an sich", in *Festschrift Albert Pinner.* Berlin: Walter de Gruyter.
NEW YORK STOCK EXCHANGE (1984) *1983 Fact Book.* New York: NYSE.
NONET, Philippe and Philip SELZNICK (1978) *Law and Society in Transition: Toward Responsive Society.* New York: Octagon Books.
RAISER, Thomas (1969) *Das Unternehmen als Organisation.* Berlin: Walter de Gruyter.
RATHENAU, Walther (1917) *Vom Aktienwesen — eine geschäftliche Betrachtung.* Berlin: S. Fischer Verlag.
SHAPIRO, Martin (1981) *Courts. A Comparative and Political Analysis.* Chicago: University of Chicago Press.
SHARP, James R. (1970) *The Jacksonians Versus the Banks.* New York: Columbia University Press.
SKOWRONEK, Stephen (1982) *Building a New American State.* Cambridge: Cambridge University Press.
STEWART, Richard B. (1983) "Regulation in a Liberal State: The Role of Non-Commodity Markets", 92 *Yale Law Journal* 1537.
— (1975) *Where the Law Ends.* New York: Harper & Row.
STONE, Christopher D. (1985) "Public Interest Representation: Economic and Social Policy Inside the Enterprise", in K. J. Hopt and G. Teubner (eds.), *Corporate Governance and Directors' Liabilities.* Berlin: Walter de Gruyter.
— (1983) "Substantive and Reflexive Elements in Modern Law", 17 *Law & Society Review* 239.
TEUBNER, Gunther (1984) "Autopoiesis in Law and Society: A Rejoinder to Blankenburg", 18 *Law & Society Review* 291.
— (1985a) "After Legal Instrumentalism?", in G. Teubner (ed.) *Dilemmas of Law in the Welfare State.* Berlin: Walter de Gruyter.
— (1985b) "Co-Determination Through Law: Social Functions of Law in Institutional Innovations", in T. Daintith and G. Teubner (eds.) *Contract and Organization.* Berlin: Walter de Gruyter.
— (1985c) "Corporate Fiduciary Duties and Their Beneficiaries: A Functional Approach to the Legal Institutionalization of Corporate Responsibility", in K. J. Hopt and G. Teubner (eds.) *Corporate Governance and Directors' Liabilities.* Berlin: Walter de Gruyter.
TEUBNER, Gunther and Helmut WILLKE (1985) "Context and Autonomy: Social Self-regulation through Reflexive Law" in G. Teubner (ed.) *Reflexive Law and the Regulatory Crisis.* Berlin: Walter de Gruyter.
THOMPSON, John B. and David HELD (eds.) (1982) *Habermas Critical Debates.* London: MacMillan.
TOCQUEVILLE, Alexis de (1945) *Democracy in America* (1838). New York: Alfred A. Knopf.

U.S. Department of Labor, Bureau of Labor Statistics (1984) (Bulletin No. 2213), *Employee Benefits in Medium and Large Firms*, 1983. Washington, D.C.

Wharton School (University of Pennsylvania) (1980) *Report to United States Department of Labor*, "The Impact of ERISA on the Investment Policies of Private Pension Funds and Capital Market Efficiency."

Wiethölter, Rudolf (1961) *Interessen und Organisation der Aktiengesellschaft*. Köln: C.F. Müller.

— (1982) "Entwicklung des Rechtsbegriffs", in V. Gessner and G. Winter (eds.), *Rechtsformen der Verflechtung von Staat und Wirtschaft*. Opladen: Westdeutscher Verlag.

— (1985a) "Materialization and Proceduralization in Modern Law", in G. Teubner (ed.), *Dilemmas of Law in the Welfare State*. Berlin: Walter de Gruyter.

— (1985b) "Social Science Models in Economic Law" in T. C. Daintith and G. Teubner (eds.) *Contract and Organization:* Berlin: Walter de Gruyter.

Winter Yale Law Review (1984) "Note: (1963) Approval of Take-out Mergers by Minority Shareholders: From Substance to Procedural Fairness", 93 *Yale Law Journal* 1113.

Cases:

Edgar v. MITE Corp., 457 U.S. 624 (1982).
Graham v. Allis-Chalmers MFg. Co., 41 Del. Ch. 78, 185 A.2d 125 (Sup. 1963).
Santa Fe Industries, Inc. v. Green, 430 U.S. 46 (1977).
Southland Stores, Inc. v. Keating, 104 S.Ct. 852 (1984).35
Weinberger v. VOP, Inc., 457 A.2d 70 (Del. 1983).

Recent Developments in Italian Corporate Law

FRANCESCO CORSI
Firenze

Contents

1. Introduction

In Italy, as in other countries, corporate law is characterized by a number of distinctive features. Disassociation of ownership and control, protection of minority shareholders, and protection of investors generally, are long-standing issues which the traditional regulation of corporations does not adequately address. Many new problems need to be dealt with as well, especially regarding the regulation of securities exchanges and groups of companies, the establishment of accounting standards, and relations between traditional corporate law and the maintenance of employment in large, but unhealthy, corporations.

Individuals, professional associations, government administrators, CONSOB (the Italian securities regulatory body), the judiciary, and Parliament are all participating in the process of developing corporate law. The new legislation is by and large mandatory. That is, parties must respect the norms of the law and cannot, even by mutual agreement, apply other rules. The new measures, however, do not always respond to actual needs, and excessive legislation is producing negative effects.

Because other legal systems share these characteristics, analytical concepts developed for them may be applicable to the study of Italian corporate law. However, comparative analyses are always difficult, and I have reservations about the applicability in Italy of some of the concepts advanced so far[1]. In particular I am dubious about the concept of "materialization"[2]. As I understand it, older legislation is considered neutral with regard to the parties whose relationships it regulates. The asserted materialization of contemporary law refers to its increasingly result oriented nature[3]. This characteristic also refers to the mandatory nature of the new legislation, in that it does not permit the parties involved to agree between themselves on other solutions.

In my opinion the more explicit instrumental character of the new legislation and its mandatory nature do not result from a new legislative style. Rather, they result from differences in the kinds of relationships which are now being regulated. In short, it is a changed socio-economic reality which is producing a different kind of legislative activity.

At least with respect to corporate law, the basic structure of this functional relationship can be identified. Commercial law, which includes corporate law, originally developed through the establishment of customary contractual practices rather than legislation. It arose in the context of the medieval guilds and was refined by magistrates temporarily designated from guild memberships.

Because of its guild origin, commercial law began by regulating contractual relationships among a homogeneous group of merchants. When nation-states began to formally adopt commercial law developed by the guilds, it was difficult for them to make obligatory the rules which had previously developed through voluntary contractual agreements. Moreover, because commercial activity was still confined to merchants who dealt with each other, there was no need to make these customary contractual rules mandatory.

Mandatory rules become necessary only when relations between parties with unequal bargaining power are regulated. Mandatory rules protect weaker parties by establishing rigid schemes which can be controlled by governmental authorities. The necessity of protecting the weaker party became obvious in the transition from a mercantile — craft economy to an industrial — capitalistic one. As part of this transition the former merchant, now industrialist, needed access to external capital in order to successfully develop mass enterprise. As long as the instrument for involving outside capital in the enterprise was a partnership among other merchants, state intervention to protect the partners providing capital may have seemed unnecessary. However, when the corporate form became that instrument and it became possible to involve relatively small investors the State was understandably forced to intervene. The purpose of its intervention has been to force relationships between unequal parties, namely the entrepreneur and small investors, into patterns that guarantee investors a minimum of protection. Given this history, it is not

1 Friedrich Kübler's contribution (*supra*), in particular, has been taken into account in preparation of this paper.

2 This terminology is inspired by Max Weber, (1967).

3 This concept has been described by Daintith and Teubner (1983) and Teubner (supra 10 ff.).

surprising that modern corporate law includes many mandatory rules. Their introduction has not been the result of a new legislative fashion, but rather of the dependence of modern industrial societies on effective capital markets.

In Italy the unification of the Civil Code and Commercial Code in 1942 caused the emergence of mandatory rules. The fusion of the two created an entity labeled "Civil Code", (approved with Royal Decree No. 262 of March 16, 1942) which actually contained the elements of a commercial code (Ascarelli, 1962; Franceschelli, 1970). Parallel to the growth of industrial activity and capitalism, the *ius mercatorum*, created and used by private agreements within the medieval guilds, became statutory law applicable not only to relationships between merchants (now industrialists) but also to relationships between merchants and nonmerchants. At the least, this regulation ought to clearly protect the weaker, nonmerchant party.

2. The Structure of the Italian Corporation

The basic structure of Italian corporate law is similar to that of French and German law. In each system, the simplest form of business organization is the partnership, which makes each partner in the enterprise personally liable for all obligations. The most complex form is that of the corporation (stock company). The autonomy of its property and the consequent limitation of shareholder liability are recognized by the grant of legal personality. The same business may be organized under either of these two forms. Indeed, it is possible for an enterprise to pass from one form of organization to another without loosing its subjective identity. Depending on the direction of the change, either a unanimous vote by the partners or an agreement by a majority of the shareholders in the assembly is necessary.

The structure of the Italian corporation, which is the form characteristic of most major businesses, follows the old French model. Its institutions include the assembly of shareholders, the *consiglio d'amministrazione* (comparable to a board of directors) and the *collegio sindacale*, which is a sort of internal auditing committee. The 1942 Civil Code established the structure of the corporation, as well as that of other forms of business organizations. The Civil Code does not differentiate between closely held corporations and those publicly traded on stock exchanges. That distinction was established by a series of later laws which altered the Code's regulation of corporations.

Modification of the Civil Code provisions began almost immediately after its adoption. For example, the Code anticipated the possibility of bearer shares, but Royal Decree No. 239 of March 29, 1942, precluded them. Modifications of the Code have become more important in recent years. They have attempted to confront, although not always with satisfactory results, the problems referred to at the beginning of this paper.

With all of this activity, it is interesting to note that only the first of the Community directives on corporate law, the one treating the right of establishment, has been explicitly implemented in Italy (Directive No. 151, of

March 9, 1968). In response to this directive, Presidential Decree No. 1127 of December 29, 1969 modified the provisions of the Code relative to the nullity of corporations and the publicity of corporate acts. It also altered the code provisions governing corporate liability to third parties for actions of corporate agents who exceed their authority and provisions governing the liability of administrators for acts not conforming to the corporate purpose.

3. Problems of Smaller Corporations and Legislative Solutions

Many special laws have been adopted in response to particular problems. Examples are Law No. 416 of August 5, 1981 on publishing houses and Law No. 91 of March 23, 1981 on soccer teams. Although these laws are too complex to consider in detail, they have had important effects. For example, the law on soccer teams requires old soccer clubs to incorporate in order to better control the subsidies they receive. However, the law contains an exception to the usual rules applicable to corporations. The obligation to distribute profits to shareholders has been reduced in order to allow the spectacular "purchase" of star players to continue. Legislative attention has focused primarily on large corporations traded on stock exchanges, which in fact do cause the most serious problems. No provisions have been adopted concerning closely held corporations except for some general rules also applicable to publicly traded ones. Provisions affecting smaller corporations include those implementing tax law modifications intended to limit the use of the enterprise for tax evasion purposes, and the raising of the minimum required capital from 1,000,000 lire (approximately 500 dollars) as established by the 1942 code to 200,000,000 lire (approximately 100,000 dollars) (Law No. 904 of December 16, 1977).

In closely held corporations the major problems relate to the protection of minority shareholders. Several provisions of the Civil Code attempt to address this problem. Under the Code the *collegio sindacale* (the internal auditing committee) controls management, but this committee is elected by the majority shareholders and is not always in a position to know the reality of the corporation's status. The Code gives qualified minorities the power to notify the judicial authorities of irregularities committed by the administrators and internal auditors. It also grants absent and dissident shareholders the right to sell their shares to the corporation if the assembly of shareholders decides to change the purpose or form of the corporation, or to move its seat abroad. Generally, these are not very effective protections. In particular, the right of withdrawal is of limited value due to the difficulty of valuing shares not traded on an exchange. Shares are therefore appraised on the basis of the corporations balance sheet. Presidential Decree No. 1127 of December 29, 1969, which implemented the first Community directive increasing corporate liability for unauthorized management actions, has in fact put minorities in a weaker position.

There are other abuses against which Civil Code provisions fail to protect minority shareholders. In many cases corporations have been purposely mismanaged by the majority in order to produce losses and thus force minority holders to cede their shares at an unreasonably low price. Another trick has been to require unnecessary increases in capital in order to dilute the relative power of minority holders who often cannot raise sufficient capital to exercise their statutory option to participate in the increase. No legislative provisions directly address these problems and the case law has only sporadically turned to administrative law concepts like *exces de pouvoir.* The major contribution of the case law has been to liberâlly accept challenges to corporate accounts, a phenomenon especially relevant to corporations traded on exchanges.

4. Publicy Traded Corporations

The problems concerning corporations traded on stock exchanges are much more numerous and complex than those relating to other corporations. Statutes enacted in 1974 (Law No. 216 of June 6, 1974), 1983 (Law No. 77 of March 23, 1983), and 1985 (Law No. 281 of June 4, 1985) have addressed these.

The 1974 law squarely confronts the disassociation of ownership and control. It recognizes the chronic separation of small shareholders from active participation in corporate affairs as an irreversible fact, and institutionalizes this recognition by allowing for the issuance of "savers' shares". These shares have no voting rights, but are privileged in the distribution of profits and in any liquidation of the corporation. Only corporations traded on exchanges may issue savers' shares, and then only up to an amount equal to half the total corporate capital. After initial hesitation the market embraced these shares, in part because they could be issued in bearer form.

The creation of these nonvoting shares limits the importance of bank efforts to collect proxy powers from the mass of disinterested shareholders. Nonetheless, the 1974 law directly limits the collection of proxies by reforming the 1942 Code. The new rules limit proxies to individual shareholder meetings, require that the delegate be named, and forbid subdelegation. To the existing ban on granting proxies to administrators, internal auditors and employees, a new rule has been added against the delegation of voting rights to controlled corporations, administrators, internal auditors, employees of controlled corporations, and banks. The ban on delegations to bankers is particularly addressed to shareholders who buy their shares and place them in bank safety deposit boxes with no intention of ever participating in control of the corporation.

There are also quantitative limits on the number of shareholders that can be represented by one delegate. For corporations traded on exchanges, one delegate may not represent more than 50 shareholders if the corporation's capital is less than 10 billion lire (approximately 5,000,000 dollars). Up to 200 holders may be represented if the corporation's capital is over 50 billion lire (approximately 25,000,000 dollars).

Although these limitations can be evaded, they have helped to control management power. However, it must be noted that Presidential Decree No. 1127 of December 29, 1969, implementing the first Community directive (No. 151, of March 9, 1968) increased corporate liability for unauthorized management actions. As already noted, these provisions in fact enlarged the power of management.

The 1974 law requires administrators, internal auditors, and directors general of corporations traded on stock exchanges to declare to their corporations and to CONSOB (to be discussed shortly), their holdings in the corporation or in other corporations directly held by it. They must declare their personal holdings as well as those of their fiduciaries, spouses from whom they are not legally separated, and minor children. They must also report any changes in their holdings. This is a first and modest step towards regulation of insider trading, a subject not otherwise regulated in Italy.

The most dramatic innovation of the 1974 law is the establishment of the Commissione Nazionale per le Societa e la Borsa (CONSOB). Modeled after the American SEC, its function is to supervise corporations whose shares are traded on stock exchanges. CONSOB can require consolidated accounts from groups of companies, as well as the publication of statistics and notices that it judges necessary for public information (those whose disclosure could damage the company or enterprise can be excluded on demand). It also has the power to perform inspections and question administrators, internal auditors, accountants, and chief executives. Finally, it may bring law suits challenging shareholder approval of corporate accounts.

CONSOB got off to a slow start. After its first five years, it took a turn for the better under the presidency of Guido Rossi as its work began to focus on forming a coherent policy of disclosure. Rossi's presidency was but two years old when he resigned in protest over the Banco Ambrosiano scandal, but the efforts which he carried forward before parliamentary commissions during his tenure significantly influenced the content of Law No. 77 of March 23, 1983. This law extended CONSOB's activity far beyond its original limits. Though initially CONSOB regulated only the trading of stocks and bonds on exchanges, its activity was expanded to cover all financial markets and the solicitation of public savings, concepts which the new law attempted to define. Previously, the 1936 banking law (Royal Decree No. 375, of March 12, 1936) had been the only legislation which expressly addressed the protection of savers.

The 1983 law extended coverage of the 1974 law to *titoli atipici*, the rapidly growing use of which was previously completely unregulated. *Titoli atipici* are a type of security undisciplined by law, and are financial instruments other than stocks or bonds.

The 1983 and 1985 laws also regulate the public sale of stocks, bonds, and other financial instruments outside of stock exchanges, a subject which was first the object of partial regulation under the 1974 law. Of particular interest is the attention given to private sales. In the five days following any private sale the buyer may withdraw with a simple telegram.

The provisions of the 1983 law that for the first time regulated mutual funds also reflect a policy of protecting savers. Although regulation of these funds had been talked about for nearly twenty years, prior to this law they operated on the fringes of the Italian legal system as entities established abroad. It is too soon to judge the results of their introduction into the framework of Italian law. Nonetheless, observers believe that the stock market seems to be showing signs of greater stability since their introduction.

5. Unsolved Problems

Despite the 1974, 1983 and 1985 legislation, there remain several areas which require legislative attention. They are the regulation of corporate groups, corporate accounting standards, co-determination, and the implementation of Community directives. With respect to the regulation of corporate groups, the 1974 law has better defined the concepts of relations and control between corporations. It regulates the acquisition of shares in controlled corporations by controlling corporations and provides for disclosure of share purchases in publicly traded corporations. Disclosure is required whenever the holdings of the acquiring corporation reach a certain percentage of the other corporation's capital. The 1985 law has extended disclosure from corporation to any person who owns more the 2% of the capital of a corporation with shares traded on a stock exchange. Sanctions available for nondisclosure include suspension of voting rights attached to the shares held by the acquiring company or person.

Sound regulation of corporate groups, however, requires much more. The concept of group emerges only sporadically in current legislation. Groups are treated by tax legislation on the payment of value added taxes. They are also treated by the provision under which CONSOB can, and frequently does, require consolidated accounts for corporate groups. CONSOB's power is diminished by the lack of principles regulating formation of group accounts. Finally, groups are treated by the law allowing "extraordinary administration" of large companies in financial crisis (Decree Law No. 26 of January 30, 1979). This law, as modified by Law No. 95 of April 3, 1979 and slightly modified by successive laws, establishes a new kind of cooperative reorganization procedure alongside the normal bankruptcy procedure. Its purpose is to restructure the enterprise in order to save jobs. To do this, it allows for a moratorium on the payment of debts while plans are formulated to restructure the enterprise. This procedure has been widely criticized for the modest results it has yielded (Libonati, 1981). Another provision of this law allows the corporations which directly or indirectly control the company in crisis to be involved in the procedure of extraordinary administration. Other corporations directly or indirectly controlled by the controlling corporation may also be involved. The law, for the first time in Italy, considers one corporation as controlling another if their managements are unified or if the first has conceded credits or guarantees to the corporation in crisis of up to a third of the value of the sales of the guaranteeing corporation. This comprehensive approach to corporate groups is a major development, but it is limited for the moment to the special case of "extraordinary administration". As already mentioned, the 1979 law limits extraordinary administration to certain major enterprises. They are identified by criteria such as the number of employees, whether their creditors are private lenders, credit institutions or the national insurance fund, and whether state subsidized financing has been offered to the corporation.

With respect to corporate accounting only minor changes have been made to the applicable provisions of the 1942 Civil Code. They relate to disclosure of relationships with controlled or related companies and to exceptions to accounting principles specified by law. The one change with major impact is the new requirement that publicly traded companies have their annual accounts certified by an accounting firm registered with CONSOB. These accounting firms are largely subsidiaries of American firms. They have consequently tended to import American procedures.

Co-determination has remained foreign to the Italian system. The Civil Code anticipates worker shareholding in corporations, and article 46 of the Constitution recognizes the right of workers to collaborate "according to the ways and limits established by law" in corporate management. However, management and labor have generally shared a desire to avoid this cooperation. Management does not want worker interference, and unions have feared that involvement in managements' problems could weaken their contractual bargaining power.

Finally, with respect to Community law, only the First Directive on corporate law (No. 151 of March 9, 1968) has been expressly implemented. This was accomplished through the 1969 law already discussed (Presidential Decree No. 1127 of December 29, 1969). Notwithstanding the lack of direct legislative response, some of the legislative reforms of 1974 and 1983 have indirectly reacted to the directives. Indeed, in some cases the directives have been twisted, as for example in corporate accounting. Article 2 of the Fourth Directive on corporate accounting requires corporate accounts to faithfully depict the financial health of the corporation (No. 660 of July 25, 1978). Article 2(5) permits exceptional principles to be applied if application of the directive's principles would yield a false picture. The exceptional principles and the reasons for adopting them must be indicated in the administrator's report. The Italian Parliament implemented this portion of the directive through article 9 of Law No. 72 March, 19 1983 on the valuation of corporate property and capital. This article interprets and modifies article 2425(3), of the Civil Code. Its phrasing, however, does not conform to the directive. It makes the use of special principles optional rather than mandatory, and fails to clearly limit them to exceptional cases. Article 2423 of the Civil Code already contains a general provision requiring that corporate accounts reveal with clarity and precision the financial position of the corporation. Given the variations in the phrasing of the directive and articles 2423 and 2425(3) as modified, it is unclear what corporate accounts must reveal. The only certainty is that this style of legislation will keep judges occupied.

6. Self-regulation

Statutory law alone does not fully describe the present state of corporate law. Although difficult to accomplish, it is necessary to evaluate the impact of nonlegislative bodies on corporate accounting. Self-regulation manifests itself through private agreements. Its power is expressed through creative contracting motivated by the needs of the market. It is especially important in Italy because Parliament is systematically tardy in confronting pressing problems. Examples of this include leasing, which is widely practiced and still not legislatively regulated, and the growth of *titoli atipici*. This latter example is closer to the area of corporate law than leasing, if only because a noteworthy share of national savings which formally went into stocks and bonds is now devoted to *titoli atipici* — limited partnership interests that have been privately sold. This nonofficial market is parallel to the securities exchanges, but until recently went without the safeguards provided for trading on exchanges. When Parliament finally reacted to this development in the 1983 law discussed earlier, it had to recognize the dimension of this new kind of financial marketing by generally regulating public solicitation of investment.

Another example of private initiative is represented by convertible bonds. These were issued for many years before being legislatively recognized in Law No. 216 of June 7, 1974 which introduced article 2420 bis into the Civil Code.

These examples support the proposition that in commercial and corporate law, legislative action has usually followed private initiative. Unlike other fields, e.g., the introduction of community property for spouses in 1975, legislation has not had a formative role. In light of the historical outline traced earlier, this is not surprising. Legislative interventions have historically occured in two phases. The first phase receives external models whose rules by their own terms apply only when the parties do not otherwise agree. In the second phase the legislature concerns itself with interests damaged by reliance on these models. In this phase the rules adopted are largely mandatory.

Rules originating from groups and associations other than Parliament are obviously not obligatory in the same way as statutes, but they do influence custom. Thus, when the professional associations of business advisors established fundamental accounting principles, these principles became points of reference for corporate management generally. CONSOB has also explicitly referred to them in its regulations.

7. Case Law

A second potentially important nonlegislative source of regulation is the judiciary. However, the judicial contribution to corporate law has been quite limited in comparison with its contribution in many other fields. It is certainly inferior to the guild judges' contribution to the *ius mercatorum*.

One reason for the difference in the contributions of contemporary judges and guild judges may be that the latter were experts in the controversies they had to resolve because they were elected from the guilds. In contrast, contemporary judges are career civil servants and decide a variety of criminal, civil, and commercial cases without the possibility of effective specialization.

In my opinion, the modest judicial contribution to corporate law largely results from lack of judicial specialization. Corporate law is a technical matter. Without a good knowledge of economic theory, it is difficult to understand the rationales underlying corporate law rules. Consequently, it is hard for generalist judges, not seriously trained in economics at any point in their careers, to adopt an informed perspective in regard to individual cases.

In other sectors of the law, where the purpose of legal rules has been easier to discern through intuitive thinking, the judiciary has successfully reworked. For example, in commercial law the judiciary has successfully adapted 1942 Civil Code provisions to the needs of modern bankruptcy practice. The rigidity of corporate law jurisprudence stands in marked contrast to this. Jurisprudence, for instance, has never allowed a corporation to participate in a partnership. Corporations are not even allowed to participate in limited partnerships. Another example is provided by the Court of Cassation's obstinacy in interpreting article 2362 of the Civil Code. This article permits unlimited responsibility for corporate liabilities when there is only one shareholder in the corporation. Until its ruling in Decision No. 6594 December 14, 1981, the Court of Cassation insisted that the principle did not apply if the sole shareholder was a corporation. Even now, the Court of Cassation refuses to apply the principle to the situation where one shareholder owns the majority of a corporation, and an insignificant fraction remains in the hands of other shareholders. In short, its jurisprudence refuses to pierce the corporate veil even when there is obvious manipulation of the protection provided by the corporate form.

Other examples are available. Many courts have adopted excessively literal readings of the restriction limiting the total value of bonds issued to a sum not exceeding the contributed capital existing "as of the last balance sheet approved". They refuse to permit an increase in corporate capital with a simultaneous issuance of bonds equal to that amount, even when the increase is fully paid in. In this situation, it is difficult to imagine jurisprudence that would recognize increases in corporate capital as protecting corporate creditors or which would hold majority shareholders responsible for corporate undercapitalization. One final example also relates to corporate capitalization. Until 1977, the minimum required capital for a corporation in Italy was 1,000,000 lire (approximately 500 dollars) — an absolutely minimal sum. With only a few exceptions, courts reviewing the regularity of a corporation's formation refused to inquire into the substantive question of whether the corporation was sufficiently capitalized. It was thus theoretically possible to have an automobile manufacturing corporation with capital of only 1,000,000 lire.

The most plausible reason for this rigidity is the inability of the judiciary to master the economics necessary to understand corporate law. The plausibility of this assertion is increased by the willingness of the judiciary to act boldly, at times too boldly, where questions of justice and the protection of particular kinds of interests, e.g., those of minority shareholders, make the right course of action intuitively obvious. This is the case with respect to challenges to shareholder votes approving improperly formulated corporate accounts.

This point merits some illustration. Until the 1960s case law was unwilling to examine the merits of corporate accounts.It was willing to invalidate them only for procedural errors in their approval. In the face of repeated manipulation of corporate accounts for the purpose of hiding profits in order to reduce dividends, the Tribunal of Milan, and later other courts, decided to enter into the merits of the accounts. It is easy to appreciate the degree of judicial adventurism inherent in this move beyond simple enforcement of the procedural requirements established by statute. The judicial creativity involved is particularly obvious in light of the indeterminate consequences of the judicial invalidation of shareholder approval of corporate accounts. Statutory law does not say whether the accounts must be reformulated and then reapproved by the shareholders. It is likewise unclear whether the invalidation of one set of corporate accounts affects successively approved accounts. These questions are still open, and to avoid them doctrinal writers are urging a return to jurisprudence focused on the liability of corporate managers who develop false accounts rather than on invalidation of the accounts themselves. In my mind, the reason for the bold advance of jurisprudence in this area is the ease with which it was possible to see the need for protection of minority shareholders.

It is worth adding that this judicial adventurism has opened the door to frivolous law suits brought only for the purpose of provoking a payment from the corporation in order to avoid the inconvenience of litigation. In response to this development Presidential Decree No. 136 of March 31, 1975 has limited the possibility of bringing such actions. The merits of accounts of publicly traded corporations can now be challenged only by shareholders representing at least 5% of corporate capital or, if the social capital is greater than 2 billion lire (approximately 1,000,000 dollars), a nominal value of shares greater than 100 million lire (approximately 50,000 dollars). The challenge can also be brought by CONSOB, which serves as protection for smaller shareholder minorities. Although requests have been made in this regard on a number of occasions, CONSOB exercised this power for the first time just a few months ago.

8. CONSOB

The establishment of CONSOB represents an example of delegalization as that concept is understood in Italy. CONSOB is a body which, in contrast to the ordinary judiciary, is composed of individuals with special competence in corporate law and thus capable of making significant contributions to its development.

Although its efforts have not been unanimously applauded, CONSOB has unquestionably played a determinative role in corporate practice and corporate regulation. Through its regulatory activity it has resolved some elementary but significant problems. For example, CONSOB's request to the managers of publicly traded corporations that they permit financial analysts to attend shareholder meetings definitively overcame the widespread belief that only shareholders and management could be present.

CONSOB's regulatory actions have focused on stock exchanges. These have included forbidding cash transactions, requiring audits of individual corporations, suspending trading in particular stocks, requiring management to clarify obscure points in corporate accounts (which must be submitted to CONSOB before presentation at shareholder meetings), requiring that the identity of the ten largest shareholders be disclosed at shareholder meetings, requiring that the transcript of shareholder meetings identify all participants by name (rather than giving only general indications of the capital present as the case law tended to require), and requiring consolidated accounts for groups of companies (even though there is still no regulation of how to compile and publish them).

The most recent exercise of CONSOB's regulatory power is its control over the acceptability of new issues of stocks and bonds for trading on exchanges. Its regulations require that the issuing corporation have a net worth of not less than 10 billion lire (approximately 5,000,000 dollars), or 50 billion for banking and insurance activities (approximately 25,000,000 dollars). In addition, corporate accounts for the previous three years must show a profit, accounts for the last year must be certified by an accounting firm, and stocks or bonds of the firm must be freely transferable. On this last point, it should be noted that CONSOB has always fought against restraints on alienability. It has even succeeded in influencing the Court of Cassation which, ignoring its previous decisions, recently accepted the nullity of restraints on alienation, at least when left to the discretion of management. The 1985 law has firmly settled this principle. CONSOB's regulations also require that at least 25% of corporate capital be represented by publicly traded stocks or bonds and that a request for the listing of stocks or bonds on an exchange be preceded by a shareholder meeting and be publicized in three national newspapers. Following acceptance of the request by CONSOB, similar publicity must be given to a prospectus prepared according to CONSOB regulations.

CONSOB's regulations apply only to the listing of stocks and bonds, but this does not mean that CONSOB intends to exclude other kinds of financial instruments from trading on exchanges. CONSOB is competent to regulate these other financial instruments under the 1983 law previously discussed (Law No. 77 of March 23, 1983). Evidently CONSOB has, for the moment, decided to develop principles for these instruments on a case by case basis.

As an institution CONSOB is not without problems, although the 1985 law has resolved some of them. Aside from inadequate funding and staffing, some of these arise from its uncertain status as a state body. As I will argue shortly, I am inclined to see CONSOB as a kind of special administrative court with corresponding guarantees of independence. However, this classification is formally prevented by article 102 of the Constitution, which bans the creation of special or extraordinary judges.

9. Other Branches of Law

Other branches of law influence corporate law. For example, the rules on administering the property of minors and incompetents influence the regulation of their shareholdings. However, these have only marginal impact. The principal body of law affecting corporate law is tax law.

Tax law is important because the government employs it as a tool of economic policy, and because of the quantity of detailed requirements it imposes. Tax law particularly impinges on the preparation of corporate accounts. Indeed, it frequently conflicts with the accounting principles of the Civil Code. For example, tax law permits accelerated depreciation, which tends to obscure the real value of entries in corporate accounts. Doctrine has extensively wrestled with how to reconcile these accounting problems. The solution is still open, and many urge the maintenance of two sets of accounts, one for tax purposes, and another for corporate accounting purposes as determined by the Civil Code. The obvious disadvantage of dual accounts is the confusion they can cause.

10. Constitutional and Administrative Influences on Corporate Law

The two remaining sources of influence on corporate law are constitutional law and the public administration. With regard to constitutional law, the Constitution does not directly address the problems of corporate law. Likewise, it does not seem that the Constitutional Court has ever had the opportunity to address these issues. The public administration's role is important, but in a negative sense. Although it does not produce regulations affecting corporations, it makes their activities more difficult.

The delay in publishing the Official Register of Corporations, for example, has at times been as great as two years. Thus, publicity through the register has only theoretical value. Under article 2441 of the Civil Code a shareholder's statutory option to participate in an increase in capital can be exercised within 30 days from the publication of the increase. It is common practice for corporations to consider that this period runs from the theoretical time of publication in the Official Register rather than from the actual publication date. In fact, when a corporation requests publication of an announcement, the office responsible for the Offical Register gives it a certificate indicating the theoretical date of publication.

The same is true regarding the publication of announcements calling together shareholder meetings. These must be published in the Gazzetta Ufficiale (analogous to the American Federal Register or the French Journal Officiel). Although the delays in issuing the Gazzetta Ufficiale are not nearly as long as those for the Official Register of Corporations, they are such that if a shareholder relied solely on the Gazzetta Ufficiale the shareholder would ordinarily be informed only a few days before each meeting.

Another example of the public administration's effect on corporate activities is the management of the corporate registry anticipated by the 1942 Civil Code. According to the Code, this register should be maintained by the clerks of tribunals, the civil courts ordinarily of first instance. This register has never been created because a law formally implementing it has not been adopted. Corporate acts are consequently deposited in the clerks' offices of tribunals according to the regulation in force under the old Commercial Code of 1882 (Law No. 681 of April 2, 1882). Since the clerks' offices have yet to discover computers, researching corporate acts is dramatically difficult. To obtain a certificate for a corporation can often require several weeks.

The public administration is a major impediment to any initiative in Italy. It creates unbelievable blockages in the most elementary applications of the law. The wide diffusion of *titoli atipici* is related to this fact. Because the *titoli atipici* resulted from private innovation, bureaucratic delays were avoided. Thus, the *titoli atipici* have an immense competitive advantage, since stocks and bonds continue to be subject to bureaucratic hurdles and tax regulation.

11. Perspectives for Research

Given the complex and continuously evolving situation I have described, it is difficult to say what insights will be achieved in the future by examining the relationships between juridification, political economy, and corporate law. For the moment, I will offer some preliminary conclusions.

I fully support the mandatory character of the recent legislation on corporate law because it responds to an important need for simplification. The need for simplification is not a novelty in commercial law. The negotiable instrument and, according to recent studies, the corporate form, both resulted from a need for simplification (Galgano, 1969).

I continue to have doubts, however, regarding assertions as to what should result from this need for simplification. Transaction costs[4] create a need for simplification, but they do not alone require that simplifying rules be mandatory. For example, the Italian experience with *titoli atipici* demonstrates that simplicity can be achieved without mandatory rules. Lack of regulation

[4] According to the *Coasean* concept, as described by Kübler (supra 220 ff.).

favored rather than impeded the diffusion of these instruments. This is true notwithstanding the fact that the lack of regulation also permitted many investors to lose everything. When the legislature finally intervened, it was not to liberalize the market for stocks and bonds in order to make them competitive with the *titoli atipici*, but to create a general securities regulation which would cover the new instruments. The new regulation does not result in greater simplicity, but to a greater degree than before it protects investors who choose to invest in *titoli atipici*.

I have noted how a phase of mandatory legislation usually follows a period in which legal rules are optional in character. I have also noted that mandatory legislation tends to adopt the models developed by the private sector. This sequence corresponds to diverse historical realities. The optional character of rules corresponds to a commercial law destined to regulate relationships among merchants. And in fact, this corresponds to the creative phase of the *ius mercatorum*. The same optional character becomes outmoded when relations between merchants and nonmerchants develop. In this phase the law must intervene with mandatory rules which dictate fixed forms and which are guaranteed by the state. This necessity corresponds to a later historical period, in which nonmerchants assume an essential role in the financing of large corporations. There is no doubt that this mandatory regulation simplifies the raising of capital and thus reduces its cost. However, it simultaneously provides greater guarantees to the investor. I believe that it is the guarantee function rather than the cost reduction function which is the primary motivation behind the mandatory character of the current regulation.

12. Policy Recommendations

Parallel to the production of mandatory rules is the phenomenon of delegating regulatory power to bodies other than the legislature. This phenomenon has been termed "proceduralization" (Teubner, supra 33 ff.), in the sense that economic policy goals are not pursued by direct imposition of legal consequences. Instead, they are pursued indirectly through the establishment of procedural rules. This picture does reflect reality to some extent. However, it must be regarded with a certain distrust by those who experience, as we do in Italy, the negative aspects of a proceduralization which translates itself into bureaucratization, hidden power, and administrative complication. This is the country in which obtaining a driver's licence for instance, or authorization to run a shop, can take months or even years. The consequence is the creation of space for administrative corruption and the kind of power that I would generically call "mafioso".

Ideally, proceduralization should involve a framework law which stimulates self-regulation by private parties. Self-regulation is certainly known in Italy, but framework laws are rare. In fact self-regulation has developed most extensively in areas where there is no law at all. It is not surprising that some would attempt to portray the renouncement of intervention by the State as a manifestation of sound judgment. However, interests which would be protected under the rule of law ought not be abandoned to the law of the jungle.

If the goal of delegalization is the absence of regulation in the sense of *laisser faire*, then in Italy we have already experienced it, partly as a result of legislative inadequacy and partly due to an inability to implement what legislation there is.

My impression is that at least with respect to corporate law, delegalization does not mean reducing regulation, but rather increasing it through specification in detailed regulations of general principles established by statute. The institution of CONSOB and its work are the best and perhaps the only example of this in Italy. By this process, Italy is achieving in corporate law what was not possible through its judiciary, i.e., the translation of legal principles into detailed rules applicable to specific cases.

In this field delegalization has been an effort to achieve effective rather than merely formal implementation of legislative principles. The complexity of modern economic relationships has made this kind of delegalization especially necessary for corporate law. For corporate law, delegalization has meant delegation. There has been a delegation of regulatory power which has resulted in an expansion of regulatory provisions rather than in their reduction. Legislative principles guide the production of specific regulations, but because they are more tied to specific cases, and because they are determined by experts, the specific regulations are more responsive to real problems than legislatively established rules could be.

The dangers and sensitivity of this work are evident. I do not believe that it should be entrusted to an administrative bureaucracy. If so, it would be subjected to the same problems of base political interference and ineffeciency that paralyze the rest of the Italian public administration. This work must be attributed to a kind of judicial body, distinguished from the rest of the judiciary by its subject matter jurisdiction, but sharing the judicial guarantees of independence. It seems to me that this is essential in order to ensure that this experience will constitute a step forward and not one back into a new dark age.

[Translated from the Italian by Patrick Del Duca]

References

Ascarelli, Tullio (1962) *Corso di Diritto Commerciale.* Milano.

Daintith, Terence and Gunther Teubner (1983) Research Project: *Law and Economic Policy — Alternatives to Delegalization.* Florence: EUI.

Franceschelli, Remo (1970) *Impresa e imprenditori.* Milano: Giuffre (ed).

Galgano, Francesco (1969) "Delle Persone Giuridiche", in: *Commentario del Codice Civile a cura di A. Scialoja e G. Branca,* sub. artt. 11-35, Bologna-Roma: Zanichelli (ed.).

Libonati, Berardino (1981) *Il Gruppo Insolvente.* Firenze: Nardini (ed.).

Weber, Max (1967) *Rechtssoziologie.* Neuwied: Luchterhand.

IV

Antitrust

Restrictive Trade Practices and Juridification: A Comparative Law Study

Klaus J. Hopt
Bern

Contents

1. Introduction: A Comparative Survey of Jurisdictions

1.1 The Most Extreme Juridification: The U.S.

Restrictive trade practices and juridification[1] constitute a problem which is presented and regarded in very different ways in various countries. The most important exponent of government intervention is undoubtedly the U.S. Since the basic law against restrictive trade practices, the Sherman Act, was enacted

[1] According to information given by the data bank JURIS at the Federal Department of Justice in Bonn the following is the annual "law production" (note the term!) for 1982 in the Federal Republic of Germany:

(1) laws	federal	130
	state	200
(2) regulations	federal	480
	state	400
(3) administrative systems	federal and state	5,000
(4) published court decisions		20,000
(5) jurisprudential contributions		
(a) jurisprudential articles etc.		20,000
(b) single printed matters		3,000
(c) dissertations and habilitations		1,000
	total	50,210

This production of law creates problems typical of all production processes: problems of control, overproduction, and quality control. If one looks at some law texts quality control evidently is functioning only to a limited extent. Maybe the time has come to introduce product liability in this area! Above all, the problem of this law production's function and significance is posed, as no-one can seriously contest the idea that 50,000 new products annually cannot be efficiently digested. Not only is an overload of the system in its various parts (law, politics, and society) risked, but an overload of the law itself as well, which should be a cause of concern for lawyers.

These problems will be investigated in relation to restrictive business practices on a comparative basis. It should be mentioned that the "flood of norms" — which represents one important aspect of juridification — should not be seen only in a positivistic perspective. If nowadays one regards "law" not only as an abstract system of norms, but as a concrete living system of interactions (law in action), then this viewpoint must find its equivalent in juridification. In other words, the social system called "law" with courts, offices, lawyers, law schools, and the like must be examined. What is at stake, finally, is the adequate role of law and of the legal profession in modern post-industrial society.

nearly 100 years ago in 1890, *American antitrust law* has expanded its stock of rules. This expansion has not relied mainly on the various statutes which have been enacted[2], though due to their comprehensive, partially unclear, primarily general clause provisions, they illustrate one of the important points of criticism in the discussion of juridification and deregulation. These acts are in fact not much more than a rough screen encompassing the vast quantity of cases and decisions[3] with which an immense legal, as well as more recently and increasingly an economic literature, is preoccupied. Instead it is the cases which constitute the bulk of American antitrust law. This is to be understood not only in the sense that they play a part in a case-law system like the American, or even in some areas have the lion's share of law-making, but also in terms of procedural and judicial sociology. Antitrust cases are frequently difficult, costly and lengthy. A typical antitrust case may last "only" two to three months, and generate 10,000 to 15,000 pages of documents, but the "monster" cases can last many years, produce mountains of paperwork consisting of many millions of pages, and create costs that can hardly be met.

In one American verdict the Court does not mince words: "The ordinary antitrust case is unmanageable, cases like the IBM and AT&T suits being in the nature of malignant growths on the judicial system" (Posner, 1976: 232). So it is not surprising that a highly specialized section of the legal profession, including some of the best lawyers, lives on antitrust law and the observer is tempted to speak of an independent subsystem within the American economy and society. Within this are two enforcement agencies, the Antitrust Division of the Department of Justice and the Federal Trade Commission, which have

[2] Notably the Sherman Act, Clayton Act, Federal Trade Commission Act, and the Antitrust Procedures and Penalties Act, together with the various reform laws such as the Hart-Scott-Rodino Antitrust Improvement Act of 1976 and the Federal Trade Commission Improvements Act of 1980.
Areeda and Turner (1978-1980); Neale and Goyder (1980); Sullivan (1977) which includes a short guide to the literature in § 4; Oppenheim and Weston (1981). As to reforms, see Handler, 1982.
Also useful is the monographic literature and the contributions in general law reviews, e.g., the *Antitrust Bulletin, Antitrust Law & Economic Review, Antitrust Law Journal* and *Journal of Law and Economics.*
Literature concerning the two problems of restraint of trade and juridification and their interplay so far cannot be found in any of the countries considered herein besides the U.S. There, the discussion of deregulation has dealt with, among other things, antitrust law. However, it is mainly concerned with specifically regulated industries and rarely raises the questions of principle which are posed here. Cf. most recently various contributions in 28 *Antitrust Bulletin* (1983 No. 1).

[3] For comparative contributions to the state of regulation and deregulation in West Germany and the U.S. see the symposium papers edited by Weizsäcker, Richter (1983); Kaufer, Blankart (1983); as to the U.S., Crandall (1983); Stewart, 1983. A comprehensive survey can be found in *Federal Trade Commission Reporter*, 5 vols. with annual issues. Between 1890 and 1974 about 1,000 civil and 723 criminal claims by the Department of Justice, and between 1937 and 1974 more than 12,000 private antitrust suits were filed. See Posner (1976: 34).

partially overlapping powers and considerable personal and financial resources[4]; the lawyers, who are sometimes grouped in large law firms which resemble large companies and need and attain corresponding turnovers; and a changing composition of courts, companies, private plaintiffs, and others. Antitrust in the United States is not only a juridified competition policy in the sense of a system of legal rules, but also an independent self-perpetuating system of legal and economic interactions. Opinions concerning this system vary. They range from the view of antitrust as part of American folklore to the emphatic view that antitrust law is, apart from the United States Constitution, the most important contribution the U.S. has made to the development of law in the world. It is true in any case that "(a)ntitrust is a banner under which many march, but for different reasons: politicians interested in combating inflation, consumer groups convinced that large manufacturers charge excessive prices, populists fearful that corporate giants corrupt the political process, businessmen threatened by the anticompetitive behavior of others, private attorneys dependent on antitrust practice as a source of income, and economists concerned with the welfare costs of monopoly and the estimated consumer gains from its elimination" (Katzmann, 1980: 1). The use of antitrust law in the take-over battles of American companies, particularly as a defensive weapon, should be included in the discussion at this point. Antitrust law can be dangerous as well as useful, but it often achieves its objectives, not so much because of the legal situation, as because of the process, cost and delay risks (Aranow *et al.*, 1977: 147 ff. Short survey of tender offer law in Hopt, 1980).

1.2 Legal Systems without Antitrust Law

While the Federal German Republic sets out in a similar direction, there are other countries which completely, or nearly completely, exclude such juridification. The reasons for this vary. In a *socialist* planned-economy system, antitrust law as such has no place *a priori.* In *Third-World countries* there are things to worry about other than antitrust law, and if antitrust law does exist it is generally a simple imitation, above all in countries under the political influence of the U.S. Such laws usually remain unenforced, or exist as a weak weapon of the host country against transnational enterprises and their home countries. Among the Western industrial nations, Italy has no antitrust law at all. There, the opinion is widespread that the international competitiveness of Italian industry could be damaged by such laws. It is believed that it may be wiser to allow Italian companies first to win back the ground which, for exam-

[4] For an introduction in German see Oehler (1976: 27-90). For comparative contributions to the state of regulation and deregulation in West Germany and the U.S. see the symposium papers edited by Weizsäcker and Richter (1983); Kaufer and Blankart (1983); as to the U.S. Crandall (1983). Accordingly the Antitrust Division had about 650 officers, and the Bureau of Competition of the Federal Trade Commission had a similar staffing, see Oehler (1976: 71). Also see in this context Clarkson and Muris (1981).

ple, German enterprises were able to gain through cartels and concentration over the decades. Furthermore, the fact that broad and central parts of the Italian economy are held by, or under the control of, large state holding companies does not favor the creation of a serious antitrust law, particularly of a type which would apply to state holdings. Only the direct validity of *Art. 85, 86* of the Treaty of Rome is relied on therefore in Italy, and one thus either unrealistically assumes this to function as the core of the national antitrust law, or, one uses this merely as a political argument for the maintenance of the *status quo*.

1.3 Less Extreme Solutions: Great Britain, France, Switzerland

Between these extremes stand some Western legal systems with a more or less developed law against restrictive trade practices. Among these, Germany and the European Community are especially well-known, but Great Britain, France and Switzerland have also developed such laws. We shall briefly discuss only the latter here. If juridification is taken not simply as an abundance of rules, but also as an implemented legal control system which produces corresponding effects (though not necessarily those aimed at by the law), then Great Britain must be mentioned first. There, a system of antitrust law, separate from the common law which had become ineffective to a great extent, has existed only since the Monopolies and Restrictive Practices (Inquiry and Control) Act of 1948 (Korah, 1982; Cunningham, 1974; Wilberforce *et al.*, 1966. More specifically Opie, 1982; and Korah 1982a). A considerable number of supplementary, amending, and completely new acts have followed[5]. This law against restrictive trade practices is enforced by the Director General of Fair Trading, by the Minister for Trade and Industry, and by the Restrictive Practices Court. More specifically, the Monopolies and Mergers Commission monitors the abuses of companies with a dominant position on the market and deals with mergers. Based on the Commission's inquiry reports, the Secretary of State, i.e. the Minister, makes orders. Private claims for compensation are provided if anticompetitive agreements have not been registered and therefore are invalid. Evaluations of this system vary above all according to sector. While the essential antitrust law itself is regarded as being quite effective, there are considerable doubts concerning the areas in which control is exercised directly by a political body. In the case of merger control for instance, since controls were introduced in 1965 until the mid-1980s, only 2.7% of some 2000 mergers falling under the Act, were submitted to the Monopolies and Mergers Commission for investigation (Korah, 1982a: 69, who includes further references. For statistical material, see Opie, 1982: 25-41).

5 Restrictive Trade Practices Act 1956, with supplement 1968; Resale Prices Act 1956; Monopolies and Mergers Act 1965; Fair Trading Act 1973; Restrictive Practices Act 1976, with supplement 1977; Restrictive Practices Court Act 1976; Resale Prices Act 1976; Competition Act 1980.

In *France* the law against restrictive trade practices is contained primarily in the Price Control Decree No. 45-1483 of 1945, which has been amended and sharpened several times, and in the 1977 Concentration Control Act[6]. Until 1977 French antitrust law was enforced only through criminal proceedings initiated by a public prosecutor before the regular courts of law. Since then the option of administrative intervention by the Minister of the Economy has been introduced. The Commission de la concurrence, previously the Commission technique des ententes, fulfils an investigatory and advisory function. Since 1977, private parties have been allowed to bring claims for compensation based on injuries resulting from restrictive trade practices through an adhesive procedure linked to criminal proceedings. Faced with a structure primarily designed for penal proceedings and political decisions, the practical relevance and efficiency of the system are necessarily limited. Even those few who take a more optimistic view as to the impact of French antitrust law consider it a relatively low-ranking instrument of state control among others[7].

Compared with the other countries examined so far, Swiss antitrust policy is not far-reaching. The Swiss federal law on cartels and similar organizations of 1962 has to be considered within the framework of the Swiss Constitution. Under this constitution the legislature has the power to enact antitrust provisions only in order to avoid negative effects on the national economy and social policy, and this only if the general interest so requires (Fischer, 1963; Schürmann, 1964; Merz, 1967; Schluep, 1982: 123-151). Consequently, the basic concept which characterizes Swiss antitrust law is that restrictive trade practices can have economically and socially desirable consequences. Thus, what is important is to ensure protection for outsiders and newcomers under private law, to maintain a minimum of competition by means of administrative law, and, if necessary, to carefully screen economic concentration by means of special inquiries. A sharpening of this antitrust law has been proposed and is a matter of controversy at this time (Schluep, 1982: 134:139).

1.4 Consequences for this Study

This comparative law survey would suggest that from the outset, any attempt to investigate juridification and restrictive trade practices is *a priori* a risky one, and even presumptuous, if more than a pure glance beyond national borders is intended. In company law, labor law, and social security law, the different legal systems may be diametrically different in their starting point and solution, but the control problems as such are fundamentally the same. This applies to

6 Azéma (1981); Burst and Kovar (1981); Glais and Lauront (1983); Gide *et al.* (1975). More specifically: Jeantet (1977: 2879); Plaisan *et al.* (1978: chr. 99); Champaud (1982: 101-121); Gavalda 1979: 473). In German: Plaisant *et al.* (1979: 551); Sonnenberger (1978: 367); Hoffmann (1978: 566); Grauel (1978: 751).

7 Möschel (1983: No. 38). Existing for more than 20 years, 1954-1977, the old *Commission Technique* made just about 130 *avis*; Azéma (1981: No. 444): *"Ce chiffre assez modeste s'explique, en partie, par la faiblesse des moyens mis à la disposition de cet organisme"*. Clement (1974: 587); Jenny and Weber (1975: 597).

the trend towards juridification as well. In contrast, opinions concerning restrictive trade practices and competition policy in the different countries vary so much that the need for antitrust law at all is sometimes disputed. In this study, however, one cannot discuss the pros and cons of a competition policy in general and of a law against restrictive trade practices in various forms. This would not be possible without discussing economic policy, and economic law as part of it, over which, even nationally, no unanimity can be achieved (Assmann, 1980: 239-341. With regard to economic law Assmann, 1980a; Mertens *et al.*, 1982; Rittner, 1979; Steindorff, 1985; EG-Kommission, 1973-1976; Hopt, 1978: 81:84). Rather the attempt will be to illuminate some aspects of the process of juridification, as well as opposite trends, with reference to the developments and reform problems of German antitrust law, taking into consideration parallel phenomena and problems of American and European law (Voigt, 1980, 1983; Gessner and Winter, 1982; Blankenburg *et al.*, 1980).

2. Stages in the Development of Juridification in the Law of Restrictive Trade Practices

2.1 Freedom of Contract with Marginal Legal Corrections

(1) Contract and Market

The starting-point of any law against restrictive trade practices is the ambivalent relationship between *contract and market.* From the beginning of modern times, starting in France with the law of March 2-17/1791 — the so-called Décret d'Allarde, then in Germany, in Prussia in particular, after 1806 when the Stein-Hardenberg reforms were introduced, freedom of trade became the basis of a new economic system, replacing previous legal regulation of markets and relying instead on free competition. Ideally these changes would allow the state to limit the objectives of the legal system to guaranteeing freedom of trade, as an institution, as well as a right for the individual. Then a self-regulative process would begin, in that individuals acting in a market would look after their own interests through a process of negotiation, based on freedom of contract. In a competitive market, the large number of private decisions would lead, via supply and demand, to optimum economic production, allocation and distribution. In this way, freedom and performance would condition one another. Social and economic functions of competition would be tied under this system.

(2) From Freedom of Trade to Antitrust Law

This ideal state of minimum juridification and state control, and maximum self-controlling processes on the market has never corresponded to reality. According to Max Weber a type of contract law exists which he calls "formal". This law has negative aspects which have led societies to abandon it in favor of other law (Weber, 1967: 129 ff., 261 ff. and more specifically 78, 92 and 206). Many people are not in a position, economically, to make use of freedom of contract and trade. Manufacturers themselves try to escape the pressures of competition by forming cartels which exert enough power over their members to make sanctions by the legal system superfluous. In addition, their power can be applied not only to these members, but against outsiders. Competition does in fact carry the seeds of its own destruction, since by excluding weaker competitors economic concentration, oligopoly and even monopoly, are encouraged. Thus the *tendencies* towards renewed *juridification* are also latent in an economic system of free competition. The only question is whether this deficiency is recognized and a need for legislature to step in is acknowledged, and if so, what legal means are used for this purpose in the various countries.

An initial stage in the development of juridification in the law of restrictive trade practices is characterized by the belief that certain marginal corrections on the freedom of contract of all, even of those forming cartels, will be enough. This was true for Germany in the 19th and early 20th centuries as shown by the judgement of the Reichsgericht of February 4, 1897 concerning the "Saxon cellulose cartel", which has become practically the symbol of German cartel policy before the First World War (Reichsgericht-Zivilsachen (RGZ) 38, 155; Möschel, 1972: 3-22; Brüggemeier, 1980: 54-64). This tendency can also be seen in Austria, France and Great Britain (see Hopt, 1984: 238-244).

2.2 Market Conduct Rules: Evolution and Complexity

Already at this initial stage of development the basic problem appears with absolute clarity. A state which chooses freedom of trade as its economic system cannot escape having to fix framework conditions for the functioning and maintenance of this economic system above and beyond this basic legal decision. Even where, as is still often the case today, for example in France or Switzerland, cartels are not regarded or prohibited as fundamentally undesirable, a distinction must still be made between *bonnes et mauvaises ententes* (useful and harmful cartels), and action taken against the latter if need be. To simply leave this to the courts, combined, under the best circumstances, with a more or less general antitrust norm, is not adequate in the long run as the similar experiences in Germany, Austria, France and Great Britain show. This is partly because the courts are overburdened by the task of evolving a clear conception of the restrictive trade practices to be prohibited, partly because they give way to the appeals of companies and branches of business which are in economic difficulties, and partly because the important cases do not even come before them, or their decisions have little actual effect.

The consequence of this is that the state itself bindingly fixes the corner-posts of its competition policy through a law against restrictive trade practices. This took place first in the U.S., with the Sherman Act of 1890, and more than half a century later in all the above mentioned European countries — first France in 1945, then Great Britain in 1948, Austria in 1951, Germany in 1957, and finally Switzerland in 1962. In all these countries when the laws against restrictive trade practices were passed, the more or less explicit objective was to retain competitive markets and to create *market conduct rules* for companies on this basis. In style and conception this was cartel law in a narrow sense. *The complexes of norms* which are found in all or some of these cartel laws were predetermined by these goals.

One important problem is that of finding a practicable legal definition of the term "cartel". This requires determination of what constitutes a restrictive trade practice and of the effects of such practices on the market. In one way or another, unacceptable and acceptable cartels must be separated from each other. German law distinguishes in a very complex manner between different types of cartels, concerning terms of trade, discount, structural crises, rationalization, specialization, export and import, special cartels, government exemptions, and cartel-free cooperation. With substantive descriptions alone this separation cannot generally be achieved. Consequently a procedure has been established through which this distinction is practised by prohibiting abusive cartels and permitting the existence of others only under continuous controls and with the option of revoking the cartel's right to exist. Control, in turn, depends on disclosure by the cartels. What is typically required is a specific form of cartel and registration in a cartel register. Finally, mandatory rights of withdrawal and termination for cartel members are a reminder of the first stage in development, during which freedom of contract was the primary starting point for regulation.

Apart from horizontal restrictive trade practices vertical ones must be taken into account. In some legal systems these are given greater attention, at least in the beginning, as in France with the central prohibition of a refusal to sell, the *refus de vente*, and prohibitions of tie-in deals. In addition, there is a prohibition of discrimination, the formulation of which as a norm with judicial precision presents great problems, and a more or less general prohibition of resale price fixing. Rules concerning exclusive dealings and licence contracts should also be noted here.

This system must be administered and executed, which is not possible, given the complexity of the subject, without a special authority like the German Bundeskartellamt, the Swiss Kartellkommission, or the British Director General of Fair Trading. In some countries, for federal or historical reasons, there may even be several authorities, as in Germany with the federal and *Länder* cartel authorities, or U.S. with the Antitrust Division of the Justice Department and the Federal Trade Commission. In a constitutional state a special authority cannot have the last word, which implies the assignment of cartel law powers to the general courts or the creation of other entities, e.g. cartel senates within the courts, or special restrictive practices courts. Administrative powers, to demand information for example, must be defined. Finally there is the question of whether a private third-party in case of loss due to a cartel should be entitled to compensation or to a cease-and-desist order, and whether his private initiative should be used as an enforcement mechanism by the system, as in the U.S. with treble damages suits, and the like.

Of course there remain countless possibilities of divergence in terms of system decisions and rules which cannot be discussed here. Even main objectives can differ, as between Germany, where personal rights are emphasized (the social policy function of competition), and France where more weight is given to ideas of economic efficiency. Instead of a system prohibiting cartels with the possibility of exceptional authorization, as in Germany, an abuse control system like the one in Great Britain can be applied, though the results would not necessarily differ for this reason alone. Even under an abuse system, the presumption could be against cartels, although it would be open to cartel members to prove this presumption wrong, as with the well-known eight gateways of the English system. Conversely, with a prohibition system exempt sectors are conceivable, for example in transport, agriculture, the credit sector, and energy, as in German law. The question of damage to competition by cartels can be decided beforehand by law, without further investigation being necessary (*per se*), or it may be decided by careful examination of the facts of the matter in each individual case (rule of reason). Cartel control can be more political, as in Great Britain and France, or more legal and administrative, as in Germany. Above all, when the political dimension predominates, but also when the assessment of facts in a matter is particularly complex, committees of experts with an advisory or investigative function can be brought in, as with the French *Commission de la concurrence*. Finally, so far as sanctions are concerned, civil, administrative and penal reactions by the legal system of the widest range are conceivable, of both a substantive and procedural type.

The difficulty of elaborating general market conduct rules beyond the conventional ones governing the effectiveness of contracts could very well be discussed in the context of the "Dyestuff" cases[8], but this cannot be done here in detail (see Hopt, 1984a: 247-251).

2.3 Market Structure Law and Merger Control

(1) Problems of Controlling Abuses by Market-dominating Companies

The problem posed by a cartel law with market conduct rules that act too late against monopolies and companies with a dominant position on the market, and in some circumstances even promote concentration, thus having a counterproductive effect, was seen early on[9]. Originally this was even used as an

[8] For Germany Bundesgerichtshof-Zivilsachen (BGHZ) 55, 104. With regard to European law, see nine decisions of the European Court of Justice: Case 48/69 ICI v. Commission [1972] European Court Reporter (ECR) 619; Case 49/69 BASF v. Commission [1972] ECR 713; case 51/69 Bayer AG v. Commission [1973] ECR 745; case 52/69 Geigy AG v. Commission [1972] ECR 787; case 53/69 Sandoz AG v. Commission [1972] ECR 845; case 54/69 Francolor v. Commission [1972] ECR 851; case 55/69 Cassella v. Commission [1972] ECR 887; case 56/69 Hoechst AG v. Commission [1972] ECR 927; case 57/69 ACNA v. Commission [1972] ECR 933.

[9] For the U.S. see Hannah (1979: 306, 312 ff.). For English cartel law before 1965 see Opie (1982: 26).

argument against any juridification by cartel law at all. However, once a cartel law has been adopted, there is no choice but to apply it to ***market-dominating companies***, whether any actual or attempted monopolizing of the market as in the U.S. is prohibited (see Section 2 of the Sherman Act), or whether as in Germany, Great Britain or France, monopolizing companies are subject to monitoring for abuse. The very considerable difficulties involved in framing legal rules result from the fact that the operations, structural changes, and market results of the self-regulating competitive system cannot be duplicated in law for a hypothetical market without competition or at least without workable competition. The general concept of an "as-if" competition is not tenable. It is more a matter of preventing a market-dominating company from acting in those ways which are open to it solely because of its market power, i.e. which would be impossible for an individual company under the rule of competition[10]. The crux of the matter however is that particular forms of conduct on the market can be judged quite differently from the point of view of competition policy depending on whether they result from companies acting in a competitive market or from companies dominating the market. What must be defined, therefore, is the kinds of conduct which endanger competition and which are open specifically to companies in a dominating position. The difficulties of such a juridification are reflected in section 22 of the German Gesetz gegen Wettbewerbsbeschränkungen (GWB) in two ways: the way the section came into being, and the substance of its rules.

The history of the origin of section 22 GWB (see Rittner, 1985: 316 ff.) demonstrates continuous experimentation by the legislature, as does the law of restrictive trade practices as a whole. Since 1957 four amendments have been made, sometimes with very substantial changes, which have not gone without criticism. Each time there was a further advance in the process of juridification.

In their content, the different national antitrust systems which provide for action against monopolizing companies show similar problems throughout. If one does not want, as for example in British law, to base oneself somewhat arbitrarily on a formal definition of a market-dominating company, i.e. a concrete 25% share of the market, then complicated criteria of a statutory or, as in the U.S., a judicial kind, are necessary in order to define monopolistic market power. Assumptions of market domination are of only limited use in this. It is particularly difficult to determine whether a plurality of (oligopolistic) companies have a dominating position, as can be seen in German, European, English and American law (Möschel, 1974). The assessment of abuse as well is a complex attempt to advance from market conduct, market structure and market result tests to specific case groups of misconduct. Such separate definitions are made even more difficult by the interdependency of different legal criteria: the relevant market, market dominance, and abuse of market power. Like moving targets they remove them-

[10] Expert opinion of the Scientific Council at the Federal Ministry of Economics, BTDrs IV/617, 1962: 96.

selves from a well ordered application of law. It is relevant here to point out that in the abuse control of market-dominating companies, competition law reaches its limits for both conceptual and practical reasons (Rittner, 1985: 318 ff.). Considering all this, it is hardly surprising that doubts have been expressed about the practical use of such abuse controls (Möschel, 1981: § 22 No. 4).

(2) Economic Concentration and Legal Control of Mergers

If this is the case, it seems logical to take into account not only market structure criteria in controlling abuses by companies dominating the market, but also at least so far as external growth is concerned, to ensure from the outset that a market structure which overstrains the legal system in its corrective intervention will not even arise. Most of the legal systems referred to have thus also completed the step towards legal *merger control*. For example, in the U.S. after the Sherman Act, as interpreted by the courts, proved ineffective section 7 of the Clayton Act was adopted in 1914. Great Britain saw the passage of the Monopolies and Merger Act in 1965, and merger control laws were passed in Germany in 1973, and in France in 1977. The European Community, in fact, has merger control powers under the Treaty setting up the European Coal and Steel Community (Art. 66), although these have remained ineffective. Since the Continental Can judgement of the European Court of Justice there is also rudimentary abuse control of company mergers under the Treaty of Rome (Art. 86)[11]. Among the other legal systems referred to, Austria has no merger control, but it does have an obligation to register certain mergers on a cartel register (Koppensteiner, 1981: 265-281). So far, Switzerland has contented itself with giving its cartel commission the power to make general investigations and, at the request of the Ministry for the Economy, specific ones concerning single lines of business. This power has been used in a whole series of cases, including an analysis of concentration in the banking sector (Schluep, 1982: 140-149).

The phenomenon of economic concentration was also the starting point for merger regulations in other legal systems. Naturally, this phenomenon was treated with much controversy in all countries concerned, starting with the question of determination and assessment and continuing through to economic and political evaluation (see e.g. Arndt, 1971; Lenel, 1968; Kaufer, 1977; Monopolkommission, 4. Hauptgutachten 1980/81, Bundestagsdrucksache (BTDrS) 9/1892,1982: VI (Ursachen der Konzentration), VII (Gewerkschaften und Konzentration); 5. Hauptgutachten 1982/83, BTDrS 10/1791, 1984: III (Stand und Entwicklung der Konzentration von Großun-

[11] Case 6/72 Continental Can v. Commission [1973] ECR 215. Recently with regard to the legal aspects of European merger control, Schmitt (1982: 169-186). For economic aspects, Jacquemin (1982: 155-168). Cf. Monopolkommission, 3. Hauptgutachten 1978/79, BTDrS 8/4404, 1980: Nos. 632-661. The proposed directive of July 20, 1973, OJ C 92/1 (Oct. 31, 1973) is reprinted in its amended form of 1984 in OJ C 51/8 (Feb. 23, 1984).

ternehmern), V (Konzentrationsentwicklung in der Pressewirtschaft)). The efforts involved, for example in the conduct of the American Hearings of the Senate-Subcommittee on Antitrust and Monopoly, documented in numerous volumes, speak for themselves[12]. In any case it can be seen from the discussion that the naive belief in the superiority of big companies which was widespread in Europe for decades following the Second World War, and which resulted in an uncritical promotion of concentration has faded (Möschel, 1983: Nos. 719-721; for France, Champaud, 1982: 104-105). Legal control of mergers need not deal with this problem directly because it is, after all, not its responsibility to limit size as such, but to prevent certain company mergers. Internal company growth, which takes place under competitive market conditions, and which is therefore preferable from the perspective of competition policy[13], remains unaffected by this. The direct motive for the introduction of merger controls was a practically overwhelming wave of mergers in the '60s and '70s, which took place in a similar fashion in different countries[14]. Problems of juridification are also evident, as with abuse control of monopolizing companies, in frequent reforms or discussion of reform, and in the content of norms.

These frequent reforms do not happen by accident, since the substantive concepts of merger control which they contain diverge widely within individual countries and internationally; this is true even in the U.S. where the Chicago School recently argued for a drastic reversal of merger control policy (Posner, 1976: 96-134, 196-201, who favors "a drastic retrenchment"; Bork, 1978: 217 ff.). These differences, which characterize the type and extent of juridification, cannot be discussed in detail here. We must limit ourselves to remarks regarding the *fundamental objective* of merger control and its basic material and procedural problems. The most important difference in principle exists between direct merger control designed to maintain competition, relied on by the U.S. and Germany (although in Germany the possibility of ministerial authorization does exist), and regulations which impose political control on mergers. The latter are relied on by Great Britain, where the decision to act lies with the Minister and is made on the basis of a general public interest test, and by France, where the decison also finally lies with the Minister, who must examine whether the merger will contribute to economic and social progress. In the latter case merger control is only part of a more

12 Economic Concentration, Hearings before the Subcommittee on Antitrust and Monopoly of the Committee on the Judiciary, United States Senate, Washington, D.C. 1965-1969, Part 1-8.

13 Cf. the well known dictum of the U.S. Supreme Court, U.S. v. Philadelphia National Bank, 374 U.S. 321 at 370/371 (1963): "corporate growth by internal expansion is socially preferable to growth by acquisition". For the reasons see Willeke (1980: 210 ff.).

14 Figures for Germany, *Konzentrationsenquête*, BTDrS IV/2320, 1964; BKartA, *Tätigkeitsbericht* 1968, BTDrS V/4236, 1969; 1972, BTDrS 7/986, 1973: 40-42; 1973, BTDrS 7/2250, 1974: 35-37; for Great Britain, Opie, (1982: 26-28); Champaud (1982: 104).

comprehensive state industrial policy oriented more or less towards *planification*. For evaluation from the viewpoint of juridification, there is a considerable difference between whether merger control juridifies a part of competition policy, and thus constitutes a self-contained legal subsystem, or whether it essentially provides a formal framework for political decisions and is thus just one among many means and objectives of industrial policy which itself is only partially or not at all juridified.

In all the legal systems concerned the central *substantive* problems of framing legal rules relate to the definition of "mergers" which, if it is to describe economic realities correctly, must take into account not only the fusion of competitors, but other types of permanent economic links as well, such as the acquisition of shares above a specific blocking minority, qualified interlocking directorates, and company agreements. This cannot be done without a catchall clause[15]. The question of from what size or threshold such mergers should be taken into account has been answered in France very cautiously, by reference to specific percentages of the national turnover (40% or 25% depending on the similarity of the products). In Germany absolute size criteria are relied on (for example, turnover proceeds of a participation company of more than 50 million DM), while in Great Britain indirect size criteria are used (25% or more than a five million pound take-over value)[16]. The central material question of criteria for prohibition depends directly on the fundamental objective of merger control. According to the German Cartel Act, the determining factor is whether a dominant position on the market arises from or is reinforced by the merger. This may be compensated for by demonstrating that there are outweighing improvements in conditions of competition. In addition, however procedurally separate, there must be the possibility of ministerial authorization of a merger on the basis of overall economic advantage or of an overriding public interest. In France the determining question is whether limitation to sufficient competition exists, but a compensating contribution to economic and social progress will bring the merger *a priori* out of the sphere of control pursuant to a legal exemption. In Great Britain, finally, the determining factor is actual or potential harm to the public interest, this being illustrated through examples in the law. According to British legislation and control practice, the protection of competition is just one among several objectives[17]. Here it can be mentioned only marginally that

15 See for Germany, GWB § 23 (2); for Great Britain, Fair Trading Act 1973, Sec. 65 (enterprises ceasing to be distinct enterprises); for France, Law No. 77-806 of 1977, art. 4 al. 1 (Concentration Control Law of 1977); for the U.S. Clayton Act § 7.

16 See for France, Concentration Control Law of 1977 art. 4 al. 4 and 5; for Germany, GWB § 24 (8), (the tolerance clause); for Great Britain, Fair Trading Act 1973, Sec. 64 (merger situation qualifying for investigation)

17 See for Germany, GWB § 24 (1) with GWB § 24 (3); for France, Concentration Control Law of 1977, art. 4 al. 8; for Great Britain, Fair Trading Act 1973, ss. 69, 73, 84; for the U.S., Clayton Act § 7 ("where in any line of commerce in any section of the country the effect of such aquisition may be substantially to lessen competition, or tend to create a monopoly").

in all legal systems a careful distinction must be made between horizontal, vertical and conglomerate mergers (Emmerich, 1982: 230-238; Möschel, 1980: 203; 1983: 855 ff.; Büscher, 1982; Korah, 1982a: 64-66). We have already referred at the outset of this study to the wide range of variations in possible legal reactions and sanctions within antitrust law in general. In the case of merger control they are limited to a narrower, primarily administrative law spectrum. Yet the different degrees of readiness of individual legal systems to enforce merger control are exemplified by how they approach divestiture (as distinct from the simple reversed transaction of a prohibited merger). In the U.S. this most extreme and furthest-going instrument of antitrust law has been known for a long time and is used in practice, while in the Federal Republic of Germany, corresponding proposals have been made but are not of immediate political interest at this time (Möschel, 1981a: 41-57; 1984: 655-678; Posner, 1981: 58-72).

One of the *procedural* problems is to choose between alternative formulations of the duty to report in the case of merger. The alternatives are prior notification, either for the purpose of simple information to the cartel authorities (as was the case until 1973 in Germany, and is still true in Austria today), or for the purpose of preventive control (as under section 24a of the German GWB in the case of big mergers), and postmerger notification (see for Germany, GWB § 23, 24a; for France, Concentration Control Law art. 5 al. 1 of 1977, and especially Champaud, 1982: 110 (*a priori, a posteriori*); for the U.S., Grauel, 1977; Neumann, 1979). Furthermore, there will be a central difference not only in conception but also in the scope of merger control if procedurally the control power is either clearly divided between a cartel authority and a political body, or if it is left, *a priori*, in the hands of the political authority. This becomes evident when German and British merger controls are compared (see Weiler, 1982: 198-199). There are also differences beween the various legal systems in the practical importance attached to informal procedures and authorizations. Finally, reference must be made to the institutional formation of politically independent or dependent cartel authorities, to the integration of advisory or investigatory commissions, and to their personal staffs, and to the role which more or less specialized courts play in merger control.

It is difficult to make a well-founded judgement concerning the efficiency of legal merger control, even for an individual country (Möschel, 1983: Nos. 831-833 "two-edged"; Hopt, 1982: 795 ff.; for France, Champaud, 1982: 107 "disappointed" "lull in the case law"; for Great Britain, Opie, 1982: 40; Korah, 1982a: 68-69: "difficult to assess"). This is even more true for the evaluation of individual parts of a material or procedural-institutional type system. In an international comparison an absolute judgement is even more difficult since the merger control systems of different legal systems have different goals. If the number of interventions and successful prohibitions of large mergers is taken as a criterion, a falling gradient is observable between the U.S., Germany and after a clear gap, Great Britain and France. By this, conclusions can be reached as to the extent of juridification (of law in action), but no value-judgement based on legal or even economic science can be made.

2.4 Problems Due to the "Coincidence" of Different Stages of Development and of Legal Systems

(1) Coexistence and Displacement of Resources within the Same Legal System

The stages in the development of juridification in the law of restrictive trade practices, which for the purposes of this study have only been sketched out roughly though they could easily be further differentiated and refined, do not take place one after the other in the sense that new regulations take over from old. Instead, partially modified old sets of norms and new ones are combined. Thus, for example, parts of the German cartel regulations of 1923 were incorporated into the GWB, and old parts of the GWB were retained during subsequent reforms of abuse controls applicable to market-dominating companies, and the introduction and reform of merger controls if only because they were necessary to prevent strategies of evasion or as further functionally essential parts of a complete cartel law system. This must be understood not only in the sense of external validity of adjacent parts, but in the individual case, in the sense of cumulative applicability. An example of this is the tendency to permit broader action against mergers by in principle applying section 1 ff. GWB and section 23 ff. GWB cumulatively against joint ventures, for example (Möschel: 1983: Nos. 200 ff.: two-barriers theory ("Zwischenschrankentheorie"); differently the majority of the scholarship: theory of separation ("Trennungstheorie")), or by activating the general clause of abuse control against mergers of market-dominating companies as well (Emmerich, 1982: 188). Older layers of norms can thus gain new dimensions of importance, even though the reverse phenomenon of loss of significance is the general rule, for example, of sections 1 and 2 of the Sherman Act for merger control after introduction of section 7 of the Clayton Act.

When different stages in development coincide with each other a further phenomenon, more important for competition policy, can be observed. Shifts towards new complexes of norms occur, generally as the result of a conscious shifting of resources by the cartel authorities. This can be observed in Germany where after the introduction of merger control, the federal cartel office started to deal with merger control in four of its nine departments. Three of these dealt in general with the control of mergers, while one specialized in the control of mergers between credit institutions and insurance companies. Since 1984 because of a new structuring of competences all departments have dealt with merger control. The Monopoly Commission has emphasized this by titling its third main report "merger control remains a priority" (Monopolkommission, 3. Hauptgutachten 1978/79, Fusionskontrolle bleibt vorrangig, BTDrS 8/4404, 1980. Cf. also 4. Hauptgutachten 1980/81, Fortschritte bei der Konzentrationserfassung, BTDrS 9/1892, 1982, 5. Hauptgutachten 1982/83, Ökonomische Kriterien für die Rechtsanwendung, BTDrS 10/1791, 1983). Similar phenomena, sometimes partially in reverse, can be observed in other legal systems. For example, a slackening of enforcement activity in the area of merger control has taken place in the U.S. under the Reagan administration, which has been influenced by the Chicago School (Katzmann, 1982: 5). There is hardly any need to emphasize that a large number of factors, not least the respective general economic situation (Berg, 1982: 336 ff.), have played a role in such shifts of emphasis and importance. This is true for antitrust law, as well as for law in general (Fischer *et al.*, 1976).

(2) International Antitrust Law: in Principle and Regarding Export Cartels

It becomes more complicated when there are not coinciding development stages within the same legal system, but whole legal systems which constitute different levels of development as far as their position towards restricted trade practices is concerned. Certainly, there are also problems between legal systems with more or less equally developed antitrust law. Nonetheless, it frequently happens that precisely for this reason an understanding of the juridified competition policy of another system exists, which can be reflected in mutual assistance in application and enforcement by governments and cartel authorities, such as that which exists between Germany, the U.S. and France[18]. With respect to transnational companies and international markets, characteristic of the pattern today, a coincidence of legal systems with different antitrust laws is absolutely necessary. From the viewpoint of juridification it is noteworthy that a fully developed antitrust law reaches out beyond national frontiers, and must do this, in the sense that it protects a domestic market from restrictive trade practices which have their origins in other countries. This can go quite far. Thus, for example, in the famous Swiss watchmaker case, an American court at first obliged the Swiss defendant, by a cease-and-desist order, to modify the articles of its export associations in Switzerland so as to exclude restrictive export regulation[19]. Similar examples are supplied by merger control. Thus, in German law the position is taken that in some circumstances major control may be applicable even to two foreign companies, which are not yet active on the domestic market and which have set up a common subsidiary abroad. Such companies must supply the federal cartel office with information about the merger even if they are only potential competitors, i.e. they are preparing to enter the domestic market. According

[18] "Abkommen zwischen der Regierung der Bundesrepublik Deutschland und der Regierung der Vereinigten Staaten über die Zusammenarbeit in bezug auf restriktive Geschäftspraktiken" of June 23, 1976, Bundesgesetzblatt (BGBl.) II 1711, also in 26 *Wirtschaft und Wettbewerb (WuW)* 578 (1976). See Grauel, 1976, 764. See also ***Abkommen zwischen der Regierung der Bundesrepublik Deutschland und der Republik Frankreich über die Zusammenarbeit in bezug auf wettbewerbsbeschränkende Praktiken***, of May 28, 1984 BGBl. II 758.

[19] U.S. v. The Watchmakers of Switzerland Information Center Inc., CCH Trade Cases 1963, § 70. 600 (S.D.N.Y. 1962), 1965, § 71.352 (S.D.N.Y. 1965). In this context see Haight, 1970: 311-363; Meessen, 1975: 186 ff.

to this position, the protective function of the GWB, which aims at maintaining domestic competition, comes into play if the effect of the foreign merger is that only one serious newcomer, rather than two, appears on the German market[20]. Conflicts which can lead to a deadlock, in the sense that two legal systems may impose contradictory requirements on the same company, are thus preprogrammed. A famous example of this is the ICI case, in which an English company was ordered by an American court under American antitrust law to hand back an exclusive patent license, whereas the same handing back was regarded by an English court as being contrary to the license agreement[21].

Such conflicts can also occur in general international private law. A national legal system can protect itself, for example, by application of its *ordre public*. In capital market law, the conflicts become particularly acute since the force of the legal system is actively supported and maintained by state authorities. A state which operates a less wide-ranging, less juridified competition, tax, or capital market policy may feel that both its policy and its sovereignty are under attack from another state, and in extreme cases react with blocking leglislation[22]. In the latter case there may then be counter-movements in the first state, either because the legal conflict is reinforced by the use of political and economic pressures, or because, conversely, there is more international cooperation, at least in the collection of information (OECD, 1984a), or the courts are inclined towards a more cautious application of the national law with respect to the interests of other states (comity considerations) (OECD, 1974). Processes of juridification and dejuridification go hand in hand, on both substantive and procedural, as well as national and international, levels.

Conversely, most national antitrust laws are extremely generous towards export cartels (See especially *Timberlane Lumber Co.* v. *Bank of America*, 549 F. 2d 597 F. 2d (9th Cir. 1976); *Mannington Mills, Inc.* v. *Congoleum Corp.*, 595 F. 2d (3rd Cir. 1979). This is based on national economic arguments that it is necessary to confirm a counterbalancing power against cartelized foreign competitors or buyers or to facilitate access to export markets for medium-

[20] Rehbinder, 1981: § 98 Abs. 2 No. 202; a different position is taken by Mestmäcker, 1981: Vor § 23 No. 60 following BGHZ 74, 322 (327) = WuW/E BGH 1613, 1615 *"Organische Pigmente"*. The latest decision is of the *Kammergericht*, July 1, 1983, WuW/E Oberlandesgericht (OLG) 3051. "Philip Morris/Rothmans"; as to the intervention of the EEC Commission on the same see BKartA, report 1983/84, BTDrs 10/3550, 1985: 62. Both cases have become moot. See generally Decision, 1984.

[21] U.S. v. Imperial Chemical Industries Ltd., 100 F. Supp. 504 (S.D.N.Y. 1952). British Nylon Spinners Ltd. v. Imperial Chemical Industries, Ltd. (1953) Ch. 19 (C.A. 1952 = (1952) 2 All E.R. 780); (1955) Ch. 37 = (1954) 3 All E.R. 88 Mestmäcker, 1974: 150 ff.

[22] E.g., the British Protection of Trading Interests Act 1980; Adolph, 1980: 181-183; Autenrieth, 1983: 15-18; French Law No. 68-678 in the form of July 16, 1980 and Law No. 80-538 of 1980. For survey of the legal situation in various countries see Pettit and Styler, 1982: 697-715; Hopt, 1977: 279-331; Note, 1979.

sized companies or to improve the currency situation of the country. Similarly, within national merger control laws the question of the international competitiveness of a national economy is regularly given considerable if not decisive importance (For Germany, GWB § 24 (3) 1; Berg, 1982; for France, Concentration Control Law of 1977, art. 4 al. 8; for Great Britain, Fair Trading Act, 1973, sec. 84 (1) (e); for the U.S., Webb-Pomerene Export Trade Association Act § 2). Thus, some states differentiate between cartel prohibition and merger control on the domestic market, and approval or even state promotion of export cartels and mergers by joint ventures on the world market. This practice is regarded as cynical and even as a form of economic aggression precisely by those countries which themselves have little or no cartel law (cf. Bundeskartellamt (BKartA), Tätigkeitsbericht 1976, BTDrS 8/704, 1977: 16). The consequence is a further hardening of the above-mentioned fronts and one more argument for defensive legislation. In some legal systems, such as the U.S. or German, the opposite juridification tendencies can be observed for these very reasons. Export cartels are judged more critically and subjected to stricter interpretations of national cartel law because they are regarded as dangerous for the domestic market and as a step towards the lessening of competition on foreign markets. According to some voices even purely international export cartels aimed at the monopolizing of foreign markets without domestic impact may be prohibited as abusive, since they go against the interests of German foreign trade (Rehbinder, 1981: § 6 Nos. 162, 184). Furthermore the U.S. and Germany are both energetic supporters of a consistent control of international restrictive trade practices through further juridification in other countries and through international law.

(3) Federal, Supranational and International Antitrust Law

Up to now we have considered how the conflict between different legal systems produces "horizontal" juridification tendencies, in the form of blocking legislation, supplementary laws and new legislation. "Vertical" juridification tendencies also arise. This would be conceivable within any national federal system. In fact in many countries competition policy is regarded as being *a priori* so important that cartel law is immediately made the object of exclusive federal legislation and put under the competency of a federal ministry. The fact that a few specific powers of lesser importance are dedicated to regional cartel authorities, as in Germany, changes nothing in the final analysis.

The first comprehensive attempt to create a genuinely supranational system was made with the Havanna Charter of 1946, which never came into force. Instead, a supranational European cartel law was created, through the European treaties, initially in the European Coal and Steel Community Treaty, and later more comprehensively in the Treaty of Rome. While the importance of Articles 65 and 66 of the former is limited, Aricles 85 and 86 of the latter, measured in terms of the number and content of decisions of the EEC Commission, of the national cartel authorities and courts, and of the

European Court of Justice, are of considerable importance[23]. From the viewpoint of juridification, one point worth noting is that with European cartel law, concepts of competition law penetrated member states which until then had no national cartel law. This sometimes had the result that these countries created a national cartel law, or endeavoured to bring the content of their law into conformity with the standard set by the European Community. For example, France in 1967 and particularly in 1977, as well as Greece in 1977 (Tzouganatos, 1983), introduced merger control which according to some was intended to prevent regulation by the European Community. The co-existence of national and supranational antitrust law does, as is well known, create considerable difficulties which have resulted in a flood of legal literature. The original concept of co-existence in the sense of the two-barrier theory has today been abandoned in favor of the clear priority of European antitrust law. This in turn makes the introduction of European merger control going beyond the Continental Can doctrine difficult, particularly for those member states which, like Germany, do not wish to substantially weaken their own more developed merger control law.

In the meantime the attempt to arrive at an international system of antitrust law continues. To be noted are the efforts and investigations of the OECD, and most recently, the Codex of the United Nations against restrictive practices in international trade[24] approved in December 1980, which has been worked out by UNCTAD and approved by industrial as well as socialist and developing countries. Although from a strictly legal viewpoint not binding (this will be discussed below (3.2 (3)), the importance of these guidelines should not be underestimated. Finally, a whole series of bilateral agreements should also be noted which may well be of considerable importance for antitrust law[25].

[23] For the most recent developments, see the list of German and EEC decisions in the activity reports of the BKartA, the latest issue 1983/84, BTDrs 10/3550, 1985:181-183. See also the Annual General Report of the EEC about its activity. A list of European Court of Justice and EEC Commission decisions is available in Gleiss and Hirsch, 1978:780-788 and 1981. Up to 1983 see Ommeslaghe *et al.* 1984.

[24] With regard to the OECD Code see the reports of the Committee of Experts on Restrictive Business Practices, e.g., OECD, 1977, 1984, 1984a. With regard to the UN Code (5.12.1980) see 31 *WuW* 91 (1981); 32 *WuW* 32 (1982); Fikentscher and Straub, 1982: 637 and 727; von Hahn, 1982: 367-380; Fikentscher, 1983: 212-249.

[25] See the convention between the U.S. and Germany, supra; the conventions between Austria and the EEC, especially ***Abkommen zwischen der Republik Österreich und der Europäischen Wirtschaftsgemeinschaft*** (ÖEWGA), Art. 23 and ***Abkommen zwischen der Republik Österreich und der Europäischen Gemeinschaft für Kohle und Stahl,*** (ÖEGKSA) Art. 19, which initiated the introduction of a national antitrust law, hereto with text: Koppensteiner, 1981: 43-44.

3. The Crisis of Growth, Proposals for Reform, Regulation and Deregulation Strategies

3.1 The Phenomenon and its Causes

(1) Differentiation and Stratification

The study of the stages in the development of juridification in the antitrust laws of different legal systems shows an increasing and apparently unstoppable *trend towards more law*. As has been shown above, the evolution of the legal and economic system starts with freedom of trade, and passes through various stages of development. The first two can be defined based on Max Weber's work, as making contract law ethical by protecting the freedom of cartel members and outsiders, and as materialization in the sense of the extension of layers of norms regulating market conduct. The third and most important stage is one of structuralization, proceduralization, and bureaucratization. Market structures are used as a criterion for legal decisions. Their worsening is to be prevented, and if possible the legal system should even, as partially postulated in the divestiture discussion, proceed to actively remedy the distortion of entrenched market structures. This process takes place within the framework of complicated lengthy and cost-intensive procedures with the participation of administrative, judicial and company bureaucracies.

The process of growth runs not only *horizontally* within a legal system, but also vertically and internationally. By horizontal is meant not only an expansion of the actual law against restrictive trade practices into the present threefold division consisting of cartel law itself, control of abuses by monopolizing companies, and merger control, as exists, for example, in Germany, but also an increasing complication of the fields of intersection between the law against restrictive trade practices and other areas of law. This applies particularly to those legal systems in which the law against restrictive trade practices forms a part of an economic law which emphasizes planning, but can also be observed in legal systems which distinguish between cartel law and planification by economic law. In the latter systems, such fields of intersection relate partially to constitutional law but, with the development of antitrust law, they relate increasingly to areas such as unfair competition, groups of companies law, and the law of special sectors such as agriculture, banks, transport, energy, etc. *Vertical* tendencies towards juridification are partly observable in legal systems with a federal structure but, above all, in the EEC with its interplay of supranational and national antitrust law. *Internationally*, juridification processes are multidimensional: national antitrust law is expanded to the limits of the national legal system, which leads to blocking legislation by other states. Subsequent reactions of legal systems without antitrust law, or with fairly undeveloped antitrust law, make themselves apparent. A genuine international cartel law based on public international law agreements and conventions, or its foreshadowing in the form of legally non-binding codes of conduct, is developing.

This process of growth in antitrust law has its price which in comparison with the alternatives recommended by state-interventionists of an economic policy which trusts less in the market and more in state control, may appear to be slight or at least bearable, but which nonetheless attracts legal, economic and political criticism. This doubt and criticism comes from very different quarters, and leads correspondingly to extremely varied proposals for reform and strategies for regulation or deregulation, as an answer to the *crisis of growth* which is increasingly diagnosed. The content of the related discussion cannot be dealt with fully here, since it ranges from discussions of ideological principles to highly professionalized discussions between experts in economics and antitrust law (the difficulties of such a discussion are shown exemplarily by the contributions of Gotthold, 1981: 286 and Möschel, 1981b: 590). Here we can only outline some of the more general directions of the discussions in relation to juridification problems.

(2) Cognitive and Policy Problems

In the center of this crisis of growth and juridification there stand *very fundamental cognitive and policy problems*, of which only a few can be mentioned here by way of example.

The central *cognitive* problem lies in the understanding of competition (Möschel, 1974: 34-48, 1978: 45). The problems of the function of competition and of the competition models and terms (to mention only "full" and "workable" competition) can be neglected in this context. With regard to the juridification discussion something else is decisive: if it is precisely this self-steering process which dynamically brings the desired results and is thus superior to planning, i.e. the limits to what is knowable are *a priori* set. These cognitive limits make it difficult to find the borderline between modes of conduct inherent in competition and those which restrict competition. In terms of competition, entrepreneurial conduct is ambivalent. One and the same mode of conduct by a company in a dominant market position can considerably affect competition, for example, price discrimination or exclusive agreements. But the same conduct followed by a company in a competitive market position can also be an instrument of sharp competition. Thus, on oligopolistic markets, tacit agreement on price reductions, i.e. secret competition, can make a whole petrified price level move. Not without good reason the rather popular market information procedures are regarded very critically by the official guardians of antitrust law. Conversely, discrimination in the hands of powerful companies can be used to hinder competitors and to restrain competition on preceding and subsequent markets. Similarly, this is true for exclusive agreements. They can result in an unbearable tying to market-dominating companies or in a competitively necessary instrument in the hands of a company which wants to penetrate a new market.

These cognitive problems are inherent in legal rules controlling abuse by market dominating companies and, particularly, in rules governing mergers. The attempt to prescribe certain actions in the sense of an as-if-competition to a company which is exposed to little or no effective competition must fail *a priori*. At best it is possible to discern and prohibit certain patterns of abusive conduct. It is with this failure of price control in Germany and the EEC that antitrust law is connected (Rittner, 1985: 348 ff.). The legal policy difficulties of merger control are even greater. It is difficult to predict the restrictive effects of mergers, quite apart from estimating their economic and social consequences and weighing the pros and cons of all these factors. This is reflected in the diametrically opposed positions of economic science, politics and law within individual countries as to merger control in general and individual mergers specifically.

Subject to such central cognitive uncertainties, equally basic *policy problems* arise. What is at stake is not only a large number of policy problems concerning the end-means relationship of the many individual rules, but also basic policy problems, which concern the general approach of guidance by law and the place of antitrust law in such an approach[26]. Such a fundamental policy decision, which in the final analysis goes back to basic economic and social theories can be found, for example, in F.A. von Hayek's system theory, according to which competition is the optimum discovery process. The legal order must restrict itself to rules of the game for this self-controlling system. According to this conception, any regulatory intervention by law is necessarily distorting, because predictions as to the organization and results of this system going beyond general pattern predictions are impossible. The concept itself is, as emphasized by Hayek, not empirically verifiable.

A contrary fundamental policy decision is that which instrumentalizes the law as such, and competition law as a part of overall law. In the center of this stands *political control*, which is thought to be necessary and of at least some practicability. Starting from this concept, it is a question of finding the policy appropriate to the respective politically selected objective. This policy may be of a legal and specifically cartel-law type, but not necessarily so. Intermediate and overall objectives other than competition, are then kept directly in view and aimed at through control. Examples of these objectives include: the favoring of a specific company size regarded as correct from a certain small and medium industry perspective, the strengthening of national industry and its position on the world market, the imposition of price controls as a consumer protection measure, the avoidance of unemployment by means of reorganization mergers, and the maintenance of structures in particular areas along with prevention of bankruptcy in these areas, such as banking, etc. Possible consequences for the design of competition law can easily be discerned, e.g. approval of certain cartels, approval or even promotion of certain company mergers (e.g. in politically important areas), systems for controlling abuses by dominant companies (e.g. price control) and handling of areas of exemption from cartel law, (e.g. banking, energy, traffic, agriculture etc.).

Between these two basic directions, there are a large number of concepts,

[26] Möschel, 1983: § 3 Wettbewerbskonzeptionen und Methodenfragen, and more specifically with regard to mergers see § 11; Assmann, 1980: 280-311; Reich, 1977: 29-66, where consideration is given to Marxist approaches. Generally as to regulation in a liberal state see Stewart, 1983.

which to some extent constitute independent starting points, and which combine certain elements. To be mentioned here are e.g., the assumption based on an economic analysis of law (e.g. Calvani and Siegfried, 1979) as represented by the Chicago School, or the so-called "theory of restrictive trade practices" which is restricted to detecting individual restrictive trade practices and endeavouring to counteract these via appropriate legal measures. The latter may once again take into account elements of economic analysis of law, or emphasize the peculiar rules governing a judgement within competition law. Often these approaches are combined with practicality considerations.

Obviously, the respective, often ideologically based, positions concerning these basic cognitive and policy problems decisively influence the way juridification in antitrust law is evaluated. There is not a single, objectively "correct" diagnosis and therapy for juridification problems. Juridification or deregulation are but after-effects of approaches and decisions which have been taken elsewhere.

(3) Difficulties of Enforcement

Apart from cognitive and policy problems, *problems of enforcement* are also responsible for the growth crisis in antitrust law, since in general they lead to demand for an expansion of legal norms and of legal personnel, and only exceptionally to an acceptance of the need for law to withdraw into areas which are more certain and easier to enforce. The problem of enforcement in antitrust law is particularly great for a variety of reasons.

For companies, prohibitions or mandatory behavior under cartel law are not just a question of legal standards which must be taken into account along with economic and other data. They often deprive companies of options in decision-making which can be of crucial importance, and in extreme cases may mean life or death for the company. This is reflected in the fact that antitrust law difficulties very rapidly go beyond the legal department and become the concern of company management itself. This fact explains why here, more than in many other areas of law, the attempt is made to sound out peripheral areas of legality and discover whether an evasion will be recognized or a violation discovered. The situation is illustrated by the bidding cartels in the German building industry, which in spite of clear legal prohibitions going back for decades and corresponding efforts to enforce them by the federal cartel office, continue to operate.

In addition, there are considerable difficulties of proof, also well illustrated by the bidding cases. Cartel agreements and other restrictive trade practices often come to light only by chance, e.g. when a company manager has not destroyed related memoranda, or an employee leaves a company on bad terms and "spills the beans". Above all, entrepreneurial conduct on the market does not clearly reflect whether restrictive trade practices are in use or not. Practically any conduct on the market can be used for restrictive purposes.

We must also remember the limited legal, personnel, and financial resources available to those bodies responsible for the enforcement of antitrust law. International comparison shows striking discrepancies in the setting of political priorities in this area. Without appropriate resources even the best antitrust law will be ineffective. In a situation of limited resources, the establishment of correct priorities by the antitrust authorities itself becomes a problem of credibility.

(4) Limits of Control by Rules of Law

The crisis of growth in the law against restrictive trade practices goes beyond the problems already discussed to the basic problem of the *limits of control* by legal norms as such. These limits may be of a legal, political or economic sort, and may combine to overload the subsystem or lead to its becoming independent from the system as a whole. As already mentioned there are trends in this direction discernible in the U.S.

Limits of a *legal* type are reached when the quantity of norms supplied by the legislature is so great that the courts hardly know how to deal with them anymore. Robert Fischer, former president of the German *Bundesgerichtshof* and of its Cartel Senate, expressed this once in the following terms: "The GWB is no longer a law, but a novel. Paragraphs which extend over three pages are no longer justifiable. The content of rules born out of political compromises makes application of the law difficult. The federal cartel office has furthermore brought forward atypical cases for judgement which do not give the federal court the possibility of reaching a decision based on legal principles. Clarification of the law by the courts is made obsolete by continuous amendments to the GWB" (Fischer, 1978). With reference to the analytically separable stages in the process of steering by economic law (Hopt, 1972: 1017, 1024) this can be described as follows: the legislative aims are already unclear in parliament due to the above-mentioned cognitive and policy problems (Elzinga, 1977: 1191). Concepts of objectives and ways and means are, in the course of the legislative process, made even more obscure by real and pretended ideals, tactical manœuvres, political compromises, and ambiguous terms. Such inconsistencies are particularly obvious in the treatment of exemption areas such as banking, insurance, transport and energy (Möschel, 1983: § 12). Essential powers of decision are thus shifted to courts, a fact sometimes admitted — more frequently minimized or even denied. In this situation central decision-making is fragmented. The field as a whole is split up into countless individual areas or even individual case decisions. The results of the interplay between companies, partially competing cartel authorities, and first instance and appellate courts, each placing their emphasis in a different place, and political bodies acting under public pressures, sometimes cannot be forecast even by experts in the field.

Political limits to the law against restrictive trade practices also exist (Pitofsky, 1979: 1051). These can be seen, for example, in the situation where a government has an interest in seeing the merger of certain public companies, and in spite of all expert criticism, is willing to push the merger through[27]. A second situation arises when unemployment becomes such a politically sensitive issue that a reorganizational merger, in spite of all evidence indicating that it will not save jobs[28], cannot be rejected. Similar limits apply to European antitrust law, the limited power of the EEC Commission, and the deadlock in the introduction of European merger control.

There are *economic* developments as well which reduce or eliminate the power of law to act against restrictive trade practices. These can be described as a shift from market processes to organization processes. This is a question on the one hand of economic concentration, against which cartel law in the narrower sense can do nothing (even the various national merger control laws have only limited impact in this regard, and in so far as internal company growth is concerned have no effect at all). On the other hand the oligopoly problem must be considered, which is hardly solvable in practice. In addition, there are developments which lead to company aims and decisions being based increasingly on criteria other than rational market factors. Examples of this are provided by discussions on the obligation of a board to set objectives other than the simple maximization of profits (Hopt and Teubner, 1985), or the still disputed concept of company co-determination (Hopt, 1984a).

The crisis of growth in the law against restrictive trade practices has spurred reform proposals and strategies aimed at more, less, or at least more flexible regulation. In many cases the approach is legal, with the aim of reducing either complexity to improve enforcement or increasing complexity to improve decision-making (3.2.1). Attempts to increase the efficiency of the system by increasing sanctioning powers, resources, and the power of enforcement and initiative have also played a large part in the discussion of reforms (3.2.2). Finally, moves towards deregulation, or at least a loosening of the grip of mandatory sanctions in favor of more flexible mechanisms can be seen in antitrust law, although these tendencies are somewhat isolated (3.2.3). These partly alternative and partly cumulative trends in cartel law correspond to the legalist, technocratic and communal responses worked out in the general international discussion of juridification and dejuridification (Galanter, 1980: 11-26).

[27] See especially the VEBA-mergers, as VEBA/Gelsenberg 1974 and VEBA/BP 1979 and in this context above all Monopolkommission, Sondergutachten wettbewerbliche und strukturelle Aspekte einer Zusammenfassung von Unternehmen im Energiebereich, 1975; Sondergutachten 8: Zusammenschlußvorhaben der Deutschen BP AG und der VEBA AG, 1979.

[28] Monopolkommission, 1. Hauptgutachten 1973/1975, Mehr Wettbewerb ist möglich, 1976: No. 933; 2. Hauptgutachten 1976/1977, Fortschreitende Konzentration bei Großunternehmen, 1978: No. 437, 478 ff.; Sondergutachten 5, 6 Karstadt/Neckermann, Thyssen/Hüller/Hille, 1977; Sondergutachten 10 Zusammenschluß der IBH Holding AG mit der WIBAU AG: 1982: Nos. 64-69; Möschel, 1979a: 487.

3.2 Reactions

(1) Reduction or Increase of Complexity

The strategy of ***reducing complexity*** in order to improve enforcement power can be seen very early in the history of the law of restrictive trade practices. Already in 1911 the U.S. Supreme Court, under the Sherman Act of 1890, developed the so-called ***per se rules*** (*Standard Oil Co. of New Jersey* v. *U.S.*, 221 U.S. 1 (1911) and *U.S.* v. *American Tobacco Co.*, 221 U.S. 106 (1911); Sullivan, 1977: § 67). According to these certain types of conduct were regarded as unreasonable ***per se*** since, due to their nature or their inevitable effects, they were particularly dangerous. Examples of activities which were unreasonable ***per se*** include price arrangements, limiting of output, sharing out of sectors and markets, collective boycotts or refusals to supply, tie-in deals, etc. The intent was to enable such conduct to be dealt with rapidly and forcefully as violations of the Sherman Act, without having to determine, in every single case, whether a restrictive trade practice in fact existed, as was necessary under the rule of reason. The company was not allowed to refute this presumption. It was accepted that in individual cases, conduct that was not really in restraint of trade might be prohibited for the sake of simplifying the enforcement of the antitrust laws.

Similar burden reducing effects can result from the establishment of cartel law norms which already cover cases of potential worsening of competition, or already contain or permit market-structure decisions instead of market conduct control relating to concrete abuse in particular cases. In the German discussion of the reform of cartel law, proposals have, for example, been made that company mergers be absolutely prohibited (Hoppmann, 1972: 59 ff.: "prohibition of mergers as a general ***per se rule***"), or at least prohibited above a certain size[29]. Reform proposals linked to absolute size criteria have also been discussed in the U.S. in relation to purely conglomerate mergers (Möschel, 1983: Nos. 53, 730). Such wide-reaching proposals have not, however, become the law in any country and rightly so, since a generalized judgement on mergers, as comparable to the ***per se rule***, is not acceptable considering the economically complex assessment required.

What has become law instead, however, are certain types of legal presumptions, as in section 23 (a) GWB, introduced by the 4th GWB amendment of 1980. Under this section, in the case of vertical and conglomerate mergers of a size aimed, above all, at turnover and market volume, the presumption exists that a dominating market position will arise or be reinforced as a result of the merger. Similar presumptions, yet related to shares of the market in section 22, (3) GWB were already introduced by the 2nd GWB amendment in 1973 in the reform of control of abuses by market-dominating companies. The legislative history of these presumptions is a good

[29] Hoppmann, 1972: 88 ff. According to Hoppmann, at least in the field of specific kinds of mergers, where developed knowledge about their adverse effect on competition exists, e.g., objective criteria of absolute size in turnover, capital, etc. in the area of superconcentration.

example of the lack of clarity in setting objectives, as mentioned above. The legal committee of the German Parliament wanted to regard the presumptions as being no more than simple bases for action, while the economic policy committee wanted to give them genuine substantive effect. The result is that today, particularly since the Kloeckner-Becorit decision of the *Bundesgerichtshof-Zivilsachen* (BGHZ 79, 62 at 65 ff. Wirtschaft und Wettbewerb (WuW)/E BGB 1749 (1754)), there is agreement that the principle of official investigation (*Amtsermittlungsgrundsatz*) continues to apply fully to cartel authorities and courts, and that a presumptive effect only follows on the reaching of a final *non liquet.* The importance of the presumptions is thus limited in practice (Möschel, 1981: § 22 No. 92).

A more frequent strategy is that of *increasing* complexity in order to arrive at better decisions. This runs like a thread through the stages in the development of juridification in the law of restrictive trade practices, as discussed above. In Germany, the continuously reformed control of abuses by market-dominating companies offers rich material for consideration which does not need to be examined here in detail. A few examples will suffice. The legislature in the 2nd GWB amendment introduced a superior market position test (section 22 (1) No. 2 GWB) as an alternative criterion of market domination. In addition to the old definition of market domination (section 22 (1) No. 1 GWB), which assumed a total absence of competitors, or at least of important competition. This does not represent, as some have assumed, a turning away from the concept of market power, but rather the expansion of an isolated market share approach. New criteria are taken into account, above all financial power and cash flow, access to supply and sale markets, interlocking relationships with other companies and advantages deriving from them, as well as legal or actual barriers to market access by new competitors. Certainly this facilitates the proof of market domination for the courts concerned, but this is precisely because the legislature has given them more comprehensive criteria to use which must be taken into account in a comprehensive view of all relevant circumstances (Möschel, 1981a: § 22 No. 54). An example of the increase in complexity in application of the law is the attempt to institute price controls within the framework of the control of abuses by companies, which has been approved in various legal systems by the courts, especially in the pharmaceutical sector. The related theoretical and practical problems have been thoroughly discussed. They concern the supplementing of market-conduct and market-structure criteria with noncompatible market-results criteria and are evident, e.g., in remarks which seem somewhat arbitrary concerning comparable markets in terms of space, nature and time, and in the granting of various surcharges as a kind of safety margin in case of uncertainty about hypothetical prices under competitive conditions[30].

[30] See for Germany BGHZ 67, 104 = WuW/E BGH 1435 "Vitamin B-12" and also BGHZ 68, 23 = WuW/E BGH 1445 "Valium I" and BGHZ 76, 142 = WuW/E BGH 1678 "Valium II"; for the EEC under Art. 86 case 27/76 United Brands Co. v. Commission [1978] ECR 207 and before Commission (Dec. 17, 1975)

The examples given relate to an increase in complexity due to increasingly far-reaching and complicated legal rules. Another type of increase in complexity occurs when analyses made by economists are given a comprehensive role in cartel law, as is the case in the U.S. Materially this results not only in a rethinking of the whole of antitrust law, but also in the direct relevance of arguments between different schools of economic thought, such as the one between the Chicago School, the Harvard School and their manifold adaptations and nuances. One example among others is provided by the widely varying positions of these schools in relation to economic concentration and the value of legal merger control (Kirchner, 1980: 563, 574 ff.). Procedurally this is reflected in calculations as to the optimization of enforcement of cartel law from welfare-economy viewpoints (Kirchner, 1980: 579-581). This has practical consequences for the role of the Federal Trade Commission as a whole and, within the latter, for the Bureau of Economics (Katzmann, 1980: 36 ff.).

(2) Attempts to Increase Efficiency

A further strategy is based on technocratic improvements. The first reaction to problems relating to the application of cartel law is frequently to demand wider competences of intervention as well as sharper powers of enforcement. Such *attempts to increase efficiency* may concern real loopholes in enforcement, but are frequently fairly superficial, and reflect an unquestioned belief in technocracy. Examples of the *closing of gaps* are provided by sections 37 (a) and (b) GWB, introduced by the second and fourth GWB amendments. Section 37 (a) GWB enables cartel authorities to execute an objective process of prohibition irrespective of individual fault. On the basis of the earlier version of the GWB it had been generally assumed that the choice of sanctions was limited to the nullification of contracts, compensation of damages, and imposition of fines. Accordingly the public authorities were very often restricted to the imposition of fines. In this situation, however, the authorities were requried to demonstrate fault, which they were rarely able to do. The federal cartel office welcomed the new objective process of prohibition and now believes that it can act more rapidly and effectively than before against companies whose conduct constitutes a form of restrictive trade practice (BKartA, Tätigkeitsbericht 1974 BTDrS 7/3791, 1975: 94). In the meantime, the fourth GWB amendment of 1980 has further extended the uses of the objective prohibition process (Bericht des Wirtschaftsausschusses zum Regierungsentwurf einer Vierten GWB-Novelle, BTDrS 8/3690, 1980: 29.). Under section 37 (b) GWB, a company with a dominant position on the market which continues an abusive practice even after a complaint from the cartel authority, can have the resulting revenues confiscated. That result would not have been guaranteed by simply extending the damage compensation obligation under section 35 (2)

O.J. 95/1 (April 9, 1976) case 85/76 Hoffmann-La Roche v. Commission [1979] ECR 461; for Great Britain the "Valium-Librium" report of the Monopolies Commission 1973; see Möschel 1974: 97 ff.

GWB (Regierungsentwurf Vierte GWB-Novelle, BTDrS 8/2136, 1978: 15, 26; Bericht des Wirtschaftsausschusses, BTDrS 8/3690, 1980: 28). The Monopoly Commission had spoken against this reform, as did most commentators, because, among other reasons, it opened up such broad scope of discretion for the cartel authority that practicability and legal control by the courts were prejudiced, and because there seemed to be no real practical need for the rule (Monopolkommission, 2. Hauptgutachten, 1978: No. 399). These arguments, which did not impress the legislature, show the difficulty of trying to solve fundamental problems by applying new sanctions. Looked at more closely, it becomes evident as well that to calculate extra profit due to excessive price demands is highly unreliable, as is already clear from the above mentioned theoretical and practical difficulties of price control where market-dominating companies are concerned (Emmerich, 1981: Nos. 18-27). Unless one simply skips over this by using a greatly simplified method of calculation, or by making an estimate according to section 37 (b) (3) GWB, (which would be very problematic), there is not much left of a tangible gain in enforcement. One example of attempts to increase efficiency which create more fundamental problems is the effort sometimes made to criminalize particular restrictive trade practices such as conspiracies in tender offers as for example in the building industry (Möschel, 1980a). Broadening the application of deconcentration instruments in German law, following the American pattern, is another example (Möschel, 1979; Oehler, 1976). This could lead to greater efficiency especially if these measures are not restriced to mergers in restraint of trade, but are aimed more generally at an improved market structure.

In any case, the enforcement agencies expect that increases in efficiency would be achieved by *enlarging personnel and financial resources.* The differences between the various national cartel law systems become particularly evident here (Schmidt, I., 1973: 100). The phenomenon in the U.S., according to which control decisions are made not only by increasing personnel and budgets, but also by cutting them back is so far not observable in Germany. It is true that large-scale reforms with new tasks usually go together with rather limited personnel and budget allocations. Here we may discern a controlling decision in the fact that the cartel authority has to organize the fashion in which it will fulfill the new functions, being obliged to reallocate resources hitherto devoted to previous tasks. This was the case e.g. with the introduction of merger control. In times of general financial shortages, cutbacks in normal increases can also be observed. However, due to the specific structures of the German system, decisive cutbacks, which would result in the drawing off and reallocation of resources allocated to cartel law, are not to be expected. This touches on the more fundamental problem of what role organizations and bureaucracies embedded in a specific system can play generally in the administration and enforcement of antitrust law (Scharpf, 1970). The question of personnel and financial resources only scratches the surface of this. A linked question, discussed in various countries, is whether an increase in the number of economists in enforcement agencies would result in efficiency gains. Interestingly enough, it is the representatives of the Chicago School who are reserved in their attitude towards the actual integration potential of such institutionalized cooperation (Dam, 1976: 385).

Finally, increased efficiency in the enforcement of antitrust law is conceivable as a result of greater use being made of ***private initiatives.*** This strategy in antitrust law comes from the U.S. Section 4 of the Clayton Act, for example, gives private persons the right to claim treble damages in a private action if they have been injured by a violation of antitrust laws. In addition, private prohibitory actions can be brought. The number of suits of this type filed by private persons is many times that brought by the cartel authorities (Möschel, 1983: No. 52). In other systems of antitrust law, private claims for damages have also been tried or discussed (Linder, 1980; Steindorff, 1974: 504, 509 ff.). In Germany in section 35, (2) GWB, inserted by the fourth GWB amendment, an attempt has been made to fill the so-called sanction loop-hole in the case of abuse orders. This loop-hole resulted from the fact that section 22 (4) GWB is not officially recognised as a protective law giving rise to damage claims. The problem of whether decisive improvements can be achieved through private initiatives, and what precautions should be taken against excessive mobilization of private individuals and their lawyers has not yet been fully discussed even in the U.S., as recent contributions from the Chicago School show (Posner, 1976: 227-232; Breit and Elzinga, 1974: 329; Kirchner, 1980: 579-581). Additional problems emerge when this strategy is transferred into the legal systems of other countries. Besides different legal mechanisms and traditions, surrounding social and cultural fields must be taken into account, as illustrated by the frequently heard claim that, for example, the British are not so "litigious" as the Americans.

(3) More Flexible Mechanisms

A set of further strategies which individually are extremely heterogeneous is on the other hand aimed at pulling back the scope and enforcement of law, or at least loosening it through ***more flexible mechanisms.*** Behind this stand to some extent considerations of pure practicability. Partially, however, there are also more fundamental positions relating to the role of law and juridification. In the U.S. these are to some extent influenced by the economic analysis of law, while some are on the bandwagon of the deregulation discussion and then proceed to demand a retreat of antitrust law in certain areas.

In various legal systems the disposal of cases by settlement or by assurances plays a considerable role. In the U.S., in antitrust law as well as other areas, *consent decrees* are of tremendous importance. One estimate is that as many as 80% of all cases which come before the antitrust division of the Justice Department are settled by consent decree (Sullivan, 1977: 758. Generally Kienast, 1978; Windbichler, 1980: 619). These consent decrees however have ambivalent effects. On the one hand, they give the cartel authority the opportunity to succeed where it might have failed before a court, and to consider and stop selected forms of conduct which are strategically more important to it than others. On the other hand, the risk to the public interest inherent in the pursuit of antitrust law violations is considerable. Quite apart from repeatedly occurring, politically motivated, or at least politically influenced settlements such as the spectacular IT&T settlement under the Nixon administration during the Watergate period (Sullivan, 1977: § 208, 243 b.), it is easy for a cartel authority, as a result of overwork and a faulty assessment of a case's importance and its chances before a court, to agree to a settlement which it subsequently comes to regret. The Antitrust Procedures and Penalties Act endeavours to establish barriers against such settlements by mandatory publicity, hearings, and judicial substantiation.

The practice of settling cartel cases by *assurances* of the companies concerned exists to some extent in the British merger control system (Opie, 1982: 35; Korah, 1982a: 63, 69; Weiler, 1982: 196). This is regarded as presenting no problems since this form of dispute settlement is in conformity with British concepts of control based on self-regulation, compromise, and out-of-court settlements (Rider, 1978: 319-348). In contrast to this, the problem of assurances within the framework of German merger control has become the object of fundamental discussions. It is even said that the assurance policy of the federal cartel office is among the most disputed matters in German merger control law (Möschel, 1983: No. 882). In the practice of the federal cartel office one can identify different types of assurances, above all assurances to divest or to sell, assurances concerning voting right restrictions, and other limitations on influence, and so-called open market assurances (for the latest cases of assurances see BKartA, Tätigkeitsbericht 1983/84, BTDrS 10/3550, 1985: 48-52). The intention of the last of these is to keep access to supplier markets open to the third party companies affected, if necessary even by participation in a joint venture, as for example with regard to the Feldmuehle AG: Kopparfors A/B and PWA Papierwerke Waldhof-Aschaffenburg AG/ Svenska Cellulosa A/B (BKartA, Tätigkeitsbericht 1979/80, BTDrS 9/565, 1980: 73-74). Apart from many more technical points, the main dispute turns on whether the cartel authority can rely on companies' assurances to carry out measures during a time which comes after the expiry of the period of prohibition of the merger. Both practice and scholarship generally allow this, but if the promises are not kept, considerable difficulties arise (Möschel, 1983: No. 884). Federal cartel office policies regarding open market assurances meet with opposition because their separation from assurances relating to company behavior, which are forbidden by law (section 24 (3) 4 GWB), is unclear. Above all, they are opposed because such assurances lead to officially promoted collaboration between the parties concerned and thus may be the seed for anticompetitive concerted actions or even cartels at a later stage[31].

Informal procedural practices, however, exist elsewhere as well. In the U.S., for example, there is the Federal Trade Commission practice of publishing industry guides on the basis of detailed hearings which offer all parties the

[31] E.g., Monopolkommission, 4. Hauptgutachten 1980/81, BTDrS 9/1892, 1982: No. 643-648 with regard to the opening clauses; generally to the practice of assurances Mestmäcker, 1981: § 24 No. 187.

chance to express their opinions, and thus give the different branches of industry points of reference regarding the practice to be expected from the Commission (Sullivan, 1977: § 243 a. See also the Department of Justice Merger Guidelines 1985). The corresponding procedure in individual cases is to give a so-called "advisory opinion" concerning specific actions intended by a company and submitted to the Commission. In other legal systems similar features can be found, e.g.: the Administrative Principles for the Assessment of Structural Crises and Rationalization Cartels, published by the German Federal Cartel Office (March 31, 1978, Bundesanzeiger (BAnz.) No. 66 of April 4, 1978. Cf. § 50 (1) 4 GWB), the leaflet of the Federal Minister for the Economy concerning the facilitation of cooperation amongst small and medium-sized companies under section 5 b GWB (Information sheet of April 15, 1975, reprinted in Immenga and Mestmäcker, 1981: Textanhang 5), and information to the press supplied by the German Federal Cartel Office concerning the handling of market information processes under cartel law (Press information of the BKartA No. 8/77 of Jan. 24, 1977, reprinted in Immenga and Mestmäcker, 1981: Textanhang 2). The activity reports of the German Federal Cartel Office also play a carefully considered role here (cf. § 50 GWB).

We are concerned here with information supplied to companies concerning current or planned enforcement practices of the cartel authority. The complementary question of information to the cartel authority, private plaintiffs, and cartel law-makers, constitutes a problem which is important to solve if the crisis of growth in cartel law is to be overcome. The instrumentalization of information and disclosure for preventive enforcement purposes (Loss, 1985), relied on in other areas such as company law, also plays a role in cartel law, although a much smaller one. Examples of this are the publication of a planned consent decree in the U.S. (Windbichler, 1981: 56), and German competition rules and cartel register (§ 9, 28 ff. GWB). Simple obligations to disclose, instead of prohibition and intervention norms, have so far proved to be transitional solutions, even when the transition period has been long, as was the case in Germany with rudimentary merger disclosure obligations (§ 23, 24 GWB (1957) until the 2nd GWB-Amendment 1973). The problem of information access for those bringing private actions, whose initiatives are to be mobilized for enforcement, is currently being discussed in the U.S. (Kirchner, 1980: 580). Finally, one should note the American practice of holding extensive inquiries and hearings before legislative bodies (for example, the Hearings on Economic Concentration, 1965-1969 in Washington, D.C.).

Institutional and organizational slackening of antitrust law enforcement is illustrated by the setting up of *advisory commissions*, which has taken place in different countries. In Germany, the Monopoly Commission is responsible for publishing biannual and special supplementary reports concerning company concentration, individual merger projects, and related problems. This provides an advisory opinion from a body independent of government, business, and labor unions, which has expert knowledge in economic and other fields (§ 24 b (1) 2, (2) GWB). The British Monopolies and Mergers Commission (Opie, 1982: 34; Korah, 1982a: 56) is similar, as is in principle the French Commission de la concurrence (Azéma, 1981: Nos. 455; Burst and Kovar, 1981: Nos. 444, 588-590) which, however, appears on the whole to be more closely tied to the administration. Striking in comparison is the German separation between legal merger control aimed at competition, exercised by the cartel authority, and political control aimed at the general public welfare, exercised by the Minister. The separation between these two levels leads to a clearer distinction between different interests, canalizes lobbying influences, and forces the Minister of Economic Affairs, if he insists on approving a merger prohibited by the cartel authority, to make a clearly justified and reasoned decision (see in this context Weiler, 1982: 199). The difference between an administrative level and a prior level of self-administration, as in the enforcement of company and capital market law where it has great importance (Hopt, 1975: 148-168), plays an inferior role in cartel law, being relevant e.g. in efforts to obtain cartel free cooperation (Kartte, 1982: 149; Veltins, 1982: 93; Emmerich, 1982: § 9, 1976: 167-187), or in the establishment of competition rules (Wolf, 1972; Baur, 1977: 293; Mees, 1981: 878). Competition is a matter of chance and risk for the individual company, not a matter for professional or sectorial organizations which naturally tend towards arrangements.

Finally we must come back to the phenomenon, already discussed above in another context, of legally nonbinding international codes and rules of conduct in the area of antitrust law (Fikentscher and Straub, 1982; von Hahn, 1982). As is the case with other extra-legal and quasi-legal principles of conduct, directives and rules (so-called *soft-law*) (Hopt, 1977: 324-331; Horn, 1980; Waldman, 1980; Kolvenbach, 1982: 381), one is initially inclined to see these as an alternative to formal legal regulation. It is precisely in antitrust law, however, that this is true only to a limited extent. Rather the problem is to formulate principles against restrictive trade practices in international law, in particular for those countries which still have no national antitrust law. The nonbinding nature of the rules is explicable therefore not in terms of the superiority or specific advantages of a cartel policy with more flexible mechanisms, but in terms of the realities of national sovereignty and international politics. This is confirmed by the observation that in the initial stages of negotiations, legally binding norms are always demanded but are not politically attainable and that after the enactment of legally nonbinding rules of conduct, attempts immediately begin to assign a certain legal force to these rules. At least in the international sphere, and in any case in antitrust law, soft law is generally a step towards more, rather than less, law (Fikentscher, 1983: 68 ff.; Meessen, 1981: 1131).

(4) Rejection of a General Criticism of Juridification and Overall Strategy of Deregulation for the Law of Restrictive Trade Practices

If we consider the stages in the development of juridification in the law of restrictive trade practices, and the proposed reforms and strategies of regulation and deregulation discussed in relation to the crisis in growth, we can see that because of the complex findings and the uniformly unsolved problems, we must be careful not to make generalizing judgements in conclusion. What is necessary, however, is to reject all general criticisms of juridification (see generally Abel, 1980: 27-47) and the dream of a general deregulation strategy in antitrust law. If we choose a market economy, we must fix and maintain its framework conditions through law. In this sense it is correct to say that competition is a creation of the state. A differentiated cartel and merger control with a corresponding apparatus for its enforcement is necessary. We can argue about the type and scope of norms and enforcement, but not about a withdrawal of the legal system in general. Order: through law, or through cartels and monopolies — for economic and social policy reasons the appropriate choice is clear.

[Translated from the German by John Hearsum]

References

ABEL, Richard L. (1980) "Delegalization, A Critical Review of its Ideology, Manifestations, and Social Consequences", in E. Blankenburg *et al.* (eds.), *Alternative Rechtsformen und Alternativen zum Recht.* Opladen: Westdeutscher Verlag.

ADOLPH, Johannes (1980) "Protection of Trading Interests Bill im britischen Unterhaus", 30 *Wirtschaft und Wettbewerb* 181.

ARANOW, Edward R., Herbert A. EINHORN and George BERLSTEIN (1977) *Developments in Tender Offers for Corporate Control.* New York: Columbia University Press.

AREEDA, Phillip and Donald F. TURNER (1978-1980) *Antitrust Law*, 5 vols. Boston: Little, Brown & Co.

ARNDT, Helmut (1971) *Die Konzentration der Wirtschaft*, 2nd Ed. Berlin: Duncker & Humblot.

ASSMANN, Heinz-Dieter (1980) "Zur Steuerung gesellschafts-ökonomischer Entwicklung durch Recht", in H.D. Assmann *et al.* (eds.), *Wirtschaftsrecht als Kritik des Privatrechts.* Königstein: Athenäum.

— (1980a) *Wirtschaftsrecht in der Mixed Economy.* Königstein: Athenäum.

AUTENRIETH, Karl-Heinz (1983) "Der britische Protection of Trading Interests Act im System des internationalen Kartellrechts", 29 *Recht der Internationalen Wirtschaft* 15.

AZÉMA, Jacques (1981) *Le droit français de la concurrence.* Paris: Presses Universitaires de France.

BAUR, Jürgen (1977) "Wettbewerbsregeln und Außenseiter", 141 *Zeitschrift für das gesamte Handelsrecht und Wirtschaftsrecht* 293.

BERG, Hartmut (1982) "Internationale Wettbewerbsfähigkeit und nationale Zusammenschlußkontrolle", in *Festschrift Arno Sölter.* Köln: Heymanns.

BLANKENBURG, Erhard, Ekkehard KLAUSA and Hubert ROTTLEUTHNER (1980) *Alternative Rechtsformen und Alternativen zum Recht.* Opladen: Westdeutscher Verlag.

BORK, Robert H. (1978) *The Antitrust Paradox.* New York: Basic Books.

BREIT, William and Kenneth G. ELZINGA (1974) "Antitrust Enforcement and Economic Efficiency: the Uneasy Case for Treble Damages", 17 *Journal of Law & Economics* 329.

Brüggemeier, Gerd (1980) "Probleme einer Theorie des Wirtschaftsrechts", in H. D. Assmann *et al.* (eds.), *Wirtschaftsrecht als Kritik des Privatrechts.* Königstein: Athenäum.

Burst, Jean-Jacques and Robert Kovar (1981) *Droit de la concurrence.* Paris: Economica.

Büscher, Rolf (1982) *Diagonale Unternehmenszusammenschlüsse im amerikanischen und deutschen Recht.* Baden-Baden: Nomos.

Calvani, Terry and John Siegfried (1979) *Economic Analysis and Antitrust Law.* Boston: Little, Brown and Co.

Champaud, Claude (1982) "Merger Control in France: Direct and Indirect Ways of Control", in K.J. Hopt (ed.), *European Merger Control, Legal and Economic Analyses on Multinational Enterprises,* Vol. I. Berlin: De Gruyter.

Clarkson, Kenneth W. and Timothy J. Muris (1981) *The Federal Trade Commission since 1970, Economic Regulation and Bureaucratic Behaviour.* Cambridge: University Press.

Clement B. (1974) "An Appraisal of French Antitrust Policy", 19 *Antitrust Bulletin* 587.

Crandall, Robert W. (1983), "Deregulation: The U.S. Experience", 139 *Zeitschrift für die gesamte Staatswissenschaft* 419.

Cunningham, James P. (1973, 1974, Supplement 1978) *The Fair Trading Act.* London: Sweet & Maxwell.

Dam, Kenneth W. (1976) "Comment", 14 *Journal of Law & Economics* 385.

EG-Kommission, (1973-1976) *Das Wirtschaftsrecht der Mitgliederstaaten der Europäischen Gemeinschaften in einer Wirtschafts- und Währungsunion,* 7 vols. Bruxelles: Amt für amtliche Veröffentlichungen der EG.

Elzinga, Kenneth G. (1977) "The Goals of Antitrust: Other than Competition and Efficiency, What Else Counts?", 125 *University of Pennsylvania Law Review* 1191.

Emmerich, Volker (1976) "Kooperationen im Wettbewerbsrecht — Kritische Bemerkungen zum gegenwärtigen Stand der Kooperationsdiskussion", 5 *Zeitschrift für Unternehmens- und Gesellschaftsrecht* 167.

— (1981) "Comment on § 37 b GWB", in U. Immenga and E.J. Mestmäcker (eds.), *Kommentar zum GWB.* München: Beck.

— (1982) *Kartellrecht,* 4th Ed. München: Beck.

Fikentscher, Wolfgang (1983) *Wirtschaftsrecht,* Vol. I. München: Beck.

Fikentscher, Wolfgang and Wolfgang Straub (1982) "Der RBP-Kodex der Vereinten Nationen, Weltkartellrichtlinien (I) & (II)", *Gewerblicher Rechtsschutz und Urheberrecht* Int. 637 and 727.

Fischer, Otto (1963) *Bundesgesetz über Kartelle und ähnliche Organisationen.* Bern: Schweizerischer Gewerbeverband.

Fischer, Robert (1978) "Kurzinformation", 28 *Wirtschaft und Wettbewerb* 6.

Fischer, Robert, Arlin M. Adams, Wolfgang Sperl and William R. Cornish (1976) *Das Entscheidungsmaterial der höchstrichterlichen Rechtssprechung. Welche sozialen Konflikte kommen vor die staatliche Gerichtsbarkeit, insbesondere die obersten Gerichte?* Frankfurt a.M.: Metzner.

Galanter, Marc (1980) "Legality and its Discontents: A Preliminary Assessment of the Current Theories of Legalization and Delegalization", in E. Blankenburg *et.al.* (eds.), *Alternative Rechtsformen der Alternativen zum Recht.* Opladen: Westdeutscher Verlag.

Garland, H. B. (1985) "Deregulation and Judicial Review". 98 *Harvard Law Review* 505.

Gavalda, Christian (1979) "Le contrôle des concentrations d'entreprises selon la loi française No. 77-806 du 19 juillet 1977", 97 *Revue des Sociétés.* 473.

GESSNER, Volkmar and Gerd WINTER (1982) *Rechtsformen der Verflechtung von Staat und Wirtschaft.* Opladen: Westdeutscher Verlag.

GIDE-LOYRETTE-NOUEL, Xavier DE ROUX, Dominique VOILLEMOT and Thierry VASSONGNE (1975) *Le droit français de la concurrence.* Paris.

GLAIS, Michel and Philippe LAURENT (1983) *Traité d'économie et de droit de la concurrence.* Paris: Presses Universitaires de France.

GLEISS, Alfred and Martin HIRSCH (1978) *Kommentar zum EWG-Kartellrecht*, 3rd Ed. Heidelberg.

— (1981) *Common Market Cartel Law.* 3rd Ed. Washington D.C.: The Bureau of National Affairs.

GOTTHOLD, Jürgen (1981) "Neuere Entwicklungen der Wettbewerbstheorie. Kritische Bemerkungen zur neo-liberalen Theorie der Wettbewerbspolitik", 145 *Zeitschrift für das gesamte Handels- und Wirtschaftsrecht* 286.

GRAUEL, Holger (1976) "Das deutsch-amerikanische Abkommen über die Zusammenarbeit der Kartellbehörden", 26 *Wirtschaft und Wettbewerb* 764.

— (1977) "Der Hart-Scott-Rodino Antitrust Improvements Act of 1976", 27 *Wirtschaft und Wettbewerb* 385.

— (1978) "Das französische Kartellgesetz vom 19. Juli 1977". 28 *Wirtschaft und Wettbewerb* 751.

HAHN, Helmut von (1982) "Kodex der Vereinten Nationen gegen Wettbewerbsbeschränkungen im internationalen Handel — Chancen und Risiken", in *Festschrift A. Sölter.* Köln: Heymanns.

HAIGHT, George W. (1970) "The Swiss Watch Case", in J. Rahl (ed.), *Common Market and American Antitrust.* New York: MacGraw-Hill.

HANDLER, Milton (1982) "Reforming the Antitrust Law", 82 *Columbia Law Rev.* 1287.

HANNAH, Leslie (1979) "Mergers, Cartels and Concentration: Legal Factors in the U.S. and European Experience", in N. Horn and J. Kocka (eds.), *Recht und Entwicklung der Großunternehmen im 19. und 20. Jahrhundert.* Göttingen: Vandenhoeck and Ruprecht.

HOFFMANN, Dieter (1978) "Einführung einer Fusionskontrolle in Frankreich", 24 *Recht der Internationalen Wirtschaft* 566.

HOPPMANN, Erich (1972) *Fusionskontrolle.* Tübingen: Mohr and Siebeck.

HOPT, Klaus J. (1972) "Rechtssoziologische und rechtsinformatorische Aspekte im Wirtschaftsrecht", 27 *Betriebs-Berater* 1017.

— (1975) *Der Kapitalanlegerschutz im Recht der Banken.* München: Beck.

— (1977) "Recht und Geschäftsmoral multinationaler Unternehmen", in *Festschrift Tübinger Juristenfakultät.* Tübingen: Mohr and Siebeck.

— (1978) "Book-review: EG-Kommission, 'Das Wirtschaftsrecht der Mitgliedstaaten der Europäischen Gemeinschaften in einer Wirtschafts- und Währungsunion'", 13 *Europarecht* 81.

— (1980) "Book-review: H. Dietrich 'Die Tender Offer im Bundesrecht der Vereinigten Staaten'", 44 *Rabelszeitschrift* 180.

— (1982) "Merger Control in Germany: Philosophies, Experiences, Reforms", in K.J. Hopt (ed.) *European Merger Control, Legal and Economic Analyses on Multinational Enterprises*, Vol. I. Berlin: De Gruyter.

— (1984) "Wettbewerbsbeschränkungen und Verrechtlichung" in H.F. Zacher, *et al.* (eds.), *Verrechtlichung von Wirtschaft, Arbeit und sozialer Solidarität.* Baden-Baden: Nomos.

HOPT, Klaus J. and Gunther TEUBNER (eds.) (1985) *Corporate Governance and Directors' Liabilities — Legal, Economic and Sociological Analyses on Corporate Social Responsibility.* Berlin: De Gruyter.

HORN, Norbert (1980) *Legal Problems of Codes of Conduct for Multinational Enterprises.* Deventer: Kluwer.

IMMENGA, Ulrich (1981) "Comment on § 1 GWB", in U. Immenga and E.J. Mestmäcker (eds.), *Kommentar zum GWB.* München: Beck.

IMMENGA, Ulrich and Ernst-Joachim MESTMÄCKER (1981) *Kommentar zum GWB.* München: Beck.

JACQUEMIN, Alexis (1982) "Concentration and Mergers in the European Economic Community: Towards a System of Control", in K.J. Hopt (ed.) *European Merger Control, Legal and Economic Analyses on Multinational Enterprises,* Vol. I. Berlin: De Gruyter.

JEANTET, Fernand-Charles (1977) "La loi sur le contrôle des concentrations économiques en France", *Jurisclasseur Périodique* (ed. G.) I 2879.

JENNY, Frederic and André Paul WEBER (1975) "French Antitrust Legislation: An Exercise in Futility?", 20 *Antitrust Bulletin* 597.

KARTTE, Wolfgang (1982) "Wettbewerb und Kooperation", in *Festschrift A. Sölter.* Köln: Heymanns.

KATZMANN, Robert A. (1980) *Regulatory Bureaucracy: The Federal Trade Commission and Antitrust Policy.* Cambridge, Mass.; London: Massachusetts Institute of Technology Press.

KAUFER, Erich (1977) *Konzentration und Fusionskontrolle.* Tübingen: Mohr and Siebeck.

KAUFER, Erich and Charles B. BLANKART (1983) "Regulation in Western Germany: the State of the Debate", 139 *Zeitschrift für die gesamte Staatswissenschaft* 435.

KIENAST, Peter J. (1978) *Consent Settlements im amerikanischen Antitrustverfahren.* Diessenhofen: Rüegger.

KIRCHNER, Christian (1980) "'Ökonomische Analyse des Rechts' und Recht der Wettbewerbsbeschränkungen (antitrust law and economics)", 144 *Zeitschrift für das gesamte Handelsrecht und Wirtschaftsrecht* 563.

KOLVENBACH, Walter (1982) "Verhaltenskodices für multinationale Unternehmen: Problem oder Hoffnung?", in *Festschrift A. Sölter.* Köln: Heymanns.

KOPPENSTEINER, Hans-Georg (1981) *Wettbewerbsrecht.* Wien: Orac.

KORAH, Valentine (1982) *Competition Law of Britain and the Common Market,* 3rd Ed. The Hague: Nijhoff.

— (1982a) "Control of Mergers in the U.K. on Grounds of Competition: Legislation, Practice and Experience", in K.J. Hopt (ed.), *European Merger Control, Legal and Economic Analyses on Multinational Enterprises,* Vol. I. Berlin: De Gruyter.

LENEL, Hans Otto (1968) *Ursachen der Konzentration,* 2nd Ed. Tübingen: Mohr and Siebeck.

LINDER, Ludwig (1980) *Privatklage und Schadensersatz im Kartellrecht.* Baden-Baden: Nomos.

LOSS, Louis (1985) "Disclosure as Preventive Enforcement", in K.J. Hopt and G. Teubner (eds.), *Corporate Governance and Directors' Liabilities.* Berlin: De Gruyter.

MARFELS, Christian (1977) *Erfassung und Darstellung industrieller Konzentration.* Baden-Baden: Nomos.

MEES, Hans-Kurt (1981) "Die Wettbewerbsregeln des GWB: Verbindlichkeit und Bedeutung im Wettbewerbsprozess", 83 *Gewerblicher Rechtsschutz und Urheberrecht* 878.

MEESSEN, Karl Matthias (1975) *Völkerrechtliche Grundsätze des internationalen Kartellrechts.* Baden-Baden: Nomos.

— (1981) "Internationale Verhaltenskodizes und Sittenwidrigkeitsklauseln", 34 *Neue Juristische Wochenschrift* 1181.

— (1984) *Kollisionsrecht der Zusammenschlußkontrolle.* Baden-Baden: Nomos.

MERTENS, Hans-Joachim, Christian KIRCHNER and Erich SCHANZE (1982) *Wirtschaftsrecht*, 2nd Ed. Opladen: Westdeutscher Verlag.

MERZ, Hans (1967) *Das schweizerische Kartellgesetz*. Bern: Stämpfli.

MESTMÄCKER, Ernst-Joachim (1974) *Europäisches Wettbewerbsrecht*. München: Beck.

— (1981) "Comment on § 24 GWB", in U. Immenga and E.J. Mestmäcker (eds.), *Kommentar zum GWB*. München: Beck.

— (1984) *Der verwaltete Wettbewerb*, Tübingen: Mohr and Siebeck.

— (1984) *Recht und ökonomisches Gesetz*, 2nd Ed. Baden-Baden: Nomos.

MÖSCHEL, Wernhard (1972) *70 Jahre Deutsche Kartellpolitik*. Tübingen: Mohr and Siebeck.

— (1974) *Der Oligopolmißbrauch im Recht der Wettbewerbsbeschränkungen. Eine rechtsvergleichende Untersuchung zum Recht der USA, Großbritanniens, der EWG und der Bundesrepublik Deutschland*. Tübingen: Mohr and Siebeck.

— (1978) *Pressekonzentration und Wettbewerbsgesetz*. Tübingen: Mohr and Siebeck.

— (1979) *Entflechtungen im Recht der Wettbewerbsbeschränkungen*. Tübingen: Mohr and Siebeck.

— (1979a) "Die Sanierungsfusion im Recht der Zusammenschlußkontrolle", in *Festschrift R. Fischer*. Berlin: De Gruyter.

— (1980) "Konglomerate Zusammenschlüsse im Antitrustrecht der Vereinigten Staaten von Amerika", 44 *Rabelszeitschrift* 203.

— (1980a) *Zur Problematik einer Kriminalisierung von Submissionsabsprachen*. Köln: Heymanns.

— (1981) "Comment on § 22 GWB", in U. Immenga and E.J. Mestmäcker (eds.), *Kommentar zum GWB*. München: Beck.

— (1981a) "Dekonzentration als Mittel der Wettbewerbspolitik", in *Kontrolle von Marktmacht nach deutschem, europäischem und amerikanischem Kartellrecht*. Köln: Heymanns.

— (1981b) "Neuere Entwicklungen der Wettbewerbstheorie, kritische Bemerkungen zu kritischen Bemerkungen", 145 *Zeitschrift für das gesamte Handelsrecht und Wirtschaftsrecht* 590.

— (1983) *Recht der Wettbewerbsbeschränkungen*. Köln: Heymanns.

— (1984) "Die erste Entflechtungsentscheidung in der Fusionskontrolle", 13 *Zeitschrift für Unternehmens- und Gesellschaftsrecht* 655.

NEALE, Alan D. and George D. GOYDER (1980) *The Antitrust Laws of the United States of America*, 3rd Ed.. Cambridge: Cambridge University Press.

NEUMANN, Jens (1979) "Anmeldepflicht bei Unternehmenszusammenschlüssen im US-Antitrustrecht", 29 *Wirtschaft und Wettbewerb* 100.

— (1979) "Foreign Nondisclosure Laws and Domestic Discovery Orders in Antitrust Litigation", 88 *Yale Law Journal* 612.

OECD (1974) *Export Cartels, Report of the Committee of Experts on Restrictive Business Practices*. Paris: OECD.

— (1977) *Restrictive Business Practices of Multinational Enterprises, Report of the Committee of Experts on Restrictive Business Practices*. Paris: OECD.

— (1984) *Merger Policies and Recent Trends in Mergers*. Paris: OECD.

— (1984a) *Competition Law Enforcement — International Co-operation in the Collection of Information*. Paris: OECD.

OEHLER, Wolfgang (1976) *Entflechtung und Kontrahierungszwang. Methoden und Erfahrungen im amerikanischen Recht der Wettbewerbsbeschränkungen*. Baden-Baden: Nomos.

OMMESLAGHE, Pierre van and B. VAN DE WALLE DE GHELCKE (1984) "Les articles 85 et 86 du traité de Rome à travers les arrêts de la Cour", *Cahiers de Droit Européen* 54.

OPIE, Roger G. (1982) "Merger Policy in the United Kingdom", in K.J. Hopt (ed.), *European Merger Control, Legal and Economic Analyses on Multinational Enterprises*, Vol. I. Berlin: De Gruyter.

OPPENHEIM, Chesterfield F. and Glen WESTON (1981) *Federal Antitrust Laws*, 4th Ed. St. Paul, Minnesota: West Publishing Co.

PETTIT, P.C.F. and C.J.D. STYLES (1982) "The International Response to the Extra-territorial Application of United States Antitrust Law", 37 *The Business Lawyer* 697.

PITOFSKY, Robert (1979) "The Political Content of Antitrust", 127 *University of Pennsylvania Law Review* 1051.

PLAISANT, R., J. LASSIER and J. EEPSTEIN(1978) "Le contrôle des concentrations en France: La loi No. 77-806 du 19 juillet 1977", *Dalloz Sirey Chronique* 99-108.

— (1979) "Die Zusammenschlußkontrolle in Frankreich", 29 *Wirtschaft und Wettbewerb* 551.

POSNER, Richard A. (1976) *Antitrust Law: An Economic Perspective.* Chicago: Little, Brown and Co.

— (1981) "Divestiture, Deconcentration and Antitrust Policy", in *Kontrolle von Marktmacht nach deutschem, europäischem und amerikanischem Kartellrecht.* Köln: Heymanns.

REHBINDER, Eckhard (1981) "Comment on § 6 and § 98 GWB", in U. Immenga and E.J. Mestmäcker (eds.), *Kommentar zum GWB.* München: Beck.

REICH, Norbert (1977) *Markt und Recht.* Neuwied: Luchterhand.

RIDER, Barry A. (1978) "Self-regulation: the British approach to policing conduct in the securities business, with particular reference to the role of the City Panel on Take-overs and Mergers in the regulation of insider trading", 1 *Journal of Comparative Corporate Law and Securities Regulation* 319.

RITTNER, Fritz (1976) "§ 22 GWB im Spannungsfeld wirtschaftswissenschaftlicher Theorien und rechtsstaatlicher Postulate", in *Festschrift G. Hartmann.* Köln: Heymanns.

— (1979) *Wirtschaftsrecht mit Wettbewerbsrecht und Kartellrecht.* Heidelberg: C. F. Müller.

— (1985) *Einführung in das Wettbewerbs- und Kartellrecht*, 2nd Ed. Heidelberg: C.F. Müller.

SCHARPF, Fritz (1970) *Die politischen Kosten des Rechtsstaats.* Tübingen: Mohr and Siebeck.

SCHLUEP, Walter R. (1982) "The Swiss Act on Cartels and the Practice of the Swiss Cartel Commission Concerning Economic Concentration", in K.J. Hopt (ed.), *European Merger Control, Legal and Economic Analyses on Multinational Enterprises*, Vol. I. Berlin: De Gruyter.

SCHMIDT, Ingo (1973) *US-amerikanische und deutsche Wettbewerbspolitik gegenüber Marktmacht.* Berlin: Duncker and Humblot.

SCHMIT, Paul M. (1982) "Multinational Corporations and Merger Control in Community Antitrust Law", in K.J. Hopt (ed.), *European Merger Control, Legal and Economic Analyses on Multinational Enterprises*, Vol. I. Berlin: De Gruyter.

SCHÜRMANN, Leo (1964) *Bundesgesetz über Kartelle und ähnliche Organisationen.* Zürich: Füssli.

SONNENBERGER, Hans Jürgen (1978) "Die Konzentrationskontrolle nach der französischen Kartellrechtsnovelle 1977", 142 *Zeitschrift für das gesamte Handelsrecht und Wirtschaftsrecht* 367.

STEINDORFF, Ernst (1974) "Gesetzgeberische Möglichkeiten zu verbesserter Durchsetzung des Gesetzes gegen Wettbewerbsbeschränkungen", 138 *Zeitschrift für das gesamte Handelsrecht und Wirtschaftsrecht* 504.

— (1985) *Einführung in das Wirtschaftsrecht der Bundesrepublik Deutschland*, 2nd Ed. Darmstadt: Wissenschaftliche Buchgesellschaft.
STEWART, Richard B. (1983) "Regulation in a Liberal State: The Role of Non-Commodity Values", 92 *Yale Law Journal* 1537.
SULLIVAN, Lawrence A. (1977) *Antitrust*. St. Paul, Minnesota: West Publishing Co.
TZOUGANATOS, Dimitris (1983) *Zur Rezeption fremden Rechtsguts im Bereich des Wirtschaftsrechts — dargestellt am Beispiel der Problematik einer Fusionskontrolle nach griechischem Kartellgesetz*. Bonn: Stollfuß.
VELTINS, Michael A. (1982) "Die Wettbewerbsgrenze bei der Zulassung von Mittelstandskartellen gemäß § 5 b GWB", 35 *Der Betrieb* 93.
VOIGT, Rüdiger (1980) *Verrechtlichung*. Königstein: Athenäum.
— (1983) *Gegentendenzen zur Verrechtlichung*. Opladen: Westdeutscher Verlag.
WALDMAN, Raymond J. (1980) *Regulating International Business Through Codes of Conduct*. Washington, D.C.: American Enterprise Institute for Public Policy Research.
WEBER, Max (1967) *Rechtssoziologie*, 2nd Ed. Neuwied: Luchterhand.
WEILER, Joseph H.H. (1982) "Discussion Report", in K.J. Hopt (ed.), *European Merger Control, Legal and Economic Analyses on Multinational Enterprises*. Vol. I. Berlin: De Gruyter.
WEIZSÄCKER, Carl Christian von and Rudolf RICHTER (eds.) (1983), "Regulation, Analysis and Experience in West Germany and the U.S.A.", 139 *Zeitschrift für die gesamte Staatswissenschaft* 375.
WILBERFORCE, Richard O., Alan CAMPELL and Neil ELLES (1966, Supplements 1969, 1973) *The Law of Restrictive Trade Practices and Monopolies*, 2nd Ed. London: Sweet and Maxwell.
WILLEKE, Franz-Ulrich (1980) *Wettbewerbspolitik*. Tübingen: Mohr and Siebeck.
WINDBICHLER, Christiane (1980) "Informal Practices to Avoid Merger Control. Litigation in the U.S. and West-Germany: a Comparison", 25 *Antitrust Bulletin* 619.
— (1981) *Informelles Verfahren bei der Fusionskontrolle*. Heidelberg: Recht und Wirtschaft.
WOLF, Heinz (1972) *Wettbewerbsregeln*. Düsseldorf: Verlag Handelsblatt.

Antitrust: Alternatives to Delegalization

RICHARD S. MARKOVITS
Austin, Texas

This paper will propose an ideal antitrust regime and compare its desirability with that of various procedural or institutional responsive alternatives. Part 2 will explore the ability of antitrust to increase economic (allocative) efficiency. Part 3 will analyze the various distributional, political, and social goals that antitrust might be designed to achieve and explain why antitrust is more able to further some of these objectives than others. Part 4 will delineate four complementary tests that our discussion of goals suggests antitrust authorities should use to assess the legality of particular business practices and explain why the performance of antitrust agencies would be improved if they were also authorized to sell the right to engage in certain kinds of conduct in appropriate circumstances. Part 5 will then examine the methodologies antitrust decisionmakers should employ when applying the tests of Part 4 as well as the sanctions and institutional arrangements that would best enable antitrust regulation to achieve its various goals. And, finally, Part 6 will explain why antitrust is to some extent a responsive approach to the problems caused by business conduct; assess the risk that in practice my ideal antitrust regime would be marked by the same deficiencies that are alleged to undermine purposive law in general and contemporary antitrust law in particular; and examine the likelihood that some more conventional "responsive" procedural or institutional approach would produce better results than my proposal.

1. The Economic Goals of Antitrust: Increasing Economic (Allocative) Efficiency

A policy is said to increase allocative efficiency if it gives its beneficiaries the equivalent[1] of more dollars[2] than it takes away from its victims. Proponents of antitrust have usually emphasized that such policies will increase allocative efficiency in this sense. In particular, antitrust supporters have traditionally argued that pro-competition policies will always increase allocative efficiency by improving relative unit output (RUO) allocation — i.e., the relative proportions in which our economy's various goods and services are produced. Antitrust proponents have based this contention on the fact that an individual monopoly will produce RUO inefficiency if the economy contains no other so-called Pareto imperfections — i.e., if (a) the whole economy is perfectly competitive (there is no monopoly or monopsony in either goods or factor

[1] The phrase "the equivalent of" reflects the fact that policies can affect parties without changing their bank balances. Thus, a policy that benefits someone by improving the quality of the air in the neighborhood in which he owns his house will generate an "equivalent dollar gain" for him equal to the number of dollars he would have had to receive (in some neutral way) to be made as well off as the policy left him. Similarly, a policy that injures someone by reducing the quality of the air in the neighborhood in which he owns his house will impose an equivalent dollar loss on him equal to the number of dollars whose (neutral) loss would have left him as badly off as the policy left him. For a further explanation (e.g., of the point of the word "neutral"), see Markovits, (1975a).

[2] One should therefore note at the outset that in the applied sense in which I will be employing it, the concept of allocative efficiency is a monetary concept. A policy that increases allocative efficiency may therefore decrease utility if the average utility generated per equivalent dollar gained is less than the average utility lost per equivalent dollar lost.

markets); (b) no real externalities are generated (nobody pollutes, for example); (c) no taxes are levied on the margin of income (no income taxes, sales taxes, value added taxes, capital gains taxes, consumption taxes, etc.); (d) no human errors are ever made (no-one ever misperceives his own interest or fails to maximize his perceived interest); and (e) no problems are ever caused by consumer surplus. In fact, however, this argument is based on a *non-sequitur*: the fact that an individual monopoly will cause RUO (and various other kinds of) inefficiency in an otherwise Pareto optimal world does not in itself even make it more likely that a pro-competition policy will increase allocative efficiency in our actual world, in which other Pareto imperfections abound. Roughly speaking, this result reflects the fact that unless one can make a special argument to the contrary one must assume that the imperfections such a pro-competition policy can remedy will be as likely to offset as to compound the other imperfections remaining in the system. In fact, it is possible to make such special arguments in relation to many specific antitrust policies (though it will not be possible to justify a general conclusion that policies that increase competition will always increase efficiency on that account).

2. Antitrust and Allocative Efficiency: A More Sophisticated Approach

In general, antitrust policies can affect allocative efficiency in two general ways. First, antitrust can affect allocative efficiency by altering the defendant's organizational allocative efficiency (OLE) — by reducing the allocative cost he generates when producing and selling a given amount of any particular product. For example, antitrust policies may alter a particular firm's OLE by giving it access to a more efficient production technique, by giving it an incentive to develop such a production technique, or (on the downside) by precluding it from using various control techniques that enable it to lower its transaction or bureaucratic costs (by prohibiting a firm from using a tying device to reduce the cost it has to incur to control the quality of the complements its customers combine or sell with its product or by forbidding the firm to engage in vertical integration when the hierarchical controls such integration would permit are cheaper than the contractual controls that are their next-best alternative).

Second, antitrust can affect allocative efficiency by changing the competitiveness of the economy. We have already seen that monopoly can cause RUO misallocation. In fact, monopoly can also cause many other sorts of misallocation: for example, misallocations of time between productive activities and leisure, misallocations that relate to the set of product types offered by the economy- quantity-vs-quality-or-variety increasing (QV) investment misallocations (that relate to the proportion of our resources we allocate to producing additional product or distributive quality or variety) and inter-industry QV investment misallocations (that relate to the amount of quality and variety we have in some industries relative to others), and misallocations of resources to cost-reducing production-process research. (For an analysis of all these possibilities, see Markovits, 1976).

Monopoly produces such misallocations by distorting the private cost of the relevant choices to the producer and sometimes the private value of such choices as well. Monopoly causes such distortions because firms that face downward-sloping demand curves normally reduce their prices to all their customers when they lower their price to marginal buyers to induce them to purchase additional units of output — because a monopolist's (X) marginal revenue is normally less than his price.

The fact that a monopolist X's marginal revenue (MRx) is less than his price (Px) has two consequences. First, since *ceteris paribus* the allocative value of the monopolist's last unit of output will equal Px (its dollar value to its consumer)[3], the fact that Px exceeds MRx implies that X's monopoly will distort the private value X receives by producing this unit of output (PVx) — in particular, will reduce PVx below the allocative value of this marginal unit of X (LVx). If all other Pareto optimal conditions were fulfilled, this distortion would lead X to produce too little of his product. Second, since the private cost some other producer, Y, has to incur to bid away from X the resources X would have used to produce a last unit of his output X equal the private value of X's last unit of output to X while the allocative cost of Y's bidding away these resources equals the allocative value of this last unit of X's product (on our assumptions, its value to its consumer — Px), the fact that MRx is less than Px also implies that X's monopoly will artificially deflate the private cost of the relevant resources to Y (and concomitantly will artificially deflate the private marginal cost of Y to its producer — MCx — below the marginal allocative cost of his producing Y — MLCx). This deflation of Y's costs will lead Y to produce too much of this output: this is the flip-side of X's monopoly leading him to produce too little X.

Of course, the same process will work in reverse: to the extent that X bids his resources away from a factor-market rival Y who is also a monopolist, the private cost to X of the resources he uses will also fall below their allocative cost. Fortunately, if we focus on X's unit output decision, the distortions introduced by Y's monopoly will offset the distortions introduced by X's own monopoly — i.e., the tendency of Y's monopoly to reduce MCx below MLCx (the marginal allocative cost of X) by artificially deflating X's private resource costs will offset the tendency of X's monopoly to artificially deflate the private value X obtains by producing additional units of his output (PVx = MRx) below the allocative value of these units (Px = MLVx or the marginal allocative value of X). That is why, in a world of multiple monopolies one cannot be sure that an individual monopolist will produce too few units of his output or concomitantly that a policy that reduces P toward MC will improve RUO allocation.

Unfortunately, although the relevant monopolies will tend to offset each other (conceivably reasonably perfectly) where RUO misallocation is

[3] This equation will hold only if the consumer has not made an error, is not a monopsonist, and does not generate any externalities when consuming the good in question.

concerned, that will not be the case where other types of resource misallocation are involved. For example, the relevant monopolies will tend to compound each other in relation to quantity-vs-QV investment misallocation: each relevant monopoly will tend to induce the economy to produce too few units of an excessively diverse, conveniently distributed, and quickly delivered set of products. In order to see why, let us focus on the economy's marginal QV investor and assume that the resources he uses to create his QV investment (to design his new product variant, to locate and construct his new distributive outlet, or to build up his capacity and inventory to increase his average speed of service through time) would otherwise have been used to increase the unit output of one or more of the economy's pre-existing product types. At least two sets of competitive imperfections (monopolies) will distort such a marginal QV investor's decision — i.e., will create a divergence between the private profits he will realize on his investment and its allocative efficiency. The first set of relevant monopolies contains the monopolistic firms from which the marginal QV investor will bid away the resources he uses to create his QV investment — e.g., to design his new product variant, to produce a prototype, to engage in preliminary market research into its attractiveness to consumers. These monopolies will artificially inflate the private profitability of the marginal QV investment by artificially deflating the private cost the marginal QV investor must incur to obtain the resources he uses to create the QV investment. The second set of relevant monopolies consists of those firms from which the marginal QV investor bids away the resources he combines with his QV investment to produce physical units of his new product (in effect, the "monopolies" with which his new product will compete — from whom it will take sales). By artificially deflating the cost of such resources to the marginal QV investor, these monopolies artificially inflate the profits the marginal QV investor realizes by using his QV investment — the amount by which he improves his position by producing his new product or operating his new outlet rather than costlessly destroying the associated QV investments. Accordingly, where quantity-vs-QV investment allocation is concerned, the two relevant sets of monopolies will tend to compound each other — i.e., both will tend to artificially inflate the private profitability of QV investments. Although a full analysis would have to consider the direction in which and the extent to which the private profitability of QV investments is distorted by the various other Pareto imperfections, I am confident that such an analysis would lead to the conclusion that all capitalist economies produce too few units of a too diversified, too conveniently distributed, and too quickly delivered set of goods. This conclusion has dramatic implications for the ability of antitrust to increase allocative efficiency.

This background should enable me to explore the various ways in which pro-competition policies can affect allocative efficiency by increasing the competitiveness of the economy. Even in our highly imperfect world, policies that increase price competition will generally tend to increase allocative efficiency in a number of ways regardless of the characteristics of the industry in question. In particular, increases in price competition will always tend to improve resource allocation by reducing the amount of our resources allocated to QV investment, will improve labor-leisure allocation by reducing the amount of time we spend on leisure activities (except when the good in question is complementary to leisure), will normally tend to improve production process research allocation by increasing the amount of resources we spend on cost-reducing research, and will usually increase allocative efficiency by redistributing income to consumers (and concomitantly to the poor) and away from such bad actors as price fixers and predators[4]. In addition, prohibitions of price fixing and predatory pricing will tend to improve resource allocation by reducing the frequency with which sales are made by firms that are not best-placed to obtain the relevant buyers' patronage (by firms that are undercutting their rivals' fixed prices or by undercut firms that are retaliating against such undercutting). Such policies may also increase allocative efficiency by deterring firms from expending resources to design and police their price-fixing rings though they might also induce the relevant defendants to use more expensive, less detectable means of policing their agreements. Of course, at least some of the above gain would be offset by the transaction costs the government and the defendants must incur to bring and try the cases in question and the misallocation that would be generated by the government's financing of its antitrust policy.

Moreover, policies that increase price competition on a more selective basis will also tend to improve other types of resource allocation. Thus, policies that (by design or incidence) increase price competition in industries with higher-than-average P/MC ratios will tend to improve RUO allocation among distant competitors on that account; and policies that increase price competition in industries whose post-tax rates of return have been inflated to a greater than average extent by Pareto imperfections will tend to improve inter-industry QV investment allocation by decreasing the proportion of total QV investment in both the industries in question and the industries with which they are unusually competitive. (For an analysis of these possibilities and others, see Markovits, 1975b).

Accordingly, even in our highly imperfect world, a strong allocative efficiency case can be made for policies that increase the competitiveness of price

[4] Such redistributions increase allocative efficiency in two ways. First, to the extent that they increase the real income of the poor, they may tend to increase allocative efficiency indirectly (1) by improving the position of some poor consumers sufficiently to make them decide not to buy misallocative, breakdown-prone, polluting cars and not to rent misallocative, disease-spreading and firespreading apartments, (2) by sufficiently improving the life which poor individuals can live without engaging in illegal activity to deter them from engaging in misallocative crimes, and (3) by giving the poor and their children the nutrition, medical resources, and housing conditions that will enable them to develop their productive capacities to an efficient degree. Second, such redistributions will increase allocative efficiency directly to the extent that various parties value for their own sake redistributions to the poor or away from price fixers and predators.

competition. Of course, the fact that such policies can generate some efficiency gains does not guarantee their allocative efficiency. As I have already noted, antitrust policies will always generate both litigation-related transaction costs and finance-related resource misallocation. In addition, certain methods of increasing price competition (for example, prohibiting internal horizontal growth or specific horizontal mergers) may generate prohibitive efficiency losses by precluding firms from taking advantage of economies of scale or from combining assets that are complementary for non-scale reasons. Nevertheless, a good allocative efficiency case can be made for attacking horizontal price fixing, and important allocative efficiency arguments can be given for prohibiting horizontal mergers that decrease price competition as well.

Unfortunately, no similar argument can be made in support of pro-competition policies that are designed to increase QV investment competition. Various antitrust policies relate specifically to the extent that firms compete away their supernormal returns by introducing additional product variants, opening up new or superior distributive outlets, or adding to their average speed of service by constructing additional capacity or accumulating additional inventory. Thus, rules prohibiting conglomerate mergers which eliminate best-placed, effective potential entrants into particular markets are often justified by the tendency of such mergers to reduce QV investment competition. On the other side, courts concerned with preserving or increasing QV investment competition might be tempted to favor mergers that increased the merger partners' ability to expand by combining complementary assets that facilitate QV investment activity.

Moreover, a sophisticated second best analysis leads to the conclusion that any resulting increases in QV investment competition would probably be allocatively inefficient. As we have seen, the existing Pareto imperfections almost certainly have led us to make an allocatively excessive amount of QV investment. Although a policy that increased QV investment competition and hence QV investment in an unusually competitive industry whose profits were taxed at an unusually low effective rate could conceivably improve inter-industry QV investment allocation by more than it worsened quantity-vs-QV investment allocation, any such result would be at best extremely rare. Hence, although a good second-best allocative efficiency case can be made for increasing price competition, no such argument is available where QV investment competition is concerned.

Thus, although pro-competition policies will be able to increase allocative efficiency when they increase price competition, they will not tend to do so when they increase QV investment competition. Moreover, although pro-competition policies will sometimes increase their addressees' organizational allocative efficiency, they will also sometimes reduce the OLE of such firms.

3. Possible Distributional, Social, and Political Goals of Antitrust

Proponents of antitrust have also tried to support such policies by citing their impact on various distributional, social, and political goals. This section will review these goals and the ability of antitrust to achieve them. Obviously, the importance of these various goals for antitrust policy evaluation cannot be inferred from the number of pages required to analyze them.

Pro-competition policies will tend to improve the distribution of income from most value perspectives. Thus, because such policies tend to redistribute real income from their addressees' stockholders (who are better-off) to their addressees' customers (who are worse-off), their distributive impact will appear desirable to egalitarians and utilitarians who believe in the declining marginal utility of money. And since many pro-competition policies will prevent people from profiting from their own wrongs or from reaping rewards that exceed the social benefits which their activities have generated, they may also appear distributionally desirable from the perspective of various "historic" values[5].

Pro-competition policies may also further the goal of preventing labor market discrimination by reducing their addressees' profits and derivatively the wages their managers and employers can realize. The effect on business profits is relevant because high profits may enable managers to sacrifice their shareholders' interests to indulge their own prejudices by helping them to conceal the fact that they have done so. The effect on manager and employer salaries is relevant because companies that pay high salaries and wages may find it more profitable to indulge such prejudices. This conclusion reflects the fact that employees may be willing to sacrifice more gross wages to indulge their prejudices if they are more highly paid for the following two reasons: (1) the net wage cost of sacrificing a given amount of gross wages will be lower for better-paid employees, who are in higher tax brackets; (2) the utility-cost of sacrificing a given amount of net wages will be lower for better-paid workers.

Pro-competition policies may also be able to achieve a variety of social and political goals to the extent that, by deconcentrating industries, they disperse political power. From a political perspective, industrial concentration is undesirable both because it facilitates lobbying for inefficient and maldistributive policies and because it leads to a concentration of political power that is inconsistent with many of the justifications for liberal democracy.

Many antitrust supporters have also maintained that pro-competition policies can produce social benefits by preserving or increasing the number of small businesses in the economy. Small business advocates believe that such enterprises should be promoted for at least three reasons that are unrelated to their traditional efficiency:

[5] An "historic" value makes the desirability of some distribution of income or welfare depend on the factors that resulted in various parties' occupying particular positions in the distribution — i.e., on the behavior, merits, or history of these parties. Historic values are contrasted with "endstate" values, which rank income or welfare distributions only according to their shape — which are indifferent to who is occupying what position in the overall distribution (which are indifferent to the histories of the people in the distribution).

1) some believe that small businesses are desirable because the experience of owning a small business leads its owners to generate various benefits outside their business proper — to be active church members, youth club athletic coaches, and participants in local political affairs;
2) others believe that small businesses are desirable because the opportunity to start such a business gives potential entrepreneurs efficient incentives to build up their skills, work hard, and save capital; finally,
3) still others believe that the preservation and stimulation of small businesses is desirable because the fact that a society gives its citizens a meaningful option to start such enterprises legitimates the society as a whole.

I am not persuaded by any of these rationalizations:
(1) I suspect that in fact small businessmen, in comparison with local managers of national chains, are too financially pressed and too politically vulnerable to take more active civic or political roles;
(2) I doubt that many people are encouraged to work and save efficiently by any increase in their perceived opportunity to form a business of their own; and
(3) I do not think that societies can or should be legitimated by their giving their members the opportunity to operate inefficient small businesses. Of course, these conclusions do not undercut the case for antitrust policies (e.g., against predatory behavior) that preserve efficient small businesses. However, they do lead me to oppose antitrust policies that try to preserve small businesses that are inefficient — e.g., by allowing them and forbidding their better-established rivals to adopt such efficient contractual control devices as vertical territorial restraints. (See for example, *White Motor Co.* v. *United States*, 372 U.S. 253 (1963)). Indeed, if I thought that inefficient small businesses should be preserved, I would oppose preserving them by forcing their larger rivals to operate inefficiently: far better to grant the small businesses direct public subsidies.

Some antitrust advocates and judges also believe that antitrust can in part be justified by its ability to secure for independent businessmen "the freedom to dispose of the goods they own as they see fit"[6]. In the name of such economic "liberty", these commentators would support antitrust rules prohibiting manufacturers from restricting the prices their independent distributors can charge; the customers to whom or territories within which they can sell; or perhaps the way in which they display their products and the goods with which they sell it. I do not understand the attraction of the value in question and suspect that efforts to secure it through antitrust would be self-defeating in any case.

The term "liberty" has been defined in many different ways. Economists often speak as if any non-budgetary restriction in the set of alternative choices available to an individual is a restriction of his liberty. Although many do use the term in this "liberty as license" or "billiard ball theory" sense, the concept

[6] The quotation comes from Mr. Justice White's concurring opinion in Continental T.V. Inc. v. GTE Sylvania Inc., 433 U.S. 36 (1977).

cannot play any significant role in political or ethical discourse unless it is defined more narrowly to refer to choices that work through or express the personality or important life-choices of the actor in question. Liberty in this sense has been called "liberty as independence". Within liberal theory, government policies that restrict liberty as independence require special justification, while policies that restrict liberty as license (for example, policies that forbid a driver from proceeding in the wrong direction down a one-way street) do not.

The argument that antitrust can promote the freedom or liberty of traders is almost always made in cases involving vertical restrictions on the way in which distributors can run their business. More particularly, such arguments are used to support the conclusion that antitrust courts should hold illegal, vertical territorial restraints, vertical customer allocation clauses, resale price maintenance provisions, and tying or reciprocal trading agreements — i.e., clauses in a contract between a manufacturer and his distributor in which the manufacturer respectively restricts the territories within which the distributor may sell; designates the customers to whom he can sell; sets a minimum price below which or a maximum price above which he may not sell the product; conditions the sale of one good on the distributor's agreeing to purchase a specified amount or his full requirements of a second good as well; or conditions the purchase of one good on its supplier's agreeing to purchase a second good in turn.

Admittedly, all these provisions do in one sense restrict the set of alternative choices available to the buyer — do in one sense (see below) restrict liberty as license. However, for three reasons it does not seem to me that such restrictions do unjustifiably restrict liberty as independence — the kind of liberty that a liberal state is supposed to protect and foster. First, even if one agrees that individuals do sometimes have a liberty as independence interest in practicing the profession of their choice that requires the state to have a special justification for restricting them in these areas (a conclusion one can share without agreeing with the German pharmaceutical decision), I doubt that even state-imposed restrictions of the kinds just described would limit distributors in ways that raised a liberty as independence issue. In part, my doubts on this issue reflect my sense that being a retailer or wholesaler is different from being a doctor or lawyer or pharmacist or cabinetmaker — that one is more likely to have a "calling" for the latter professions than for the former. In part, my doubts also reflect my sense that partial restrictions on the customers whose patronage a distributor may seek, the prices he charges, and the identity of the goods he buys may not prevent him from practicing his profession in a way that raises a liberty as independence issue. Admittedly, however, my sense of these matters may be different from that of many Europeans: I suspect that in general, Americans do identify less with their occupations than Europeans. Let me therefore turn to my second and third reasons for rejecting the liberty argument in this context.

Second, even if such state-imposed restrictions were thought to restrict the ability of a distributor to practice his profession in a way that does raise the liberty as independence issue, the state might very well be able to provide justifications for such restrictions that make them permissible in a liberal regime. As we shall see, many of the vertical restrictions just described do perform valuable functions such as reducing the cost of allocatively efficient quality control, encouraging allocatively efficient pre-sales advice, or reducing the cost of providing buyers with allocatively efficient warranties of quality. Even if distributors did have a right not to be restricted in these ways without a sufficiently good reason, they would not have a right to practice their professions in ways that caused allocative inefficiency — i.e., the tendency of a relevant restriction to promote allocative efficiency would be a good enough reason to justify the restriction.

Third, even if state-imposed restrictions of the kinds just described did restrict liberty as independence and could not be justified, the antitrust courts are not being asked to rule on state-imposed restrictions: the question is whether the relevant distributors should be allowed to escape from restrictions to which they voluntarily agreed. I indicated before that the relevant clauses restrict the distributor's liberty in only one sense — in the sense that a decision to buy one product restricts the choices available to the buyer post-purchase. In fact, it does not seem to me that voluntary choices which reduce options in this way do restrict liberty in any sense worth pointing out. All the manufacturers in question would be willing to allow any distributor the relevant freedom of choice if he were willing to pay for it — to pay the cost which his free choices would impose on the manufacturers. The fact is that the distributor was not willing to pay for it. Admittedly, the manufacturer in a given case may not have formally given the distributor the option of buying his way out of the restriction. But the manufacturer's failure to do so reflects his knowledge that no distributor would have exercized such an option — that none would have been willing to pay the costs involved. Certainly, individuals do not have a right to practice their distributive trade when they are willing to do so only if subsidized by their supplier.

For all these reasons, then, I do not think that antitrust laws should be used to protect whatever interest distributors have in disposing of their goods as they see fit: one should not prohibit the kinds of vertical restriction described above to protect the supposed economic liberty of distributors.

Indeed, even if it were appropriate to pursue such economic liberty through antitrust, I doubt that antitrust prohibitions on resale price maintenance agreements, vertical territorial restraints, tie-ins, and other restrictive contracts would be likely to promote the number of free choices made by independent businessmen. The producer's response to such prohibitions has been and almost certainly will continue to be to consign rather than to sell the goods in question or to integrate forward into distribution. Hence, attempts to preserve this supposed liberty interest of independent businessmen are likely to be self-defeating as well as pointless.

Finally, a given country's antitrust policies may also be designed to enable it to improve its ability to exploit its trading position in foreign markets. Part 4.1 (4) will analyze some of the ways in which competition among a given manufacturer's distributors can reduce the joint profits they realize from producing and selling the products. Precisely the same problems can arise from the perspective of a given country or political community (henceforth a "polity") when various companies within it compete for the patronage of foreign buyers. Thus, such companies' competition can reduce the polity's total profits by reducing the prices foreign buyers have to pay for its products; by producing a sale for a seller who was not best-placed to make it; by reducing the number of visits the companies' sales representatives make to foreign buyers below the jointly optimal level (when each company is deterred from covering the relevant territory by a mistaken belief that others were already doing so); by raising the amount of advertising or sales representation to a jointly excessive level (when some of the sales taken come from other intra-polity rivals); by reducing pre-sales advice to jointly sub-optimal levels (when the buyers who receive the advice from one company can use it while purchasing another company's products); by reducing post-sales service to jointly sub-optimal levels (when the reputation and effects of such service spreads to other companies within the same polity); and by preventing exchanges of information about effective sales techniques or product uses (when each company fears that its intra-polity rivals' possession of such information will improve their competitive position vis-à-vis itself).

Accordingly, just as a manufacturer will often find it profitable to restrict competition among its own distributors, a polity will often be able to increase its profits from foreign trade by allowing its own companies to cooperate with each other when seeking foreign sales. Unfortunately, however, it is difficult to confine such cooperation (read — agreements not to compete) to foreign markets. Although government-run joint sales agencies, staffed by personnel who are forbidden to work subsequently for any of the companies they represent, may be able to reduce anti-competitive feedbacks within the national or community economy, such state-run foreign trade departments will probably also tend to be less effective at securing foreign business than the sales representatives of the individual companies concerned. If, as I expect, therefore, the state sales-agency approach is not satisfactory, the nation or community must decide whether giving an antitrust exemption to companies in relation to their cooperation on foreign trade is likely to increase the polity's gains from such trade sufficiently to offset the undesirable consequences of any associated decrease in domestic competition (the concomitant allocative inefficiency, undesirable income redistribution, added labor-market discrimination, and increased concentration of domestic political power).

The decision that is optimal from the individual polity's perspective will undoubtedly vary with the proportion of the relevant polity's sales that are made overseas. The greater that proportion the better the case for granting such an exemption. In crude terms then, such exemptions probably make less sense in general for the U.S. than for Japan and, for the same reason, they make less sense for the European Community as a whole than for any of its individual members. In what follows, I will assume that antitrust exemptions of this sort (or indeed general pro-monopoly policies that seek to improve the nation's or community's foreign trade profits by preventing intra-polity competition) would not make sense for the U.S. or the EEC. This conclusion is based primarily on the argument just delineated though it is strengthened by the possibility that any such pro-monopoly decision by the U.S. or the EEC might lead their respective foreign trading partners to adopt similar policies that would cost the U.S. or EEC more than any gain their own decision would otherwise have generated. (Obviously, from a world rather than nation-state perspective, the argument against such antitrust exemptions or pro-monopoly policies is even stronger: at least some of the gains we are discussing are purely private. Thus, although a pro-monopoly policy which prevents competition that would have reduced the prices a given nation's companies obtain in foreign markets may increase that nation's profits, it will normally do so only by reducing the allocative efficiency of the world economy.)

4. Standards for Ideal Antitrust Decisionmaking

This part will delineate four tests that antitrust authorities should employ when deciding whether to allow or prohibit particular practices and will then proceed to explain why and how such authorities could produce better results by selling the right to engage in some transactions for appropriate prices.

4.1 Four Tests for Antitrust Illegality

Antitrust's various goals would best be served if the law made it illegal to violate any of the following four tests: (1) an anti-competitive intent test; (2) a natural oligopolistic interaction test, which might be qualified to cover only natural oligopolistic pricing; (3) a qualified competitive impact test; and (4) an unnecessarily misallocative vertical practice test.

(1) The Anti-Competitive Intent Test

The anti-competitive intent test condemns all behavior whose profitability depends on its reducing the attractiveness of the offers against which the actor or actors must compete: in other words, this test condemns all behavior the relevant actor believed would not have been profitable but for its tendency to reduce the attractiveness of such competing offers. Given its requirement of such specific intent, this "but for profitability" test is probably more suitable than any of the others for inclusion in a criminal antitrust statute. The anti-competitive intent test would condemn both predatory and contrived oligopolistic practices. It would also condemn horizontal mergers and joint ventures whose profitability depended on their freeing the merger partners or joint venturers from each other's competition.

Predatory behavior is behavior whose profitability depends on its reducing the attractiveness of the offers against which the predator must compete by driving one or more of his rivals out of business or by deterring a rival QV investment (where the deterrence's profitability depends on the fact that the deterred investment would have reduced the profits generated by the predator's pre-existing capital more than they were reduced by his deterring act). Many different kinds of acts can be predatory: pricing strategies; QV investments, advertising policies, refusals to deal, and long-term requirements contracts can all be predatory though they can all be perfectly legitimate as well.

Contrived oligopolistic pricing behavior is conduct whose profitability depends on its inducing an existing rival to offer less attractive terms to the contriver's customers. Oligopolistic interactions always involve the contemplation of behavior sequences that would contain at least three acts. Thus, a party is said to behave oligopolistically whenever his choice is affected by his realization that his rival anticipates the party's reacting to the rival's response to the party's decision. Oligopolistic sequences can be either "contrived" or "natural". The relevant distinction turns on the reasons why the rival anticipates the initiating party's reacting to his decision. If the rival expects a reaction because it will be inherently profitable for the initiating party to react — i.e., because the reaction would be profitable even if it did not affect the probable future responses of the party's rivals to his choices, the oligopolistic interaction is said to be "natural". If, on the other hand, the rival anticipates such a response despite the fact that it would be inherently unprofitable for the initiating party to react — i.e., because he believes that the initiating party will sacrifice what would otherwise be his interests in order to teach the rival and his future counterparts a lesson (to deter them from competing with him in the future), the oligopolistic interaction is said to be "contrived".

Oligopolists can contrive both oligopolistic price increases and oligopolistic QV investment restrictions. In the former case, the oligopolist is attempting to charge higher prices than he could otherwise obtain by deterring undercutting, by threatening or carrying out threats of retaliation or by promising or carrying out promises of cooperative reciprocation. In the latter case, the oligopolist is attempting to induce others to restrict their QV investments in his area of product space by making or carrying out such anti-competitive threats and/or promises. Obviously, retaliation and reciprocation can take many forms. Thus, an oligopolist can retaliate by lowering his prices to inherently unprofitable levels in order to reduce his target rival's returns; by engaging in advertising that is inherently unprofitable to attract away the target rival's customers; or conceivably by making an inherently unprofitable QV investment near the target's position in product space. Similarly, an oligopolist can reciprocate by failing to lower his prices in circumstances in which it would be inherently profitable for him to do so; by eschewing an advertising campaign that would increase his profits at his beneficiary's expense; or by choosing not to make an inherently profitable QV investment that would injure his cooperating rival. The anti-competitive intent test would prohibit all contrived oligopolistic moves since their profitability depends on their reducing the attractiveness of the offers against which the relevant actors will have to compete.

Some horizontal mergers and joint ventures would also violate this anti-competitive intent test. By definition, all horizontal mergers will tend to reduce competition by freeing the merger partners from each other's competition. And although joint ventures need not have such anti-competitive effects, many will in fact do so either because they contain (possibly legitimate) ancillary provisions which restrict the parents' ability to enter into each other's and the joint venture's markets or because the joint venture deters each parent from investing in the venture's market by giving each a stake in holding down QV investment in that area of product space. However, not all horizontal mergers and joint ventures would violate the anti-competitive intent test on this account. Thus, the profitability of many horizontal mergers that do decrease the competition the merger partners give each other will not depend on their producing such effects. Similarly, many joint ventures will not restrict the competition the venturers give each other, and the profitability of many of the joint ventures that restrict such competition will not depend upon their doing so. On the other hand, it should be clear that the profitability of some horizontal mergers and some joint ventures will depend upon their restricting the competition the merger partners or joint venturers give each other. The anti-competitive intent test would make all such mergers and ventures illegal.

(2) The Natural Oligopolistic Interaction Test

As I have just indicated, in many situations, oligopolistic pricing and investment sequences can take place naturally — i.e., without any anti-competitive threats or promises having been communicated or carried out. There is very little difference between the consequences of natural and contrived oligopolistic conduct.

Both natural and contrived oligpolistic pricing will misallocate resources in a variety of ways — e.g., by increasing QV investment and reducing unit output, will redistribute income in an undesirable direction and will promote labor market discrimination by raising the income of the oligopolists' managers and employees. Moreover, a decision to prohibit natural as well as contrived oligopolistic pricing will have the further advantage of reducing the transaction costs generated by the operation of the antitrust laws: condemning natural oligopolistic pricing makes it unnecessary to determine whether oligopolistic prices could have been set naturally. Hence, although natural oligopolistic pricing is somewhat less undesirable than contrived oligopolistic pricing, it would clearly be advantageous to condemn both. Moreover, although the reductions in QV investment to which contrived and natural oligopolistic investment restrictions might lead might themselves be allocatively efficient, the relevant oligopolistic interactions will often dis-serve the other goals of antitrust sufficiently to make them undesirable overall. In fact, even when they do not, a decision to sell the right to engage in the relevant conduct would probably be superior to a simple decision to allow it.

(3) The Qualified Competitive Impact Test

Behavior that is neither predatory nor oligopolistic may still violate the competitive impact test which I think an ideal antitrust law would contain by injuring the buyers directly concerned through reducing the attractiveness of the offers they received from their inferior suppliers. I will first explain why behavior that would not fail my first two tests could violate this third one and then explain how and why I would qualify this test either by introducing an organizational allocative efficiency defense or by authorizing the antitrust authority to sell the right to engage in anti-competitive mergers for an appropriate price.

The distinction between my anti-competitive intent and anti-competitive impact tests can best be explained by focusing on a horizontal merger case. The profitability of such a merger could be assured by the economies it generated for the merger partners by enabling them to take advantage of economies of scale or by enabling them to combine assets that were complementary for non-scale reasons (as might occur if one merger partner had excess managerial capacity in its production department and the other had excess managerial capacity in its distribution department — capacity that without the merger would either be under-utilized by the individual partners or reallocated to alternative producers for whom it would be less productive, since the productivity of managers often depends on their understanding of their particular employer's personnel, communication networks, and market strengths and weaknesses). However, despite the fact that such efficiencies would tend to improve the position of the relevant buyers in the short run in various ways — by enabling the merger partners (MPs) to improve their offers on their original products to customers whom they were originally not best-placed to serve and by inducing the MPs to make additional QV investments, such a horizontal merger might still injure such buyers on balance. Thus, even in the short run, horizontal mergers will tend to injure buyers by (a) freeing the merger partners from the competitive pressure they originally placed on each other's pricing decisions (particularly when they were originally respectively best-placed and second-best-placed to obtain some buyer's patronage), (b) increasing the MPs' ability to contrive oligopolistic prices (in circumstances which might enable them to escape subsequent detection), (c) increasing the MPs' ability to obtain oligopolistic margins naturally (in similar circumstances), (d) increasing the ability of the MPs' rivals to contrive oligopolistic prices (for example, by making the MPs more vulnerable to rival retaliation), and (e) facilitating investment restrictions in the product space area concerned (by internalizing to the merged company the damage each MP's QV investment would otherwise have done to the other and by facilitating contrived oligopolistic investment restrictions in various ways). (For a complete analysis of the competitive impact of horizontal mergers, see Markovits, 1978).

Thus, horizontal mergers that do not violate the anti-competitive intent test can still reduce competition. Indeed, horizontal mergers that do not reduce competition in the above ways may still reduce competition in the long run by leading one or more of the MPs' rivals to exit. This result could obtain without the merger's inducing the MPs to engage in predatory pricing if it improved their position sufficiently for their conventional profit-maximizing prices to make it unprofitable for some rival to continue. The merger could produce this result both by enabling the MPs to take customers away from the rival in question and by reducing the profits he realized by supplying other customers he retained post-merger — both by making the MPs the privately best-placed supplier of some buyers the exiting rival would otherwise have been best-placed to serve and by improving the MPs' position in relation to buyers that rival was still best-placed to serve post-merger. However, mergers that reduced competition in this way might not violate my *qualified* competitive impact test: if no other approach were available, I would gualify my competitive impact test with an organizational allocative efficiency (OLE) defense i.e., by permitting MPs to exonerate themselves by proving that their merger would not have induced a rival to exit had it not improved their position in relation to the rival's customers by generating efficiences that were allocative as well as private. I should add, though, that such a defense might very well be less preferable than a system in which the antitrust authority sold MPs in the situation described above the right to engage in the relevant merger for a price that would reflect *inter alia* the extra gain their merger generated by freeing them from their exiting rival's competition.

The qualified competitive impact test would enable the antitrust authority to prevent many activities that have undesirable consequences. Thus, even if their anti-competitive impact is not essential to their profitability, transactions that reduce price competition will tend to cause various kinds of QV investment and other misallocations on that account. Moreover, although participants in transactions that reduce competition without violating our first test are not so culpable as predators or contriving oligopolists (indeed may not be culpable at all from some value perspectives), from utilitarian, egalitarian, and various historic perspectives, such transactions will still redistribute income in an undesirable direction. Relatedly, by increasing the profits of the participants and hence the salaries of their managers and employees, such transactions will also tend to increase labor market discrimination. In addition, to the extent that such transactions concentrate the relevant markets, they will probably tend to generate various undesirable economic, social, and political consequences by increasing the political power of their participants. Indeed, these latter consequences lead me to conclude that prohibiting transactions that primarily reduce QV investment competition may often be preferable to allowing them despite the allocative efficiency of reductions in such competition. In most cases, however, the ideal government response to such conduct would be to require defendants to pay for the right to engage in the relevant transaction. Such a solution would permit one to obtain the relevant improvement in QV investment allocation while substantially reducing the extent to which the relevant transaction would redistribute income undesirably and increase labor market discrimination.

(4) The Vertical "Unnecessarily Misallocative" Test

This test would apply to all the various (non-predatory) ways in which sellers seek to influence their customers' behavior (or vice versa) other than conventional single price profit-maximization. In particular, it would apply to such practices as lump-sum pricing (perfect price discrimination); conventional price discrimination; tie-ins; reciprocity agreements; vertical territorial restraints; and resale price maintenance agreements. Antitrust authorities currently prohibit many practices of this kind in varying circumstances on the dubious assumption that they reduce competition. In fact, although these practices will rarely if ever have such an effect[7], some will decrease allocative efficiency (a) by expending resources to convert buyer into seller surplus; (b) by reallocating goods to customers to whom they have a lower dollar value; and

[7] The competitive impact of vertical practices must be assessed by examining the consequences of a rule allowing all competitors to engage in them. To do otherwise would be to adopt a *pari mutuel* approach of handicapping well-established firms from employing particular pricing or control devices by prohibiting them and allowing their marginal and potential competitors to use such strategies. The fact is that none of the practices with which we are now concerned will ever be predatory. Moreover, they will not violate my qualified anti-competitive impact test unless two conditions are fulfilled: (1) they must be more privately profitable to well-established firms than to marginal or potential competitors, and (2) the associated reduction in the absolute rate of return which marginal or potential competitors can realize must reduce competition in my third test's sense by inducing a marginal competitor to exit or raising the barriers to entry faced by an effective potential competitor. In reality, the first condition will probably rarely be satisfied: many of the functions such practices perform (e.g., the function that tie-ins perform by reducing the cost of controlling the quality of the complements a seller's customers use in conjunction with his product) tend to be more important for marginal and potential competitors than for well-established firms, and marginal and potential competitors tend to have less attractive alternative ways of getting these functions performed. Moreover, the second condition will often not be satisfied even if the first condition is: the marginal competitor who has been disadvantaged by a decision allowing everyone to engage in some such practice may not be induced to exit, and the potential competitor who has been disadvantaged by such a decision may not have been an effective force in the "market".

Indeed, even if a practice does reduce competition in the sense of my third test, the defendants will often be able to exonerate themselves by making out an OLE defense: since several kinds of such practices are allocatively efficient (e.g., quality control tie-ins reduce the allocative cost of performing an allocatively efficient function — quality control), their well-established employers will be able to establish an efficiency defense by demonstrating that the practice disadvantaged their marginal and potential competitors because it increased the OLE of the well-established firms by more than it increased the OLE of these rivals. In fact, although I would not prohibit a plaintiff from trying to establish a *prima facie* case under my qualified anti-competitive impact test by demonstrating that the first two conditions were fulfilled, I suspect that in practice virtually no such suits would be brought. For a complete analysis of the competitive impact of tie-ins and reciprocity, see Markovits, (1980).

conceivably (c) by inducing additional expenditures on advertising, sales-coverage, and pre-sales advice that may be allocatively undesirable.

Let me illustrate each of these possibilities in turn. "Full-line forcing" tie-ins involving goods that are not substitutes provide a good example of the first possibility. Under a "full line force", a seller X of a differentiated product A reduces the unit price he charges some customer Y for this product on condition that Y also agrees to purchase from X his full requirements of a second, typically undifferentiated product B for more than its prevailing market price. In comparison with the independent sale of A, such an agreement uses up resources (a) by increasing the cost of drafting and negotiating the relevant contract; (b) by increasing the cost X has to incur to prevent Y from engaging in arbitrage on A (by increasing Y's incentive to engage in such arbitrage by lowering the unit price he must pay for A); and (c) by forcing X to incur additional expenses to police the full requirements contract on B (which Y will obviously find advantageous to violate). In addition, to the extent that such an arrangement increases the amount of arbitrage in which Y actually engages, it will misallocate resources by increasing the cost of delivering A to its eventual consumer Z (by routing A to Z via Y). Nevertheless, when the shapes of the relevant demand and marginal cost curves are appropriate and the demands for the two products are correlated in the relevant way, X (and perhaps Y as well) may find such full-line forces profitable, for they may increase X and Y's joint profits by reducing the extent to which X's supra-marginal cost pricing induces Y to lower their joint gains by reducing his purchases. However, in our worse-than-second-best world, agreements of this kind that do not involve substitutes will be unlikely to generate any allocative gains to offset the allocative costs just described — i.e., the savings in buyer and seller (transaction) surplus they generate are likely to be purely private and not allocative. (For a complete explanation, see Markovits, 1980: 1386-1400, 1441-42).

Conventional price discrimination provides a good example of a practice that misallocates resources by allocating goods to parties to whom they have a lower dollar value as well as by increasing the transaction costs generated by the relevant seller's pricing of his product. Price discrimination generates transaction costs because the discriminator normally has to incur extra expenses to identify his "high-valuing" and "low-valuing" customers, to charge them different prices, and to prevent those who are charged the lower price from selling the relevant goods to others from whom he wishes to extract the higher price. In addition, as we have seen, to the extent that price discrimination produces arbitrage, it will also misallocate resources by increasing the cost of getting the goods to the eventual consumer. For present purposes, however, we are more concerned with the tendency of price discrimination to allocate goods to the wrong parties from the perspective of allocative efficiency. To see why price discrimination will tend to do this, let us compare the effects of price discrimination with those of conventional single pricing. Assume, for example, that a seller who is charging some customers \$16 and others \$12 would charge a uniform per unit price of \$14.25 if he could not discriminate. Presumably, at the price of $14.25, the product would be purchased by buyers who valued it at $14.25 or more and would not be purchased by any buyer who placed a value below $14.25 on the product in question. Thus, under conventional uniform pricing, all buyers of the product will place a higher dollar value on it than will all non-buyers. This result will not obtain under price discrimination, for sellers will rarely be able to discriminate perfectly — i.e., will rarely be able to charge each potential buyer precisely the price he was willing to pay. Thus, in our example, some of the potential buyers who are charged $16 will choose not to purchase the product despite the fact that the value they place on it exceeds the $12 price other buyers are asked to pay. Hence, under price discrimination, some of the buyers who pay the $12 price will have placed a lower dollar value on the product than some of the non-buyers whom the seller tried to charge $16. In other words, the discrimination misallocates resources in comparison with its uniform pricing alternative because it allocates the product away from some buyers who would have purchased it at the uniform price of $14.25 but were not willing to pay the $16 they were charged under discrimination and to other buyers who did purchase it at the $12 discriminatory price but would not have been willing to pay $14.25. To the extent that price discrimination produces this result, it will cause a kind of allocative inefficiency that economists label "consumption optimum misallocation".

Finally, although I think that this judgment is clearly contestable, some vertical practices may also misallocate resources by inducing independent distributors to place more advertisements, to make more sales trips, and to offer more pre-sales advice. Vertical territorial restraints or customer allocation clauses produce this effect by raising the probability that the distributor who makes such expenditures will get the additional sales they generate by forbidding others from dealing for the customers they attract (by giving him exclusive access to particular buyers or territories). Resale price maintenance produces the same effect by prohibiting other sellers of the same product from giving the buyers whom the advertiser (advisor) contacts any price reason to take their patronage elsewhere. The claim that such consequences are misallocative is open to serious question for two reasons. First, many would challenge the underlying premise that profitable advertising, sales trips, or pre-sales advice could be allocatively inefficient. However, this premise can be supported not only by arguing that much of such information is misleading or uninformative but also by pointing out that, to the extent that rival prices exceed marginal costs, the private profits that any such activities yield by generating additional sales will exceed the allocative gains the shift in patronage permits[8]. Second, others would maintain that even

[8] The argument for this conclusion is similar to the argument on which I based my conclusion that QV investment was likely to be excessive in our worse-than-second-best world. The profits the advertiser will realize by "using" his advertising by making and selling the units of his output it enables him to sell will be artificially inflated because his product market rivals' supra-competitive prices artificially deflate the cost to him of the resources he uses to produce the additional units of his output.

if any such increase in advertising, sales trips, or pre-sales advice were misallocative, prohibitions of the vertical contractual arrangements that generate them will not increase allocative efficiency by reducing them. Such critics maintain that the prohibition of such contractual control devices will lead to vertical integration — i.e., to the substitution of privately and hence presumably allocatively more expensive hierarchical controls and not to the abandonment of any attempt by producers to induce their distributors to engage in the relevant activities. Since I suspect that producers will often respond to the prohibition of various contractual control devices by integrating forward into distribution, this second argument has real force for me.

Now that I have explained how vertical practices can cause additional misallocation not necessitated by the monopoly power of their employers, I will proceed firstly, to delineate the test I propose to apply to such practices and secondly, to explore the implications of this test for the legality of various kinds of pricing and contractual control strategies.

In theory, my unnecessarily misallocative vertical practice test is quite simple. Some complicated pricing procedures and vertical coordination strategies misallocate resources in comparison with conventional single pricing. Under the fourth test, the antitrust authority would condemn any such practice that is less allocatively efficient *than the (weighted average) alternative that would be likely to be substituted for it.* The test includes the italicized clause because it would obviously be counterproductive for an antitrust authority to condemn one practice on the ground that it is less allocatively efficient than a second practice when such a prohibition would result in the relevant defendant substituting a third practice which is allocatively inferior to the first. Hence, under my scheme, whoever is assessing the allocative efficiency of a vertical practice must consider the possibility that its prohibition will lead its employer to change his behavior in a variety of other ways. Thus, an antitrust authority, in assessing the legality of resale price maintenance, might have to consider the possibility that its prohibition would lead its employer to integrate forward into distribution — i.e., to assess the allocative efficiency of such RPM by comparing its effects with those of both vertical integration and less fancy non-integration, weighted by the respective probabilities of these two responses.

Limitations of space preclude me from analyzing the relevant vertical practices in detail. A complete analysis would lead to the following conclusions:
(a) it would be desirable though perhaps not politically feasible to forbid each firm to charge higher prices than it would have found profitable had its rivals charged its customers prices equal to their marginal costs;
(b) it would not be desirable to forbid firms from charging "extremely high" or "abusive" prices since such an approach would also be likely to cause all the problems which currently afflict American "fair rate of return" regulation;
(c) pure or mixed lump-sum pricing of separable goods should be held unlawful unless the defendant can demonstrate that its profitability was increased by its ability to reduce the sum of the seller's and buyer's risk costs;

(d) lump-sum pricing (outright sales) of the right to use a durable machine or idea should be *per se* lawful;
(e) price discrimination should be *per se* unlawful if practiced by a seller in relation to customers he would be privately best-placed to serve if contextual marginal costs were ignored;
(f) price discrimination should be lawful if the discriminatorily low price is charged to a buyer whom the discriminator would be privately worse-than-best-placed to serve if contextual marginal costs were ignored;
(g) the following types of tie-ins should be *per se* lawful: (i) tie-ins that function by controlling the quality of the complements the buyer combines with the seller's product; (ii) full-line forces involving substitutable inputs, substitutable outputs, or one substitutable input and another used in fixed proportion to output; (iii) tie-ins that reduce the cost of implementing lawful meter pricing; and (iv) tie-ins that reduce the cost of preventing arbitrage, the risk of which is created by lawful pricing strategies;
(h) the following types of tie-ins should be declared *per se* unlawful: (i) full-line forces that do not involve the kinds of product described above; (ii) tie-ins that facilitate or conceal illegal price discrimination; and (iii) tie-ins that conceal other antitrust violations or tax or contract frauds;
(i) the legality of reciprocity agreements should depend on the same functional factors that determine the legality of tie-ins; and
(j) RPM, VTRs, and vertical customer allocation clauses should be lawful unless they implement illegal reseller or manufacturer price fixes.

4.2 Selling the Right to Engage in Conduct That Has Some Undesirable Consequences

In at least two different kinds of situation, antitrust authorities would be able to achieve better results if, in addition to prohibiting or allowing various types of business conduct, they could sell the right to engage in the conduct in question. The first such situation is defined by the presence of two conditions: (1) the conduct in question must yield more profits than it is thought that the actors deserve, and (2) the sale of the right to engage in the conduct in question must be preferable to a simple decision to prohibit it. When the first condition is fulfilled, a sale at an appropriate price will be preferable to a simple decision to allow the relevant conduct both because it may improve the overall transaction's distributional impact and because, by reducing the actor's profits and hence the salaries of its managers and employees, it may reduce the amount of additional labor market discrimination that the transaction generates. The point of the second condition should be obvious although an example might be helpful. The relevant conditions might both be fulfilled by a horizontal merger. Such a merger might fulfill the first condition because it increased the merger partners' profits *inter alia* by freeing them from each other's price competition (by doing something that actually made the transaction less allocatively efficient than it otherwise would be). The same merger might simultaneously fulfill the second condition because it also generated private efficiencies that increased allocative efficiency both directly by reducing the allocative cost of production and indirectly by increasing the intensity of price competition (by improving the merger partners' positions in relation to customers they were not originally best-placed to serve). In such a case, a decision to sell the right to merge for a price that reduced the private gains which the merger partners realized from the transaction to the social gains they generated (the increase in allocative efficiency minus an equivalent dollar valuation of the attendant increase in labor market discrimination and political process losses) would both improve the overall transaction's effect on the distribution of income from the relevant historic perspective and reduce the merger's tendency to increase labor market discrimination by raising the salaries of the MPs' managers and employees.

In other circumstances, sales of the right to engage in transactions may also be desirable for a different reason. Assume, for example, that a horizontal merger would clearly have undesirable consequences if it did not generate any efficiencies, but that its net impact could be desirable if such efficiences did result (both because some such efficiencies are desirable in themselves and because they make the merger increase price competition more or decrease it less than would otherwise have been the case). An antitrust authority that was restricted to prohibiting or allowing the relevant merger would have to estimate the size of the relevant efficiencies, but one that was empowered to sell the right to engage in the merger might be able to proceed in a somewhat different way. Specifically, such an authority could offer to sell the merger partners the right to merge with each other for a price that equalled the profits the merger would yield them if it generated enough efficiencies to make it desirable overall, given the sale of the right to merge. If the authority set the price accurately[9], the MPs' refusal to buy the right to merge would indicate

[9] I should hasten to admit that it will not be simple to calculate this price. On the assumption that the antitrust authorities will always be able to detect and prosecute the kinds of transactions with which we are now concerned without incurring significant costs, the ideal price will be equal to the profits the transaction would generate for its participants if it created enough efficiencies to be socially neutral in its effects. For a variety of reasons, this price cannot be represented as the sum of various areas in conventional economic diagrams. In part, this conclusion reflects the fact that the private gains which the transaction generates by reducing the competition its participants face will bear no easily representable relationship to the misallocation it causes on this account; in part, it reflects the fact that the private gains which the transaction generates by increasing the competitive pressure its participants place on their rivals bear no simple relationship to the allocative gains it generates on this account — for example, a merger that improves resource allocation by inducing the MPs' rivals to reduce their prices by improving the MPs' position in relation to buyers they are still not best-placed to serve post-merger will not generate any private gains on this account for the MPs; and in part, it reflects the fact that the allocative gains which a merger generates by reducing the costs the MPs have to incur to produce their original products bear no simple relationship to the private cost savings the merger permits on this account — e.g., the allocative savings will

that their paid-for merger would not be beneficial while their decision to pay for the right to merge would indicate that a paid-for merger would be preferable to no merger at all. In fact, since the sale of the right to merge would usually improve the merger's distributional consequences (given that the merger itself would probably yield more profits than its participants deserved) and would always reduce its tendency to lead to labor market discrimination, the sale would almost always be preferable to a simple decision to allow the merger — even if one ignored the cost savings this technique achieves by obviating the authority's estimating the efficiencies the merger would generate. Of course, these cost savings will be offset by the costs the authority must incur in setting the appropriate price. However, I think that such costs would generally be lower than the cost of estimating the relevant efficiencies. In fact, I suspect that this technique would be able to reduce both the cost of making antitrust decisions and the number of erroneous antitrust decisions (or, more significantly, the costs such erroneous decisions generate).

In short, antitrust authorities that are empowered to sell the right to engage in certain transactions could use this power to improve the consequences of the transactions in question, to reduce the cost of making their decisions, and to reduce the losses they generated by making erroneous decisions. An ideal antitrust statute should therefore empower such authorities to sell the right to engage in transactions in the situations I have just described and should require them to set the prices in question in one of the two ways just delineated (i.e., according to whether they are trying to reduce certain undesirable consequences of the relevant behavior by setting a price that eliminates the divergence between its private profitability and overall desirability or to avoid having to estimate the size of the efficiencies the merger partners would be willing to pay only if their merger would generate enough efficiencies to be desirable when paid for).

exceed the private savings to the extent that the resources saved are used by a monopolist to increase his unit output and will be less than the private savings to the extent that they are used by such a producer to increase his QV investment. Admittedly, when the antitrust division cannot detect all such violations without incurring substantial costs, the sort of price I have described may not in fact be ideal: although it will produce the right business decision in the instant case (assuming that is an issue — that the merger is not a *fait accompli*), the uncertain prospect of having to pay such a price will not induce future possible merger participants to reduce their certainty equivalent profit estimates to the extent that would be desirable. For this reason, the price I have described will be efficient only if participants in the relevant transactions are always required to pay it.

5. Methodologies, Sanctions, and Institutional Arrangements

5.1 Methodology: Doing Antitrust Without Defining Markets in Traditional Ways

Although antitrust litigation cannot always be made simple, it should be possible to simultaneously reduce the cost and increase the accuracy of antitrust adjudication in cases in which the courts have tried to predict the competitive impact of the relevant practices from facts (such as market share and concentration data) that presuppose the definition of traditional markets. Market definition has caused enormous trouble because, in our monopolistically competitive world in which product and locational differentiation abound, there is no nonarbitrary way to define the kind of relevant market that both American and European courts have been trying to establish for antitrust purposes. All such courts have made the mistake of trying to define markets in terms of products rather than buyers. In particular, they have tried to define markets by placing the relevant products into a series of nonoverlapping groups such that all members of the same group will be equally and substantially competitive with each other and such that no members of different groups will be significantly competitive with each other. In our monopolistically competitive world, however, products cannot be grouped in this way: different, partially overlapping sets of products are well-placed to obtain the patronage of different sets of buyers. The appropriate response to this fact is to focus not on products but on the buyers who purchase them. If markets are to be defined at all, each should be defined to include all buyers whose tastes and locations are sufficiently similar for a particular group of suppliers to be well-placed to compete for their business. Under this definition, each product would be placed into several markets and each seller would be competitive with different groups of rivals in the various "markets" in which he was placed. Because it ignores this reality, the traditional market definition approach increases cost and decreases accuracy.

I will now illustrate this contention by criticizing, and proposing alternatives to, the standard approach both American and European courts have taken in analyzing the competitive impact of horizontal mergers. I will focus more specifically on the American courts' approach to such horizontal merger analyses.

Captured by the traditional market paradigm, the American courts have tried to predict the competitive impact of horizontal mergers on the basis of such traditional market-oriented data as the relevant industry's concentration and the merger partners' market shares. In essence, this approach takes disaggregated data about the competitive positions of various sellers in relation to different groups of buyers that has predictive significance and, at great expense, uses it to produce market definitions and aggregate market share and concentration figures that have less predictive power than the disaggregated data from which they were derived.

The American courts' acceptance of the traditional market paradigm has distorted their approach to determining the legality of horizontal mergers in two different ways. First, their belief in traditional markets has led them to assume that market share and concentration figures can be used to predict the various determinants of a merger's competitive impact, including the frequency with which and the amount by which the merger partners were each other's closest competitors and the premerger profitability of price fixing. Second, the American courts' belief in traditional markets has led them to ignore other factors that affect the competitive impact of a horizontal merger but have little to do with the structure of "the relevant market". The static and dynamic efficiencies the merger would produce fall into this category.

Put crudely, a horizontal merger's competitive impact will depend on whether it injures consumers — for example, by freeing the merger partners from each other's price competition, by facilitating their and their rivals' practice of price fixing, or by making each merger partner's investment decisions depend on their impact on the other merger partner's profits — more than it helps consumers — for example, by generating static efficiencies that improve the merger partners' position in relation to customers they were not originally privately best-placed to serve and by generating dynamic efficiencies that permit the merger partners to make QV investments that neither they nor anyone else would otherwise have found profitable. The merger partners' market shares and the concentration of the relevant market are not good predictors of any of the factors that relate to these possibilities. Thus, one cannot use the merger partners' market shares to determine the frequency with which or the amount by which they were each other's closest competitors because (1) there is little inter-industry correlation between the frequency with which a firm is best-placed and the frequency with which it is second-best-placed to obtain particular customers' patronage; (2) firms that are second-best-placed to make X percent of the sales in a given "market" are not second-best-placed to obtain X percent of the sales of each of their in-market rivals; and (3) firms are not equally or proportionally competitive with each of their in-market rivals.

Moreover, there is no reason to believe that the merger partners' market shares are good predictors of (1) the amount of efficiencies the merger is likely to generate; (2) the frequency with which the merger partners were a remaining rival's closest competitor; (3) the frequency with which and amount by which the merger's static efficiencies exceed the amount by which one merger partner was worse-than-second-best-placed to obtain the patronage of a remaining rival's customer; or (4) the likelihood that the merger's dynamic efficiencies will enable the merged firm to expand more easily than any of its established or potential competitors. Similarly there is no reason to believe that the concentration of the relevant market will be a good predictor of other relevant factors such as the original profitability of price fixing in the market in question or the likelihood that potential competition was effective in the relevant area of product space.

In short, there is no reason to define relevant markets in horizontal merger cases; one can produce competitive impact predictions more accurately and more cheaply if one does not try to define relevant markets. Instead, competitive impact predictions should be based on the disaggregated data one now collects to define the relevant markets (the frequency with which and the amount by which various firms were each other's close competitors) as well as on other facts (such as data on the size of the efficiencies the merger would generate) which competition theory suggests are relevant. Although the cost of this approach could be reduced by allocating to plaintiffs the burden of proving the frequency and amount by which the merger partners are each other's closest competitors and by allocating to defendants the burden of establishing the size and character of the efficiencies their merger would generate (or by selling to defendants the right to engage in their merger for an appropriate price), the approach would still be expensive. I have no doubt, though, that some more or less refined version of this system would be more cost-effective and less costly than the traditional market definition-market share-market concentration approach[10].

Before proceeding, I should emphasize the cost advantages of my approach. Lawyers always hesitate to reject traditional legal approaches in favor of more economically sophisticated proposals because of their fear that the more sophisticated approach will prove unworkable in practice — will not be operational in litigation. However, this fear is unfounded in the present context: a large part of my point is that the traditional legal approach is itself unworkable — that the search for an inevitably arbitrary market definition whose choice may make a difference of millions of dollars leads counsel on both sides to make antitrust litigation almost inconceivably expensive not only by flooding the courts with enormous amounts of data but also by making interminable arguments about the characterization of the market. The fact is that the decision about how to define the relevant traditional market(s) consumes a huge amount of resources and succeeds only in reducing the predictive value of the data on which it is based — i.e., succeeds only in permitting courts to base their decisions on aggregated market concentration and market share figures that have less predictive value than the disaggregated data on which the courts based their underlying market definitions.

Economists are fond of telling the story of the drunk who is encountered one night down on his hands and knees searching for something under a

[10] For a complete analysis, see Markovits, (1978). The approach that I have described will not only enable courts to produce more accurate answers more cheaply, it will also provide better guidance to businessmen. Thus, executives should be able to determine the facts that my approach makes relevant with sufficient accuracy to assess the legality of a proposed merger before they act. These facts include the frequency and amount by which the merger partners were each other's closest competitors, the size of the efficiencies their merger would generate, the frequency with which they were either second-best-placed to obtain a rival's customer or worse-than-second-best-placed by a small enough margin for them to become second-best or best-placed post-merger, the original profitability of contrived oligopolistic pricing for the relevant firms, and the extent to which the merger would increase the profitability of such pricing.

streetlight. When asked what he is looking for, he responds — "My wallet, I lost it up there." — and points to a dark alley. "But why, then, are you looking for it under the streetlight?" his interlocutor inquires. "Because the light's better down here." comes the response. In fact, to my mind, the courts are even more misguided in this area than the drunk of this story. They are searching at night in a dark alley for a wallet they lost under the streetlight. Not only are they unlikely to find what they seek, they are likely to spend a great deal of unnecessary time and resources in the search. Reasonable men can differ about the optimal amount of data to collect when analyzing individual cases using my non-market-oriented approach. This approach can be executed with data on more or fewer variables and with data of more or less accuracy. However, I have no doubt that my approach would be far more cost-effective than the traditional approach. In fact, I suspect that the optimal version of my approach would be cheaper as well as more accurate than the traditional market definition-market share-market concentration approach but even if it is not, any additional cost would be well worth the expense.

5.2 Sanctions and Victim Compensation

The cost-effectiveness of my ideal antitrust regime can also be increased by adopting an appropriate set of policies regarding sanctions and victim compensation. The deterrent effect of a given law depends on the extent to which its sanctions reduce the certainty of equivalent profits which its addressees expect to realize *ex ante* from the behavior it covers — i.e., the dollar value they place on the probability distribution of possible outcomes the behavior may generate, the weighted average expected value of that distribution minus the negative value its evaluators plan in the risk they confront. Accordingly, even if the law's addressees were risk neutral, an antitrust agency could reduce its enforcement expenditures sufficiently to halve the probability of an offender's being detected, prosecuted, and convicted without reducing the law's deterrent impact if the legal sanction were doubled. In fact, since businesses tend to be quite risk averse, doubling the sanction would more than double the deterrent impact, other things being equal. Admittedly, not all the *ceteris* would be *paribus*: the deterrent effect of doubling the sanction and cutting enforcement expenditure would be reduced to the extent that such a policy would lower the offender's expected *ex ante* litigation costs, make it profitable for him to increase his litigation expenditures when he is prosecuted, and make fact finders reluctant to convict him by making them operate in a situation in which convicted defendants have to pay disproportionate fines. And, of course, all our societies are committed to notions of rights or distributional values that respectively limit the extent to which we can make an example of those we do convict — the extent to which we can use them as means rather than as ends (can make the punishment not fit the crime)[11] — and make it distributionally costly for us to treat the

[11] Admittedly, such distributional principles may have less force when defendants are companies rather than individuals.

convicted in certain ways even within those limits. However, there is no doubt that the desirability of my regime could be enhanced by an appropriate sanctions-enforcement cost policy.

I also think that antitrust can be improved if the victims of antitrust violations are treated appropriately. More particularly, I would require antitrust authorities to compensate victims appropriately for providing information that leads to the conviction of antitrust violators and authorize victims to bring antitrust suits themselves if the government decides not to proceed with a suit after it has received all relevant information from the victim. In fact, I would allow judges in such private anitrust suits to grant victim-plaintiff supra-compensatory damages to the extent that the plaintiff in question's marginal or incremental litigation expenses would be likely to increase his normal *ex ante* expected damage award by less than the social value they would generate. No doubt, the authorization of such private suits and supra-compensatory damages would produce some undesirable results — would induce some businesses to attack their rivals' legitimate competition, to delay their attacks on antitrust violations, and/or to fail to mitigate damages. However, I think that the costs associated with these possibilities would be lower than the benefits that private suits would generate by combatting the tendency of low antitrust budgets and political influence to prevent antitrust agencies from bringing socially desirable suits.

5.3 Governmental Institutional Arrangements

The preceding economic analysis should have made clear that optimal antitrust decisions cannot be made without (1) a sophisticated theoretical understanding of the functions, competitive impact, and allocative efficiency of the transactions or practices in question; (2) detailed factual information about the transaction or practice under scrutiny; and (3) detailed factual background information about the many variables that would affect the competitive impact and allocative efficiency of practices with given known functions and effects on price, QV investment, etc. Such information is necessary both to determine whether a given transaction or practice should be allowed or condemned outright and to determine the optimal price to charge a business for the right to engage in conduct that does have some bad effects but is alleged to have offsetting good effects. Accordingly, regardless of the kind of institution that is authorized to initiate antitrust interventions, a large, sophisticated staff of economic analysts and data collectors would have to be provided. In fact, my own preference would be to establish a body that would collect the information necessary to evaluate given practices or transactions on a continuous economy-wide basis, i.e. to have such data collection be independent of individual prosecutorial or "permit pricing" decisions.

The next question is the character of the body that should be authorized to initiate antitrust actions. Two considerations influence my institutional preferences in this context: (1) my desire to put decisions in the hands of experts and (2) my desire to insulate decisionmakers from political influence.

In relation to prosecutorial decisions, specialized agencies or prosecutorial offices are more likely to develop the necessary expertise than non-specialized prosecutorial offices. However, they are also likely to be more vulnerable to capture by the businesses whose conduct they are trying to control. On balance, I would prefer the decision to be placed in the hands of the experts, in part because the diversity of the relevant business interests reduces the risk of capture. The choice between an antitrust agency and an antitrust division within a department or ministry of justice would depend on the political traditions within the country in question — on whether independent regulatory agencies really are independent and on whether significantly-placed lawyers in departments of justice are civil servants who prize their independence or are political appointees who value their ability to respond to their political leaders' political preferences. As I have indicated, my preference in this area would always be for the institutional arrangement that minimizes political influence in the antitrust area.

My preference for political insulation also leads me to reject any proposal that initial prosecutorial decisions be subject to presidential or ministerial review or veto. I can imagine situations in which ministers would believe that, in the special circumstances that prevail, the public interest requires the reversal of an antitrust prosecutor's decision to attack some business decision. However, in virtually all such cases, the minister will be able to respond to the special circumstances both more openly and more productively in other ways. Take, for example, the case of an anti-competitive horizontal merger that a minister does not want to prohibit because it would induce the MPs or their rivals to maintain an additional plant or outlet (to increase their QV investments) in an area in which there is substantial unemployment. Rather than allowing the merger to go forward, the minister could respond to this problem by offering to pay companies to hire additional workers or construct new facilities in the relevant area. Although the wisdom of such a regional policy could also be called into question, I would prefer the government to make its case for such an approach directly and openly rather than to pursue it indirectly and perhaps covertly by vetoing antitrust prosecutorial decisions. At least in part, my preference on this issue reflects my fear that presidents and ministers would often want to use such arguments to rationalize political interventions in the antitrust area whose motivations are far more venal (either personally or politically). Accordingly, in addition to selecting the prosecutorial institution that was most likely to be able to withstand informal political pressure, I would deny government ministers the formal right to veto the government's antitrust prosecutors' prosecutorial decisions.

Many Europeans may find this solution unacceptable. Even those who share my fears about political venality may prefer a process in which antitrust prosecutors are required to announce publicly their formal antitrust decisions but in which ministers have the right to reverse such decisions for stated reasons after their announcement. In fact, my system does not prevent political reversals of prosecutorial decisions: it simply forces the government in a parliamentary system or the president and congress in a congressional system to reverse such decisions by passing new legislation. Admittedly, that process is more cumbersome than direct minsiterial review, but that is why I like it. My respect for expertise, fear of political venality, and related doubts that a properly trained and informed antitrust office will often make decisions that ought to be reversed before trial make me want to increase the difficulty of political reversals of antitrust intervention decisions. If it is any consolation, my system would increase the difficulty of such reversals less in parliamentary systems than in congressional systems (where congress and the presidency are often controlled by different parties and party members are less controllable from the top in any case).

Precisely the same issues arise in relation to the final decisions about particular business practices, i.e., about whether they should be permitted or prohibited, about whether the right to engage in the relevant conduct should be sold, about the size of the fine that should be levied, the private recovery that should be awarded where past conduct is deemed to be illegal, or about the price for which the right to engage in some transaction should be sold. Once more, my preferences largely reflect my desire to have decisionmakers who have the relevant expertise and political independence. My concern about expertise would lead me to reject the idea of placing such decisions in the hands of lay juries or judges in courts of general jurisdiction. My concern about both expertise and political independence would lead me to reject any attempt to authorize the president or some minister to reverse or even alter any decision of the judge or commissioner of last resort. And my belief that judicial traditions, life tenure, and the requirement that judges justify their decisions in writing help to make judges more politically independent than commissioners leads me to prefer to give final antitrust decision making authority to life-tenured judges, sitting in specialized courts, and subject to the normal judicial requirement of offering written reasoned justifications for their conclusions.

6. Antitrust, Delegalization and Their Alternatives

In this concluding part, I will discuss 1) the relationship between antitrust and delegalization, 2) the risk that in practice my ideal antitrust system would be marked by the same deficiencies that are said to afflict juridification in general and contemporary antitrust law in particular, and 3) the possibility that one could produce better results by rejecting my proposal in favor of a more "responsive" approach which (a) would require business conduct of certain types to be approved by industry-wide producer organizations, (b) would place consumer, labor, and minority representatives on corporate boards of directors, or (c) would require businesses that propose to engage in various kinds of conduct to gain the approval of an external organization that has consumer, labor, and minority as well as business representatives.

6.1 Antitrust as a Form of Delegalization

Welfare economics teaches that an "unregulated" economy will maximize allocative efficiency if there is (a) universal perfect competition (no monopoly and no monoposony); (b) no externalities; (c) no human errors — no misperceptions of value and no failures to maximize, given the maximizer's perceptions of value; (d) no taxes on the margin of income; and (e) no problems caused by consumer surplus.

Put simply, the economy will be allocatively efficient if these so-called Pareto optimal conditions are fulfilled because their satisfaction will guarantee (a) that the dollar gains any consumer or producer realizes by making some allocative choice equal the allocative value the choice will generate; (b) that the private dollar costs any consumer or producer will incur by making such choices will equal their allocative counterparts; and (c) that the private dollar gains any such choices generate will exceed the private costs.

In fact, the simultaneous fulfillment of all five conditions help to achieve various other antitrust goals as well: (a) will facilitate the deconcentration of political power; (b) will reduce the amount of labor market discrimination due to monopoly-inflated wages (though it will not eliminate such discrimination since the market does not distinguish between prejudices and other tastes); and (c) will reduce the inequalities of income caused by monopoly (though it will produce substantial inequalities since it will distribute income according to the vastly different marginal allocative products of the last worker in each job).

However, it is obviously misleading to say that the economy that would produce these results is unregulated in the sense of being untouched by governmental processes. To the contrary, the relevant conditions cannot be fulfilled unless the government is very active — unless it (a) has an active antitrust policy that eliminates imperfections in competition; (b) has a property law system that assigns rights to anything of economic value to single property-right holders, a contract system that enforces all promises, and a tort system that corrects the failure of the property system to provide and protect such universal, individualized property rights; (c) has a consumer protection system which guarantees that consumers will be properly informed of the attributes of each product or service and provides them with cost information and general education that eliminate the possibility of their making mathematical maximization errors. In fact, juridification that seeks to satisfy the Pareto optimal conditions may suffer from the same defects as juridification that tries to offset Pareto imperfections, for example, by regulating a monopolist's pricing and QV investment decisions; by regulating production processes to prevent misallocative externalities; by imposing effluent taxes; or by banning or taxing goods whose value may be exaggerated by their likely consumers. Still, it is important to note that antitrust in its classical form is an attempt to avoid such regulatory interventions — to produce an economic structure which will guarantee that the actions of individuals engaged in market bargaining will be socially desirable.

Admittedly, the antitrust regime I have proposed would be both broader in scope and more selective than a classical universal pro-competition policy. As we saw, my ideal system differs from such a classical counterpart both because behavior that is not anti-competitive may still be undesirable and because (for both second-best and OLE reasons) behavior that is anti-competitive may be socially desirable. Still, even my antitrust regime seeks in part to structure markets in a way that makes it socially efficient to take advantage of the efficiencies that markets can generate by placing decisions in the hands of people who have best access to the information that determines their social (as well as private) desirability. In that sense and to that extent, the antitrust regime I have proposed is an alternative to regulatory juridification — a "procedural" or "institutional" attempt to structure the economy in a way that results in the public interests being served by the market bargains made by people who are seeking their own interests.

One can obtain socially optimal decisions from people who do not care about the "social effects which their strategies for the maximization of their specific rationality trigger." (Teubner, supra: 38). In particular, one can obtain desirable decisions from individuals or institutions without making them "sensitive" (the word is Teubner's, supra: 38) to these social effects — without structuring them so that they have a social "organizational conscience" (the phrase is Teubner's, supra: 38) by arranging matters so that their private interests coincide with the social interest. The traditional rationale for the market is that it achieves this result. The rationale I have offered for my ideal antitrust regime is that it enables the market to achieve this result by restructuring incentives rather than institutional motivations.

6.2 My Proposal and the Conventional Critique of Juridification

Throughout this paper, I have argued that the various proposals I have made would increase welfare primarily by increasing allocative efficiency and improving the distribution of income but also by reducing labor market discrimination and in most cases deconcentrating political power. In this section, I will explore the extent to which the conventional critique of juridification applies to my proposal as well — whether my scheme is likely to fail for the same reasons that other "purposive" legislation is alleged to have failed.

Gunther Teubner (supra: 19 ff., 27 ff.) lists four general deficiencies of purposive law that some might think could be found in my ideal antitrust regime as well. Although I have dealt with each at appropriate points in the preceding text, it might be helpful for me to summarize my responses here.

First, Teubner points out that government regulation sometimes leads to a reduction in freedom, to a shift of attention from the preservation of autonomy to the pursuit of various other purposive ends, (supra, 15) and indicates that this "problem" is certainly posed by the kind of antitrust approach I am proposing (supra, 15). As I have already indicated, I believe that if these concepts are defined in a way that enables them to play a significant role in moral, political and legal discourse, "autonomy," "freedom," and "liberty" will rarely if ever be undermined by the kind of antitrust policy I have proposed. Although state regulations that are designed to prevent allocative inefficiency, maldistributions of income from the perspective of value systems that are not inconsistent with notions of autonomy, labor market discrimination, and concentrations of political power may undermine liberty as license, they will not undermine liberty as independence: individuals simply do not have the right to pursue their own interests in the relevant sort of matters without regard to the social consequences of their choices.

Second, Teubner argues that the effectiveness of many purposive law systems is undermined by their inevitable tendency to become increasingly complex and incomprehensible and cites two studies of antitrust which suggest that this tendency has created a kind of "growth crisis" in this field (Teubner, supra: 22; Hopt, supra: 315). Since limitations of space have reduced the extent to which I can argue for this conclusion here, I must simply assert that the four tests of legality I have proposed and the two standards for selling the right to engage in particular conduct I have delineated are not incomprehensible and could be employed at non-prohibitive cost.

Third, Teubner argues that purposive law in general runs the risk of preventing desirable behavior that would have taken place in its absence (supra, 24 ff.). As I have indicated, that is a real problem where antitrust is concerned: to the extent that legal information imperfections make it risky for firms to engage in lawful competition, antitrust may deter socially desirable competitive conduct. However, because I believe that properly-trained decisionmakers would be able to distinguish illegal from legal behavior, I doubt that substantial losses would result on this account. In fact, it may be recalled that I am sufficiently optimistic about this issue to allow private parties (including competitors) to bring antitrust suits in appropriate circumstances.

Finally, Professor Teubner notes that purposive law regimes are often undermined by regulatory capture or political intervention (supra, 30 f.). This is certainly a risk for antitrust as well. In the United States, the Antitrust Division of the Department of Justice does have some political insulation, though Presidential or Executive Office interventions are definitely not unknown. My own inclination is to try to weaken such political pressures by eliminating formal presidential or ministerial reviews of antitrust decisions, by allowing private antitrust suits, and by giving antitrust jurisdiction to specialized courts whose members have life tenure. Although the specialization of the relevant decisionmaking bodies increases the risk of capture, life tenure, judicial traditions, and the juridical requirement that courts justify their decisions in written opinions make the associated risk acceptable to me.

In short, although some of Teubner's concerns apply to my antitrust regime as well, I do not find them sufficiently weighty to justify either the delegalization of antitrust or the substitution of one of the various responsive approaches to which we will now turn.

6.3 Alternatives to Antitrust: A Review of Some Other "Responsive" Institutional Options

I have already suggested that my ideal antitrust regime is "responsive" to the extent that it represents an attempt to make it unnecessary for the government to allocate resources itself to order others to allocate resources in particular ways, or (with the partial exception of my proposal that antitrust offices be authorized to sell the right to engage in conduct that has some undesirable consequences) to attempt to offset various Pareto imperfections by imposing appropriate taxes or granting appropriate subsidies. Ideally, antitrust should obviate the government's engaging in any of these activities by restructuring the economy to eliminate the private incentives which private actors might otherwise have to make socially undesirable decisions.

However, one might also try to prevent businesses from engaging in socially undesirable conduct in a number of other ways. This section will be concerned with other "procedural" or "institutional" alternatives to antitrust.

The first and least promising such alternative would be to try to increase the social consciousness of business organizations by requiring them to conform with codes of business conduct promulgated by each industry's members organized as a trade association. I would be surprised if such an institution would produce desirable results. The businesses themselves would obviously have every reason to pursue their own interests in the many cases in which they conflict with the welfare of their customers; the goal of promoting allocative efficiency; the value of preventing labor market discrimination; or the goal of preventing harmful agglomerations of political power. Indeed, often a majority of an industry's voters will find it advantageous to prevent one or more of their colleagues from engaging in socially desirable legitimate competition. It should therefore be no surprise that the American experience with such industry self-regulation (under the National Recovery Act of the Great Depression of the Thirties) was almost uniformly disastrous. Nor can any comfort be gained from the American or the European experience with professional self-regulation by lawyers, doctors, and dentists.

A second, more promising institutional or procedural alternative would be to try to increase the social consciousness of business organizations by changing the composition of their boards of directors to include workers, consumers, minority, and general public interest (democratic) advocates. I doubt the wisdom of this approach for several reasons. First, since conduct that increases allocative efficiency may injure the actor's customers and conduct that helps the actor's customers may reduce allocative efficiency, standard consumer representatives (who view their role as being one of protecting the buyers directly involved) are unlikely to provide the necessary pressures toward allocative efficiency. Second, since a company's consumers and workers will often have common interests that conflict with that of the public at large, it will be difficult to structure boards of directors to provide the necessary inclination to pursue the social welfare. Third, since management will often be better-informed about the relevant alternatives than the other sorts of representative described (and may be of higher status as well), the non-ownership directors may be too willing to accept the management's position. Fourth, since many of the social effects of particular kinds of conduct can be predicted only through sophisticated analysis in relation to which there are substantial economies of scale, the directors will be unlikely to have either the personal expertise or the staff help (though this might be provided by the state) necessary to enable them to evaluate the social desirability of alternative courses of action even if they are disposed to pursue the social good. And fifth, since investors will often be harmed by the socially conscious decisions of their company's board, it may seem unfair for their losses to be determined by the social diligence or intellectual skills of the advocates who happen to be appointed to their company's board of directors. All these arguments lead me to prefer an antitrust policy that attempts to bring private and social incentives into line with each other rather than a more conventional "responsive" policy that tries to make organizations sacrifice their owners' interests for the public good.

The third constitutional alternative to antitrust would be to create a kind of business conduct commission external to the businesses in question and to authorize the commission to prohibit business conduct that it finds socially undesirable in the circumstances in question. Since such a commission could adopt the various tests and standards I have proposed, this alternative would be different from my own ideal only to the extent that its personnel and procedures differed from those I have recommended. I suspect that this more conventionally responsive version of my proposal would in fact be quite different in these respects. Instead of the technical experts I would appoint to decisionmaking positions, advocates of responsive law would tend to prefer representatives of the various interests involved (business, labor, consumers, minorities, democrats). Instead of institutionalizing "rational calculation," advocates of responsive law would prefer to institutionalize negotiation. The first four of my arguments against changing the composition of boards of directors apply here as well: I oppose such a commission both because I think that expertise is needed at the highest level of decisionmaking and because I doubt that the relevant interests would receive adequate representation (in either the structural or the performance sense) in any real-world commission. Such a commission would be incapable of adequately applying my tests and standards and would be unlikely to adopt them in the first place.

In short, I am confident (1) that the antitrust regime I have proposed would produce desirable results, (2) that it would not be prevented from doing so in practice by the various tendencies which are alleged to undermine purposive law in general and contemporary antitrust law in particular, (3) that my antitrust regime would be preferable to such conventional "responsive" procedural or institutional innovations as industry self-regulation, the appointment of non-ownership members to boards of directors, or the creation of a business conduct commission whose members are chosen to represent various affected interests, and (4) that my regime would in one sense itself be responsive in that it would obviate the government's taking a more directive or regulatory role by bringing private and social incentives into line with each other.

References

MARKOVITS, Richard (1975a) "A Basic Structure for Micro-Economic Policy Analysis in Our Worse-than-second-best World", *Wisconsin Law Review* 950.

— (1975b) "The Allocative Efficiency and Overall Desirability of Oligopolistic Pricing Suits", 25 *Stanford Law Review* 45.

— (1976) "The Causes and Policy Significance of Pareto Resource Misallocation: A Checklist for Micro-Economic Policy Analysis", 28 *Stanford Law Review* 1.

— (1978) "Predicting the Competitive Impact of Horizontal Mergers in a Monopolistically Competitive World: A Non-Market-Oriented Proposal and Critique of the Market Definition- Market Share-Market Concentration Approach", 56 *Texas Law Review* 587.

— (1980) "Tie-ins and Reciprocity: A Functional, Legal and Policy Analysis", 58 *Texas Law Review* 1303.

V

Social Welfare

Juridification in the Field of Social Law*

Hans F. Zacher

Munich

Contents

* My special thanks are due to Professor Roger Lawson and to Mrs. Eva Lutz to whom I am greatly indebted for their help with the English version of the present text. Finally, I should also like to thank Professor Martin Partington for his comments on the English translation.

1. Preliminary Definition of Terms

1.1 What is Social Law?

(1) The German View as Starting Point

A report on the phenomenon of juridification in the field of social law[1] requires a basic understanding of what is meant by "social law"[2].

In the German Federal Republic there is a growing feeling that the concept of social law refers to law characterized by its socio-political objectives. In the social welfare state, however, such objectives are omnipresent, i.e., they potentially characterize all law. It is also obvious that socio-political objectives are found to a varying degree in different areas of regulation and that law is characterized by social aims to a widely varying extent and intensity. We can

[1] See here above all Tennstedt (1976); Widmeier (1976: 21ff., 101ff., 151); von Bethusi-Huc (1976: 256ff); Henke (1980); Pitschas (1980); Reidegeld (1980); Habermas (1981, Vol. 2: 522ff.; 1985: 203ff.); Luhmann (1981a: particularly 94); Mayntz/Flick (1982); Voigt (1983a).

[2] See here and with reference to the following, Schmid (1981). With reference to the multiple international findings see also the older literature quoted in this work.

therefore approach a definition by saying that law increasingly becomes social law the more it is shaped by a socio-political purpose and vice versa. Such an open definition suggests a core of distinct meaning, with qualificatory force that is lost the further we move away from the center. When defining a term, however, it is precisely in this core meaning that we are interested, and thus we must be more precise about it. The fact that some areas of law owe their origin to social policy *a priori* (primary social law), while other areas preceded social policy and were later altered by it or were used in other ways to serve its aims (secondary social law) facilitates this task. Primary social law in this sense is the law relating to social benefits and services (social assistance law, social insurance law, etc.) (Zacher, 1983b: 9). Secondary social law includes labor law, fair rent legislation, etc. The extent to which law outside primary social law has a social purpose, or can at least be regarded as socially problematic or socially effective varies, however, depending on subjective experience and evaluation, so that it is impossible to sort the areas of law into those which are social and nonsocial. In light of these considerations, it would seem appropriate, first, to define as secondary social law or social law in the widest sense, that body of law which is characterized by social intentions and which is in practice inseparable from other bodies of law, and, second, to define the legislation relating to social benefits and services, that is primary social law, as social legislation, or more precisely as social law in the narrower sense (see also Zacher, 1982a, 1983a, especially, 953).

What has been said up to now has been based on the assumption that the expressions "social" and "socio-political" are not in themselves problematic. This is indeed the case as the more general notions of "social" used in the sense of "societal" or "bound to society" (Zacher, 1980b: 18) do not apply in this context. Here we are dealing with the narrower, political, socially critical meaning of "social", which emerged in the 19th century and corresponds to the usage of the term "social movement". With the welfare state of the 20th century this notion was finally incorporated into the Constitution (Dürig, 1953: 196). Social policy (Pankoke, 1970: 167) — which is derived from this definition of "social" — historically originated as a form of aid for underprivileged groups. A prime example of this is the way the social question was equated with problems of the workers (*Arbeiterfrage*). It was not possible to help these groups generally but only in regard to certain situations. Social policy, therefore, took up situations where risk as well as the possibility of remedy manifested themselves in a special way. The basic risks of social insurance (such as sickness, old age, invalidity, etc.) may be quoted as an example of this phenomenon. The number of new groups and social situations necessitating intervention increased however, so that social policy in the end has come to be regarded as a matter of general concern for the well-being of the individual and his social group — and especially for the economic condition of people within society (Lampert, 1980: 166). At the same time different principles of social intervention arose, such as the basic maxim of combatting need (or granting a minimum level of existence), the egalitarian one of reducing differences between varying levels of material conditions (by relief, reduction or control of economically determined dependence, by giving equal opportunities and by redistribution) and the one of social security (of protection against the so-called "vicissitudes of life") — maxims which are ambiguous and overlapping.

In general it is easy to illustrate what is social. The peripheral areas, however, are broad and often remain uncertain (Luhmann, 1981a: 7). It is important to emphasize this since, according to different circumstances (groups and situations) and principles of social intervention, certain problems and solutions tend to be regarded as social ones whereas others, of similar importance are not given that title. Historically, the selection of what is social has depended on the complex constellations of societal and political conditions and their formulation. What is social is not a self-contained domain. It is the sum of potential social problems and solutions which, through polemic articulation and a more or less far-reaching consensus of opinion, are brought into consciousness as being social and which are designated as such. This was true at the very beginning when the "workers' problem" was articulated along with the "social question" while other forms of need were not so perceived and taken up — or at least were not treated as social; and this still applies today. With respect to politics and constitutional law, the title "social" is — despite the change in trends — one of the most imposing titles. It is not only claimed by those to whom it is objectively applicable but also by those who have acquired it by mere usurpation or political action, while certain needs are still waiting to be classified as "social" (Groser and Veiders, 1979).

This fundamental uncertainty about the very meaning of the term necessarily embraces the social law definition derived from the social character of the law as well. It even applies to the narrower domain of legislation relating to social benefits and services (i.e., social law in the narrower sense or primary social law), the clear-cut nature of the latter being due only to the distinction made between the regulation of benefits and services (cash benefits, social services or payments in kind) granted by the state to the individual for social purposes, and the mere modification of existing law (secondary social law, e.g., housing law). It certainly does not depend on benefits and services being defined as social and nonsocial ones. When, for example, may a medical treatment be regarded as a social service and when not? The answer turns upon various details concerning regulation and administration as well as one's societal and political viewpoint.

(2) National Differences

Both the definition and essence of social law differ from country to country (Schmid, 1981). At times a comparable word does not even exist, and in some cases only the later, narrower definition of "social security" has been taken up. In French usage, "*droit social*" is an established term which involves the equating of the "workers' problem" with the "social question". This embraces both labor law and the social security system, i.e., the provisions for employees relating to social benefits and services. With respect to the English usage, it is *a priori* difficult to determine a specific meaning when speaking of "social law". Within Anglo-Saxon countries both "welfare law" and "social security law" correspond in the first place to what is understood in the Federal Republic of Germany (FRG) by *Sozialrecht*, i.e., "social law".

It is the problems that have arisen within Anglo-Saxon countries in particular which make us realize that both terms, "social" and "law" and the connection between them, can be viewed in different ways. The English expression "social" and the German *sozial* simply do not correspond to one another (Zoellner, 1982: 7). The English concept of "social policy" emerged rather late (Cahnman/Schmitt, 1979). The German *Sozialstaat*, for example, is translated into English as "welfare state". When translating the term *sozial*, "welfare" remains an alternative to "social" in other contexts as well. Hence differences depend very much on judgments and on the ways the terms are used. Not every legal system can, however, be used to serve social policy in the same way; nor do they bear the same social characteristics. When, as is the case in Great Britain, "law" corresponds to a set of rules and institutions which in principle have developed autonomously and may be distinguished from "statute" (i.e., politically fabricated law) a distribution of roles takes place within the legal system according to special social functions (Brooke, 1979; Williams, 1979: 101). But this does not mean that it is impossible to locate the different elements of what is called *Sozialrecht* in the Federal Republic of Germany in a country with Anglo-Saxon stamp as well. What corresponds to this *Sozialrecht* will however be expressed in different terms and will be subject to another kind of demarcation, coordination, accentuation, classification and assignment.

1.2 The Question of Juridification in Social Law

(1) In General

The question of juridification (see, replacing all previous literature, Voigt, 1983, 1983a, 1983b; Habermas, 1981; Schlicht, 1982) is generally posed in critical terms. The implication is that the law has proliferated unduly, that it has moved into areas which it cannot or should not cover, and that it has been subject generally to excessive intensification and differentiation. Depending on the viewpoint of the observer, such an excrescence of law may also develop when sets of regulations, legal institutions, legal methods, and even legislators and those who apply the law leave their "proper" territory and encroach on foreign domain. Juridification in this sense implies a hybrid and misplaced evolution of law in relation to nonlaw — the area either completely free of regulation or subject to nonlegal rules — or of some species of law (authorities, institutions, methods) compared with other kinds of law. To this extent, juridification is based on a notion of the proper role of law, though this need not necessarily be clarified before discussing juridification. The issue of juridification can also be related to a feeling of unease about the consequences of law. This in turn is part of a syndrome according to which a sense of dissatisfaction about social conditions, which are subject to legislation or sets of legal rules, is linked with the suspicion that the evolution of law has something to do with these conditions.

The discussion of juridification is thus surrounded by uncertainties. In the final analysis, as has been said, it assumes an idea of "correct law", of its "proper" evolution and of a "proper" distribution of roles within law and between the law and other control mechanisms, as well as between legal norms and other rules. Where does this notion come from? How is it derived? Who is competent to define it? If we start with the syndrome relating to unsatisfactory social conditions, we must first of all determine the criteria for their evaluation and then ask the crucial question of whether the unsatisfactory conditions are due to the evolution of law or to other reasons. To talk about juridification is thus just as hazardous as it is important. It involves extremely complex relationships and the discussion covers widely different viewpoints.

If it is social law which is being discussed in this context, these difficulties are increased even more. From where can the correct picture of social law be derived? As well as the already outlined problems of defining social law, there are the complications due to its continually changing character, its late arrival as a science (Zacher, 1979a) and the difference between the proper social content of law and the right legal configuration. If it is the syndrome which is being discussed, the likelihood that judgment will be prejudiced is increased in that social law — like the social policy which helps mold it — has, of course, conditions which are *a priori* unsatisfactory as its object, and its aims and methods are controversial even in the prelegal stage. When are adequate or inadequate, possible or impossible demands made on law when dealing with juridification? And when is the right social objective aimed at, and when the wrong?

(2) The International Dimension

These difficulties are readily apparent in the comparative dimension. In the Federal Republic of Germany the debate over juridification in social law is conducted on the basis of three given conditions: first, the far-reaching development of the social state; second, the intensely legal form of this development, as evident in the close interconnection of social law and the rule of law; and third, in the discrepancy between unfulfilled social wishes on the one hand and actual political possibilities on the other, the latter lagging even behind the established norms. In other countries the extent to which these conditions exist differs widely, especially in regard to the first two conditions. This is partly because in some countries social policy has not evolved to the extent it has in West Germany, and partly because the law does not perform the role of medium and instrument of implementing social policy which it has been allocated in West Germany. In such cases the question of juridification has not arisen either because socio-political objectives have not been attained, and may yet be attained with the help of law, or because the law has made only a limited contribution in social policy, or for both reasons together.

To carry the juridification debate over into a foreign social law, where it has hitherto not been taken, is thus rather complicated. If the special nature of social law already makes it *a priori* difficult to speak of "correct" social law and to separate misgivings about social policy from legal unease, it would appear to be quite impossible to do this from the outside without the most thorough research and without making explicit all those features which are self-evident and implicit for the national observer.

1.3 About the Following Discussion

The following discussion is intended primarily to demonstrate the *variety of perspectives* from which juridification in the field of social law can be examined. There is a danger that such a discussion may be one-sided in reviewing certain aspects, while overlooking others. It is especially important from a comparative perspective to try and counteract this tendency. However, it would be outside the scope of this report to list these aspects in all their detail, particularly the corresponding relationships for various legal systems. Criteria of evaluation also appear to be secondary. As has already been said, the discussion of juridification has been triggered by a feeling of unease. It is associated with a syndrome in which neither the values which are to be applied, nor the nature of the relationships which are to be criticized on the basis of these, are or can be sufficiently clarified and explained. It therefore seems advisable to give priority to a problem survey as broad as it is differentiated.

With respect to the problems of social law, there appear to be two possible approaches which complement each other in grasping the overall phenomenon of juridification in social law.

— The question of the "location" of social law and thus the "location" of juridification in social law (Section 2).

— The question of the manifestations of juridification (Section 3).

Although this results in overlapping, it seems to be advisable to make parallel use of these two approaches. Finally, aspects of evaluation will be outlined (Section 4).

2. The Location of Social Law and Juridification in Social Law

2.1 Internalizing Versus Externalizing Solutions to Social Problems in Law

A process of juridification which has a long history is one under which law has been modified increasingly in line with social intentions, and has become more differentiated, complicated and vigorously enforced. Furthermore, a new tier of law, legislation on social benefits and services, has come more and more to complement in a social sense the already existing law relating to work, income, property, maintenance, and the general field relating to the satisfaction of needs. This new law for its part radiates in many ways into preexisting law, and gives a "second order" to those conditions of life which were initially regulated by the preexisting law[3].

[3] See with reference to the following Voigt (1983a; 1983b); Habermas (1981); Schlicht (1982); see also Henke (1980); Zacher (1981a), with further references. From the Anglo-Saxon literature in particular, Stone (1966: particularly 144 and 152ff. and references).

(1) Problem Areas of Social Benefits and Risks

Social law has evolved from the basic assumption that every adult has the possibility as well as the responsibility to earn a living for him or herself plus family (spouse and children) by working (either employed or self-employed). This basic assumption is no more than a general rule, i.e., something which embraces the possibility and reality of exceptions. It permits the taking into account of a variety of exceptions as deficits, which can be evaluated and remedied. Social law is, to begin with, the part which the law plays in defining the exceptions to the prescribed rule as social deficits, and compensating these to a greater or lesser degree, in one way or another.

The basic assumption of the general rule: that work provides income and that income is adequate to meet the needs of the income earner and the dependents of the earner, reveals three central problem areas.

(a) *Work and income*: the social organization of work and the earning of income by work.
Here of course the element of *property* must be mentioned, which considerably complicates the picture. *Assets*, i.e., active capital, can supplement and replace income and in particular act as a "safety-net" for losses of earnings. *Liabilities*, i.e., passive capital can, on the other hand, reduce assets and income and thus put the satisfaction of needs and subsistence requirements at risk.

(b) *Coverage of needs*: the social organization of the private and public supply of commodities to cover needs.

(c) *Family unit*: in which not only income for maintenance is required, but also the satisfaction of active needs for education, care, etc.

The basic rule — that work provides income and that this serves to satisfy needs, including those within the family unit — involves, however, *risks* (due to lack of independence or particular circumstances, e.g., hazardous occupations, risky medical treatment, etc.), and its realization is thus circumscribed. This is where social *deficits* become evident. Risks and deficits are the challenge to and object of social intervention. Such social problems — social risks and deficits — can be discerned in all three of the above-mentioned areas. But they can only seldom be restricted to these. The *majority* of social problems arise from the *interdependence of the areas*, or at least derive a particular significance from this interdependence.

Reduced ability to work and thus reduced income means a reduction in the ability to meet needs and provide maintenance.

The death of a wage-earner cuts off the link which he supplied between the "work-income" field and the family unit. At the same time, the consequences for the ability of the family-unit to satisfy its needs are evident.

The problem of need has one aspect when the need (e.g., medical treatment in case of illness) means a deficit in work, and another when the need (as with the illness of a child) imposes a burden on the breadwinner.

(2) Necessity for Externalizing Solutions

Problems cannot always be satisfactorily resolved in the fields in which they arise. If a handicapped person for example is permanently unable to work, in the social welfare state there is no other solution than to replace his income by social security benefits. Where solutions to problems are sought and found in the "natural" problem fields, the solutions are internalized in the sense that they are based on a connection with the "natural" problems. Together with these kinds of solutions we also have externalizing problem solutions: thus *internalizing* arises when given regulatory systems such as the organization of work, housing, or education are themselves socially corrected or modified, and *externalizing* when the social correction is removed and isolated from this relationship.

Safety of work and the liability of the employer for work accidents constitute an internalizing solution approach within labor law to the problem of work hazard. Accident insurance is an externalizing solution approach to the same problem.

The enlargement of maintenance obligations to cover the extended family is an attempt at an internalizing remedy for inadequacies within the family unit. Children's allowances, old-age pensions, survivors' pensions, etc., are externalizing solutions.

Free university education is an internalizing solution to the problem of providing education. The provision of educational grants and allowances as a social service is an externalizing solution to the related problems of income and maintenance.

Social deficits and their correction thus form a whole which contains two dimensions, i.e., the assignment to problem fields and the choice between an internalizing and externalizing solution. It is true that social risks arising out of dependency have their fixed location, in work life, in the family unit, in the satisfaction of particular needs (e.g., education or care) [4], and, as soon as they exist, in the social benefits systems themselves[5]. For deficits, however, such as inability to work, failure of income or maintenance, or increased needs as in the case of illness, there arises a further choice between several modes of compensation: between the different problem fields (work and income; coverage of needs; family unit) on the one hand, as well as between internalization and externalization on the other hand. With externalizing solutions there is also the question of which existing problem fields they should be assigned to. The history of social policy is precisely a history of trial and error in selecting the right means.

[4] Whereby it must not be overlooked that externalising solutions may relieve dependencies (as e.g. sickness benefits relieve the tensions which arise in the work relationship due to the incapacity for work of the employee, and give the employee a greater freedom to come to terms with his incapacity for work).

[5] What is meant here is in particular discriminations and relationships of dependency in the supplying of social benefits and services (particularly social services and payments in kind).

(3) Internalizing versus Externalizing Solutions in Law

The elementary structures of work and income, coverage of needs and family unit, and the alternatives of internalizing and externalizing solutions, with the social problems which lie within and between these, have two main corresponding relationships in law:

— See under a), on the one hand in the law as it relates to (i) work, income and property, (ii) the production and redistribution of consumer goods and (iii) the family maintenance units, i.e., the sphere of internalizing solutions.

— See under b), on the other hand, the legislation relating to social benefits and services, genuine social law, i.e. the sphere of externalizing solutions.

a) Existing Legal Systems

(i) To consider existing legal systems first, in the field of *work and income*, we find labor law (relating to work for an employer) and also all the regulations concerning independent employment (contract law for services, partnership law, the law relating to agriculture, the liberal professions, commercial enterprises, and others).
As regards *property*, we must take into consideration law, such as copyright law, which guarantees the long-term use of earnings and law which permits the accumulation of income as well as the investment and utilization of assets (land law, joint-stock company law, credit system law, law on savings and capital formation, etc.). To this list also belongs the regulation of liability and debt (reduction of liability under labor law in the case of hazardous work, limits on liability, exemptions from seizure, etc.).

(ii) In the field of *needs and their satisfaction* we encounter the finely graduated system of rules of public and private law, which constitute the framework for the private provision of foodstuffs, clothing, services, housing, etc. These range from the elementary and general rules of private law to the specific provisions of professional law and consumer protection. In addition, there are the areas in which greater weight is attached *a priori* to collective responsibility, e.g., the provision of education, training and extrafamilial care, of medical and hospital treatment, etc. Here we find in some cases a rigorous public control of the supply of private services (for example, law governing doctors in countries which have no comprehensive national health service) and in other cases the institutional provision of public services (e.g. school and national health services), with the latter also covering many socially completely nonspecific commodities such as water, transport services, etc.[6].

[6] On the relationship between provision for existence *Daseinsvorsorge* and social intervention see Zacher (1980b: 37ff., with further references). For a widening of the spectrum of intervention from the particularity of the social state to the universality of the welfare state see Luhmann (1981a: 7ff., 25 ff.). In the 1960s and 70s this expansion was discussed in particular also with reference to the slogan of "quality of life".

(iii) The field of the *family maintenance unit* is simpler. Here it is essentially family law which is involved.

All these areas of law have the social task of insuring, through efficient and purposeful organization, that a basic harmony of work, income, needs (satisfaction of needs), and maintenance, is preserved as far as possible, and of reinforcing the ability of the individual to deal with changes (e.g., by his own provisions and by family solidarity). It is this task which itself already leads to modifications, differentiations and intensifications of law, i.e., to a type of juridification.

b) Law Relating to Social Benefits and Services

Where, however, functional failures in the basic structures of work, income and maintenance or a mismatch between needs, income and maintenance can only be adequately compensated and corrected, by either the collective provision of income and maintenance, with supplementation according to needs, or by satisfying needs through public services offered at little or no charge, a threshold of fundamental importance is crossed. General (state, local authority, etc.) or specific (e.g., social insurance institutions) bodies assume the task of compensating for deficits. In this way not only deficits from existing fields can be met, but new deficits relating to more general norms of social well-being can be taken into account, defined and compensated. In this upper echelon of social correction, everything is equally infinitely possible and limited. What happens depends on a decision, generally one involving the law.

In more concrete terms, we are entering the area of social benefits and services (in particular social security and social advancement), which means in law the area of social legislation or social law in the narrower sense (see supra 1.1). In the German system this refers to the law of social insurance (health, pension, accident, and unemployment insurance), social compensation law (war victims pensions, compensation for victims of crime, etc.), law relating to special assistance and advancement schemes (children's allowances, maintenance allowances, youth welfare, promotion of training and employment, and housing allowances) and to the general assistance and services provided by social assistance (See for exemplification Zacher, 1983b). It is important to note that these systems link together very different types of service, i.e., cash payments on the one hand and payments in kind and other services on the other. It is precisely with respect to the law, and more particularly in terms of an international comparison, that we need to consider not only the subject of social intervention (such as sickness, old age, disability), but also its content and methods (differences here are clearly manifested in the contrast between cash payments, particularly income maintenance payments on the one hand, and payments in kind and services on the other)[7].

[7] Fournier and Questiaux (1980: 76ff., 1091): there social intervention is divided into three spheres: 1) the regulation of private activities, 2) the transfer of monetary resources and 3) the supplying of goods and services. Within the meaning of the

Two areas of law where there are similarities and dissimilarities as regards the externalizing solution to social problems are *private insurance law* and the *law of private — at least voluntary (i.e. nonstate) — charity.* Both can be only mentioned here in passing.

c) Overlapping Legal Areas

Part of the socially-politically relevant law can, however, not easily be assigned to these elements. The *taxation law* (Kirchhof, 1983), for example, can be used with respect to all legal areas in the sense of exacting taxes, tax exemption and as a mode of contribution. To exempt from taxation is, in general, an alternative to direct subsidies (Parker, 1982; Birk, 1979); and exacting taxes is a necessary precondition which makes benefits possible. Exempting may increase the ability for self-provision, and specific forms of taxation (e.g., contributions) may aim at externalizing provisions (Zacher, 1980a).

Criminal law (Stolleis, 1980: 125) gives support to all the outlined orders, but it also necessarily creates social damage.

In comparison to the externalizing solutions of social policy and the existing legal systems, these overlapping legal areas are closely linked to the legal system; unlike primary social law, they, too, have more general objects and functions which do not depend on a social designation.

(4) Location and Territory of Juridification

This map of social law shows that the processes referred to under the heading juridification have come or are coming into being in very different terrains and environments. Moreover, the conditions under which *internalizing solutions* are adopted are determined by the constitution and organization of the respective areas (work and income; need coverage; family unit). Put very simply, in the case of an internalizing solution two processes of juridification come together. On the one hand, there is the legal framework which existed in a particular area before any social intervention took place, the subsequent development of this framework as a result of changing social conditions, the need to exercise control over a particular sphere of life, and the general development of the legal order. On the other hand, there is the additional juridification which results specifically from social intervention if and in so far as it employs the law. In reality, these developments naturally take place in a complex way. It is quite possible, for example, that it is social intervention through law in a particular sphere of life that first makes its legal ordering necessary. Overall, we are faced with a wide range of possibilities. At one extreme we find an independent private life lived in interchange with more or less intensely regulated economic and social systems. At the other extreme

above text, the regulation of private activities corresponds to the social penetration of existing fields of law. The transfer of monetary resources and supply of goods and services, however, corresponds to the law relating to social benefits and services.

there is maximum regulation of the economic and social systems surrounding private life, culminating in a law which penetrates increasingly, with ever more differentiation and comprehensiveness into private areas of life (see Habermas, 1981, Vol. 2: 471ff., 510ff. See, with respect to the phenomena discussed, Burman and Harrell-Bond, 1978).

By contrast, *externalizing* solutions (social law as such) are *a priori* artificial solutions, which require at least an organizational and institutional representation. To what extent they also require legal ordering appears initially to be a question of their content and form, and then of the framework of constitutional and other law. But even where these do not impose a particular legal framework, there is inherent in externalizing solutions a built-in compulsion towards legal regulation, as an elementary necessity. Externalization is thus very much a manifestation of juridification. The creation of new risk-sharing communities which take charge of these externalizations, together with the generation and guaranteeing of those expectations, by which social security makes life more secure is in the final analysis only possible through law. Naturally, we cannot speak of uniformity. Externalizing solutions have their normative side (steering behavior, opening up expectations, and guaranteeing their fulfillment) and their institutional (organizational, actionist) side. What emerges is a question of both their form and also their political and legal environment. It is, however, conceivable that the normative element may retreat far into the background and the institutional "actionist" aspect becomes conceptually decisive. For social intervention via social work this is essentially the case, as we see clearly in the Federal German Republic today. In France, the comprehensive *action sociale*, i.e. social work and other related socio-political activities (Alfandari, 1974; Lory, 1975), is considered in a sense as supplementing the law, i.e., as being related to the law, but as well, independent and not defined by it. In Anglo-Saxon usage, terms such as "program" and "service" still apply very much today in the language of social service systems even though these are regulated by law[8]. But however that may be, in a democratic and constitutional state — whether it is called that or not — externalizing solutions require legitimization by the law, and only via rules of law do they achieve a certain degree of general validity and reliability. In most cases, however, the law goes beyond the minimum established in this way, not least because the artificiality of externalizing solutions, which are designed to complement or replace natural spheres of living, leads increasingly to further and repeated demands for clarification and modification, and the most effective instrument for dealing with these consists of legal rules. Externalizing solutions are thus inherently liable to lead to increased juridification.

[8] Partly this is also a reminder that there was a wish to exclude the old classical law (not decreed and in the hands of a limited circle of judges) from social policy, in order to replace it by a new instrumental law, by statutes, the interpretation of which was to be in the hands of tribunals. See also Brooke (1979); Williams (1979).

Juridification of this kind connected with externalizing solutions spreads out in many different directions (Dupeyroux, 1981: 264; Nef, 1981). Life has a new standardization imposed upon it. Facts of life such as sickness, old age, reduced earning capacity, or unemployment, which initially exist in an infinite number of different forms and constellations, become objects of law on which whole systems of service, financing, and organization, are built up. Further, they become objects of law and all interested parties are involved in negotiating over them (Habermas, 1981: 532; 1985: 209 "redefinition of everyday situations"). They also effect existing legal orders in the areas of life with which they are concerned. One need only think of the interrelationship between labor law and social insurance law (Binder, 1980; Kremalis, 1982), social assistance law and maintenance law (Ruland, 1973; Gitter and Hahn-Kemmier, 1979), and tort law and social service law in order to find examples (see von Maydell, 1981; Nef, 1981). Familiar patterns of living are changed following the introduction of educational grants and benefits, old age pensions, survivors' pensions etc. (see Kaufmann, 1982a). With the building up of externalizing solutions, life is shaped by law into two moulds, by direct law as such and by developed social benefit legislation.

Furthermore, out of externalizing solutions new areas of social interaction emerge, both in and between organizations, and between organizations and their public[9]. They are subject to processes of juridification going in opposite directions. On the one hand, they owe their existence to the social intervention of the law. On the other hand the growing needs for control and more regulation which develop from them lead to a further proliferation of law.

In a simplified way, the following periods in the progress of juridification in the field of social law can be distinguished:

[9] A really extreme example of juridification as a consequence of the diversity of the administrative authorities is provided in the history of social assistance law in Germany. Up to the time following the Second World War, the individual was not granted a legal right to social assistance, so that no interpretative legal culture could arise out of the complaints of those receiving social assistance. But the limitation on the obligation to supply social assistance of the social assistance institutions, and the claims for reimbursement made by the institutions not finally competent against the finally responsible institutions led to disputes between the institutions which resulted in a high judicial and literary level of interpretation — such as might not have been expected against the background of lack of legal entitlement. There is rich documentation to be found in the literature relating to the *Unterstützungswohnsitzgesetz* of 1870 and the *Reichsfürsorgepflichtverordnung* of 1924. Another example of juridification as a consequence of organisational differentiation which is very different not only because it concerns a different country and time, but also because of the facts, is supplied by the Greek social security system, information concerning this was supplied orally by Prof. Dr. Kremalis (Athens). This is distributed over 376 institutions. Allocation, however, is insufficiently regulated. Thus there are many disputes concerning allocation both between the institutions and also between citizens and the institutions.

— The life spheres of work and income, coverage of needs, and family unit, are reinforced and surrounded by corresponding systems of law.
— These legal systems may, irrespective of any social intervention, be subject to a natural process of internal and external growth. In other words, they have their own process of juridification. The social responsibility of the Community and of the legal order leads in any case to (possibly additional) regulations. These make the legal regulations governing work and income, coverage of needs, and maintenance, appear as social law in a broader sense. The socialization of existing law[10] is thus very much itself a process of juridification.
— If these modifications of existing law do not fulfil the social purpose, however, social service systems arise. Generally these are constituted by legislation, and their fabricated nature produces a continuous process of clarification, differentiation and expansion through legal rules. Social law (in this narrower sense) is thus genuinely both — *a priori* and as a consequence — a phenomenon of juridification.
— This juridification by social legislation then spreads out in the form of further juridification of areas of life, which are embraced by preexisting laws (labor law, maintenance law, etc.)[11].

2.2 Degrees of Juridification in Social Law

The phenomenon of juridification by social law has so far been introduced in a general way. We must now discuss it in more detail. This will be done first of all by examining more closely the objects and locations of regulations. By contrast, we shall then (in Section 3) seek to clarify the differences in forms and methods of law.

(1) Cash Benefits Versus Social Services and Payments in Kind

Juridification and monetarization (i.e., an emphasis on monetary benefits) are closely related phenomena of social policy (Tennstedt, 1976; Luhmann, 1981: 31 footnote 20, 94 and 105) and cash payments are very much an object of juridification. Cash payments attract more juridification than payments in kind and other services, and are more easily regulated by statutory legislation than the latter. Thus a social policy which relies heavily on the instrument of legislation also concentrates on cash payments (monetary bias of social policy). Payments in kind and other benefits, however, tend to be more resistant to standardizing control (Krause, 1981; Kaufmann, 1982b). A social policy which places payments in kind and other services and benefits (e.g.,

[10] The term "socialisation of law" (Stone, 1966) is, just as with the term *Sozialisierung des Rechts* (Henke, 1980), used in a broader sense also embracing externalisation.

[11] See Habermas (1981: 539; 1985: 214). Regarding the result of the development described, its interpretation and evaluation, see the thorough discussion with interesting further material in Rehbinder (1971).

medical care under a national health service) in the foreground, therefore shows *a priori* a lesser degree of juridification. With respect to services in kind and other benefits, the law is practically restricted to the regulation of entitlement and to the institutional conditions under which these services and benefits can be offered and supplied[12]. Of course, the specifically German faith in the normative availability of money (sanctioned at the highest judicial level by the Federal Constitutional Court (BVerfGE)), which has recognised claims to cash payments under social law particularly pension claims — as property protected under constitutional law (Decisions of the Federal Constitutional Court, Vol. 53: 257; 289ff.; see also Krause, 1982; Stober *et al.*, 1982)) can lead to very specific problems. If the state becomes unable to supply what has been promised, the state has the choice of either disavowing the promise of the law or giving rival needs priority over the fulfilment of legal entitlement[13].

(2) Normative Versus Institutional Style

As already mentioned, in the distinctions in regulations between cash payments on the one hand, and payments in kind and other services on the other, there is a difference in style of juridification which is of wide-ranging importance: the difference between normative and institutional social policy. By normative social policy is meant law which directly regulates conduct (e.g., the promise of a specific pension, the fixing of minimum wages, etc.). Institutional social policy refers to the establishment of a framework of conditions for specific social functions (the supplying of social services, social control within existing legal systems, etc.). Normative social policy is *a priori* a matter of law and thus already on the road to juridification. Whether institutional social policy requires normative rules, or needs an ordering of the institutions by law, depends on more basic principles of law, and in particular on the Constitution[14]. In the Federal Republic of Germany institutions are themselves largely a matter of the law (See Art. 84ff. of the Constitution of the Federal Republic of Germany). However, in other countries solutions which have a very slight legal content are conceivable. Under such conditions the institutional style can develop, in the extreme case, into socio-political actionism.

[12] This is taken to a particular extreme in Canadian social law (particularly in the social law of Quebec). Here a sharp distinction is made between guaranteeing access to sickness benefits and other social services on the one hand, and those social benefits on the other hand which are intended to cover the costs arising from social requisition. See Lajoie *et al.* (1981: 83ff., 97ff.).

[13] With respect to this dilemma, see Isensee (1982). Concerning the conflict between acquired rights and needs, see from an English viewpoint, Pinker (1975: 19ff.).

[14] Art. 22 § 4 of the Greek Constitution of 1975 requires that the scope of social security be determined by the law.

Nevertheless, even where in principle institutional solutions are the (necessary) task of the law, institutional law controls the actions of the parties concerned only indirectly. Looked at more closely, however, behind this dialectic between normative and institutional styles is the synthesis that both styles depend on each other. An institutional solution poses the question of which norms should determine how the different parties conduct themselves, and what should be done in and by the institutions. Where the law does not regulate this, the question arises as to alternative control mechanisms (e.g., in the form of professionalization, or bureaucratization taking the place of law, filling out the margins of action left by the law and determining its concrete implementation). We also must not neglect the question of what institutional conditions bring about normative solutions (Pitschas, 1977). It is precisely in the area of social law that the question of perception of the law, of access to the law, of maintaining a balance as regards ability to use the law, etc., is of key importance (Igl *et al.*, 1981, in particular Zacher, op. cit.: 259 and Igl, op. cit.: 274; Kaufmann, 1982b: 75).

(3) Excursus: Economization, Professionalization, Bureaucratization, and Juridification

The phenomena of juridification, monetarization, economization, professionalization and bureaucratization may be described as the most significant sources of disequilibrium in modern socio-political developments. This is certainly true of West Germany, which is no doubt in the foreground in this respect. These disequilibriums are evident, however, to a varying extent, in other countries. Monetarization has already been mentioned, and it is important now to discuss economization, professionalization, and bureaucratization in more detail.

With respect to *economization*, monetarization is a particular expression of economization in social policy. The interrelationship between monetarization and juridification also reflects the close proximity of economization to juridification[15]. Economic goods are made available by a system of law in a different way from noneconomic goods. By the same token, economic disadvantages can be compensated for by the law in a different way from noneconomic disadvantages. "Functions which require the cooperation of people to change their circumstances, e.g. education, rehabilitation, secondary socialization, education for the retired, etc.", are "by their nature not fulfilled with law and money". "This area of work requires resources such as personal effort, commitment and flexibility of interaction, which cannot be made available by law and money, and which cannot therefore be made centrally available either, and not centrally monitored for errors" (Luhmann, 1981: 109). In addition to this, however, there are also the natural limits which the yearning for equality comes up against: the unsurmountable contrasts such as those

[15] See in particular Tennstedt (1976); Luhmann (1981a: 94ff.,107ff.). With respect to the economic list of social policy and social law see also Zacher (1981a: 759ff.).

between the healthy and sick, intelligent and dull, sociable and unsociable, beautiful and ugly[16]. Both economics and the law are equally at a loss here. In the final analysis as well, it is in human interest itself if the individual nature is not infringed in this repsect[17]. Moreover, it is unfortunate that the welfare state can be of more effective service to those who can be helped with money and law than those who can only be helped with services and personal intervention (Zacher, 1981a: 759). This is why there is not only a distinction in the different degrees of juridification between cash payments and other services, but also in the degrees of juridification between normative and institutional solutions. Noneconomic needs can be helped — if at all — only through services, and these services must be made available primarily by institutional means. From both viewpoints the power of the law is limited.

Where social policy cannot be helped with law and money, in other words where it must supply services, in the form of social welfare institutions or by ensuring access to the assistance available within society[18], there arises the problem of the regulation of these services. Only rarely can they be left solely to the individual supplier of the service, i.e., to his personality, education, experience and good will. From many different perspectives, a standardization or normalization seems necessary: How is this achieved? (See also, and with respect to the following, e.g. Kaufmann, 1982b). Somewhat informal means are constituted by education, further training, exchange of experience, and the formation of opinion among those supplying the same type of service. Formal means are rules of conduct in professional codes, the articles of professional organizations, and finally statutory regulations. Notwithstanding the way in which roles are distributed amongst the individual elements within this range of instruments, the result will be *professionalization* (Reidegeld, 1980; Blankenburg, 1980). The relationship between professionalization and law is extremely complicated. The informal elements of professionalization can relieve the burden on law, but they may just as easily work against the law. If they are too weak or if they go in a false direction, correction by formal means — particularly by statutory law — may be necessary. Formal instruments may, however, run riot. Professionalization can then manifest itself as a process of juridification. Even the informal instruments can lead to a hardening of professional attitudes, the disadvantages of which are no less than those of formal juridification. Professionalization and juridification are related to each other, in other words, like two intersecting circles. And the relationship between the two circles may be considered in a particular context to have a positive value as well.

[16] Luhmann (1981a: 97): "The inclusion principle seems to have its limit where people themselves have to be changed in order to be able to avail themselves of the opportunities that society offers them."

[17] Luhmann (1981a: 97) "Changing people is in any case the most dangerous objective that a policy can set itself".

[18] With respect to the distinction between insuring access on the one hand and the financial ability on the other hand to bear the costs of social requisition, see Lajoie *et al.* (1981).

The phenomenon of *bureaucratization* goes a lot further (see also Reidegeld, 1980 and his references; Habermas, particularly, 470ff.; Luhmann 1981a: 103ff.), and the relationship between bureaucratization and juridification is much more complex. Bureaucracies arise in order to apply the law. They arise in order to administer monetary social policy. They also arise wherever the legal instruments are weak, and where cash payments are not appropriate, i.e., whenever payments in kind and other benefits must be provided institutionally. Even where the ideal of personal care and individual help is intended, the personnel employed to this end may tend to become bureaucratic, professional, or both. If bureaucracies arise, then regulations also arise. Where the law has not established and controlled a bureaucracy from the beginning, the law can only give free rein to the norms inherent in the bureaucracy, or endeavor to establish its rule over the bureaucracy. Thus in the broader sense bureaucracy always means juridification. The question of juridification can only be put in terms of how the regulations of the bureaucracy arise, how they can be justified, and how they are perceived by the public concerned.

(4) *Juridification and Hierarchies of Rules of Law*

a) Hierarchies of Rules of Law

Developed law involves a differentiation into hierarchies of rules (Zacher, 1978c: 21, 30). Such hierarchies of rules of law may be of a purely qualitative nature (e.g., constitution — law — and rules and regulations dependent on legislation). This presupposes that the hierarchy of rules of law is based on the authority (sovereignty) of a single lawgiver. Hiercharchies of rules of law can, however, have the task of handling the relationship between several lawgivers (states — supranational community; states — international community; member states — central state in a federal state). Then several maxims of conflict settlement coincide with one another. Apart from the formulae which determine the relationship between the layers of rules within a purely qualitative hierarchy of rules of law (e.g., whether being in contradiction with the constitution makes a law invalid or contestable, or not), we find formulae for the settlement of disputes between different entities of law (e.g., whether a violation of international law makes a national law invalid, and whether within a federal state a central state law breaks a member state law or not). The sum of all conceivable hierarchies of rules of law thus forms a complex structure of overlapping basic models. The difficulties multiply when we consider the diversity of maxims of conflict settlement such as the invalidity of a lower rule which contradicts a higher rule for everyone, or at least for every judge, the concentration of examination in a single court (a constitutional court), the solely external sanction (e.g., violation of international law), or the internal effect of invalidity, etc. The picture is no less complicated when we examine the difference between law made by the state and the bodies incorporated within the state (local authorities, social insurance institutions, etc.), and the law established by private institutions (associations, societies, companies, factories, parties to wage agreements, parties in collective agreements etc.). It is not our task here to establish absolute clarity, nor does this lie within our reach. We must content ourselves with pointing out that, fundamentally, all rules of law exist within an open system involving several hierarchies of rules. Discussions of juridification within the field of social law must not ignore the fact that this juridification at some levels of these hierarchies is like a river in full flood, whilst at other levels there are simply trickles and streams; and at the higher levels it occurs not infrequently merely as clouds. Any attempt to draw uniform and generally valid conclusions would fail here because of the multiple hierarchies of rules, particularly the diversity of national conditions, which of course always has two sides, i.e., the diversity of the law and of social policy, and hence the diversity of contents and designs of social law.

b) Borderline Between State-Made Law and Law of Society

The last point throws special light on the *demarcation between state-made law and law immanent within society*, the paradigm of which is found in the contrast between statutory law on the one hand and law relating to collective agreements on the other hand. Externalizing solutions (social benefit systems) are only at the disposal of state legislation. Collective agreement law comes up against a boundary problem here. Its genuine field consists of the internalizing solutions of labor law. Externalizations by collective agreements can only result in private insurance solutions or solutions enforced by the joint parties to collective agreements, but not solutions which are the responsibility of the body politic (the state authority or particular public bodies for which the state is responsible such as public social insurance institutions). Naturally, statute law can give appropriate authority to collective agreement law; it can, to some extent, push open the door to an externalization (for example, sec. 4 (2) Tarifvertragsgesetz für sog. gemeinsame Einrichtungen (collective agreement law for so-called joint bodies)). An autonomous collective agreement is by itself not capable of doing this. This is even more evident at the company level. The demarcation between law existing within society and state-made law thus has a great deal to do with the distinction between internalizing and externalizing solutions. It must not be forgotten, of course, that this applies only in one direction. State-made law can create internalizing solutions, whereas "law within society" cannot create externalizing solutions on its own. Juridification which runs along the paths of collective agreement law, company agreements, etc., is thus fundamentally juridification within the field of social law in a broader sense, and not within the narrower field of social legislation.

c) Distribution of Roles in State-Made Law

If we concentrate our examination on state-made law we must ask whether in social law the functional division between different layers of law (e.g., constitutional law, statutory law and subordinate law) is absolute, or whether gradations are evident. This again is a question which cannot be answered in a uniform way. Clearly it is appropriate to grant a natural priority to formal parliamentary law — or whatever corresponds to this in the different constitutional and legal systems. This applies especially wherever this law acts as the central medium in the general evolution of law and political decision-making and, in particular, where the legislature also has power over the budget. But there are many factors which invalidate this rule. What often happens is that parliamentary law (framework or enabling law) and government "law" (concretizing or authorizing regulations) jointly participate in the legislative function[19]. In Switzerland, *Volksgesetz* and *Parlamentsgesetz*, share in the crucial legislative formation of social policy[20]. In the East European countries it may be said that the law tends to have the character of a "framework" in relation to what is determined by the state-planning bodies or the trade unions as state-authorized institutions of the social security bureaucracy (Zacher, 1982b). In the final analysis, however, all the levels in the legal hierarchies are employed in socio-political tasks. The question is only that of the distribution of roles and their mutual relationship, in general, as well as with respect to social law. Thus there emerges out of these legal hierarchies a demand for rules to organize the interplay of roles, i.e., to juridify them. Given the present state of research into these matters, especially of comparative research, (for law in general as well as for social law), it seems pointless to speculate further. Only the problem of regulatory weakness with respect to social law requires closer examination.

d) Weakness of Higher Ranking Law in Regulating Social Law

By this is meant the ***difficulty*** which constitutional law (or simiar international instruments, e.g., European Social Charter, ILO-conventions, UN-treaties), has in ***programing social law*** in a binding way. Such control of (lower) law by (higher) law is very much intended or assumed to be a function of constitutional law (Zacher, 1980b), and international instruments of law, particularly in the field of social law (Zacher, 1978a). However, the actual effects of control are difficult to foresee. This difficulty is most directly and readily apparent with constitutional programs of a social character (the principle of

[19] According to Art. 34 Para. 4 of the French Constitution of 1958, it is the responsibility of the parliament to provide framework legislation for social security, to be filled in by the council of ministers and the president (Art. 13 Para. 1). The complementarity of parliamentary framework legislation and presidential (by president and government) decrees also characterises the most recent development in Greece. It should be noted within the context of German social law history that during the Weimar period, essential social reforms were undertaken only via administrative law-making. Most exemplary of this is the *Reichsfürsorgepflichtverordnung* of 1924. This was a government regulation the authorisation of which did not lie in a law, but in the *Dritte Steuernotverordnung* of 1924.

[20] In Switzerland, the "plebiscitarian legislation" has given a very individual stamp to social policy, see Maurer (1981, particularly, 742ff., 823ff.). The relative slowness of the plebiscitarian legislation led, however, to a greater split within legislation between the plebiscitarian legislation and delegated legislation through parliament and government see Maurer (1979: 126ff.).

the social state (Zacher, 1977a) and its specific constitutional provisions and basic social rights (Isensee, 1980; Lücke, 1982), and corresponding international guarantees (Zacher, 1978a)). It applies however also to classical higher ranking law, e.g., basic constitutional rights relating to personal liberties. Whereas these rights can be used quite effectively as a protection against direct encroachments by the state they remain unreliable as regards the indirect kind of state action which regulates life via social interventions[21]. Even equality as a general principle has not been able to fully permeate the development of social law, contrary to the assumption arising out of the egalitarian impulse within social policy. Only prohibitions of individual types of discrimination can themselves produce lasting effects (Zacher, 1968). The reasons for this weakness in regulating social law are diverse. The most general are: the chain of realities and their evolution, to which social law aiming at altering realities is linked; the necessity in social law for detailed regulations where precise rights are to be established (and not simply vague claims within the discretionary power of the official or rights of access to institutions); the unfulfillable and infinite nature of desirable social improvements and the need for a corresponding discretion in order to determine what is ultimately feasible; the inner conflicts of aims within social policy (prevention of want versus provision of a share in prosperity, increase in equality versus maintenance of unequal standards of living etc.); and the fluctuations in definitions of, and solutions to, problems between the existing legal systems and possible areas for externalizing solutions, which is precisely what has a laming effect on the principle of equality. With respect to the weakness in personal and civil liberties, there is also the contradiction between greater freedom brought about by libertarian social provision and control of freedom resulting from the conditions for implementing these policies[22].

Nonetheless, despite this weakness of higher-ranking law in regulating social law, it must not be forgotten that social policy and social law are subordinate to such law. The socio-political discussion has to take this higher-ranking law into account and social law is subject to its sanctions. Wherever constitutions are sanctioned by constitutional courts this has in fact

21 See Luhmann (1981a: 37): "While in older social formations with hierarchically structured politics the danger of despotism, of arbitrariness, of abuse of power, grew to such a pitch that politics became a problem and a danger for itself, in the welfare state there are additional problems resulting from the self-referential way of working. This does not render the issue of misuse of power obsolete, nor the rule of law and the constitutional state set up to deal with it superfluous. But the drawbacks of a risky structural development are no longer fully covered through these categories, and there are symptoms of developments that give cause for concern in quite different directions". For the derivation of benefit claims from the constitution see Rüfner (1981b).

22 On the "ambivalence of guarantees of and denials of freedom" see Habermas (1981: 531 with further references; 1985: 208-9). For a different and supplementary view to the above, see Zacher (1977b).

led to an involvement of the constitutional courts in social policy and socio-legal development[23]. However, the committees of experts set up to monitor observance of the conventions of the International labor Organisation and the European Council (Zacher, 1978a) have not been able to achieve comparable importance [24].

3. Manifestations of Juridification

3.1 The Thematic Extension of the Law

(1) The Replacement of the Natural Society by a Society Ordered by Social Law

With the development of social law — and especially of social law in the narrower sense — the law has cast its net ever more widely. Areas of life now covered which formerly were not, or at least not directly, the object of law include sickness, old age, number of children, cost of housing, disablement, reduced ability to earn a living, failure of physical and mental faculties, etc. Alongside a concern with securing essential subsistence needs, new alternative social provisions have emerged, i.e., where social benefits are designed as a substitute for income from work or for maintenance obligations. All this has meant a broadening of the law, so that social life has been standardized to an unprecedented extent and in a variety of ways. The law, in turn, has altered the patterns of behavior of its (potential) subjects. Former worlds have been destroyed, changed or defunctionalized; and with the increasingly artificial nature of social conditions the possibilities and responsibilities of the law still continue to grow[25].

This cannot and should not be taken to mean that all those developments in social conditions which are collectively fabricated are the product of law, or under the control or responsibility of law. Politics contain many other means of changing conditions and exerting pressures. Systems of state domination where there are state ruling parties, mass organizations, or bureaucracies are designed precisely to function without law. Viewed in this way, it is generally good fortune when social development occurs through law.

[23] See for the FRG the reports by Rüfner (1979; 1980; 1981a; 1982); Katzenstein (1982). For Italy, the contributions in Angeli (1978). For Austria, Schrammel (1983).

[24] On the other hand, the case of the European Court of Justice is fundamentally different. It has evolved a comprehensive effectiveness, see Schulte/Zacher (1979; 1980; 1981); Schulte (1981). The European Court of Justice is less concerned with the regulation of social law by higher-ranking law than with the carrying through of the (specific) European system of social law vis-à-vis the (more general) national social laws.

[25] See supra 2.1; see also Tennstedt (1976); Widmeier (1976: 21ff., 101ff., 151); von Bethusi-Huc (1976: 256ff.); Henke (1980); Pitschas (1980); Reidegeld (1980); Habermas (1981, Vol. 2: 522ff.; 1985: 203ff.); Luhmann (1981a, particularly 94ff.); Mayntz/Flick (1982); Voigt (1983a).

(2) The Proliferation of Social Law

Intervention, however, generates further intervention. Thus with the establishment of social law there emerges a new range of tasks for the law which, as it were, serve to control the consequences of social law. This second generation of juridification in social law can be divided roughly into two dimensions: the internal integration of social law, and the external conditions necessary for its effective operation.

a) Inner Integration of Social Law

The internal integration function of social law becomes increasingly evident the more social law develops from being a corrective for social conditions into a determining influence over them, i.e., broadly speaking, as it changes from being an exception into the rule. In the corrective phase, the reliefs and advantages brought about by social law tend to be in the foreground. By contrast, in the phase of institutionalization and generalization, it is the shortcomings of social conditions which are given prominence.

— Such shortcomings may be ***needs which have not yet been met.*** The issue of marginal groups is a typical phenomenon of this type. However, defects specific to certain systems of provision also belong here. When social insurance was introduced, for example, particular stress was placed on the fact that those persons who were able to insure themselves were those who could pay social insurance contributions. As people became increasingly accustomed to the progress of this principle, more and more concern was expressed for those who could not insure themselves because they were unable to pay.The secondary social risk of being unable to insure oneself was discovered. Various techniques were used to remedy this (e.g., taking into account periods of unemployment in pension insurance or payment of pension contributions for recipients of unemployment benefits).

— With the increasing structuring of conditions of life through social law, forms of ***discrimination*** have come to be perceived, ***which themselves can be seen to result from social law.*** Reforms to achieve equality between men and women in social insurance represent a broad reaction to this.

— The requirements for an ***inner coordination of social law*** are seemingly unlimited. First of all, we must consider the illogical results that arise within social benefit systems (see as an example the title of Gitter, 1969) from incorrect prognoses, unanticipated developments in implementing provisions or the conditions with which they are concerned, and similar causes. No less important are the inconsistencies between different social benefit systems, such as the objectively unjustifiable granting of privileges to some groups and disadvantaging of others. A number of areas of conflict occur: cumulations of benefits, allocations of individuals to systems and vice versa, problems in dealing with different national legal systems, above all however — and this is particularly significant considering the mobility of social law — problems of intertemporal collision. These all require consideration and solution.

— More in the background are those discrepancies which arise from the inherent contradictions in what is social, i.e., the combatting of basic want and ensuring of a minimum subsistence level; concern for greater equality; reduction of dependency; the balancing out of differences in levels of prosperity; security against the vicissitudes of life; security of living standards; more freedom through the provision of the means to make use of this freedom; and finally, a share in prosperity for all. All these aims are inherently ambiguous and conflicting in character. A desire for reform is frequently the starting point of an attempt to realise neglected objectives of this kind, and is almost inevitably at other people's cost. The older the welfare state becomes, the more a different kind of inner contradiction becomes evident. Social justice was always — though not always at the same time — manifested in three forms: as justice in relation to needs, as justice in relation to achievement, and as justice in relation to property. The welfare state initially evolved out of the aim of achieving justice in relation to needs; it then came to terms with justice in relation to achievement, and finally developed vis-à-vis property. The tension between these three types of justices is obvious. It is precisely in times when the potentialities of the welfare state are dwindling (see in particular, Pinter, 1975; Sensee, 1982) that the conflict between justice in relation to need and justice in relation to property becomes particularly evident.

— Finally, experience with social law gives rise to requirements for order and regulation which result in ***procedural rules, control mechanisms, means of facilitating access to law***, and so on. (Igl *et al.*, 1981; Kaufmann, 1982b). In the Federal Republic of Germany discussions about the specific legal relationships referring to social protection and social benefits and services (see in particular, Krause *et al.*, 1980; Maurer, 1979: 254ff; Krejci, 1982) and to social care and nursing are examples of such resultant problems. (See e.g. Krause *et al.*, 1978; Schmitz-Elsen *et al.*, 1978; Igl, 1983 with further references).

  Calls for a simplification of social law are a general reaction to the overabundance of such problems. They seldom meet with success.

b) External Conditions for the Effectiveness of Social Law

In this ***second generation*** of juridification in social law, altered patterns of behavior appear to play a central role. Whereas social law was originally developed under the assumption that the risks which it combatted, and the deficits which it met, constituted inescapable needs for those to whom help under social law was addressed, it is precisely here that changes have taken place. The most important of these may be said to be the following:

— Whenever social law proceeds from the assumption that the avoidance of the situation to which its remedial measures refer may be left to the persons involved, it turns out that, after taking the remedial measures, the alternative "no deficit situation plus no remedy" or "deficit situation plus remedy" can become ***calculable and steerable*** for the parties involved (Wulfhorst, 1982). The discussion of the "abuse of social benefits" (Eichenhofer, 1982) is thus directed at a further differentiation of legal facts, technically conceivable in the widest range of ways.

— Social law remedies aim as well, via more equality (e.g. security for all in the case of sickness), at more freedom (reduction of the consequences of conduct harmful to health not only for the richer, but also for the poorer sections of society). Among those concerned this leads to a new question of equality, i.e., the *equal sharing of burdens where there is unequal use of freedom.* The discussion concerning the self-responsibility of the socially insured (Braun *et al.*, 1981; Ecker, 1981; Faude, 1983) thus also aims at a refinement of legal facts.

— An important additional change is that alongside the *emergency services* an increasing number of *opportunity-related services* have been provided (educational benefits, occupational training, to some extent rehabilitation, preventive measures, etc.). In such cases social law does not assume that the qualifying conditions for benefits can not be manipulated, but rather that certain conditions can be established, even if arbitrarily (precisely by the readiness to make use of the offer of such services). The difficulties in distinguishing between opportunity-related services and emergency services appear to be great for all those concerned (politicians, social service institutions, beneficiaries, etc.). They create confusion and hence a feeling of unease, which leads to a need for further clarification and a possible increase in law.

3.2 The Dismantling and Replacement of Existing Orders and Control Systems by Positive Law

The process of juridification has developed in numerous and overlapping ways:

— in the transition from an ordering of life which is not consciously structured or deliberately regulated but accepted as given, to social control (Luhmann, 1970), e.g., by training, instruction, indoctrination;

— by the establishment of legal frameworks for autonomous groups (e.g. the family), for control mechanisms (e.g. the market), or for alternative regulating mechanisms (e.g. the school);

— by increased material intervention in these frameworks and control mechanisms;

— by law designed to regulate behavior and substantive law (from economic incentives to direct instructions);

— and finally by the providing of a safety-net for social deficits by means of social legislation.

Social law was initially "entwined" in this process mainly by materializing interventions which had the effect of deepening and supplementing existing legal frameworks (e.g. of employment contract law). As the density of these interventions grew, another process occurred involving a structuring of life through the expansion of social benefit legislation (social law in the narrower sense).

Thus social law has contributed in a twofold way to reduce the scope of the not consciously structured or deliberately regulated orders in a concerted or indirect way (expected or unexpected), as well as for autonomous areas. Here there are perhaps two fundamental turning points which are of special significance:

— the step from not conscious to deliberate structuring (whether by legal framework, by intervention, or by comprehensive materialization),
— and the step from the single-level social law design with an exclusively internalizing corrective action, to a two-level design emerging from this development of externalizing solutions.

The first turning point can be illustrated to some extent by the changes which take place when a traditional ordering of family life accepted without question is given a framework in the form of a positive, decreed ordering of family life. Even if the legal framework was designed to maintain the *status quo*, the old order will no longer be what it was because of an awareness of the now deliberately structured order, even though only in the form of a framework. The second step is evident in the change which occurs when the maintenance of a family is taken over by the alternatives of state provided educational promotion, pensions, etc., and when the capacity to maintain is modified by benefits such as childrens and housing allowances, and when the role of the bread-winner is replaced and continued beyond its natural period by survivors' pensions, etc.

The development referred to here is initially a phenomenon of legal and social history. It is worth noting that this development occurs with the differentiation of the problem fields referred to above (see 2.1). In the old society there is only the deliberately regulated but accepted as given order, in which is found the family unit, with the work and income unit and the need coverage unit. The effective differentiation of these spheres broadly parallels the development of corresponding legal orders. The final step takes place when externalizing social problem solutions are added to the internalizing corrections of the relevant orders.

This development still has a topical interest for two reasons. In the first place, we find these stages of development normally belonging to different historical periods that occur simultaneously in developing countries. We can also witness with particular clarity the altering — not to say the destructive — effect of the later phase on the remains of the earlier phase[26]. Tanzania, for example, recently passed a regulation under which the modern judge has a duty to clarify the premodern maintenance obligations if their nonfulfillment leads to the claiming of social benefits. The second reason this development is of topical interest is that the retroactive effect of the alternatives to social

[26] See the report on a discussion on social law and social policy in the developing countries in Fuch *et al.* (1983).

benefits and services legislation on the primary rules and regulations is far from being clarified in the developed countries as well. We only need to think, to leave the family sphere as an example for once (see with respect to all the above once again the contributions in Kaufmann, 1982a), of the countless changes due to social law that have an influence on the "health market", in that market mechanisms which in fact regulate themselves are now practically nonexistent (see for example, Überender, 1983).

Another question, of no less importance, is the extent to which law is at all capable of replacing other mechanisms of regulation and guidance, at least in a meaningful sense. Personal social services (e.g., social work) cannot be controlled primarily by legal instructions, but only by other guidance mechanisms (education, further training, rules of art, professional ethics, etc.). However, this does not mean that the law is simply superfluous. A pedagogic intervention (Kaufmann, 1982a: 80) left to itself cannot substitute for undecreed orders. It decrees them itself and usurps their formulation. In the final analysis the law is indispensable to again clarify a social consensus where this has been lost. What is of decisive importance is the correct interaction of all competent control mechanisms.

3.3 Metamorphosis of Social Law

Finally we must look at what juridification in social law perhaps most obviously expresses, i.e., the change of form in social law (in the broader sense).

(1) Formulation of Law

It can already be termed juridification when unformulated rules are replaced by formulated rules[27]. To this extent the formulation of codes of conduct for social workers, or the drawing up of rules for medical treatment within health insurance, constitute juridification. In this sense, it is also juridification when in international law the legal opinions of bodies which are not authorized to legislate in the conventional sense are set out in resolutions and declarations designed to take effect as "soft law" (Simma, 1975; Frowein, 1976). It is precisely when we disregard the exact qualifications of such sources of law that it becomes clear what importance the formulation of rules already has by itself. Access to law becomes different, the fight for law changes, as does the process of evading the law when rules are written. If this constitutes the step linking non-law to law, this change becomes all the more significant.

In this connection we may also consider the question as to the relevance of codifications[28]. Their position in the process of juridification differs widely.

[27] Habermas (1981, Vol. 2: 524; 1985: 204): "The expression 'juridification' refers quite generally to the tendency towards an increase of written law which can be observed in modern society".

[28] See Zacher, 1981b. It should be added that Law 825/81 empowers the minister for social affairs to collect into a compilation the laws relating to the insurance of the employees.

Social law in the narrower sense is generally *a priori* written law. Codifications thus either summarize written law (compilations), refine it and take it further (consolidation), or give basic new structures and contents to social law (codifications in the narrower sense). Depending on their nature, they modify the state of juridification only slightly or not at all (compilations), they are attempts to control the proliferation of social law (consolidations), or they increase the quantity of rules over a period of time (codifications in the narrower sense). The classical codification of private law generally had a different significance. In adopting legal traditions (judge-made law, scientific doctrines, etc.) and laying them down, it transformed not only unwritten into written law, but also transferred legal developments from jurisprudence and the courts into the hands of a formal legislature, and transferred long-term evolutions into momentary decisions. This may still take place today in social law (in the wider sense), e.g., in labor law. For social law in the narrower sense it is of rather marginal importance. Here codification may, however, contribute to an "increase in written law"[29]. Codification does not however have a uniform and essential significance in the juridification process in social law.

(2) Juridification as a Shift in Power and Complication of Procedures

Juridification is often referred to when the formal legislature and/or the judge become competent in situations where they previously were not. Where the formal legislature becomes competent, this can primarily signify that an unwritten (possibly collected, but not textually fixed) law is transformed into written law. It can mean that the development of law has shifted from the administration to the formal legislature or from the judge to the formal legislature. It can also — possibly vis-à-vis the parties to collective wage agreements — mean that the state takes over decisions where these were previously left to social forces. The extent to which the margin for action of the administration is restricted depends generally on the content of the law. Where the judge is competent, as a rule this means that the administration has, more or less to its disadvantage, to share with him its authority to use and interpret the law. In this way, the higher courts gain their own function of forming law, in that they compete with the formal legislature. We can only mention this in passing here. Looked at in detail, the processes differ very widely in form and consequence.

A striking example of the extent to which juridification processes of this type are characterized by national peculiarities is the British debate on the relationship between law and social services (Brooke, 1979; Williams, 1979). Law in this case is regarded as the traditional law dominated by an inner circle of lawyers and judges. On the assumption that this exclusively is law, it was for a long time held that the law should be kept out of social services. Develop-

[29] See e.g. the laying down of law not previously formulated or only specially formulated, in Part I and X of the *Sozialgesetzbuch* (Social Code) of the FRG.

ments followed the path of regulation by statutes and numerous other instruments, as well as of legal protection by tribunals (Fulbrook, 1978). From a Continental viewpoint, this is naturally regarded as merely the development of an "other law" [30]. From the British viewpoint, the gulf which was originally seen to exist and to be desirable between law and the courts on the one hand and social legislation and tribunals on the other, seems to be narrowing.

In the Federal Republic of Germany, juridification has certainly evolved as social legislation has broadened in scope and as parliamentary acts have increasingly become a precondition for the legitimate administrative supply of social benefits and services (Wertenbruch, 1978). At the same time the power of judicial control over the administration has been made universal and maximalized[31] through the authority given to the constitutional courts, particularly the Federal Constitutional Court, to monitor rules of law, and the legislature has also been subjected to judicial control (see again for the FRG the reports by Ruefner, 1979, 1980, 1981a, 1982; Katzenstein, 1982. For Italy the contributions in Angeli, 1978. For Austria Schrammel, 1983). There remain, of course, striking differences between juridification resulting from legislation and juridification resulting from the power of the judges. (See here, and with respect to the following Zacher, 1981a: 732ff. and the references given). The formal legislature, who is at the same time responsible for the budgetary legislature, has within social service law a very different margin for action compared with the judge (even if the latter regards himself as being fundamentally called upon to develop further law). Again and again, e.g., the formal legislature has "cut back" expansions of services resulting from decisions of the Federal Social Court (Rappe and Pohl, 1979: 68). A further distinction is that the weakness of the Constitution as higher-ranking law regulating social law is also reflected in the intervention of the Federal Constitutional Court in social legislation. The Federal Constitutional Court (which originally was only permitted to declare acts invalid) has, for example, developed the technique of simply objecting to social legislation which it considers unconstitutional and leaving it to the legislature to produce a constitutional version (Ipsen, 1983). To an increasing extent this socio-political "homework" which the Federal Constitutional Court has passed on to the legislature has not been dealt with.

30 Here again differences can be observed between the different jurisdictions. See Dutheil de la Rochere (1979). Koebl (1979) gives, not a differential diagnosis, but is nonetheless interesting as a comprehensive discussion of the methods of a special jurisdiction.

31 On the one hand, by the blanket clause saying that the violation of rights can always be brought before a court (Art. 19 Para. 4 of the Constitution Law of the FRG), and on the other hand by the principle, indirectly taken from the Constitution, that the legal system must also guarantee a legal entitlement as of right as regards the public authorities observing the provisions which also affect the individual sphere of the citizen.

(3) *Juridification as a Process of Concentration, Differentiation, and Intensification of Rules of Law*

The following phenomena may also be regarded as juridification within the field of social law:

a) Refinement and Concentration of Rules

The network of rules and controls has been increasingly refined and condensed. German social law certainly constitutes an extreme example of this process. Looked at internationally, a correlation between the development of social law and extreme refinement does not necessarily have to exist. However such intensity and refinement is characteristic of many socio-legal cultures. It should be noted here that the difference in regulations between cash payments on the one hand and payments in kind and services on the other is clearly revealed in this process of refinement. While an institutional style dominates with respect to payments in kind and other services, a normative style is both possible and cultivated within the field of money payments. The discrepancies become larger and larger (see once again supra 2.2(1) and (2)).

b) Diminution of Discretion

With the intensification of law, the scope for administrative discretion is reduced (see a comprehensive discussion of this in Adler and Asquith, 1981; and Bogs, 1969). First-line social service systems (social insurance, demogrants, etc.) tend to be genuinely opposed to discretion. Their "invention" is based on the view that the social condition of people should be kept as free as possible from official discretion. Discretion was and is a matter of the simple subsidiary systems (of public assistance). Gradually, of course, there has been an overall reduction in discretion.

What we are talking about here, however, is a highly complex phenomenon. The above comments apply directly only to legal decisions. Wherever — and in whatever connection — there is a question of payments in kind or other services, expert evaluation by the supplier of the services would appear to be indispensable. But once again this is true to a varying degree. Training norms, professional agreements, service instructions and the rules of occupational law also intervene here (Smith, 1981). A totally different question is whether juridification can also be discerned in the fact that the law does in fact leave certain margins for action but that judicial control of the administration then lays claim to this as its territory (Dupeyroux, 1981: 775). Another aspect is revealed if we take into account that similar incalculabilities and dependencies, corresponding to discretion, arise if the law does indeed exclude discretion but makes the decision largely dependent on precise conditions. The difference between a precise assessment of need (a means test) and a decision based on discretion is at most a difference of degree. We shall, however, return to this contradiction between concrete and abstract regulations.

c) Instruments of Control and Execution

What has been said up to now has been based on the standard model of the separation of powers, i.e. on the fact that regulative power and executive power exist, and that juridification takes place to the extent and in a way in which the executive power is controlled by the regulative one (and in which the judicial power lays emphasis on the regulations, and supplements them in some way). The executive power, however, disposes of instruments allowing self-control, and these instruments are of a regulating nature, that is, they are part of juridification. This kind of juridification, inherent in administration, is no less important than actual legal juridification. Seen from the perspective of the legal order, it is difficult, even in theory, to make this differentiation. Even where it exists *de facto*, the citizen often is unable to tell whether his interests refer to a legal rule or to an instrument of control inherent in the administration. In the sense of excessive growth of regulations both the legal as well as administrative ones correspond to juridification.

Many different phenomena are involved here. The general administrative provisions of the central bodies (such as ministries and the managerial organs of the self-governing bodies) that bind lower authorities represent the modality most similar to law. They are established like the legal rules and may only be distinguished by their validation since they are solely, or at least in the first place, legitimated by the administrative managerial power. Starting from this core definition, differences arise in three dimensions. The first arises from the diminution of the degree of standardization, which is partly due to the limitation on clarifying details, and partly to indefinite statements (e.g., general appeals). The second dimension depends on the managerial nature receding into the background behind the agreements made between the administrative bodies enjoying equal rights. When bodies with equal rights (such as self-governing bodies, associations or individual states in a federal state) must fulfill parallel duties, they are able to coordinate the administrative practice as mentioned above. On the strength of managerial power, the instruments of coordination may also affect the lower authorities once the respective leading bodies have agreed upon them. It is however also possible that, with respect to such coordination, bodies of parallel competence join up to form associations, as is generally the case with the social insurance institutions of the Federal Republic of Germany. The third dimension diverging from the core definition of the administrative provision does not so much refer to the executive administration but to the party directly concerned, i.e., to the citizen him or herself (via broadsheets, informative pamphlets, application forms, etc.).

It is not possible, within this study, to systemize the various existing forms and produce evidence for them; neither is it possible to clarify by means of definitions which phenomena deserve to be called juridification and which do not. Attention must, however, be drawn to the fact that the instrumentarium in question shows parallels to juridification by parliamentary acts and by instruments similar to them. In this respect, one should also note the extent to which the execution of law can be affected by other existing forms — even if the typical elements of law-making are missing, such as publicity and generality of the legal orders *(Rechtsbefehl).* This may signify that the role of law recedes into the background with respect to the role of administrative instruments and may even reach the point of juridification being replaced by formally inconceivable indoctrination.

d) Legal Entitlement as of Right

Another phenomenon of juridification is also constituted by the supplementing of normative social service programs and institutional tasks (in other words, of procedures which must be initiated by official action — *Amtsprinzip*) by a legal entitlement as of right (Habermas, 1981, Vol. 2: 531; Luhmann, 1981a: 103; Luhmann, 1981b). This phenomenon has many layers.

Thus, for example, a basic legislatorial and technical sense has to be distinguished. The basic legislatorial sense refers to designing the allocation of social benefits to the beneficiaries as *Eigentum* (Federal Constitutional Court, Vol. 53: 257 (289ff.); see also Krause, 1982; Stober *et al.*, 1982), as property (Reich, 1964), as acquired right, etc., and may be inherent in this phenomenon despite of all different aspects. The technical sense is inherent in the phenomenon when rights are conceded on social benefits and services in order to guarantee a comprehensive legal protection via the judiciary to the beneficiary. To a large extent, both may coincide. What is certain, however, is that legal protection via the judiciary can be guaranteed without granting a right. It is sufficient to provide the possibility of making complaints and bringing actions within positive law[32].

A further difference is that of whether the legal entitlement as of right is concerned with the fulfillment of a definitive normative program, or whether it requires the exercise of discretion or even depends in the first instance on the availability of necessary resources, services and institutions. Rights are then also possible. But their effect remains extremely varied (Marshall 1981, especially The Right to Welfare: 83; Thevenet, 1979: 179).

Here we also must not overlook the complications arising from the function of those who must fulfill this right. In this respect an interesting development has taken place in German social law. The right of entitlement to social

[32] See Maurer (1979: 273ff., footnote 668): "The difficult question whether the entitlement to social insurance is a subjective public right, or merely a reflex effect of the objective right, cannot be dealt with here, especially since in view of the highly elaborated judicial practice it is scarecely of practical importance". At first glance Art. 113 Para. 1 of the Italian Constitution would also appear to belong here: "Judicial protection of legitimate rights and interests before ordinary or administrative judicial bodies against acts of the public administration shall always be available". Looked at more closely it becomes evident that, in the sense of the German system, this does not refer to the equivalent of law and non-law, but to two kinds of right. In this connection, however, the legal situation in Italy does nonetheless constitute a confirmation of the text: Granting access to substantive law and granting access to adjective law are difficult to separate from one another.

assistance was recognized, but the principle involving procedures which have to be initiated by official action (*Amtsprinzip*) also had to be retained. The duality of the institutional task and legal claim, however, remained problematic. Obviously it is not possible to demand of one and the same official that s/he look out for those who are entitled and at the same time carefully reject those who are not (Leibfried, 1976). This has led to a kind of "division of powers" in the social welfare offices. The bureaucratic administrative decision is limited to a negative screening of the claims made. The *Amtsprinzip* is entrusted to the social workers, welfare associations, etc.[33]. Here again we are presented with the question of the paths of juridification specific to social law.

e) Juridification and Abstraction

The contrast between concrete and abstract appears in all the phenomena of juridification we have been describing. Social law is always faced with a choice between the alternatives of concrete granting of what is concretely right and general granting of what is generally right (Zacher, 1977c: 214; Zacher, 1982a: 333). In a sense, this represents the basic relationship between social assistance and social insurance. Social assistance gives what is concretely necessary — no more, no less. This implies a precise decision and continuous monitoring regarding what is required. Social insurance gives a pension, once certain conditions are fulfilled (invalidity, old age), on the basis of earned contributions and irrespective of whether the pension is adequate, or whether it is needed. What is concretely justified is not taken into account. The decision is limited to a few standard conditions and facts. Checks on the continued correctness of a decision are either not made or only made at intervals. Related to this is the contrast between giving priority to need or to security — security first of all of expectations, and then in the sense of stability (e.g., the pension as a basis for planning a life in retirement). This latter is of course only a security regarding what has been promised, and does not imply that real needs will be covered. The objective of effectively covering true needs is associated with flexibility and in turn with insecurity and instability.

From a technical legal viewpoint, this contrast corresponds to the alternatives of differentiated standardization of facts and legal effects on the one hand, and a vague open standardization (by general clauses, unspecific legal terms, and discretion), on the other hand, it corresponds as well to the alternatives of directly calculable rights and law describing the duties of the competent institutions. Abstraction is thus "more law", more juridification. Concrete social law implies a feeling of unease at being subject to the judgment of those implementing the law. Abstract social law means a feeling of unease at the discrepancy between the general rule of law and the conditions to which the law is applied[34]. But abstraction also creates those

[33] With respect to the difficulties which social workers experience in directly delivering welfare benefits, see Hill (1979).

[34] Re abstraction as a decisive point in social intervention by law see Noerr (1981: 359ff.).

difficulties of social law which are evident, for example, in the discussion concerning the evasion of social law, the abuse of social benefits, and the weakening of self-responsibility (see literature indicated in 2nd and 3rd paragraph of 3.1 (2b)). One of the most important questions of juridification in the field of social law can be considered to be contained in this opposition between concrete and abstract legal design.

(4) Juridification as a "Rising Tide" of Law

Finally, we must refer to a foreground phenomenon which is indeed the most powerful impulse of the debate on juridification, the "rising tide of law" (Out of a large number of relevant publications see e.g. Berner, 1978; Maassen, 1979; Vogel, 1979; Stark, 1979; Sendler, 1979; Buelow *et al.*, 1980). Here it is important to emphasize that this is a question not only of an increase in the above sense (of decreed law, written law, statute law, judicial law, etc.), not only of a narrowing of the margins of action of existing law and alternative social guidance mechanisms, not only of an increasing differentiation of law, but also and above all of an increase in change within the law (Zacher, 1979b). A rising tide of law has both a synchronous and diachronous dimension. With respect to the synchronous dimension we can more or less refer back to most of the terms already used. The diachronous dimension however is also of importance to social law — indeed it has the greatest conceivable importance. The principal reasons are:

— Social law aims to change realities and to guide such changes. It must therefore continuously adapt itself to such changes;
— Social law is based on social conditions (e.g., work life, family life, etc.). Sometimes social law aims to influence social conditions by supporting and altering; and hence a change in social conditions also requires an adaptation of social law.
— The various fields of regulation of internalizing solutions are just as interdependent as the already existing orders of work and earnings, covering of needs and the family unit with the externalizing problem solutions of social law. Any change in the state of the law can therefore produce wide-ranging consequences.
— Social law (in the narrower as well as the wider sense), such as social policy, is unable to create an ideal social condition fulfilling all wishes. The more social law strives for direct realization of an ideal state the less it is capable of a perfect, definitive and satisfying order. The remaining imperfections always leave behind expectations of change. This *a priori* inadequacy of the order of social law is kept tolerable by means of a continuous reshaping of advantages and disadvantages (whereby the advantages must be as conspicuous, and the disadvantages as inconspicuous as possible). In this sense, the more perfect it aims to be, the more the welfare state has to continuously recycle its imperfections (Zacher, 1978b).

It is precisely with respect to the rising tide of social law that important national differences become evident. These are probably due to the gradient in juridification between normative and institutional styles, as well as between cash payments on the one hand, and payments in kind and other benefits on the other. They also have something to do with the degree of differentiation attained by social law, and something to do with the institutional framework conditions as well. They depend very much on the readiness of a society to give priority to the stability of an order and not to its (probably only apparent) higher level of justice[35].

4. Aspects of Evaluation

4.1 The Impossibility of Drawing Conclusions

It is not possible to make a conclusive judgment concerning the state of juridification in the field of social law. Developments have been and continue to be very different in various countries. Thus one cannot define the state of development with adequate differentiation without a proper national discussion of the subject within a number of countries, which would only be possible as the product of comprehensive research for which in this connection neither the time nor the resources are available.

What the preceding discussion was intended to indicate and hopefully has expressed, is that juridification is a highly differentiated phenomenon, particularly in the field of social law. This applies first of all to the phenomenon of juridification itself, and the accent here has been placed on its manifestations. It applies as well, however, to evaluation of the phenomenon of juridification.

4.2 Grounds for Juridification

Such an evaluation can at best be hinted at here. With all the reservations which have been expressed in the preceding discussion, and to which of course the juridification debate as a whole is subject — it must be emphasized that underlying juridification there exist not only blind or even destructive forces,

[35] As an example of a "calm" social law, the Swedish law is especially typical. This has general reasons which lie in the Swedish legislative procedure. This legislative procedure is extremely disciplined, see Kindermann (1983). There are also reasons specific to social legislation however. In the Scandinavian countries, social security legislation is understood primarily as programmes granting benefits and services and is adopted as such. It is not designed to settle conflicts. It is executed rather than interpreted. The execution is called upon, not disputed over. From this side also, there is thus no pressure for continuous correction of social legislation as is typical for the FRG. For the effect of direct democracy on the Swiss legislative procedure, see the literature indicated in the 3rd paragraph of 2.2(3). A continuous debate concerning the threat to the correctness of the law as a result of the rising tide of rules is taking place above all in Poland. In 1972 a special legislative council was set up by the prime minister, which was obviously intended to improve the quality of legislation. In 1979 a draft law — not yet passed — on legislation was brought in. The discussion is also taking place in the literature. For detailed information about this I have to thank Dr. Herbert Szurgacz (Wroclaw).

but also good intentions. Juridification by law is an instrument of democracy. Juridification by judicial protection of the law is an instrument of the division of powers. Without law freedom cannot be guaranteed and equality cannot be achieved. Law is certainly no sufficient instrument on its own, but it is undoubtedly a necessary one for opening up expectations and making their fulfillment as certain as possible. Social security without the security of the law is inconceivable in a developed society.

The law is an essential and proven instrument for the clarification of politically legitimate desires and for disclosure of the results of the political decision-making process. The law gives optimum possibilities to different interests within society to work out the conflicts between them. This applies not only to interests, but, to put it simply, to the coexistence of different opinions[36]. The less matters are self-evident in a society, the more necessary the law is in order to eliminate intolerable contradictions. Law also supplies information, or at least well-made law can do so. Finally, the entitlement as of right is the classical instrument for raising the citizen from an object of governmental and administrative activities to the level of an individual able to use and realize legal possibilities as of right.

All this is also a necessity within the sphere of social policy. Here we even find a pent-up demand for "correct" juridification. This applies in a sense to a correct ordering of the conditions for care (see Igl, 1978; Krause *et al.*, 1978, report by Peter Krause; Schmitz-Elsen, *et al.*, 1978), concentrating on what is essential, or a correct ordering of social work (Hoerz, 1984; Haberkorn, 1984; Schroeder, 1982). The juridification debate must not forget that the same amount of social policy with a lesser degree of juridification would not show defects which today go under the name of juridification, but would reveal other defects which would result from the law lagging behind social policy. These defects would probably be worse. For a society which is accustomed to have, use, produce and distribute goods within the framework of the law, as in the case of the Western industrial society, it would be intolerable not to go the other way also within the framework of law, i.e., the way of supplying and distributing goods, of socio-political redistribution, and of reservation and allocation. It would be a deep and damaging break if within the sphere of socio-political redistribution reservation and allocation, society did not find again the legal power of the individual to pursue his own interests (the individual's entitlement), if it did not see again how law makes behavior calculable, and did not again receive expectations opened up by the law and experience these as protected. The law must be retained as a factor in the social climate even if the citizen moves from the sphere of market economy to that of social policy. The unity of the medium of law through social policy and market economy is a necessity which also holds true for the sake of the market

36 As to the functions outlined above, these cannot be replaced in some way by the technique of social indicators either (a technique for which, at one time, there was high expectation). See Zacher (1974).

economy. Law for the economy with simultaneous lawlessness in social policy would make the law of the economy sick as well.

One of the further grounds of juridification is that where it has developed the law is in most cases without an alternative. (Re the research for alternatives which cannot be discussed and assessed in detail here, see Voigt, 1983c). Would it be in some sense an alternative to give the expert — the technocrat — more room than he has (Galanter, 1980; Voigt, 1983b; see also a critical view in Habermas, 1981: 533ff.)? Does not the technocracy again and again constitute a challenge to the law to protect those concerned from the excessive power of the technocrats? Would it be conceivable to leave social necessities to altruism alone?[37]. Would it be an alternative to reinforce human communities (Badura/von Ferber, 1981; Nokielski/Pankoke, 1982; Institut für soziale Arbeit e.V., 1982)? In fact it seems to be necessary for interhuman groups and interactions to relieve the community and its law. But can this aim be reached other than by appropriate changes in the law? Cooperatives, self-help groups, etc., cannot flourish without the law, but only with the "right" law. (Re automation as an alternative to law, see Garstka, 1980; Horn, 1980).

4.3 Risks of Juridification

But naturally reservations remain. Law can be made, and to make social changes by means of the law is one of the temptations of politics (see particularly, Luhmann: 1981a: 121 ff.). Naturally, social policy which was not essential has been made again and again (while social policy which was necessary, but politically would not have been effective, was not made). Naturally as well, each of these interventions have produced a new intervention. The law has increased the temptations of social policy.

Certainly the law can miss the point of social policy. The certainty of the law takes its life from abstraction. Correct abstraction, however, is an art. Social law is always pioneering into new territory. Social law, like social policy itself, aims to help people. By abstracting offers, and by granting rights to this, it often opens itself up to inappropriate use by those to whom help should not be granted. The law creates possessions. In that it protects trust and peace within the law, the law serves the culture of social policy. But the law can also be blind to the need for balanced judgment. The history of social law is still extremely young. Experiences follow in rapid succession and there is surprisingly little scientific energy expended in making use of these experiences and in improving the strategies and tactics for converting social policy into social law. Thus there is, in addition, risk of juridification for social policy.

The greatest dangers, however, threaten the law itself. It is being excessively

[37] See Tennstedt (1976); Widmeier (1976: 21ff., 101ff., 151); Gräfin von Bethusi-Huc (1976: 256ff.); Henke (1980); Pitschas (1980); Reidegeld (1980); Habermas (1981, Vol. 2: 522ff.; 1985: 203ff.); Luhmann (1981a, particularly, 94ff.); Mayntz/Flick (1982); Voigt (1983a). Re the problem of "soft power relationships" in care and nursing, see also Zacher (1976: 35).

increased and changed. The closeness of social law to the realities of life and to social conditions, the interdependence between social law and related law (labor law, family law, tax law, etc.), and the continuous reorientation of socio-political requirements, result in the law being subject to incessant modifications after it has set itself to work in the service of social policy. This puts the clarity and certainty of the law at risk. An increase in a differentiated and constantly shifting law, finally, no longer seems to be an improvement but a worsening of social policy. One great danger is that the law is used to fulfill expectations which social policy cannot fulfill. This applies not only to a retirement pension income which is not supplied from the national product. It is true much more generally:

"The sense of law in Germany today is characterized above all by the expectation that the law must be able to make life more calculable, i.e. less threatened by fate. People hope in the state as the entity which bears responsibility for the law and shift over onto it the task of defending them against the injustice of fate. The attitude of protest against what we call fate is part of the modern attitude. The law administered by the state is called on to be opponent of fate." The sense of law of our citizens today inclines very much towards the attitude that "state and the law have the responsiblity of compensating the individual for the blows of fate which he had suffered through no fault of his own. The formula of fate as an actionable loss of right describes the situation as broadly as an election slogan. In previous periods of history fate was a problem for the individual with which he had to come to terms on religious or other philosophical grounds... The Job of today under the blows of fate looks for someone from whom to claim compensation. Generally he finds this someone in the state... He demands compensation for the fate which he feels to be an injustice. This is not a question of vague emotions and resentments, but of concepts of law". "Not only the concept of fate is brought into legal thinking. The sense of law is increasingly inclined to also include the desire for prosperity and a high standard of living in the sphere of the law" (Werner, 1966).

The question as to how juridification in the field of social law should be evaluated thus allows no simple blanket answer. It cannot be a simple question of being either for or against juridification. The search must be for the "right" juridification (see contributions and references in Voigt, 1983a). Law must learn to be the golden mean between the security and the freedom of the individual[38].

[Translated from the German by John Hearsum]

[38] See Maihofer (1969b: 9ff; 1969a: 44ff.). The difficulty, of course, becomes clear when we find the following statements in Eichenhofer (1981): "The ideal of justice in social law: transcendence of the contradiction between distributive and commutative justices". "The concept of freedom in social law: transcendence of the contradiction between right and duty". — "Social law as transcendence of the contradiction between public and private law". In addition to all the other references made, the reader's attention should also be drawn to Cranston (1985) which, because of its recent date of publication, has not been included in this study.

References

AALER, Michael, and Steward ASQUITH (eds.) (1981) *Discretion and Welfare*. London: Heinemann.

ALFANDARI, Elie (1974) *Aide Sociale — Action Sociale*. Paris: Dalloz.

ANGELI, Franco (ed.) (1978) *Il lavoro nella giurisprudenza costituzionale*. Milano: Angeli.

BADURA, Bernhard, and Christian VON FERBER (eds.) (1981) *Selbsthilfe und Selbstorganisation im Gesundheitswesen. Die Bedeutung nicht-professioneller Sozialsysteme*. München/Wien: Oldenbourg.

BERNER, Georg (1978) "Inflation im Recht", 24 *Bayerische Verwaltungsblätter* 617.

v. BETHUSI-HUC, Viola, (1976) *Das Sozialleistungssystem der Bundesrepublik Deutschland*, 2nd Ed. Tübingen: Mohr.

BINDER, Martin (1980) *Das Zusammenspiel arbeits- und sozialrechtlicher Leistungsansprüche*. Wien: Braumüller.

BIRK, Dieter (1979) "Steuergerechtigkeit und Transfergerechtigkeit", 12 *Zeitschrift für Rechtspolitik* 221.

BLANKENBURG, Erhard (1980) "Recht als gradualisiertes Konzept. Begriffsdimensionen der Diskussion um Verrechtlichung und Entrechtlichung"; in *Alternative Rechtsformen und Alternativen zum Recht*, 6 Jahrbuch für Rechtssoziologie und Rechtstheorie. Opladen: Westdeutscher Verlag.

BOGS, Walter (1969) "Von der Freiheit durch das Gesetz. Bemerkungen über Anspruchs- und Ermessensleistungen im Sozialrecht", in *Festschrift Hans Achinger*. Berlin: Duncker und Humblot.

BRAUN, Hans (1981) "Das Verhältnis des Bürgers zur sozialen Sicherung", in *Selbstverantwortung in der Solidargemeinschaft. Das Recht der sozialen Sicherung und der Verantwortungswille des Bürgers*. Baden-Baden: Nomos.

BROOKE, Rosalind (1979) *Law, Justice and Social Policy*. London: Croom Helm.

BUELOW, Erich, Hermann MAASSEN, Dieter SIMON, Helmut SIMON and Spiros SIMITIS (1980) "Gesetzesflut — Gesetzesperfektionismus", in *Verhandlungen des 53. Juristentages*, Schlußveranstaltung, Part Q.

BURMAN, Sandra, and Barbara HARRELL-BOND (1978) *The Imposition of Law*. New York: Academic Press.

CAHNMAN, Werner, and Carl M. SCHMITT (1979) "The Concept of Social Policy", 8 *Journal of Social Policy* 47.

CRANSTON, Ross (1985) *Legal Foundations of the Welfare State*. London: Weidenfeld and Nicolson.

DÜRIG, Günter (1953) "Verfassung und Verwaltung im Wohlfahrtsstaat", 8 *Juristenzeitung* 193.

DUPEYROUX, Jean-Jacques (1981) *Droit de la Securité Sociale*, 8th Ed. Paris: Dalloz.

DUTHEIL DE LA ROCHERE, Jacqueline (1979) "Social Security Law in France: Decision-Making and Judicial Control", in M. Partington and J. Jowell (eds.), *Welfare Law and Policy*. New York: Nichols; London: Pinter.

ECKER, Walther (1981) "Das schadenstiftende Verschulden gegen sich selbst und die soziale Sicherung", in *Selbstverantwortung in der Solidargemeinschaft. Das Recht der sozialen Sicherung und der Verantwortungswille des Bürgers*. Baden-Baden: Nomos.

EICHENHOFER, Eberhard (1981) "Soziales Recht und Sozialrecht", 19 *Vierteljahresschrift für Sozialrecht* 19.

—(1982) "Mißbrauch von Sozialleistungen", 29 *Die Sozialgerichtsbarkeit* 137.

FAUDE, Michael (1983) *Selbstverantwortung und Solidarverantwortung im Sozialrecht. Strukturen und Funktionen der sozialrechtlichen Relevanz des Selbstverschuldens des Leistungsberechtigten*. Bonn: Röhrscheid.

FOURNIER, Jacques, and Nicole QUESTIAUX (1980) *Traité du droit Social*, 3rd Ed. Paris: Dalloz.

FROWEIN, Jochen (1976) "Der Beitrag der internationalen Organisationen zur Entwicklung des Völkerrechts", 36 *Zeitschrift für ausländisches öffentliches Recht und Völkerrecht* 147.

FUCHS, Maximilian (1983) "Der Stand der Forschung auf dem Gebiet des Sozialrechts in den Entwicklungsländern", 11 *Vierteljahresschrift für Sozialrecht* 5.

FULBROOK, Julian (1978) *Administrative Justice and the Unemployed.* London: Mansell.

GALANTER, Marc (1980) "Legality and its Discontents: A Preliminary Assessment of Current Theories of Legalisation and Delegalisation", in *Delegalization: Alternative Rechtsformen und Alternativen zum Recht*, 6 Jahrbuch für Rechtssoziologie und Rechtstheorie. Opladen: Westdeutscher Verlag.

GARSTKA, Hans Jürgen (1980) "Automation rechtlicher Verfahren als Entrechtlichungsprozeß", in *Organisation und Recht*, 7 Jahrbuch für Rechtssoziologie und Rechtstheorie. Opladen: Westdeutscher Verlag.

GITTER, Wolfgang (1969) "Zweckwidrige Vielfalt und Widersprüche im Recht der Sozialversicherung", *Schriftenreihe des Deutschen Sozialgerichtsverbandes*, Vol. 6. Wiesbaden: Chmielorz.

GITTER, Wolfgang and HAHN-KEMMLER, Jutta (1979) "Die Verdrängung des Zivilrechts durch das Sozialrecht — dargestellt am Unterhaltsrecht", 26 *Die Sozialgerichtsbarkeit* 195.

GROSER, Manfred, and Wolfgang W. VEIDERS (1979) *Die neue soziale Frage.* Melle: Knoth.

HABERKORN, Rolf (1984) *Die Rechtsstellung des Sozialarbeiters in England.* Berlin: Duncker und Humblot.

HABERMAS, Jürgen (1981) *Theorie des kommunikativen Handelns*, 2 Vols. Frankfurt a.M.: Suhrkamp.

—(1985) "Law as Medium and Law as Institution", in G. Teubner (ed.), *Dilemmas of Law in the Welfare State.* Berlin/New York: de Gruyter.

HENKE, Wilhelm (1980) "Die Sozialisierung des Rechts", 35 *Juristenzeitung* 369.

HILL, Michael (1979) "Social Workers and the Delivery of Welfare Benefits", in M. Partington and J. Jowell (eds.), *Welfare Law and Policy.* New York: Nichols; London: Pinter.

HÖRZ, Armin (1984) *Die Rechtsstellung des Sozialarbeiters in Frankreich.* Berlin: Duncker und Humblot.

HORN, Ulrich (1980) "Normvollzug in einer automatisierten Massenverwaltung. Ein empirischer Beitrag zur Rechtswirksamkeit in öffentlichen Organisationen", in *Organisation und Recht*, 7 Jahrbuch für Rechtssoziologie und Rechtstheorie. Opladen: Westdeutscher Verlag.

IGL, Gerhard (1978) "Rechtliche Gestaltung sozialer Pflege- und Betreuungsverhältnisse", 6 *Vierteljahresschrift für Sozialrecht* 201.

—(1983) "Der Heimvertrag als Regelungsgegenstand, Nachrichtendienst des Deutschen Vereins für öffentliche und private Fürsorge", 63 *Vierteljahresschrift für Sozialrecht* 110.

—(1981) "Die Lage der Behinderten — Eine Aufgabe des Sozialrechts", 35 *Zentralblatt für Sozialversicherung, Sozialhilfe und Versorgung* 257.

INSTITUT FÜR SOZIALE ARBEIT e. V. (1982) "Alternativbewegung, Jugendprotest, Selbsthilfe. Dokumente, Materialien und Kommentare", 5 *ISA-Schriftenreihe.* Münster: Selbstverlag.

IPSEN, Jörn (1983) "Nichtigkeitserklärung oder 'Verfassungswidrigerklärung' — zum Dilemma der verfassungsgerichtlichen Normenkontrollpraxis", 38 *Juristenzeitung* 41.

ISENSEE, Josef (1980) "Verfassung ohne soziale Grundrechte", 19 *Der Staat* 367.
—(1982) "Der Sozialstaat in der Wirtschaftskrise. Der Kampf um die sozialen Besitzstände und die Normen der Verfassung", in *Festschrift Johannes Broermann*. Berlin: Duncker und Humblot.
KATZENSTEIN, Dietrich (1982) "Das Sozialrecht in der neueren Rechtsprechung des Bundesverfassungsgerichts", 10 *Vierteljahresschrift für Sozialrecht* 167.
KAUFMANN, Franz-Xaver (ed.) (1982a) *Staatliche Sozialpolitik und Familie*. München: Oldenbourg.
—(1982b) "Elemente einer soziologischen Theorie sozialpolitischer Intervention", in F.X. Kaufmann (ed.), *Staatliche Sozialpolitik und Familie*. München: Oldenbourg.
KINDERMANN, Harald (1983) "Aktuelle Probleme der Gesetzgebungslehre — ein Diskussionsbericht", *Theorie und Methode der Gesetzgebung*. Frankfurt a.M.: Metzner-Verlag.
KIRCHHOF, Paul (1982) "Steuergerechtigkeit und sozialstaatliche Geldleistungen", 37 *Juristenzeitung* 305.
KÖBL, Ursula (1979) "Allgemeine Rechtstheorie. Aspekte der Gesetzesbindung", in *Sozialrechtsprechung — Verantwortung für den sozialen Rechtsstaat*, 2 Festschrift zum 25jährigen Bestehen des Bundessozialgerichts. Köln: Heymanns.
KRAUSE, Peter (1978) "Empfiehlt es sich, soziale Pflege- und Betreuungsverhältnisse gesetzlich zu regeln?", in 1 *Verhandlungen des 52. Deutschen Juristentages*, part E.
—(1980) "Das Sozialrechtsverhältnis". *Erste Sozialrechtslehrertagung 1979, 18 Schriftenreihe des Deutschen Sozialgerichtsverbandes*. Essen: Selbstverlag.
—(1981) "Rechtsprobleme einer Konkretisierung von Dienst- und Sachleistungen", in *Festschrift Georg Wannagat*. Köln/München: Heymanns.
—(1982) *Eigentum an subjektivem öffentlichem Recht*. Berlin: Duncker und Humblot.
KREJCI, Heinz (1982) "Das Versicherungsverhältnis", in T. Tomandl (ed.), *System des österreichischen Sozialversicherungsrechts*. Wien: Manz.
KREMALIS, Konstantinos (1982) E koinoniki asfalisi ton ergazomenon. Athens: Selbstverlag.
LAJOIE, Andrée, Patrick MOLINARI and Jean-Marie AUBY (1981) *Traité du Droit de la Santé et des Services Sociaux*. Montreal: P.U.
LAMPERT, Heinz (1980) *Sozialpolitik*. Berlin: Springer.
LEIBFRIED, Stephan (1976) "Armutspotential und Sozialhilfe in der Bundesrepublik", in 9 *Kritische Justiz* 377.
LORY, Bernard (1975) *La Politique d'Action Sociale*. Toulouse: Selbstverlag.
LÜCKE, Joerg (1982) "Soziale Grundrechte als Staatsziel, Bestimmungen und Gesetzgebungsaufträge", 107 *Archiv des öffentlichen Rechts* 15.
LUHMANN, Niklas (1970) "Positivität des Rechts als Voraussetzung einer modernen Gesellschaft", in *Die Funktion des Rechts in der modernen Gesellschaft*, 1 Jahrbuch für Rechtssoziologie und Rechtstheorie. Opladen: Westdeutscher Verlag.
—(1981a) *Politische Theorie im Wohlfahrtsstaat*. München: Olzog.
—(1981b) "Subjektive Rechte: Zum Umbau des Rechtsbewußtseins für die moderne Gesellschaft", in N. Luhmann, *Gesellschaftsstruktur und Semantik*, Vol. 2. Frankfurt a.M.: Suhrkamp.
MAASSEN, Hermann (1979) "Die Freiheit des Bürgers in einer Zeit ausufernder Gesetzgebung", 32 *Neue Juristische Wochenschrift* 1473.
MAIHOFER, Werner (1968) *Rechtsstaat und menschliche Würde*. Frankfurt a.M.: Klostermann.
—(1969) "Ideologie und Recht", in Werner Maihofer (ed.), *Ideologie und Recht*. Frankfurt a.M.: Klostermann.

MARSHALL, Thomas Humphrey (1981) *The Right to Welfare and Other Essays*. London: Heinemann.

MAURER, Alfred (1979) *Schweizerisches Sozialversicherungsrecht*, Vol. 1. Bern: Stämpfli.

—(1981) "Landesbericht Schweiz", in P. A. Köhler and H. F. Zacher (eds.), *Ein Jahrhundert Sozialversicherung*. Berlin: Duncker und Humblot.

VON MAYDELL, Bernd (1981) "Der Wandel des Sozialversicherungsrechts im allgemeinen Rechtssystem in den letzten 100 Jahren", 28 *Die Sozialgerichtsbarkeit* 412.

MAYNTZ, Renate, and Jürgen FLICK (1982) "Zur Diskussion um die Normenflut", 15 *Die Verwaltung* 281.

NEF, Urs C. (1981) "Der Einfluß des Sozialversicherungsrechts auf das Privatrecht", 77 *Schweizerische Juristenzeitung* 17.

NÖRR, Dieter (1981) "The Matrimonial Legislation of Augustus: An Early Instance of Social Engineering", 16 *The Irish Jurist* 350.

NOKIELSKI, Hans, and Eckart PANKOKE (1982) "Familiäre Eigenhilfe und situative Selbsthilfe", in F.X. Kaufmann (ed.), *Staatliche Sozialpolitik und Familie*. München: Oldenbourg.

OBERENDER, Peter (1983) "Mehr Wettbewerb im Arzneimittelbereich der Gesetzlichen Krankenversicherung: Eine Alternative zum staatlichen Dirigismus", 1 *Medizin, Mensch, Gesellschaft* 26.

PANKOKE, Eckart (1970) *Sociale Bewegung, sociale Frage, sociale Politik: Grundfragen der deutschen "Socialwissenschaft" im 19. Jahrhundert*. Stuttgart: Klett.

PARKER, Herminione (1982) *The Moral Hazard of Social Benefits*. London: Goron Pro-Print.

PINKER, Robert (1975) "Soziale Politik und soziale Gerechtigkeit", 6 *Archiv für Wissenschaft und Praxis der sozialen Arbeit* 1.

PITSCHAS, Rainer (1977) "Formelles Sozialstaatsprinzip, materielle Grundrechtsverwirklichung und Organisation sozialer Dienstleistungen", 5 *Vierteljahresschrift für Sozialrecht* 141.

—(1980) "Soziale Sicherung durch fortschreitende Verrechtlichung? — Staatliche Sozialpolitik im Dilemma von aktiver Sozialgestaltung und normativer Selbstbeschränkung", in R. Voigt (ed.), *Verrechtlichung*. Königstein/Ts.: Athenäum.

RAPPE, Hermann, and Klaus-Peter POHL (1979) "Das Bundessozialgericht und die Arbeit des Bundestages", in *Sozialrechtsprechung, Verantwortung für den sozialen Rechtsstaat, Festschrift zum 25jährigen Bestehen des Bundessozialgerichts*, Vol. 1. Köln: Heymanns.

REHBINDER, Manfred (1971) "Wandlungen der Rechtsstruktur im Sozialstaat", in E. E. Hirsch and M. Rehbinder, *Studien und Materialien zur Rechtssoziologie*, 2d Ed.. Köln, Opladen: Westdeutscher Verlag.

REICH, Charles (1964) "The New Property", 73 *Yale Law Journal* 756.

REIDEGELD, Eckart (1980) "Vollzugsdefizite sozialer Leistungen: Verrechtlichung und Bürokratisierung als Grenzen der Sozialpolitik", in R. Voigt (ed.), *Verrechtlichung*. Königstein/Ts.: Athenäum.

RÜFNER, Wolfgang (1979) "Das Sozialrecht in der Rechtsprechung des Bundesverfassungsgerichts", 1 *Jahrbuch des Sozialrechts der Gegenwart* 59.

— (1980) "Das Sozialrecht in der Rechtsprechung des Bundesverfassungsgerichts", 2 *Jahrbuch des Sozialrechts der Gegenwart* 21.

— (1981a) "Das Sozialrecht in der Rechtsprechung des Bundesverfassungsgerichts", 3 *Jahrbuch des Sozialrechts der Gegenwart* 33.

—(1981b) "Grundrechtliche Leistungsansprüche", in Festschrift *Georg Wannagat*. Köln/München: Heymanns.

—(1982) "Das Sozialrecht in der Rechtsprechung des Bundesverfassungsgerichts", 4 *Jahrbuch des Sozialrechts der Gegenwart* 35.

RULAND, Franz (1973) *Familiärer Unterhalt und Leistungen der sozialen Sicherheit.* Berlin: Duncker und Humblot.

SCHLICHT, Joachim (1982) *Verrechtlichung der Gesetzgebung.* Bad Honnef: Bock und Herchen.

SCHMID, Felix (1981) *Sozialrecht und Recht der sozialen Sicherheit. Die Begriffsbildung in Deutschland, Frankreich und der Schweiz.* Berlin: Duncker und Humblot.

SCHMITZ-ELSEN, Josef, and Otto Ernst KRASNEY (1978) "Empfiehlt es sich, soziale Pflege- und Betreuungsverhältnisse gesetzlich zu regeln?" in 2 *Verhandlungen des 52. Deutschen Juristentages,* Sitzungsberichte, part N.

SCHRAMMEL Walter (1983) "Das Sozialrecht in der Rechtsprechung des österreichischen Verfassungsgerichtshofes", 11 *Vierteljahresschrift für Sozialrecht* 213.

SCHROEDER, Leila (1982) *The Legal Environment of Social Work.* Englewood Cliffs, N.J.: Prentice Hall.

SCHULTE, Bernd (1981) "Das Sozialrecht in der Rechtsprechung des europäischen Gerichtshofs", 4 *Jahrbuch des Sozialrechts der Gegenwart* 439.

SCHULTE, Bernd, and Hans F. ZACHER (1979) "Das Sozialrecht in der Rechtsprechung des europäischen Gerichtshofs", 1 *Jahrbuch des Sozialrechts der Gegenwart* 353.

—(1980) "Das Sozialrecht in der Rechtsprechung des europäischen Gerichtshofs", 2 *Jahrbuch des Sozialrechts der Gegenwart* 359.

—(1981) "Das Sozialrecht in der Rechtsprechung des europäischen Gerichtshofs", 3 *Jahrbuch des Sozialrechts der Gegenwart 419.*

SENDLER, Horst (1979) "Normenflut und Richter", 12 *Zeitschrift für Rechtspolitik* 227.

SIMMA, Bruno (1975) "Methodik und Bedeutung der Arbeit der Vereinten Nationen für die Fortentwicklung des Völkerrechts", in W. Kewenig (ed.), *Die Vereinten Nationen im Wandel.* Berlin: Duncker und Humblot.

SMITH, Gilbert (1981) "Discretionary Decision-Making in Social Work", in M. Adler and S. Asquith (eds.), *Discretion and Welfare.* London: Heinemann.

STARK, Christian (1979) "Übermaß an Rechtsstaat?" 12 *Zeitschrift für Rechtspolitik* 209.

STOBER, Rolf (1982) "Verfassungsrechtlicher Eigentumsschutz sozialer Rechtspositionen", 2. *Sozialrechtslehrertagung,* 23 Schriftenreihe des Deutschen Sozialrechtsverbandes. Wiesbaden: Chmielorz.

STOLLEIS, Michael (1980) "Strafrecht und Sozialrecht", in K. Lüderssen and F. Sack (eds.), *Seminar abweichendes Verhalten,* Vol. 4. Frankfurt: Chmielorz.

STONE, Julius (1966) *Social Dimensions of Law and Justice.* Sydney: Maitland.

TENNSTEDT, Florian (1976) "Zur Ökonomisierung und Verrechtlichung in der Sozialpolitik", in A. Murswieck (ed.), *Staatliche Politik im Sozialsektor.* München: Piper.

THEVENET, Amedée (1979) *L'Aide Sociale d'Aujourd'hui,* 3rd Ed. Paris: Les Ed. ESF.

VOGEL, Hans-Jochen (1979) "Die Diskussion um die Normenflut", 34 *Juristenzeitung* 321.

VOIGT, Rüdiger (1983a) "Gegentendenzen zur Verrechtlichung. Verrechtlichung und Entrechtlichung im Kontext der Diskussion um den Wohlfahrtsstaat", in R. Voigt (ed.), *Gegentendenzen zur Verrechtlichung.* Königstein/Ts.: Athenäum.

—(ed.) (1983b) *Gegentendenzen zur Verrechtlichung.* 9 Jahrbuch für Rechtssoziologie und Rechtstheorie. Opladen: Westdeutscher Verlag.

WERNER, Fritz (1966) "Wandelt sich die Funktion des Rechts im sozialen Rechtsstaat?" in *Festschrift Gerhard Leibholz.* Tübingen: Mohr.

WERTENBRUCH, Wilhelm (1978) "Gedanken zum Vorbehalt des Gesetzes (Art. 31 SGB-AT — Social Code, General Section) aus verfassungsrechtlicher Sicht", in *Festschrift Horst Schieckel.* Percha, Kempfenhausen: Schulz.

WIDMEIER, Peter (1976) *Sozialpolitik im Wohlfahrtsstaat.* Reinbek: Rowohlt.
WILLIAMS, D.G.T. (1979) "Judicial Restraint and Judicial Review: the Role of the Courts in Welfare Law", in M. Partington and J. Jowell (eds.), *Welfare Law and Policy.* New York: Nichols; London: Pinter.
WULFHORST, Traugott (1982) "Leistungssteigerndes Verhalten der Berechtigten im Sozialrecht", 10 *Vierteljahresschrift für Sozialrecht* 1.
ZACHER, Hans F. (1968) "Soziale Gleichheit", 93 *Archiv des öffentlichen Rechts* 341.
—(1974) "Soziale Indikatoren als politisches und rechtliches Phänomen", 2 *Vierteljahresschrift für Sozialrecht* 15.
—(1976) "Grundfragen theoretischer und praktischer sozialrechtlicher Arbeit", 4 *Vierteljahresschrift für Sozialrecht* 1.
—(1977a) "Was können wir über das Sozialstaatsprinzip wissen?", in *Festschrift Hans-Peter Ipsen.* Tübingen: Mohr.
—(1977b) "Freiheits- und Sozialrechte im modernen Verfassungsstaat", in S. E. Szydzik (ed.), *Christliches Gesellschaftsdenken im Umbruch.* Regensburg: Pustet.
—(1977c) "Gleiche Sicherung von Mann und Frau. Zur gesellschaftspolitischen Relevanz der Rentenversicherung", *Deutsche Rentenversicherung* 197.
—(ed.) (1978a) *Sozialrechtsvergleich im Bezugsrahmen internationalen und supranationalen Rechts.* Berlin: Duncker und Humblot.
—(1978b) "Der Sozialstaat als Prozeß", 134 *Zeitschrift für die gesamte Staatswissenschaft* 16.
—(1978c) "Einleitung: Horizontaler und vertikaler Sozialrechtsvergleich", in H. F. Zacher (ed.), *Sozialrechtsvergleich im Bezugsrahmen internationalen und supranationalen Rechts.* Berlin: Duncker und Humblot.
—(1979a) "Rechtswissenschaft und Sozialrecht", 26 *Die Sozialgerichtsbarkeit* 206.
—(1979b) "Das Sozialrecht im Wandel von Wirtschaft und Gesellschaft", 7 *Vierteljahresschrift für Sozialrecht* 145.
—(ed.) (1980a) *Die Rolle des Beitrags in der sozialen Sicherung.* Berlin: Duncker und Humblot.
—(1980b) *Sozialpolitik und Verfassung im ersten Jahrzehnt der Bundesrepublik Deutschland.* Berlin: Schweitzer.
—(1981a) "Sozialrecht und soziale Marktwirtschaft", in *Festschrift Georg Wannagat.* Köln: Heymanns.
—(1981b) "Die Kodifikation des Sozialrechts im Ausland", in *Festschrift Theodor Maunz.* München: Beck.
—(1982a) "Zur Anatomie des Sozialrechts", 29 *Die Sozialgerichtsbarkeit* 329.
—(1982b) "Sozialrecht in sozialistischen Ländern Osteuropas, Nachwort", 23 *Jahrbuch für Ostrecht* 331.
—(1983a) "Der Sozialstaat als Aufgabe der Rechtswissenschaft", *Gedächtnisschrift Leontin Constantinesco.* Köln: Heymanns.
—(1983b) *Einführung in das Sozialrecht der Bundesrepublik Deutschland.* Heidelberg: C.F. Müller.
ZÖLLNER, Michael (1982) *Welfare — das amerikanische Wohlfahrtssystem.* Köln: Bachem.

The Juridification of Social Welfare in Britain*

MARTIN PARTINGTON
Brunel, London

Contents

1. Introduction

In preparing this paper, I was confronted by two fundamental problems:

(1) understanding what is involved in the complex range of issues covered by the concept of juridification; and

* For helpful comments, I am particularly indebted to Professors G. Teubner and H. Zacher.

(2) deciding precisely what should be the scope of the substantive topic of "Social Welfare Law", which is to be the main focus of this paper.

In Part 2, therefore, I set out my views on both these issues; this provides a backdrop against which the rest of the paper may be set. Having discussed these problems of definition, the paper goes on, in Part 3, to offer a description of the structure of social welfare in Britain; part 4 examines the characteristics of social welfare law in Britain; part 5 asks why the law has developed as it has; and in a concluding section, the question is asked as to whether the juridification of social welfare in Britain is, in fact, a problem.

2. Problems of Definition

2.1 Juridification

It would not be appropriate here to provide a detailed analysis of the concept of juridification. This has already been the subject of a considerable literature (For an introduction to this literature see Teubner, supra: 6 ff.). However, it is clearly necessary for me, at the outset of a paper focusing primarily on the juridification of social welfare law in Britain, to draw out from this rich and complex literature my own interpretation of what seems to me to be the main issues that are implicit in the concept.

This is not a straightforward task, since the concept of juridification is not precise and different writers have developed their own variations on the meaning of the term. However, I think that it is clear that, in considering juridification, we are not being asked to consider simply a *quantitative issue*, i.e. the fact that there is now much more law than, say, fifty or a hundred years ago. That may be interesting but, of itself, is thought to be intellectually a rather trivial matter.

Rather, discussion of juridification involves us in noting this increase in the volume of laws, and then engaging in an analysis of the *nature* of this law as it has been developed in the mixed economies of the Western World. Such analysis includes consideration of a range of questions including: how does the newer regulatory ("materialized") law differ from earlier notions of "formal" law; what are the factors which may help to explain the growth of this regulatory law and what factors may be identified which may explain the limitations of the effectiveness of this materialized law; what impact does this explosion of laws have on people's lives; and, if society is truly suffering from a surfeit of such regulatory law, what alternative strategies may be devised to cope with this problem while, at the same time (presumably), enabling the social policies implicit in such materialized law to be advanced?

The concept of juridification is thus intended, as I understand it, to provide the basis for an analysis of the relationship between three groups of issues: law, legal forms and legal values; the social, political and economic policies that may be said to characterize the present Welfare States of the West; and the impact of those policies, as transformed into legal forms, on the lives of ordinary people. It is in this sense that the term will be used in this paper.

Before turning to the definition of social welfare law, however, two further points need to be made in relation to juridification. First, it has to be noted that, as the term is used by Habermas (1985) and Teubner (1985), juridification appears to be regarded not simply as an analytical tool, but also as implying a value judgment — that there is too much law, that the "life-world" of the individual is being "colonialized", that there is a "reality" which is "ugly". I think it important that, at least in the first analysis, these value judgments about the phenomenon of juridification should not be accepted without question.

A second series of more fundamental questions also needs to be posed here: why does the debate focus on the question of *juridification* at all? Why does *law* seem to be the problem? Is it not the case that, though law clearly exists as some kind of social reality, it is nonetheless the product of the work of human actors — politicians, civil servants, judges, citizens? May not the focusing on law and the problems of juridification which are said to relate to the quantity and quality of laws which exist in modern western societies be mere diversions from rather more fundamental issues about the social *policies* and the processes of creating and implementing those policies which underpin the law itself and which are merely reflected in the law?

I do not intend to address these two points at this stage of my paper. Rather they are put down as problems which must be discussed further and to which I shall return in the concluding section.

2.2 Social Welfare Law

The second area of definitional difficulty relates to the scope of the substantive area of social welfare which is to be the primary focus for discussion in this paper.[1] When asked to participate in the work on which this volume is based, I was originally asked to write on "social security". The particular difficulty with this is that, in the British context, "social security" has a rather closely defined meaning; it relates *only* to cash payments paid by the state to individuals in particular, defined circumstances: e.g., unemployment, sickness/disability, retirement, birth, death, industrial injury, war injury (for details see, e.g. Ogus and Barendt (1982)). This rather precise concept — focusing exclusively on the techniques developed for providing income to particular groups at risk — is too narrow for a series of papers which, at base, seeks to analyze rather wider issues relating to the relationship between law and economic policy.

On the other hand, too broad a concept of "social welfare" or "social welfare law", referring to all those areas of law which relate to the implementation of social welfare or social policy, may be too extensive to be helpful. For example, it *could* be argued that *all* public policy was designed to promote

[1] Much of the argument that follows in this section is developed from a similar discussion by Partington (1985), an as yet unpublished paper prepared by the author for the (British) Economic and Social Research Council. See also Cranston (1985).

social welfare.[2] (Indeed some would argue that any form of human endeavor — whether promoted by the state or otherwise — could, or even should, advance the sum of human happiness and thus, in that sense, promote social welfare). Although it is important to remember the existence of such debates, completely open-ended uses of the concept of "social welfare" are likely to prove too wide for the purposes of this paper.

What does seem to be important here is that our concept of "social welfare law" should not focus exclusively on those areas of law which are the basis for the administration of social security benefits (as narrowly defined); nor should it be limited to a consideration of other social policies that are promoted for and delivered to individual citizens *directly* by agencies of the state. A discussion of the juridification — as sketched out above — of social welfare law must include a consideration of the relationship between the private and public sectors of the economy in relation to matters of social policy. Indeed, in the present political environment in Britain (and no doubt elsewhere) one must appreciate that patterns of social welfare provision are changing and becoming increasingly complex and that, as a consequence, any consideration of the legal context of social welfare provisions is also becoming increasingly complex (There is a rapidly developing literature on this issue: see, e.g. the essays in Le Grand and Robinson (1984)).

For the purpose of this paper, therefore, I have decided not to focus on "social security" in the narrow, technical British sense, but to offer an analysis of the nature of British social law based on a rather broader concept of "social welfare" which may be regarded as comprising *all those areas of social policy that are designed or intended to assist or enhance the quality of life of those groups or individuals in society who can be described as disadvantaged* (for the argument that much "social policy" is, in fact, bound to keep the disadvantaged in their disadvantaged position, see Los (1981). Cf. George and Wilding (1984)).

This rather broad definition will assist us both to recognize the great variety of agencies, bodies and individuals that may be said to promote social welfare as thus defined, and to consider the wide scope of services that are offered. This, in turn, will help us to identify the areas of law that relate to the advancement of those areas of social policy which is an essential preliminary to any analysis of the nature of that law.

3. The Scope of Social Welfare Policy in Britain

Having set down the basic definitions on which this paper is to be built, we may begin to consider some of the essential features of social welfare law in

[2] There is, indeed, a vast literature on definitions of "social welfare", its ideological bases, and on strategies for promoting the advance of social welfare; see e.g. George and Wilding (1976); Weale (1978); Pinker (1979). Such discussions are frequently linked to the even more elusive concept of "social justice"; see e.g. Miller (1976).

Britain. Rather than start from a purely abstract or theoretical position, it may help if, as a first step, we offer a brief sketch of the scope of social welfare provision in Britain.

3.1 The Structure of Social Welfare Delivery

If we ask, first, what is the structure of welfare provision, or to put it another way, who actually administers social welfare in Britain, it can quickly be seen that an extensive range of individuals and agencies is involved. The following table offers, albeit in a crude diagrammatic form, a summary of the various categories of welfare provision.

TABLE

Welfare Agencies	Benefits Provided
Individuals	**Family Support** (e.g. for the sick/elderly/disabled) **Self-help**
Central Government	**Benefits in cash** (e.g. Social Security; housing benefits) **Indirect benefits** (e.g. tax allowances) **Benefits in kind** (e.g. National Health Service; provision of cars for disabled)
Local Government	**Personal Social Services** (e.g. child care, mental health, social work) **Community Services** **Benefits in cash** (e.g. payments under s. 1 of Children & Young Persons Act, 1963) **Benefits in kind** (e.g. subsidized housing)
Charities/Voluntary Groups	**Benefits in kind** (e.g. housing, children's homes) **Cash benefits** (e.g. adoption, advice agencies)
Private Companies	**Cash Benefits** (e.g. pensions, sick-pay, life assurance, redundancy pay) **Other** (e.g. employment benefits such as maternity leave)

Three immediate points need to be made in relation to the table:

(1) it does not include *all* the kinds of agency/service that could be included in an even broader definition of "social welfare". Thus, for example, the table does not mention specifically anti-discrimination agencies, or the providers of educational services that *could* be argued to be part of the welfare state system. However, it is hoped that it does identify the main groups providing social welfare within the definition of "social welfare" given above;

(2) it should always be remembered that the structure of welfare provision is not carved in stone but is a *dynamic* structure.

The boundaries between the different categories of providers, and thus the shape of the structure is always changing: at some periods in time more dramatically than at others[3];

(3) furthermore it must always be remembered that the present structure is the result of years of *political and social struggle* and that all changes and tensions within the structure are still the subject of continuous refinement and debate. Questions relating to the extent of welfare provision, the responsibility for welfare provision, the relationship of welfare provision to other aspects of social and economic policy are still controversial — particularly in the present age of fiscal crisis, "monetarist" economic policy and the attack on Keynesian economic principles.

3.2 The intricate web of social welfare policy: direct and indirect social provision.

One lesson that is immediately apparent from the table is that the implementation of social welfare policy involves an exceedingly complex mix of individual/family responsibility, direct provision by the agencies of the state at both the central and local government level, and indirect provision, sometimes by government but also via charities and corporations. To adopt the slightly different language used by Zacher, it can be seen that, as in Germany (and other countries), British social policy also employs both "internalising" and "externalising" solutions to the social problems with which it has to attempt to cope (Zacher supra 379 ff.).

It is not possible in a paper of this length to sketch a comprehensive picture of social welfare policies in Britain, but the following examples may help to illustrate the complexities mentioned above:

(1) It is still the case that the primary responsibility for acquiring the monetary resources with which the essential commodities of living may be purchased rests with wage-earners working in the employment field. In the case of low wage earners, this may be supplemented by government policies in

[3] For example, there is a number of benefits that have been negotiated on behalf of workers by their trade unions which are not currently regarded as a part of formal social policy but which might develop as such over the years. See Cunningham (1981); and for a more general discussion Field (1981).

relation to taxation relief, direct subsidies of wages (family income supplement) or indirect subsidies (legislation relating to low wages).

(2) Again, if the ability to acquire such monetary resources is diminished as a consequence of unemployment or redundancy (retrenchment), there are varieties of forms of social policy that may be relevant: the direct payment of social security benefits (unemployment benefit) or legal requirements on employers to make (subsidized) redundancy payments. Indirect policies may relate to the retraining of the unemployed or the redundant in order to acquire new skills. There have also been a number of measures, e.g. the Temporary Short Time Working Compensation Scheme, (Freedland, 1980) designed to try to encourage employers not to make workers unemployed or redundant.

(3) Primary responsibility for caring for the sick, disabled, and (probably also) the elderly still resides in the family. This too is supplemented by social policies affecting the sick and the elderly which relate to the direct replacement of earning (e.g. social security payments or, of increasing importance, private sickness insurance and pensions), health care (the National Health Service) and other support services for the sick and the elderly (such as social workers, "sheltered accommodation", residential care establishments, and the like). In addition, there is a gradual recognition in social welfare policy of the need to provide support for the carers of certain categories of the chronic sick and disabled and elderly (e.g. social security payments such an invalid care allowance and attendance allowance, and also certain forms of privileged treatment through the taxation system).

(4) In a more specific area of social policy, primary responsibility for industrial safety rests with the individual worker. But this is supported by direct social security payments for injuries suffered at work — industrial injuries benefits — which are partly compensation and partly earnings substitution. Where negligence or breach of statutory safety duties are found such payments may be supplemented by common law awards of damages. And there is an extensive range of statutory duties imposed on employers and employees to provide and adopt safe systems of work under Health and Safety (and related) legislation, supplemented or reinforced by more or less adequate agencies of enforcement. Such measures include specific legal requirements on employers to work with employees' organizations in order to enhance safety at work.

(5) A further example of the intricate web of social policy measures may be seen in the context of the birth and care of children. Again, primary responsibility for this rests with families/parents who have decided to have children. But this is supplemented by cash assistance for the expense of a new baby (maternity benefits and defined provisions in the social assistance/supplementary benefits scheme) and a state contribution towards the costs of rearing children (child benefit — formerly a mix of family allowances and tax relief). In addition, increasing attention has been directed towards protection of the employment opportunities for women (statutory rights to maternity leave and maternity pay). There is also much talk though less action in relation to other

welfare policies such as the provision of child-minding/crèche facilities and the appropriate means for regulating and maintaining standards in relation to such services.

Many other specific examples could be given of the complexities of British social welfare policy and provision. Four important points may, however, be made at this stage:

(1) Social welfare policy in Britain is delivered through a vast variety of agencies, both government and private including, most importantly, the family. In considering the public role of the state, it is vital not to underestimate the more private role of the individual.

(2) The objectives of apparently "social" policies must not be considered in isolation from other policy objectives. For example, there is an increasingly clear interaction between much social security policy and manpower policy. Benefit levels are determined at least in part not on the basis of objective considerations of social needs but to reflect the wage levels of those in employment and to provide "incentives" for those not in work to return to work. Furthermore, social security contributions payable by employers have recently been restructured in order to encourage employers to hire more low paid workers. Similar interactions could be found in the interface between social welfare policy and other areas such as family or education or health policy.

(3) The social policies themselves which are delivered through such a variety of agencies and which are embedded in the complexities of other policies may not, in fact, complement those other policies and may, indeed, even be counter-productive.[4] The policies have not developed as a coherent whole, and should not be viewed as though they had developed in this way.[5]

[4] The most obvious area of confusion and inconsistent policy which has been noted by academics for many years and which is now attracting some political attention is the tension between social security policy and taxation policy as means for assisting those on low incomes, and the problem of the "poverty trap", which helps to keep the low paid in a state of poverty see, e.g. Dilnot *et al.* (1984). Another area of inconsistency and conflict, not specifically highlighted in the main text, is in the area of subsidies for housing costs: see e.g. Ermisch (1984).

[5] Some attempt at developing a coherent strategy may be seen in the seminal Beveridge Report on Social Insurance which stressed that social insurance had to be linked with other social policies, e.g. full employment opportunities, and preventive health care; but any coherent strategy, unless constantly revised and updated, is unlikely to be able to achieve coherence because of the constant pressure on politicians to respond rapidly, piecemeal and in the short-term to problems that truly need more comprehensive treatment. The sheer vastness of the social welfare "system" now makes such a task a daunting one (though an interdisciplinary team operating with sophisticated computer modelling might be of value). Certainly the recent review of certain aspects of social security policy, which the relevant government minister has described as the most important overview of policy since Beveridge, is likely to prove anything but that: constraints on their timing and methods of

(4) The policies are by no means all designed to advance "social welfare", at least not in the sense offered earlier in the paper. Much social welfare policy, particularly in relation to the unemployed but in other areas as well, has a clear disciplinary/social control purpose as well as the more generous welfare purpose (see, e.g. Piven and Cloward, 1971; Jordan, 1981).

4. The Characteristics of Social Welfare Law in Britain

Having looked in outline at the providers of welfare policy and the range of policies they are called upon to administer, it is now possible to identify a little more precisely the types of law, and legal form, which underpin such policies and in so doing suggest some of the characteristics of such law to see how far they may be fitted into the framework for analysis that has been developed by Teubner (infra).

4.1 The Common Law: "Formal" law

Although, perhaps, not immediately apparent, there are aspects — albeit limited — of the common law which in practice relate to the advancement of social welfare policy (as now defined in the context of the late twentieth century) which derive from older principles of common law, that is to say those principles of law that have been devised through the formal legal processes of judicial decision-making in an hierarchical court structure.

Most significant is the area of *tort* law, where principles of the law of negligence in particular have developed in such a way as to be the basis of the provision of compensation for accidents and other forms of personal injury.[6] A further important development in the common law, which followed on and was an important supplement to the late nineteenth and twentieth century interventionist policies of the state, is the tort of *breach of statutory duty*, which today forms a basis for civil litigation in the courts in cases where no other form of statutory remedy is provided.

A second area of importance is *contract* law, in particular — in the context of social welfare law — the contract of employment and the legal recognition of terms and conditions that may be negotiated or bargained as between employee and employer. Such forms of private welfare as contractual sick pay

operation mean, almost inevitably, that their analysis and proposals for reform will continue to be of a patchwork and relatively short-term character.

More critically, some would argue that social welfare policy cannot, by definition, be completely coherent, since in a market economy, it is necessary for there to be some measure of inequality to encourage people to work harder, and to provide those out of work with "incentives" to undertake paid employment.

[6] It is not proposed to rehearse here the now familiar critique of tort law, that a system of compensation based on the principle of "fault" transforms the operation of tort law into a "forensic lottery"; See Ison (1967); Atiyah (1980. See also Harris, *et al.* (1984).

schemes, or health insurance, or premature retirement insurance are part of what may properly be characterized as "private welfare" but are nonetheless important in any analysis of the totality of public welfare.

A third area of "formal" law of great relevance to our considerations here is *charity* law. Charities were the early forerunners of the modern welfare state and are still (and perhaps increasingly) an important aspect of the welfare delivery system today (for a most helpful analysis of charity law in the context of social welfare policy see Chesterman (1979)).

What the common law in Britain has not achieved, despite the attempts of well-intentioned pressure groups and public interest lawyers (Prosser, 1983), is any kind of substantive "floor of welfare rights". (There have been indications in other common law countries, particularly in those countries with written constitutions, Bills of Rights or similar statements of fundamental normative principles, that some kind of basic system of "rights in welfare" might be created by the courts.[7]) The plea for the development of the common law to recognize basic rights to an income, or family security, or housing (advanced e.g. by Lord Scarman, 1975), has not made progress in the courts in Britain. Substantive welfare rights — legally enforceable claims to the provision of cash or services from the state by the citizen — have been, almost exclusively, the creation of statute law, i.e. the result of political debate and the subsequent endorsement of policies by politicians through the parliamentary process. It is to this second, and much more important class of legal rule (both quantitatively and qualitatively) that we now turn.

4.2 Public law or "materialized law": State provision of social welfare

Since the bulk of contemporary social welfare policy is delivered via various agencies of the state, and given the fundamental principle of government that public officials must be able to point to direct statutory authority whenever they are required to operate official policy in relation to members of the public, it is not surprising that the bulk of the "materialized" law of the welfare state should be contained in statutory provisions (for a most valuable and detailed account of the history of social security legislation in Britain see Ogus (1982)). These have varied in their detail and complexity. Such variations are, to a large degree, the consequence of rather broader political/constitutional debates about the necessity for detailed legislative control over the circumstances in which public expenditure may be authorized. Two areas of social policy will be considered in this section: social security, and other social welfare programs.

[7] See in the context of the U.S.A., Reich (1964; 1965); cf. Scheingold (1974). Even in the U.S. context there is now widespread scepticism as to the ability/willingness of the *courts* (as opposed to agencies of government) to create basic welfare rights, recognizable and enforceable as legal rights: see also Horowitz (1977).

(1) *Social Security*: Although the history of social security law in Britain must properly be traced back in many respects to the Elizabethan Poor Law of 1601, and beyond (aspects of the Poor Law can still be found in social security law to the present day), it is with Acts of Parliament such as the Workmen's Compensation Act 1897, the Old Age Pensions Act 1908 and the National Insurance Act 1911 that the legislative basis for the modern welfare state was created. All these Acts, particularly the last-named, were very detailed in nature, reflecting the view that the demands for public control over public expenditure necessitated detailed regulation. Over the years, it is increasingly the case that detailed primary legislation (Acts of Parliament) has been replaced by much more detailed secondary legislation (Statutory Instruments) whose legitimacy depends on rather vague power-conferring rules now found in much primary legislation. Notwithstanding this technical change, the principle of legislative detail remains firmly entrenched.

Interestingly, the area of British social security law that was most ill-defined and lacking in statutory detail was the law relating to the Supplementary Benefit (Social Assistance) scheme. Until 1980, this system was based on a rather small number of statutory rules conferring entitlement to benefit, which were combined with very broad discretionary powers (permitting payments in "exceptional circumstances" or to meet "exceptional needs") which were in turn the subject of detailed administrative (rather than statutory) guidance from a semi-independent government agency — the Supplementary Benefits Commission. From November 1980, this loose discretion-based scheme has been replaced by a much more formalized rule-based scheme of breath-taking complexity. Government assertions (made before the November 1980 scheme came into effect) that the new rule-based scheme would be "simpler to understand" were not borne out in reality. (Partington, 1980). (The desire for simplification is still very much on the formal political agenda in Britain in that the official reviews of aspects of the social security system which are in progess as this paper is being written are stated, *inter alia*, to be looking for a more "simplified" scheme.)

At first glance, it might be thought that the overall complexity of social security law in Britain, and the more recent debate about complexity versus simplification which has occurred in the context of social assistance is a manifestation of the "problem" of juridification. To a certain degree this may be so, but it is important to realize that the debate about simplification also raises other, and in my view, much more fundamental questions. In particular, a social security system that attempts to offer a highly individualized range of social security benefits, directed at satisfying a high variety of clearly defined individual needs (which might be thought to be an appropriate, even laudable, objective for a social security system) is likely to be extremely complex; by contrast a system which offers "rough justice" may be simpler, because less individual cases need to be satisfied and thus be the subject of specific rules. In the present political and economic climate in Britain it must be stressed that the overt quest for simplicity also masks a more or less covert search for ways to cut (or at least prevent rises in) levels of social security expenditure.

(2) *Other social welfare programs*: In addition to social security, there is a variety of other social welfare programs delivered by the state. An important, though sometimes neglected, source of social welfare is that delivered through the *taxation* system. Unlike the social security system, which delivers direct cash benefits to those claimants who are entitled to them, the taxation system works in a "negative" fashion, by granting allowances for various kinds of social disadvantage. Most significant is the basic "tax threshold", a defined sum of money on which there is no liability to income tax. This has the purpose of relieving many of the poorest paid from taxation. A more detailed taxation "benefit" is found in the special assistance granted to blind persons. These allowances and exemptions are not, in legal terms, especially complex (though their social policy impact certainly is); nonetheless successive Finance Acts have had to contain statutory provisions to legitimate these reliefs from the burden of taxation.[8]

A second general area of social welfare policy comprises the variety of social services offered by social workers. These relate to family support, the care of children, care of the mentally ill and handicapped, and the elderly. In many areas (e.g. child care and mental health), where the implementation of policy may well involve questions of an individual's civil liberties, the powers of the relevant officials are spelled out in some detail in legislation (see, e.g. Hoggett, 1977; 1984). In such cases, detailed legal provisions would be widely regarded as the appropriate basis for making decisions. In other areas, where the powers of local authority social workers are of a rather more general and supportive kind, the legislation will, in turn, be rather less detailed (for a more general introduction to the work of social workers see e.g. Barclay (1982)).

4.3 Public Law: The Public Regulation of Private Welfare Provision

In addition to the direct provision of welfare by agencies of the state, British social policy also depends, to some extent, on the provision of welfare through the private sector, subject to the regulation of basic standards by the state. This policy direction seems likely to increase in the coming years. Such forms of regulation are manifest in a number of different contexts, of which the following are, perhaps, the clearest examples:

(1) Provision of cash benefits

The most obvious example of the public regulation of private benefit is in the context of *private pensions*. Since the Social Security Pensions Act 1975 was

[8] As noted above (4) there has been a complete failure at the governmental level, to come to grips with the complexities of the interaction of the taxation and social security systems. There was a debate, early in the 1970s on the desirability or otherwise of introducing a system of Negative Income Taxation, or a Tax-Credit system, but this came to nothing. There are indications that there is some revival of official interest in this, but it is hard to predict whether this will lead any further. Certainly the current review of British social security policy has not taken the issue on board.

passed, retirement pensions have been based on the following structure: the state continues to provide a basic flat-rate *retirement pension*, but this is to be topped up by an occupational (earnings-related) pension. Employers who provide a private occupational pension scheme, that conforms to certain basic statutory minima, may contract out of the state-run occupational pension scheme; the state-run scheme then applies to workers who are not in an employment with a private contracted-out pension scheme. The scheme, which will take twenty years to come into full operation, is intended to ensure that, eventually, on retirement all workers will receive an earnings-related pension. In this way it is hoped that the continuing reliance of retired persons on social assistance will, at last, be substantially reduced.[9] This tendency toward statutory (public) schemes nonetheless provided through the private sector of the economy is likely to be enhanced still further if current proposals relating to the *transferability of occupational pension entitlements* from one employment to another — at present the subject of considerable debate amongst employers, workers and the pension funds — are brought into effect.

More recently, a *statutory sick pay* scheme has been introduced whereby workers who fall sick will, in the normal case, lose entitlement to the state sickness benefit (and also the basic industrial injury benefit) and instead receive, for the first eight weeks of illness, sick pay under a statutory scheme, but paid out by employers (though refunded in full by the government).

Another example of the public regulation of private welfare provision can be seen in the area of *redundancy* where — again — employers are required, in defined circumstances, to pay employees' redundancy pay in accordance with a detailed statutory scheme (Grunfeld, 1980). Similar points can be made in relation to provisions regarding statutory *maternity pay.*

(2) Welfare in Employment

Another area of the public regulation of private welfare is to be found in the area of the employment relationship. The most comprehensive aspect of social welfare policy under this heading is health and safety legislation which attempts to offer all employees a safe working environment in which, it is hoped, injuries resulting from accidents will be kept to a minimum. This legislation imposes on employers (and also employees) a wide range of duties to make their plant safe, which is enforced by a public sector agency — the Health and Safety Executive.

More specific social welfare rights which employers are obliged by law to provide to their employees relate to, e.g. provisions for maternity leave. There has also been legislation, in certain industries, relating to low wages, though

[9] Of course this new scheme has caused further policy problems. One important matter, not of direct concern to this paper, is the economic impact of the vast amount of cash now in the hands of the pension funds, swelled as a result of participation in the pension scheme. A second important issue is the extent to which the state can be said to be able to afford this scheme; doubts have been raised as to its viability in the long run.

the present government is committed to the repeal of the relevant legislation in the near future (an example of dejuridification?).

(3) The Public Regulation of Private Welfare Agencies

A third type of public law applied to the private sector of welfare provision relates to the regulation of privately run providers of welfare services. Thus, e.g. private hospitals, private homes for the elderly, private nursing homes, privately-run adoption agencies, and the like, are all required to comply with statutorily defined standards of care and provision of facilities, or they may run the risk of closure or other forms of intervention by governmental enforcement authorities (See e.g., Freeman and Lyon, 1984).

4.4 Procedural Law in Relation to the Implementation of Social Welfare Policy

So far we have concentrated on identifying, with examples, the main areas of *substantive* law relating to the operation of social welfare. This section would not, however, be complete, without mentioning the *procedural* law of social policy, by which is meant those specific parts of the law which prescribe the procedures by which claims to various forms of social welfare must be asserted by members of the public and the methods of adjudication upon those claims by officials and other appellate/review bodies. Just as the policies themselves are of the utmost complexity, so too is the variety of means for taking decisions and appealing against adverse decisions.

In general, decisions arising from the implementation of welfare policies will be the responsibility of designated officials: central government officers, local authority employees and the like. In certain cases, initial decisions must be taken by a panel, or a board, or some kind of tribunal, rather than by an official acting on his/her own.

In addition, there has long been established a political convention that there should be opportunities for dissatisfied parties to an initial decision to appeal against that decision to a higher authority.[10] In some cases (as with Workmen's Compensation), appeal may be to the courts. In others, and more commonly, appeals will be to specially constituted tribunals; in the case of social security, there is even a two-tier appellate structure, first to a locally based Social Security Tribunal then to a Social Security Commissioner (Micklethwait, 1976). A more recent development in Britain is the creation of both central government and local government ombudsmen to hear and investigate complaints of official maladministration (e.g. Williams, 1979). And, even where not given a specific statutory jurisdiction, the courts retain an inherent, if sometimes restricted and often very technical supervisory jurisdiction to

[10] Decisions to create appeal procedures have, at least on occasion, been as much the result of calculated political judgment as any adherence to conceptual principles regarding the need for social appeal structures: see Lynes (1975); for a more recent example, see Partington, *et al.* (1984).

rule on interpretations of the law and to strike decisions down that may not have been reached in accordance with legally developed norms of decision-making (de Smith, 1980).

In the context of adjudication, particularly appellate adjudication, it is possible to argue that there has been an increase in juridification of the welfare system. Despite the stated aim that tribunals should provide a cheap, speedy and informal system of justice, they have not been able to operate effectively in this way (Street, 1968). Indeed, the tendency in recent years has been for tribunals to adopt a rather more formal approach to their decision-making and this is likely to have emphasized the legal nature of this part of social welfare administration. However, it should be remembered that the number of cases that are appealed in any year is only a minute proportion of claims made and adjudicated upon by officials. The increase in this area of juridification of the appeal structure has made rather little impact on welfare claimants as a whole.[11]

5. Reasons for the Juridification of Welfare in Britain

Parts 3 and 4 sketched out some of the main features of current British social policy, and have noted the main characteristics of the legal provisions which underpin such policy. However, as discussed at the beginning of the paper, juridification involves not just a quantitative analysis, but also a *qualitative* analysis of the legal structure of social welfare in Britain. This statement also involves, in some degree, an analysis of the reasons why British social policy (and hence its legal forms) has emerged in the way that it has.

It would be quite impracticable in this paper to offer any detailed account of the history of the development of social policy in Britain. Fortunately there are some good general histories of this development (Fraser, 1973; Thane, 1982) and an increasing number of more detailed accounts of the development of policy in particular areas of social welfare, (Gilbert, 1966; Harris, 1972; Bartrip and Burman, 1983). At the risk of over-simplification, these accounts describe and analyse the types of social problem that were thrown up by the increasing industrialization of Britain in the late eighteenth and nineteenth centuries. They show how what would now be described as the social welfare policies of private charities and other private mechanisms proved wholly inadequate to meet the hardships experienced by so many people. Fear of disease, fear of social unrest, and the increasing politicization of workers, combined with the enlightenment of particular employers and notable social reformers led to demands for increasing state intervention. However, early attempts to alleviate social distress merely by giving powers to local authorities did not provide an adequate basis for effective action. Thus the

[11] It might, of course, be the case that claimants are deterred from appealing by what they perceive as an increasingly juridified and alienating appellate structure; there is, however, no empirical evidence for such an assertion.

making of direct provision of welfare on a collective basis by the state and its agencies ultimately came to be regarded as an acceptable feature of political life. The authority of the state was needed to provide the bases of social policy which individuals, left to their own devices, would either not wish to subscribe to or, through poverty, would not be able to afford. Although attacked by some as an example of "socialist" doctrine, social welfare policy, is perhaps, more accurately characterized as a response by capital to the failures of the market and to the threats which increasingly organized labor might have posed to the private enterprise system.

Thus, the *principle* of state intervention derives from the social, economic and political context of the industrial revolution of Victorian Britain. The *forms* of intervention were always very varied. *Workmen's Compensation* imposed statutory duties on private employers, which were ultimately enforceable in the ordinary courts. *National Insurance* provided a scheme of benefits, which was originally developed from models of private working-class insurance schemes and the friendly societies, but which increasingly came to be administered by agencies established by the state. *Private charities* continued to provide much important back-up, and to develop new welfare services. *Local authorities* became increasingly important in the provision of newly developing social work services, particularly involving oversight of the care of children and the elderly. In addition, after World War II, a *National Health Service* was established. These developments were not part of any single co-ordinated social plan, but were very much a reflection of the realities of political life whereby existing institutions became expanded or developed to meet newly emerging needs.

The variety of *forms of law*, therefore, is a result of the variety of types of policy initiative and development which have occurred over the last hundred years. The juridification of British social welfare policy has not been the result of the work of the courts, but that of politicians (and civil servants). The principal way in which the law has *directly* influenced such policy development derives from the (unwritten, and thus court-created) principle that authority for the activities of public servants must be found in legal, and in particular, statutory authority. The twin principles of the "Rule of Law" and the "Sovereignty of Parliament" have resulted in the particular (and some might say peculiar) legal edifice that currently underpins the law of social welfare in Britain.

In addition, legal considerations have had a direct impact on the way welfare appellate authorities exercise their jurisdiction. Apart from these, however, law has been much more the reflection of social welfare policy developments in Britain than the determinant of such policy developments.

6. Concluding Remarks: Is Juridification a Problem?

At the outset of this paper, I indicated some rather fundamental problems I had in using the notion of juridification, but I offered a view of what I thought it meant and have tried to look at British social security and social welfare law in that light. I would not like to end this paper, however, without posing the question; is juridification a problem? Should juridification be seen as a problem? Whose problem is it?

Attempting answers to these questions raises two rather different lines of argument. First, at least in the British context, the concept of juridification seems to miss the mark. Certainly there is much more law relating to social welfare policy than fifty or a hundred years ago. But, it is conceded by all commentators that the mere fact that quantitatively there is more law, though interesting, is not a matter of profound moment.

Throughout this paper, I have sought to stress that, in most areas, law is the reflection of social policy, is the means by which social policy is given effect, and is not a major determinant of it. There is a danger that concentrating on the law, the politics of welfare will be forgotten or, at least, down-played. (Griffith, 1979). To some degree, it may need to be conceded that this is a particularly British response, since in Britain there is no written constitution or other form of "basic law" which has been used in other countries as the basis for major developments in social welfare law. Nonetheless, I would argue that, even in countries with written constitutions or basic laws, social welfare must at base be a matter of politics, not of law. In so far as juridification suggests that there is a problem which is legal or jurisprudential in nature, it seems to me to be inappropriate.

However, even if it is accepted that juridification at least raises political rather than legal issues, there is a second line of argument that needs to be addressed, which is more controversial. Implicit in the concept of juridification are questions, coming both from the left and the right of the political spectrum about the legitimacy and desirability of state intervention. There is a feeling, on the part of some, that the state is too interventionist, with the result that individual freedom is under threat; others would argue that too much state intervention is affecting the operation of free markets and capitalist enterprise. Perhaps there are specific contexts, such as labor relations or the regulation of corporate structures, where such suggestions may have some validity. I am not at all certain, however, that the same can be said in the area of social welfare.

To be sure, even here arguments can be heard that state intervention has gone too far: that the state shoulders too much responsibility for the protection of the welfare of the individual; that social welfare undermines the integrity of the family unit; that social welfare policy saps the will of people to work and contribute to the creation of wealth in a society and so on. However, this would seem to me to ignore the lessons of history that, unless the state is careful, the social consequences of the operation of the market on the weak or the disadvantaged are liable to be so severe that more social problems are likely to emerge from rolling back the boundaries of the welfare state, than by keeping them (more or less) as they are. (It is, perhaps, not unimportant that, despite the massive level of unemployment that has affected the Western World in recent years, the level of social disorder has been remarkably low.)

Of course, there may need to be some fine tuning; some adjustments between, say, the public and private sectors as to the means of delivering particular welfare policies. There are also specific complaints that much social welfare legislation is unnecessarily complex; that not enough people take advantage of their legal entitlements (e.g. Corden, 1983); that many "means-tested" benefits stigmatize claimants (Deacon and Bradshaw, 1983); that where public enforcement of private agencies is required, these mechanisms are undermined by inadequate numbers of staff, or insufficiently aggressive enforcement policies. These specific complaints, however well made, should not detract from the overall benefit to society of current social welfare provision. The social advantages of the collective provision of a basic system of social welfare rights, funded and organized through the state rather than founded on individual initiative, seem to me to be the only effective way of ensuring that the victims of the economic system of the Western World are given some protection against the otherwise unbearably harsh realities of social life, and that whatever defects may be found, and whatever fine-tuning may be suggested, that juridification of the welfare state, far from being a crisis, on balance represents a social achievement of profound importance in a civilized world.

In short, although the analysis of Habermas (1985) has focused attention on a general problem of social welfare policy that has to be considered, it is submitted here that the consequences of the impact of social welfare policy on the lives of ordinary people are not as great, and certainly not as deleterious, as Habermas appears to be suggesting. And, at least in the British context, if there is a problem, it is essentially a *political* problem, not a problem for the law.

References

ATIYAH, Patrick Selim (1980) *Accidents, Compensation and the Law.* London: Weidenfeld and Nicolson.

BARCLAY, Peter (Chairman) (1982) *Social Workers: Their Role and Tasks.* London: Bedford Square Press.

BARTRIP, Peter and Sandra BURMAN (1983) *The Wounded Soldiers of Industry: Industrial Compensation Policy, 1833—1897.* Oxford: Clarendon Press.

CHESTERMAN, Michael (1979) *Charities, Trusts and Welfare.* London: Weidenfeld and Nicolson.

CORDEN, Anne (1983) *Taking up a Means-Tested Benefit — The Process of Claiming Family Income Supplement.* London: Her Majesty's Stationery Office.

CRANSTON, Ross (1985) *Legal Foundations of the Welfare State.* London: Weidenfeld and Nicolson.

CUNNINGHAM, Michael (1981) *Non-Wage Benefits.* London: Pluto Press.

DEACON, Alan and Jonathan BRADSHAW (1983) *Reserved for the Poor: The Means-Test in British Social Policy.* Oxford: Basil Blackwell and Martin Robertson.

DE SMITH, Stanley A. (1980) *Judicial Review of Administrative Action,* 4th Ed. by J.M. Evans. London: Stevens and Sons.

DILNOT, A.W., J.A. KAY and C.N. MORRIS (1984) *The Reform of Social Security.* Oxford: Clarendon Press for the Institute for Fiscal Studies.

ERMISCH, John (1984) *Housing Finance: Who Gains?* London: Policy Studies Institute.

FIELD, Frank (1981) *Inequality in Britain: Freedom, Welfare and the State.* Glasgow: Fontana.

FRASER, Derek (1973) *The Evolution of the British Welfare State.* London: Macmillan.

FREEDLAND, Mark (1980) "Leaflet Law: The Temporary Short-Time Working Compensation Scheme", 12 *Industrial Law Journal* 220.

FREEMAN, Michael David Alan and Cristina M. LYON (1984) *Law of Residential Homes and Day Care Establishments.* London: Sweet and Maxwell.

GEORGE, Vic and Paul WILDING (1976) *Ideology and Social Welfare.* London: Routledge and Kegan Paul.

— (1984) *The Impact of Social Policy.* London: Routledge and Kegan Paul.

GILBERT, Bentley B. (1966) *The Evolution of National Insurance in Great Britain: The Origins of the Welfare State,* 2nd Imp., (1973). London: Michael Joseph.

GRIFFITH, John Aneurin Grey (1979) "The Political Constitution", 42 *Modern Law Review* 1.

GRUNFELD, Cyril (1980) *The Law of Redundancy,* 2nd Ed. London: Sweet and Maxwell.

HABERMAS, Jürgen (1985) "Law as Medium and Law as Institution", in G. Teubner (ed.), *The Dilemmas of Law in The Welfare State.* Berlin: Walter de Gruyter.

HARRIS, Donald Renshaw, Morris MACLEAN, Hazel GENN, Sally LLOYD-BOSTOCK, Paul FENN, Peter CORFIELD, and Yvonne BRITTAN, (1984) *Compensation and Support for Illness and Injury.* Oxford: Oxford University Press

HARRIS, Jose (1972) *Unemployment and Politics: A Study of English Social Policy, 1886—1914.* Oxford: Clarendon Press.

HOGGETT, Brenda (1977) *Parents and Children.* London: Sweet and Maxwell.

— (1984) *Mental Health Law,* 2nd Ed. London: Sweet and Maxwell.

HOROWITZ, Donald (1977) *The Courts and Social Policy.* Washington D.C.: Brookings Institution.

ISON, Terence (1967) *The Forensic Lottery.* London: Staples Press.

JORDAN, Bill (1981) *Automatic Poverty.* London: Routledge and Kegan Paul.

LE GRAND, Julian and Ray ROBINSON,(eds.), (1984) *Privatisation and the Welfare State.* London: Allen and Unwin.

LOS, Maria (1982) "The Concept of Justice and Welfare Rights", *Journal of Social Welfare Law* 4.

LYNES, Tony (1975) "Unemployment Assistance Tribunals in the 1930s", in M. Adler and A.W. Bradley (eds.), *Justice, Discretion and Poverty.* Abingdon: Professional Books.

MICKLETHWAIT, Robert (1976) *The National Insurance Commissioners.* London: Stevens.

MILLER, David (1976) *Social Justice.* Oxford: Oxford University Press.

OGUS, Anthony I. (1982) "Great Britain", in P.A. Kohler and H.A. Zacher(eds.), *The Evolution of Social Insurance (1881—1981).* London: Frances Pinter.

OGUS, Anthony I. and and Eric M. BARENDT (1982) *Law of Social Security,* 2nd Ed. (Supplement, 1984). London: Butterworths.

PARTINGTON, Martin (1980) "Rules and Discretion in British Social Security Law", in Franz Gamillscheg, Jean de Givry, Bob Hepple, Jean-Maurice Verdier (eds.), *In Memoriam Sir Otto Kahn-Freund.* Munich: C.H. Beck.

— (1985) "Socio-Legal Studies and Social Welfare". Unpublished literature review prepared for the Economic and Social Research Council, and presented in March 1985.

PARTINGTON, Martin, Helen BOLDERSON and Karen SMITH (1984) *Housing Benefit Review Procedures: A preliminary analysis.* Uxbridge: Brunel University.
PINKER, Robert (1979) *The Idea of Welfare.* London: Heinemann.
PIVEN, Frances Fox and Richard A. CLOWARD (1971) *Regulating the Poor: The Functions of Public Welfare.* New York: Vintage Books.
PROSSER, Tony (1983) *Test-cases for the Poor: Legal Techniques in the Politics of Social Welfare.* London: Child Poverty Action Group.
REICH, Charles (1964) "The New Prosperity", 73 *Yale Law Journal* 733.
— (1965) "Individual Rights and Social Welfare — The emerging Legal Issues", 74 *Yale Law Journal* 1245.
SCARMAN, Lord (1975) *English Law — The New Dimension.* London: Stevens.
SCHEINGOLD, Stuart (1974) *The Politics of Rights.* New Haven: Yale University Press.
STREET, Harry (1968) *Justice in the Welfare State.* London: Stevens.
THANE, Pat (1982) *The Foundations of the Welfare State.* London: Longmans.
WEALE, Albert (1978) *Equality and Social Policy.* London: Routledge and Kegan Paul.
WILLIAMS, David (1979) "Social Welfare Consumers and their Complaints", *Journal of Social Welfare Law* 257.

Authors' Biographical Sketches

BERCUSSON, BRIAN, Senior Lecturer in Laws; born 1947; LL.B. 1969, London; LL.M. 1970, McGill University; Ph.D. 1974, Cambridge University; Research Fellow of Christ's College, Cambridge 1973-1977; Teaching Fellow, Osgoode Hall Law School, York University, Toronto, 1973-74; Lecturer in Laws, Queen Mary College, London University, 1978-1983; Senior Lecturer 1983-; Jean Monnet Fellow, European University Institute, Firenze, 1983-84. *Author*: Fair Wages Resolutions, 1978; (with C.D. Drake), The Employment Acts 1974-1980, 1981; Legislation Editor of the Encyclopedia of Labour Relations Law.

BUXBAUM, RICHARD M., Professor of Law; born 1930; A.B. 1950, LL.B. 1952, Cornell University; LL.M. 1953, University of California, Berkeley; Private Practice, 1953-61; Professor of Law, School of Law, University of California at Berkeley 1961-; Visiting Professor, University of Michigan School of Law 1965, University of Köln, Faculty of Law 1966, University of Frankfurt, Faculty of Law 1970, 1979. *Author*: Corporations — Cases and Materials, 5th ed. 1979; Die Bedeutung der privaten Klage als Mittel zur Durchsetzung wirtschaftspolitischer Rechtsnormen, 1972; (with Hopt), Legal Harmonization and the Business Enterprise, 1986; various articles in American and European professional journals.

CLARK, JON, Senior Lecturer in Industrial Relations; born 1949; B.A. 1972, Birmingham University; Research Fellow in Industrial Relations, London School of Economics and Political Science, 1976-1977; Visiting Research Fellow, Groupe de Sociologie du Travail, Paris, 1977-1978; Dr. phil., University of Bremen, 1979; Lecturer/Senior Lecturer in Industrial Relations, University of Southampton, 1978-. *Author*: (with H. Hartmann, C. Lau, D. Winchester), Trade Unions, National Politics and Economic Management, 1980; (with Lord Wedderburn and R. Lewis), Labour Law and Industrial Relations: Building on Kahn-Freund , 1983; Bruno Schönlank und die Arbeitersprechchorbewegung, 1984; (with I. McLoughlin, H. Rose and R. King), Technological Change in the Workplace 1986.

CORSI, FRANCESCO, Professor of Commercial Law; born 1933; Dr. in law 1956 University of Firenze; qualified as Lecturer 1968; Lecturer on industrial property and commercial law, University of Firenze, 1971; Associate Professor of commercial law, University of Calabria 1976; Associate Professor of commercial law, University of Firenze, 1976; Professor of commercial law, University of Firenze, 1979; Private practice from 1958;

Advocate from 1964-. *Author*: La revocatoria ordinaria nel fallimento, 1965; Il concetto di amministrazione nel diritto privato, 1974; Regime patrimoniale della famiglia, 1984; La società in accomandita per azioni, 1985; Revision of "Gli imprenditori e le società" di F. Ferrara, 1984; various articles in professional journals.

Ewald, François, Chargé de recherche, Centre National de la Recherche Scientifique; born 1946; diplomé en philosophie et en droit, University of Paris; Assistant at Collège de France, Chaire d'Histoire des Systèmes de Pensée (Professor: Michel Foucault) 1977-1984. *Author*: L'accident nous attend au coin de la rue, 1982; L'Etat-providence, 1985; various articles on social legislation and history of social security in professional journals.

Giugni, Gino, Professor of Labor Law; born 1927; Professor of Labor Law, University of Bari, 1960-1975; University of Rome, 1975-; Honorary Dr. of the University of Nanterre; Visiting Professor at the University of California, Los Angeles (UCLA) and Paris; Chairman of the Italian Association for Labor and Social Security Law; Chairman of the Committee on Labor of the Senate; Member of the National Council for the Economy and Labor, 1977-1983. *Author*: Introduzioni allo studio dell'economia collettiva, 1960; Mansioni e qualifiche nel rapporto di lavoro, 1964; Il sindacato tra contratti e riforme, 1972; Diritto sindacale, 6th ed., 1984 (Spanish translation, 1983). *Editor*: Giornale di diritto del lavoro e delle relazioni industriali. *Co-editor*: Lavoro informazione; various essays in professional journals; writes for La Repubblica, Mondo Operaio, Il Mulino.

Kübler, Friedrich, Professor of Law; born 1932; Dr. iur. 1961, Habilitation 1966, University of Tübingen; M.A. (hon.) 1985, University of Pennsylvania; Professor of Law, University of Giessen, 1966-1971; Teaching Fellow, Harvard Law School 1968-1969; Professor and Dean, University of Konstanz, 1971-1976; Visiting Professor, University of Pennsylvania, 1975 and 1983; Professor of Law, University of Frankfurt, 1976-; Professor of Law, University of Pennsylvania, 1985-. *Author*: Feststellung und Garantie, 1967; Gesellschaftsrecht, 2nd ed. 1985; Medienverflechtung, 1982; articles in various professional journals.

Hopt, Klaus Jürgen, Professor of Commercial and Business Law; born 1940; Referendar, University of Tübingen, 1963; M.C.J., New York University, 1965; Dr. iur., University of München, 1968; Dr. phil., University of Tübingen, 1969; Assessor, München, 1969; Habilitation, University of München, 1973; Associate Professor, University of München, 1973-74; Professor of Law, University of Tübingen, 1974-78, 1980-85; Dean of Law Department, 1982-83, Professor of Law, European University Institute, Firenze 1978-80; Head of Law Department, 1979-80; University of Bern, 1985-; Visiting Professor, University of Pennsylvania, Philadelphia, 1979; European University Institute, Firenze (Italy, 1981, 1983); Judge at State Court of

Appeals of Stuttgart (senate for commercial law and trade regulation), 1981-85. *Author*: Schadenersatz aus unberechtigter Verfahrenseinleitung, 1968; Die Dritte Gewalt als politischer Faktor, 1969; (with Will) Europäisches Insiderrecht, 1973; Der Kapitalanlegerschutz im Recht der Banken, 1975; Gutachten für den 51. Deutschen Juristentag, 1976; (with Hehl) Gesellschaftsrecht, 1979, 2nd ed. 1982; Handelsgesetzbuch (Baumbach-Duden-Hopt), 27th ed. 1986; (with Buxbaum) Legal Harmonization and the Business Enterprise, 1986. *Editor*: (with Mössel) Handelsrecht, 1985; European Merger Control, 1981; Groups of Companies in European Laws, 1981; (with Teubner) Corporate Governance and Directors' Liabilities, 1985; articles in various professional journals and collective publications.

MARKOVITS, RICHARD S., Professor of Law; born 1942; B.A. 1963, Cornell University; Ph.D. 1966, London School of Economics; LL.B. 1968, Yale University; Lecturer, Department of Economics, Yale University, 1966-68; Visiting Professor, Department of Economics, Cornell University, summer 1967; Assistant and Associate Professor of Law, Stanford University, 1968-75; Visiting Professor, Departments of Law and Economics, University of Konstanz, 1972; Professor of Law, University of Texas at Austin, 1975-; Co-Director (Centre for Socio-Legal Studies), Governing Board Fellow (Wolfson College), Member (Faculty of Law, Oxford University), 1981-83; Fellow, Wissenschaftskolleg zu Berlin, 1985-86. *Author*: Putting Us in Our Place, forthcoming; Predatory Conduct — A Policy and Legal Analysis, forthcoming; various articles in law journals, economics journals, and collections of essays on (1) antitrust, (2) the economic analysis of contract law, tort law, environmental law, property law, and tax law, (3) the relationship between economic analysis and legal or moral analysis, and (4) jurisprudence in general.

PARTINGTON, THOMAS MARTIN, Professor of Law; born 1944; B.A. University of Cambridge, 1965; LL.B. University of Cambridge, 1966; Assistant Lecturer in Law, Bristol University 1966-1969; Lecturer in Law, Warwick University, 1969-1973; Lecturer in Law, London School of Economics, University of London; 1973-1980; Professor of Law, Brunel University, West London, 1980-; Dean of the Faculty of Social Sciences, 1984-. *Author*: Landlord and Tenant Social Security Benefits, 1978. *Co-author*: (with Andrew Arden) Housing Law (1983; lst Supplement, 1985; 2nd Supplement, 1986); (with P. O'Higgins) Bibliography of Social Security Law, 1986; numerous articles in academic and professional legal journals on social security law, welfare law, housing law, and legal services.

SIMITIS, SPIROS, Professor of Law; born 1934; Dr. jur. 1965, University of Marburg; Professor, University of Giessen 1964-69; University of Frankfurt 1969-; Visiting Professor London School of Economics 1966; University of California Berkeley 1976; University of Pennsylvania, Philadelphia 1979; Yale University since 1980. *Author*: Grundlagen der Produzentenhaftung 1965;

Informationskrise des Rechts 1970; (with Gisela Zenz) Familie und Familienrecht, 1975; (with U. Dammann/Mallmann/Reh) Kommentar zum Bundesdatenschutzgesetz, 3rd Ed., 1981; articles in various professional journals.

TEUBNER, GUNTHER, Professor of Private Law and Legal Sociology; born 1944; Referendar, University of Tübingen, 1967; Dr. iur., University of Tübingen, 1970; Assessor, Stuttgart 1971; M.A., Sociology of Law, Berkeley, 1974; Habilitation in law, University of Tübingen, 1977; Privatdozent, University of Frankfurt, 1977; Professor of Law, University of Bremen, 1977-; Visiting Professor, University of California at Berkeley, 1980-81; Professor of Law, European University Institute, Florence, 1981-; Head of Law Department, 1984. *Author*: Standards und Direktiven in Generalklauseln, 1971; Public Status of Private Associations, 1974; Gegenseitige Vertragsuntreue, 1975; Organisationsdemokratie und Verbandsverfassung, 1978. *Co-author*: Alternativ-Kommentar zum BGB, 1979-81. *Editor*: (with Hopt) Corporate Governance and Directors' Liabilities, 1984; Dilemmas of Law in the Welfare State, 1985; (with Daintith) Contract and Organisation, 1986; Autopoietic Law, 1987; various articles in professional journals and collective publications.

LORD WEDDERBURN OF CHARLTON, Professor of Commercial Law; born 1927; B.A., 1948; LL.B., 1949 (Chancellor's Medallist); M.A. 1951; F.B.A., 1981; Fellow of Clare College and Lecturer in Law, University of Cambridge, 1952-64; Barrister, Middle Temple, 1953; Cassel Professor of Commercial Law, London School of Economics, University of London, 1964-; Visiting Professor, Harvard, 1969-70; University of California, Los Angeles, 1967, 1971; Chairman T.U.C., Independent Review Committee; Member of Bullock Committee on Industrial Democracy. *Author*: Cases and Materials on Labour Law, 1967; (with P. Davies) Employment Grievances and Disputes Procedures in Britain, 1969; The Worker and The Law, 1965, 3rd ed., 1986; (with B. Aaron) Industrial Conflict: A Comparative Legal Survey, 1972; (with R. Lewis and J. Clark) Labour Law and Industrial Relations, 1983; (with W.T. Murphy) Labour Law and the Community, 1983; various articles in English and foreign journals and collective publications. *Co-author*: Politica e Democrazia Industriale, 1978; Discrimination in Employment (ed. Folke Schmidt, 1978). *Editor*: Modern Law Review. *Co-editor*: Clerk and Lindsell on Torts, 14th ed., 1975, 15th ed. 1982; Gower's Modern Company Law 1969, 4th ed. 1979.

ZACHER, HANS F., Professor of Law; born 1928; Dr. iur., University of München 1952; Professor, Saarland University 1963-1971, University of München, 1971-; Director, Max-Planck-Institut für ausländisches und internationales Sozialrecht, 1980-. *Author*: Freiheit und Gleichheit in der Wohlfahrtspflege, 1964; Freiheitliche Demokratie, 1968; Sozialpolitik und Verfassung im ersten Jahrzehnt der Bundesrepublik Deutschland, 1980; Einführung in das Sozialrecht der Bundesrepublik Deutschland, 3rd ed. 1985; Numerous articles on social legislation, social policy, constitutional law, administrative law and law of economics in periodicals and compilations.

Subject Index

Bei Fragen zur Produktsicherheit wenden Sie sich bitte an:
If you have any questions regarding product safety,
please contact:

Walter de Gruyter GmbH
Genthiner Straße 13
10785 Berlin
productsafety@degruyterbrill.com